James P. Cannon and the Early Years of American Communism

Titles in the *Prometheus Research Series*

• No. 1 *Guidelines on the Organizational Structure of Communist Parties, on the Methods and Content of Their Work,* 94 pages, August 1988.

A new English translation of the definitive German text adopted by the 1921 Third Congress of the Communist International. ($6.00)

• No. 2 *Documents on the "Proletarian Military Policy,"* 101 pages, February 1989.

Includes rare materials from the Trotskyist movement in the U.S. and Europe during World War II, as well as an analytical introduction by the International Executive Committee of the International Communist League (Fourth Internationalist). ($9.00)

• No. 3 *In Memoriam, Richard S. Fraser: An Appreciation and Selection of His Work,* 108 pages, August 1990.

Fraser pioneered the Trotskyist understanding of black oppression in the United States, fighting for the perspective of Revolutionary Integration. Contains material from entire span of Fraser's political life, including seminal 1953 lectures, "The Negro Struggle and the Proletarian Revolution." ($6.00)

These bulletins in 8½" by 11" format are available from Spartacist Publishing Company. Prices include shipping and handling.

A brochure describing the Library is available from:

Prometheus Research Library
Box 185 Canal Street Station
New York, New York 10013

James P. Cannon and the Early Years of American Communism

Selected Writings and Speeches 1920–1928

PROMETHEUS RESEARCH LIBRARY

1992

NEW YORK CITY

Cover: 1926 Passaic strike support rally in New York's Union Square, International Newsreel photo courtesy of American Labor Museum, Haledon, New Jersey; photograph of James P. Cannon is from 1928 Labor Defender.

Cover design by Bruce Mishkin

Prometheus graphic from a woodcut by Fritz Brosius

Library of Congress Catalog Card Number: 92-82578

Publisher's Cataloging in Publication

Cannon, James Patrick, 1890-1974.

James P. Cannon and the early years of American Communism: selected writings and speeches, 1920-1928 / James P. Cannon.

p. cm.

Includes bibliographical references and index.

ISBN 0-9633828-0-2 (cloth)

ISBN 0-9633828-1-0 (pbk.)

1. Communism–United States–1917–Sources. 2. Socialism–United States–Sources. I. Title.

HX86.C159 1992 335'.43'0973

QBI92-1301

Prometheus Research Library books are published by:

Spartacist Publishing Company
Box 1377 G.P.O.
New York, New York 10116

Printed in the United States of America

The paper used for the text of this publication meets the minimum requirements of American National Standard for Information Sciences–Permanence of Paper for Printed Library Materials ANSI Z39.48-1984. ♾

To George Breitman (1916-1986), general editor of Writings of Leon Trotsky *and of* James P. Cannon: Writings and Speeches, *who goaded us to produce a representative collection of Cannon's writings and speeches in the 1920s. This led into the research which underlies this book.*

To Louis Sinclair (1909-1990), for his work over many years in meticulously cataloging Trotsky's works, as well as for his index of international Trotskyist internal bulletins. His pioneering Trotsky: A Bibliography *serves as an inspiration.*

To Martha Phillips (1948-1992), a field representative for the Prometheus Research Library, whose achievements as a revolutionary included being an able and energetic educator for the heritage of James P. Cannon. She was murdered at her post in Moscow, 9 February 1992.

Contents

1920-22

1923

1924

1925

1926

1927

1928

"James P. Cannon was the finest communist political leader this country has yet produced. In his prime he had the evident capacity to lead the proletarian revolution in America to victory."

Workers Vanguard No. 52, 13 September 1974

About James P. Cannon

James Patrick Cannon was born on 11 February 1890 in Rosedale, Kansas, which is now a part of Kansas City. Won to socialism by his father, an Irish Republican and Populist who had come over to the Socialist movement in 1897 with Eugene V. Debs, Cannon joined the Socialist Party (SP) in 1908 at the age of 18. In 1911 he quit the SP to join the syndicalist Industrial Workers of the World (IWW). From 1912 to 1914 he traveled the American Midwest as an agitator and organizer for the IWW; from 1914 to 1919 he was active in the local Kansas City chapter.

Galvanized back into political action on the national field by the Russian Revolution, Cannon rejoined the SP in order to hook up with its developing pro-Bolshevik left wing. In April 1919 Cannon helped to launch a communist newspaper in Kansas City, *Workers' World.* In June Cannon was Kansas City delegate to a national caucus of the SP left wing held in New York City. At an August 1919 convention in Chicago, the left wing split from the Socialist Party, and two communist parties were formed. Although he did not attend the convention, Cannon and the entire Kansas City left wing joined John Reed's Communist Labor Party (CLP) rather than the rival Communist Party of America. Cannon was elected CLP secretary for Missouri and organizer for the Nebraska, Kansas and Missouri district.

The two communist parties eventually merged their forces and founded the Workers Party of America. This was the name the party retained until 1929. Cannon was the chairman of the Workers Party from its founding in December 1921 through its third convention in December 1923. He was a member of the Central Executive Committee (Central Committee) from 1920 to 1928 and the Executive Council (Political Committee) from 1922 to 1928. Cannon was assistant executive secretary of the party from December 1923 until August 1925; throughout this period Cannon was a prominent public party spokesman, as well as the party's education director. He was the Workers Party candidate for governor of New York in the fall of 1924.

In July of 1925 Cannon was instrumental in founding the International Labor Defense (ILD), a united-front defense organization. Cannon was secretary and chief administrator of the ILD from its foundation until his 1928 expulsion from the Workers Party. He was a frequent public speaker on behalf of the ILD, which organized mass agitation against the execution of the anarchists Sacco and Vanzetti, among other campaigns.

Cannon first went to Moscow to serve as the American delegate to the Executive Committee of the Communist International (ECCI) in June 1922. He spent seven months there, first as a member of the Presidium of the ECCI from June through November and then as a delegate to the Fourth Congress of the Communist International. He made four other trips to Moscow later in the decade: in 1925 he was delegate to the Fifth Plenum of the ECCI; in 1926 he attended the Sixth ECCI Plenum; in 1927 he was a delegate to the Eighth ECCI Plenum; and finally, he was a delegate to the Sixth World Congress, July-August 1928. It was at the Sixth Congress that Cannon was won to Leon Trotsky's Left Opposition. In October 1928 he was expelled from the Workers Party for Trotskyism, along with Martin Abern and Max Shachtman. At the time of his expulsion Cannon was the party's candidate for Congress in New York's Second District.

For the next 25 years Cannon was the principal leader of American Trotskyism, retiring as National Secretary of the Socialist Workers Party (SWP) in 1953. At the time of his death in August 1974 Cannon was still the National Chairman of the SWP; however the party had abandoned the Trotskyist program more than ten years earlier. The SWP's Pathfinder Press distributes a posthumous series of Cannon's writings as a Trotskyist, *James P. Cannon: Writings and Speeches.* Four volumes in the series have been published, covering the years 1928-31, 1932-34, 1940-43, 1945-47. Pathfinder also distributes a number of books by Cannon that were published during his lifetime, including *Notebook of an Agitator,* which includes many of his popular, agitational articles from 1925 to 1928, as well as *The History of American Trotskyism* and *The First Ten Years of American Communism.*

Editorial Note

This book was a struggle to create. We began to compile the material in 1984 under the tutelage of George Breitman, who had been the Pathfinder Press editor responsible for both the Leon Trotsky and James P. Cannon writings series. We had collected most of Cannon's published articles by September 1985, when George wrote us a memo urging that we make the book a top priority, noting "mainly it is a matter of selecting what will go into the book and what will have to be excluded." We had little experience in this kind of editorial work, however, and George's death in April 1986 caused us to put aside the ambitious Cannon book project in favor of the more modest goal of publishing a few library research bulletins. It was only after we had published three bulletins in our *Prometheus Research Series* that we were able to continue work on this book.

The bibliography lists all the writings and speeches by James P. Cannon which we were able to locate in published and unpublished sources, from 1912 through Cannon's expulsion from the Workers Party in the fall of 1928. We were able to review material from the James P. Cannon and Rose Karsner Papers, 1917-1924 which were recently deposited by the Socialist Workers Party in the Archives Division of the State Historical Society of Wisconsin. These papers were opened to researchers only in July 1992; they contain some items which were unavailable from other sources, including personal political correspondence. We have thus searched the bulk of open archives likely to contain documents or speeches by Cannon from the 1920s; however it is possible that the files of the Communist International in Moscow contain additional material.

We have edited all the Cannon material included in this volume, modernizing spelling and correcting obvious typographical errors and inconsistencies. Where possible we have checked the accuracy of quotations cited. We have also provided explanatory introductions and footnotes to Cannon's texts. However, the available documentation of the early American Communist movement is very partial. We have not been able to identify all of the individuals mentioned by Cannon. Nor have we been able to provide background information on all the issues under dispute in the Workers Party.

An extensive glossary of names, organizations and terms possibly unfamiliar to the contemporary reader is provided at the end of the volume. Abbreviations are listed in the index.

A section of photographs can be found in the middle of the volume, a list of sources appears on page 572. We would like to thank the New York Reference Center for Marxist Studies for allowing us to copy the *Workers Monthly*, *Labor Herald* and *Labor Defender* photographs which appear in this section.

We thank Theodore Draper for making available to us his research papers deposited at the Hoover Institution Archives in Stanford, California, and at the Robert W. Woodruff Library at Emory University. The librarians at both these institutions were extremely helpful, as was Dorothy Swanson and the staff at the Tamiment Institute Library in New York. We thank Frank Lovell, Albert Glotzer, Harvey Klehr and Morris Lewit for their assistance in identifying some of the individuals named in this volume. We thank Anne Stillwaggon for her advice on book publishing.

Unless otherwise stated, all unpublished transcripts, letters and manuscripts published here are from originals or photocopies in the collection of the Prometheus Research Library.

The compilation and selection of the material for this book, as well as the introduction and editorial notes, were centrally the work of Emily Turnbull and James Robertson; Lisa Diamond, Jonathan Lavine and Diana Kartsen were responsible for copy-editing. The glossary was prepared by Keith Anwar; the index was compiled by Jonathan Lavine; the bibliography of Cannon's writings was prepared for publication by Steve Miles; Cory Pearson was the photographer; Maria Gianotten designed the photograph pages. Héctor Cornejo, Bree Conover, John Heckman, Diana Kartsen, and Carl Lichtenstein were centrally responsible for production.

Introduction

On 27 October 1928 James P. Cannon, a member of the Political Committee of the American Communist Party—called at that time the Workers (Communist) Party—was expelled for attempting to organize within the party in support of Leon Trotsky's Left Opposition. The Trotskyist opposition was fighting to return the Soviet regime and the Communist International to the revolutionary internationalism of Lenin's day, insisting that the fate of the Soviet regime depended on the international extension of the October Revolution and that the forging of Leninist vanguard parties was key to that extension.

By the time of Cannon's expulsion Trotsky and other leading members of the Left Opposition had already been expelled from the Soviet party and the Communist International. Many had been sent into internal exile in the Soviet Union; Trotsky himself was in Alma Ata in Soviet Central Asia. Most of those fighting against the Stalinist degeneration of the Russian Revolution learned only much later that their fight had found support in the adherence to their cause of a senior American party leader.

More importantly, they learned that Cannon did not stand alone. Expelled along with Cannon were fellow Central Committee member Martin Abern and alternate member of the Central Committee Max Shachtman, both of them close associates of Cannon since the early days of American Communism, leading members of the longstanding "Cannon group" (or faction) within the party, and leaders, along with Cannon, of the International Labor Defense. Over the next few months more than 100 members of the Workers Party were expelled, some for making forthright statements in support of Cannon, Abern and Shachtman, most for simply questioning the propriety of the expulsions. The newly expelled had almost all been supporters of the Cannon faction, and they included Arne Swabeck, another full member of the Central Committee, as well as Vincent R. Dunne, most of the Twin Cities leadership, and Cannon's companion Rose Karsner, a founding member of the party and a central administrator of the ILD. Expelled from the Canadian Communist Party was Maurice Spector, party chairman and member of the Executive Committee of the Communist International, along with a small band of supporters.

Not all of the Cannon faction opposed the expulsions. In particular Cannon's closest friend and associate, William F. Dunne—a full Central Committee member and candidate member of the Political Committee who was on foreign assignment for the Communist International at the time of the expulsions—stayed in the party and denounced Cannon. Manuel Gomez, alternate member of the CC and head of the party's Anti-Imperialist League, testified against Cannon in the Political Committee. In all, probably only about half the members of the faction—which was composed almost entirely of party cadre and was thus the smallest of the three major factional groupings in the party—were expelled, and not all of these became members of the Trotskyist Communist League of America (CLA) when it was founded in May 1929. But a solid majority of those who founded the American section of the Left Opposition were Cannon faction supporters of long standing.

The genesis of the CLA from an established grouping within the Communist Party, with years of political collaboration and agreement behind it, gave it an organizational stability and political cohesion lacking in other International Left Opposition sections outside of the Soviet Union itself. Most other leaders who came over to the Left Opposition from parties of the Communist International did so only after they had been discredited and stripped of all supporters. Cannon stands out as the only one expelled while he was still a credible party leader, able to win others to his political course.

The material presented in this book is designed to shed new light on the unique origins of American Trotskyism by providing a documentary record of the political evolution of Cannon and his faction within the Workers Party. Though we have been able to include some of the popular agitational pieces, our selection of Cannon's writings and speeches is heavily weighted toward internal factional material. We include here many documents coauthored by Cannon, and others which he cosigned but probably had no part in writing. In most cases it was impossible to determine the actual authorship of the jointly signed material, and the political profile of the Cannon faction would have been severely skewed if we had not included the major coauthored statements. Where necessary we have also supplemented this material with excerpts from the party's Executive Council (Political Committee) minutes.

Yet it would be a mistake to look at this material simply as a prelude to Cannon's later emergence as the authoritative American Trotskyist leader. For Cannon was also one of the most able Communist leaders in the 1920s, a period when the party was not yet homogenized into a rigid Stalinist orthodoxy. This was a time of real, necessary and inevitable debate about the tasks facing Communists in the United States. From 1924 these debates were increasingly dominated, and increasingly deformed, by a Communist International which was losing its revolutionary perspective. The American party, feeling the pressure of an expanding and stable American imperialism, readily followed in the International's wake. Thus the experience of building a Leninist party in the United States in the 1920s was largely negative. But if Cannon, feeling at a dead end in the internal factional wars, was able to make the leap in 1928 to Trotsky's programmatic and international understanding of Stalinism, it was in large part because he had *tried*, in the preceding period, to chart a path for the party based on revolutionary communism.

This book does not stand alone but supplements the excellent two-volume history of the American Communist Party (through 1929) written by Theodore Draper, one of only two "reasonably adequate histories" of Comintern sections, according to the historian E.H. Carr (the other being J. Rothschild's history of the Bulgarian party).[1] An ex-Communist if anti-Communist, Draper had a sympathy and feel for the subject usually lacking

---

[1] Joseph Rothschild, *The Communist Party of Bulgaria, Origins and Development 1883-1936* (New York: Columbia University Press, 1959). E.H. Carr recommended the Draper and Rothschild histories in *Socialism in One Country 1924-1926*, Vol. III, Part 1 (New York: Macmillan Company, 1964), v-vi.

in professional historians. Moreover, he was able to interview many former party leaders in preparing *The Roots of American Communism* and *American Communism and Soviet Russia.*[2] Cannon, in semi-retirement, was able to devote considerable time to answering Draper's questions about the Communist movement. His letters were a major independent contribution to Draper's researches, and they were later published as *The First Ten Years of American Communism.* Draper wrote a preface for Cannon's book, and in it he paid tribute to Cannon's excellent memory of the period:

> For a long time, I wondered why Jim Cannon's memory of events in the Nineteen-Twenties was so superior to that of all the others. Was it simply some inherent trait of mind? Rereading some of these letters, I came to the conclusion that it was something more. Unlike other communist leaders of his generation, Jim Cannon *wanted* to remember. This portion of his life still lives for him because he has not killed it within himself.[3]

Draper contrasted Cannon's letters with other autobiographical efforts: "Official American communists have published so-called autobiographies, but they have been largely spurious. Cannon's letters are the real thing."[4] It hardly needs to be noted that the documentary record presented here, culled from the published press of the Communist International and the Workers Party as well as from unpublished archival sources, fully validates Cannon's *First Ten Years,* even as it amplifies and augments it. Such a documentary record—even a highly selective one—cannot be said to exist for the accounts of many leading ex-Communists, to say nothing of the official histories penned by Stalinist hacks. William Z. Foster's tendentious *History of the Communist Party of the United States* writes Cannon, among others, almost entirely out of the party's early years, while Earl Browder and Benjamin Gitlow portray Cannon—in their own image—as simply an unprincipled

---

2 Theodore Draper, *The Roots of American Communism* (New York: Viking Press, 1957) and *American Communism and Soviet Russia* (New York: Viking Press, 1960). They will henceforth be cited in the footnotes as Draper I and Draper II.

3 Theodore Draper, preface to James P. Cannon, *The First Ten Years of American Communism* (New York: Lyle Stuart, 1962), 12. Henceforth Cannon's book will be referred to as *First Ten Years.*

4 Ibid., 11.

and power-hungry intriguer.[5] Bertram D. Wolfe, on the other hand, disingenuously disappears his own role as Jay Lovestone's chief factional hatchet man and anti-Trotsky expert.[6] These accounts—written by those who contributed greatly to the Stalinization of the Workers Party and its destruction as a revolutionary organization—often make unintentionally hilarious reading. We could supplement Draper's observation: if Cannon had reason to remember, he also had nothing to cover up. Cannon went on to become the finest communist political leader the United States has yet produced.

Cannon in the IWW

Cannon was one of those who came to Lenin's communism by way of the syndicalist movement. But Cannon's syndicalism was not the "boring from within the American Federation of Labor" variety espoused by William Z. Foster, who also joined the Communist movement. Cannon had been a member of the Industrial Workers of the World (IWW), a "Wobbly." He had quit the Socialist Party (SP) at the age of 21 to champion the "one big union" envisioned by the IWW, which eschewed the electoral political activity of the SP in favor of what it called "direct action." Cannon was part of a great exodus of left-wingers from the Socialist Party at that time—many quit after the SP adopted a constitutional clause against the advocacy of "sabotage" in 1912 and many more left when the SP removed IWW leader "Big Bill" Haywood from its Executive Board in 1913.

In many ways Cannon was typical of the revolutionary-minded proletarian youth who flocked to the early IWW, disgusted with the middle-class reformism of the dominant SP leadership. The IWW believed in dual unionism—the strategy of building new revolutionary unions from the great mass of non-unionized, largely unskilled workers, rather than "boring from within" the

---

[5] William Z. Foster, *History of the Communist Party of the United States* (New York: International Publishers, 1952); Benjamin Gitlow, *I Confess* (New York: E.P. Dutton & Co., 1940); Earl Browder's undated and unfinished manuscript, *No Man's Land*, which positively drips with rivalry toward Cannon, is deposited in the Earl Browder Papers, George Arents Research Library, Syracuse University. The Earl Browder Papers are also available from the Microfilming Corporation of America.

[6] Bertram D. Wolfe, *A Life in Two Centuries* (New York: Stein and Day, 1981).

existing conservative American Federation of Labor (AFL) craft unions. The dual-unionist ideology heavily influenced the nascent American left wing, and it was to plague the early Communist movement.

Cannon had made a special study of public speaking in high school (he had dropped out of school at the age of 12 to help support his family by working in a meatpacking plant, but he returned to high school in 1907 and attended for three years). It was his ambition to become a soapbox agitator for the IWW, and he did indeed become a popular speaker at 6th and Main in downtown Kansas City. He was a delegate to the seventh national convention of the IWW in Chicago in 1912. He served as secretary of the convention and took an active part in its proceedings. He caught the eye of IWW leader Vincent St. John and after the convention he became a protégé of St. John.

Cannon cut his teeth in the labor movement as a Midwest organizer and speaker for the IWW from 1912 to 1914. After the convention St. John sent Cannon to Jackson, Michigan, where an auto strike was on. But the strike fizzled and Cannon ended up in New Castle, Pennsylvania, working on the IWW journal *Solidarity*. The winter of 1913 saw Cannon make a speaking tour of the Midwest in support of the Akron rubber strike; he spent two weeks in jail in Peoria, Illinois toward the end of that year for his activity in support of the Avery manufacturing strike. Cannon learned as he went along during this period of itinerant organizing. His experience was characteristic of the IWW at the time, as he later noted in a tribute to Vincent St. John, who was widely known as "the Saint":

> "The Saint," of affectionate memory, was a wonderful man to learn from. He was short on palaver and had some gaps in his theory, but he was long on action and he was firmly convinced that the water is the only place where a man can learn to swim. His way of testing, and also of developing, the young militants who grew up under his tutelage was to give them responsibility and shove them into action and see what happened. Those who acquired self-confidence and the capacity to make decisions under fire on the spot, which are about 90 percent of the distinctive quality of leaders and organizers, eventually received credentials as voluntary organizers and thereafter enjoyed a semi-official status in the strikes and other actions which marked the career of the IWW in its glorious hey-day. The shock

troops of the movement were the foot-loose militants who moved around the country as the scene of action shifted.[7]

After Cannon was released from the Peoria jail, St. John sent him to Omaha, then to Duluth, where he worked with Frank Little in an ore dockers strike. Later on in 1914 Cannon was a delegate to the IWW's eighth convention. Afterward he returned to Kansas City, joining his first wife, Lista Makimson, who was a schoolteacher there. Lista had come to visit Cannon when it looked like he might face a long jail term for his activity in the Avery strike; they were married in Pekin, Illinois. Cannon remained active in the Kansas City IWW; during World War I he registered for the draft as a conscientious objector and was known as a vocal opponent of the war.[8] It was the Russian Revolution which galvanized Cannon back into political action on the national field. He was far from the only one so affected. A pro-Bolshevik left wing was developing inside the Socialist Party; Cannon, disillusioned by the IWW's failure to grasp the significance of the workers revolution in Russia, rejoined the SP in order to hook up with this left wing. In 1919 Cannon and Earl Browder, who had been a local supporter of William Z. Foster's syndicalist organization, launched a pro-Bolshevik journal in Kansas City, *Workers' World.*

The Birth of American Communism

The year 1919 saw the crest of the wave of labor radicalism which swept Europe in opposition to the great carnage of World War I and in support of the 1917 Russian Revolution. 1919 was the year of the Spartakist uprising in Germany, the short-lived Hungarian Soviet Republic, the founding of the Communist Third International. Even on the distant and politically backward shores of the United States the wave sweeping Europe made its ripples. More man-hours were lost due to strikes in the United

---

7 "Spirit and Technique of the Pioneers," in the California Socialist Party's *Labor Action* (San Francisco), 28 November 1936 (reprinted in *Notebook of an Agitator*, New York, Pioneer Publishers, 1958, p. 104). Cannon also paid tribute to St. John in his 1961 essay, "The IWW: The Great Anticipation," *First Ten Years*, 277-310.

8 Transcript of Joseph Hansen interview with James P. Cannon, 5 October 1956, in the James P. Cannon and Rose Karsner Papers 1919-1974, Archives Division, State Historical Society of Wisconsin, Box 25. This collection is hereafter referred to as the Cannon Papers.

States in 1919 than in the next six years put together. In February a solidarity action in support of higher wages for shipyard workers in Seattle grew into a citywide general strike, and for five days the labor unions ran the city. Later that year the Seattle longshoremen refused to load arms shipments bound for the White Guard counterrevolutionary troops in Siberia. The coal miners went out on national strike; so did the steel workers. The ranks of the Socialist Party swelled, mostly through an influx of foreign-born workers, those most affected by events in Europe. The Socialist Party's pro-Bolshevik left wing had the support of two-thirds of the party's more than 104,000 members. In September the American Communist movement was born. Unfortunately, most of the members of the SP's left wing did not make the transition to the Communist movement.

The American bourgeoisie did not leave this wave of labor radicalism to recede on its own. Race-hate was the bourgeoisie's first line of defense: in 1919 there were 70 lynchings and 25 anti-black pogroms, including a crucial one in Chicago which broke the back of an interracial union-organizing drive among the meatpackers. The young Communist movement was also subjected to massive state repression, beginning in November, only two months after its birth. Dubbed the "Palmer Raids" after then-Attorney General A. Mitchell Palmer, the persecution lasted for over four months. Communist offices and newspapers were raided; over 6,000 Communists were arrested in nationwide raids in the first week of January 1920. Foreign-born Communists were deported *en masse* (249 deported to Russia in December 1919 alone). Many leading Communists were jailed and/or faced trial on "criminal syndicalism" charges.

The repression had the desired effect, driving away many of the left-wing SPers from the young Communist movement. But this movement had other problems. It was crippled from birth by a bitter organizational split. The Communist Party of America (CPA) of Louis Fraina, dominated by seven large and insular East European foreign-language federations, lacked both a sense of American social reality and any real desire to affect it. The Communist Labor Party (CLP) of John Reed was more concerned with actual American conditions—Cannon and the entire Kansas City left wing had joined it. But both parties carried the ideological baggage of the sterile ultraleftism of the old SP left wing, which had been strongly influenced by the theories of Socialist Labor Party leader Daniel De Leon and the Dutch theoreticians Anton Pannekoek and Hermann Gorter. Cannon later explained the problem:

> The traditional sectarianism of the Americans was expressed most glaringly in their attempt to construct revolutionary unions outside the existing labor movement; their refusal to fight for "immediate demands" in the course of the class struggle for the socialist goal; and their strongly entrenched anti-parliamentarism, which was only slightly modified in the first program of the Communist Party.[9]

Both the CLP and CPA went underground in reaction to the Palmer Raids. Both decided, on principle, to remain there, eschewing public political activity as the postwar revolutionary tide swirled above them.

Cannon in the Underground

It was only the influence of the Communist International (Comintern) that persuaded the American Communists to overcome the ultraleftism which infected the early movement. Cannon also explained how this occurred:

> All that hodgepodge of ultra-radicalism was practically wiped out of the American movement in 1920-21 by Lenin. He did it, not by administrative order backed up by police powers, but by the simple device of publishing a pamphlet called *Left-Wing Communism: An Infantile Disorder*....The "Theses and Resolutions" of the Second Congress of the Comintern in 1920 also cleared up the thinking of the American communists over a wide range of theoretical and political problems, and virtually eliminated the previously dominating influence exerted by the sectarian conceptions of De Leon and the Dutch leaders.[10]

Cannon was one of the first to grasp Lenin's message. He first entered the national arena in the Communist movement when he gave a powerful speech against dual unionism to the founding convention of the United Communist Party (UCP) in May 1920. This convention was the first small step on the road to uniting all the forces in the U.S. that stood for the Third International: it

9 Cannon, *First Ten Years*, 318.
10 Ibid.

united the Communist Labor Party with a C.E. Ruthenberg-led split from the Communist Party of America. The UCP was not yet ready to shed its ultraleftism and adopt the Bolshevik position of working within the reactionary American Federation of Labor where necessary. But Cannon's status as an ex-Wobbly and therefore a "reformed" dual unionist so impressed the delegates that he was elected to the Central Committee and appointed organizer for the St. Louis/Southern Illinois Coal District.[11]

Though they were few, the syndicalists who came over to the Communists were crucially important. For they made the American party rich in its acquired inheritance. Not only SP party men like Ruthenberg and foreign-language federation sectarians, but also trade unionists who knew the score in the American labor movement—all these currents endeavored to assimilate Lenin's communism. The cross-fertilization that resulted gave a vitality to the early American party, a vitality totally lacking in, for example, the early British Communist Party, which failed to win over the syndicalists and Celts of the Socialist Labour Party and was left with only former members of H.M. Hyndman's sterile British Socialist Party.[12] The IWW withered to a shell of its former self after 1919, but Cannon remained concerned with winning its remnants to Leninism. It was Cannon's ties to the pre-WWI radical movement that impressed the young Max Shachtman, among others:

> He made an enormous impression upon me, which never really died....He was known as an excellent orator, a very smooth writer, an exceedingly intelligent and shrewd politician; and he had what comparatively few of the then leaders of the Communist party had: namely, he had a living, personal connection with the pre-Bolshevik revolutionary radical movement in this country.[13]

In the fall of 1920 Cannon was named editor of *The Toiler,* the UCP's weekly newspaper published in Cleveland. It was around this time that he started spending most of his time in New York instead. Many of the prominent party leaders, including Ruthen-

[11] Cannon was always very proud of his speech to that UCP convention. See Cannon, *First Ten Years,* 197-198. Unfortunately we could find no transcript.

[12] See Raymond Challinor, *The Origins of British Bolshevism* (London: Croom Helm, 1977).

[13] Reminiscences of Max Shachtman (1963), Columbia University Oral History Research Collection, 24.

berg, were in jail as a result of the Palmer Raids. Cannon himself was under indictment. In April 1920 he and Charles Baker, the National Organizational Secretary of the CLP, were charged under the Lever Act for obstructing the production of coal during the 1919 miners strike—Cannon had spent two months in jail for his support activities—but the 1920 indictment never came to trial (charges were dropped in February 1922). So Cannon was one of the few available communist leaders who had the English-language ability and office skills necessary for party administration. Cannon later described how, as much as he preferred to leave the major decisions to others, he soon recognized that they were politically unqualified: "I knew then that I had to fight for the leadership."[14]

And fight he did. The two Communist parties were finally united, upon the Communist International's insistence, in May of 1921. Cannon and the young Jay Lovestone became the main axis of the leadership which steered the newly united, but still underground, party into legal political activity. They were aided by the development of a new pro-Communist group within the Socialist Party, organized around the journal *Workers' Council.* In December 1921 the Communists merged with the Workers' Council forces and founded the Workers Party as a legal party (a parallel "illegal" Communist Party apparatus remained until April 1923). James P. Cannon was the Workers Party's first chairman and its major public spokesman.

Not surprisingly, there exists today very little record of the internal deliberations of the American Communist movement from the underground period. We have found a few articles on the IWW signed by Cannon in late 1920, when the Communists were trying to intersect an intense discussion among the Wobblies on relations with the Communist International. We also found an extensive article, published in *The Liberator*, on Kansas miners leader Alexander Howat. All these articles reflect Cannon's origins in the IWW and Midwestern labor movement, and they are included in this book. However, the record of Cannon's activities as an adept and skillful Communist politician begins with his

---

[14] Quoted in Harry Ring's reminiscences of Cannon in *James P. Cannon As We Knew Him* (New York: Pathfinder Press, 1976), 169.

address to the founding convention of the Workers Party, also included here.

The United States in the 1920s

The political climate of the United States had shifted dramatically by the time the Workers Party emerged from the underground. The intense repression of the Palmer Raids was very short-lived—the raids were over by the summer of 1920. But this was because the bourgeoisie soon realized that the force used was out of all proportion to the threat. The revolutionary sentiments that seemed to have gripped the working class were fading.

In the fall of 1920 Republican Warren Harding, running on a program of returning the country to "normalcy," was elected president with a landslide majority of 61 percent. The vote represented a massive repudiation of Woodrow Wilson's overseas crusading and of the liberal reform movement known as "Progressivism" which had swept through both major bourgeois parties on and off for most of the previous two decades. Harding pardoned Socialist Party leader Eugene V. Debs, who had been sentenced to 16 years in prison for his opposition to WWI, as well as many IWW activists similarly imprisoned.

Even as Harding softened the political climate, he refused to pardon the Communists under indictment. The Workers Party was tolerated, but the underground Communist Party convention at Bridgman, Michigan was broken up by the police in August 1922 and many of the party's leaders, including C.E. Ruthenberg, were arrested. The bourgeoisie remained vigilant against the "Bolshevik menace," and the rest of the decade was one of legal reaction. At the same time as the Bridgman raid Harding's administration sought, and got, a sweeping injunction which was used to outlaw the railway shopmen's strike. This set the tone for the period, which saw the repeated use of the Sherman Anti-Trust Act against the unions. The Supreme Court outlawed minimum-wage laws and declared "yellow dog" contracts, which made the promise not to join a union a condition of employment, perfectly legal. At the end of the decade Supreme Court Chief Justice and former President William H. Taft said that the aim of it all had been "to prevent the Bolsheviki from getting control."

The grip of Jim Crow racial segregation had consolidated across the South in the decades before World War I, and the Ku

Klux Klan, reborn in 1915, was recruiting by the thousands in the 1920s. Anti-immigrant and Asian-exclusion sentiment ran at an all-time high. In 1921 an emergency bill was passed limiting annual immigration from any nation to 3 percent of the number of that country's nationals who had been living in the United States in 1910. The National Origins Act of 1924 changed that to a percentage of nationals *resident in 1890,* further discriminating against the more recent East European immigrants. The act prohibited further Japanese immigration (Chinese immigration had been banned in 1882) and it barred the entry of women from China, Korea, Japan and India, so that Asian males already resident in the United States could not bring their wives into the country and start families here. The shortfall in the labor pool caused by the slowing down of foreign immigration was made up by an exodus from America's farmlands, particularly the migration of black workers northward. Agricultural prices had collapsed in 1921; they never recovered.

The business of America was business. A speculative economic boom fueled government corruption (like the Teapot Dome oil scandal) and led to the 1929 stock market crash, but the watchword of the early decade was "scientific management," and its symbols were the stopwatch and the timeclock. There was massive mechanization of basic production processes: output per manhour in manufacturing rose 72 percent from 1919 to 1929. For the first time a mass market developed for consumer durables like cars, radios, refrigerators, vacuum cleaners.

But the benefits of the increase in productivity barely trickled down to the American working class. The stock dividend proportion of national income rose by over 64 percent; wages and salaries advanced by only slightly more than 20 percent. *Real* wages grew only 9.1 percent on average from 1923 to 1928, but the increase for those at the bottom of the wage scale—newer immigrants and blacks—was much lower. Wage differentials in the United States were at the time among the highest in the world. High wages for craft workers was the price that the job-trusting bureaucrats at the top of the American Federation of Labor exacted for attempting to ensure labor peace.

The decade was one of decline and demoralization of the trade-union movement. Membership in the AFL peaked at slightly more than 5 million workers in 1920. By 1929 it was less than 3.5

million. Almost 20 percent of the non-agricultural workforce was unionized in 1920; the figure had fallen to just over 10 percent by 1930. Many unions virtually disappeared. Especially hard hit were the miners and the textile unions; it is no accident that the Workers Party maintained a substantial base of support in these two industries for most of the decade. The craft unions came more and more to dominate the AFL. Blacks had no choice but to work in open shops, if they worked: 24 of the major AFL unions discriminated against blacks by statute; most of the others did so informally. And the union leaders made no bones about their enlistment in the war against godless communism. Photo-Engravers leader Matthew Woll, a member of the AFL Executive Council, declared, "It is no secret that the American Federation of Labor is the first object of attack by the Communist movement. Consequently the American Federation of Labor is the first line of defense."[15]

Cannon's Seven Months in Moscow, 1922

Even after the founding of the Workers Party in December 1921, the ultraleftist disease lingered in the American Communist movement. Diehard undergrounders insisted on maintaining the parallel illegal apparatus of the Communist Party, even after it became clear that the Workers Party could function openly. Soon a fight was raging between the undergrounders-on-principle (known as the "Goose Caucus") and those who wanted to abolish the underground party (who were known as the "Liquidators"). Cannon was one of the principal "Liquidators." Freed of major administrative responsibility for the party by C.E. Ruthenberg, who became secretary of the Workers Party after his release from prison in the spring of 1922, Cannon was designated to represent the "Liquidators" before the Executive Committee of the Communist International (ECCI) in Moscow. He left New York in May and spent the rest of the year in Moscow.[16]

---

15 Quoted in Irving Bernstein, *The Lean Years* (Boston: Houghton Mifflin, 1960), 141. The facts and figures on the American labor movement cited in the preceding paragraphs also come from this source.

16 Caleb Harrison had been elected Workers Party secretary, but he did not have the skills for office administration and most of the tasks had fallen to Cannon,

(continued)

Cannon had to fight hard to convince the Comintern leadership of the necessity for abolishing the underground party. The black poet Claude McKay, who also attended the Comintern's Fourth Congress and participated in the discussion around the American question though he was not formally a member of the Workers Party, described Cannon's demeanor:

> I listened to James Cannon's fighting speeches for a legal Communist party in America. Cannon's manner was different from Bill Haywood's or Foster's. He had all the magnetism, the shrewdness, the punch, the bag of tricks of the typical American politician, but here he used them in a radical way. I wondered about him. If he had entered Democratic or Republican politics, there was no barrier I could see that could stop him from punching his way straight through to the front ranks.[17]

But Cannon's Midwestern American "bag of tricks" was hardly going to sway the leadership of the Communist International. In a letter to Draper, Cannon described how the tide was finally turned in favor of the "Liquidators" after Cannon, Max Bedacht and Arne Swabeck were able to present their position directly to Leon Trotsky.[18] We publish here the famous document on "one sheet of paper—no more" where Cannon and his cothinkers summarized their position for the Russian leaders. Unfortunately, we have been unable to locate any other record of Cannon's 1922 interventions in the ECCI, American Commission or other bodies. We do publish here "In the Fifth Year of the Russian Revolution," the speech Cannon gave on his tour of the United States upon his return.

In Moscow Cannon served as American party representative on the Presidium of the ECCI, a post which put him in intimate touch with the day-to-day workings of the Communist International and its leaders. He also worked on the executive body of the Red International of Labor Unions. This experience was crucial, for in 1922 the International was still infused with the

---

who viewed Ruthenberg's release from prison as "a godsend." See Theodore Draper, Interview with James P. Cannon, 24 April 1956, Theodore Draper Research Files, Robert W. Woodruff Library, Emory University (hereafter cited as Draper Files), Series 3, No. 7.

17 Claude McKay, *A Long Way from Home* (New York: Arno Press and The New York Times, 1969), 178.

18 See Cannon, *First Ten Years*, 64-73.

revolutionary will and spirit that had animated its founding. The experience instilled in Cannon a deep and abiding internationalism, and a respect for Zinoviev, in particular, which was later to prove crucial in Cannon's evolution to Trotskyism.[19] The "Liquidators" succeeded in carrying the day and the International's salutary intervention prevented another pointless split in the American party. The trust Cannon developed toward the Comintern made him slow to realize later in the decade that things had fundamentally changed with the ascendancy of Zinoviev, Stalin and Bukharin in the Russian party.

The Degeneration of the Comintern

Even in 1922 the clouds were gathering for the storm that was to break in the Russian party in late 1923 and early 1924. Lenin was already sick and Cannon saw him only once, when Lenin spoke to the Fourth Congress. The Bolsheviks had won the bloody civil war, but the country was devastated, and large sections of the working class had virtually disappeared. The New Economic Policy (NEP) allowed for a necessary breathing space, but the revival of trade brought with it the newly wealthy "Nepmen," and this petty-bourgeois layer had its effect upon the old tsarist administrators who were still ensconced in many areas of government.

All this weighed heavily on the relatively small layer of Bolshevik cadre. Already at the 11th Party Congress in Moscow in March 1922 Lenin had asked the question "Who is running whom?" in the state administration. In December 1922 Lenin made a bloc with Trotsky to fight Stalin and dictated his famous "Testament," adding a postscript calling for the removal of Stalin from his post as General Secretary in January 1923. But Cannon would have learned little of this during his stay in Moscow. Lenin's Testament was kept hidden, and Trotsky compromised with Stalin at the 12th Party Congress in April 1923.

1923 was the year of transition in the Soviet Union. When the

19 Cannon pointed to the importance of Zinoviev's 1926-27 bloc with Trotsky in his *First Ten Years of American Communism* (p. 186): "It was Zinoviev's bloc with Trotsky and his expulsion, along with Trotsky, that first really shook me up and started the doubts and discontents which eventually led me to Trotskyism. I have always been outraged by the impudent pretensions of so many little people to deprecate Zinoviev, and I feel that he deserves justification before history."

German Communist Party let slip a promising revolutionary situation, putting an end to all hopes of immediate international extension of the proletarian revolution, this gave the increasingly conscious bureaucratic layer atop Soviet society an impetus to action. In the fall of 1923 the Russian party had its last open and full discussion, threatening the incipient bureaucratic consolidation. In the discussion leading up to the 13th Party Conference in January 1924 the loose "Trotskyist" opposition obtained 20 to 30 percent of the vote in the Moscow and Leningrad party organizations, but Stalin's apparatus rigged the elections to the conference and won its decisive victory there.

Trotsky had sounded the alarm about the German situation in the Comintern; the troika of Zinoviev, Kamenev and Stalin, fearing he might be successful, refused to let him go to Germany. In the aftermath of the botched uprising Trotsky demanded a full accounting of the role of both the German leadership and the Comintern in the defeat. But Zinoviev made a scapegoat of the German leadership and denied the decisive nature of the defeat. The discussion of the German question in the ECCI Presidium in January 1924 was dishonest, deformed by the troika's attempt to justify its rule and discredit Trotsky. So were the discussions at the Fifth Comintern Congress in the summer of 1924. In December 1924 Stalin advanced the program of "socialism in one country." Over the next decade and a half, while the cadres of Lenin's party were first purged and then physically destroyed in the course of bureaucratic consolidation, the Comintern was made into the Kremlin's instrument to betray other countries' revolutions. The full evolution of Trotsky's views on the degeneration of the Soviet Union and CI, and the developments foreseen in later works such as *The Revolution Betrayed* (1936), are only today being fully played out in the final cowardly collapse of Stalinism within and outside the ex-USSR.

After 1924 it was the expediencies of the fight in the Russian party which more often than not determined the political line of the Communist International. The terms of political debate shifted, and issues were no longer debated on the basis of intrinsic merit but increasingly according to what looked "correct" vis-à-vis the fight against Trotsky and his allies in the Russian party. The pseudo-leftism and glorification of the peasantry under Zinoviev in late 1924 and 1925 gave way in 1926-27 to the general rightism of Bukharin's reign after Zinoviev and Kamenev recoiled from their erstwhile ally Stalin and formed a bloc with Trotsky. All Workers Party documents written in 1924 and after, especially those written for consumption in Moscow and including those written by Cannon and his cothinkers, can only be fully understood in this context.

The Comintern's degeneration was not the only thing pushing against the revolutionary will of the Workers Party, however. For if the Russian Revolution waned, enthusiasm for a revolutionary policy on the part of leaders of the sections of the Communist International did as well. The appetite to repeat the experience of the Soviet Revolution diminished as the stabilization of the capitalist world grew in the aftermath of the German defeat of 1923. An expanding and self-confident imperialism weighed particularly heavily on the American party, as Cannon later explained:

> "Moscow domination" did indeed play an evil role in this unhappy time, but it did not operate in a vacuum. All the conditions of American life in the late Twenties, pressing in on the unprepared infant party, sapped the fighting faith of the party cadres, including the central leaders, and set them up for the Russian blows. The party became receptive to the ideas of Stalinism, which were saturated with conservatism, because the party cadres themselves were unconsciously yielding to their own conservative environment.[20]

John Pepper Comes to America

The Communist International began its degeneration just as the American party was finally making the turn toward the working class. The task of winning the majority of the active proletariat for communism confronted all the parties of the International, even those that were qualitatively larger than the American one, for in most of Europe the Social Democracy had retained the allegiance of substantial sectors of the working class. The Third Comintern Congress had been held in 1921 under the watchword "To the Masses!" and the tactic of the united front had been introduced shortly afterward; the Communist parties were to propose joint actions to the reformist parties of the Second International, exposing in practice their failure to act in the interest of the working class.

---

20 Cannon, *First Ten Years*, 25.

In the United States, however, the vast majority of the working class remained under the sway of the two main *bourgeois* political parties. During the first decade of the 20th century the American Socialist Party had won the support of a substantial working-class minority, but that support dissipated after 1912, the year Eugene V. Debs won almost one million votes in the U.S. presidential elections. Hillquit's purge of the SP left wing around Big Bill Haywood had driven many militants into the IWW, where they were unfortunately isolated from the mainstream craft unions.

In purging the SP left wing, Hillquit was merely following in the shadow of Samuel Gompers. The November 1911 confession to the bombing of the *Los Angeles Times* building by the structural iron workers' unfortunate McNamara brothers had severely embarrassed Gompers, who had publicly and repeatedly insisted on the brothers' innocence. The case had galvanized pro-labor sentiment in the country, resulting in the near election of a Socialist mayor in Los Angeles. In the aftermath Gompers took great pains to dissociate the AFL from anything approaching labor militancy and independent working-class political action. As a result, the step which Frederick Engels in 1886 had called "the first great step of importance...the constitution of the workers as an independent political party, no matter how, so long as it is a distinct workers' party," had not been taken on a national level.[21]

The newly founded Workers Party began agitation for a labor party in late 1922, attempting to form a united front with the preexisting "Farmer-Labor" movement. The major advocate of the new labor party orientation was one József Pogány, known as John Pepper, who had become a figure of the party leadership during Cannon's Moscow sojourn. Pepper, one of the leaders of the 1919 Hungarian Workers Republic disaster, was part of a Comintern delegation sent to unite the various Communist forces in the U.S. in the summer of 1922. The delegation was led by the Pole Henryk Walecki (known in the U.S. as Valetski), a post-WWI convert to Bolshevism whose later career in the Comintern caused

21 Frederick Engels, Letter to F.A. Sorge, 29 November 1886. Published in Karl Marx and Frederick Engels, *Letters to Americans 1848-1895* (New York: International Publishers, 1953), 163.

Trotsky to remark: "People of Walecki's calibre will never conquer anything. But they are perfectly capable of losing what has been conquered."[22] Walecki hesitated to take a strong side in the fight between the Goose Caucus and the "Liquidators." He did, however, manage to get all the forces claiming allegiance to the Comintern to finally unite in one party.

Pepper had evidently been assigned to the U.S. simply to work with the party's Hungarian-language Federation, but he passed himself off as some kind of permanent official Comintern "representative" and was elected to the party's Central Committee at the 1922 Bridgman convention. An unprincipled adventurer who was a frequent target of Trotsky in internal Comintern disputes, Pepper became a major destabilizing factor within the American party: "He was a phony, but by far the most brilliant phony I ever knew. He sparkled like an Arkansas diamond," wrote Cannon in later years.[23] Having arrived in the country knowing nothing of the language, Pepper wrote in English the party's first pamphlet for a labor party in October 1922, only three months later.[24]

The Workers Party was a small party by Comintern standards —it claimed only slightly more than 12,000 members by late 1922. Nonetheless, the growing predominance of American imperialism in the world made the U.S. party of strategic concern, and the party was given a representative on the International's Executive Committee. But while many Russian leaders had spent years in exile in Europe and felt they knew something about France, Germany, or even Britain, none of the major Comintern leaders had spent more than a few months in the United States. They did not presume to dictate where they did not know the situation; there was no one to give the American party the attention that, say, Trotsky gave the French Communist Party in the early years. People of the calibre of John Pepper were able to storm into the breach and they were the sort who also adapted well as the Comintern degenerated. Pepper plunged the party onto a political

---

22 Leon Trotsky, "Who Is Leading the Comintern Today?", *The Challenge of the Left Opposition (1928-29)* (New York: Pathfinder Press, 1981), 187.

23 Cannon, *First Ten Years*, 80.

24 The first edition of the pamphlet, *For a Labor Party*, was published as "a statement by the Workers Party." Subsequent editions in 1923 were signed by John Pepper.

course that was both organizationally sectarian and politically opportunist.

The Farmer-Labor Party

November 1919 had seen the formation of a reformist national "Labor Party" in Chicago. Max Hayes, president of the new party, was a confirmed anti-Communist—he had already quit the Socialist Party in Cleveland after the left wing led by C.E. Ruthenberg had taken control. But the driving force of this Labor Party was the head of the Chicago Federation of Labor, John Fitzpatrick. Fitzpatrick was an Irish nationalist with a reputation as a radical trade unionist opposed to AFL chief Samuel Gompers. He had been an opponent of U.S. entry into WWI, and he and his chief assistant, Edward Nockels, had given AFL backing to William Z. Foster when he organized the 1919 steel strike.

Fitzpatrick had run for mayor of Chicago on a local labor ticket and garnered 56,000 votes in the spring of 1919. His national Labor Party united the local labor parties that had sprung up in a number of U.S. cities, including Seattle in the aftermath of the general strike, and New York City. While the labor tops were in large part trying to undercut pro-Communist sentiment, the parties also reflected the real political ferment within the working class.

The Communist movement was too infected with ultraleftism to take much notice of the labor party movement in 1919. By the time the party woke up in late 1922 Fitzpatrick's Labor Party was no longer an unambiguously working-class organization. In July 1920, prior to its second convention, the Labor Party leadership had entered into negotiations with the bourgeois Committee of 48, inheritors of Theodore Roosevelt's "Bull Moose" Progressive Party tradition. The negotiations did not produce agreement, but the forces of the Committee of 48 nonetheless merged their convention with that of Fitzpatrick's party. They sought the nomination for the presidency of the United States of the Progressive war-horse "Battle Bob" La Follette, Governor of Wisconsin from 1900 to 1906 and then U.S. Senator from Wisconsin. La Follette was a longstanding Republican, but an anachronism in a party which had abandoned the short-lived "Progressive" tradition for Harding's "normalcy."

Though there were already far fewer trade unions represented at the Labor Party's 1920 convention (Gompers was moving to strangle it), Fitzpatrick was not yet ready to completely junk his party's "labor" identity by supporting so openly bourgeois a candidate as La Follette. Instead the party nominated Parley Parker Christensen of Utah, a lawyer and supporter of the Committee of 48 who had defended the IWW in the past. The party's class identity was further watered down when the convention changed the party's name to the Farmer-Labor Party, seeking the vote of rural populists.

At the time the chronic disaffection of the American family farmer had been captured by the Non-Partisan League, an organization that advocated cheap rural credit and state ownership of grain elevators. The League was the last gasp of a Western agrarian radical populism which went back to the Grange of the 1870s, a current which had always in the past been co-opted by bourgeois "Progressivism." The Non-Partisan League was strong in the Western states, particularly Minnesota and the Dakotas. Its strategy was to take over either of the local bourgeois parties (usually the Republican) through election primaries.

Farmer-Labor Party candidate Christensen polled a quarter of a million votes in the 1920 elections. He did particularly well in Non-Partisan League states like the Dakotas and Montana, as well as Washington where the memory of the Seattle general strike remained strong. The agrarian Western states remained the electoral bastions of the "Farmer-Labor" movement through the 1924 elections.[25]

Fitzpatrick's Farmer-Labor Party joined the Conference of Progressive Political Action (CPPA), an organization founded by the railroad union tops in February 1922, hoping to pressure it into founding a party modeled on the reformist British Labour Party. The CPPA was explicitly *not* a party, but an agency to support "Progressive" candidates of any party in state and local elections. When the CPPA voted to keep this "non-partisan" orientation at its conference in December 1922, Fitzpatrick split in disgust. The Workers Party, whose delegates the CPPA conference had refused to seat, went with him.

---

25 Nathan Fine, *Labor and Farmer Parties in the United States 1828-1928* (New York: Rand School of Social Science, 1928), 363-397.

Fitzpatrick then agreed to call a conference to found a new party and to work with the Workers Party in building the conference, which was called for 3 July 1923. The Workers Party eagerly and enthusiastically entered into the bloc with Fitzpatrick. The fact that Fitzpatrick's Farmer-Labor Party had already taken a giant step backward from its original stand for independent working-class political action did not concern the Workers Party leadership, which accepted the "Farmer-Labor" orientation and designation. In this they may have been adversely influenced by Zinoviev's confused formulations on possible "workers and peasants governments" at the Fourth Comintern Congress.

But the Workers Party leadership was also exhibiting a woeful and willful ignorance of recent American political history. In 1912 Socialist Party candidate Eugene V. Debs had run *against* Teddy Roosevelt's Progressive Party, pulling almost a million votes in the presidential elections. The Progressive current had sought, since that time, to co-opt working-class and petty-bourgeois socialist currents into the movement for a third bourgeois party. The Communist leadership was blind to this danger. The party did not attempt to draw a clear class line in its propaganda by insisting that the new party be unambiguously *working-class* in character. Nor did they insist that the new party make a complete break with bourgeois political currents, including La Follette's.

The Split with Fitzpatrick

The Workers Party did not combat Fitzpatrick politically but it flouted his organizational concerns at every turn. The story of the precipitous and ill-conceived break with the Fitzpatrick forces at the July 3 conference is well told by Theodore Draper.[26] Given the growing conservative mood in the country, a split was probably inevitable sooner rather than later. Fitzpatrick was under intense and immediate pressure from the AFL to split with his Communist allies. Most of the AFL unions refused to send delegates to the July 3 conference. At the first meeting of the united-front conference preparations committee, Fitzpatrick's line to the Workers Party was: "Let's get the record straight—we are willing to go along, but we think you communists should occupy

26 Draper II, 38-51.

a back seat in this affair."[27]

What was not inevitable was the weight of the forces on each side of the split. If the Workers Party had tried to polarize Fitzpatrick's party on a programmatic class basis, they might have come out of the venture with augmented forces. Instead, under the leadership of Pepper, they viewed the conference as a get-rich-quick scheme. They accepted the two-class "Farmer-Labor" designation, muddying the political waters, while organizing to take control of the conference completely away from Fitzpatrick. In the end the independent trade-union forces in attendance went with Fitzpatrick, leaving only the Workers Party and a few petty-bourgeois Non-Partisan League populists in the newly founded Federated Farmer-Labor Party (FFLP).

Fitzpatrick was furious; he became a bitter, vengeful enemy of the Workers Party, which now lost the protection the alliance had provided them in the national AFL. The effect was immediate on William Z. Foster's Trade Union Educational League (TUEL), which had become the party's trade-union arm. In August 1923 Morris Sigman, newly elected head of the International Ladies' Garment Workers' Union (ILGWU), declared TUEL membership incompatible with membership in his union. By the end of 1925 most major unions had done likewise. John L. Lewis revoked the charter of the Nova Scotia United Mine Workers (UMW), which had applied for membership in the Comintern's Red International of Labor Unions.[28] In November 1923 William F. Dunne, prominent party member and delegate from Butte, Montana, was refused his seat at the annual AFL convention in Portland. The UMW motivated Dunne's expulsion; only six delegates voted against it.

Cannon had almost no part in the deliberations of the Workers Party leadership leading up to the July 3 convention. Immediately after his return from Moscow in January 1923 he had been sent on national tour to speak about the situation in Soviet Russia, probably a conscious maneuver on the part of Pepper to get

27 Arne Swabeck, unpublished and untitled autobiography (photocopy of manuscript in Prometheus Research Library), Chapter VII, 7. Swabeck was one of the chief negotiators for the Chicago Workers Party.

28 David M. Schneider, *The Workers' (Communist) Party and American Trade Unions* (Baltimore: Johns Hopkins Press, 1928), 48-49.

him out of the way. But in May he passed through Chicago and got wind of how things were going when Arne Swabeck and other Chicago leaders complained to him. Cannon fired off a letter to Ruthenberg, which we publish here, complaining about the stupidity of attempts to pack the conference. Needless to say, his advice was ignored.

The Fight Against "Pepperism"

Cannon described how, in the aftermath of July 3, he made a pact with William Z. Foster to fight against Pepper's leadership of the party.[29] The Foster-Cannon faction won control of the Workers Party at its Third Convention in December 1923, moving the party headquarters from New York to the proletarian center of Chicago. They retained control of the Central Executive Committee (CEC or Central Committee) up until the party's Fourth Convention in August 1925. The Cannon faction was born as an integral part of the Foster-Cannon faction of this period. We publish here Cannon's opening shot in the campaign against Pepper, "The Workers Party Today—and Tomorrow," as well as the theses on the labor party submitted by Foster and Cannon to a CEC plenum in November 1923.

John Pepper did not stand alone against the Foster-Cannon forces. He had carefully built up a base of support in the party, based largely on the ex-ultraleftists of the Goose Caucus, and had found a willing pupil for his unique brand of opportunism/adventurism in Jay Lovestone. Moreover, party secretary C.E. Ruthenberg lent his significant credibility to the Pepper faction, as did Max Bedacht.

While the two factions may have initially differed on their evaluation of the split with Fitzpatrick, in the aftermath there were few differences on the orientation of the party. *Both* the Pepper-Ruthenberg and the Cannon-Foster factions compounded the party's initial error in failing to polarize the Fitzpatrick Farmer-Labor Party around a class axis. They proposed that the Workers Party enter into an ongoing political alliance with the "Progressive" forces.

What remained of the petty-bourgeois agrarian populists and

---

29 Cannon, *First Ten Years*, 84-94.

trade-union "Progressives" in the Federated Farmer-Labor Party were already lining up behind the proposed candidacy of Robert M. La Follette for the 1924 presidential elections. It was clear that the AFL, the Socialist Party and the pathetic remnants of the Non-Partisan League were all going to participate in the attempt to found a new "Progressive" party. In his inimitable fashion, Pepper saw in this a "La Follette revolution" which "will contain elements of the great French Revolution, and the Russian Kerensky Revolution. In its ideology it will have elements of Jeffersonianism, Danish cooperatives, Ku Klux Klan and Bolshevism. The Proletariat *as a class* will not play an independent role in this revolution."[30] So, Pepper argued, the Workers Party had to go along with La Follette and separate itself out at some unspecified later date. This strategy of ongoing political blocs with bourgeois forces would ultimately be perfected by the Communist International under Stalin as the "Popular Front" or "People's Front."

Foster and Cannon held no brief for Pepper's anti-Marxist theoretical schemes. But they feared the party's further isolation in the trade-union movement if they attempted to swim against the political tide for La Follette. Even before the December 1923 Workers Party convention, Foster and Cannon had come to essential political agreement with the Ruthenberg faction on this question. In November Foster and Cannon had withdrawn their theses, which condemned the formation of the FFLP, and voted instead for a new, conciliatory set of theses by Ruthenberg-Pepper. The new "November Theses" stressed the necessity of a continued bloc with the "Progressives" even as it hailed the formation of the FFLP.

Both major factions were thus in agreement as the Workers Party embarked on an opportunist course which led it close to open support for La Follette. Their policy of building a party with La Follette's supporters, without openly advocating—or strongly opposing—La Follette's candidacy, was known as the "third party alliance." Cannon's writings from the fall of 1923 through May 1924 fully support the "third party alliance," wrongly painting the La Follette "Progressives" as working-class centrists rather than as a bourgeois political current with supporters in the workers move-

---

30 Cited in Draper II, 83.

ment. In later years, Cannon noted the essential unity that existed at the top of the Workers Party on the La Follette question:

> The cold fact is that the party which had proclaimed itself at its inception as a revolutionary party of the working class, and had adopted a corresponding program, became, for a period in 1924, the advocate of a "third party" of capitalism, and offered to support, under certain conditions, the presidential candidacy of the petty-bourgeois demagogue La Follette....
>
> The bewildered party disgraced itself in this affair, and all the prominent leaders without exception, myself included, were in it up to our necks, with no excuse save that of ignorance and no reason except perhaps the foolhardy ambition to outwit ourselves. If I can force myself to return to this leap into political irrationality, even now—30 years later—it is only because a bad experience, honestly evaluated and accounted for, may serve a useful purpose in immunizing the movement against similar abnormalities in the future.
>
> Foster's role in this sorry business was the same as mine and that of all the other American leaders at the time. Pepper—interpreting what he took to be the Comintern line—formulated the policy; the rest of us went along. Considering the fact that Pepper had been defeated and put in the minority at the party convention, at the end of 1923, this says a lot for his resilience and continuing influence, but it doesn't say much for the rest of us.[31]

The only Workers Party leaders to oppose the "third party alliance" were Ludwig Lore and Moissaye Olgin, whose bases were, respectively, in the German Federation cadre and the Jewish workers in the garment unions. Both Olgin and Lore were well enough schooled in pre-Leninist Social Democratic Marxism to recognize that an ongoing alliance with the Republican La Follette was not the road to the "distinct workers party" that Engels had written of. Lore's New York group held the balance of power between the Foster-Cannon and Pepper-Ruthenberg factions at the December 1923 convention. The Cannon-Foster faction won the day only by getting the Lore group's support. This they managed to do *without* abandoning their faction's support for the "third party alliance." By common agreement, the question was referred to the Comintern.

The support of the Finnish Federation was also key to the

31 Unpublished notes by Cannon, written for Theodore Draper, ca. 1959, Cannon Papers, Box 7.

Cannon-Foster victory. The Finnish Federation had come over to the Workers Party from the Socialist Party only in 1921; it was a clannish group, based on agricultural and cultural cooperatives. The Finnish membership gave their allegiance to Soviet Russia but wanted little part in American politics. They were a pivotal group within the Workers Party because they comprised about 50 percent of the membership: 6,509 out of a total party membership of 12,394, according to figures prepared for the Workers Party's 1922 convention. In contrast, total membership of the English-speaking branches at the time was only 1,276.[32]

It was Cannon who carefully built up support for the Foster-Cannon faction, masterminding the coup against Pepper-Ruthenberg at the party's December 1923 convention. In winning Lore's and Olgin's support, Cannon was also able to finally bring about unity between the warring factions of Alexander Bittelman and Moissaye Olgin in the Jewish Federation. Cannon's immense skills as a factional politician were later described by Bittelman:

> As I became better acquainted with Jim, I began to notice and appreciate his skills in internal party politics....He seemed fully aware, not alone of the political differences between the two groups, but also of the individual and personal frictions and incompatibilities between, say, Salutsky and myself, or between Olgin and Shachno Epstein, by way of example.
>
> These skills in intra-party politics, the playing of which he obviously enjoyed very much, were unquestionably a source of strength to Jim himself as well as to our party, or parties—the Communist Party and the Workers Party. I remember a certain image of him that I acquired after a while. It was the image of a caretaker of a large experimental institution or laboratory, moving about the various machines, tools, gadgets, testing tubes, etc., making sure they operate properly, oiling, fixing, changing, improving and adjusting. That was Jim Cannon's main contribution in our party; and, for the particular phase in its development a very important contribution. His humor and wit played no small part in all of that.[33]

Cannon's skills as a politician were not universally appreciated. In a letter to the ECCI defending John Pepper, who had

---

32 "Report of the Central Executive Committee to the Second National Convention, New York City, Dec. 24-25-26, 1922," Draper Files, Box 22, Folder 19.

33 Alexander Bittelman, *Things I Have Learned*, Alexander Bittelman Collection, Manuscript 62, Tamiment Library, New York University, 358-359. Bittelman's

(continued)

been recalled to Moscow, Jay Lovestone complained in early 1924: "The seeds of the present factional struggle were sown when Comrade Cannon returned from the Fourth Congress of the Comintern."[34] But the aim of Foster-Cannon had been to put an end to "Pepperism," not to push aside Pepper's American backers. Ruthenberg remained secretary of the party even after the Foster-Cannon victory. Cannon became assistant secretary, while Foster was party chairman. In the period after the convention Cannon was at great pains to build a collective at the top of the party, as is evident from a letter he wrote in the spring of 1924 to a Lore supporter and leader of the Jewish Federation in New York:

> 2. *Jewish Affairs* The unification effected in the leading strata will gradually spread to the ranks if the leading comrades will work to that end consciously and patiently. The most important thing to strive for, of course, is *ideological unity on a broad basis....*
>
> What you do not see clearly yet is that the party is in the midst of a profound *crisis of growth.* It is going through a *transition period.* The *old* party, which was a loose collection of warring groups without a single authoritative, leading group, is working its way, with much travail, into a homogeneous body led by a support and confidence of the great majority of the party members. [emphasis in original][35]

Factional Gang War

Nonetheless the factional lineups hardened, leading to the factional gang warfare which plagued the party for most of the rest of the decade. Personal antipathies and social factors certainly played a role in the developing factional war, as Alexander Bittelman, himself a member of the Cannon-Foster inner circle, explained:

> Most of the Cannon-Foster circle were a rather rough-and-ready group of individuals. There was among them much camaraderie, plain spoken talk and few niceties in mutual relations. In group discussions they would use what they chose to call "trade union language," in which variations on "damn it" were of the more

---

rambling autobiographical manuscript stands in stark contrast to the usual dishonest accounts by ex-Stalinists. It was written in 1963 after he had been expelled from the Communist Party.

34 Jay Lovestone, Letter to the ECCI, Draper Files, Box 10, Folder 22.

35 Letter to Noah London, 29 April 1924, Cannon Papers, Box 1.

innocent expressions. And candor compels me also to say this: in our own circle four-letter exclamations were a dime a dozen and sometimes cheaper. Whereas Ruthenberg, in circumstances which tempt one to resort to some such exclamation, would merely say: "Goodness gracious." I can never forget the expression on the faces of some of my comrades in the Cannon-Foster circle on such occasions.[36]

Ruthenberg saw in the Foster-Cannon bloc a bunch of upstart trade-union opportunists who threatened communist orthodoxy. Max Bedacht, who was, like Ruthenberg, a proper and straight-laced German (he never got over the antipathy he felt because Cannon was chewing tobacco when they first met), thought likewise.[37] Though "C.E." Ruthenberg (no one ever called him by his first name) had an honorable history as an SP left-winger and was the faction leader with mass appeal among the Workers Party rank and file, he was an aloof individual who by all accounts left to others the details of the internal factional struggle. Pepper was Ruthenberg's factional operative until Pepper was recalled to Moscow in May 1924; after that Jay Lovestone played the role. Lovestone became the dominant force within the Ruthenberg faction, even before Ruthenberg's untimely death in March 1927.

Pepper was "the consummate type of the man who knows how to adapt himself, a political parasite."[38] Lovestone was a man molded in Pepper's image. If the search for a get-rich-quick road to mass influence through the Farmer-Labor movement was the political basis of the early Ruthenberg faction, Lovestone's corrupt and cynical organizational methods were the internal counterpart. His factional cohort, Benjamin Gitlow, wrote accurately (if bitterly), at least on this question:

He was unmarried, as far as anyone knew, but beyond that not a man in the Party knew anything more about him. But Lovestone knew everything about everybody in the Party. He was a walking Walter Winchell of the lives and scandals of the important Party members. To him many Party comrades would confide their innermost secrets, yet he confided nothing. The leaders of the Party

36 Bittelman, op. cit., 407.

37 Max Bedacht to Theodore Draper, 9 December 1954, Draper Files, Box 10, Folder 15.

38 Trotsky, "Who Is Leading the Comintern Today?", op. cit., 185.

> feared and hated him more than any other man because he knew too much. His personal file was the talk of the Party. Whenever he could get a leader of the Party down in black on white, it went into his file, and when one least expected it, the letter, foolishly written, the remark, damaging to one's character, was publicly used if the occasion demanded it.[39]

Antipathy to Lovestone characterizes all those who were on the other side of the factional divide in the Workers Party. Bittelman later wrote that "Lovestone's way was ruthless, unscrupulous and iron-fisted."[40] "In intimate circles," according to Cannon, "Foster remarked more than once that if Lovestone were not a Jew, he would be the most likely candidate for leadership of a fascist movement. That was a fairly common opinion."[41]

There was nothing that Lovestone wouldn't do in the fight to put his faction in control of the Workers Party. Cannon explained why Lovestone was the predominant figure in the Ruthenberg faction:

> Wolfe was a more serious student, he was better educated and more effective both as a speaker and a writer than Lovestone himself. And Bedacht, a product of the old pre-war German school, knew far more about formal Marxist doctrine and took it more seriously. But both of them lacked Lovestone's will, his ruthless and driving ambition, to say nothing of his truly diabolical passion for intrigue and his indefatigable energy in setting men against each other and fouling things up generally.[42]

"I don't know whether you can get a comprehension of what it meant to fight with a son-of-a-bitch like Lovestone," Cannon later told Draper.[43] But if Lovestone kept the factional pot boiling in the American party, it was the increasingly Stalinized Comintern that provided the heat.

Trotsky Fights the "Third Party Alliance"

It was Leon Trotsky in Moscow who insisted on pulling the Workers Party back from the opportunist course of the "third

---

39 Benjamin Gitlow, op. cit., 325.

40 Bittelman, op. cit., 474.

41 Cannon, *First Ten Years*, 156.

42 Letter by Cannon to Theodore Draper, 4 August 1954, Cannon Papers, Box 7.

43 Draper interview with Cannon, 24 April 1956, Draper Files, Series 3, No. 7.

party alliance" in 1924. Trotsky's views were already being censored by the triumvirate; he was not able to publish any articles attacking the policy of the American party in the English-language Comintern journals. But a collection of his Comintern writings between 1919 and 1923 was soon to be published in Russian. He took the opportunity to write an introduction on current Comintern problems. Attacking the attempt to downplay the significance of the 1923 German defeat, Trotsky pointed out that there had been an international turn toward stabilization of the capitalist world. He insisted that the Comintern's European sections must pay more attention to combatting reformist and bourgeois trends within the workers movement. He particularly lambasted the Workers Party leadership:

> For a young and weak Communist Party, lacking in revolutionary temper, to play the role of solicitor and gatherer of "progressive voters" for the Republican Senator La Follette is to head toward the political dissolution of the party in the petty bourgeoisie. After all, opportunism expresses itself not only in moods of gradualism but also in political impatience: it frequently seeks to reap where it has not sown, to realize successes which do not correspond to its influence. Underestimation of the basic task—the development and strengthening of the proletarian character of the party—here is the basic trait of opportunism!...The inspirers of this monstrous opportunism, who arc thoroughly imbued with skepticism concerning the American proletariat, are impatiently seeking to transfer the party's center of gravity into a farmer milieu—a milieu that is being shaken by the agrarian crisis. By underwriting, even if with reservations, the worst illusions of the petty bourgeoisie, it is not at all difficult to create for oneself the illusion of wielding influence over the petty bourgeoisie. To think that Bolshevism consists of this is to understand nothing about Bolshevism.[44]

Trotsky's preface was dated May 20. The same day, the Comintern issued its decision on the question. Zinoviev had finally conceded the main point to Trotsky: "An alliance with the La Follette movement would not serve the liberation of the petty-bourgeois masses from domination by capital." But Zinoviev could not adopt Trotsky's hard line against a two-class party without undercutting the triumvirate's campaign against Trotsky for "underestimating" the

---

44 Leon Trotsky, introduction to *The First Five Years of the Communist International*, vol. I (New York: Pioneer Publishers, 1945), 13-14.

peasantry. The decision accepted the need for a farmer-labor party in America:

> These two independent tasks—the task of building around the Communist Party a broad class labor party and of establishing a bond between the labor party and the poorest elements of farmers—have developed in the United States, thanks to the peculiarities of historical evolution, as one problem, namely, the building of a common party of workers and exploited farmers.... The American Communists must establish within the Farmer-Labor Party a strong consolidated labor wing including the agricultural wage workers.[45]

Subsequent Comintern decisions on the labor party question in the United States only compounded and amplified the confusion on the question of the "two-class party" exhibited in this declaration.

The Comintern decision accepted the Cannon-Foster contention that the split with Fitzpatrick's forces had been a disaster. (Even Israel Amter, a hard Ruthenberg-Pepper supporter, had been forced to admit in the Comintern's journal that "experience demonstrates that the conception of comrades Foster-Cannon was correct.")[46] But the ECCI was careful not to endorse either faction, and it criticized Cannon by name:

> If the group represented by comrades Ruthenberg and Pepper has made the mistake of not realizing sufficiently the dangers besetting the party on the long path leading to securing the co-operation of the petty-bourgeois masses, the comrades gathered around the other group, such as comrades Hathaway and Cannon, have made a number of declarations which show that in their efforts to secure influence on the petty bourgeoisie they failed to maintain the Communist position.[47]

In his capacity as secretary of the Farmer-Labor Federation of Minnesota, Hathaway had signed a statement against the imposition of communist "utopias," an act attacked by both Trotsky

45 "Workers Party Issues Declaration of Policy," *Daily Worker*, 20 August 1924. This Workers Party declaration incorporated most of the ECCI May 20 decision.

46 Israel Amter, "Neue Perspektiven der Einheitsfronttaktik in den Vereinigten Staaten" ("New Perspectives of the United Front Tactic in the United States"), 16 April 1924, in *Kommunistische Internationale* No. 34-35, 128. Translation is by the Prometheus Research Library.

47 "Workers Party Issues Declaration of Policy," op. cit. This is probably the condemnation that Cannon referred to in *History of American Trotskyism* (New York: Pioneer Publishers, 1944), 35-36.

and the ECCI decision as a particularly egregious example of opportunism. No specific declaration of Cannon's was mentioned, but the singling out of Cannon was no doubt due to Pepper's Comintern influence. In effect, the attack on Cannon served to deflect attention from the fact that *both* factions had "failed to maintain the Communist position." The public criticism had to have affected Cannon's standing in the party. Readers will note a marked shift toward Communist orthodoxy in Cannon's writings in the summer of 1924. While other party leaders viewed the Comintern's decision as only a temporary setback, Cannon sought to assimilate its full significance for communist strategy.

The 1924-25 Faction Fight

Cannon wasn't the only one who shifted gears in the summer of 1924. The entire Workers Party awkwardly and abruptly changed course after receiving the Comintern decision. La Follette issued a ringing denunciation of the Communists just at that time, making the party's sudden change in orientation a bit easier to explain to the radical public. The June 17 St. Paul convention of the Farmer-Labor movement did not nominate La Follette for president. In the end the Workers Party ran its own candidates in the elections: William Z. Foster for president and Benjamin Gitlow for vice president. They polled slightly more than 33,000 votes, a respectable showing considering that the party was able to get on the ballot in only a few states. La Follette's third party polled far fewer votes than expected—only 4.8 million. His supporters viewed the election results as a defeat. Republican candidate Calvin Coolidge, Harding's successor, won by a landslide.

The faction fight rekindled in the Workers Party almost as soon as the polls closed. The basic issue was the evaluation of the election results: Cannon and Foster insisted that the Farmer-Labor movement had been co-opted by La Follette and was now dead. Nothing was to be gained by continuing to raise the labor party slogan; the party should concentrate on united-front campaigns around concrete issues in the trade unions. Ruthenberg-Lovestone argued that the La Follette forces had won a great victory in the elections, that the party had to continue to orient to the movement which had supported him, and that agitation for a labor party should remain on the party's agenda.

Both sides could, of course, claim to stand on the muddled May 1924 Comintern decision. Cannon and Foster were, unwittingly, emphasizing Trotsky's thrust while Ruthenberg-Lovestone, taking advantage of the Comintern's acceptance of the two-class Farmer-Labor Party, were pushing for what was basically a reversal of the anti-La Follette decision. The fight consumed the party from December 1924 right through to the party's Fourth Convention in August 1925.

We publish here most of Cannon's polemics from this crucial fight in the Workers Party, both those he wrote in his own name and those he coauthored. As the fight progressed, the issues in dispute in the American party were further muddled by Zinoviev's anti-Trotsky campaign. But it is no less true that the anti-Trotsky campaign in the American party was muddled by the party's preexisting factional lineup.

The Fight Against Lore's "Two and a Half Internationalism"

Foster had succeeded in having Pepper recalled to Moscow in May 1924. But Pepper was all the more dangerous there, working in the Comintern apparatus as an agent for Ruthenberg-Lovestone. Trotsky's May 1924 essay was not available in English, and Cannon later told Draper that he was not aware of differences between Trotsky and Zinoviev on the American question. But John Pepper certainly was. Trotsky's victory on the central issue of La Follette's candidacy had been Pepper's defeat. Pepper recognized that Stalin's ascendancy meant that this defeat was reversible, and this fueled the American faction fight.

The only tendency in the Workers Party that opposed the "third party alliance" was that of Ludwig Lore. Moreover, in early 1924 Lore, writing in the party's German-language *Volkszeitung*, which he edited, had painted the victory of the Foster-Cannon faction as a victory for Trotsky's opposition. Lore had a great deal of personal sympathy for Trotsky, but he was no Trotskyist; the *Volkszeitung* also supported the expelled rightist German leader Paul Levi, and Lore's public complaints about the zigzags of Zinoviev had more in common with Levi than with Trotsky. The 1924 Comintern decision on the American question had directed the party leadership to wage a struggle against Lore's "Two and a Half Internationalist" tendency, even as it propounded Lore's position against the La Follette alliance.

In order to avoid losing Lore's support, Foster and Cannon had initially refused to take a position in favor of the Stalin-Zinoviev-Kamenev "Old Guard" in the Russian party when Pepper tried to force the issue in the Central Executive Committee in March 1924. But Foster, who went to Moscow in May to put forward the case for the "third party alliance," quickly realized that opposition to Trotsky was the *sine qua non* for favor in the eyes of the Zinoviev leadership. After Foster's return he and Cannon began voting for the anti-Trotsky resolutions proposed by Ruthenberg and Lovestone, but their slowness to endorse the "Old Guard" was a key weapon in Pepper's arsenal. After Pepper's advantage became clear, both Foster and Cannon moved quickly to separate themselves from Lore and remedy the situation. Nonetheless, Lovestone took to referring to the Foster-Cannon faction as the "Foster-Lore Group."

Lore's real crime, as far as Zinoviev was concerned, was his support to Trotsky. But there was truth to the charge that Lore remained a social democrat who, like Kautsky with his short-lived "Two and a Half International," was trying to straddle the fence between reformism and communism. Lore's group of party supporters were definitely a rightist bunch, centered on a layer of trade-union officials like needle trades leader Charles Zimmerman. In June 1924 Cannon had labeled Zimmerman "a dangerous opportunist who has to be watched"; Zimmerman's later trajectory would indicate that this was not an exaggeration on Cannon's part.[48] The needle trades leaders soon broke with Lore, and they retained membership in the Workers Party even after Lore was expelled in 1925. Their opportunism remained a frequent target of Cannon.

As is apparent from the material we publish here, Cannon energetically took up the ideological struggle against Lore's "Two and a Half Internationalism." He also pushed Zinoviev's "Bolshevization" campaign. But even as he promoted these cam-

---

48 Zimmerman was part of Lovestone's Right Opposition in 1929 and ended his days as a simple trade-union bureaucrat. Zimmerman quotes Cannon in a letter to Foster, 16 June 1924, Charles S. Zimmerman Records, Box 45, Folder 6, ILGWU Archives, New York State School of Industrial and Labor Relations, Cornell University.

paigns, which were code words for anti-Trotskyism in the Comintern as a whole, he remained essentially a passive supporter of the broader anti-Trotsky campaign. He was able to take this position in part because Loreism was a real right-wing tendency within the American party.

Though they turned against their erstwhile supporters in the Lore faction, the Cannon-Foster faction hardly had the profile of a left wing. They correctly insisted on the necessity of a *proletarian* majority in any farmer-labor movement, but they did not criticize the party's failure to insist on the working-class character of the party formed at the July 3 Chicago convention. Their documents reveal a tendency to adapt to the backward prejudices common in the AFL unions. There is little emphasis, for example, on the need for the party to aggressively wage a fight against the racist Jim Crow restrictions in most union constitutions. And they said little about American imperialism's increasingly restrictive and racist immigration policies.

The decision against support to La Follette had been part of a general left turn by the Comintern in 1924-25. Afraid that Trotsky might pick up support, Zinoviev maneuvered to outflank him on the left. The years 1924-25 were later described by Trotsky as "the years of Left mistakes and putschist experiments."[49] Under the general rubric of "Bolshevization," most of the established sectional leaderships were replaced by figures loyal to Zinoviev and hence more willing to spout the leftist rhetoric he demanded. The ascendancy of Ruth Fischer and Arkadi Maslow in Germany was symptomatic of this trend. Pepper knew how to couch the Ruthenberg faction's orientation in terms of the pseudo-leftism that was the political currency of the Comintern under Zinoviev. It was this, combined with Pepper's skillful playing of the Trotsky card, that ensured the defeat of the Foster-Cannon faction at the Comintern's Fifth Plenum in March-April 1925.

The 1925 Decision on the Labor Party Slogan

The dispute on the labor party slogan was fought out in the American Commission which convened in Moscow around the

---

49 Leon Trotsky, *The Third International After Lenin* (New York: Pioneer Publishers, 1936), 118.

ECCI Fifth Plenum in March-April 1925. We publish here transcripts of some of Cannon's remarks to American Commission sessions, as well as the Foster-Cannon article "Controversial Questions in the Workers Party of America," which was published in the Russian- and German-language *Communist International* around the time of the plenum. Foster and Cannon were roundly defeated in the commission.

The plenum declared, "it must be recognized that in the elections La Follette gained an important victory," and decreed the urgent necessity of continued agitation around the labor party issue. The ECCI did not correct the party's former position in favor of a two-class farmer-labor party even though it reversed it: "Our slogan itself should now be revised insofar that we no longer agitate for a 'farmer-labor party' but only for a 'labor party,' since in the changed conditions the premises for the formation of a joint party of workers and small farmers are lacking."[50] Political clarity was beside the point to the ECCI.

As a propaganda slogan, the demand for a labor party could have had a place in the communist arsenal at this time. But to insist on the need for an agitational campaign around the slogan was tantamount to insisting on a continued orientation to the bourgeois "Progressive" forces. An unsigned article in the March English-language *Communist International* had argued this explicitly: "The La Follette movement is an inevitable stage in the process of the revolutionization of the American proletariat....The chief political task of the American Communists now consists in breaking the proletarian and poor farmer elements, away from the La Follette movement...."[51] The La Follette third party movement was dead, however, so the opportunist orientation demanded by the Comintern remained a dead letter in the next period, except in a few states like Minnesota, where small "Farmer-Labor" remnants survived.

The Comintern leadership clearly favored the Ruthenberg-Lovestone faction. But the Cannon-Foster faction still had the

---

50 "Decision of the Communist International on the American Question," *Daily Worker*, 19 May 1925.

51 "The Future of the La Follette Movement," *Communist International* No. 9, March 1925.

votes in the American party: they won a majority of delegates in the elections to the party's Fourth Convention, held in August 1925. Both Cannon and Draper describe how a cable from Moscow intervened to change the verdict of the American party.[52] The Comintern cable declared that the "Ruthenberg Group is more loyal to decisions of the Communist International and stands closer to its views," demanded that the hated Lovestone remain a member of the Central Executive Committee and insisted that the Ruthenberg faction get at least 40 percent of the seats on the incoming CEC.

The Cannon-Foster Split

Cannon and Foster split over how to respond to the cable. Cannon wanted to comply with the sense of the cable and give each faction 50 percent of the incoming CEC. Foster wanted to flout the Comintern and wash his hands of the new CEC by giving the Ruthenberg group an absolute majority. Cannon carried a bare majority of the Foster-Cannon caucus and the faction followed his proposal. But the Comintern representative to the new CEC, S.I. Gusev—a Russian who had followed Stalin's line in the Russian party since the Civil War days—declared his intention to vote with the Ruthenberg faction, giving them the majority in any case. In the aftermath, the following joke reportedly became popular among the more cynical party members: "Why is the Communist Party of the United States like the Brooklyn Bridge? Because it is suspended on cables."[53]

But Cannon was not at all cynical where the Communist International was concerned. He was a loyal "Cominternist" and, as he later told Draper, he had "been convinced in our discussions with the Russians, that we had made a political error in our estimate of the prospects of a labor party in the United States, and I was most concerned that we make a real correction. With inadequate theoretical schooling I was already groping my way to the conception, which later became a governing principle, that a correct political line is more important than any organizational

---

52 Draper II, 127-152; Cannon, *First Ten Years*, 131-138.

53 Gitlow, op. cit., 187.

question, including the question of party control."[54]

For Foster, however, the question of party control remained paramount. The split in the Cannon-Foster faction hardened and became permanent because Foster and Bittelman insisted on appealing the Comintern cable after the convention and sought to mobilize the base of the Cannon-Foster faction against the Comintern. Such an opposition was necessarily based on the rightism of the Finns and of Lore's supporters (who remained in the party even though Lore himself was expelled by the convention). Cannon had already written a polemic against the anti-internationalism of the leader of the Finnish Federation, Henry Askeli. In later years Shachtman described the thinking of Cannon and his supporters when they broke with Foster:

> The kind of support we would necessarily rally, the kind of support that would come to us whether we rallied it deliberately or not, would be of a kind that first would mobilize all of the right-wing elements of the party against the Comintern, and in mobilizing them behind the appeal, we would be placed increasingly at the mercy of these right-wing elements. They would constitute more and more of our troops. And, willy-nilly...a split would ensue. Why willy-nilly? Because nobody really felt the Comintern would reverse its decision.[55]

The break between Cannon and Foster became final when Cannon spoke out against the Foster-Bittelman appeal in a speech, which we publish here, to the Young Workers League conference in October. Foster retained the support of the Finns and the core of the TUEL apparatus—his group had the bigger rank-and-file base. But the Cannon-Foster cadre had split down the middle. Cannon won the youth, including Shachtman, the party leaderships in Detroit and Minnesota, as well as Abern, Swabeck, Gomez and Cannon's best friend and collaborator, William F. Dunne.

Cannon and his supporters blocked with the Ruthenberg faction in the period after his split with Foster, trying to forge a collective pro-Comintern leadership. Their joint resolution "Unify the Party!" is included here. But even as Cannon broke with Foster, he and Dunne were compelled to register a protest in the Political Committee against Ruthenberg's attempts to undercut

---

54 Cannon, *First Ten Years*, 132-133.

55 Shachtman, op. cit., 95-96.

Foster's Trade Union Department. Their bloc with Ruthenberg-Lovestone did not last very long.

The International Labor Defense

The International Labor Defense (ILD) was the center of Cannon's public political work from August 1925 until his expulsion in 1928. In a letter to Draper, Cannon told the story of how the ILD was conceived in Moscow in 1925 with ex-Wobbly "Big Bill" Haywood. Rose Karsner, at the time head of the International Red Aid campaign in the United States, was also in Moscow and participated in the discussions. Cannon detailed the proud history of the ILD's non-sectarian defense of class-war prisoners.[56] Such defense had been a theme of Workers Party propaganda since the party's inception, but the ILD gave it flesh and blood.

It appears that only the timing of the ILD's founding allowed it to survive the vicissitudes of the internal party struggle. Just before the Fourth Convention Cannon was able to force his plans for the establishment of the ILD through the Executive Council (Political Committee) over Ruthenberg's objections, as indicated in the 26 June 1925 minutes, excerpts of which we publish here. If Ruthenberg had prevailed and Max Bedacht had been appointed ILD secretary, the entire project would probably have been scuttled since Cannon's personal ties with the IWW and ex-Wobbly milieu were key: the Wobblies demanded that Cannon be secretary of the organization as a condition for cooperation.[57]

By late August Ruthenberg-Lovestone had a majority on the Executive Council, but the ILD was protected (as Foster's TUEL was not) by Cannon's initial alliance with Ruthenberg. Cannon had time to build it into the party's largest and most successful united-front organization. Its monthly magazine, the *Labor Defender*—edited by Max Shachtman and managed by Martin Abern—had a circulation of 22,000 by July 1928. Cannon wrote frequently on ILD matters in both *Labor Defender* and the party's *Daily Worker.*

In 1958 Cannon published a selection of his popular, agi-

56 Cannon, *First Ten Years*, 160-165.

57 James P. Cannon, unpublished interview with Harry Ring, 15 August 1973.

tational writings over the years, *Notebook of an Agitator*.[58] He included most of his ILD material and all of his major articles on the campaign against the execution of the anarchists Nicola Sacco and Bartolomeo Vanzetti in 1927. *Notebook of an Agitator* also includes some other popular pieces Cannon wrote while in the Workers Party, including his tribute to C.E. Ruthenberg. This book is still readily available; we therefore publish none of these articles here. We include here only one ILD article which was not in Cannon's selection: "The Red Month of November" (November 1927).

The American Negro Labor Congress

The International Labor Defense was not the only united-front organization formed by the Workers Party in 1925, though it was the most successful one. In October the American Negro Labor Congress (ANLC) was founded at a conference in Chicago attended by some 40 black Communists and close sympathizers. But despite the extensive propaganda the party devoted to the need to fight for black rights and against Ku Klux Klan and lynch mob terror, the ANLC remained a paper organization for most of the decade.

The founding of the ANLC represented a radical departure from the traditional attitude of the American left wing toward the oppression of the black population. The Socialist Party had included open racists; its best element was represented by Eugene V. Debs' famous statement that the Socialist Party had "nothing special to offer the Negro."

The syndicalists were significantly better than the SP on this question; they actively fought Jim Crow in the labor movement. In its first decade the IWW made significant headway in organizing an integrated timber workers union in the South. Cannon's account of the 1912 IWW convention takes special note of the fact that two black delegates attended the convention, including one from the Brotherhood of Timber Workers, calling the integrated meeting "proof that we have surmounted all barriers of race and color."[59] The Chicago Stockyards Labor Council, organized by

---

58 James P. Cannon, *Notebook of an Agitator* (New York: Pioneer Publishers, 1958).

59 James P. Cannon, "Seventh Convention, Harmonious Gathering of Young Men Fighting for Industrial Freedom," *Solidarity*, 28 September 1912.

Foster and Johnstone in 1919, made some headway in organizing black workers as well as white. On the eve of the July 1919 Chicago race riot the Stockyards Labor Council tried to organize an integrated packinghouse workers' march through the black neighborhoods of Chicago's South Side. When the packing bosses succeeded in having the march banned (on the pretext that it might foment racial tension!), Foster and Johnstone organized two separate marches—one black and one white—both of which marched the planned route, to the cheers of the black community which lined the parade route.[60]

But even the best of the syndicalists did not hark back to Marx and Engels' writings on the revolutionary nature of the American Civil War. No one in the American left wing saw the fight against the oppression of black people as a motor force for the American socialist revolution.

The Workers Party in the 1920s broke with this tradition of lack of attention to the unique racist structure of American capitalism. The Russian Bolsheviks had developed their party in intense opposition to the Great Russian chauvinism of the tsar's empire, and they understood that the demands of oppressed minorities could be a powerful revolutionary force. Cannon recalled in his 1961 essay, "The Russian Revolution and the American Negro Movement," how important the Russian influence was in reorienting the American Communist movement:

> The best of the earlier socialists were represented by Debs, who was friendly to all races and purely free from prejudice. But the limitedness of the great agitator's view on this far from simple problem was expressed in his statement: "We have nothing special to offer the Negro, and we cannot make separate appeals to all the races. The Socialist Party is the party of the whole working class, regardless of color—the whole working class of the whole world" (Ray Ginger, *The Bending Cross*). That was considered a very advanced position at the time, but it made no provision for active support of the Negro's special claim for a little equality here and now, or in the foreseeable future, on the road to socialism.
>
> And even Debs, with his general formula that missed the main point—the burning issue of ever-present discrimination against the Negroes every way they turned—was far superior in this regard, as in all

60 James R. Barrett, *Work and Community in the Jungle, Chicago's Packinghouse Workers 1894-1922* (Urbana: University of Illinois Press, 1987), 205-206.

> others, to Victor Berger, who was an outspoken white supremacist....
>
> The difference—and it was a *profound* difference—between the Communist Party of the Twenties and its socialist and radical ancestors, was signified by its break with this tradition. The American communists in the early days, under the influence and pressure of the Russians in the Comintern, were slowly and painfully learning to change their *attitude*; to assimilate the new theory of the Negro question as a *special* question of doubly-exploited second-class citizens, requiring a program of special demands as part of the over-all program—and to start doing something about it.
>
> The true importance of this profound change, in all its dimensions, cannot be adequately measured by the results in the Twenties. The first ten years have to be considered chiefly as the preliminary period of reconsideration and discussion, and change of attitude and policy on the Negro question—in preparation for future activity in this field.
>
> The effects of this change and preparation in the Twenties, brought about by the Russian intervention, were to manifest themselves explosively in the next decade. The ripely favorable conditions for racial agitation and organization among the Negroes, produced by the great depression, found the Communist Party ready to move in this field as no other radical organization in this country had ever done before.[61]

Many of the initial black cadre of the American Communist movement came from the milieu around A. Philip Randolph's journal, the *Messenger*, and his Harlem Socialist political club. Randolph sided with the reformist SP majority in the 1919 split; those blacks who saw the Russian Revolution as the way forward gravitated to the African Blood Brotherhood (ABB), founded late in 1919 by Cyril Briggs. The ABB's initial aim of "African liberation and redemption" was later expanded to that of the "immediate protection and ultimate liberation of Negroes everywhere" and it became a recruiting ground for the Communist movement by the summer of 1921. Claude McKay, who had worked with the British Communists in London from 1919 to 1921, played a role bringing the Harlem ABBers into the orbit of the American Communists.

The Brotherhood sent a fraternal delegation to the founding convention of the Workers Party in December 1921 and many

61 Cannon, *First Ten Years*, 230-233.

ABB members joined the new legal party. While the ABB retained a separate existence and identity through 1924, it was closely associated with the Workers Party; its remaining local organizations were advised to join the Workers Party in 1925. In New York the ABB was based mostly among political activists of West Indian extraction, while in Chicago it had a significant base among the Southern-born skilled building tradesmen organized in the American Consolidated Trades Council (ACTC). Edward Doty, a plumber by trade, was the Chicago ABB post commander and also the founder of the ACTC.[62]

In discussions on the question of the oppression of the American black population in the early congresses of the Communist International (such discussions took place at the Second, Fourth and Fifth World Congresses in 1920, 1922 and 1925 respectively), the question was viewed primarily as an extension of the colonial question. The early Comintern laid great emphasis on the leadership role American blacks were destined to play in the liberation of the African colonies. Concomitantly the American party tried to influence and recruit from Marcus Garvey's back-to-Africa Universal Negro Improvement Association; in the mid-1920s the party supported the anti-Garvey opposition as the UNIA fell apart following Garvey's 1922 arrest.[63] Both the party and the ABB participated in an ill-fated "All-Race Negro Congress" in Chicago in February 1924, but the majority of black middle-class delegates were resolutely opposed to a pro-labor, communist perspective.[64]

With the formation of the American Negro Labor Congress in 1925, the party's orientation shifted to organizing American blacks as part of the working class, taking into account the beginning of the mass migration which was to transform the predominantly Southern agrarian black population of sharecroppers and tenant farmers into a key component of the urban American

62 Philip S. Foner and James S. Allen, eds., *American Communism and Black Americans: A Documentary History, 1919-1929* (Philadelphia: Temple University Press, 1987), 16-27; Mark Naison, *Communists in Harlem During the Depression* (Urbana: University of Illinois Press, 1983), 5-11; Harry Haywood, *Black Bolshevik: Autobiography of an Afro-American Communist* (Chicago: Liberator Press, 1978), 121-131.

63 Naison, op. cit., 9; Foner and Allen, op. cit., 76-86; Political Committee Minutes, 21 September 1926.

64 Foner and Allen, op. cit., 38, 53-63.

proletariat. But the ANLC still reported to the Comintern's Eastern Department, and the black Americans who went to Moscow to study in the 1920s were sent to the University of the Toilers of the East, an institution established expressly for educating Communists from the colonial world.[65]

Perhaps because the fight for black liberation was not seen as strategic for the *American* socialist revolution, the party's line on the fight against racial discrimination, and the work of the ANLC after 1925, were not issues in the factional struggles that racked the Workers Party in the 1920s. There is little on the question in the Cannon factional writings we publish in this book.

It is notable, however, that at least according to Harry Haywood, most of the party's black members supported the Ruthenberg-Lovestone faction. This factional lineup was not to change until the Comintern's Sixth Congress in 1928 when Haywood, then a student at the Lenin School in Moscow, joined the Foster-Cannon factional bloc. Haywood was then the only black member of the American party supporting Stalin's position that blacks in the Southern United States "black belt" formed a nation whose right to self-determination the party should champion. The Foster-Cannon opposition, with Foster and Dunne in the lead, jumped on the self-determination bandwagon early, in order to use this as a club against the Lovestone faction. Most of the black American party members initially resisted the self-determination slogan, arguing that the party should continue to champion full social and political equality for blacks—Haywood's brother, Otto Hall, who was also a student in Moscow, accused Haywood of seeking to provide grist for Foster's factional mill.[66]

While support for the post-1925 CEC majority does not appear to have netted the ANLC leaders access to greater party resources or attention—the minutes of the Political Committee meeting of 7 December 1927 reveal that Lovestone simply dismissed an ANLC request that the party fund two full-time ANLC organizers

65 The ANLC's founding documents are reprinted in Foner and Allen, op. cit., 109-129. The ANLC was to report to the Eastern Department, according to the 8 April 1926 minutes of the Workers Party Political Committee. See Haywood, op. cit., 148-175, for an account of his studies at the University of the Toilers of the East.

66 Haywood, op. cit., 140-147, 245-280.

—this was nonetheless a real element in the internal dynamics of the party. Haywood reports that Robert Minor's attention to the black members, as well as his writings on the question of black oppression, played a role in winning the black members to the Ruthenberg-Lovestone group. Haywood also remembers that the Ruthenberg-Lovestone faction was seen as pro-Comintern, while the Foster-Cannon supporters were seen as "opportunist, narrow-minded trade unionists lacking in Marxist theory."[67]

It was the Foster-Cannon faction which was most closely identified with the party's exclusive emphasis on "boring from within" the reactionary AFL unions. Most of these unions actively *refused* to admit the blacks who had streamed into the Northern factory cities during WWI. The AFL orientation of the Workers Party in the 1920s meant, in practice, that the party *could not* organize black workers. While Cannon was never personally committed to the exclusively AFL trade-union policy, Cannon's lieutenant Bill Dunne leaned more in Foster's direction. And Dunne was the Cannon-Foster faction "expert" on what was then called the "Negro question."[68]

Dunne was the Workers Party's representative to the Fifth Congress of the Comintern in 1924, and to the Third Congress of the Red International of Labor Unions (Profintern) which followed. When the head of the Profintern, A. Lozovsky, suggested at the congress that the American party should organize separate unions of black workers where the AFL unions refused to organize blacks, Dunne adamantly opposed this perspective. Pointing to the racial integration in the UMW, where the party actually had a significant base, Dunne basically alibied the racist policies of the AFL bureaucracy. His words speak volumes about the limitations of the American party at the time:

> The fact that black workers are unorganized is not due to racial antagonism, but is because the American workers are unorganized in general. In those industries where Negroes work, they are admitted

67 Haywood, op. cit., 141.

68 See William F. Dunne, "Negroes in American Industries," *Workers Monthly*, March-April 1925; "Negroes as an Oppressed People," *Workers Monthly*, July 1925; "Our Party and the Negro Masses," *Daily Worker*, 13 August 1925; "The NAACP Takes a Step Backward," *Workers Monthly*, August 1926. Three of these are reprinted in Foner and Allen, op. cit.

> into the unions as members with equal rights; this is the case in the miners union, the largest organization in the American Federation of Labor; this is the case in the building trades. There are unions which encompass only skilled workers and they, of course, do not admit Negroes. But when Negroes appear in these industries in significant number, and compete with the members of the unions, then they will be accepted as members with equal rights. If we are opposed to dual unions in general, then we cannot be in favor of parallel Negro unions. Certainly racial antagonism exists, but the best way to fight it will be by accepting white and black workers into one organization, not by mobilizing the Negroes on one side of the barrier and whites on the other.[69]

Dunne's speech contrasts sharply with the urgency Trotsky conveyed on the question of fighting race prejudice in the American labor movement, in a letter to Claude McKay published the year before Dunne spoke:

> In North America the matter is further complicated by the abominable obtuseness and caste presumption of the privileged upper strata of the working class itself, who refuse to recognize fellow workers and fighting comrades in the Negroes. Gompers' policy is founded on the exploitation of such despicable prejudices, and is at the present time the most effective guarantee for the successful subjugation of white and colored workers alike. The fight against this policy must be taken up from different sides, and conducted on various lines. One of the most important branches of this conflict consists in enlightening the proletarian consciousness by awakening the feeling of human dignity, and of revolutionary protest, among the Negro slaves of American capitalism.[70]

The Communist International eventually prevailed over the leadership of the American party, and the resolution adopted by the Workers Party's Fourth Convention in August 1925 included the proviso: "Where Negroes are not permitted to join the existing 'white' trade unions, it is the duty of the Communists to take the initiative in the formation of organizations of Negro workers, declaring in principle against dual unionism and

---

69 *Protokoll über den Dritten Kongress der Roten Gewerkschafts-Internationale, abgehalten in Moskau vom 8. bis 21. Juli 1924* (Berlin: Verlag der Roten Gewerkschafts-Internationale Auslieferungsstelle, n.d.), 99-100. Translation by the Prometheus Research Library.

70 Leon Trotsky, "A Letter to Comrade McKay," first published in *International Press Correspondence*, 13 March 1923, and reprinted in *The First Five Years of the Communist International*, Vol. II (New York: Pioneer Publishers, 1953), 355-356.

against racial separation, and declaring as a primary purpose the struggle for admission into the existing unions, but functioning as full-fledged Negro unions during the struggle."[71]

This policy remained a dead letter, however, so long as Foster's exclusive emphasis on the AFL dominated the party's trade-union work. Taking note of A. Philip Randolph's success in organizing the Pullman Porters, Dunne proposed to the Political Committee on 21 September 1926 that the ANLC take the initiative in calling a national conference on organizing black workers. But nothing appears to have come of this initiative. It was only when the party finally broke out of the AFL straitjacket and put the struggle for black rights at the center of the struggle for the American revolution (the discussions at the Comintern's Sixth Congress in 1928 at least accomplished this task, though they also resulted in the adoption of Stalin's ridiculous theory, most often ignored in practice, that blacks in the Southern "black belt" constituted a nation) the party was able to make significant gains among the black population.[72] The groundwork for the gains made by the party during the early 1930s was painstakingly laid in the discussions and accretion of black cadre during the 1920s.

The TUEL and the Sixth Plenum of the ECCI

Cannon was in Moscow for the ECCI's Sixth Plenum in February 1926, but he seems to have taken no part in the proceedings. The fight against the joint Trotsky-Zinoviev-Kamenev opposition was already in the air. Bukharin was beginning to eclipse Zinoviev in the Comintern, though he did not take over as secretary until the Eighth Plenum in November of 1927. Ultraleftism was now seen as the "main danger" in the Comintern parties; Fischer-Maslow had already been deposed as German party leaders. The turn to the right might have been expected to benefit Foster, but

71 "The American Negro and the Proletarian Revolution," in *The Fourth National Convention of the Workers (Communist) Party of America* (Chicago: Daily Worker Publishing Co., n.d.), 117.

72 See Dan T. Carter, *Scottsboro, A Tragedy of the American South* (Baton Rouge: Louisiana State University Press, 1969), Robin D.G. Kelley, *Hammer and Hoe, Alabama Communists During the Great Depression* (Chapel Hill: University of North Carolina Press, 1990), and Naison, op. cit., for accounts of the Communist Party's work during the 1930s.

Bukharin was a personal friend of Lovestone; under his leadership the Comintern would continue to favor the Ruthenberg-Lovestone faction.

Foster and Bittelman had gone to Moscow to appeal the Comintern cable in the fall of 1925. They met personally with a sympathetic Stalin, who was apparently already looking to keep the Foster group in reserve for any future moves against Bukharin.[73] While Foster and Bittelman were not successful in overturning the new Ruthenberg majority, they did succeed in getting some Comintern protection against the worst of Ruthenberg-Lovestone's factional excesses. This was largely because of the intervention of RILU head A. Lozovsky. Cannon later explained to Draper:

> Lozovsky supported Foster, was hostile to the Ruthenberg faction and vigorously opposed all the attempts of the Ruthenberg leadership to cut down Foster's latitude in trade union work. But at this time, as I recall it, the issues on which Lozovsky's interventions were based were not differences of party policy in the trade union movement but the work itself. He knew that Foster was serious and thoroughgoing in his approach to trade union work, and he thought the Ruthenbergites merely dabbled with it. In that he was dead right.
>
> But even here it must be assumed that Lozovsky's interventions for the protection of the Foster group were not independent operations on his part. The way things worked in the relations of the Profintern and the ECCI, it is quite inconceivable that Lozovsky acted without the knowledge or approval of the leaders of the Russian CP. Indeed, his support of Foster *in trade union work*, which was the field to which he limited his intervention, seems in retrospect to coincide with the consistent policy of the Russians at that time. This policy was to give the edge to the Ruthenbergites politically but to emphasize Foster's priority in trade union affairs and to push back the Ruthenbergian invasions of the field. [emphasis in original][74]

The persecution by the AFL leaders had driven the TUEL underground in most unions; party members had been forced to deny TUEL affiliation or face expulsion. After he gained control of the party Ruthenberg had sought to destroy the TUEL, and Foster's base of party support along with it. Benjamin Gitlow was pushed as the new "trade-union" expert, and a plan was ex-

---

73 See Alexander Bittelman, op. cit., 440, for a description of the meeting with Stalin.

74 Letter by Cannon to Theodore Draper, 19 July 1955, Cannon Papers, Box 7.

pounded to "convert" the TUEL into a broad "left bloc" organization through a new national organizing committee and national conference.

Cannon supported the move to broaden the TUEL, as is evident from his remarks at a Moscow discussion on the American question (the only record found of his trip to Moscow) which we publish here. In late 1925 Cannon and Bill Dunne, who was the Cannon faction's trade-union operative, had generalized their break with Foster into a critique of the party's trade-union work, arguing in fact for the complete liquidation of the TUEL:

> Conceived as the progressive bloc, the TUEL consists now almost wholly of Communist fractions. The existence of such a bloc between us and the broad progressive movement is a source of endless confusion, and the TUEL in its present status serves to prevent rather than encourage the building of a national oppositional bloc in the American trade union movement.
>
> As already pointed out, our party's trade union work achieved its best results when the TUEL was in fact a left bloc movement. But the TUEL is now so identified with the party that its usefulness as a left bloc organization has been destroyed completely.[75]

The move to liquidate the TUEL embodied an inherent contradiction. On the one hand, the move away from Foster's exclusive emphasis on "boring from within" the AFL was a step forward. It was under the banner of a non-AFL united-front organizing committee that the Workers Party led the great Passaic textile strike in early 1926, which began while Cannon was in Moscow. On the other hand, the liquidation of the TUEL could also have been an excuse to put an end to an open Communist presence in the trade unions. While Cannon had emphasized the crucial role of open Communist work in the trade unions in his 1924 speech, "Our Aims and Tactics in the Trade Unions" published in this volume, Dunne tended to put the stress on the liquidationist aspects of their position.

In any case, the ECCI refused to get rid of the TUEL. The Sixth Plenum decision decreed that the Foster group was to have

75 "Draft Resolution on Trade Union Policy and Tactics," Cannon Papers, Box 8. No author is indicated on the typed manuscript, but "1925 Bill Dunne Draft" had been written in pencil across the top. A number of mimeoed Foster faction circulars from late 1925, found in the same file, also support the contention that Cannon and Dunne wanted to liquidate the TUEL.

a majority on the party's leading Trade Union Committee. Foster was to remain head of the TUEL and his policy of eschewing *all* attempts to organize outside of the framework of the AFL was endorsed (the Passaic strike was settled after Foster's return from Moscow by turning the organizing committee over to the AFL). But the Comintern ordered the TUEL to enlarge its base of support within the AFL; the TUEL was to drop its explicitly communist program and broaden itself into a united-front organization.

Whatever the differences over the TUEL, all factions were committed to the strategy of searching for "Progressive" trade-union allies with whom to make united fronts. Cannon and Dunne not only endorsed the strategy but actively pushed it in the numerous discussions around trade-union questions which occurred in the Political Committee, as is evident from Cannon's motions on the TUEL at the 29 October 1926 Political Committee meeting, which we publish in this book.

By that time "Progressive" was an ambiguous term in Workers Party parlance. With La Follette's party dead, the term encompassed everything from authentic militant trade unionists like Alex Howat of the miners, to left-talking bureaucrats on the make like David Dubinsky in the ILGWU and supporters of the Minnesota Farmer Labor Party (which became a shill for the Democratic Party). The Workers Party did not always distinguish between an action-oriented united front and an ongoing political bloc. The strategy of seeking to always enter into united fronts with so-called progressives therefore tended to cut across the clear communist perspective for trade-union work which Cannon laid out in "Our Aims and Tactics in the Trade Unions."

While the Foster faction bitterly resented what they regarded as Cannon's defection to Ruthenberg, Cannon did not view himself in this light. In a letter written from New York, where he stopped en route to the Sixth ECCI Plenum, Cannon urged his supporters in Chicago to "remember the attitude we agreed upon: no indication of any preferences, decision on all questions as they arise according to our main political line, regardless of who is for or against."[76] After he returned from Moscow, Cannon embarked on a campaign to end factionalism in the party.

---

76 Letter to Comrades from Jim, 16 December 1925, Cannon Papers, Box 1.

Anti-Trotskyism in the Mid-1920s

Cannon later wrote that in the spring of 1926, by accident, he got hold of a Left Opposition document about the Anglo-Russian Trade Union Unity Committee. It was under the cover of this committee that the reformist British trade-union bureaucrats scuttled the May 1926 General Strike, and Cannon was won over to Trotsky's position condemning the Anglo-Russian Committee, though he kept quiet about it.[77] It should be noted that to hold a private opinion on Trotsky at variance with the public party position was by no means unusual in the Comintern at the time. It is important not to read back into the Communist movement of the mid-1920s the anathema that Trotsky later became, as Max Shachtman explained:

> Although everybody voted *pro forma*, as I said before, against Trotsky, nevertheless our respect and admiration for Trotsky as the organizer of the Bolshevik revolution and next to Lenin the principal leader of the Communist International was pretty much undiminished. I mention this in connection with Dunne only for this reason. On one of his visits to Moscow as a representative of the American Party...he wrote back a letter to our faction which we circulated as a faction letter that he and with him all of Moscow was delighted that Trotsky's pictures were back in the windows again. That was the period when the Stalin-Zinoviev combination was breaking up, and Stalin modified at that time and almost abandoned an active attack against Trotsky in order to concentrate his fire upon Zinoviev....
>
> It was characteristic of many of us in the movement at that time—this was in the middle of the '20s—that while we didn't consider ourselves Trotskyists—God forbid; that was unorthodox—the reaction of Dunne to the fact that Trotsky, at least so far as his picture was concerned, was no longer considered a heretic aroused a good deal of delight in all of us. We were relieved. We felt: all right, so he is wrong; we know he is wrong, but still he is not the scoundrel that they had made him out to be. That, by the way, was very true of many people in Europe in the Communist International, who had also gone along without enthusiasm in voting against Trotsky.[78]

Antoinette Konikow, a veteran of the Marxist movement going back to the 1880s, who in 1927 *openly* supported Trotsky's

77 Cannon, *The History of American Trotskyism*, 46. Some of Trotsky's writings on Britain were published in *International Press Correspondence* and *Communist International* in 1926 and it may be these that Cannon is referring to.

78 Shachtman, op. cit., 53-54.

Left Opposition in the Workers Party's Boston branch, was even tolerated up until the expulsion of Trotsky, Zinoviev, et al. from the Soviet party at the end of 1927. Even then she was only removed from her post as an instructor in the local party school.[79] Konikow was not expelled from the Workers Party until *after* Cannon was (see her letter to the Political Committee published here in Appendix I).

Cannon certainly voted for all of the ritual anti-Trotsky resolutions. He was distinguished, however, by his failure to actively take up anti-Trotsky polemics. Both Foster-Bittelman and Ruthenberg-Lovestone tried to take advantage of the fight against the Left Opposition to further their own factions and their own careers within the Workers Party. Foster continually quoted Stalin; Lovestone was one of those who proposed Trotsky's expulsion at the Eighth Comintern Plenum in 1927. Cannon refused to take part in this cynical game.

In the spring of 1925 Max Eastman had published a book in support of Trotsky, *Since Lenin Died.* On 18 October 1926 he succeeded in getting Lenin's "Testament" printed in the *New York Times.* The party had advance warning of the impending publication; at a Political Committee meeting on October 16, Lovestone reported that the *Daily Worker* would prepare a response. Though Trotsky had been obliged to denounce Eastman's efforts, the episode could not have failed to increase Cannon's unease on the question. This may have been one of the reasons he requested to be a delegate to the Seventh Plenum of the ECCI in late 1926, which was to debate Stalin's program of "socialism in one country." The Ruthenberg majority voted him down.[80]

Ruthenberg's Sudden Death

Cannon voted independently within the Political Committee for most of 1926 and early 1927, blocking on the basis of the particular issue with whatever faction he happened to agree with, campaigning against the factionalism of both other groups. Relations with the Ruthenberg group must have worsened considerably after Ruthenberg proposed in the summer of 1926 that the

79 Minutes of Political Committee No. 13, 14 December 1927. Cannon voted with the PC majority for Konikow's removal.

80 Minutes of Political Committee No. 97, 29 October 1926.

party headquarters and *Daily Worker* move back to New York City. Cannon and Dunne vigorously opposed the move.[81] With support from Moscow, Ruthenberg was able to move the *Daily Worker* back to New York by January 1927; Dunne, as one of the editors, moved with the paper. Cannon did not move until the party headquarters did, later that year.

Working from Chicago in the fall of 1926 Cannon was able to make an important recruit to his campaign against factionalism: New York district organizer William Weinstone, long a supporter of Ruthenberg-Lovestone. It was Lovestone's corruption which evidently pushed Weinstone in Cannon's direction.[82] Weinstone brought with him a few other leading members in New York, including Jack Stachel, and together with Cannon's supporters they sought to build "a faction to end factions."

Cannon cemented his alliance with Weinstone in a trip to New York in January 1927. In a letter to his factional supporters, Cannon reported that, as regards the "Weinstone-Stachel group —its break with the Ruthenberg group can be regarded as absolutely definite on ideological and political grounds. They are in direct conflict with them on the external as well as the internal line of the party *not less than we are* and for precisely the same reasons."[83] Cannon told his supporters that the Weinstone group was also working closely with the New York Foster faction, and that there had been significant discussion of the possibility of forming a "triple alliance" against Ruthenberg-Lovestone. But Cannon adamantly opposed the perspective of the triple alliance, as he told his supporters in a subsequent letter:

> I do not quite remember how I expressed my point of view on one aspect of the question in the previous letter, and to avoid any possible misunderstanding I want to state and underscore here the opinion that it would be absolutely wrong for us to give anyone the impression that we are advocates of the "triple alliance" or the "reunification of the old majority group." On the other hand, we

81 "Statement on the Question of Moving Party Headquarters and the *Daily Worker* to New York," and "Supplementary Statement to the Political Committee on the Question of Moving the Headquarters and *Daily Worker* by James P. Cannon," Cannon Papers, Box 8. See also Letter to Comrades from Bill Dunne, 3 August 1926, Cannon Papers, Box 1.

82 *Militant*, 1 January 1929.

83 Letter to Comrades, 10 January 1927, Cannon Papers, Box 1.

> should not be so stupid as to neglect to utilize any sentiment that may exist for such ideas for the purpose of discussing policy and for propagating the idea that policy must be the decisive question governing all important actions in the party.[84]

Cannon's campaign against factionalism may have been making headway, as revealed by the summary of a 7 February 1927 discussion between Cannon and Ruthenberg and his leading supporters, which we publish here. In the next period, Cannon coauthored with Ruthenberg a major Political Committee statement designed to stop the faction fighting over the party's work in the various cooperative movements.[85] Ruthenberg's sudden death on March 2 upset the equilibrium in the party and opened a particularly frenzied period in the internal party faction fight.

Draper gives a full account of the brawl which ensued as Lovestone attempted to assume Ruthenberg's mantle.[86] Cannon and Weinstone made a bloc with Foster to support Weinstone for party secretary, and they had a majority of the CEC. Dunne, who had always had a closer political affinity than Cannon with the narrow trade unionists of the Foster faction, pressed for a broader political agreement with Foster in a 2 April 1927 telegram to Cannon. In his draft reply to Dunne, Cannon remained adamant in his opposition to the "triple alliance":

> No combination now either faction STOP Next period one of independent principal struggle STOP Relations other groups can ensue only when Jays dictatorship and Fosters hegemony are smashed by fight and we have consolidated sufficient organized strength and influence to guarantee against danger compromising line or weakening organizational position STOP Absolutely opposed any agreements or commitments either faction before or at plenum STOP All energy must be concentrated now on consolidation own forces on external internal and critical program and coming out openly and militantly as independent group STOP[87]

Lovestone flouted the CEC and ran off to Moscow, followed by Foster, Cannon and Weinstone. Yet another American Com-

---

84 Letter to Comrades, 15 January 1927, Cannon Papers, Box 1.

85 The statement was attached to the minutes of Political Committee No. 119, 24 February 1927. We do not publish it here.

86 Draper II, 248-267.

87 Draft Reply to 2 April 1927 Telegram from Bill Dunne, written in pencil on back of Dunne's telegram, Cannon Papers, Box 1.

mission was convened in Moscow and we publish here some of Cannon's remarks to it. It was pressure in Moscow that finally forced Cannon to agree to the bloc with Foster, as is evident from the 26 June 1927 Cannon factional circular which we publish here. Though Cannon was not the author, the letter is based on his reports from Moscow. Such private circular letters, supplemented by faction caucus meetings, were used by all three factions to keep their members informed of internal developments. We also publish the joint Cannon-Weinstone-Foster letter to the American Commission, as well as excerpts from the original theses Cannon and Weinstone prepared for the plenum.

In 1927 there were few differences over political program between the various factions. The documents we print here strain to manufacture issues based on Moscow's concerns at the time. One of these was the "war danger": the British had just broken diplomatic relations with the Soviet Union, and Chiang Kai-shek's Chinese armies had just crushed the Shanghai workers' commune. Stalin used a war scare to help deflect attention from the disastrous results of his two-class "workers and peasants" alliance with Chiang's Kuomintang.

The fight for control of the American party was no less vicious for the lack of political differences. The initial Comintern decision did not, however, favor either side. It was only after the hapless Alexander Bittelman, who had remained in the United States, formed an ill-advised "National Committee of the Opposition Bloc" within the Workers Party that Lovestone was able to unambiguously win the Comintern's support. An excerpt from a Lovestone circular, which "explains" the Comintern condemnation of the National Committee of the Opposition Bloc, captures the flavor of most Lovestone polemics:

> The Communist International considers this factionalism without political differences the "WORST OFFENSE AGAINST THE PARTY" particularly in the "present objective situation"—the WAR situation, which demands the CONCENTRATED attention of the Party....
>
> The opposition is spreading fake cables from Foster, which the next day they "correct" with another fake cable. Now we know that the Comintern refuses to support such tactics and has given the group a sound slap in the face.
>
> You will notice that Cannon-Weinstone are not mentioned at all. They are, as we predicted, completely ignored by the Comintern.

> They had no reason for existence in the Party and the Comintern refuses to be fooled by them. They declared that the Party situation could not be settled without their going to Moscow. They have gone —and will come home with their tails between their legs—unless their tails have been cut off in Moscow.[88]

The fight was bitter right through to the American party's Fifth Convention in August 1927. Even the campaign against the execution of Sacco and Vanzetti became a factional football—Cannon was thwarted in his attempts to organize a national Sacco and Vanzetti conference before the execution on August 23, as well as in his attempts to have the party convention postponed to allow for full participation in the last-minute agitation against the execution. He was forced to protest the *Daily Worker*'s downplaying of the ILD's role in the campaign.[89] It is a tribute to the ILD that the campaign mobilized as much protest as it did.

Lovestone won a majority of the Fifth Convention, which opened August 31. The Opposition Bloc demanded a minority credentials report, questioning the honesty of the elections organized by Lovestone's apparatus. But it was useless to appeal. Weinstone soon abandoned the Opposition, but Cannon and Foster maintained their bloc against Lovestone.

Lovestone Becomes Lovestone

Lovestone's ascendancy shifted the political center of the old Ruthenberg faction. Lore's old supporters in the needle trades leadership issued a formal statement of affiliation to the Lovestone group. Ruthenberg's chief ideologist, Max Bedacht, was thrown aside. Lovestone's chief lieutenant was his old CCNY chum Bertram Wolfe, a man who had *twice* fled his posts in the old underground movement in the face of government persecution and who owed his office only to Lovestone's patronage.[90] Wolfe became Lovestone's chief anti-Trotsky expert and ideologist. Under their tutelage the party began to develop the theme that the Workers Party was the true heir to the tradition of the

88 Unsigned circular headed "Very Latest!!!, Most Important!!!, To Be Given to *Every* Member of the Party Without Affiliation!!", 7 July 1927, in the collection of the Prometheus Research Library.

89 Minutes of Political Committee No. 148, 11 August 1927.

90 Bertram Wolfe, op. cit., 232-248; 261-275.

American Revolution of 1776. They also expounded the thesis that conditions were unfavorable for the class struggle in general and for an independent party election campaign in 1928 in particular.

As is evident from Cannon's speech to the American party's February 1928 plenum, which we publish here, Cannon tried in the aftermath of the Fifth Convention to mitigate the factional struggle. But he found himself forced to fight some of the more egregious examples of the party's right turn. In particular, he opposed the support Weinstone's New York organization had given to the Socialist Party candidate for judge, Jacob Panken, who had a major base, not uncoincidentally, in the needle trades unions.[91] Cannon also insisted that the party organize aggressively against John L. Lewis in the miners union, calling for a national miners conference which would lay the basis for a new union. In this period the Cannon faction took on the coloration of a genuine left opposition, while the Lovestone group fully evolved into the American version of Bukharin's Right Opposition.

The winds were, of course, already changing in Moscow by early 1928. The domestic policies advocated by the Bukharin right wing had led to the disaster Trotsky had predicted: the wealthier peasants (kulaks), encouraged by Bukharin to "enrich" themselves, had begun to hoard grain, trying to force a price rise and threatening to starve Soviet cities. Stalin moved with brutal violence to forcibly collectivize the peasantry. His left flipflop in domestic politics was bureaucratically paralleled by a turn to the left by the entire Comintern, as Stalin took the opportunity to both undercut Trotsky's Left Opposition and eliminate Bukharin as an authoritative figure.

Stalin was moving against Bukharin by the Comintern's Ninth Plenum in February 1928. But the official political line moved only slowly to the left, toward the dual unionism and ultraleftist rhetoric of Stalin's "Third Period." In the beginning the Comintern simply criticized the American party for adapting to the AFL bureaucracy and called for new unions only where the AFL refused to organize the unorganized. Even this was too much for Lovestone, and initially Foster, who resisted the abandonment of

91 Cannon, Foster and Bittelman all voted against this policy in the Political Committee; see minutes of Political Committee No. 4, 12 October 1927.

his "boring from within" policy until it became clear that he had to either accept the dual unionism of Stalin's Third Period or give up his post as a leader of the party. (That he would abandon long-held political views in favor of his party post had long been a given.)

Cannon had always been opposed to Foster's AFL fetishism; he had also been an enthusiastic proponent of a more active Workers Party orientation to organizing the unorganized. Thus for a brief period during the Comintern's swing to the left, its formal positions coincided with Cannon's own. He was the only major party faction leader to support the new anti-AFL orientation, and he had to fight within the Political Committee even to get his 1928 article on the trade-union question published. (Bittelman, who could read Russian and knew which way the political wind was blowing in Moscow, soon broke with Foster on the question and blocked with Cannon.) Within the Political Committee Cannon also insisted that the party run in its own name in the upcoming elections, while Lovestone initially resisted, desperate to find some "labor party" gimmick. We publish here Cannon's articles on both these questions.

Cannon's star was thus actually *rising* within the Comintern as it zigzagged left in 1928. But Cannon was far from a cynical factional games player and he was not heartened by the Comintern's left turn. He was, by all accounts, increasingly disaffected. He had come to a total dead end in his campaign to end the party's factional wars, and he knew it. At the February plenum he refused to speak on the Trotsky question, despite William Dunne's urgent pleas that this failure would hurt the standing of the faction. It was at this plenum that he and Canadian Communist Party leader Maurice Spector also first spoke to each other of their doubts about the dirt being heaped on Trotsky.

After the plenum, Cannon went on a two-month national tour for the ILD. In Minnesota, Carl Skoglund and Vincent Dunne, local party leaders who later became founding members of the CLA, asked Cannon what he thought about the expulsion of Zinoviev and Trotsky. Cannon replied, "Who am I to condemn the leaders of the Russian revolution."[92] Cannon did not make

92 Cannon, *The History of American Trotskyism*, 47.

much of a pretense of hiding his views from his faction partners. Alexander Bittelman recalled a frequent saying of Cannon's in private conversations at the time: "Stalin makes shit out of leaders and leaders out of shit."[93]

Cannon initially resisted going as a delegate to the Sixth Congress of the Communist International which opened in August 1928, horrifying his top factional lieutenants. Cannon argued that with the party engaged in major campaigns in the miners union, in the textile union and in a national presidential campaign, *some* of the party leadership should stay home. He agreed to go only at the last minute, as he indicated in the statement he submitted to the Political Committee, which we publish here.

Cannon Becomes a Trotskyist

At the Fourth Congress in 1922 Cannon had been appointed a member of the commission assigned to develop a program for the Communist International. In 1928 Bukharin finally submitted a draft program and Cannon was again made a member of the commission at the Sixth Congress, as was Maurice Spector. Trotsky, already in internal exile at Alma Ata in Soviet Central Asia, had written a critique of Bukharin's draft program which he submitted to the congress. For some reason the Comintern apparatus translated large parts of the first and third of the three sections of Trotsky's critique. This was submitted to members of the Program Commission, who were not notified that only part of the document had been translated.[94]

It's not hard to imagine the profound impact even this partial version of Trotsky's document had on Cannon. Trotsky's condemnation of the Comintern's political zigzags since the adoption of Stalin's reactionary program of "socialism in one country" powerfully corresponded to Cannon's own personal experience. Trotsky's scathing attack on John Pepper's "third party alliance," which Trotsky explained as part of a general Comintern turn to two-class parties in 1924-25, must have been a revelation:

> The most caricature-like character in this respect was assumed by the Workers' Party of America in its efforts to support the candidature

93 Cited in Bittelman, op. cit., 510.

94 The entire critique is published in English as *The Third International After Lenin* (New York: Pioneer Publishers, 1936).

> of the bourgeois, "anti-Trust" Senator La Follette, so as to attach, in this manner, the American farmers to the wheel of the Social Revolution. Pepper, the theoretician of the maneuver, who is one of those who has ruined the Hungarian Revolution and who failed to notice the Hungarian peasantry, made here a great effort to ruin the Workers' Party in its first stages of activity....This confused idea had its followers and half followers among the leaders of the Comintern. In the course of a few weeks the scales vacillated from one side to the other until finally a concession was made to the letter of Marxism. Having been taken off its feet the American Party had to be cut off from the noose of the La Follette party which died even before its founder.[95]

Cannon's experience with Pepper and the La Follette disaster predisposed him to accept Trotsky's condemnation of Stalin's policy of building up the bourgeois-nationalist Kuomintang as a supposed "workers and peasants" party in China, a policy which had strangled the Chinese Revolution. Now Trotsky explained that the degeneration of the Russian Revolution by early 1924 was itself the root of the problem; the change Cannon had seen occur in the Communist International since the Fourth Congress was explained.

Cannon and Spector paid little attention to the formal congress proceedings as they read and studied Trotsky's document which offered Cannon a programmatic way out of his impasse in the internal faction fight. Both he and Spector resolved to take up the fight for the Left Opposition.

Cannon did speak once during the Sixth Congress and his speech is reprinted here. The faction fight in the American party did not stand still while Cannon studied. Dunne had re-cemented the Cannon faction's bloc with Foster before Cannon arrived in Moscow. The bloc went on the offensive against Lovestone and submitted a document to the congress, "The Right Danger in the American Party." We have not included this lengthy document here.[96] As rumors of a split between Stalin and Bukharin spread

---

95 This quote is taken from the translation serialized in the CLA's newspaper, the *Militant*. See "The Draft Program of the Comintern: A Criticism of Fundamentals," *Militant*, 1 July 1929. The *Militant*'s introduction to the series drew readers' attention to this passage on La Follette and noted that Trotsky had led the fight against the "third party alliance."

96 "The Right Danger in the American Party" was serialized in the *Militant*, 15 November 1928-15 January 1929.

through the congress, the Foster-Cannon supporters had every reason to believe that control of the American party would soon be coming their way. Everyone in the Comintern knew that Bukharin's—and therefore Lovestone's—days were numbered. Stalin confirmed this by granting Foster and Bittelman an audience during the congress.

If private sympathy for Trotsky had been tolerated in the Comintern in the past, it was clear by the Sixth Congress that this was no longer to be the case. Cannon and Spector were wisely and necessarily cautious about their adherence to Trotsky's Left Opposition, as Cannon later explained:

> Our chief concern was to get the document out of Russia and use it in working for the Opposition in our own parties. We did not want to risk exposure and possible detention in Moscow by probing around in the other delegations on this explosive subject....I can't recall that Spector and I ever speculated about possible sympathizers with our own views in the other delegations. We took it for granted that they considered Trotskyism a closed question.[97]

Nonetheless, Cannon did seek to approach his cofactionalists. Manuel Gomez, a key Cannon factional lieutenant at the time, later told Draper that Cannon was very cagey in approaching him on the subject:

> Cannon talked at great length about it in Moscow without talking about it. He talked a great deal about Trotsky without supporting Trotsky and without opposing Stalin—but raised questions in a very ambiguous way that made one ask himself, "Why is he talking like that anyway? There is something peculiar going on here."[98]

It is hard to believe that Cannon would not also have approached Bill Dunne, who was also a delegate to the congress. Dunne's response must also have been strongly negative. Cannon never spoke about this in later years, though in 1929, according to one source, Cannon did "admit" that he "was in a great measure responsible for the estrangement of Dunne."[99] Dunne went to China on Comintern assignment after the congress; from

---

97 Letter by Cannon to Theodore Draper, 28 May 1959, Cannon Papers, Box 7.

98 Theodore Draper interview with Manuel Gomez, 18 February 1964, Draper Files, Series 3, No. 9.

99 Letter from Albert Glotzer to Max Shachtman, 13 September 1929, Cannon Papers, Box 1.

Hankow he sent a cable denying rumors that he supported Cannon. But Dunne's three brothers in Minneapolis became founding members of the Trotskyist Communist League of America.

Cannon needed to get a copy of Trotsky's critique back to the United States where he would have a chance to recruit others. But the copies handed out to Program Commission members were individually numbered and the members were required to turn them in at the congress's end. It is unclear how Cannon and Spector managed to get a copy out of the Soviet Union. Shachtman later retailed the story that they stole a copy from one of the Australian delegates. According to another account, they smuggled the document out of the country in a child's teddy bear with the help of an Irish delegate, George Weston.[100] Cannon himself was always very close-mouthed on the subject.

Nonetheless Cannon's interest in Trotskyism was not such a secret in Moscow. On the floor of the congress Lovestone supporter Harry Wicks attacked Cannon for using Trotsky's words to criticize Pepper.[101] Swabeck reports that rumors of Cannon's Trotskyism preceded him back to the United States. Swabeck also reports that William Z. Foster, who was the first of the American delegates to arrive back from Moscow, also praised the "masterful contents" of the Trotsky critique in a joint meeting of the Foster-Cannon caucus.[102]

Foster's position in the party was then at a low ebb—his own faction had rebelled against his leadership in Moscow and offered to support Cannon for future party leader.[103] Perhaps Foster figured Cannon knew something he didn't. More likely, there was a widely held supposition in the Comintern at the time that Stalin had Trotsky's document distributed to the congress because he was planning to rehabilitate Trotsky to use against Bukharin. Foster was certainly a man to hedge his bets.

But Bittelman knew better, and it became clear soon after Cannon's return to New York on September 23 that Cannon him-

100 Shachtman, op. cit., 153-154; Sam Gordon in *James P. Cannon As We Knew Him*, 55-56.

101 *International Press Correspondence*, 11 August 1928, 850.

102 Swabeck, op. cit., Chapter XII, 1.

103 Cannon, *First Ten Years*, 210-215.

self was not hedging his bets, but actively organizing to win adherents to the Left Opposition. Cannon, Shachtman and Abern were expelled from what had been the joint Foster-Cannon Opposition on October 5. On October 16 charges were preferred against them in the Political Committee by Foster, Bittelman and Philip Aronberg. Cannon, Abern and Shachtman were removed from their posts in the ILD on that same day, but by that time they had managed to get a copy of the complete subscribers list of the *Labor Defender* (they later mailed everyone on it a copy of the first issue of the *Militant*, dated 15 November 1928). Over the next week and a half they temporized, trying to gain new adherents. Only on October 27 did they submit a statement in support of the Left Opposition. Cannon was extensively questioned in the Political Committee before he was expelled that day, and we publish excerpts from the transcript here.[104] At that time Cannon saw his adherence to the Left Opposition as the logical and natural end result of his entire history in the Workers Party.

The material presented in this book shows that there were factors in the political profile of Cannon's faction that militated against his leap to the Left Opposition: a parochial concern for American questions, insistence on the strategy of a bloc with the "progressives" in the trade unions, lack of emphasis on the fight against special oppression of blacks and minorities in the United States. Shachtman and Abern were soon to ridicule the idea that the American Left Opposition had undergone a period of "gestation" within the old Cannon faction:

> On every fundamental question of principle, the Cannon group stood upon the platform of international Stalinism sometimes a little to the Right of it and sometimes a little to the Left of it....If anything, it was the least "international" of all the party groups, and concerned itself less than any others with such questions as the British general strike, and the Anglo-Russian Committee, the Chinese Revolution, the struggles within the Russian Party although the interests of the other groups were purely factional....To the extent that we have developed towards the full and basic views of the Left

104 The statement submitted by Cannon, Abern and Shachtman is available in James P. Cannon, *The Left Opposition in the U.S. 1928-31* (New York: Monad Press, 1981), 29-35.

Opposition, we have had to break both politically and organizationally with the old Cannon group.[105]

Shachtman was not being candid. Insofar as any member of the Cannon faction had written about international issues, especially China, it had been Shachtman—it was he who had unthinkingly spouted the Stalinist line. Moreover, in 1925 Shachtman had linked the fight against Lore to the fight against Trotsky more explicitly than Cannon did in his own writings. Shachtman wrote that it was necessary to fight not only Lore, but also "those who avow themselves of Loreist tendencies...while formally repudiating any connection with right-wing deviations. As Bukharin pointed out: many comrades who raise their hands in holy terror at being associated with Trotskyism and vehemently assert their opposition to it, nevertheless follow a purely Trotskyist policy in the peasant question, for example."[106]

When, in 1932, Shachtman and Abern led a rebellion against Cannon's leadership of the Communist League of America, they were only interested in telling one side of the story. The material presented here also tells another, one that *predisposed* a deliberate and considered workers' leader like Cannon to turn away from high office within the American party in favor of remaining true to the revolutionism that had animated his youth and continued to animate the program of the Left Opposition.[107]

Abern, Shachtman and Glotzer weren't the only ones who in later years tried to revise the record of the Cannon faction for

---

105 Martin Abern, Albert Glotzer and Max Shachtman, "The Situation in the American Opposition: Prospect and Retrospect," 4 June 1932, 14-15.

106 Max Shachtman, "A Communist Milestone. The Fourth Convention of the Workers Party of America," *Workers Monthly*, August 1925, 452. For Shachtman's articles on China see "China and the Imperialist Struggle," *Workers Monthly*, July 1925; "The Limitations of American Imperialism," *The Communist*, March 1927, 25-31; and "American Imperialism Shall Not Throttle the Chinese Revolution," *Labor Defender*, July 1927. In the spring of 1928 Shachtman went on a national speaking tour for the ILD on the subject of China.

107 Shachtman, Glotzer and Abern remained in the Trotskyist movement only until 1940, when they caved in to the anti-Soviet hysteria caused by the Stalin-Hitler pact and abandoned the military defense of the Soviet Union. By the early 1960s Shachtman was defending the U.S. imperialist-backed Bay of Pigs invasion of Cuba, and functioning as a sort of grey eminence behind Albert Shanker's crusading Cold War bureaucracy in the American Federation of Teachers. When Shachtman died in 1972 ILGWU bureaucrat Charles Zimmerman, whose opportunism

(continued)

their own political purposes. In 1949 William Z. Foster rather pathetically tried to tar Cannon with Lovestone's brand of "American exceptionalism":

> Cannon, who for several years had been a member of our Party's Central Committee, expressed his American exceptionalism, his fear of the "overwhelming power of American capitalism," by an acceptance of Trotskyism, with all its radical phrases, its pseudo-revolutionary programs, and its treachery to Socialism and the working class.[108]

Foster was just echoing his mentor, Stalin, who had made American "exceptionalism" a major crime in a speech to the Comintern's American Commission in May 1929. Stalin argued that communist internationalism is based on "the general features of capitalism, which are the same for all countries." This line was used to justify the simultaneous turn by all sections of the Communist International to "Third Period" ultraleftism.

Trotsky had polemicized against Stalin's absurd thesis that specific national features are "'merely supplementary to the general features,' like warts on a face." "In reality," wrote Trotsky, "the national peculiarities represent an original combination of the basic features of the world process. The originality can be of decisive significance for revolutionary strategy over a span of many years."[109]

Even by the time of the "Third Period" the Communist International had buried any concern for revolutionary strategy in the "socialism in one country" grave. But after 1935 the peculiar

---

had been such a frequent target of the Cannon faction in the 1920s, was a featured speaker at the memorial meeting. Abern died in 1949; Glotzer supported Shachtman in his political evolution.

In *The Prophet's Army, Trotskyists in America, 1928-1941* (Westport, Connecticut: Greenwood Press, 1977, 199) Constance Ashton Myers claims that at the end of his life Shachtman came to "hold an abiding respect for Stalin and for what he viewed as an essential wisdom in the Communist party," in particular for Stalin's handling of the Chinese revolutionary movement in the 1920s.

108 William Z. Foster, "Cannon, Lovestone, and Browder," *Political Affairs*, September 1949, 17.

109 Leon Trotsky, "Introduction to the German Edition" of *The Permanent Revolution*, translation published in *The Permanent Revolution and Results and Prospects* (New York: Pathfinder Press, 1969), 147. The quotation from Stalin's speech to the May 1929 American Commission is taken from the same source; the speech does not appear in Stalin's *Collected Works*, though it was printed in *The Communist* (June 1930).

"warts" of various national capitalisms became all-important to Stalin, as the Soviet Union vainly sought to make a deal with French, British and American imperialism in order to stave off the threat posed by Hitler's Germany. "Communism is 20th Century Americanism" proclaimed the American Communist Party, and William "Zigzag" Foster went along without a peep as the CP uncritically supported Franklin Roosevelt, the WWII no-strike pledge and U.S. imperialism's war aims. The material published here reveals Cannon to be concerned with revolutionary strategy throughout the 1920s, despite the party's internecine factional struggles and despite the Stalinization of the Communist International, giving the lie to Foster's ludicrous attempt to paint Cannon as an "exceptionalist" quaking before the power of American imperialism.

The fight of the Cannon-Foster faction against an orientation to La Follette's bourgeois third party movement after the 1924 elections; Cannon's insistence on the leading role of the working class in any farmer-labor party; the strong, if skewed, internationalism that made Cannon break with Foster and refuse to lead a rightist revolt against the Communist International in 1925; Cannon's attempt to reverse the dead-end factional wars which crippled and deformed the party after 1925; his willingness to break with the party's adaptation to the AFL unions in 1928: all this predisposed Cannon to make the leap to the Left Opposition when that option presented itself. Cannon, unlike the other Workers Party leaders had not been made cynical by the corrupt maneuvering inside the degenerating Comintern. The fact that a number of Cannon's factional supporters, including Abern and Shachtman, made the leap to Trotskyism with Cannon, only reinforces this point.

In order to give the reader an idea of the breadth of experience and political profile of the broader Cannon faction, we include in Appendix I some material by Martin Abern and Arne Swabeck from the summer of 1928. Cannon's supporters ran a good deal of the party's public work while the party leadership was in Moscow attending the Sixth Comintern Congress. Their reports and letters on the ILD and the campaigns for new unions among the miners and textile workers serve to illustrate the point that Cannon's supporters were not mere factional games players like most of Lovestone's supporters. The Cannon factional leadership had roots and experience in the workers movement. They had been around, involved in all the hot spots, and the contacts they made and the experience they gained stood the Trotskyist movement in good stead later on.

Lovestone's Political Committee was so worried about Arne Swabeck's base of support among the party miners in southern Illinois that it sent Foster himself to tour the area in early December 1928.[110] They evidently had reason to worry. The response of one puzzled miner was reportedly: "I don't know Mr. Trotsky and I don't know Mr. Cannon; but I know Arne Swabeck, and you can't tell me that he is a traitor to the working class."[111] The CLA played a role in a campaign to establish the Progressive Mine Workers of America in the area a few years later.

In Appendix II we publish a transcript of Lovestone henchman Jack Stachel's report on the Trotskyists to the Workers Party Political Committee on 25 December 1928. Cannon's apartment had been burglarized and most of his correspondence stolen on December 23. If there was ever any doubt as to the identity of the culprits, Stachel's report removes it: he quotes many of the stolen letters and crows about the great "blow" that had been struck against the Trotskyists. His report reveals the broad extent of Cannon's support in the party up until that time.

In early 1929 Lovestone and a shrunken band of supporters were also expelled from the party. They passed through the Bukharinite international Right Opposition on their road to becoming paid agents for the American labor bureaucracy and the U.S. government. The expulsion of Lovestone completed the Stalinization of the Communist Party—the Workers Party's name had been changed to Workers (Communist) Party in 1925; it was finally changed to Communist Party in 1929. After 1929 there was only one faction—Stalin's faction—in the U.S. party, as in the Comintern as a whole. The American party leadership no longer had any say in determining its political line or perspectives.

But it was different in the earlier period, and that history belongs to American Trotskyism more than it does to today's pathetic Stalinist supporters of whatever the current version of the

110 Minutes of Political Committee No. 71, 1 December 1928.

111 Swabeck, op. cit., Chapter XII, 3.

La Follette "third party alliance" happens to be. This was the perspective Cannon himself defended:

> The important thing to remember is that our modern Trotskyist movement originated in the Communist Party—and nowhere else. Despite all the negative aspects of the party in those early years...despite its weaknesses, its crudities, its infantile sicknesses, its mistakes; whatever may be said in retrospect about the faction struggles and their eventual degeneration; whatever may be said about the degeneration of the Communist Party in this country—it must be recognized that out of the Communist Party came the forces for the regeneration of the revolutionary movement....Therefore, we should say that the early period of the Communist movement in this country belongs to us.[112]

Each political generation in the communist vanguard will have to ascribe its own significance to the material we publish here. But it had better be assimilated, along with much else. This was certainly Cannon's hope, when he wrote about the publication of *The First Ten Years of American Communism*:

> I don't care so much about the public reception this book may receive, but I do hope that the activists in our movement will study it attentively and reflect on the lessons I had to learn so painfully in the early years of American communism—without benefit of instruction and advice from others who had had previous experience with the problems of factionalism which so bedeviled all the pioneer American communists, who had to start from scratch, and play by ear, and try to learn as they went along. Very few of them learned in time, and that was one of the main causes of their catastrophe.[113]

The core questions addressed by Cannon in the 1920s have not gone away: the political relationships between the working class and the petty bourgeoisie; the tension between the trade-union bureaucracy and the working class, organized and unorganized; the struggle against the oppression of ethnic minorities in the U.S., centrally the struggle against the oppression of black people. Only a proletarian revolution, based upon recognition of these questions, can begin to effect a solution.

Prometheus Research Library
August 1992

---

112 Cannon, *The History of American Trotskyism*, 39.

113 Letter by Cannon to Gerry Healy, 8 February 1961, Cannon Papers, Box 7.

The IWW at Philadelphia

Published 27 August 1920

The following article by Cannon was published in The Toiler, *the United Communist Party weekly journal produced in Cleveland, Ohio. The UCP had been founded at a convention in May which united the Communist Labor Party (CLP) with a C.E. Ruthenberg-led split from the Communist Party of America (CPA). The convention had adopted a position of support to the Industrial Workers of the World (IWW) as opposed to the reactionary business unionists of the American Federation of Labor. This policy was, however, controversial and Cannon opposed it. Cannon used the pseudonym "Dawson" at the convention and his role in the dispute on the trade-union question was described in the convention report written by Y.F. (*The Communist, *12 June 1920):*

"The CPA convention had passed up the question of the IWW because it was apparent that this question could not be settled by agreement. Perhaps two-thirds of the CPA delegates favored a direct endorsement of the IWW and a program of cooperation, reserving criticism of the IWW theorizing. The other CPA delegates considered the IWW as essentially no better than the AFL, citing the reactionary character of the IWW in some of the Eastern cities. All of the CPA delegates were agreed upon an absolute stand against the AFL as an inherently anti-revolutionary organization which must be destroyed.

"On the other hand, there was a strong current in the CLP ranks for a treatment of the subject of industrial unionism from a general viewpoint which would neither include direct endorsement of the IWW nor absolute condemnation of the AFL. The lead in this debate was taken by Dawson who argued that the AFL must be considered from the angle of the local unions, not from the side of the Gompers officialdom; that industrial unionism was having a development in many fields aside from the IWW; that the need was for a call to a new general industrial union, a new One Big Union."

Cannon had adopted his new position of opposition to dual

unionism under the influence of V.I. Lenin and the leadership of the Communist International. This position was finally adopted by the American Communist movement at the convention which fused the UCP and CPA in May 1921.

Throughout 1920, the UCP attempted to woo the IWW for communism, and by the summer there was a current in the IWW, including some members of its General Executive Board, which favored affiliation to the Third International. The August 1920 issue of One Big Union Monthly, *which published the General Executive Board statement Cannon quotes in this article, was entitled "Special Bolshevik Number."*

Nothing has so stirred the radical labor movement of the East for many a day as the rumor, later verified and admitted to be a fact, that members of the IWW were loading high explosives at Philadelphia to be shipped to Poland and used in the infamous war against Soviet Russia.[1] It seemed unbelievable that the IWW of Frank Little, the IWW that has always been in the vanguard of the class struggle, bearing the brunt of the fight in America and inspiring the whole world's movement by its heroic deeds and sacrifices, could now be engaged in this nefarious enterprise—this high treason to the international working class.

The information reached New York members of the organization (from an outside source, not from protesting members at Philadelphia) on August 6, and, as a result of their prompt intervention and vigorous protest, the matter was brought before the General Executive Board and the Philadelphia branch of 7,000 members expelled. The contention that this dastardly work was done by new members, who are unfamiliar with the principles of the IWW, is not borne out by the facts. The Philadelphia Transport Workers branch is an old one, having been in existence continuously since 1913, and many well-known and influential

[1] In May 1920 the Polish army, backed by French imperialism and under the leadership of the fascistic dictator Józef Pilsudski, invaded Soviet Russia. The Red Army soon drove out the Polish forces, but the Soviet government, hoping to spark a revolutionary uprising in Poland and link up with unfinished revolutionary developments in Germany, decided to follow the retreating Poles across the border. Unfortunately, Soviet hopes proved unfounded. The Red Army was defeated by the Poles in the battle of the Vistula in mid-August. In October the Soviet government signed a provisional peace agreement with Poland.

members of the organization are in Philadelphia at the present time taking active part in the affairs of the union. No satisfactory explanation has yet been made of their failure to take quick and decisive action. True revolutionary men, confronted with such a situation, would have prevented the loading of the ships even at the cost of their own lives.

Statement of Executive Board

The General Executive Board has issued a statement in which the actions of the Philadelphia members are severely condemned as being diametrically opposed to every principle of working class honor that the IWW has "stood for, fought for and bled for from its inception." It sounds a new note in the current literature of the organization, in refreshing contrast to the "evolutionary bunk" printed in their official organ, the *One Big Union Monthly.* The statement, in part, reads as follows:

"The IWW has proved by deeds that it is willing and eager at all costs to fight and sacrifice for the cause of international solidarity. It still keeps the faith.

"The organization was designed to make it impossible for one group of workers to be used against another group in the great struggle of the classes. We do not want and will not tolerate in our membership men who can stoop so low as to aid and abet any capitalist government or any other national or international section of the common enemy in keeping the working class in slavery.

"We look with horror and disgust upon the action of the Philadelphia longshoremen in loading high explosives on ships for the purpose of butchering our brave fellow workers in Russia who have established the first working class government in the world.

"The IWW has stood the brunt of the fury of master class hatred in America. More of our members have been imprisoned, murdered and brutalized than all other revolutionary organizations combined. The reason is that we stand and have always stood for the use of militant direct action to overthrow the dictatorship of the capitalist class.

"The IWW wishes to keep its fair name untarnished in the eyes of the world's proletariat.

"We call upon the membership of our organization to use their utmost power to assist the Soviet government of Russia in fighting the world's battle against capitalism."

Appeal to Communists

"We pledge ourselves and our organization to help overthrow capitalism and everything that stands for capitalism.

"We appeal to the working class in general and the United Communist Party in particular to take a stand in industry and help build up a revolutionary organization that will make forever impossible a repetition of the dastardly action of the Philadelphia longshoremen.

"The IWW holds out the clean hand of brotherhood to the revolutionary workers of the world."[2]

---

[2] The decision expelling the Philadelphia local of Marine Transport Workers Industrial Union No. 8 was reversed in the fall when a new leadership, opposed to relations with the Communist International, took over administration of the IWW. The Philadelphia IWW local was an unusual one, made up largely of black workers. In July it had led a militant strike on the Philadelphia docks. But it functioned increasingly as a job-trusting business union, maintaining a closed shop and charging an initiation fee of $25 in order to keep out casual laborers. This was an offense against the revolutionary principles of the IWW, whose usual initiation fee was only $2. In December 1920 the new General Executive Board expelled the Philadelphia Marine Transport Workers local again—this time for charging such a high initiation fee.

Another Renegade

Published 11 December 1920

The following article by Cannon was published in The Toiler, *the United Communist Party's weekly journal which Cannon had begun to edit in the fall of 1920. The August 1920 "Special Bolshevik Number" of the IWW's* One Big Union Monthly *had published a lengthy appeal to the IWW by the Executive Committee of the Communist International, which explained: "Soviet Russia is on strike against the whole capitalist world. The social revolution is a general strike against the whole capitalist system. The dictatorship of the proletariat is the strike committee of the social revolution." This appeal had an impact on the IWW membership —after he finished reading it, Big Bill Haywood exclaimed, "Here is what we have been dreaming about; here is the IWW all feathered out!" But support for Soviet Russia and Communism remained a very controversial question in the IWW.*

In the fall a new, anti-Communist General Executive Board took over IWW administration. The new leadership opened up a 90-day discussion period on the question of whether the IWW should affiliate to the Third International. They also submitted the question to a membership referendum, recommending against affiliation. During the discussion the pages of the Chicago-based IWW weekly paper Solidarity *were full of pro-Bolshevik articles, while the Seattle* Industrial Worker *published an editorial, quoted by Cannon below, which opposed affiliation until the IWW received "accurate information as to the actual condition of the workers of Russia."*

The results of the referendum, announced in mid-December, shortly after Cannon's article was published, were murky. The proposal for unconditional affiliation to the Third International lost, 602 votes to 1658. But a motion for affiliation so long as the IWW would not have to take part in "parliamentary action" was passed. In any case, the General Executive Board declared the proposal to affiliate to the Third Inter-

national defeated, and the 13th IWW Convention, which met in May 1921, declared the referendum null and void.

The counterrevolution has set up a new outpost in this country at Seattle, Washington. Mr. H.F. Kane is the officer in charge and he occupies the exalted position of editor of the *Industrial Worker*, western organ of the IWW. Mr. Kane is too far away from Soviet Russia to lend a hand to General Wrangel. But that doesn't prevent him from doing his little bit behind the lines, after the manner of the stay-at-home patriot who couldn't go to war but made four-minute speeches to help it along.

The question of affiliation with the Third International is before the membership of the IWW and Mr. Kane's particular job, it appears, is to see to it that the outlawed and persecuted direct actionists of the IWW make no alliance with the outlawed and persecuted direct actionists of the Third International. The Russian Revolution, which is the Third International in action, is the object of his attack. He warns the members of the IWW to think twice before they make an entangling alliance with a working class government which, he says, is "propped up by bayonets and which has sent invading armies into other countries." For the Russian workers and peasants to defend themselves, like the IWW men at Centralia,[1] with weapons in their hands, and make good with it and beat off all their oppressors: this is what Mr. Kane condemns.

In the issue of October 30th, which has just come to our notice, he propounds a series of questions for the western lumberjacks to answer before they join hands with the roughneck Bolsheviki. This is one of them:

"Are the workers of Russia permitted to freely travel through the interior looking for employment?"

There you have it, fellow workers! If you line up with the Third International you are in danger of sacrificing your dearly bought privilege of chasing a job from one place to another, the employment sharks will be put out of business, and the whole country will go to hell! Of course, you may have more time to hunt and fish, or look around for decent homes to live in. But your own government, "propped up by bayonets," will deprive

[1] For an account of the Centralia massacre, see Cannon's article, "The Red Month of November," page 472.

you of the pleasure of searching for a master.

This is old stuff, of course. We have read it many times in capitalist papers and magazines. John Spargo and Charles Edward Russell explained it all to us long ago, and the *New York Times* seldom lets a day go by without mentioning it. The last convention of the AFL sounded a warning to the same effect, and Lloyd George talks with tears in his voice about the "blood and terror" of the Bolsheviks. But we doubt if the international bourgeoisie, in their most sanguine moments, ever counted on such help from the press of the IWW.

Renegades come and go, and one more or less makes but little difference in the final summing up. Harold Lord Varney made quite a little splash, but he has already sunk beneath the black waves of oblivion.[2] But there is one thing to be said for Varney. He broke with the IWW before he sold out to the master class. He didn't play the double game. He didn't say industrial freedom and counterrevolution in the same breath. He renounced Frank Little before he shook hands with his assassins.

We have confidence that the western members of the IWW will deal promptly with this man Kane who has attacked the revolution in their name. A plain man of the rank and file has already answered him in a masterful article in the issue of November 20. They may be confused by queer and crooked arguments of the *One Big Union Monthly* against the Third International. They may want to study it over a while before they undertake the heavy responsibilities of affiliation. But you can't fool them about the Russian Revolution, Mr. Kane! They know, as the workers all over the world know, that the workers republic of Russia represents their highest hopes and aspirations. They know that the enemies of the Russian Revolution are the enemies of the working class!

---

[2] Harold Lord Varney had joined the IWW at the age of 18 in 1912. By 1919 he was one of the organization's major propagandists and the author of a history of the IWW. Just before the Palmer Raids began in Chicago in early January, he suddenly moved to New York. After he was indicted on criminal syndicalism charges in Chicago, he wrote a renunciation of the Wobblies which appeared in the New York *Sunday World* on 8 February 1920. Varney claimed that the IWW's only aim now was to destroy the AFL and wrote that "The system which we revolutionists have called capitalist is regnant today because it has shown itself practical, workable and human." Varney wrote in the same vein for other bourgeois journals, including the *New York Times*.

The Story of Alex Howat

Published April 1921

The following article by Cannon was published in The Liberator. *Though the Kansas United Mine Workers membership numbered only 12,000, making it one of the smaller districts in the union, the Kansas miners were among the most militant sectors of the American labor movement. Their leader Alexander Howat had been imprisoned in 1919 for refusing to call off a local strike, and frequent wildcats finally caused the state to set up a special Industrial Court in 1920.*

Alexander Howat is the president of District 14 of the United Mine Workers. He has been an officer of that union for the most of 19 years, and has not yet learned the profession of labor leadership. He still thinks like a coal digger. The Southwestern Coal Operators' Association has had a 20 years' struggle with the coal miners of Kansas and has never been able to deal with the president of the union in the manner in which professional labor leaders are habitually dealt with.

This alone went far to bring about the famous Kansas contribution to statecraft. The legislature was called into special session for the purpose of passing the Industrial Court law, which forever puts an end, legally, to all strikes in the state of Kansas. Unions are permitted, of course, but they must be strikeless unions. Disputes between employer and employees are legally to be settled by three judges of the Industrial Court appointed by the governor. Thus the function of the state—"to moderate the collisions between the classes"—reaches its ultimate in the state of Kansas. Even on the organized industrial field there shall be no active class struggle. An Industrial Court shall settle disputes "with justice to all concerned" and without stopping production.

Then the coal diggers met in district convention and "repealed" the Industrial Court law, so to speak. District 14 of the United Mine Workers made it "illegal" under union law for its officers to have any dealings whatever with the Industrial Court law of the state. The miners union statute provides heavy penalties against members who may recognize the state Industrial Court statute.

It has been something more than a year since these two conflicting laws were enacted, and now the population of Kansas is split between the two authorities—the government of Kansas and the miners union of Kansas.

Last winter the Industrial Court summoned Alexander Howat, as district president of the union, to come before it to testify in a labor dispute. Not only did he and his Executive Board refuse to appear, but Howat published a statement denouncing the Industrial Court for attempting to interfere with the affairs of the miners union and to "chain men to their jobs like slaves." For this Howat and the other officers of the union were sent to jail for contempt of court. The coal miners of Kansas went out in a mass on a protest strike until their representatives were released on bond.

Since the passage of the anti-strike law, it has been the custom for the miners to walk off the job when occasion demanded, without waiting for a formal strike order from the Executive Board. The Industrial Court has not proceeded against the miners involved in these local strikes. Neither has it attempted to prosecute the miners for the protest strikes which they engaged in each time Howat and the Executive Board members were arrested.

In February an old dispute came to a head at the H&J mines of the Mackie Fuel Company over some back pay amounting to about $200 which the union claimed to be due a boy named Carl Mishmash. President Howat and the District Executive Board called a strike to compel the company to make a settlement.

Howat and the other officers of the union were arrested, for calling strikes in violation of the Industrial Court law. All the mine workers went on a protest strike again, and most of them came into Pittsburg to attend the trial.

"I hope Alex tells them to go to hell," said an Italian boy who couldn't get past the steps of the courthouse. The courtroom only held a fraction of the miners who wanted to hear Howat talk to the judge. They packed the hallways and stood in clusters around on the sidewalk and the street corners. They gathered in the poolrooms, restaurants and cigar stores, all talking about the case.

The Attorney General and the county attorney wanted Howat to make "damaging admissions." He made plenty of them without concern. Howat was asked if he didn't think it would be better to take the grievance of young Mishmash into the Industrial Court. His answer was emphatic:

"No. I never did see any good for labor come out of courts."

"Will you call off the strike now?" inquired the Attorney General.

"No. We will not call off the strike until the Mackie Fuel Company pays that fatherless boy and his widowed mother the back pay that is due them."

"Do you not intend to obey the law?"

"The Industrial Court law is unconstitutional."

After a day of argument of attorneys, Howat, Vice President August Dorchy and Executive Board members John Fleming, Willard Titus, James McIlwrath and Hearl Maxwell were sentenced to a year in jail. The miners in the courtroom were silent for a moment. Then one standing in the back of the room cried out:

"Jail one year, no work one year!"

This expression in various forms was repeated throughout the room. Most of the miners waited at the courthouse until the appeal bonds were made out and the men released.

Soon after the court adjourned I saw Howat, who told me:

"Governor Allen said the Industrial Court law would stop strikes. We said it wouldn't. And the fact that there is a strike now on in this district proves that it can't stop strikes. The best they can do is to put men in jail. And we are not afraid of that. We know what we are up against. We will stay in jail until we are carried out in boxes before we will yield an inch in this fight. The miners of Kansas cannot fight this battle all alone. But I have confidence that the miners of America and organized labor generally will come to our aid, because we are fighting for them as well as for ourselves."

The bankers and businessmen and most of the professionals are on the side of the state of Kansas. They express themselves freely in private conversation, but few of them will say anything about the fight for publication. Several indiscreet merchants have felt the heavy hand of the union boycott, and their experience has made the others cautious. Pittsburg is a union town. The miners have assisted and inspired the organization of most of the other trades. The jitney drivers, the cooks and waiters, the streetcar men, the office workers, the telephone girls—all have functioning unions. The girls who work in the ten-cent store are organized and they went out with all the other unions in a one-day protest strike when Howat was first arrested. The spirit of the miners strongly influences the other unions of the town. They have learned to act together.

A tea and coffee salesman was delivering a set of dishes as a premium from his company the day of the Howat trial. The woman customer asked him what he thought about it.

"They ought to give him life—"

He didn't finish what he was going to say. At that point the lady raised the dishes and broke them over his head.

During the great coal strike in the fall of 1919 Governor Allen undertook to get the Kansas miners back to work. A court order was secured which placed all the miners under temporary control of three receivers appointed by the court on recommendation of the governor. To make it fair for all concerned, one receiver was selected from the coal operators, one from what is called the public, and one from the miners union—a sort of coalition government of industry. Governor Allen had just returned from Red Cross service in Europe. He learned something over there of the weakness of Socialists for bourgeois cabinets. He appointed Willard Titus, a member of the Mine Workers' District Executive Board and an old-time Socialist, to represent labor on the Board of Receivers.

It was a clever stroke on his part. But Titus is not that kind of a socialist. He sent a short note to the governor, informing him that he could not serve the state of Kansas as a receiver for the reason that such an action on his part might conflict with the constitution and bylaws of the United Mine Workers of America, which was the only body authorized to call off a strike of miners.

This is a point of view that is widely held among the miners of District 14. They have no literature on the subject. It is not stated in their preamble or declaration of principles. But when the union orders a strike and the court orders no strike, the miners are not troubled by a divided loyalty. They lay down their picks and go home until further orders from the union.

This looks like a new philosophy which regards a union as an authority higher than any other institution. It is a philosophy which not only turns gray the hair of Kansas employers, but also shocks the sense of propriety of the national heads of the United Mine Workers of America. The national officers of the UMW were fighting Bolshevism in Kansas many years before Gompers heard of Bolshevism in Russia. They never got along well with Howat and always maintained that he carried things too far in his fights with the operators. Howat brought his ideas with him regularly to the national conventions of the union, and this tended to introduce class feeling.

Seven years ago the Southwestern Coal Operators' Association involved itself in a civil suit which required that its books be examined in court. A mysterious entry on their books was an item of $25,000, which they, with apparent hesitation, explained represented a bribe paid to Alexander Howat. John P. White, who was then the International president of the United Mine Workers, was terribly agitated and demanded that Howat resign until he had proved his innocence.

Howat went back to the mines. He stayed there, working as a coal miner for 21 months. The systematic campaign to destroy his influence with the miners began. National organizers were sent into District 14 to undermine him. The national president wrote letters periodically to all the locals denouncing him as a betrayer of the workers. Each time Howat, at his own expense, circularized the locals with his answer. The controversy culminated in a challenge by Howat to debate the issue before mass meetings of the members in his district. White accepted. A series of debates in the different towns of the district was arranged.

The first and only debate took place in the Opera House of Pittsburg, Kansas. The miners still talk about it. Standing room was not available to half of those who wanted to hear it. White spoke and Howat answered him. The miners voted confidence in Howat and demanded that he be provided with his own attorney for a libel suit against the Operators' Association. White agreed. The next debate was scheduled for the following evening at

Frankfort, in the heart of the Kansas coal fields. Several thousand miners were waiting, but White did not appear.

Frank Walsh was engaged by Howat, and the case finally came to trial in May 1916 in Kansas City. By tracing the bank checks and vouchers, Walsh accounted for all of the mysterious $25,000 and proved that Howat had not received a cent of it. Howat was awarded $7,000 damages by the jury.

But the Kansas miners had not waited for the verdict of the jury before bringing in their own. Prior to the trial they re-elected him district president by an almost unanimous vote. He has had no serious opposition since.

Howat was a candidate for the International vice presidency in the last election.[1] A great deal more of electioneering and ballot-box stuffing than usual was required to beat him. Three hundred national organizers, 26 International board members and 65 traveling auditors campaigned against Howat, the coal digger.

The International officers of the United Mine Workers of America will not lose anything if the Kansas organization is broken up and Howat and the other officers are put in jail. The Illinois miners sent $100,000 direct to the Kansas miners, but the International treasury has sent them nothing.[2] Unlimited support was promised as one of the considerations of the Kansas miners going back to work during the big general strike, but it was never made good.

"The International is against us," one of the local leaders in

---

[1] Howat ran on a slate headed by R. Harlin of Washington state, who challenged John L. Lewis for the UMW presidency. Lewis defeated Harlin by 60,000 votes, but Howat was defeated by Lewis' running mate, Philip Murray, by only 11,000 votes.

[2] Alexander Howat was among those who opposed Lewis in his bid to unseat Samuel Gompers as head of the AFL in June 1921, and was the first of the oppositionists to be drummed out of the UMW by Lewis. Later in 1921 the entire Executive Board of District 14 was suspended from the union for refusing to order an end to a strike at a small Kansas concern, where 40 miners had ignored the legal requirement to submit a dispute over work conditions to arbitration. The September 1921 UMW convention upheld the suspension, and shortly thereafter Howat was jailed for violating the Kansas Industrial Court law. At the February 1922 UMW convention Lewis only narrowly defeated another challenge by Howat. Though Gompers' AFL supported Howat, the District 14 leader spent the rest of the decade fighting for his reinstatement.

District 14 told me, "and that is the hardest thing we have to contend with. The coal operators and the Industrial Court of the state of Kansas would have given up their fight long ago if they hadn't known that they could depend upon the secret support of the International. Instead of backing us up to the limit like real leaders of the union ought to do, they are always threatening to revoke our charter and looking for a pretext to enable them to do it."

The Political Prisoners

Published 1 May 1921

The following article by Cannon was published in The Red Album, *a special pamphlet issued for May Day and published by* The Toiler. *A copy of this rare pamphlet is in the collection of the Reference Center for Marxist Studies in New York City.*

Every war has its hazards: the class war more than any other, for the organized workers wage it for the largest stakes in all the world's history—for the Earth and all its fruits, for the complete expropriation of the present-day ruling class. In this worldwide struggle there is no compromise and no quarter. The aim of the workers is nothing less than the complete abolition of the capitalist system. Both classes are organizing on an international scale.

The list of the prisoners of the class war—the Workers' Roll of Honor—is a long one and it increases steadily in spite of all the predictions that "normal conditions" of civil liberty will be restored. There can be no more normal conditions. This is the era of the world revolution. The war is on and there will be no more peace until the workers triumph everywhere.

It is to be expected that many will fall in battle and many be taken prisoner by the enemy before the final goal is reached. The ruling class today is the capitalist class. They maintain themselves in power by force and violence. They make the laws according to their own class interests. The revolutionary movement is a menace to their system. Therefore it is an outlaw movement. Everyone who takes an active part in the struggle for the liberation of the working class takes a chance of going to prison. When the workers get on top they will reverse the order of things. The workers will make the laws then according to their class interests. They will outlaw their class enemies and put them in jail. That is what they are doing in Russia today. It is a very simple proposition. Absolutely natural, absolutely necessary.

The ruling class of America used to laugh at the talk about socialism. They didn't take it seriously. But the Russian Revolution created a panic amongst them. It demonstrated that the thing can be put over quickly if the time is ripe and the workers get the right idea. When they saw the conditions for working class revolt developing here in the United States, they began to search for agitators to put in their jails. They wanted to lock up their ideas.

At first they grabbed everybody who talked "radical"; but after a while they decided that some kind of talk doesn't hurt much. They learned to discriminate between the dangerous ideas and the harmless ones, and to recognize certain propaganda as legal. Some ideas are not legal according to capitalist laws and never will be.

The Communists have an idea that the masters fear, therefore it is illegal and the persecution of the Communists continues. The New York State prison holds five of them; twenty more at Chicago were convicted during the last year of "peace."[1] Revolutionary unionism is a dangerous idea, so the IWW men stay in jail and others go to join them.

There is a definite purpose behind this persistent and systematic railroading of working class agitators. The money-sharks who rule America thought they would be able to break up the movement by taking away the leaders and intimidating the rank and file. But the revolutionary movement grows up out of the life needs of the workers and there is no power that can break it. Persecution is but the fire in which it is tempered and hardened. When leaders go to prison others come forward out of the ranks

---

[1] The anti-Communist persecution known as the "Palmer Raids" began first in New York, where hundreds of Communists were arrested in November 1919. Over 75 were prosecuted but only five—C.E. Ruthenberg, I.E. Ferguson, James Larkin, Harry Winitsky and Benjamin Gitlow—were convicted of criminal anarchy. They received sentences of five to ten years, though most served only about two years. Larkin, a leading Irish Socialist and labor leader, had remained in America after a November 1914 U.S. lecture tour, helping to found the Communist movement. He served almost three years before being pardoned and deported back to Ireland.

The Palmer Raids began on 1 January 1920 in Chicago and were expanded nationally the next day. While hundreds of Communists were arrested in Chicago, only 20 were convicted, among them L.E. Katterfeld, Charles Krumbein and Max Bedacht. They all received sentences of one to five years.

and take their places. When fainthearted followers desert, new recruits, better suited for the stern requirements of the class war, are enlisted.

The men who have gone to prison for the workers' cause know this. That knowledge enables them to bear their confinement without complaint, oppressive as it is to men of independent spirit. They see the proletarian revolution still triumphant in Russia; they see it rising in all the countries of Europe where capitalism has played out its string and cannot reorganize production; they know that we, who are on the outside of the jails, have not forgotten them nor our sacred obligation to appeal to the all-powerful workers in their behalf.

The day is coming when the toiling masses of America will hear that appeal and act upon it. Then the prison doors will be opened and the prisoners set free, for the masses have an authority higher than that of any court. To redouble our efforts to hasten on the day of liberation is the pledge we make to our imprisoned comrades on this First of May.

Who Can Save the Unions?

Published 7 May 1921

The following article by Cannon was published in The Toiler.

The Central Trades and Labor Council of Greater New York has just adopted three recommendations of a special committee of 25 appointed to devise ways and means to combat the "open shop" campaign of the bosses. The unions cannot fight the open shop by the measures proposed; in that respect they have no value. But as striking examples of what not to do they may serve a useful purpose and, from that viewpoint, should be considered and analyzed. This is what the special committee recommended:

1. To organize a speakers bureau which will present the case for unionism to civic bodies, church forums and similar organizations.

2. To amend the constitution of the central body, permitting the seating of fraternal delegates from non-labor organizations interested in unionism.

3. To seek greater cooperation with such bodies as the Interchurch World Movement, and other organizations felt to be working for union labor.[1]

All three of these undertakings are based on a misconception of the nature of the struggle. The impression seems to be that labor's troubles in the present crisis are mainly due to a "misunderstanding" as to the aims of the labor movement on the part of some pious people who don't work for a living, but who are "felt to be working for union labor." But the real misunderstanding is in the minds of the delegates who adopted this program.

[1] The Interchurch World Movement was a Christian social reform organization initiated in 1919 by John D. Rockefeller, Jr., a devout Baptist. It functioned in the early 1920s, and among other activities issued an influential report on the 1919 steel strike.

Civic bodies, church forums, "non-labor organizations"—the elements who go to make up such groupings are poor props for the unions to seek to lean upon. They may "feel" for organized labor, but the organized workers never feel it in the shape of substantial support in their fight.

The "open shop" campaign is one of the manifestations of a state of war that exists in society between two opposing classes: the producers and the parasites. This war cuts through the whole population like a great dividing sword; it creates two hostile camps and puts every man in his place in one or the other. Those to whom the New York unions would turn for aid are beneficiaries of the present system of labor exploitation. Their interests lie with the system and, as a general rule, people do not allow their sympathies to interfere seriously with their interests. They live in the camp of the enemy. Their material welfare is bound up with those who aim to destroy the unions.

No, the labor unions can get no help in their struggle outside of the working class. More than that, they need no other support. The working class has the power not only to defeat the effort to destroy the unions, but to end the system of exploitation altogether. The principal thing lacking for the quick development of this power is the mistaken point of view illustrated by the program of the New York central body.

Let the labor unions put aside their illusions; let them face the issue squarely and fight it out on the basis of the class struggle. Instead of seeking peace when there is no peace, and "understanding" with those who do not want to understand, let them declare war on the whole capitalist regime. That is the way to save the unions and to make them grow in the face of adversity and become powerful war engines for the destruction of capitalism and the reorganization of society on the foundation of working class control in industry and government.

Workers Party of America Born

23 December 1921

The following speech was delivered by Cannon as greetings to the founding convention of the Workers Party of America, held in New York City, 23-26 December 1921. This transcript was published in the 6 January 1922 issue of Voice of Labor, *a Chicago weekly edited by William Z. Foster and others.*

Comrades, after our long struggle to unite our forces, we have succeeded. We have brought together into a convention practically every important left wing element in America. We have brought them together to unite them, and we will not listen to any man who speaks any other word than unity in this convention. (Applause.) We have had for two years many struggles and much strife in our ranks. This was inevitable after the great upheaval of the World War and the Russian Revolution that shook all of our organizations to their foundations and put every one of our old theories and dogmas to the acid test of how it measured up to the crisis. Every one of us was compelled to revise some of our theories and some of our plans. It was no more than natural, I might say it was inevitable, that in the beginning we should have some confusion and some disorganization. Many of us who are here in this convention responded and reacted very quickly to the call that came from Russia. Many who are here in this convention answered the call for the Third International the first day its banner was raised. Others moved slowly. Others at times became impatient with us because they felt that we were too impatient. But we have all moved steadily and consistently to the position where we stand today, where I think there is not a single man or woman in this convention who is not ready to say in categorical terms that he looks for leadership and guidance of the world proletariat, not to the Second International that betrayed the workmen and led them into the universal slaughter, not to the compromisers and evaders of the revolution of the Two and a Half International, but I think every man and woman in this hall will say with me that we look for our guidance to the inspirer, the organizer and the leader of the world proletariat, the Communist International. (Loud, prolonged applause.)

I say, comrades, we have come here by different roads. Some moved by one, some by another. By many methods and as a result of many struggles, we have come to a common ground where we shall unite. There are no fears upon our part, and there need be no fears upon the part of anyone about the character of the party we are launching today, because the people who are here to do it are not men who have sprung up overnight.

It is not an artificial gathering manufactured by our Conference Committee. The men and women who are here to make the Workers Party are the men and women who for many years past have been in the vanguard of the movements that have led to it. They have struggled and suffered and they bear the scars of the battle, and that is the guarantee of the revolutionary integrity of this organization. Now, I think that there is no one here who is more optimistic about the task before us than the circumstances warrant. I think we know enough, comrades and fellow workers, of the colossal tasks ahead of us not to take them lightly, not to take them in a spirit that we are going to solve them by resolutions or by an excessive amount of phraseology in our programs. We know that we are going to solve them only if we try in a true Marxist spirit to analyze them and understand them and then face them and fight out the issues. The task is before us.

We have a labor movement that is completely discouraged and demoralized. We have an organized labor movement that is unable on any front to put up an effective struggle against the drive of destruction organized by the masters. We have a revolutionary labor movement which, until this inspirational call for a Workers Party convention, was disheartened, discouraged and demoralized. Our labor unions, upon which the workers build their first line of resistance—and I want to say right here, comrades, that you must face it as the most menacing thing on the horizon—the labor unions of America are being broken up because there is not sufficient unified understanding, because there is not sufficient leadership to save them, and I say that unless we comrades, unless we, the revolutionary workers, we who know that only on a program of the class struggle can they mass and fight victoriously, unless we organize and prepare to unify and direct them, to lead their struggles, then I say, the American labor movement will be destroyed and black reaction will settle upon this country. We have a responsibility upon us, and we must find the way out. Yes, reaction is in full sway in America.

Many of our finest spirits, our bravest boys, our best fighters languish their lives away in the penitentiaries of America. The boys that threw themselves into the struggle during the war, those who did not take down their flag when the persecution became severe, the very cream of the movement, have languished in prison for over two years, and I say it is a shame and a disgrace that we have not made any effective protest against it. It is a pitiful thing that for two years the campaign for release of our fellow workers and comrades, which should have been carried on upon the basis of the class struggle, which should have been the rallying cry to arouse the workers and inspire an irresistible campaign for amnesty, has been left almost entirely to such as the American Civil Liberties Bureau on the one hand, the Socialist Party's Amnesty Committee on the other, and the IWW lawyers on the third, and there is very little difference between them.

Now, I say, we are going to change the rout the workers are confronted with. We are going to try to stop the stampede by putting up a program and plan of action with a set of fighting leaders, and give out the rallying cry: Fellow workers, stand and fight! It is better to die in the struggle than to be driven to death and crushed without effective resistance. (Applause.)

I think that everyone who was present at our meeting last night had ample reassurance and an ample answer to the question upon everybody's lips: Is this real unity, is this at last an effective getting together?

At last night's meeting the question was answered, as it is today. There came to that meeting fighting men and women from all fields, from all movements. From the IWW for the Red International of Labor Unions came George Hardy. From the American Federation of Labor came J.W. Johnstone. From the Socialist Party, from the left wing, from those who long ago left the Socialist Party, from all parts of the country they came, they, the battlers, came, showing the marks and scars of conflict and persecution. They came to submit in the name of unity, and they sealed and guaranteed our pledge to present a unified movement to the workers of America.

There are only a few things I wish to touch upon further. They are a few suggestions on the nature of our organization. In our Convention Call you will notice we are not very verbose. We did not put in very many revolutionary words or foreign phrases, because that period is past and the time is here for action—revolutionary action is here. We are prepared to meet this need on the basis of the definite and emphatic principles upon which we stand. One of these is a fighting party, and that, I say, is the difference between us and other political organizations claiming the support of the workers. The difference between us and the Socialist Party or the Farmer-Labor Party, or the Gompers bureaucracy, will not be alone in the fact that we declare for the final revolution and they do not, not because we are willing to hold before the workers the final goal and all of these others are not, but because in terms of class struggle, on questions of bread and butter, on housing, on labor organization, wages and hours, they are afraid to fight, and the Workers Party says it will fight on every single one of these issues. That is the difference between a betrayers' organization, a cowardly organization, as against a workers' organization. I have talked to comrades who have fears of reformist tendencies. They are afraid we did not put enough revolutionary words in our program, and I say, comrades, there is no danger of reformism in a party that is organized and led by class-conscious fighters. Reformism comes only from those who do not want to fight, and the guarantee that our organization will not be reformistic is not alone in our program, but in the personnel of the delegates who have fought consistently and determinedly on the basis of the class struggle in the past, and that is the guarantee of our activity in the future.

With regard to the form of organization, we also speak specifically. We want a centralized party. Now what do we mean by that?

We want to build a serious movement that will be bound together by enough discipline to enable it to act as a united body. We are not going to have an excessive amount of referendums in our organization, because those go with organizations that are more concerned with talk than with activity. We want an organization able to move as one man and effectively in the right direction, and for that purpose we build it up on the basis of democratic centralization. We bind it together by discipline, and we call upon every man and woman to enter it in the spirit of the soldier, ready to give everything the organization asks, and willing to do everything the organization says. We want to make it consequently a party of action, a fighting party, a centralized party. These are our slogans, comrades. If we will follow them, we will build up an organization to which the disheartened and demoralized workers of America will rally. They will hail it as a morning star. They are looking for it. I say, comrades, they are looking for it with longing eyes. The workers do not like division. There is nothing that dispirits them more than to see their own battle front divided, their own leaders demoralized. In the past we were not able to give them unified leadership. Let us move quickly away from past mistakes. The first step in the right direction is to take out of our minds the last bit of small personal malice against individuals or organizations which might militate against the best fraternal spirit in which we must meet and unite forces. Let us, every one of us, in the true spirit of revolutionary comradeship, join together in this work. The past is dead. Let the dead past bury its dead. We have come together to face the future. Let us judge each other upon the activities of the future and not upon the activities that lie behind us.

The final word is for unity, unity of the revolutionary workers. Down with those who speak against us! Down with those who seek to divide the revolutionary movement! Long live the unification of revolutionary forces! Long live the Workers Party to be! Long live the workers republic that the Workers Party fights for. (Long and loud applause.)

The American Question

ca. November 1922

The following unpublished and undated document was written at the behest of Leon Trotsky during the Fourth Congress of the Communist International (held in Moscow, 5 November-5 December 1922) by Cannon and other American Communists who were struggling against the maintenance of the dual structure of a clandestine Communist party alongside the legal Workers Party. It played a crucial role in winning Comintern support for the liquidation of the underground party. Among the document's signers were delegates Cannon, Max Bedacht and Arne Swabeck, under the names Cook, Lansing and Marshall. The other signatories have not been identified, though one of the Young Communist League delegates is probably Martin Abern who was in Moscow at this time. This is a translation of a German-language copy in the Theodore Draper Papers, Special Collections Department, Robert W. Woodruff Library, Emory University. A slightly different English translation was published in Spartacist *No. 40 (Summer 1987).*

In the United States the objective preconditions for revolution are not yet fully developed. In addition, the class consciousness of the American workers is still undeveloped; they have not even risen to the point of undertaking independent political action.

However, there is developing within the trade union movement a rapidly increasing rebelliousness against the official union bureaucracy and, linked to this, a steadily growing tendency in favor of a labor party. Our main task at present is to develop these tendencies, to crystallize and organize them; tactics must be oriented toward making us an integral component of the labor party when it is founded.

The illegality of the Communist Party of America is a major obstacle in its work. In addition, American workers are still dominated by democratic illusions, so that they grasp neither the aim nor the reasons for conspiratorial, clandestine organizations. We must therefore wage a determined struggle for a legal Communist party. A large part of the organized workers movement will support us in such a struggle. If we win, the party will enjoy the enormous advantages of legal party organization, at least for a time. But if we lose, the fact of our defeat will greatly contribute to destroying the democratic illusions of the masses; at the same time they would come to grasp the necessity of illegal organization.

This struggle must be carried out with the legal party that already exists. Every function which can be carried out openly and legally must be transferred to it; its program must gradually be strengthened and clarified; the duties of members must be increased and their discipline must be tightened; all with a view toward the goal of making it a real Communist party.

We are hindered in carrying out these tasks by the fact that the great majority of members are comrades born abroad, mainly of Russian origin, who judge things not from the standpoint of the objective conditions prevailing in America, but on the basis of their subjective conceptions, which are based on events in Europe. This is why they oppose every attempt to realistically apply the Comintern's tactical guidelines to American conditions.

The simultaneous existence of these two irreconcilable elements in the party is the real cause of the ineffectiveness and sterility of the American movement. The bitter disputes and splits which develop in the American party over every fleeting question are merely symptoms of the more deep-seated sickness in the party. The unity imposed by the Comintern has not resolved the problem in America, but only aggravated it.

We ask the Comintern for a clear presentation of its guidelines concerning the questions mentioned above and request, in the event that a new split occurs in the course of realistically implementing these guidelines in America, that the Comintern not again insist on a mechanical formula for unity.

Signatures follow:

Marshall, Cook and Lansing
Minority of the delegation to the Comintern

By signing, the following comrades declare that they are in complete agreement with the above:

Starr and Marlow
Delegates of the Young Communist League of America to the Congress of the Youth International

Godfrey, Brooks and Knowles
Delegates of the Trade Union Educational League to the Congress of the Profintern

Harrow
Communist Party of America regional organizer

The Fifth Year of the Russian Revolution

Early 1923

When Cannon returned from Moscow in January 1923, he undertook a five-month speaking tour around the U.S. This lecture on Soviet Russia was published by the Workers Party in a 1923 pamphlet.

Russia Through the Shadows

The story of Soviet Russia for the first four years after the revolution was a story of desperate struggle against tremendous odds. The fight of the Russian workers did not end with their victory over the bourgeoisie within Russia. The capitalist class of the entire world came to the aid of Russian capitalism.

The workers republic was blockaded and shut off from the world. Counterrevolutionary plots and uprisings inside of Russia were financed and directed from the outside. Mercenary invading armies, backed by world capital, attacked Soviet Russia on all sides. On top of all this came the terrible famine which threatened to deal the final blow.

In those four years Soviet Russia indeed went "through the shadows." But now, after five years of the revolution, we can tell a brighter story. In 1922 Soviet Russia began to emerge from the shadows and started on the upward track. The long and devastating civil war was at an end and the counterrevolution stamped out. The great famine was conquered. The last of the invading foreign armies—except the Japanese in the Far East—had been driven from Russian soil; and the workers government, freed from the terrible strain and necessity of war, was enabled, for the first time, to turn its efforts and energies to the great constructive task of building a new Russia on the ruins of the old.

While I was yet in Russia the Red Army drove the Japanese out of Vladivostok and set up the soviets again. And before the Fourth Congress of the Communist International was ended, we had the joy of hearing comrade Lenin say that all the territory of Russia was at last living in peace under the red flag of the soviets.

I reached Moscow on the first day of June. Signs of recuperation from the long travail were already noticeable. The streets and sidewalks were being repaired and buildings were being painted; for the first time in five years, they told me. During the war all resources and all energies went for bitter necessity; everything else had to wait. Even the buildings in the Kremlin got their first coat of paint this year.

I was riding on a Moscow streetcar one day soon after my arrival, with a comrade who had once been in America and who now holds a responsible position in the Soviet government. I spoke of the good appearance and condition of the car; it had just been newly painted, and looked very pretty. They know more about blending colors than we do; and they care more about it, too. He told me that the Moscow streetcar system had been greatly improved during the past year. The number of cars in operation had been greatly increased, the trackage extended and a fairly reliable schedule maintained. The Moscow streetcar workers were very proud of their achievement; especially so because the improvement in the service had brought with it a corresponding improvement in their own living conditions.

The famous Genoa Conference was still alive at that time, the conference which Lloyd George called to settle the problems of Europe, but which didn't succeed in settling anything except the career of Lloyd George. France and Belgium, you will remember, were demanding that the property in Russia which had been confiscated by the revolution should be restored to the original foreign owners. Russia had not yet given her final answer, and I asked my friend in the streetcar what he thought it would be.

He said, "Most of the big industrial plants in Russia, and even a part of the railroad system, belonged to foreign capitalists before the revolution. Russia was practically a colony of European capitalism."

"Do you know," he asked me, "who used to own the streetcar system in Moscow—it belonged to the poor Belgian capitalists, and they are trying to get it back at Genoa."

I asked him what chance the poor Belgian capitalists had to get their streetcars back. He answered, "No chance at all."

He told me as soon as that demand became known the Moscow streetcar workers—as well as the workers in the other important industries—called meetings and passed resolutions to this effect: "The foreign capitalists tried for four years to take these industries away from us by armed force, and they couldn't succeed. Now we are certainly not going to let them talk us out of them at the diplomatic table."

Before I went to Russia I had read much about the impending collapse of the Soviet government. A story of this kind used to appear on an average of about once a week in the *New York Times* and other capitalist newspapers; and no doubt you have all read them. Here lately the capitalist press has dropped that story and the Socialist Party and the IWW papers have taken it up. I spent seven months in Russia, and I assure you that I looked diligently for the signs of this famous "collapse," but I couldn't find it. On the contrary, the more I investigated, the more I saw of the attitude of the Russian workers, the more I became convinced that the Soviet government under the control of the Communist Party is firmer and stronger now than at any period in its history.

I saw the power of the Russian Communist Party tested by an historic conflict with another party which challenged its control. The occasion was the trial of the leaders of the so-called Social Revolutionary Party.

These Social Revolutionaries were brought to trial before the proletarian court and when I was in Moscow, I was present, with an interpreter, on the day it opened in the Labor Temple, and at many of the other sessions. It was a fair trial—nothing like it ever occurred in America. The defendants were allowed to talk as freely and as much as they pleased. There was no restriction whatever on their liberty to speak in their own defense. The trouble with them was that they had no defense. The Soviet government had the goods on them. A number of the prisoners had repented of their crimes against the revolution, and they testified for the Soviet government.

The case was clear. These leaders of the SR Party, defeated in the political struggle with the Communist Party, resorted to a campaign of terror and assassination. They murdered Uritsky and Volodarsky. They dynamited the building which housed the Central Committee of the Russian Communist Party and killed fourteen people. They had Trotsky and Zinoviev marked for assassination. It was an SR bullet that brought Lenin down and from which he still suffers today.

They went even further than that. They went to the point that all the opponents of the Soviet system go in the end. They collaborated with the White Guards and they took money from the French government to do its dirty work in Russia. All this was clearly proven in the trial; most of it out of the mouths of men who had taken active part in the campaign.

While the trial was in progress occurred the anniversary of the assassination of Volodarsky, one of the most beloved leaders of the revolution, who had been shot down by the SRs; and the Communist Party called upon the workers to honor his memory by a demonstration for the Soviet government and against the SR Party. The Communist speakers went to the factories and requested that no worker march except of his own free will.

I stood in Red Square and watched that demonstration. Practically the whole working class population of Moscow marched that day, carrying banners which proclaimed their solidarity with the Soviet government and the Communist Party, and demanding the death penalty for the leaders of the counterrevolutionary, White Guard SR Party.

I was standing in the reviewing stand with the members of the Executive Committee of the Communist International. It was five o'clock in the evening. The demonstration had commenced at noon and the workers of Moscow were still marching in wide streams from all directions through Red Square. One of the leaders of the Russian Communist Party turned to us and said, "Comrades, this is the funeral of the counterrevolution in Russia!"

So it was. The counterrevolution in Russia is as dead as the King of Egypt. The only places there is any life left in it are Paris, London and the East Side of New York.

Economic Reconstruction

Politically, the Soviet regime, under the leadership of the Communist Party, greatly strengthened itself in the past year. And economic progress went hand in hand with political improvement. Much of this economic progress, and its reflection in the field of politics, was due to the timely introduction of the New

Economic Policy, or, as they say in Russia, the "NEP."

Early in 1921 it became evident that some of the drastic economic measures taken by the Soviet government, under the pressure of political and military necessity, could not be adhered to. The backward social and industrial development of Russia, together with the failure of the European proletariat to succeed in making a revolution, compelled the Soviet government to make a retreat on the economic field.

The Soviet government had been forced to adopt many of these extreme economic measures by political and military necessity. But Lenin did not hesitate to say that they had been going too fast. The economic development of Russia did not permit the direct transition to a system of pure socialist economy.

When this frank and obvious statement was made by Lenin, the yellow socialists of the Second International, as well as some so-called "Marxians" of this country who have been against the Russian Revolution because it wasn't made according to their blueprint, find much satisfaction. They say: "Ha! Ha! We told you so. The Bolshevik Revolution was a mistake!" Their conclusions are that the workers of Russia should give up the political power and go back to capitalism.

But the Russian Bolsheviks are practical people. They have made the revolution once and they don't intend to go back and do it over again. They say: "No, the revolution was not a mistake, and we will not go back to capitalism. We will make a retreat on the economic field, but we will keep the political power in the hands of the proletariat and use that as a lever to develop our industry to the point where it can serve as a base for a system of socialist economy. And if we can't find anything in the books to support this procedure, we'll write a book of our own."

There are people who say that Russia has gone back to capitalism, but that is not true. In Russia they say, "It is neither capitalism nor communism, it is 'NEP'!" Trotsky described the present situation in Russia as follows:

"The workers control the government. The workers government has control of industry and is carrying on this industry according to the methods of the capitalist market, of capitalist calculation." I think that is the best concise definition of the NEP.

The state controls commerce and has a monopoly of foreign

trade. The state owns all the land, and from the peasants who cultivate the land it collects a tax in kind of approximately 10 percent of the crop. Free trade is permitted. The peasants may sell or exchange their surplus products after the tax has been paid.

Private enterprises exist alongside of state enterprises. The workers in both state and private enterprises are paid wages in money and the medium of calculation and exchange is money. That is the NEP.

The New Economic Policy was first introduced in the spring of 1921; but it was not until 1922 that the effects of it began to be felt on a wide scale. During the period that I was in Russia the positive and beneficial results of the NEP could be seen in all fields.

The paper money of Soviet Russia, like that of all countries ruined by the war, was greatly inflated. But in 1922 it was stabilized for a period of six months as against three months in 1921. The peasants were able in 1922 to overcome the famine and they voluntarily brought their tax in kind to the government elevators and warehouses. Only in the most exceptional and isolated cases was it necessary to use force to collect the tax.

Before the revolution the Russian peasant had the landlord on his back. Today the landlord system is done away with; there is not one landlord left in the whole of Russia. All that the peasant produces, above his tax in kind of approximately 10 percent, is his own, to do with as he sees fit. The result is a very friendly attitude toward the Soviet government.

1922 marked the beginning of a general revival in trade industry. The revolution inherited from the old regime an industrial system that was poorly developed, inefficiently managed and badly demoralized by the strain of the imperialist war. The long civil war, the interventions and the blockade dealt still heavier blows to Russian industry and almost brought it to complete ruin.

To try to do anything with it seemed a hopeless task. Agents of other governments, industrial experts, went to Russia, investigated her industries and reported that they couldn't be revived without assistance from the outside. It was reports of this kind that bolstered up the hope of European and American capitalists and their political agents that the Soviet government was certain to fall.

These gentlemen reckoned without the Russian working class and the Communist Party that leads and inspires it.

In the revolution and the war which followed it for more than four years, the Communist Party dared the "impossible"—and accomplished it. The same courage and determination characterize its attack on the problem of industry. Seval Zimmand told me a story of a meeting which he had an opportunity to attend in the Ural industrial district. It was a conference of engineers, factory managers and trade union leaders presided over by Bogdanov, the commissar of the Supreme Council of Public Economy. After discussing all features of the situation with the engineers and managers and hearing their reports, Bogdanov said, "I know that it is hard to improve the industries in the Ural. But the industries of the Ural can be improved and the industries of the Ural must be improved."

There, in one word, is a definition of the Communist Party of Russia—the party of MUST! While others say, "It is impossible," and, "We had better wait," or, "It can't be done," the Communist Party says, "It must be done!"—and the Communists go ahead and do it.

Russian industry, on the whole, in 1922 registered a general increase of production of more than 100 percent. This brought the standard of production up to 25 percent of the pre-war condition. This condition is bad enough, but the Russian workers lived through a worse one, and they have begun to make headway.

Russian exports in 1922 were six times greater than the year before. In 1921 the exports were only 5 percent of the imports. Last year they were brought up to 25 percent. All the light industries, that is, those which produce for the market, improved remarkably last year and are now in pretty fair shape. The heavy industries, that is, the coal, iron, steel and oil industries, whose product goes mainly to the other state industries—only about 10 percent of it being sold in the market—recover more slowly. Here the problem is a colossal one. For a long time after the revolution, all these basic industries were in the hands of counter-revolutionary armies. The iron region in the Urals, the coal, iron and steel in the Donets Basin—the Pennsylvania of Russia—and the oil fields around Baku, were all held by hostile armies. When the Red Army recaptured these territories, the industries were in ruins.

The Soviet government bent itself to this task and in 1922 made substantial headway. Coal production was increased 25 percent over 1921, naphtha 20 percent, cast iron 42 percent, while iron and steel production in 1922 doubled that of the year before. In 1913, before the imperialist war began, the Russian railroads loaded 30,000 cars a day. In 1918, at the low tide of the revolution, when the blockade was still in effect and hostile armies surrounded Russia with a ring of steel, the number of railroad cars loaded daily dropped to 7,590. By 1921 this figure was brought up to 9,500. In 1922 the improvement was continued and 11,500 cars were loaded; this is more than one-third of the prewar volume.

Russia's great problem today is the problem of heavy industry. The leaders of the Russian Revolution recognize this and are concentrating all their energies on that task.

The Soviet government is saving on everything in order to help the heavy industry. All state appropriations, even those for schools, are being reduced for this purpose. When some sentimental people complained that the reduction of school appropriations was a backward step, Lenin answered that the chance for Russia to become a really civilized and cultured nation depended on the improvement of the heavy industry. That is the foundation.

The Soviet government last year made a profit of 20 million gold rubles on its trading activities. That is the equivalent of ten million dollars, and the whole of it was given by the government as a subsidy to heavy industry. Likewise a considerable portion of the tax collected from the peasants and from the Nepmen engaged in commerce goes for that purpose.

One way of attracting outside capital, which has attained some degree of success, is through the formation of so-called mixed companies. The Soviet government goes into partnership with private capitalists in commercial enterprises, such as putting up part of the capital and sharing in the management and the profits. Lenin told us that by this means a large number of workers are enabled to learn from the capitalists how to carry on commerce; and the Soviet government retains the right to dissolve the companies later.

The wages of the Russian workers kept pace with the improvement of production, increasing in just about the same proportion. Wages are not yet up to the pre-war standard. The Russian shoe workers today get 33.3 percent of pre-war wages. The metal workers get 42.9 percent, the textile workers 42.1 percent and the wood workers 57.9 percent. Wages vary according to the conditions of the various industries. The foodstuff industry is pretty well on its feet and the bakery workers get 81.9 percent of pre-war wages, while the tobacco industry pays 13.1 percent. These figures do not tell the whole story. Because the workers, under the Soviet government, get many special privileges such as cheap rent, food at cost, etc.

The Russian worker, after five years of the revolution, is not as well off materially today as he was under the tsar. But his condition is now steadily improving and the political and spiritual gains of the revolution are beyond calculation. There is no sentiment among the workers for a return to the old regime. To those who measure everything in terms of concrete, immediate material gains, and who ask the Russian workers what they have to show for their five years of revolution, they answer: "The revolution is not over yet."

Trotsky pointed out at the Fourth Congress of the Communist International that the French standard of living, ten years after the great revolution which smashed the feudal system and opened the way for the development of the capitalist mode of production, was far below that which prevailed immediately before the revolution. Revolutions destroy before they can build anew, and in this destruction the people suffer. But the destructive phase of the Russian Revolution is already past and in five more years, at the present rate of progress, there is no doubt that the material conditions of the Russian workers, as well as their spiritual, intellectual and political conditions, will be far better than ever before.

Since private industrial and commercial enterprises exist alongside of state enterprises, the question naturally arises—and it certainly is a most important question—what is the relative strength of the two? This question is answered by the figures on the number employed by each. The state controls all means of transport, including the railroads, and in this transportation industry 1,000,000 are employed. The state trusts—these are corporations organized by the state for the commercial and financial management of the various industries under its control—employ 1,300,000. And in non-trust state enterprises another half million workers. This brings the total of state employees up to 2,800,000. Private enterprises employ only 70,000.

There is little danger in this ratio. The danger is still lessened by the fact that the state holds all the big and important industries which are the bases of power while private capital is confined to smaller factories and to commerce. The average number of workers employed in state enterprises is 250 while private plants have an average of only 18.

Trade Unionism in Russia

Practically all the workers employed in both state and private undertakings are organized into the Russian trade unions. These trade unions are organized according to the industrial form; there is but one union for each industry. The membership of the Russian trade unions is three million. Before the revolution the total membership of all the trade unions of Russia was only 1,385.

The trade unions have played a great part in the revolution. During the period of "war communism" they were closely united to the apparatus and took upon themselves a number of government responsibilities. But under the New Economic Policy they have completely separated from the state machinery and have reorganized as independent bodies, having for their main functions the defense of the interests of the workers in the factories.

Strikes were never prohibited by law under the Soviet government, but during the period of the civil war the Trade Union Congress voluntarily decided to forego that method of struggle. Under the New Economic Policy, however, the right to strike has been reaffirmed. Strikes are discouraged and do not occur very often. Boards of conciliation, courts of arbitration and mutual agreements are first resorted to, and as a rule all controversies are settled by these means.

I never saw a strike in Soviet Russia and never heard of one taking place while I was there. But comrade Melnichansky, the head of the Moscow trade unions, told me of a few that had occurred under his jurisdiction. In those cases all the methods and forms of industrial warfare familiar to European and American labor movements automatically developed, such as strike committees, pickets, strike benefits, etc. There had been rare cases, he told me, when unscrupulous employers had tried to operate the struck plant by means of ignorant peasants recruited from the villages. The government gave no favor to this "freedom of contract" so popular with our own government. And a visit from the pickets usually sufficed to convince the strikebreakers that they had better go back where they came from. I asked comrade Melnichansky if they had encountered any strike injunctions. He laughed and answered, "My dear comrade, you must understand that this is not America!"

I attended the Fifth All-Russian Trade Union Congress. It is analogous to the national convention of the American Federation of Labor, but it was quite a different looking delegation from the sleek, fat, overdressed "men of labor" who meet once a year under the chairmanship of Gompers. There were more than a thousand delegates present at this congress, and I saw only one man who appeared to be overweight.

The congress was held in the Moscow Labor Temple which, in the old days, was the Nobles Club. It is a gorgeous place, with marble pillars, crystal chandeliers and gold leaf decorations. One could imagine that the "Nobles" had many a good time there in the "good old days." But, in the words of the comic strip artist, "Them days is over." The workers are the ruling class today and they have taken all the best places for their own purposes.

I saw something at that congress that never yet happened in America. Zinoviev and Rykov came to the congress to make a report on behalf of the government. I thought how natural it was, in a country ruled by the workers, for the government to report to the trade unions. It is just as natural as it is in America for the government to report to the Chamber of Commerce. The same principle applies. Governments have the habit of reporting to those whom they really represent. The old proverb says, "Tell me whose bread you eat and I'll tell you whose song you sing."

The Soviet government is a labor government and it makes no secret of the fact that it is partial to the working class. It doesn't pretend to be fair or neutral. They frankly call the government a dictatorship. "It's just like your own government in America," they told me, "only it is a dictatorship of a different class."

"Otherwise the two governments are much alike," they said. "They are both dictatorships. But there is another difference. The Russian government says it is a dictatorship and makes no camouflage about it. The government of the United States pretends to be fair and democratic, to represent both the workers and the capitalists, but whenever you have a big strike the government soon shows whom it belongs to."

Ninety-eight percent of all the delegates to this Fifth All-Russian Trade Union Congress were members of the Communist Party. Those figures constitute another answer to the question: "How does the Communist Party keep in power?" When more than a thousand trade union delegates come together from all parts of Russia, and more than 98 percent of them are Communists, it is a pretty reliable indication, I think, that the Communist Party has its roots very deep in the basic organizations of the workers.

Referring to the fact that wages of the Russian workers had been increased 100 percent during the past year, keeping even pace with the increased production, Zinoviev laid before the congress the program of the Communist Party on the question of wages and production. He said the two must go forward together, hand in hand.

"Every country in the world," he said, "outside of Russia has built up its industrial system at the price of an impoverished and exploited working class. The capitalist countries have built a marvelous industrial system; they have erected great structures of steel and stone and cement; they have piled up wealth that staggers calculation. And alongside of all this they have a hungry and impoverished working class which made it all. For all their toil and accomplishments the workers have reaped a harvest of poverty and misery." "Russia," he said, "must not go that way. We are a working class nation and we must not forget that the interest of the workers must be our first concern, always. We will strain all energies to increase production, but here at the beginning let us lay down an iron rule for our future guidance: that every improvement in industry must bring a corresponding improvement in the living standards of the workers in the industry.

We want to build a big industry and we want to build it quickly. But we also want to build a bigger and better human race."

The Workers and the Red Army

Between the trade unions and the Red Army there is a close and fraternal unity that does not prevail between the labor movement and the army of any other country in Europe. The trade unionists regard the red soldiers as the protectors and defenders of the labor movement, and they treat them with the highest honor.

There is a reason for this attitude. When some of the industrial districts of Russia fell into the hands of the counter-revolutionary armies, the first thing the White Guards did, after dissolving the soviets, was to break up the trade unions, shooting or jailing the leaders; it was something like West Virginia. And when the Red Army reconquered those territories, the trade unions were immediately reorganized under the protection of its bayonets. This is the reason for the brotherly solidarity between the unions and the army.

It was not surprising, therefore, that the Red Army should send a representative to the Trade Union Congress. General Budenny, the head of the famous Red Cavalry, was there and he was given a tumultuous reception. I was thinking of the time a general of our army visited the American trade unionists, the time that General Wood came to Gary.[1] For several minutes they applauded and shouted for General Budenny. He was embarrassed and had difficulty getting started. His speech consisted of only one sentence, but it was enough. Drawing himself up to a military posture, he clicked his heels together and saluted the delegates and said, "Comrades, just tell us what you want us to do, and we'll do it!"

The Red Army is a new factor in the international situation, and a very important one. The diplomats cannot meet today to partition off the earth without asking, "What will the Red Army

---

[1] A reference to the occupation of Gary, Indiana by federal troops under the command of Major General Leonard Wood during the 1919 steel strike. Martial law was declared, and hundreds of strikers were arrested and deported as the troops helped break the strike.

do?" The red soldier is present at all the councils of the war makers. He puts his fist on the table and says, "I am in on the war game in Europe from now on!"

The Red Army is something new under the sun, a proletarian army, made up exclusively of workers and peasants, with most of its officers drawn from the working class. It proved its mettle in the long and successful struggle against the interventionist armies. It has a morale, spirit and discipline unknown to the military history of Europe. There is not an army on the continent of Europe that, man for man, can stand up against it.

When I was in Russia the size of the Red Army had been reduced to 800,000 men. Since I left, it has been still further reduced to 600,000. But that is not its full strength by any means. The standing army of 600,000 is only a skeleton around which five million men, already trained for service, can be quickly organized.

The Red Army is a powerful military machine, but that is not all. It is a school, the greatest school on earth. The great bulk of its soldiers come from the peasantry, and 80 percent of the Russian peasants are illiterate. But in the Red Army they are all taught to read and write. Last May Day they celebrated the liquidation of illiteracy in the Red Army. Trotsky made the statement that on that day there was not a soldier in the army who was not able to read and write. The Russian Bolsheviks have taken an instrument of destruction and utilized it for a great constructive purpose.

I visited some Red Army camps and learned something about the spirit of the soldiers at first hand. I had read something about it and wished to check up on what I had read. I asked Trotsky about it and he said, "Go to the camps and see the soldiers themselves. Then you will understand it." I asked him why the red soldier has a different attitude toward the government from that of the other soldiers of Europe, and he answered, "The attitude of the red soldier toward the Soviet government is determined by the attitude of the Soviet government toward the red soldier."

That is the secret of it. That is the reason for the intense loyalty of the red soldier which the old-school militarists cannot understand. The red soldier is respected and honored in time of peace as well as in war. He is not heroized as he marches off to battle and then chased up a back alley when he comes home. He is not given a medal when he is needed and refused a job or a handout when the war is over. In the working class society of Russia the red soldier has a place of dignity and honor. In Russia the soldiers and the workers are the real "people of importance."

I saw another phase of the educational work of the army in one of the camps. It was a moving picture show attended by about two thousand soldiers. It was a moving picture of large-scale grain farming in Canada. Most of the soldiers in the audience were peasant lads. They had come from the villages and their idea of agriculture was founded on the primitive, individualistic methods they had always known. Most of them had never seen a farming implement larger than a one-horse plow. Here on the screen before them was flashed a picture of modern farming on a big scale, with tractors, gang-plows and great threshing machines; a single working unit covering hundreds of acres at a time.

They drank in that picture very eagerly. As I watched them I saw another picture. I saw those peasant lads going back home when their service in the army would be ended, with their newly acquired knowledge and their vision of the great world outside their little villages, telling their friends and their old folks of the great farming machinery which the city worker will manufacture for the peasants and which will be the means of developing large-scale communal farming instead of small-scale individual farming, and which will transform the individualist peasant of today into the Communist peasant of tomorrow.

I found the red soldiers pretty well informed as to what is going on in the world. They spoke of the prospects of revolution in Germany with the air of men who had read and talked much about it. That is part of their education; Trotsky keeps them fully informed about international developments, and there are special Communist detachments in all regiments who carry on a constant propaganda for internationalism.

Capitalist journalists write a great deal about the intense national patriotism of the Red Army. These stories are usually written by journalists who sit around in Moscow hotels and cook up stories about it, and, as a rule, they are very far from the truth. As a matter of fact, the main effort of Communist propaganda in the army is to overcome tendencies toward Russian national patriotism and to develop a patriotism to the international proletariat.

Since the army quit singing *God Save the Tsar* it has had no national official hymn. The official air played in the Red Army is the *Internationale.* Internationalism is the watchword.

This was impressed upon us very vividly by a speech we heard at the graduation exercises of the school of Red Cavalry commanders at Moscow. A number of international delegates attended those exercises and spent the entire day with the young students who were just finishing their studies. For several hours we watched them perform hair-raising feats on horseback and late in the afternoon we had dinner with them in the mess hall. After dinner the delegates from the various countries each spoke a few words of greeting to the graduates and then they put up one of the graduates to respond. He was lifted upon the table from which we had just eaten our dinner, a young Communist lad who only a short time before had been taken from the factory, put through an intensive course of instruction and on that day was being turned out as a red commander.

"Comrades," he said, "we greet you as comrades and brothers in the same army with us. We do not want you to think of us as soldiers of Russia, but as soldiers of the international proletariat. Our army is a working class army and the working class of the world is our country. We will be very glad when the workers of Europe rise in revolt and call on us for assistance; and when that day comes they will find us ready."

The Workers and Internationalism

It is not only the red soldiers in Russia who are internationalists. Internationalism permeates the entire working class. When the Russian workers rose in revolt five years ago and struck the blow that destroyed Russian capitalism they were confident that the workers throughout Europe would follow their example. They have been waiting five years for the international revolution and they still believe it is coming. Nothing has been able to shake that faith. They believe in the workers of Europe as they believe in the sun.

Ah, the faith of those Russian workers! It is so strong that it communicates itself to others. All of us who saw and felt it came away with our own faith surer and stronger. One afternoon I heard a band playing in the street outside the hotel where I was living. I looked out the window and saw a big parade marching with banners flying. I took a Russian comrade with me and we followed the parade. It wound up at the Labor Temple with a mass meeting. There were enthusiastic speeches, the band played the *Internationale* and the crowd sang it. It was a demonstration of the bakery workers of Moscow with the bakers of Bulgaria who were out on a general strike. And those bakery workers of Moscow, from their meager wages, raised a fund to send to their comrades in faraway Bulgaria to cheer them on in the fight.

On the fifth anniversary of the revolution the delegates of the Communist parties and red trade unions were the guests of the proletariat of Petrograd.[2] A great throng of workers met us at the station. We symbolized to them the international labor movement and they gave us a warm and generous welcome. Red Army troops were drawn up before the station, the streets in all directions were packed with workers who had come to greet us, and from every building and post flew banners, proclaiming the fifth anniversary of the Russian Revolution and hailing the international revolution.

That day we saw a demonstration of the workers of Petrograd. I shall never forget it. They had built a special reviewing stand for us before the Uritsky Palace and we stood there and watched them march by in detachments according to the factories where they worked. They carried the same old banners which they had carried five years before, many of them torn by the bullets that flew during the decisive battle.

I never saw before such an outpouring of people, nor such enthusiasm. The parade commenced at eleven o'clock in the morning. Hour after hour we saw them come in wide streams across the square. The afternoon wore away and turned to dusk. It was six o'clock and we grew tired of standing and had to leave, and still the workers of Petrograd were coming by the thousands, carrying their revolutionary banners and singing the *Internationale.* All the workers of Petrograd marched that day to show their solidarity with the international proletariat and to prove to us that

---

[2] The name of the city was changed to Leningrad after V.I. Lenin's death in 1924. It had been called St. Petersburg before 1914 and was renamed Petrograd during World War I by the tsarist government as an anti-German gesture.

they still believe in the revolution they made five years before.

The next day, as though to show us that the Russian Revolution and the International has not only spirit and solidarity on its side, but military power also, they let us see a parade of the Red Army.

It was a cheering and inspiring sight to see the red soldiers on the march with their rifles over their shoulders and their bayonets shining in the sun. They marched in perfect step, with heads erect, the picture of physical prowess. As they passed the reviewing stand they all shouted, "Long live the Communist International!" and we shouted back, "Long live the Red Army!"

In the reviewing stand that day were delegates of the Communist parties of other countries; and beside us sat the diplomats of foreign governments in Russia. It is the custom to invite them whenever there is a parade of the Red Army. They say that when the diplomats see the red soldiers march, it cools their enthusiasm for another war against Soviet Russia.

Before we left Petrograd we made a pilgrimage to the Field of Mars, where in one great grave are buried the victims of the November Revolution.[3] Five years before it was the scene of desperate battle. The air was torn by rifle fire and the cries of those Petrograd workers who had risen in revolt and staked their lives on the issue. On the 7th of November, five years before, the workers of Petrograd fought there the battle of the human race and of the future. Many of them fell, never to rise again.

We stood there, with heads uncovered, in a cold, drizzling rain. The once noisy battlefield was quiet. There was no sound but the soft music of the *Funeral Hymn of the Revolution*, and the very ground, once spattered with the blood of our heroic dead, was banked high with flowers, placed there in gratitude and love by the delegates of the Communist parties and red trade unions of all lands.

Those Petrograd workers put their lives in the scale. They had lived lives of misery and oppression, but they were possessed by a

---

[3] The Bolshevik Revolution occurred on 7 November 1917 according to the modern calendar. However, the old-style Julian calendar was still in use in Russia in 1917, and its dates are 13 days behind the modern calendar. By the Julian calendar, the revolution occurred on October 25. Hence the revolution is generally referred to as the October Revolution.

daring vision of the future when the lives of all men will be better and fairer. They were the heralds of a new day in the world when there will be no more masters and no more slaves, and they gave their lives to hasten on that day.

There is an end now to their labor, their struggle and their sacrifice. They rest beneath the Field of Mars and their mouths are stopped with dust. But still from the grave they speak, and their voices are heard all over the world. They lighted an everlasting fire in the sky which the whole world is destined to see and follow.

Those Petrograd workers struck the blow which shattered the capitalist regime in Russia and put the working class in power. But they did more than that, because the Russian Revolution did not stop in Russia. It found its way over the borders. It broke through the blockade and spread all over the earth. The Russian Revolution was the beginning of the international revolution.

Wherever there is a group of militant workers anywhere in the world, there is the Russian Revolution. The Russian Revolution is in the heart of every rebel worker the world over. The Russian Revolution is in this room.

Comrade Trotsky told us, just before we left Moscow, that the best way we can help Soviet Russia is to build a bigger trade union movement and a stronger party of our own. Recognition by other governments will be of some temporary value, but the real recognition Soviet Russia wants is the recognition of the working class. When she gets that she will not need the recognition of capitalist governments. Then she can refuse to recognize them!

For, after all, Soviet Russia is not a "country." Soviet Russia is a part of the world labor movement. Soviet Russia is a strike—the greatest strike in all history. When the working class of Europe and America join that strike it will be the end of capitalism.

What Kind of a Party?

Published 3 March 1923

The following article by Cannon was printed in the 3 March 1923 issue of The Worker, *weekly newspaper of the Workers Party.*

What kind of a party—that is the question. We are turning a new page in the history of the American movement and it is important that we agree amongst ourselves now as to what we wish to write upon it. Two fortunate circumstances have conspired together to give us this opportunity; the one being the favorable political development in America, and the other the intervention of the Communist International which has prodded the party forward to take full advantage of this favorable development.

We are fighting our way, as a party, back into the open. After long argument and a push from Moscow—we are undertaking to establish and maintain an "Open Communist Party." What kind of a party do we want it to be—large or small, broad or narrow? The next future of the party depends, to a large extent, upon the answer we give to this question.

It faces us at every turn. Every time we discuss a question of policy it has to be considered. New contacts we are making with radical trade unionists compel us to think about it. It was brought to the front again by the recent declaration of Scott Nearing, in which he showed a very friendly attitude toward us. Some party members, myself among them, have frankly welcomed the prospect of such additions to our ranks, on the condition, of course, that they agree to our general statement of principles. Others, with equal frankness, express fears about admitting those who may not be 100 percent "kosher" into the party, which, according to their view, already has too many "centrists." They think the party suffers now for lack of purity; we say its main weakness is that it is not big enough and not broad enough.

Which point of view is correct? The answer depends upon

another question: the one asked at the beginning of this article—What kind of party? If you have the small party idea, if you think the "million masses"—to borrow a phrase from De Leon—can be led by a clever clique, you will very naturally fear the influx of new elements. On the other hand, if you see things as we see them, you will prop the door wide open and, if necessary, kick out the window. We try to look at the American situation as it really is, and to shape our tactics accordingly. We see the best organized and most powerful capitalist class on earth; we see a highly developed labor movement and a strongly entrenched bureaucracy at the top of it, and we say: Only a big party can cope with this situation. Our greatest danger, from which we must flee as from a pestilence, is the tendency toward sectarianism, the tendency to let the party degenerate into a small, self-satisfied, exclusive circle of narrow partisans without influence on events about it and without receiving any control from them.

Scott Nearing and the large group whom he, to a certain extent, typifies and symbolizes—former Socialists, former IWWers and trade union radicals—are very close to us. We can assimilate the bulk of them if we really make the effort. They have no set prejudices against us; no opposition in principle. They are separated from the party mainly by doubt, hesitation and pessimism. And they lack confidence in the party. All these difficulties can be overcome by systematic work and a friendly, sympathetic attitude toward them.

For us it is a life and death proposition to draw in these new elements; to start a definite movement toward the party within the next year. The party has big tasks before it and it must grow bigger to meet them. We must get more members into the party. We must get them quickly. Our failure to do so, with external conditions so favorable, will prove there is something wrong with us.

The membership of the Trade Union Educational League is much broader than that of our party. It embraces many elements who are far from understanding the fine points of Marxian theory. Yet it works. It is causing Gompers more concern than any small group of pure disciples ever did. The reasons for its success are clear enough. One reason, and not a small one either, is that it set out at the start to be a broad movement, a sweeping movement, drawing in everyone who wants to fight the labor fakers and the bosses. Another reason is that it has its feet on the solid ground of reality. The revolutionary implications of its propaganda and activity are clear and unmistakable; but it does not deal exclusively or mainly in the ultimate. It is taking hold of the workers in the trade unions because it has something to say and do concerning the concrete problems which press hard against them in their daily lives. Incidentally, and for these reasons, the Trade Union Educational League is a revolutionary factor of great importance. The man in the shop will listen to a little talk about the final revolution from a man who works and fights beside him in a practical way; the propagandist who hurls an abstract proclamation at him from somewhere "above the battle" gets no attention.

Everyone in our party recognizes the great importance of the Trade Union Educational League. It is undoubtedly true that with many this recognition is as yet theoretical and platonic; it does not result in any serious consequences. It is sufficient now to note this. I intend to speak about it more fully in another article. We are dealing here with theories of the movement; and since we are all united on the question of the Trade Union Educational League—in theory—we can proceed from a common point.

The question is: What shall be the future relation between the party and the League, and what can we learn from the experience of the League? Up to the present time we have taken it as a matter of course that the League should organize the militant left wing of the trade unions into a broad organization while the party should aim only to be a small nucleus within it, supporting it in every way and trying to exert an influence on its general policy. This theory has been pretty generally accepted and has worked out fairly well so far.

Now, since we are "starting a new chapter in our work" we ought to ask ourselves whether this theory is the best one possible, or whether this relation between the party and the trade union left wing is necessarily permanent. Undoubtedly it was the only thing possible at the start, in view of the weakness of the party and the strength of the left wing. But I am of the opinion that we can and should now take a leaf from Foster's book. I think we should set to work with the conscious purpose of making the party as broad as the militant left wing in the trade unions and identical with it. The party should not be always a small nucleus within the left wing but it should aim to become, in time, the left wing itself.

Is there anything startling in this proposal? There shouldn't be. In almost every other country the situation which I have set up as a goal to strive toward has already been reached. The Communist Party, being the only revolutionary party, has quite naturally become the undisputed leader of the revolutionary left wing in the world labor movement. Everywhere, except America. Here the party was so small, so obscure, so unequal to its task, that the leadership of the left wing passed over to a non-partisan body. We must admit that this non-partisan body has done a very good job so far, with our help. But he who is satisfied for the party to be a helper in a big enterprise doesn't think much of the party; and he forgets its historic mission, which is to be the leader of the majority of the working class through the revolution. We are far from that now. Long before we reach that point we must prove that we are able, as a party, to lead the revolutionary minority in the trade unions. The party can fill this more modest role only on one condition: that the party grows much bigger, broader, and more realistic and practical in its work.

During the six months I was in Moscow I studied the tactics of the International on this point with special interest because I already had the opinion that our party was much smaller and narrower than it needed to be and that the fault lay, partly, with our own conceptions. That opinion was strengthened and confirmed by what I learned there. The expression "mass party," which the great leaders never tire of hammering into the young Communist parties, means what the words say. The Communist Party must not only aim to be the leader of a mass movement; it must itself be a mass movement.

It is a great mistake to think that all the parties in the Comintern are already thoroughly Communist in their activity as well as in their programs. I had a pretty good chance to see them as they really are—the actions of one or more of them were being constantly considered by the Executive Committee—and I came to the conclusion that there are few which are "purer" in the doctrinary sense than our own. There is no group in our whole party that ever went so far to the right as the center of the French party, which represented at that time a majority of the members, or the ruling faction of the Norwegian party. Yet the International did not start a "centrist" hunt. They demanded the exclusion only of those individuals who were clearly anti-Communist—bourgeois agents in our ranks. They dealt very patiently and carefully with those who, while far from being thoroughgoing Communists, showed the will to move in the right direction. The International tried in every way to hold on to those who, as Zinoviev said, "want to be Communists."

The meaning and the purpose of this strategy became very clear to me. The leaders of the Comintern start out with the idea that we must get large masses of workers into our party and still larger masses to follow its leadership. That is the main idea behind all of their maneuvers and they never lose sight of it. We must have the masses, so they reason; otherwise we are bound to lose, no matter how good our intentions. We must break ever-larger numbers from the influence of the reformists and the bourgeoisie and get them under our influence. And we must swell the membership of the party; make it a "mass party." That is the sine qua non, the condition without which the victory of the proletariat is impossible.

Germany is a smaller country than the United States and the struggle for power there will certainly be no harder than here. Yet the German Communist Party, with its 250,000 members, is not yet large enough or influential enough for the task. Zinoviev suggested to the German comrades the slogan of "A million members for the party!" Those who have the small party idea in America might very profitably reflect on this.

We hear it stated often, in support of the small party theory, that the Bolsheviks of Russia had but ten thousand members "at the time of the revolution." This is true—if you mean the Kerensky revolution, which put the bourgeoisie in the saddle. But during that same speech where he suggested the slogan to the German party, Zinoviev pointed out that the Bolshevik Party had a quarter of a million members at the time it led the struggle for power in October. Of course, he made it clear that the influence of the party is not measured exactly by its size. The fundamental requirement is the support of a majority of the working class. The German party may accomplish this with less than a million members, but it will be more apt to accomplish it with them.

It is claimed that there is danger in a conscious effort to broaden the party, a search for large numbers of new members quickly, and an adaptation of the party's tactics to facilitate this end. These questions are asked: "If we run after members will not centrists, even opportunists, find their way into the party? Is there not danger that our doctrine will be diluted and the party lose its firm Communist character?"

To the first question we must frankly answer, yes. As the party broadens itself it will undoubtedly attract some elements who cannot be assimilated and whom we will eventually have to discard. But we will easily cope with that danger if we have confidence in ourselves. A healthy body does not avoid disease germs; it throws them off. Besides, that danger is only incidental; it is one of many that we cannot possibly avoid if we are going to be a serious party playing a serious part in the class struggle. The real danger before the American movement at the present time is that we may allow it to remain small and doctrinaire—a little clique of personal friends and partisans, running no risks because it is afraid of them.

The second danger, that our own doctrine will be diluted, we need not fear at all. Communist principles and tactics, as taught by the great leaders, are made of the stuff of life: they live and thrive on contact with reality. They have no meaning except as they are put to constant use and to every test. Communist principles are living things. They have no significance standing alone. They are made to mix with the mass labor movement and from that mixture fruitful issue comes. If you believe in the principles and tactics of Communism, put them to work! Give them a real chance to show how strong they are. The result will be, not to weaken and dilute the party, but to build and strengthen it and clarify its purpose and multiply our own faith and confidence a thousand times. The movement to broaden the party, in its membership and its activities, is not a departure from Communist principles and tactics. On the contrary, it is based on the desire to really begin to apply them in America.

Broaden the party!—that is our slogan. It represents in a word the will of those who are dissatisfied with the present, but who are filled with confidence for the future. We believe that our party, after four years of experience and with the help of the International, is finding the right road. That road leads to a bigger and broader party, working and fighting realistically in the heat of the daily struggle, and extending its influence over an ever-widening circle of conscious workers. This is not merely a pious aspiration on our part. The conditions for the making of the kind of a party we want are already at hand. The conditions are at hand for the making of such a party within a comparatively short time. We cannot fail unless we ourselves fail to understand what it is we have to do.

Don't Pack the July 3 Conference

25 May 1923

In the spring of 1923 the Workers Party joined with the Farmer-Labor Party, led by Chicago Federation of Labor leader John Fitzpatrick, in organizing a convention for a nationwide party of workers and farmers to be held 3 July 1923 in Chicago. When Cannon passed through Chicago on his speaking tour, the local Workers Party leaders told him of their fears that the policies of the national party leadership were inexorably leading to a break with the Fitzpatrick forces. In response Cannon addressed the following letter to Workers Party national secretary C.E. Ruthenberg in New York.

Dear Comrade:

We sent you a wire today regarding the question of party delegations to the forthcoming conference here. We have also noted the elaborate preparations for big delegations from the party local units and fraternal organizations to this affair. We think it is absolutely necessary to come to some understanding as to what we are trying to do and this cannot be done without knowing the developments in the situation from day to day.

As you have very probably been informed by comrade Lovestone, we had an informal discussion the other day with the other people here. He surely must have impressed you with the danger of our making serious errors if we are not careful.

The refusal of the Socialist Party to accept the invitation to participate has created quite a serious situation which perhaps is felt much more strongly here by those in touch with the other people than it is by you comrades in New York. Everyone here is of the opinion that the greatest tact and caution is necessary by our party to avoid giving the enemies of the conference an opportunity to brand it as a Workers Party affair. This will have the effect of blowing it up entirely.

I am under some difficulty in writing to you on the question because I have received absolutely no information about the committee's discussions and decisions on this whole question, and do not know just what your point of view is about the conference except as it is reflected in the apparent effort to get a big party delegation. In this respect all the active comrades here including myself hold an absolutely contrary opinion. What is it we expect this conference to do? Do we look upon this conference as an opportunity for a big public forum for the advertisement of the Workers Party wherein we will have a hard struggle with the other elements in it? If that is the case, of course, we are working chiefly for party advantage and advertisement at the conference itself. Then we want to pack in as many delegates as we can possibly muster up. But that is not our view of the conference. We think the chief significance of this conference consists in the possibility of laying there the basis for the organized drive towards a labor party and our party cooperating in it as an integral unit from the start. The thing that we want is the launching of an organization campaign in the trade unions towards the center which is created by that conference.

Having already gained the right for our party to participate in the conference, the next question we have to consider is the single one of how we can best act to make the conference a success and to give its enemies as few weapons as possible when it gets under way.

It seems quite obvious to us that the failure of the SP to accept the situation has a meaning which we cannot fail to take into account. It is certainly not far-fetched to assume that with the SP out of it, Gompers will feel free to attack the conference as a red proposition and try to scare all of the conservative elements away from it. If we flood the conference with Workers Party delegates, we simply lay the conference open to such a successful attack and thereby defeat ourselves by defeating the conference; and it will be no consolation to us that we had a lot of strength at the conference and got a lot of newspaper publicity.

We are not the only ones that see the tremendous dynamic possibilities of this conference, you can be sure. It would be a tragedy indeed if through our overzeal in the matter, we give a weapon into the hands of the enemies of the labor party. The whole situation is so tense and will be so much affected by the turn of every event between now and the time of the conference that we think it is absolutely impossible for our party to steer the right course and avoid costly mistakes unless it has authorized representatives here on the ground in daily touch with the situation, so that the decisions made by our committee in all matters pertaining to the conference from now on be based on a very close knowledge of the actual situation and in agreement with those who are cooperating with us for the main purpose of the conference. A subcommittee located in Chicago should be appointed at once to keep in consultation with the other parties to the enterprise. I suggest for this committee comrades Browder, Swabeck and Krumbein. If it is possible to send one or more from New York to serve on this committee, so much the better.

In fact, I think the Political Committee of the party should by all means try to find a way to come to Chicago and sit here while all these delicate questions are being handled from day to day.

We all here feel the tenseness and importance of the situation and await the reply of the CEC to this communication with the greatest anxiety.

Fraternally yours,
James P. Cannon

Another point. It can safely be assumed that a number of Internationals and other labor organizations which come to the conference will not commit themselves there. That is another reason for not giving the conference too much of a WP color. This letter has been shown to Swabeck, Browder, Krumbein and others and is endorsed by them. Please send the answer to Swabeck and a carbon copy to me on the road.

The Workers Party Today—And Tomorrow

Published 25 August-22 September 1923

The following five-part series by Cannon was published in the party's weekly journal, The Worker. *The articles marked the opening salvo in Cannon's struggle against Comintern "representative" John Pepper, whose policies had led to the disastrous break with John Fitzpatrick's "progressive" forces at the July 3 Chicago convention. The Federated Farmer-Labor Party formed by Workers Party supporters at that convention obtained little in the way of independent trade-union support.*

Part I. Some Aspects of the Labor Party Campaign

The struggle for a labor party in America is still in its infancy, and so is the career of the Communists. Both, however, have progressed to the point where lessons may be drawn from the tactics employed; and this is one of the chief gains of both. It was nobody's theory, but the decree of history, that these two developments—the beginning of the organized fight for the labor party, and the appearance of the Communist Party in the open arena of the class struggle—should take shape simultaneously. And it requires no prophet to say that the two will be henceforth interlocked. The question of the labor party cannot be considered separately from the role of the Communist Party in it any more than the Communist Party can be considered independently of the labor party.

The recognition that the awakening to class consciousness of the American workers would be reflected in the movement toward a labor party marked a decisive turning point in the life of the Workers Party as well as in the struggle for a labor party.

As soon as we saw that our fate as a Communist nucleus was indissolubly bound up with that of the broader movement of conscious and semi-conscious workers for political expression, the revolutionary changes in our conceptions and activities began. Consciousness on the part of the party leaders initiated these changes, but necessity was the driving force. The very nature of the demands made upon the party compelled it to bend and shape itself to the requirements of the new task. Sectarian conceptions could not live in this atmosphere.

And if our participation in the broader movement has exerted a powerful influence on our own party, no less can be said of the labor party itself. The Chicago conference, which, as comrade Pepper truly said, was "not the end, but rather the beginning of the formation of a genuine labor party," reflected the deep impression already made by the Communists. The genuine labor party—that is, the party formed and supported by the organized masses—lies in the future. There will be much propaganda, many conferences and a long, hard struggle before it is a reality. But the Chicago conference threw a searchlight on the road that leads toward it.

It showed that the movement for a labor party has reached a new stage since the Communists have acquired an influence in it. An organized form and a militant character—this is what the Communists are giving to the labor party movement. The labor party is no longer an issue to play with, a means of recording one's sentiments and marking time. At Chicago the Communists showed that they intend to go forward with the fight for the labor party regardless of who drops by the wayside, and the rank and file delegates there, who really want the labor party, showed that they will go with those who lead the fight for it, even at the risk of being called Bolsheviks.

Before Chicago we said the movement for a labor party would get no help from the reactionary leaders, but that it inevitably takes the form of a struggle against them. After Chicago we can also say that even many "progressive" officials, who have been "standing" for the labor party, are not willing now to make a serious fight for it, and that for the present, if we want to remain true to the labor party, we must go ahead without them. The Chicago conference brought out clearly, and emphasized more than ever, the essential rank and file character of the present stage of the labor party campaign, and, therefore, enlarged the role of the Communists.

The attack on the rank and file conference at Chicago showed that the reactionaries will fight any serious move toward a labor party so fiercely, and draw the line so sharply, that there will be no middle ground to stand on. All those who want to be friends with the reactionary officials will have to take their stand against the labor party and against the rank and file workers. And those who want the labor party will have to fight with the rank and file against the present leaders. The "friends" of the labor party and the advocates of nebulous "independent political action" will be rejected by the rank and file, as they were at Chicago, and by the reactionaries, as they were at Albany.[1] The labor party issue is rapidly dividing the entire labor movement into two distinct camps for the greatest battle in American labor history.

The left wing, i.e., the class-conscious elements of the rank and file, versus the reactionary officialdom—that is the lineup. The very idea of the appearance of the working class as an independent party in the political arena implies a certain degree of class consciousness. And for that very reason class consciousness is the only sound basis upon which the genuine labor party can be built or the present struggle for it organized. There is plenty of evidence already to prove that the size and strength and stability of the labor party movement is equal to the size and strength of the militant left wing. And from this evidence we draw the conclusion that the organization of the labor party must begin with the organization of the left wing into a separate political body.

The workers of America have made many attempts in many places at independent political action, and, while this experience has not been uniform, it shows in every case that such action has no stability unless it is led by an organized body of class-conscious workers. Any other condition results in a mushroom growth which only lives for a day.

Labor parties formed with the hope of quick political success begin to disintegrate with the first failure. Most of the state units of the old Farmer-Labor Party collapsed after the first campaign.

---

[1] A reference to a meeting of the Conference for Progressive Political Action held in late July in Albany, New York. The railroad union leaders walked out of the conference rather than countenance any talk of independent political action.

Where they lived longer and made a stubborn effort to keep in the field it was invariably due to their control by a body of militant workers who were committed to the labor party as a principle. The state of Washington provides the classic illustration of both these points.

The Farmer-Labor Party in this state has been organized for several years and has weathered several campaigns, local, state and national. At one time it had the backing of the whole labor movement of the state, but failure to win in its first election soon deflated the movement to its natural size. Pressure from Gompers on the one hand, and overtures from the capitalist parties on the other, soon brought about the defection of the state labor machine. In its later campaigns the party was supported only by the most advanced local unions and the organizations of the poor and exploited farmers, the conservative unions and the organizations of well-to-do farmers having withdrawn their support. There the movement crystallized into a stable minority party of the left wing of the farmers and city workers.

It will gain the official support of the labor movement again only when the class-conscious elements become dominant or gain sufficient strength to force the leaders into line. The leaders of this party are not Communists, but they have learned by their own experience that the labor party has to fight for its life, not with the conservative leaders but against them. That is why, when the showdown came at Chicago, they did not hesitate for one minute to break with the old leaders to go with the new ones who stood for militant struggle.

Those who form their theories about the labor party from British experience overlook the fact that America has already accumulated some experience, such as this cited here, and that this American experience is vastly different from the British. We are much more "American" than the Socialists and "progressives" who attack us for "taking orders from Russia," because we base our policy on an analysis of the struggle in America, and on deductions drawn from concrete American experience.

We are bound to the labor party by principle and, while we have not sought to control it, our duty will not allow us to shirk the responsibility of leadership, when other leaders retreat. But this puts upon us the double responsibility to watch carefully where we are going. It is necessary to rouse the enthusiasm of all our party members and sympathizers for an aggressive and militant campaign for the labor party; but it is also important not to let our enthusiasm lead us to overestimate the rate of radical development, and rush into premature actions. And we must guard against the danger of isolation, and take special care that the semi-conscious and honest progressive workers are not alienated from us by any fault of ours, by foolish mistakes, by what may appear to them as our own narrow party interests, or by overanxiety for quick results.

The interests of the Workers Party are identical with the interests of the wider circle of radical workers who are seeking for expression through the labor party. Unless our party plays an active part in the labor party movement, it is bound to wither into a futile sect, and the developing class struggle will pass it by. And those overzealous "friends" of the labor party who are willing to subordinate the Workers Party, or eliminate it entirely, would rob the labor party of an element indispensable to its life and growth. The presence of the disciplined body of Communists within the labor party is the one and only guarantee that it will not be killed by its savage enemies from without, or sabotaged and betrayed by its unreliable friends within. The labor party will have a stable and healthy growth from now on only to the extent that it becomes organized, develops a militant character, and carries on an uncompromising struggle against the capitalist parties and their agents in the labor movement. The Communists will assist the labor party to follow this line.

The weakness and lack of aggressiveness of some of the elements who have hitherto played an important part in the labor party imposes a double task upon the Communists. We are obliged by the new developments to take a much larger share of responsibility in the labor party campaign, and to give more of our time and energy to it. And these increased duties and responsibilities demand that we build and strengthen the Workers Party, for our effectiveness in the broader movement is measured by the strength and discipline of our own independent party of Communism. The campaign we are now starting to increase the membership of the Workers Party is one of the most important immediate steps in the struggle for the labor party.

Part II. A Look at the New Movement

After I returned from Moscow I started out on a cross-country speaking tour with two questions uppermost in my mind. They were: first, how quickly will the party be able to assimilate the decisions of the Fourth Congress, and, second, how soon will the results begin to manifest themselves?

My propaganda tour lasted nearly five months and took me to every section of the country where we have party connections. I had been pretty familiar with the party since it was organized in 1919, as well as with the socialist and syndicalist movements from which it sprang. Then the six months I spent on the Executive Committee of the Communist International, where the problems of the various affiliated parties were dealt with almost daily, enabled me to get a clearer understanding of what the great leaders mean by the term Communist party. I was, therefore, able to look at the party today, in comparison with the party in its first three years, and with the older movements which preceded it; and also to form an opinion as to the progress we are making towards becoming a genuine Communist party.

First of all, on the basis of what I saw and learned on the long trip, I have no hesitancy in saying that, in all respects, we are making great headway. And with equal certainty the reasons for it can be stated: the advice of the Communist International, and the increased activity in party affairs, and influence on party policies, of a number of experienced and practical trade union men.

Anyone who knew the real condition of the party only a year ago cannot but regard the progress as phenomenal. From all standpoints we are in better shape than ever before: the party has stronger discipline, closer unity, more homogeneity, wider influence and more of the characteristics of a real Communist party.

But when I make these statements, it must be understood that I am speaking comparatively. I have in mind the fact that the life of the American Communist movement, for the first three years, was mainly an internal one, poisoned with sectarian dogmas and paralyzed by factional disputes. I do not mean to say that we have capitalism by the throat, or that our party has become the leader of a big proletarian mass movement. To expect this of a party that is just finding its legs, and of a class that is showing only faint signs of awakening to class consciousness, would be to expect a miracle. And Communists, by official decision of the Enlarged Executive, are not allowed to believe in miracles.

The real progress the party has made, especially during the past year, is indicated principally by the nature of its activity. The main activity of the party today is external, not internal. From a small sect of abstract theory and routine propaganda it is striving to become a party of campaigns and actions over concrete issues, and it is doing this without falling into the theoretical errors, confusion and opportunism which wrecked the older movements in America when they tried to broaden the scope of their work.

These changes in the character of the party, more than the increased amount of influence it has gained, represent the advancement it has made. The class struggle is not a slot machine which automatically returns a package of influence for the first penny of real, practical effort we insert into it. The results are sure, nevertheless, and we need not worry if the party has not become popular overnight. Such a party as we are striving to become will inevitably extend its prestige by leaps and bounds. Of this we can be confident.

A year ago we could all say that sectarianism was our greatest danger. Now it is quite clear that we are overcoming that trouble, and doing it much more rapidly and with less internal travail than the most optimistic amongst us hoped. We have taken deeply to heart the advice of the International, and are trying with all our zeal and energy to become a body of realistic fighters in the daily struggle, without forgetting for one minute the revolutionary aims of the movement. The whole party has learned, in theory at least, that revolutionary work in America today is daily work, the work of leading the fight for regeneration of the labor movement and raising the level of working class consciousness, of carrying the war to the capitalists and their labor lieutenants on questions which press hard against the workers today.

We are at the very beginning of this work and, taking into account the present stage of the class struggle in America, we can see, surely, that many years of pioneer work are ahead of us. For that reason we ought to carefully study the situation and the part we are playing in it. A constant and fearless self-criticism is the only thing that will prevent the little mistakes that inevitably occur in the daily work from growing into big ones. Thoughtless mistakes are a luxury which a revolutionary party cannot well afford.

Our campaigns for amalgamation and the labor party have deeply stirred the trade unions, without a doubt, and have already produced a number of results which should be noted. We have to face the fact that the expected increase in party membership has not yet materialized; but, in the real sense of the word, the party has grown. We have succeeded, through these campaigns, in drawing into the party quite a number of well-connected trade unionists. These elements are like nuggets of gold to the party. If we had nothing else to mark up to the credit side of these campaigns we would be repaid a thousandfold for the energy we put into them.

In several localities our party has been able to set the whole labor movement in motion through the instrumentality of a few of these strategically situated individuals. Lenin, in one of his books, speaks very warmly of the "eminent workingmen" who, in the days of blackest reaction in Russia, got themselves so situated that, in spite of all difficulties and obstacles, they could carry out the party's work in the labor organizations. The dynamic possibilities of a party made up principally of such elements, and armed with the tactics of Leninism, staggers the imagination. That would be a real Bolshevik party!

Besides drawing a number of these workers directly into the party, we have also succeeded in organizing around us a much wider body of sympathizing workers than we ever had before. But it must be admitted that our propaganda and agitation has run far ahead of our organization. Many of our well-aimed bullets turn out to be blank cartridges for this reason. With such a small party we are only able to fight successfully if a much larger body of sympathizing workers stands with us. When we get too far ahead we run into trouble. Many of the fights which appear to be very spectacular have more smoke than fire, as far as we are concerned.

Organized opposition confronts us all along the line. The

fights we have started in several of the big unions, and especially the formidable showing of our party at the Chicago Farmer-Labor conference, have greatly alarmed our old enemies, and united them with some new ones against us. In one way this can be taken as a proof that we are active and that the reactionaries fear us.

The united front against the capitalists is still a propaganda slogan; but the united front against the Communists is a reality. We seem to be organizing our enemies faster than we are organizing our friends.

An old sickness of the American party—a psychological one—is not yet completely cured. That is the tendency to get unduly excited, to overestimate the radical development, and plunge into premature actions which bring disastrous defeats and paralyzing reactions in our own ranks.

We have progressed earthward during the past year, but we are still too much up in the air. We still throw more bluffs and make more noise than our strength warrants. This would not matter if we were not the ones who suffer by it. Many times during the past year delicate situations which might have been matured by quiet work have been shot to pieces by too much advertisement and boasting of our intentions. Lincoln's story of the river steamboat is not a bad one to remember. This boat had a small engine which could not generate enough power to move the boat and blow the whistle at the same time. Our engine is not very large either.

An aggressive, fighting policy is, of course, the breath of life to a party such as ours. And in our general propaganda our demands should not be modest ones. We can be as bold as the "SLP" in this respect and demand "the unconditional surrender of the capitalist class." But when we take up specific fights on concrete questions of the day, and raise slogans of action in regard to them, we have to take into account the relative strength of our forces with those of our enemies, and endeavor to regulate the tempo of our campaign somewhat by the rate at which the struggle is naturally developing.

When we fail to do this, we overstimulate the movement, run away ahead of our own sympathizers and bring the issue to a head prematurely. Then we suffer from the consequent reaction, and the isolation of our comrades who, in such cases, often have to hunt for cover and keep still for a while in order to regain their contacts.

Outside of the defects noted here which, after all, are the result mainly of the busy life we have been living, and the lack of time for self-examination, there is very little to find fault with in the party. It is on the right road, its general line of tactics is correct, and it has excellent prospects for healthy growth. If we cannot find the grounds for the optimistic hope expressed by comrade Zinoviev in his letter that "In the near future the Workers Party will mature to one of the truly Communist mass parties of the world," we can say, confidently, that the party is going forward at a good rate of speed, and that it will give a good account of itself in the next year.

Part III. The United Front Against the Communists

The united front is a very good slogan, and everybody nowadays seems to be in favor of it. Our united front slogan has been such a good success that our enemies have adopted it, with an amendment of their own. Those who are unwilling to make a united front against the capitalists are making a united front against the Communists.

Look at them: Farrington and Lewis, after calling each other crooks and grafters and proving it, unite to fight the "Reds," while indictments against our active comrades in Pennsylvania dovetail neatly into their plans. The Socialist Party makes peace with Gompers and war on us. The "progressive" leaders of the old Farmer-Labor Party take up the fight against us with Gompers' slogans of "Red," "Force and Violence," etc. While these big dogs spring at our throat the little ones snap at our heels, the Socialist Labor Party, Proletarian Party, etc.

We were never short of enemies. Quite a number of "progressives" have been in a sort of coalition with us. Now even some of these are joining in an effort to isolate us. An analysis of the make-up of the American labor movement, however, will show that this situation is not a permanent crystallization, and that it is possible, by using the right tactics in the developing class struggle, to break up the present anti-Communist front and bring about realignments of various kinds which will advance the movement as a whole and strengthen our position in it.

No European Analogy

The American movement has no counterpart anywhere else in the world, and any attempt to meet its problems by the simple process of finding a European analogy will not succeed. The key to the American problem can be found only in a thorough examination of the peculiar American situation. Our Marxian outlook, confirmed by the history of the movement in Europe, provides us with some general principles to go by, but there is no pattern, made to order from European experience, that fits America today.

In all the European countries the workers movement has matured to class consciousness and is committed, in theory, to socialism. The working class is organized politically and does not support the capitalist parties. The three factions of the movement, right, center and left, each have a political party organization, all of which are professedly anti-capitalist.

How different is the situation in America. Here the dominating element in the labor movement defends the capitalist system in theory as well as in practice, and the great body of workers still support the capitalist parties. The immaturity of the American working class is nowhere more clearly revealed than in the fact that only a minority support the labor party. A working class without a party of its own is an infant that has not yet celebrated its first birthday.

Beside the Communists, who, of course, are an organized party with a clearly defined revolutionary program, four other elements make up the American labor movement; and all four of them are now centering their chief opposition on the Communists. These four elements are: 1) the right wing bureaucracy; 2) the Socialists; 3) the revolutionary sects; 4) the "progressives."

The Right Wing

The right wing, the ruling bureaucracy, is by all standards the most reactionary in the world. Its philosophy is capitalistic, not socialistic as is the case in the European countries. It is organized and has a definite program of systematic opposition to all radical proposals. It fights all progress under the very same slogans used by the capitalistic press.

Gompers denounces the Trade Union Educational League on patriotic grounds, and accuses the Communists of wanting to overthrow the United States government, with the same moral indignation that inspires a prosecuting attorney who speaks against us in court. Lewis, of the miners union, goes one step farther in defense of capitalist institutions. He crosses the Canadian border and expels the Nova Scotia miners, one of his charges against them being that they went on strike to undermine the "constituted authorities" in Canada. His devotion to capitalism is not confined within the narrow limits of national boundaries.

The leaders of the labor movement lean so far backward in support of the profit system that many politicians in the capitalist parties appear to be revolutionaries in comparison with them. Senator Wheeler, of Montana, made the statement that "the bankers in Montana are more radical than the labor leaders in Washington." These bureaucrats are our natural enemies. They belong in the united front against us.

No Peace with Socialist Party

The Socialists are also an organized party with a definite program of reformism. Fortunately for the working class it is a small party with a dwindling influence, and its miserable role is not an important one. It crawls before the black reactionaries, but against the left wing it is militant and venomous. War to the knife is the only attitude a revolutionary party can have toward it. We fight the reformist Socialist Party because we know from the bitter experience of the European workers that reformism is poison to the labor movement.

If we can prevent such a party from ever getting a grip in America it is quite possible that the working class will be able to cross the bridge to revolutionary understanding much quicker and less painfully than the workers of Europe have done. There is no possibility of peace between the Communist left wing and the Socialist Party unless it completely changes its present character and attitude. There is no sign of this, so we can say that it also has its proper place in the united front against us.

We need not devote much time here to the third factor enumerated above: the little, voluble, chattering sects of revolutionary phrasemongers who take no real part in the struggle, and whose energy is expended in snapping and barking at our heels. The struggle will dispose of them. It will sweep into the ranks of the fighting party all of them who honestly want to fight against capitalism. As for the others, to whom super-radical phrases are merely a cloak to hide behind, they have already shown that in action they are against us.

The "Progressives"

The fourth element—the so-called "progressives"—is one that, like the right wing, is peculiar to America. Altogether it makes up a considerable section of the movement, a vague, indefinite, unorganized group shuffling back and forth between the organized militant right and the organized militant left. They are the American "centrists"; but for several reasons they cannot be dealt with precisely according to the formula which the Communists use in dealing with the centrists in Europe.

They are not nearly so definite a grouping nor so highly developed politically as the classic centrists of the international movement. For one thing, they have practically no organization, no systematic and consistent political philosophy, and they have no recognized, authoritative leaders of the highly trained, professional European type. They do not represent a crystallized movement, but a hazy sentiment which, speaking in terms of America, where anything resembling a class viewpoint is progress, is really progressive.

This "progressive" element is already quite large, and it is growing. It has not yet acquired sufficient consciousness to develop an organized form; that is why it is so uncertain, inconsistent and non-militant in action. But at bottom it is a revolt against Gompersism. This is plainly indicated by its general support of such proposals as the labor party, amalgamation, recognition of Soviet Russia, etc., wherever it is not called upon to fight too hard for them.

Present Alignment Only Temporary

Up until recently most of these progressives were going along in a rather loose alliance with us in support of these measures. At the Chicago conference, and in some localities before the

Chicago conference, through no fault of ours in a single case, a number of these "progressives" broke away from this alliance and joined the united front against us. But I do not think the bulk of them naturally belong there, or that we should take it for granted they will stay.

The rapidly developing class struggle will not permit any elements which stand for progress to stay united with the dead reaction of the Gompers regime. The "progressives" cannot do it without repudiating all the things they have been standing for up till now. Some of the leaders may be willing to do this, but the progressive movement cannot so easily change its character overnight.

It is more a drifting movement than a conscious one, and the intensifying struggle accelerates the drift toward the left, not toward the right. This situation offers tremendous possibilities for the Workers Party, and it should certainly be a part of our strategy in the labor movement to look forward to the possibility of a rapprochement with the "progressives," at least with those who have not consciously betrayed the movement and gone over to Gompers.

In next week's article I will undertake to analyze the "progressive" movement, and the reasons which brought about the break between some of the leaders and the Communist left wing, and, also, to set forth what, in my opinion, our tactics toward them should be in the future.

Part IV. The Workers Party and the Progressives

Why did some progressives break with us, and what does it signify? This is an important question for us because it has a vital bearing on our future strategy in the labor movement. It affects our fight for the labor party, for amalgamation and, most of all, for the recognition of our party as an integral part of the labor movement. In order to find the answer we have to analyze the progressive movement, and if we analyze it correctly we should have little difficulty in arriving at the proper attitude toward it.

The great mass of the awakening workers whom we classify under the heading of "progressives"—those who have broken away from the ruling bureaucracy and who have not yet joined the left wing—are not under the control of an organized party. And it is precisely this situation that makes our task of strengthening and extending the Communist influence immeasurably easier than that of our comrades in Europe, who are confronted at every turn by the opposition of powerful Socialist parties.

It is our good fortune to have already created a clearly defined, if small, Communist party which is operating in an intensifying class struggle with a politically undeveloped, but rapidly fermenting labor movement. These features of the American situation give the Communists their supreme opportunity. By following the right line of strategy, correctly appraising the other elements and adopting the correct attitude toward them, our party can drive forward with the speed of a locomotive.

Defining the Progressives

In order to talk about the other elements in the movement we must first define and label them. The word "progressives" is both a definition and a label for those with whom we are principally concerned in this article. We cannot speak of them in any of the classic terms of the class struggle, because they are only partly class-conscious. From the standpoint of the international proletarian movement they are neither right, left nor center. They are not Socialists, Communists, centrists, anarchists, or syndicalists. They are—progressives.

This is a very vague word, it is true; but the section of the American labor movement it describes is, as yet, very hazy in its outlook, and its composition is a hodgepodge. It is altogether too loose and indefinite a body to be spoken of in precise socialist terminology. And that is the crux of the question.

Progressivism is a revolt against Gompersism that has not yet developed a systematic philosophy or an organized form. It is not as yet a conscious movement and it does not show a uniform development in all parts of the country, and in all the International unions. The administration of the Amalgamated Clothing Workers is not the same thing as the administration of the Seattle Central Labor Union. There is some difference between Fitzpatrick of Chicago and Cramer of Minneapolis. The Detroit Federation of Labor is not the West Virginia Federation of Labor. But all of them, and the hundreds of thousands of workers whom they represent and typify, have certain things in common: they are not a part of the Gompers machine, they are not Socialists, and they are not Communists.

For several years this progressive movement has been drifting comfortably along, putting itself more or less formally on record for progressive measures, but creating no real disturbance in the labor movement. Gompers, the militant reactionary, had little difficulty in beating it back. It was not aggressive enough to cause any sharp collision anywhere. It was not submitted to any real tests and, for that reason, it was not easy to discover its real nature.

Their Uncomfortable Position

But the rapid rise of the Workers Party, and the organization around it of the militant left wing, have introduced a new and most dynamic factor into the situation. The progressives, who are disposed to move ahead slowly and peacefully, find themselves in a most uncomfortable position. Between the militant left wing, which tries to hurry them forward at a faster rate of speed, and the militant reactionaries, who launch fierce counterattacks in order to drive them back, the progressives have no more peace. Under this pressure from the left and right the progressive movement is revealing its true character quite clearly.

The recent startling actions of different sections of this progressive movement—the big step forward here, the panicky retreat there; the open support of the Michigan Communist cases at first, and the denunciation of them a few months later; the joint campaign with the Communists for the labor party before the Chicago conference, and the sudden, unprovoked break at the conference—all these inconsistent actions are nothing more nor less than the first reactions of the progressive movement to the war between the left and right wings in the labor movement, and the propaganda and pressure each side exerts upon it. That is the real meaning of these recent events.

The progressives do not constitute a homogeneous body, and its lack of consciousness and organization robs it of militancy and certitude, rendering it very susceptible to propaganda and pressure from the right as well as from the left. Under pressure from the left it supports the amalgamation movement. Under counterpressure from the right it abandons even the labor party. It oscillates between the right and the left, and whenever it has a minute's peace it stops at its own position—mild support of the labor party and recognition of Soviet Russia, and still milder support of amalgamation.

Chicago Break No Accident

What took place at Chicago was not an isolated, unexplainable accident. The happenings at Chicago merely dramatized and gave prominence to a ferment in the ranks of the progressives which, prior to the Chicago conference, had unmistakably manifested itself in several localities where the struggle between the right and the left brought matters to an issue.

If any of us were greatly surprised at what occurred at Chicago and elsewhere it was because we had overestimated the political consciousness and stability of the progressives, and expected too much of them. Such shakeups will serve a good purpose in the long run if they prompt us to make a more thorough examination of the whole question and bring us to a better and clearer understanding of our own task in regard to it. These events will be worth whatever they cost if we do not deceive ourselves as to what really happened and what it signifies.

At Chicago, when the crisis came, our program made the stronger appeal to the great majority of the convention delegates, including a big section even of the Farmer-Labor Party, and they came along with us. But that did not make them Communists. With others, the secret pressure of the Gompers machine and the fear of an open struggle with it were the dominating factors, and at the crucial moment they broke with us. But that single act does not make them reactionaries, even if, in stress of the occasion, for want of an argument to justify their acts, they turned on us with the stale accusations of Gompers, which, in turn, are only a variation of the capitalists' indictments of those who challenge their rule.

An individual amongst them, here and there, may have already consciously decided to go back to Gompers. Even in these cases, however, we can well afford to wait for a consistent series of actions to remove all doubt, before we classify them as reactionaries. Likewise there is a strong probability that some of them have made up their minds to go all the way to the left. This also will have to wait for proof. There has been a shuffling of individuals to the right and to the left, but the progressive movement, as a whole, remains practically the same as before the recent shakeups. Only the onward-driving class struggle, and the greater intensification of the war between the right and the left, will be able to substantially change its character.

Our Attitude Toward Progressives

The progressive movement remains practically the same as before, and our attitude toward it prior to Chicago, which was essentially correct, still holds good. But two points have to be especially emphasized now. First, we must continue to approach the progressives in a friendly and patient manner, and, second, we must exert all our energy to build the Communist left wing as an independent power.

The progressives have shown themselves to be a confused and unreliable body, and for that reason we cannot count too much upon any alliance with them, not even as much as we did before Chicago. Our real ability to influence the labor movement depends, first of all, not on an alliance with the progressives, but on our independent power as a party. Not only that, but our ability to affect the course of the progressives, to give any meaning to an alliance with them, also depends upon it.

Only where we have a strong party organization does the coalition with the progressives represent a real force.

In such localities as Minneapolis we have had experience to show that the unity of the left wing and the progressives, where the left wing is not organized as an independent power, is a house of cards that collapses under the first volley from Gompers' guns.

The confusion and instability the progressive movement has revealed, which makes it doubly necessary for us to build our own party as an independent power, is also the reason why we cannot adopt a sharp or hostile attitude toward it. It cannot be put into the same category with the Socialist Party, which carries on a systematic ideological war against us. The progressive movement, in spite of its glaring defects, represents a sound, healthy, honest impulse of hundreds of thousands of workers. It offers great possibilities for us, and it must be our aim to effect an alliance between it and the left wing whenever it is possible, and by careful, patient and friendly work to lead the progressive workers to the platform of Communism.

Part V. The Workers Party and Its Rivals

In my recent trip across the country I made inquiries in every locality as to the strength and influence of the various radical parties which are rivals to the Workers Party. The information I obtained in this way, supplementing the knowledge we already have as to their national influence in comparison with that of our party, enabled me to get a clear view of the actual situation. It can be summed up by this statement, which, in my opinion, is unquestionably true: the Workers Party is rapidly outstripping the whole field; it is going forward and its rivals are declining; in many places the other parties have become practically liquidated by the assimilation of their best elements into the Workers Party. The Workers Party is the only one that is showing any aggressiveness or driving power in the class struggle. It has already put itself at the head of militant rank and file movements locally as well as nationally. And these, of course, are the fundamental reasons why it is pushing its rivals to the wall.

There are not many consciously radical workers in America but there are very many radical organizations. The whole radical labor movement of America looks pitifully small in comparison with most of the European countries, but we can challenge any country in the world to show a greater number of radical and revolutionary organizations, factions, sects and cliques. Except for the Proletarian Party, which is a sectarian split-off from the Communist movement, our party is the youngest in the field. We are only four years old as a party. The Socialist Party is 23, the Industrial Workers of the World is 18, and the Socialist Labor Party is a middle-aged lady who doesn't speak of her age anymore. The Proletarian Party, if we remember rightly, is three years old, but it is manifestly an abnormal child which sits listlessly in the library reading books which it doesn't understand, and suffers from lack of exercise. It doesn't seem to run and play enough to get the proper development.

These bodies are not much given to agreeing with anybody about anything, but they all agree with each other that the Workers Party is no good. They have a united front on that issue. Those who used to spend most of their energy fighting each other now center their main fire on us, and, strangely enough, they all use pretty much the same arguments and accusations.

As a revolutionary party which aims to represent the entire class interests of the proletariat, our real fight is against the capitalists and the capitalist government first, and next against the agents of the capitalists in the labor movement—the Gompers machine. But in marshaling the revolutionary workers for this fight against the class enemies of the proletariat we have to insist on sound revolutionary policies and principles; otherwise the fight would not be successful. These rival radical parties who espouse false doctrines have only a harmful effect on the movement. To the extent that they have influence they create divisions in the ranks of the class-conscious workers and introduce confusion into the struggle. This brings us into collision with them. Our fight against them is a fight against division and confusion.

The Collapse of the Socialist Party

I was especially struck by the obvious moral and organizational collapse of the Socialist Party. The fight with it in New York City, where it is still entrenched in the needle trades unions and buttressed on a number of property institutions in its control, has a tendency to give us an astigmatic view of its real status. In the country at large it has practically ceased to exist as a vigorous rank and file movement. The young blood has left it and joined the Communists, many thousands have quit the movement, and only a handful of tired old men hold the fort here and there for the Socialist Party, talking about the past but doing very little today.

The Socialist Party of America could be more accurately called the Socialist Party of New York and Milwaukee. In these cities it represents a real power and it is a real stumbling block to the revolutionary movement. In these places we find it necessary to wage a direct fight against it not only because of its false philosophy, but also because of the treasonable conduct that springs logically from that philosophy. But in other localities, where it has no property institutions, no newspapers and no established professional officialdom, the tendency of our party is to sweep past it completely. The constructive work of our party, its united front tactics, give it the leadership of the radical workers. The necessity for direct struggle with the Socialist Party does not arise for the simple reason that the Socialists are not in the field.

The Socialist Labor Party

We have skirmishes now and then with the Socialist Labor Party, but they are never of a very serious nature because the SLP is not a serious factor in the fight. The official organ attacks us very heatedly and excitedly nearly every week, but we could not afford to spend much time in answering them. We fight them, nevertheless, and the difference between their method of fighting and ours reveals very clearly the difference between a dogmatic clique and a realistic political party.

We proceed on the theory that a party which has a false theoretical foundation, and which takes the wrong position regarding the revolutionary goal of the movement and the way to realize it, will not follow a revolutionary policy in the daily struggle. We have no objection to theoretical arguments now and then, but the average worker does not take much interest in such combats. So, as a rule, whenever the SLP meets us in the field with a challenge to debate the merits of the late Daniel De Leon, we answer with a proposal that they make a united front with us against the common enemy, against the capitalists, the capitalist government and the reactionary labor leaders. The SLP is a sterile sect that does not understand any life except abstract controversy. Marxism to it is only a collection of dogmas. It is not a party of the class struggle, and against proposals to really fight in the class struggle it is absolutely helpless.

A few months ago I was speaking to a crowd of miners in southern Illinois. There is a little nest of chronic SLP fanatics in that section, and after I finished speaking they offered to start an argument with me about the dictatorship of the proletariat. I answered them in this way:

> I would be glad to discuss this question with you, but it is quite possible that most of these miners here have not made a sufficient study of revolutionary theory to be able to conclude from our debate

> which party they want to support. Suppose we put the question in another way that will make the case simpler. Right now these miners are suffering a great oppression at the hands of Farrington and Lewis, who are nothing but the agents of the mine owners in the miners union. I will invite you to make a united front with us against Farrington and Lewis, and for a program that will improve and strengthen the miners union and make it a revolutionary instrument in the hands of its members. We can still have debates once in a while over theories, but in the meantime let us make a common fight against the common enemies of the working class.

When the SLP members refused this proposition the miners would not let them talk anymore. They came to the natural and logical conclusion that a party which will not fight today is only bluffing when it talks about fighting in the future.

The Proletarian Party

The Proletarian Party is not a political party in the true sense of the word because it does not have a national character, takes no part in the general political struggle and has never undertaken any kind of a campaign on a national scale. It appears to be a loose collection of groups and study classes located in about a half dozen cities. Its activity consists almost exclusively of conducting and holding study classes, street meetings and heckling Workers Party speakers. They are quite militant in their fight against the Workers Party but we have never been able to get much help from them in the fight against the labor fakers. They call themselves Communists, and, taking them at their word, we have made many efforts to get them to unite with us into one Communist party. But they have always refused on one pretext or another. Even the direct appeal of the Communist International could not avail with them. They are sore at us and they refuse to play in our yard—that is about all we can make out of their childish behavior.

We cannot say what the real object of the Proletarian Party is. But if they thought they could seriously injure the Workers Party by their bitter and senseless attacks on it they have failed most miserably. The Workers Party has stood the test of action far better than the Proletarian Party, and it has already succeeded, by the constructive nature of its activity and its energetic campaigns for the labor party, amalgamation, etc., in bringing into its ranks quite a number of former members of the Proletarian Party who could not accept a Communist program as a substitute for Communist work.

They are amongst the most valuable members of our party at the present time and the fact that they have come over to us is the best proof that our attitude toward the Proletarian Party has been correct. We have refused to engage in a mud-slinging campaign with them. We simply have set up our actions against their words, and let all those who call themselves Communists take their choice.

Amalgamation—The Burning Question

Published 20 September 1923

The following article by Cannon in favor of industrial unionism appeared in the Chicago weekly, Voice of Labor, *one of whose editors was William Z. Foster.*

One of the biggest questions on the agenda of all labor conventions these days is amalgamation. The demand for it is steadily growing, despite all official opposition. It is a powerful movement from below, born of the actual need of the hour, and nothing can stop it.

The amalgamation proposition is very simple, and has been stated in classic form by the Chicago Federation of Labor in the resolution adopted on March 19, 1922. After pointing out that under the present conditions of craft divisions, "the unions are unable to make united resistance against their employers, constantly suffer defeat after defeat, with heavy losses in membership and serious lowering of the workers' standards of living and working conditions," the resolution says:

> The only solution for the situation is the development of a united front by the workers through the amalgamation of the various trade unions so that there will remain only one union for each industry.

A Bad Year for Labor

Despite the optimistic talk of officials, the open shop movement of the bosses is still smashing forward, wrecking one union after another and depriving ever-larger numbers of workers of hard-won conditions. The year between the Cincinnati convention of the American Federation of Labor and the one about to be held at Portland has been a disastrous one for the workers. This is the bitter truth, and even Gompers will not be able to juggle figures enough to hide it.

Since the Cincinnati convention we have had the opportunity to see the full effect of the open shop war on the railroad shop crafts, once the stronghold of American unionism. On many roads the seven shop craft unions have been completely wiped out, and in their place has come the "Company Union." Even on those roads where settlements were secured, the old-time power of the unions is gone. The "settlements" were really surrenders on the part of the strikers in practically every case. This crushing defeat, the manifest inability of the shop crafts alone to cope with the consolidated power of the railroad companies, has robbed all the railroad unions of militancy and aggressiveness. They take what they can get, because they have not the power to take what they want.

The defeat of the railroad shopmen had a widespread effect outside the railroads; it dealt a heavy moral blow to the entire labor movement. So depressed and paralyzed have the trade unions become under the crushing effect of the open shop campaign that they were not able to show a noticeable recuperation during the industrial revival. In previous periods of "prosperity" the trade unions have greatly increased their membership and pressed home their advantage; big and successful organization campaigns have been the rule in every trade. But in the period just closing the trade unions have not been able to hold their own, to say nothing of making headway. What will happen when the coming depression gets under way and millions of unemployed workers flood the labor market?

Bosses Wage Real War

The employers are waging a real war against the unions. By new mergers and consolidations they are eliminating all competition amongst themselves and presenting a solid front against labor. They have the government, the police, the army and the courts all on their side absolutely. The great daily papers are just so many organs of lying propaganda for them. They are assembling every conceivable weapon for the attack against unionism. The trade unions, with their present antiquated craft form of organization, cannot defend themselves against this attack. It is a matter of life and death for them to be amalgamated into industrial unions without delay.

Gompers and the whole officialdom of the American Federation of Labor are united against amalgamation. They fight it by all unfair means of falsehood and misrepresentation. They cover its advocates with slander and abuse. They resort to every form of trickery and deception and intimidation in order to "kill" amalgamation. But all to no avail. Amalgamation rises up ever stronger. Where they suppress it temporarily in one place it springs up in another. While they were concentrating all their forces to defeat it at the convention of the Illinois Federation, it was being passed at Utah and West Virginia. They defeated it at the American Federation of Labor convention a year ago, but when they meet this year at Portland it will confront them again. They cannot kill amalgamation, but amalgamation will kill them if they continue to fight against it.

A Rank and File Movement

The leadership of the trade union movement today is the enemy of all progress, and every proposal to strengthen and regenerate the trade unions and make them a mighty power for the interests of the workers has to be advanced in the face of their opposition. Every forward movement is a movement from below, from the rank and file. This is particularly true of the amalgamation movement.

Despite the opposition of the Gompers officialdom, the rank and file has pressed the issue so hard that several International unions, 15 state federations, scores of city central bodies and thousands of local unions have already declared for it. Some idea of the tremendous sweep of the movement may be gained from the report of O.H. Wangerin, secretary of the International Committee for Amalgamation in the Railroad Industry, that 3,377 local lodges, including all the 16 standard railroad unions, have endorsed the program of amalgamation for the railroad industry.

It is no exaggeration to say that the majority of rank and file trade unionists already favor amalgamation. The officials are the big obstacle. They will only move in response to tremendous pressure from below. Rank and file workers everywhere must make their voices heard on this burning issue. Put your local union on record for it. Raise the question in every central body and convention, and develop a mighty wave of sentiment that will sweep all obstacles aside and bring about the complete amalgamation of the trade unions before they are annihilated by the bosses. Amalgamation or annihilation is the issue. Fight for amalgamation.

Statement on Our Labor Party Policy

November 1923

The following statement was written by Cannon and William Z. Foster for Workers Party internal discussion. It argues against a set of theses written by John Pepper and C.E. Ruthenberg for the Central Executive Committee majority—the "August Theses"—which hailed the July 3 formation of the Federated Farmer-Labor Party as a great victory, despite the fact that the Fitzpatrick forces had refused to go along. The statement is from the Theodore Draper Papers in the Special Collections Department, Robert W. Woodruff Library, Emory University.

Soon after Cannon and Foster submitted this statement, Ruthenberg and Pepper submitted a new, conciliatory set of theses which emphasized the necessity of maintaining a bloc with the "progressives" in the trade unions. This prompted Cannon and Foster to withdraw their statement. However, the Foster-Cannon opposition continued their fight against the Ruthenberg-Pepper leadership, and they went on to win the majority of delegates to the Third Convention of the Workers Party, December 1923. For the next year and a half the Foster-Cannon group held the majority on the CEC.

1. The outstanding feature of the present political situation in America is that the great masses of industrial workers and exploited farmers are beginning to take their first determined steps in independent political action. The industrial workers are being driven to this course by the ever-growing oppression of the employers and the increased use of the centralized governmental powers against them in their struggles, while the farmers are forced into political action in their own behalf by the complete bankruptcy of agriculture. The two great groups of producers are being united in their fight against the common oppressor. This uprising of the workers and exploited farmers, and their combination for a joint struggle, is of tremendous significance in the development of the class struggle in America.

2. The participation of the industrial workers in this movement is an instinctive, elementary expression of their awakening class consciousness. The growing labor party is not an artificial creation but on the contrary it is the natural, healthy reaction of the workers to the pressure of their environment. It is a profound rank and file movement, steadily gaining in scope despite the opposition of the labor bureaucracy. Gompers and all his reactionaries are unable to block the expanding movement. Likewise, reactionary leaders of the farmers are being swept aside.

3. Many labor unions, representing a large section of the organized workers, have already declared in favor of the labor party. Two of the most important additions to the list recently are the Iron, Steel, and Tin Workers' Union, and the Iron Molders' Union, both of which have long been noted as among the most conservative unions in America. The West Virginia State Federation of Labor, within the past couple of months, has decided by unanimous vote to organize a state labor party. The farmers and workers of Minnesota are the backbone of the Farmer-Labor Party which has already elected two United States senators. Similar parties are now being organized in a series of states, such as California, Montana, Utah, etc. All signs lead to the conclusion that a mass labor party, based on the trade unions and farmers organizations, is in process of formation.

4. The fate of the Workers Party is bound up with this mass movement of the rank and file workers and farmers towards a labor party. Our policy on this question is of supreme importance. With the right policy, especially while the mass movement is just taking shape, our party can drive forward rapidly to a position of leadership over wide masses of awakening workers. On the other hand, a wrong policy will isolate our party from this mass movement and condemn it to sterility.

5. We see three tasks for the Workers Party in this situation: (1) To develop and unify the labor party sentiment, and help it to take organized form, locally and nationally; (2) To defeat the efforts of liberal bourgeois politicians and their labor and farmer henchmen to divert the genuine labor party sentiment into a nondescript third party; (3) To permeate the labor party movement with Communist ideas and to strengthen the Workers Party, morally and organizationally.

Our Labor Party Campaign

6. Before the organization of the Federated Farmer-Labor Party, on July 3-4-5, 1923, our labor party policy, as we declared many times, was simply the application of the united front policy of the Communist International. This policy was absolutely correct, and so long as we held to it we made great headway. Our campaign for a united front labor party met with a wide response. We drove the labor party movement forward and our party advanced along with it, gaining great prestige. The united front policy enabled us to penetrate deeper into the labor movement than ever before and to establish our comrades in many strategic positions. The united front labor party, along with amalgamation, was the most dynamic issue in our hands, and the most powerful weapon against the reactionaries. Under this slogan the left wing was on the offensive and advancing all along the line.

7. The united front labor party policy was the basis of an effective alliance between the Communists and the progressive trade unionists, with the Communists everywhere furnishing the driving force of the powerful combination. The alliance was of the greatest advantage to us, yet to maintain it we did not have to give up anything in principle. It yielded the maximum that any united front arrangement can ever yield to our party. We were able to broaden the mass movement of the rank and file, strengthen the position of the Workers Party, and throw an ever-increasing force against the Gompers machine. The program of the alliance was our own program. We were turning the whole fire against the reactionaries and widening the breach between them and the progressives, and we had complete freedom of independent party action.

8. This united front policy, which proved so successful, not only to the labor party movement as such, but especially to the Workers Party, practically came to an end with the formation of the Federated Farmer-Labor Party. The July conference was called upon the initiative of the Farmer-Labor Party, of which the

Chicago Federation of Labor was the controlling group. The policy of the majority of the WP Central Executive Committee towards this conference was entirely wrong and inevitably led to the split which there took place. The situation was a very delicate one. Many factors contributed to make this so. The growing activities of the Communists prompted the Gompers machine to bring strong pressure to bear upon the progressive elements in Chicago, and the latter showed unmistakable signs of weakening. But the contention that this attack of Gompers would have brought about the split anyway between the Communists and progressives is unjustified. Gompers' opposition to the passage of the amalgamation resolution by the Chicago Federation a year earlier was far more intense and determined than his attack upon the labor party move, and he came to Chicago to lead the fight against it personally, but the Communist-progressive bloc stood unbroken against him. In fact the attack of the Gompers machine has not yet succeeded in splitting the alliance of the Communists with the progressives in other centers, such as Minneapolis, Buffalo, Detroit, etc., where the Federated Farmer-Labor Party issue has not been pressed by us.

The False Policy of the CEC

9. Nevertheless, the situation in Chicago was critical. The danger of a split was manifest weeks before the July 3 conference. This should have prompted the CEC to use extreme care to prevent such an eventuality. They were given adequate warning that the Farmer-Labor Party was weakening under the attacks of Gompers and the refusal of the Socialist Party and the large International unions to participate in the conference, and that a careful and conciliatory attitude would be necessary to hold the alliance together. But the majority of the CEC turned a deaf ear to all appeals for caution. It was animated by a false policy which was a deciding factor in causing the split of July 3. This policy, which is endangering our whole movement, was based upon two misconceptions: first, an overestimation of the tempo of revolutionary development; second, a greatly exaggerated idea of the present strength of the Communist forces.

10. Guided by this policy, the majority of the CEC drove headlong toward the split of July 3. Its attitude towards the FLP was hostile and intransigent; the discussions in the CEC at this time were so belligerent towards the FLP that one would believe that this organization was our bitterest enemy. In the critical days before the conference, the CEC's negotiations with the FLP were casual, inadequate, and most unsatisfactory. It went into the conference without any real understanding with the progressive leaders as to what was to be done, and thus left the door wide open for a split. The CEC, which was located in New York 1,000 miles away, had no confidence in the comrades located in Chicago, the headquarters city of the FLP, and refused to appoint a single one of them on the negotiations committee, notwithstanding their intimate knowledge of the situation. Proceeding upon the assumption that either the FLP had to go along with the immediate formation of the Federated Party, or that it would not matter if they did not, the CEC practically forced the issue and burned its bridges behind it. It rejected the compromise proposal of the FLP, made weeks before the conference, that the organization of the Federated Party be deferred until the movement could take on more volume, and that for this purpose the conference organize an affiliation committee to which the Workers Party could be affiliated. Acceptance of this proposal would have meant that the Workers Party could have continued to pursue the policy that had proved so successful in the preceding months pending the time when the Federated Party could have been launched under more favorable conditions. The statement of the majority in their August Theses that the break with the FLP could have been avoided only by sacrificing the role of leadership of the Workers Party in the fight for the idea of the labor party, and by the betrayal of the confidence of the rank and file, was a gratuitous assumption and not borne out by the actual situation. The fact is that the Political Committee of the CEC voted unanimously on October 30, 1923, almost four months after the July 3 conference, to accept a practically identical affiliation committee arrangement in connection with the proposed national labor party movement initiated by Minnesota. The trouble was that the CEC had committed itself completely to the slogan of "Organize the Federated Farmer-Labor Party on July 3, or betray the working class." The inevitable result of this intransigent attitude, in view of the delicate situation, was the split at the conference.

11. To condemn the CEC for the split on July 3, it is not necessary to defend the Farmer-Laborites. Their actions throughout were weak, hesitating and inconsistent, and, at the crucial moment, treacherous. But such qualities are characteristic of centrist elements, especially such weak centrists as the American "progressives," and must be taken into account in all our dealings with them. This does not change the fact that alliance with them is of the greatest value to us at the present time. The combination of the Communists with the progressives is a historic necessity in the struggle to overthrow the Gompers machine and build the labor party. To split with them on the grounds that they are not good revolutionary militants is to reject the idea of alliance of the Communists with other elements in the labor movement, and to repudiate entirely the principle of the united front.

Results of the July 3 Split

12. Since the formation of the Federated Farmer-Labor Party the situation has been radically changed. We have departed from the principle of the united front and have gotten onto a sectarian basis in the national labor party movement. Our former offensive fight for the labor party, consequently, has been turned into a defensive struggle wherever the Federated Farmer-Labor Party has been made the issue of the fight. Wherever we raise the issue of the Federated Farmer-Labor Party we are immediately confronted with a split. The drastic effects of this are shown, for example, in Chicago and the state of Illinois, which was the center of the Farmer-Labor Party movement and where the split is definitely accomplished. In this district, which was once our chief stronghold, our alliance with the progressives has been broken. We have lost the issue of the united front labor party and are fighting now for our own labor party, the Federated. As a consequence our comrades are largely isolated, and face a united front of all other elements against them. In the Chicago Federation of Labor and, to a great extent in the Illinois Federation of Labor, the controlling element was a bloc of Communists and progressives against the reactionaries in support of many immediate slogans of the Communists. Today, however, these bodies present the spectacle of a united front against the Communists and against the entire program of the Communists. Our position has been weakened and that of the reactionaries immeasurably strengthened. The progressive program, industrial as well as political, is defeated, and the progressives are forced into the arms of the reactionaries and subordinated to them. Since the July 3 split the leadership of Fitzpatrick has been practically destroyed through his retreat to the right. His position as leader is being taken, not by a stronger progressive or by a Communist, but by Oscar Nelson, an agent of Gompers. The Chicago Federation of Labor, once the leader of the opposition movement in the AFL, is again fast becoming a stronghold of the Gompers machine. The body which refused by unanimous vote to criticize the Soviet government for the prosecution of the Social Revolutionaries (a criticism in which even Debs joined) is no longer a friend of Soviet Russia. For the first time in many years its sessions are marked by hysterical attacks upon revolutionaries, customary in other AFL organizations. The policy of the majority of the CEC in dealing with the FLP has entrenched the reactionaries and isolated the Communists. A similar policy in dealing with the progressives in other labor party centers will produce similar results.

13. The sweeping advance that the Communists were making under the united front policy in the Chicago unions, and the heavy losses that followed the abandonment of it, are graphically illustrated in the following table, given in the report of the Chicago District Executive Committee. The delegates referred to in the table as "non-party" are not the Fitzpatrick group but are left wing delegates that went the whole way with the Communists. [see table next page]

14. The harmful effects of the July 3 split have been manifested in many ways. Despite the fact that, due to the primarily local character of the FLP, the split did not spread organizationally throughout the country, nevertheless the apparent break of the Communists with the progressive wing of the labor movement emboldened the reactionaries for a great counteroffensive against the Communists, which continues to be one of the most pronounced features of the present labor situation. The administration of the International Ladies' Garment Workers' Union commenced their drive to break up the TUEL immediately after

	Delegates from Unions		Number of Local Unions	Total Membership
	Party	Non-Party		
WP United Front Conference, May 1, 1922	6	6	8	2,500
FLP Cook County Convention, Oct. 1922	12	10	17	9,000
FLP Cook County Convention, Jan. 1923	19	15	24	12,000
WP United Front Conference, May 1, 1923	22	11	26	17,000
FLP Cook County Convention, June 10, 1923	33	38	45	25,000
July 3-4-5, 1923 Conference, Chicago	55	45	51	40,000
Affiliated to Federated Farmer-Labor Party since July 3, to Oct. 30			6	2,500

the July 3 split. They centered their fight in Chicago and found their ablest assistants in the Fitzpatrick group, our erstwhile allies. The opposition to the League and its policies has greatly intensified since that time. A striking illustration of this was the Decatur convention of the Illinois Federation of Labor. The AFL bureaucracy rallied all its forces to beat the Communists there. The struggle was of national significance. Had there been no July 3 split, the Gompers machine would have had to confront a Communist-progressive bloc strong enough to have defeated or checked it. But as it was, the Communists were almost completely isolated and the Gompers machine, in conjunction with the progressives, rode roughshod over the Communists and turned what should have been a progressive convention into one of the most reactionary conventions in recent years. The climax of the "anti-red" drive came in the spectacular attacks upon the Communists and the expulsion of Wm. F. Dunne at the Portland convention of the AFL.

The Failure of the Federated

15. Since the July 3 conference the Federated Farmer-Labor Party has proved itself a failure and has discredited the CEC theory which brought it into being. Immediately after the conference, and proceeding upon the assumption that the FFLP was a real mass labor party, the CEC ordered all its connections to secure immediate affiliations to the FFLP. This policy resulted in so many defeats for our militants in the unions that the CEC was compelled to abandon it as a mandatory policy and to adopt, two or three weeks later, the following alternative policies: (1) affiliation with the FFLP, (2) endorsement of the FFLP, (3) sending of delegates to the coming January convention of the FFLP. This second elastic policy has fared little better than the first. In practice it has been proved virtually impossible to even raise the question of the FFLP.

16. The record of our activities in the main labor party centers shows that we have been compelled to abandon the whole FFLP program, although it is still retained in the theory of the majority. The complete domination and control of the FFLP by the Communists could not remain a secret of our own. It gave an excellent weapon into the hands of our enemies and they were not slow to take advantage of it. The combined attack launched against the FFLP by the capitalist press, the labor bureaucracy, the Socialists and the Farmer-Laborites, has succeeded in branding it before the labor movement as merely another name for the Workers Party. When we fight for it, therefore, our enemies are able to take the issue of the labor party out of our hands and fight the FFLP on the issue of the Communist International. The result is that labor organizations which are ready for the labor party, but which are not ready openly to join a party definitely labeled "Communist," do not join it. The great bulk of the rank and file delegates who attended the July 3 conference have not been able to affiliate their organizations to the FFLP, or even to endorse or to send delegates to its coming convention. We are told that the organization of anything short of the Federated Farmer-Labor Party on July 3 would have meant a betrayal of the rank and file. But we have seen how, in actual practice, one of the two following results of its formation almost invariably occurred: either the delegates themselves, frightened by the terrific attack and the united front against them, changed their minds about the question, or they were repudiated by their organizations. We captured the delegates for three days, but we did not capture their organizations for the FFLP. The claim that the FFLP is a mass party with approximately 600,000 members has absolutely no foundation in fact.

17. The campaign to affiliate the important organizations represented at the conference met with decisive defeat all along the line. The Amalgamated Clothing Workers withdrew during the conference; likewise large sections of miners. The West Virginia Federation of Labor has since formed a state labor party, but it would not entertain the question of affiliation to or endorsement of the FFLP. In the friendly Detroit Federation of Labor—*with the administration supporting us*—we were defeated by a vote of 2 to 1. In Buffalo, where our comrades hold leading positions in the local labor party, they cannot afford to even raise the issue of the FFLP, because the issue would certainly split that body. Practically all of the Farmer-Labor Party delegates who came over to us at the conference have been repudiated by their own organizations: this is the case in Ohio, Kentucky, and other places; even the FLP of the state of Washington has not been affiliated to the FFLP. Practically the only organizations to join the FFLP are unions directly under Communist leadership. Vague endorsements and promises to send delegates to the next convention of the FFLP are the best we have been able to do even in the places where we are strongest. None of the important organizations represented at the July 3 conference has joined the FFLP with the single exception of the Los Angeles Labor Party, and the affiliation there represents a real danger to us. It exposes our comrades to the next onslaught of the Gompers machine, in such a way that they will not be able to fight upon the issue of the labor party which would unite the rank and file behind them, but on the issue of the FFLP, which will divide the rank and file. Our single victory thus paves the way to a future defeat.

18. The places where the labor party sentiment is most developed and has taken organized form are precisely the places where the FFLP has the least possibility to gain affiliations. This is strikingly illustrated by the case of Minnesota. In the Farmer-Labor

Federation convention there, our comrades, notwithstanding their strong position, won by their careful and systematic work, could not even mention the question of affiliation to or endorsement of the FFLP, and the mild proposal to send delegates to the January convention had to be withdrawn without being put to a vote, so strong was the prejudice against the FFLP. Farmer-Labor parties are now being formed in California, Utah and Montana, but the non-Communist elements participating in their organization will not go along with the FFLP and an attempt to force affiliation means a split. The CEC does not dare now to propose a fight to affiliate any of these local or state mass labor parties to the Federated unless it is ready to say openly that it wants to split these parties. The splitting of the labor party forces throughout the country and the isolation of the Communists, as in Chicago, is prevented only because the majority, while stubbornly clinging to its exploded theory of organizing the FFLP as a mass labor party, does not attempt to apply it concretely in the real centers of the labor party movement. The "elastic tactics" of the CEC majority have meant the practical abandonment of their theory in every case of real importance. In the face of this record of failure with the FFLP, the August Theses of the CEC majority appear ridiculous and show complete inability to estimate the situation when it says: "In a whole series of cities and states we can immediately organize the FFLP." Equally absurd is the attempt to establish an "alibi" with the charge of sabotage within the party.

19. Driven out of the main centers of the labor party movement, the majority theory is now trying to find a footing for the FFLP as a mass party by organizing branches in "unoccupied territory"; and it claims a victory for the theory for a special Communist labor party in New York City, where we have organized a group of Communist-controlled unions as a branch of the FFLP in opposition to the American Labor Party. But this tactic will not stand analysis. The FFLP is a positive handicap to our work even in this restricted field. In New York City there is not a natural labor party movement springing up from the trade unions. The American Labor Party of New York City was merely an attempt of the Socialist Party to appropriate the labor party idea and to adapt it to its own special interests; it is based upon the conception of a special labor party organized around a particular group, being a collection of SP-controlled unions and SP branches, with the latter dominating absolutely. We very properly attacked the American Labor Party at its conception as a caricature of the bona fide labor party movement. The organization of the FFLP in New York City is merely an imitation of the Socialist Party tactic, but it is not the best way to fight the SP in New York City. As a fighting measure against the Socialists to force the admission of the WP into the Labor Party, it is proper in the case of New York City to organize our trade union forces into a local labor party. The slogan by which we fight the SP in New York City should be: "Unity of both labor parties into one organization." This fight can be more effective if our labor party there is not a branch of the FFLP, but a separate unaffiliated local party. If we lay aside the issue of national affiliation entirely for the time being, the slogan of unity will be a powerful weapon in our hands and we can eventually succeed with it. The SP theory of special labor parties controlled by the various political groups is a theory which is incorporated in the August Theses of the CEC majority.

20. As for the "unoccupied territory," here too the FFLP is a source of weakness rather than of strength. In such places as Washington County, Pennsylvania, where we have organized a branch of the FFLP, we are laying the young movement open to attacks from the reactionaries on grounds most favorable to them. They will be able to attack the newly formed party, not on the broad issue of the labor party, where we can well afford to meet them, but on the narrow issue of the FFLP being a Communist party. It can be put down for a certainty, on the basis of abundant experience already accumulated, that many unions, which join the party before the fight develops because they really stand for a labor party, will weaken under this attack and either withdraw or develop a split. Where it is possible to organize a branch of the FFLP, it is possible in almost every case to organize a much larger body of workers into an unaffiliated local or state party in which our influence and control would be strong and of much more value to us. The same forces that drove the FFLP from the organized centers of the labor party movement will also inevitably drive it from the unorganized fields which the majority of the CEC now want it to invade. The place for the FFLP is neither here nor there.

FFLP as Liability to the WP

21. Besides being a failure as a mass party, the FFLP is a positive handicap, as at present conceived, to all phases of the WP work for the labor party. For one thing it is a heavy drain on the funds and energies of the WP and exercises a distinct liquidation tendency upon the latter. Practically all the work done for it has to be done by our members at the expense of the WP. Our trained workers are very few, and our financial resources are already strained to the breaking point. They should both be conserved for the most vital propaganda and agitational activity of the WP, and we should aim to put upon the broader movement the task of finding most of the administrative forces and their upkeep. Every man taken from party work for the FFLP diminishes the forces of the WP. The funds we have been already obliged to contribute necessitate the neglect of party undertakings. We cannot go ahead on this basis. With our small party and limited resources, such small items as the foregoing become very important. We can do some of the work to make the labor party, but we cannot do all of it. We can donate our share of the funds, but we cannot subsidize the whole enterprise. In most of its present functions, the FFLP is a rival of the WP. The identity of the WP in the labor party movement is submerged in the FFLP, and to the extent that the FFLP is pushed into the foreground, the WP has to be pushed into the background. The sending of a trained party worker into Oklahoma, for example, to organize the FFLP before the WP is organized there, means that all our potential forces there will be diverted from our proper task of first founding the WP. We hold that our most important revolutionary task is the building of a mass Communist party, based upon individual membership, which is the WP. The building of a labor party not only must not interfere with, but must directly assist, this process. The August Theses of the majority point out that a Communist party based on individual membership is far superior to a party based on the loose affiliation of trade unions, yet this same thesis and the practice of the CEC contradictorily tends to sabotage the WP, the real

Communist party based upon individual membership, for the sake of their proposed mass Communist party based upon loosely affiliated trade unions.

22. A further disadvantage of the FFLP to the WP is that the former prevents the latter from getting proper credit for our work in the establishment of the labor party movement. In almost all the local and state parties springing up throughout the country, the Communists are actually doing the bulk of the organization work and acting as the driving force. But our party is getting little or no credit for it with the masses, and it does not stand out as the leader. The result is a great loss of prestige for us, which is an essential element for the building of our party. The reason for this failure to get credit for the work we are doing is that nationally we stand committed to the FFLP, whereas the local and state parties that we are organizing are unaffiliated to the FFLP and their failure to affiliate gives all the appearance of being a defeat for us. In the eyes of the masses the FFLP stands for the split idea. Its existence as a separate party brings upon us all the hostile criticism that naturally is directed against the split policy in a situation that so clearly demands the united front policy. Thus we are in the anomalous position of actually building the labor party throughout the country, while our enemies are able to point to the FFLP which is our special charge, and accuse us of being a stumbling block in the way of the formation of the labor party.

23. The August Theses make the argument that the FFLP can be developed into a mass Communist party. There is no foundation for such an assertion. The conditions for the building of a mass Communist party are the existence of a closely knit Communist nucleus operating within the broadest mass organizations of the workers, permeating them with its doctrines and sweeping the most advanced of them into its ranks. The WP is such a Communist nucleus, and the naturally developing labor party movement is such a mass organization. By working within this mass organization and pushing it forward, the WP is bound to expand and extend its influence. The organization of the FFLP does not facilitate this development, but interferes with it. Wherever it takes organizational form it separates the Communists and their closest sympathizers from the main body of the movement and creates the conditions for a sectarian Communist party controlling a sectarian labor party. The argument that the FFLP will become a mass Communist party is an abandonment of the theory expounded in the same theses, that it will become a mass labor party. It can be neither the one nor the other.

Conflict Between Theory and Practice

24. In addition to the conflicting theories within the August Theses of the CEC majority, there is a flat contradiction between the labor party theory and practice followed since July 3. The theory of the majority that the Communists alone, in the present stage of the class struggle in America, can and should organize and control a mass labor party of their own—the theory that is crystallized in the FFLP—is the theory of splitting with the progressives in the labor party movement, a split which would inevitably spread to all phases of our activities in the labor movement. But this splitting theory runs so counter to the crying needs of the present situation that the CEC does not dare apply it in practice. Due, however, to its theoretical confusion, the whole time and effort of the CEC has to be devoted from week to week in the various labor party developments to the effort to twist the prevailing splitting theory into realistic practical applications of the united front principle. The whole committee is thus paralyzed between the tendency, inherent in the theory of the majority, to extend the split in the labor party movement, and the conscious struggle of the opposition to prevent it. The outcome is that the splitting theory is not being put into practice in spite of the theory to the contrary. This basic conflict between the practice and theory of the CEC is destroying the morale of the party and its capacity for straight thinking. The comrades in Minnesota, for example, are told that they are following the theory behind the organization of the FFLP, when it is obvious that the instructions given to them by the CEC amount to a complete repudiation of that theory insofar as the Minnesota situation is concerned. The adaption of the CEC theory, which is fundamentally a theory of splitting, to the requirements of the concrete situations, where we do not dare to put it into practice for fear of outlawing our comrades in the labor movement and destroying their influence—

and where, therefore, the majority is compelled to accept the program of the opposition—necessitates so much sophistry and self-deception that a general state of confusion prevails throughout the party. An even worse feature of this confusion between theory and practice is that the CEC is constantly confronted with practical situations which it must conform to in spite of its contrary theory, and to adopt makeshift solutions. The effect of this is to entirely deprive the party of the initiative which comes from a correct theoretical grasp of the problems and which would provide a uniform policy in regard to them. A correct theory must give us the initiative and leadership in the labor party movement, while the present confusion compels us to follow after and fit into the developing movement. The sum and substance of the practice of the CEC since the July 3 conference is a retreat from the split policy set up by its theory, to a begrudging and ill-understood practice of the united front principle. The only remedy is the complete rejection of the disastrous split theory, and the unification of our theory and practice by the adoption of a clear-cut united front policy.

Preventing the Spread of the Split

25. The CEC majority claims that the split between the Communists and progressives has already taken place throughout the country and that we proceed upon that basis. But this is not the case. It is true that the split of July 3 has taken full effect in Chicago and the state of Illinois, but it has not yet spread to other important centers. The reason for this is that the Farmer-Labor Party, as a tightly knit organization, was restricted pretty much to the state of Illinois, and for the split to take place elsewhere it was necessary that the issue of the FFLP should be pressed in those centers. This the CEC has not ventured to do. Had the FLP been a really national party the Communists would have been isolated all over the country as they now are in Chicago. The splendid position we have gained in Minnesota is clearly the result of the united front policy we have followed there of working within the broad labor party movement and not as a separate party. This policy in Minnesota produced three good results: (1) It has the effect of uniting and strengthening the labor party against its enemies; it was demonstrated that even a small group of Communists can play a very important role in steering the labor party along the right course and protecting it against disintegration. (2) Our policy enabled the Communists to penetrate deeply into the movement and entrench themselves in strategic positions from which it will be difficult to dislodge them; the prestige of the WP rose greatly and many valuable new members were added to our ranks. The third result of our tactic in Minnesota was to bind the progressive elements closer to us, and to bring them nearer to the left position; Mahoney and Cramer, for example, who stood far apart from us only a few months ago, are working hand in hand with us today. The Minneapolis *Labor Review* and the Minnesota *Labor Advocate* are outspokenly defending the Communists against the attacks of the Gompers machine. The wavering of Cramer a few months ago was sufficient for the theses of the majority of the CEC to say he had gone to the right and united with Gompers and to accept this as a working basis. There is no doubt that we could have made a complete split with him and other progressives there, just as we did in Chicago, if we had not used the most careful tactics to avoid it. The results in Minnesota strengthened our position while the results in Chicago weakened it, because in the former case we used the united front tactic and in the latter the splitting theory of the majority of the CEC.

26. It was possible to avoid the split in Minnesota only because we did not raise the issue of the FFLP. The same thing is true of practically every other labor party center. We have had to choose in each case between the unity of the labor party forces on the one hand, and the organization of the sectarian FFLP, carrying with it our isolation, on the other. Fortunately in most cases, so far, the CEC has been constrained to violate its theory and sacrifice the FFLP. But this has put us in the anomalous position of claiming to have a national labor party without trying to give it an organizational base in the main labor party centers where the movement is best developed. Such a position is untenable. The FFLP cannot be a real party unless it gains the affiliation of local and state parties, and it cannot fight for this affiliation without breaking our alliance with the progressive elements and thus splitting the labor party movement. The continuance of our efforts to organize the FFLP as a separate labor party renders our whole position unstable. It holds the constant menace of a needless and disastrous split between the Communists and the progressives in their fight against the Gompers machine. This standing threat of a split weakens the influence of our militants everywhere in the labor party movement and demoralizes the movement itself.

27. To spread the Chicago split throughout the country would be the greatest disaster to our party. The class struggle in America has not developed to the point, and the issues are not of such a nature, that the Communists must fight alone against the entire field. We can profitably leave that conception to the SLP. Gompers' tactic is to isolate the Communists, to have them standing alone, in order that he may expel them from the labor movement before they get a strong footing there. Our Communist forces are as yet but few and scattered. The period of "collecting the Communist forces" is not finished in America; it is only beginning. Our members in the trade unions have had but little experience in realistic trade union work, and they are only now beginning to establish themselves in the labor movement. In the face of the tremendous offensive of Gompers against us, and with our forces so weak and inexperienced, it would be little less than criminal folly for us deliberately to break the alliance with the progressive trade unionists who are inclined to stand with us in the immediate fight for the issues which we ourselves proclaim. Under the very best conditions we are in a position where the most careful strategy is necessary. The split with the progressives would play right into the hands of Gompers. Not only would it compromise the labor party fight, but it would lead to the wholesale expulsion of the Communists from the trade unions, and shatter the left wing movement in the trade unions which only now, for the first time in the history of America, is taking an organized and conscious form. For us it is a life and death question to organize as wide a bloc as possible in the trade unions for the fight against the Gompers machine. The CEC opposition will fight against the needless split with the progressives and against any policy that leads to it at this time, with all its power. The FFLP as now conceived represents a theory that makes for this split, and that is one of the many reasons why we must give up the idea of attempting to organize it as a separate labor party.

The Labor Party Movement in America

28. The attempt to transfer European labor party analogies to America is bound to lead us astray for the simple reason that there is no real analogy. The labor party movement in America, rising out of conditions that have no counterpart anywhere else in the world, is developing along lines marked out for it by the peculiar American situation. The course of its own natural development is indicted by the experience so far. This experience completely blasts the Socialist Party theory that the labor party will be organized from the top by the labor bureaucracy. And it likewise disposes of the made-to-order theory that it can be artificially imposed from the top by a prematurely formed national organization under the control of the Communists. The existence at the present time of "our own" labor party—the FFLP—does not arise out of the normal course of events; it is the result of our own misconceptions and foolish maneuverings.

29. The basic labor party movement in America as it has developed thus far reveals the following characteristics: (1) it is organizing from the bottom on a local and state basis; (2) it is a real mass movement of the rank and file and not simply the artificial creation of politicians; (3) it is almost uniformly a combination of city workers and farmers, with a sprinkling of the middle class elements who invariably attach themselves to all such movements.

30. The labor party movement in America is a united front movement and we must return to that platform. We dispute the contention of the CEC majority that the normal development of the labor party movement is the growth of a number of competing labor parties under the control of rival political groups. We must abandon the idea of trying to maintain a labor party of our own which is definitely labeled as a Communist organization, and become again the champions of the mass labor party, the united front labor party. The genuine labor party, as we see it developing in the various centers, is based on the trade unions, workers' political parties, and farmers' organizations. It is essentially a mass party, and a strong class sentiment among the rank and file workers in the given city or state is a necessary condition precedent to its formation. The attempt to mechanically measure the possibilities of local organization by an arbitrary ratio of ten workers to one member of the WP puts the whole question of the labor party upon an artificial basis and disregards entirely the essentially united front character of the labor party. The organization of premature and artificial labor parties, as the theses of the majority virtually propose, makes a caricature out of the very idea of the labor party and runs the danger of discrediting it. The Workers Party cannot assume the responsibility for such undertakings without injuring its standing in the eyes of the workers. As against the theory of conflicting labor parties controlled by the rival political groups, we advocate the mass labor party organized on a united front basis.

31. One of the fundamental errors of the CEC majority is their confusion in the use of the term "left wing," which occurs all through their conception. On the one hand, they state that only the "left wing" elements will comprise the labor party at its inception, which is correct if we bear in mind that these elements represent a broad "left wing" from the standpoint of the labor movement as a whole. On the other hand, they consider the FFLP as synonymous with this broad "left wing," which is incorrect, as the FFLP is only the revolutionary section of that left wing. In other words, the organizational basis of the "left wing" which goes to make up the labor party is much wider than the "left wing" which is found in the FFLP. The former is composed of workingmen and farmers from the mildest progressives to the most advanced revolutionaries, while the latter consists almost entirely of revolutionary elements. The one is a united front organization and the other is a revolutionary group. A striking illustration of the fact that the "left wing" which naturally makes up the labor party movement is much broader than the "left wing" which comprises the FFLP is to be found in Minnesota. There the Farmer-Labor Federation is so much more conservative than the FFLP that it will not even affiliate with the latter. The same condition prevails in West Virginia and other centers. The policy of trying to build the labor party on the basis of the narrow "left wing," which is found in the FFLP, instead of the broad "left wing" which is always found in the labor party movement wherever it has taken an organized mass character, is a sectarian policy that leads directly to the isolation of the Communists. To speak of the broad movement of workers and exploited farmers which stands for the class party as the "left wing" and then to use the same term interchangeably, as the CEC majority constantly does, to describe the forces of the FFLP, is to presuppose an identity between the two which does not exist.

32. Our position is not based on the assumption that the entire labor movement must join the labor party at once, or that even a majority is necessary. But we hold that wherever it is formed, it must unite the labor party forces and have a genuine mass character. We want it to be organized upon as broad a base as possible with as large a mass of workers as can be gotten together upon the issue of a labor party, and not merely those who can be organized on the issue of Communism which is raised by the FFLP. Our militants should endeavor to take a leading part in all these mass parties, entrench themselves in strategic positions and lead the workers by degrees to the platform of Communism.

33. Neither do we expect the reactionary leaders to form the labor party. It has to be done by a bloc of the radical and progressive workers in which the Communists are the driving force. It is essentially a rank and file movement and our aim should be to gradually extend the Communist influence and leadership in it, and at the same time to preserve its mass character. Communists in America, at this stage of development, thrive best within a broader mass movement and especially within a mass labor party. It is foolish for us to form a little labor party of our own in order to be the leaders of it.

34. Important as the revolt of the bankrupt farmers is in the present political situation, and necessary as it is that a close alliance be cemented between the exploited farmers and the industrial workers, there is a great danger in the tendency, displayed by the CEC majority, to base their labor party policy upon the farmers' revolt, and to relegate the role of the industrial workers to second place. In Oklahoma, for example, it disregarded the organized workers and based its decision to organize the FFLP there upon fragmentary information of the farmers' unrest;

whereas further investigation, urged by the opposition, has shown that even in this agricultural state the organized workers in the State Federation of Labor are now making the most significant move for independent working class political action, by taking the initiative in a statewide conference of all labor party forces. A similar tendency is manifested in the consideration of the labor party problem in other states. It is a fundamental of a sound labor party policy that the organized industrial workers, particularly in our present historical stage, shall occupy the leading position and be the organizational and ideological basis for the labor party. We must keep our eye on Pittsburgh as well as Fargo.

35. It is incorrect to raise the question of a conflict of interest between the Workers Party and the labor party as such, as the CEC majority does. At the present stage of class development in America the formation of a mass labor party represents a revolutionary advance on the part of the working class. The breaking away from the capitalist parties and the entrance into politics under their own standard signifies nothing less than the awakening of class consciousness on the part of the workers. It represents their conscious entry into political life and consequently increases their receptivity to Communist propaganda and agitation. Above all it offers to the Communists a tremendous opportunity to entrench themselves among the masses and to seize positions of leadership. The experiences in Buffalo, Los Angeles, Minnesota and elsewhere demonstrate that the mass labor party provides the very best field for the operations of the Communists. In Minnesota the organization of the Farmer-Labor Federation gave the Workers Party the opportunity for the greatest advances in its history in that section, despite the fact that it has not yet been admitted to the Federation as an organization. The formation of the labor party means political activity for the workers. In Minnesota we have seen that this political activity gave the Communists the opportunity to penetrate deeply into the labor movement in a very short time, and there cannot be a doubt that if the comrades in Minnesota continue their present realistic work and are guided by a sound united front policy, they will in good time succeed in permeating the entire movement with the ideas of Communism. The Workers Party will not only gain admittance to the Farmer-

Labor Federation, but it will become the leader of it. The labor party movement is not a danger in itself to the Communist movement, but a tremendous opportunity for it. The danger lies only in our adopting a wrong policy towards it.

36. The labor party sentiment is at once the most healthy current in the American labor movement, and the most dynamic issue in the hands of the Communists. It is the issue by which the Gompers machine can be smashed and the ground broken for the leadership of the Communists. It is the greatest folly for us to caricature this basic issue and reduce it to a sectarian or factional basis. When we set up our own labor party we lose the main issue entirely. Our enemies are able to wave the red flag and scare the mass of immature rank and file workers away from us. The working masses are not yet ready to rally to the standard of Communism openly displayed in definitely labeled Communist organizations, but ample experience proves that they will accept Communist leadership in mass labor parties. Under the slogan of the labor party we can organize them and lead them into conflicts which will inevitably sharpen their understanding and draw them closer to a consciously revolutionary attitude.

37. The CEC majority falsely put the question this way, "Shall we assume leadership?", and try to make it appear that the opposition is based upon defeatism and lack of confidence in the party. This is nonsense. The real question is, "*How* shall we assume leadership?" There is only one way to gain the leadership of the masses, and that is to push ourselves and our doctrines deeply into their ranks. We can lead large masses now, but we cannot do it by setting up our own organization and calling them into it. Such a procedure presupposes a highly developed consciousness among the masses that does not yet exist. The setting up of a separate labor party organization, such as the FFLP, known to all the world as the special party of the Communists, breaks our connections with the half-awakened masses and defeats our efforts for leadership. What the CEC opposition wants is not simply leadership of our own organizations, but leadership of the masses. And since the masses will not come to us and join our labor party, our policy is to go to them and join forces with them in a broad labor party and gain leadership of it. The question of Communist contact with the masses of workers is inseparable from the question of Communist leadership. The road to leadership does not lead through the swamp of isolation.

38. The probable organization of a "third party" by such bourgeois politicians as La Follette or Henry Ford presents a danger to the immature labor party movement; it is obvious that an effort would be made, with the assistance of labor politicians, to sweep large sections of the Farmer-Labor Party movement into the "third party." We must fight resolutely against this all-class third party tendency and insist upon a genuine class party of workers and exploited farmers. While we are bound to favor the formation of a "third party" as the result of a split in the ranks of the capitalist parties, our main task is to prevent the stultification of the Farmer-Labor movement to such an end. This fight can be made successfully only on the condition that we and our closest sympathizers are not isolated in a separate party of our own, but that we have attached ourselves inseparably to the mass movement. The separate existence of a small labor party under the direct control of the Communists jeopardizes the main labor party movement by separating it from the one element, the Communists, that can safeguard it from the machinations of traitorous politicians.

39. The healthy impulse behind the labor party movement is manifested by the large number of local and state labor parties springing up on every side. We should foster this development in every way. Wherever there is a genuine sentiment for the labor party idea the Communists must attempt to give it an organized form. While always propagandizing the necessity of a national labor party, the formation of local and state parties should not wait for the unification of existing organized movements on a national scale. They should be organized at once wherever possible. The opposition repudiates as ridiculous the charge of the CEC majority that we advocate mere propaganda "for the labor party, and not its actual organization."

40. The next necessary great step in the development of the labor party is the unification of the movement into a genuine national organization on a mass basis. All efforts must be put forward for the establishment of this national organization for the next presidential campaign. The participation of the main body of the existing state and local parties is a necessary condition for the building of a real mass organization. Because of its known control by the Communists, the FFLP cannot serve for this purpose. It must be our policy to support and foster bona fide plans for national crystallization, as, for example, the one proposed by the Minnesota party. We should participate wholeheartedly in this effort of the Minnesota party, or in any others of a similar character if this one is a failure. As soon as the national labor party movement takes organized form of a genuine mass character, we should merge all our labor party forces in it, and, if necessary, accept minority representation in its directing bodies for the time being. When such national conferences are held, our policy should be to fight for: (a) the establishment of a closely knit national labor party to include the WP and the FFLP, and (b) that the newly established united front national labor party should set up united front party branches in all states and cities, to which the WP should be affiliated. Our aim should be to get the practical control in building these united front parties, national and local.

Immediate Program

Our conception of the FFLP is that of a means to organize the labor party and to unite the left wing forces within that party. To carry out this policy the following shall be its function and method of operation:

(a) The FFLP should not be a separate labor party, rival to other labor parties, but an organizing and propaganda instrument for the building of a united front labor party. It is not necessary to liquidate the FFLP but to transform its functions.

(b) The FFLP, to unite the left wing forces, shall carry on a campaign for the direct affiliation to itself of all trade unions, farmers' associations, workers' political parties, and other organizations except mass labor parties, in harmony with its program of organizing the labor party movement.

(c) The FFLP shall carry on a militant campaign everywhere for the organization of local and state mass labor parties.

While not accepting the affiliation of these labor parties officially, the FFLP shall maintain the closest possible connection with and control of them, thus uniting the whole into a coordinated national movement under its direction.

(d) The FFLP shall agitate and move for the organization of an official national mass labor party at the earliest possible opportunity. When such a national movement develops upon a genuine basis the FFLP shall merge into it all its official and unofficial connections and groups.

(e) In the national mass labor party the FFLP shall serve as a left-bloc medium to unite all the left wing forces against the reformists and reactionaries in order to revolutionize the mass movement.

(f) Our aim shall be to gradually transform, as quickly as possible, this control and leadership of the left wing forces in the national mass movement by the FFLP into direct and acknowledged leadership and control of these forces by the Workers Party itself.

What Happened at Portland?

Published 24 November 1923

The following article by Cannon concerns the refusal of the American Federation of Labor convention in Portland to seat Montana delegate and Workers Party leader William F. Dunne. It was published in The Worker.

Only six delegates, representing a voting strength of 130, voted against the expulsion of "Bill" Dunne, the Communist, at Portland, while 27,888 votes were cast for it. On the face of this showing, two conclusions are being drawn from the convention. The labor officialdom sees the labor movement again made safe for capitalism by this holy war against the Communists; while some elements in the radical labor movement, like the IWW and the OBU,[1] claim it proves their contention that the Communist policy of working within the conservative trade unions is a failure. They point to the shamelessly reactionary character of the entire convention, its open and cynical declaration of partnership with the masters against the revolutionary workers, its expulsion of the lone Communist, and say: "There is no hope here, no sign of progress." Both of these conclusions are false.

The triumph of reaction at Portland appears only on the surface. The real victor was the Communist movement.

Communism was the victor because it was raised there into a living issue of the labor movement. It was the victor because it has

[1] Evidently a reference to the syndicalist organization, One Big Union, formed in Western Canada in early 1919. OBU members were active in the May-June 1919 Winnipeg general strike, and the organization claimed over 41,000 members by the end of 1919. A small American offshoot was formed in June 1920. But by 1923 the entire North American organization was probably down to a few thousand members. In contrast to the IWW, the OBU eschewed all talk of direct action and violence; it organized its membership on a territorial, rather than industrial, basis.

penetrated in so short a time into the very citadel of the reactionary officialdom and made them recognize it as their most deadly enemy. It was the victor because the message of Communism was called to the attention of millions of workers by the tremendous amount of publicity given to the expulsion of Dunne. The Portland convention did not prove the falsity of the Communist tactics in the trade union movement. On the contrary, it proved that they are already beginning to register decided results.

Anyone who paid attention to the convention could see that these labor leaders are hand in glove with the bosses. Never before was the complete identity of their interest and viewpoint with those of the capitalists so clearly and dramatically revealed as it was at Portland. Major George Berry comes there directly after breaking the strike of the members of his own union in New York City. He is given a warm reception and Gompers calls on him for a speech. He boasts of his dastardly work in siding with the employers, and the convention votes approval of his actions. John L. Lewis gets up and tells how many district organizations of mine workers he has disrupted in his war against the militant rank and file, and the convention agrees that it was a good thing. The convention adopts a set of "principles" enunciated by strikebreaker Berry, the central point of which is the "recognition of the right of property in industry." Amalgamation, the labor party, the recognition of Soviet Russia and every other proposal calculated to strengthen and regenerate the pitifully weak labor movement are defeated. Finally, Wm. F. Dunne, the Communist, the most hated enemy of the Anaconda Mining Company, the well-tried, intelligent and courageous fighter for the cause of labor, is expelled from the convention amid the plaudits of the open shop press. Many thousands of workers will look at this record and say that there is no difference between the men who made it and the employers. Many of them will look a little further and see that Communism, personified by comrade Dunne, stood there as the champion of everything these men were against.

Some workers are able to see only one side of the Portland convention. They say: "It is easy to see that these men are not workers at all and have nothing in common with the workers. What is the use to bother with them? You can't expect to convert them to Communism, and as soon as you begin to carry on your work they will expel you from the unions. Why not leave them now and start new unions without them?" That looks like a simple and easy way out of the difficulty, but it does not solve the problem. These men dominate and control the official machinery of the trade unions which embrace the overwhelming mass of the organized workers in America. The problem is how to free the great mass of the rank and file from their influence. This cannot be done by leaving the old unions, because the rank and file workers do not follow. It can only be done by working amongst them in the old unions, and winning them over, by degrees, to a revolutionary position. Intelligent and systematic work, combined with the historical developments, which are all in our favor, will eventually do it. It is a process, and the events at Portland are a part of that process.

We have to expect that the reactionaries will go to extreme lengths before they will give up the control of the labor movement. The history of the world movement shows that they will not hesitate to split and disrupt the unions when their treacherous leadership is challenged. But these tactics avail nothing in the end. They can expel Communists but they cannot expel Communism. The Communists are destined to win because their platform corresponds to the actual needs of the working class. Splits and expulsions did not save the yellow leaders of the Russian unions and it is not saving the yellow leaders of the German unions. It will not save them in America if the revolutionary workers keep their heads and follow the right tactics.

Comrade Dunne's service to our cause at Portland was a double one. He not only raised the issue of Communism there and forced it to be discussed, but he gave a splendid example to the whole working class of America of how a Communist conducts himself in the fight. He stood there in that den of business men and told the truth about them to their teeth. Even the capitalist reporters had to pay tribute to his brave and manly attitude. They said he was "bold and audacious"; that is to say, he was a Communist. He indicted the traitor leaders in burning words, pouring out the scorn that honest workers feel for them. He made the issue clean and sharp, standing proudly by his own good record and the principles of his party. One labor writer said about his speech: "It was a splendid, fearless answer, retracting nothing, apologizing for nothing."

Is anyone so foolish as to think they killed comrade Dunne by expelling him from the convention? Even the capitalist press has some uneasiness on that score. The *New York Times* said: "The Federation action makes a new hero among the Communists and may give that propaganda a new impetus among the workers." We can say that comrade Dunne is no new hero to us, but an old fighter in the ranks. The stupid reactionaries have now made him known to a much wider circle. By expelling him they have only given more life to the party they sought to kill. They have centered attention of thousands of workers on him, and the Workers Party, which he personified there, in such a way that the Workers Party in their minds will be identified with the picture of a working man standing there in that vast gang of agents of the capitalist class, fighting for the rank and file of labor and denouncing the traitors to their faces, putting forward all constructive proposals to better the trade unions and yielding not an inch in the camp of the enemy. There can be no doubt that the event will give the Communist propaganda a "new impetus among the workers." Communism, after Portland, will have a stronger propaganda. It will not be eliminated from the trade union movement but will penetrate deeper into it. And comrade Dunne will play a bigger part in this work than ever before. The expulsion at Portland did not signify the end of Communism in the trade unions but the real beginning of it.

The IWW and the Red International of Labor Unions

Published 1 December 1923

The following article by Cannon was published in The Worker. *The IWW had decided against affiliating with the Comintern in 1920; its fourteenth convention in 1922 had decided against affiliation to the RILU. Nonetheless, some elements in the organization remained sympathetic to the Communists through 1924.*

The Fifteenth General Convention of the Industrial Workers of the World, which is scheduled to remain in session for three weeks, devoted 30 minutes of its time to hearing representatives of the Red International of Labor Unions appeal to them to send delegates to the forthcoming World Congress in order to discuss there the basis of a working program upon which all the revolutionary elements in the American labor movement may unite their forces for the common struggle. Without exaggerating the immediate results accomplished, I venture to say that this act of the convention was the most significant one in all its deliberations. The Red International appeared there as the advocate of unity in the struggle of all revolutionary labor unionists of America and the world. There is no bigger question before the working class than this, and the mere discussion of it, even though it leads to no immediate result, is an event of major importance.

The friendly approach of the Red International toward the convention of the IWW does not signify any change of policy on its part. It simply represented another step in its efforts to unify all the militant elements in the labor movement on a common platform of revolutionary struggle. It has already accomplished much toward this end. The Red International has been the leading and inspiring force in the organization, for the first time in history, of the left wing of the American trade unions into a compact, unified body. It has gained a decisive influence in many of the radical independent unions, and has been the greatest power making for the harmonious cooperation of the members of these unions with the revolutionary workers in the conservative trade unions. The next necessary task is to bring about a unity of purpose between these elements and the IWW. It must be acknowledged that this will be a tremendous task. Thick walls of prejudice and misunderstanding stand in the way. But the Red International turns to it with such a record of real achievements to its credit as to give the promise that it will find the way to overcome all difficulties and achieve its purposes in good time.

It would be foolish to think this will be a simple or easy thing to accomplish. Real and serious differences stand in the way, and they will not disappear merely because we might wish them to. But it is worthwhile now to begin a serious discussion of the whole question. The Red International does not cover up real differences, it brings them out into the open and talks about them frankly. This is what we must do.

There are two main conflicts, one theoretical and the other practical, which have so far not only prevented unity between the IWW and the revolutionary trade unionists and the Communists, but which have charged the whole atmosphere with hostility and led to the most bitter controversies. All sorts of controversies have complicated the situation, but they are all subordinate to the main questions and spring from them. The main points of controversy are these two: first, the conflict in philosophy between Communism and syndicalism, or industrialism which is its American variant, over the role of the state, the necessity for a proletarian party and the question of the dictatorship of the proletariat; second, the conflict between the Red International program of working within the conservative unions, wherever they exist as mass organizations, in order to revolutionize them from within, and the IWW program of organizing branches as rivals to the other unions. These conflicts are of such a deep-seated nature as to absolutely preclude the possibility of an immediate complete agreement and organized unity between the IWW and the Communists on the one hand and between the IWW and the trade unions on the other. But it does not follow from this that a state of war must exist between them along the entire front, with no cooperation anywhere. On the contrary, an examination of the concrete situation will show that a working agreement and cooperation in action is immediately possible in most places and on many questions of great importance.

For example, there is no valid reason to prevent a joint fight of the IWW and the Communists and adherents of the Red International for the release of class war prisoners, against criminal syndicalism laws and injunctions, in support of Workers Germany, etc.[1] Each organization could join in such a united front without sacrificing any principle or jeopardizing its organizational integrity in any way. All that is required to bring it about is an alliance for the specific purpose, not a unity of the organizations. Such a joint fight would be of the greatest agitational value; it would multiply the power behind the drive and make for its success. The movement generally, and the IWW in particular, has much to gain from it. A campaign of this nature can be carried out without regard to the points in dispute between us. Its effect would be to strengthen and stimulate the movement as a whole and to promote a feeling of friendship and solidarity which would make it much easier to work for a basis of united effort on other questions. To say that because we do not all agree on the question of the state, we cannot make a joint fight for the class war prisoners, is tantamount to saying that we can never work together as long as there is one point at issue between us. Such a view is dogmatic and unreasonable. The united front on the questions mentioned above is an immediate practical possibility. If we are serious revolutionists who put the interests of the working class above everything, we have to say this united front is a necessity.

Turning to the field of organization, it can be shown that the differences between the IWW and the adherents of the Red International are not nearly so great as to prevent cooperation in most cases of real importance. The story has been persistently

[1] Despite the decisive nature of the defeat in Germany earlier in 1923, when the Communist Party of Germany (KPD) let slip a promising revolutionary situation, the Executive Committee of the Communist International continued to insist into early 1924 that "The basic appraisal of the German situation given by the Comintern Executive last September remains in essentials unchanged....The KPD must not strike from the agenda the question of the insurrection and seizure of power" (ECCI "Statement on the Events in Germany in October 1923," 19 January 1924).

circulated, and is believed by many members of the IWW, that the Red International wants to "liquidate" the IWW, and that it makes a fetish of the AFL. There is no truth in this story. The Red International does lay it down as a cardinal point that the revolutionary workers must not isolate themselves from the masses, that they must join the unions to which the masses belong, no matter what their affiliation may be, and work there in good faith to build them up, to strengthen them in every way and to inspire them with the spirit of militant struggle. But this does not mean that the Red International has a special love for the unions affiliated to the AFL, as such, and is opposed on principle to the IWW and independent unions. The Red International works according to the concrete facts as it finds them, not according to a cut and dried formula. It surveys each industry separately, and in each case asks the question: "Where are the masses of the workers?" The answer to that question determines its program for that industry. In the coal mining industry it naturally supports the United Mine Workers, an AFL organization, because the organized workers are there. For the same reason, in the men's clothing industry it supports the Amalgamated Clothing Workers, an independent union, and in such industries as lumber and agriculture it supports the IWW. In an industry having two or more rival unions it works for the unification of all of them into a single industrial union for the entire industry. Its approach to the question in each case is practical, not simply theoretical.

This realistic attitude of the Red International does not suit those who take a dogmatic view of the labor movement, who want to move always along a straight line and meet all its complex problems by the simple process of saying yes or no. They point to this flexible program as proof of their contention that it is impossible for the IWW to even speak to the Red International, to say nothing of affiliating with it. But a sober consideration of the question for five minutes is sufficient to completely explode this theory. It is true that this policy of the Red International conflicts with the IWW program of universal organization in such fields as the coal mining industry, the needle trades, building trades, etc., where the workers are already organized in large numbers into other unions. In these fields there is a real conflict, but it is a conflict more of theory than of practice. In the daily struggle the question hardly ever arises for the simple reason that the IWW does not exist there as a functioning labor organization. And the conflict there does not preclude the possibility of unity in other fields where the practical situation is different. If we will turn to those fields where the IWW functions as a labor union we will find that there is no real conflict between it and the Red International.

The financial report of the general office of the IWW for the fiscal year ending October 1, 1923, shows the average number of dues-paying members for the year to be approximately 38,000. This report also shows conclusively that, in spite of all theories of universality, the IWW is predominantly an organization of migratory workers. The great bulk of its membership consists of lumber workers, agricultural workers and general construction workers. In these three industries it has about 21,000 members. In these industries, as in practically the whole field of migratory labor, the IWW is the only real labor union. The question of a conflict between the IWW and other unions does not arise here, and consequently there is no conflict between the IWW and the program of the Red International. The Red International can come to a complete agreement with the IWW in this field on the basis of all of its supporters joining and supporting the existing unions of the IWW. At the very beginning we see that complete unity between the Red International and the IWW can be realized immediately in the main fields of IWW organization. The very first discussion of the problem will dispose of the charge that the Red International wants to "liquidate" the IWW and it will also eliminate at least 75 percent of the organizational conflicts.

In the metal mining industry and the marine transport industry the IWW also has some organization. The problem is not quite so simple in these industries because rival unions exist and the great majority of the workers are unorganized. The total number of dues stamps issued to the Metal Mine Workers' Union of the IWW (which also includes a small number of coal miners) by the general office during the past year was 2,680, while the total number of dues stamps issued to the marine transport workers was 6,426. The real problem in these industries is the problem of organizing the workers. A necessary preliminary to this is the cooperation of all the militant elements. It cannot be said offhand what precise form this cooperation would take; that could only be arrived at after the most thorough discussion and consideration of the whole situation on the part of all concerned. One thing is certain: friction between the militant elements could be reduced or eliminated entirely, and their whole energy concentrated on the fight against the bosses. In any event the question of "liquidation" does not enter.

It may be argued that this article deals only with a part of the differences which have caused the bitter controversy in the past, and that it leaves many points of conflict untouched. This is true enough. We have no patent prescription by which complete unity with the IWW can be achieved at one stroke. Argument alone is not sufficient to erase the longstanding antagonisms. The struggle itself is the great unifier that welds all truly militant elements in the working class into one body and hammers all their theories into a unified system. My purpose here has been to bring to the front those questions upon which agreement can be reached, and to throw some light on the great possibilities for future cooperation opened by the proposal of the Red International that the IWW send delegates to the next World Congress in order to discuss the whole question there. It is my contention that the differences of theory and doctrine between the IWW and the Communists, real and serious though they be, do not justify a continuous state of war along the whole front. This war is all the more harmful to both because it is unnecessary, and, more than that, it is harmful to the interests of the working class as a whole. The conflict in the camp of militant labor, which goes to the point of preventing solidarity and unity in the class struggle, serves the capitalists and them alone. A thorough discussion at the World Congress may not succeed in settling all matters in dispute. But it will lay the basis for unity of action in the struggle. That is the important thing now. The rest will follow.

The militant labor movement of America is nearer to unity than ever before, and the greatest power making for this unity is the Red International of Labor Unions. Here in America, as everywhere else in the capitalist world, the Red International is fulfilling its great historic role. It is uniting the militant workers into a mighty army and marshaling them for the struggle. It has already won the devoted allegiance of the revolutionary workers in all the American labor organizations except the IWW. The members of the IWW still stand aside from the Red International only because the flood of misrepresentation has prejudiced them against it. But the Red International will not accept this attitude as final. It is a fighting body, but it is willing to fight only against the capitalist class and its agents. To the IWW, as to all organizations of rank and file workers, it holds out the hand of brotherhood. Its answer to the narrow dogmatists who have misrepresented and slandered it, and to those members of the IWW who have been deceived thereby, is to turn again to the IWW with an appeal for a friendly discussion of all differences in order to find a basis for unity. The time is surely coming when the rank and file of the IWW will hear that appeal and act upon it. And the result of their action will be to bring about a greater solidarity than the American movement has ever known, a tremendous stride forward of the movement as a whole and its unity under one banner, the banner of the Red International.

The IWW Convention

Published January 1924

The following article by Cannon was published in Labor Herald, *journal of the Trade Union Educational League.*

The IWW has just finished its Fifteenth General Convention. It lasted for 18 days and was attended by 26 delegates representing a membership of approximately 38,000. The great bulk of the members represented are migratory workers, nearly two-thirds being engaged in three industries—lumber, agriculture and general construction. All the delegates were from the rank and file, coming directly from the job. It can be pretty safely assumed, therefore, that the convention was a fairly accurate reflection of the present state of mind of the IWW. It will be of interest to consider some of the outstanding decisions of the convention and see what that state of mind is.

The question of international relations has been "settled" several times already by the officials of the IWW, but, in spite of all, it came up again at this convention and was the biggest issue before it. This is natural and inevitable. There was a plainly manifested desire on the part of most of the delegates to have done with this troublesome question which has vexed them so much since the formation of the Red International of Labor Unions. But such an issue cannot be put aside today by any body of militant workers. It came before the convention in three separate proposals: 1) To send delegates to the forthcoming World Congress of the Red International; 2) To affiliate with the so-called Syndicalist International; 3) To regard the IWW itself as the only International. All three propositions were defeated. The present position of the IWW on the question of the International is no position.

Nevertheless the convention marked a distinct step forward on the road that cannot but lead the IWW to the Red International. It advanced from an attitude of open hostility to an attitude of neutrality. And, for the first time in the long controversy, a representative body of the IWW listened to an argument for the Red International made by its accredited representatives. In response to a cablegram from the Executive Bureau at Moscow the convention, after a sharp struggle, granted the floor to Robert Minor and the writer to speak for the acceptance of the invitation to send delegates to the World Congress. Although the invitation was rejected, the action of the convention in consenting to hear the question discussed cannot represent anything else than a step *forward* from its past attitude of opposition and hostility and a step *closer* to the Red International. Several of the delegates made the statement on the floor that they had never heard before the side of the Red International. This is the real explanation of the bitter antagonism of the past. The members of the IWW have been prejudiced against the Red International by misrepresentation of its program and purpose.

Other actions of the convention showed a commendable moderation of attitude and give the hope that the black night of dogmatism and intolerance is passing in the IWW, and that its rank and file membership is drawing closer to an appreciation of the need of friendly cooperation with other revolutionary groups and tolerant consideration of the rights of minority elements in its own ranks. One of these was the decision of the convention in the case of Ralph Chaplin, Forrest Edwards, Richard Brazier, and a number of others who accepted President Harding's conditional commutation from Leavenworth, and the other was the case of Harrison George who was put on trial for "Communism." This "trial" was conducted by a Chicago branch during the sessions of the convention and the spirit of the convention undoubtedly had a determining effect on its outcome.

A majority of 15 out of 26 IWW prisoners at Leavenworth, including Ralph Chaplin, Forrest Edwards and other old and tested militants, accepted the commutation last June, while a minority of 11 rejected it. A sharp factional controversy then arose within the IWW over the demand of some of those who rejected the commutation that those who accepted it be excluded from the right to take part in any of the work of the IWW General Defense Committee in behalf of class war prisoners. This demand was pressed at the convention by H.F. Kane and F.A. Blossom who, with others, had even gone to the point of issuing circulars against Ralph Chaplin and attempting, by this and other means, to disrupt meetings addressed by him. This controversy raised a question of no little importance. The excellent standing and long-proven revolutionary integrity of the men involved made their case of concern to the entire radical labor movement. Any official action to discredit them and to exclude them from activity would have been a decidedly reactionary step and would have produced a most unfavorable impression.

The convention, fortunately, took the right viewpoint. After thoroughly going into the whole matter, it exonerated those who had accepted the commutation and declared them to be eligible to any responsible post assigned to them by the General Defense Committee or the General Executive Board. More than that, it condemned those who had resorted to public agitation against them.

Harrison George is an outspoken Communist, a member of the Workers Party, and the charges against him involved directly the right of a member of the IWW to hold Communist opinions and to openly express them. He had written an article in *The Worker* against the censorship of the IWW press. For this he was put on trial by the branch to which he belonged. A number of points were included in the charges against him, including charges of "dishonesty" and "insubordination"; but everybody knew that his only crime was the self-confessed one of being a Communist. Harrison George acted like a real Communist. He did not run away, but resisted the attempt to expel him and conducted a militant defense, turning it into an offensive attack against the whole policy of censorship and heresy-hunting in the IWW. His long record as a fighter in the class struggle and his years of imprisonment for the IWW, bravely borne, were in his favor. He was able to prove beyond question that his activity had not been of a disruptive character and that the charges of dishonesty had no foundation. The sessions of the trial were attended by many delegates to the convention and became a forum for the discussion of the great questions involved in it.

This historic trial ended in a complete vindication of Harrison George on every point of the indictment against him. He was acquitted by the unanimous vote of the trial committee and by the unanimous vote of the branch members attending the meeting. Of course, the vote for him was not a vote for Communism, but a vote for the right of a member of the IWW to be a Communist. And, since many well-known anti-Communists participated in the decision, the outcome gives every indication of the beginning of an end to the policy of suppressing and persecuting Communists in the IWW, and that henceforth they will enjoy the same rights of opinion and political activity that are enjoyed by other members. The IWW will never have cause to regret the adoption of this attitude toward the Communists. It will go a long way to overcome the bitter conflicts of the past, and it will very soon be demonstrated that Communists work constructively in all labor organizations and that their destructive activities are aimed only at the capitalist class and its institutions.

Two communications from the Workers Party were read to the convention. One of these was a proposal that the IWW make a united front with the Workers Party and all other working class organizations for the defense and support of the impending German Revolution. The other was an invitation to the IWW to make joint campaign with the Workers Party for the release of class war prisoners and the repeal of criminal syndicalist laws. The need for joint action on these questions is quite manifest and was freely admitted by a number of individual delegates. But the convention took no official action on the matter. This is to be regretted, but the reason for it is quite clear. The IWW has an unholy fear of "politicians," and is very apprehensive about any dealings with them, even though the "politicians" in this case happen to be revolutionary workers who have nothing in mind except the organization of the working class for the struggle against capitalism. The IWW has not yet come to the point where it makes a distinction between capitalist politics which are aimed against the working class and Communist politics which are aimed against the capitalists. This prejudice is one of the biggest stumbling blocks in the way of cooperation between the IWW and the other revolutionary workers in America, and one of the foremost tasks of the Communists in relation to the IWW is to overcome it.

Paradoxical as it may seem, the IWW is an intensely political organization. This is what complicates the problem of unifying its activities with those of the other revolutionary workers. The IWW is not simply a labor union. In the real sense of the word it is also a political party, and the fact that it decries politics and has nothing to do with elections does not alter the fact. Its very creed of "anti-politics" stamps it as a political body, that is, a body dominated by ideas and conceptions and not simply by immediate economic interests like an ordinary union. The IWW functions as a labor union in the real sense of the word only in a very restricted field. The convention representation, as well as the annual financial statement, revealed the fact that the unions of the IWW are almost exclusively unions of migratory workers. Its membership in the main fields of conservative labor organization is so negligible as to present no real organizational problem in relation to the other unions, but only a theoretical problem, a conflict of theory between the IWW and the Communists as to how the revolution will be made in the future, and a conflict of ideas about immediate work as to whether it is better to work within the established conservative unions in order to revolutionize them or to undertake at once to build new unions of the IWW. The conflict is thus a conflict of ideas and not a conflict between rival labor unions. In these industries, the record shows, the IWW does not exist as a labor union, but only as a small nucleus bound together by certain ideas.

In the field of migratory labor, however, the situation is somewhat different. Such organization of the workers as there is here is in the IWW. The great mass of migratory workers, like the majority of workers in all industries of America, are unorganized. But the fact that the IWW is the principal or exclusive labor organization amongst the migratory workers greatly simplifies the problem there. The adherents of the Red International take all labor unions as they find them and adapt their program accordingly. Their aim is not to arbitrarily favor one organization and oppose another, but to build the existing unions, to unify the militant workers, to bring rival organizations together and to organize the masses of unorganized workers. The practical basis of work in every case, in every industry, is and must be the already existing labor unions in the given industry.

The beginning of a more tolerant and friendly attitude of the

IWW toward the Communists, as it was manifested by the recent convention and the trial of Harrison George, ought to pave the way for a better understanding and, eventually, for real cooperation between the IWW and the Communists, at least in the field of migratory labor which, as we have seen, is the field where the IWW is functioning as a labor union.

Reply to the Thesis of Comrades Lore and Olgin

Published 12 April 1924

The following article was written by Cannon and Alexander Bittelman for the CEC majority and published in the Daily Worker *magazine supplement. It answers a thesis published by Ludwig Lore and Moissaye Olgin in the same magazine. Lore and Olgin opposed the developing "alliance" of the Workers Party and its Federated Farmer-Labor Party with forces supporting a new third party, insisting that "It is absurd to assume that we can have common campaigns with the third bourgeois party for its bourgeois candidates and at the same time conduct an independent campaign for our program."*

Cannon and Bittelman project the possibility of the Workers Party supporting the candidates of the new third party, but they do not mention that this party was being built around support to the presidential candidacy of Republican Senator Robert M. La Follette.

The thesis of comrades Lore and Olgin on the Workers Party policy in the elections for 1924 is based upon two fundamental errors.

1. A misconception of the strategy and tactics of the Communist International.
2. A wrong analysis of the economic and political forces operating within the framework of present-day America.

Strategy and Tactics of the Communist International

The strategy of the Communist International consists of the mobilization of the working class and all other oppressed groups that can be allied with it for an aggressive struggle against capitalist exploitation, for the destruction of the capitalist state, and the establishment of the dictatorship of the proletariat.

From this it follows that a Communist party, which is the one to carry on this strategy, must itself be a fighting organization linked up with every phase of the class struggle and moving along consciously and persistently in the direction of the final proletarian struggle for power.

The class struggle does not develop along straight lines. Its ways are devious and complicated. As Trotsky said, "In politics the shortest distance between two points is a zigzag." The thesis does not follow the method of Lenin when it attempts to speak of a "straight," and "direct" and "unyielding" policy as opposed to *a policy of devious ways, political machinations or obscure paths.*

A policy is correct, Communist and revolutionary if it promotes, deepens and intensifies the class struggle, if it accentuates class divisions and solidifies the working class as against the capitalist class and if it strengthens the Communist Party and broadens its influence over the laboring masses.

A policy which satisfies the above requirements is a good Communist policy, irrespective of whether the line of its path is straight, broken or circular. The shape of the line of our tactics is determined, not by our free will but by the prevailing conditions of the class struggle.

The thesis is wrong and non-Marxian, and manifests a failure to understand the fundamentals of Communist strategy, when it attempts to dump all non-proletarian groupings into one reactionary heap which is to be condemned and fought against always in the same measure and with the same tactics. The established strategy of the Communist International, which is based on a Marxian conception of capitalist society, always differentiates between the immediate interests of the various groups and strata of the non-proletarian classes for the double purpose of (1) mobilizing at a given moment the greatest possible force of anti-capitalist opposition, and (2) winning over all the exploited and oppressed elements to the proletarian cause, thereby bringing about the isolation of the capitalist class. The thesis sins heavily against this principle of strategy and also against the actual facts involved in the third party movement when it proposes to treat this movement, which is a revolt against big capital, precisely as we treat the Republican and Democratic parties, which are the parties of big capital.

And, lastly, the whole thesis is pervaded with a spirit of pessimism, passivity and fear of tackling a complicated situation, which is altogether out of proportion to and unjustified by the known facts of the present situation and the established policies of the CI. This spirit is peculiarly reminiscent of an attitude formerly shared by certain sections of our movement that the beginning and end of all Communist activities is propaganda of Communism, straightforward, unyielding preaching of Communist principles. It is this attitude that prevented for a time some of our members from accepting the labor party policy of the Workers Party.

The Present Situation

The thesis of comrades Lore and Olgin does not disprove the fact that we are witnessing now in the United States a growing revolt of the working masses on the one hand and of the petty-bourgeois elements on the other hand against the domination of the two old parties. The thesis is very careful to avoid the use of the term revolt. It says instead: "growing tendency, growing influence, marked dissatisfaction," etc. But this difference in terminology, which is important, of course, does not, however, alter the fact that there is afoot a growing movement involving large masses of workers, farmers, and petty-bourgeois elements tending to split away from the two old parties. This is the most important cardinal fact in present-day American politics. Therefore, no strategy can be correct which fails to put this fact in its proper light and to analyze its basic factors. The thesis of comrades Lore and Olgin is deficient in both. It fails to probe down to the real economic basis of the insurgent movement, inside and outside of the two old parties, and therefore misses its true volume, scope and significance.

The Economic Situation

The thesis admits "the economic situation is gradually approaching a crisis" and that "the economic depression has been on the increase throughout the latter part of 1923." This is correct but the present crisis is not of the type of the periodic, pre-war capitalist crises and herein lies its significance. It is not a temporary or passing affair. It is a manifestation here in the United States of the general critical state of world capitalism. This crisis may have its ups and downs but its lasting and permanent nature cannot be disputed.

It is this lasting and permanent nature of the present economic depression, plus the recent political developments, which have unmasked the American government as the tool and sergeant of big capital, that is responsible for the acuteness of the class relations prevailing at present in the United States.

The Political Situation

The thesis of the CEC which is to be submitted to the Communist International speaks of the mass revolt in the United States against the domination of the two old parties *as a revolt against the economic and political rule of big capital*. And that is what it is, but this fact the thesis of comrades Lore and Olgin fails to take note of. It speaks of a "growing dissatisfaction," "bitter restlessness" of the workers, farmers and petty-bourgeois elements without realizing that what we are confronted with now is a movement and not merely a state of mind. A movement of large masses against the present rule of the bankers and big industrialists, and that this movement is tending unmistakably in the direction of a third petty-bourgeois liberal party. Whether this party materializes —if it does—as a petty-bourgeois liberal party or as a regular capitalist party similar to one of the old parties is still somewhat problematical. It may eventually turn either way, which does not in the least change the present nature and significance of the movement. As to our tactics and attitude towards a third party, the thesis of the CEC provides for either case. The thesis of the Central Executive Committee lays down clearly and definitely the conditions and terms for a possible election alliance between the Farmer-Labor Party and the third party.

Our Attitude Toward the Third Party Movement

The thesis of the Central Executive Committee bases its attitude toward the third party movement on three sets of considerations.

1. The third party movement accelerates the development of the class struggle, produces a clearer crystallization of political groupings on the basis of real economic interests,

and weakens the united capitalist front against the working class.

2. The third party movement involves and is followed by large masses of workers and exploited farmers who are revolting and struggling against the domination of big capital. *For these masses the third party movement is objectively a transitory stage to the class farmer-labor party.* The successful development of the third party movement will seriously affect if not shatter the domination of the Gompers machine in the AFL, thereby opening the way for favorable changes in the labor movement.
3. The movement toward and the formation of a third petty-bourgeois party creates a favorable situation for the development of a class farmer-labor party which is the main objective of our present strategy.

The thesis of comrades Lore and Olgin fails to take cognizance of any of these considerations. It admits that this movement "is important for the working class mainly through the general political agitation it creates in the country and particularly through the attacks it levels at the old capitalist parties." But it fails to understand the far-reaching implication even of this statement. What it does see is the probable coming into existence of "a third bourgeois party, which would be no more than a united front of the big bourgeoisie and the mass of the middle and petty bourgeoisie which would become an obstacle for the creation of a proletarian party and may subsequently be much more difficult to combat than an open and avowed enemy of the working people."

What this third party movement may eventually materialize into, nobody knows as yet. For the present, however, it is not a united front of the big bourgeoisie with the middle and petty bourgeoisie but a movement of revolt of the workers, exploited and well-to-do farmers and various elements of the petty bourgeoisie against the rule of big capital.

That the third party movement carries with it serious dangers for the success of the Farmer-Labor Party movement goes without saying. The thesis of the Central Executive Committee clearly points out these dangers, and proposes definite measures to meet them.

After setting forth the conditions under which it is possible for the Farmer-Labor Party to support the candidates of the third party in the 1924 elections, the thesis of the CEC says the following:

> If under the conditions set forth above an election alliance, either national or local, is made the Farmer-Labor Party must maintain a distinct organization and carry on an independent campaign for its own program and utilize the situation to the utmost to crystallize in the definite form of an organized Farmer-Labor Party all those workers and exploited farmers who can be brought to the support of a class party.
>
> Throughout any campaign in which we maintain an alliance with the third party, we must constantly criticize and expose it and its candidates, show up the futility of its program, and make it clear to the workers who are reached by our own campaign that the third party will bring them no salvation and no relief. We must make it clear that the whole campaign is simply a starting point in the struggle for the establishment of a workers and farmers government, which in turn is a step towards the proletarian dictatorship, the one and only instrument for their liberation.
>
> All the elements of the classes which are participating in the revolt against and split from the old capitalist parties will be represented in the St. Paul convention on June 17th. But the probability of the class farmer-labor elements—the rank and file workers and poor farmers—predominating will be greatly increased by the aggressive role of the Workers Party in the campaign for the convention and the tendency of the third party elements (including the labor bureaucrats, who are ideologically a part of the petty bourgeoisie) to turn to the Cleveland conference of the CPPA or to some other center which may be created by the La Follette group to serve as the nucleus of the third party.
>
> Our task at the June 17th convention will be to strengthen and clarify its class character, fight for the adoption of a class program, organize it into a class party separate and distinct from the Cleveland conference or any other third party conference which may be held. The party formed there shall negotiate, through committees, with other conferences on the question of common campaigns or common candidates only as an organized body.
>
> At the St. Paul conference we shall nominate and fight for proletarian candidates as against any other candidates at the conference. We shall utilize the conference to lay the basis for the organization of the Farmer-Labor Party throughout the country and also advance

there the proposal and plans for an economic organization of farmers to serve as the foundation for their political organization.

This step of supporting the candidates of a petty-bourgeois liberal third party, under the conditions laid down in the thesis of the Central Executive Committee, is a correct one; not only because it is in accord with the general strategy of the CI (as manifested in its attitude to the British Labour Party and the Mexican presidential elections), but also because it offers the best tactical move of eventually separating the masses of workers and exploited farmers from the leadership of petty-bourgeois liberalism and bringing them into the ranks of the class farmer-labor party, which is a step along the road to Communism. On the other hand the position toward the third party movement taken by the thesis of comrades Lore and Olgin offers the best means of perpetuating petty-bourgeois influence over the masses of workers and exploited farmers that are now following this movement.

The thesis of comrades Lore and Olgin takes the position of no support for the candidates of the third party under any circumstances, and this for five reasons:

1. Our support would be futile because we do not command large numbers of voters who actually influence the outcome of the election.

And suppose we did command large numbers of voters? Would we then be justified in supporting candidates of the third party? Obviously not, according to the general strategy of the thesis of comrades Lore and Olgin. Then where is the point of this argument?

2. It would "perturb the class vision of our membership and cause among them great consternation, appearing to them as an obvious deviation from the straight line of class struggle."

This argument figures very prominently in the thesis that the working class in America as a whole, being disgusted with the political game, will not follow, let alone approve, the tactical move involved in the support of a third party candidate.

If this argument has any validity at all, then the only conclusion to be drawn is: Total abstention from politics! Boycott all capitalist institutions! No compromise! No dealings with the enemy until we come to the final direct struggle for power and until then—preach Communism!

This is the straightest possible line of the class struggle. The only trouble with it is that it is wholly imaginary.

3. Support of third party candidates would make it impossible for us to explain our refusal to support a "Friend of Labor" on the ticket of the Democratic Party.

By this argument the thesis shows that it is dealing not with social forces, classes, and parties, but with individuals.

The conception of "labor friends," which underlies the non-partisan policies of Gompers and the CPPA, can be exploded only on the basis of class relations and the social analysis of political parties. It is our duty to teach the workers to think in terms of classes and parties and not individuals. Until we have succeeded in this, nothing will help much, not even a policy of straight lines.

We analyze before the workers the social make-up of the two old parties and thereby show that they are controlled and dominated by big capital—the master and enemy of the working class. Candidates on the tickets of the two old parties will either do the biddings of the capitalists or fail. In either case, the workers are the losers. Therefore, don't support candidates of the old parties.

We then analyze the social make-up of the third party and if we find that it is controlled by a petty-bourgeois liberalism, we say so. And we explain what it means in terms of the economic interests of the workers, poor farmers, wealthy farmers, other petty-bourgeois elements, and big capital. In other words, we explain the political aspirations of the third party by means of its social-economic basis.

In doing this, we will find that the "friendliness" to labor of a third petty-bourgeois party rests on an economic basis. The middle classes revolting against big capital need the assistance of labor and are, therefore, compelled to offer some concessions to labor. And it is here that we point out the limitations of these concessions and the general unreliability of the election promises.

We proceed further to explain that the workers and exploited farmers can best utilize this division in the ranks of the bourgeoisie by organizing their own party and fighting their own battles, at the same time giving their organized support, as an independent class farmer-labor party, to candidates of the third party where such support will assure the defeat of the old parties or increase the divisions in the ranks of the bourgeoisie, or assist in splitting away large masses of workers and farmers from the two old parties.

4. The sense of the fourth argument is that it is impossible to support and criticize third party candidates at one and the same time, which is the same as saying that the Farmer-Labor Party cannot support a third party candidate and at the same time carry on an independent Farmer-Labor campaign.

If this were true, then how could a Communist party support candidates of a farmer-labor party and at the same time carry on an independent Communist campaign? And again, how could the Communists of Mexico, on the advice of the Comintern, support Calles (petty-bourgeois candidate) and carry on an independent campaign?[1] And finally, how could the Comintern support the colonial struggles of the oppressed nationalities (petty-bourgeois in character) against European and American imperialism and at the same time carry on among the proletarian elements of the same nationalities a class campaign along Communist lines?

The answer is that of course it can be done, as we have shown above. That it is difficult and even dangerous no one can deny, but this is no reason for not doing it.

5. Support of third party candidates "would make it appear to our members that we put all our hopes in parliamentary re-

---

[1] In a letter to the Communist Party of Mexico (PCM) of 21 August 1923, the Executive Committee of the Comintern wrote that "the Communist Party must participate in the elections on behalf of Calles." In the maneuvering leading up to the 1924 vote, former Mexican treasury minister Adolfo de la Huerta opposed the appointment of General Plutarco Elías Calles as designated successor to General Alvaro Obregón, then in power. Despite the lack of a clear left-right, let alone class, polarization between the contending forces, the ECCI argued that "the overwhelming majority of the workers and peasants will support the candidature of Calles."

During 1923-24, the PCM was increasingly under the sway of Jay Lovestone's chief crony, Bertram Wolfe, who had fled to Mexico to avoid arrest in the United States. In December 1923, De la Huerta led an abortive military uprising against Obregón. While Mexican party leaders had previously been aligned with De la

(continued)

> forms and that all our propaganda of mass action is no more than a phrase."

The direct opposite is true. It is those who cannot appreciate the real mass nature of the present revolt against the two old parties and who refuse, by adopting elastic tactics, to divert the class elements of this mass movement into the channels of a class farmer-labor party, that are making a mockery and empty sound of the Communist conception of mass action. Mass action is not something static, immovable and unchangeable. It is a process and a development which has its beginning in such mild occurrences as the present movement of large masses of workers and exploited farmers away from the old parties and in the direction of independent political action and culminating, through various changes and developments (not always running in a straight line) in a direct struggle for power.

This is the Communist conception of mass action and it is such mass action that we will assist in developing by adopting the tactics of the Central Executive Committee.

Restating Our Objective

Our immediate objective is the unification and consolidation of all politically mature farmer-labor forces in the United States for an independent campaign along class lines in the coming presidential election. Our aim is the formation of a mass party of workers and farmers, and the advancement of Communist influence within it.

Huerta, at Wolfe's insistence the PCM backed the Obregón government. Soon after, the party offered to support Calles in the elections if he accepted certain minimum "worker and peasant" demands (presented to him on its behalf by the radical painter Diego Rivera). Calles "accepted" the demands and Communist support.

The call for support to Calles reflected the general confusion on the question of two-class "worker-peasant" parties then current in the Communist International. The ECCI letter was published in English by the Workers Party as a pamphlet under the title *Strategy of the Communists*, and the American *Daily Worker* gave prominent coverage to the Mexican party's support to Calles. After Calles won the election but before he took office, the Obregón government gave diplomatic recognition to Soviet Russia. When the Comintern swerved to the left later in 1924, the PCM began denouncing Calles' bonapartist, pro-imperialist regime. Wolfe was expelled from the country by the Calles government in 1925.

The convention of June 17th is the next point of concentration.

In striving toward this objective we find ourselves confronted with a petty-bourgeois third party movement which is neither of our making nor under our control. It is clearly a revolt of large masses of workers, farmers and petty-bourgeois elements against big capital and thus runs somewhat in the same general direction as the Farmer-Labor Party movement. This third party movement contains in its ranks large masses of workers and exploited farmers. Hence, the bigger the volume of this movement, the better the chances for a class farmer-labor party, provided we meet the situation as it is and do not run away from it.

This situation creates a problem for us. The problem is to develop our labor party policy in such a manner as to increase the volume and scope of the split-away movement from the two old parties, at the same time carefully and after proper preparation diverting the class elements into the channels of the class farmer-labor party. The thesis of comrades Lore and Olgin misses completely this central problem of our whole labor party policy. The thesis of the Central Executive Committee states the problem, analyzes its factors, and gives the best solution of it.

St. Paul–June 17th

Published May 1924

The following article by Cannon was published in the Trade Union Educational League journal, Labor Herald. *Though the Workers Party was willing to enter into an "alliance" with the third party forces of Republican Senator Robert M. La Follette, it sought to maintain a modicum of "independence." The St. Paul Farmer-Labor convention was called in competition with a Conference for Progressive Political Action convention set for Cleveland on July 4—after the finish of both the Democratic and Republican conventions—where it was projected that La Follette would be nominated for U.S. president on the Progressive Party ticket. In May the Communist International directed the Workers Party not to support La Follette. When the St. Paul convention met in June it therefore nominated an independent Farmer-Labor Party ticket: mine union official Duncan MacDonald for U.S. president and William Bouck of the Washington state Federated Farmer-Labor Party for vice president.*

A city and a date—St. Paul, June 17th—represent at the present time the central point around which all the forces of the awakening industrial workers and poor farmers are organizing. The great national farmer-labor convention called by the joint action of the Minnesota Farmer-Labor Party, the Federated Farmer-Labor Party and practically all other existing bona fide farmer-labor organizations, will meet in St. Paul on June 17. Neither the city nor the date is accidental. They, as well as all the other facts about this convention, which distinguish it from the July 4th convention of the CPPA at Cleveland, have reasons for their being which arise from class relations and the present stage of development of the class struggle.

The Northwest Politically Awake

It is in the Northwest, especially in Minnesota, that the masses of workers and farmers have made the greatest advancement in political life. Their political development has already reached the point of definite organization and a degree of success, even, in the elections. Practically the whole labor movement of Minnesota is participating in the affairs of the Farmer-Labor Party. More than that, the bulk of the trade unions have advanced to the point of leading in the organization of the Farmer-Labor Federation, an organization within the Farmer-Labor Party which aims to put it on a definite foundation of workers' and farmers' economic organizations, and control it in this way. It is natural, therefore—one might almost say inevitable—that the other sections of the American labor movement which are striving towards an independent party should turn towards St. Paul and look upon it as the logical center for the crystallization of the national movement. The date of the convention, before the Republican convention will be adjourned and before the Democratic convention will be convened, illustrates the determination to act there without regard to the decisions of these two conventions of the capitalist parties.

Those officials and leaders in the ranks of the labor and farmer movements who are trying to head off the sentiment among the rank and file workers for an independent party of their own, and steer it back into the old parties of the big capitalists, or, failing that, into a third party of the petty bourgeoisie, lost no time in opening fire on the St. Paul convention. They turned against it just as naturally and automatically as the conscious and awakened workers and poor farmers turned towards it. The St. Paul convention and all its surroundings—the city, the date, the participants, the program and the determined spirit of it—stamp it unmistakably as a real and genuine convention of workers and farmers bent on organizing an independent political party on class lines. The $10,000-a-year labor leaders do not want such a party. That is why they are fighting the St. Paul convention.

The widespread revolt of the masses of workers and farmers against the Teapot Dome[1] government is taking a number of

[1] A reference to the financial scandals that rocked the Harding administration, generally known under the rubric of "Teapot Dome," which was the name of the Wyoming naval oil reserve leased in 1922 to Harry F. Sinclair by Harding's

(continued)

forms and showing various manifestations which can only be understood if they are analyzed from the standpoint of class relations and the class struggle. One question especially arises in the minds of many workers. It goes something like this: What is the difference between these two gatherings and what is the reason for the split between them? Why the devil don't they all get together into one convention? And why do I have to be in favor of one and not of both?

The answer to this question is that between the two conventions there are basic differences of composition, purpose, and viewpoint. The two conventions are not striving towards the same goal. That is the reason why they exist separately. An analysis of the make-up and actions of the two bodies makes this very clear.

CPPA Against Rank and File

The Conference for Progressive Political Action only talks vaguely about independent political action but, in practice, participates in and supports the capitalist parties. It is true that among many of the workers who have been following the CPPA there is a decided sentiment for a labor party but this sentiment does not exist among the leaders of the CPPA. They play the part of "lightning rods." They pose as favoring independent action only as a concession to the sentiment of their followers, in order to catch it and direct it into the ground. Their "sympathy" for the idea of a labor party is a disguise to hide their actual allegiance to the capitalist parties. These "leaders" of labor cannot lead a fight to form a working class party because they do not have a working class point of view. They do not live like the workers and they do not think like the workers.

Moreover there will be no chance for the rank and file workers who want a labor party in spite of the officials to make a fight for it at the Cleveland convention. It is a convention of leaders and officials. The rank and file is not welcome there. Local unions are not admitted. City central bodies have only one vote.

Secretary of the Interior, Albert Fall. It was later revealed that Sinclair had given Fall a herd of cattle, $85,000 in cash and $223,000 in bonds to clinch the deal. In 1929 Fall was convicted of bribery, fined $100,000 and sentenced to a year in jail—the first U.S. Cabinet officer to serve time in prison.

Local organizations of farmers are not invited. The International unions, which will be represented by their bureaucratic and reactionary officials, together with some national organizations of farmers, businessmen, liberals, and the traitor Socialist Party, have drawn up a set of rules and apportioned the voting in the convention in such a way as to make it absolutely proof against rank and file interference with their plans. It is needless to add that the Workers Party is not invited to Cleveland. The Workers Party has been leading the fight for a real class party of workers and farmers, and it could not be expected that those who oppose this idea would invite it to their gathering. If the Workers Party were admitted to the Cleveland convention, the game of the treacherous leaders would be brought out into the open and exposed. If Communists were in the convention they would press the labor traitors to the wall, and organize a fight against their treachery in the convention itself.

St. Paul of and for Real Workers

The St. Paul convention, on the other hand, is a convention of the rank and file. It is committed in advance to the program of putting up independent farmer-labor candidates in the coming election *regardless* of the decisions of either the Republican or Democratic parties. The bodies which constituted the preliminary conferences and issued the call for the convention consisted of seven already existing farmer-labor parties including the Federated Farmer-Labor Party, to which last the Communists of the Workers Party are affiliated. The class idea was the dominant idea in the conference and the sentiment for welding the whole movement into one national farmer-labor party on June 17th is strong and growing among the participants in the arrangements for the convention. That both these factors will grow stronger there can be no doubt. The presence in the convention of the Communists, who stand squarely and fight aggressively for the organization of a national party and the domination in it of the class idea, is the best guarantee of this.

This St. Paul convention holds out tremendous possibilities. If we succeed in our aims there and crystallize in one body the revolting elements of the workers and tenant and mortgaged farmers, formulating a class program and establishing an aggressive leadership, the political revolt of the oppressed masses will move forward with giant strides. A successful convention at St. Paul on June 17th will mean that the workers as a distinct class, in alliance with the poor farmers, have stepped onto the political stage in America for the first time. Such an event will have a profound influence, not only upon America but upon the entire world.

We are not alone in this appraisal of the significance of June 17. The enemies of the independent working class political movement are alive to the dynamic possibilities of this convention in St. Paul. They have commenced to fire a tremendous volley of denunciation and misrepresentation against it. The capitalist press, and that part of the labor press which serves the capitalists, are fighting the St. Paul convention with all their power. Their aim is to defeat the rank and file movement for an independent class party, to steer the workers back into the capitalist parties, or into a third party dominated by the petty bourgeoisie. There is no mystery in the fact that they single out participation by the Communists in the June 17th convention for particular attack. The presence of the Communists—the driving force in the genuine labor party movement—assures that a real fight will be made for the formation of a national party on a class basis, dominated by the workers and poor farmers. This is what the capitalists and their labor agents fear the most. This is why they are making such a fight against the Communists in connection with this convention.

St. Paul Means Class Struggle

For the conscious and militant workers and tenant and mortgaged farmers, the fight for the St. Paul convention is the most important question on the order of the day. This convention, and the struggle for it, concentrates on one point, for the time being, the whole struggle of the rank and file of exploited labor against the capitalists, the capitalist government and the agents of the capitalists in the labor movement. It represents the beginning of the union between the workers of the cities and the farms—which is an indispensable prerequisite to the final victory. The size and strength of the St. Paul convention, and the extent to which the conscious class elements dominate and shape it, will be the best and most reliable measure of the political development of the exploited workers and farmers of America. The militant trade unionists have to realize all these facts and make the fight for the June 17th convention the biggest issue in the labor movement.

Our Aims and Tactics in the Trade Unions

27 July 1924

Cannon delivered the following speech to a conference of Workers Party coal miners in St. Louis, Missouri. It was first published in the Daily Worker *magazine supplement, 2 August 1924.*

Comrades:

These conferences of party members in the important trade unions in which representatives of the Central Executive Committee take part are becoming frequent occurrences. We must regard this as a healthy sign. It indicates that we are maturing as a party of theoretical and practical revolutionists, and getting a firm grip on our basic tasks. The close collaboration between the active comrades in the field and the leading organ of the party has a beneficial result all the way around.

The close and intimate contact with the practical problems of the daily struggle, and with the comrades who directly face them, serves as an unerring corrective to any tendency there might be in the party to deal with these problems in an abstract or purely doctrinaire fashion. On the other hand, the participation of the party representatives insures that the fundamental political aspect of the trade union struggle will be brought to the front in these trade union conferences. The importance of this cannot be overestimated. Otherwise there is constant danger of the work of our trade union comrades being influenced too much by expediency and so-called practicality. One-sided conceptions, purely trade union points of view, take the upper hand and the general class issues of the struggle are pushed into the background. Such a state of affairs must be guarded against. We know too well that it leads to reformism and futility.

We are meeting here today to consider the problems of the particular trade union you belong to, from the standpoint of the party, which is the standpoint of all Communists. And I think I will be proceeding in the proper order if I put forward as a premise the revolutionary aims of our party and propose that we weigh and judge every trade union question that comes before us, no matter how small or practical it may appear to be, in the light of our final aims.

A Revolutionary Party

Our party is a party of the proletarian revolution and the dictatorship of the proletariat. The proletarian revolution is the only solution of the labor problem and all our work must lead to this goal. This is our starting point in the trade unions, as in every field of activity in the class struggle. It is this fundamental conception that distinguishes us from all other parties and groups in the labor movement. It is the band of steel that binds us together into one party.

Our revolutionary goal shapes our policy in the daily struggle. The revolutionary aspirations of our party comrades generate the enthusiasm and self-sacrifice that give the party its driving power. Woe to us if we become so "practical" as to forget this for one moment. All our work must lead toward the proletarian revolution. If we keep this always in mind and measure all our daily work by this standard we will keep on the right road. The revolutionary principles to which we are committed put upon us responsibilities and duties which cannot be shifted or evaded if we are to live up to our conception of the party as the vanguard of the workers. We have to stand up and fight for the true interests of the working class as a whole, at every turn of the road.

With the Masses, But Leading Them

We want to be with the masses, but we must also be ahead of the masses, and not be afraid to take an unpopular stand, when it is necessary in order to combat their prejudices. Take for example the Ku Klux Klan. Here is an organization that is anti-labor in its very character—yet large numbers of coal miners are misled into supporting it. To fight the Ku Klux Klan, to expose its reactionary nature and win the workers away from it, is a difficult and somewhat hazardous task in certain sections of the country, but it is our duty to the working class to make such a fight. We would not be worthy of the proud name our party bears if we evaded such a fight on any pretext.

Our work in the trade unions is developing. Evidence of this can be seen on every side. Such conferences as this are proof of the rapid strides we are making. We have already accumulated rich experience, and this experience is bringing to light both positive and negative sides in our work. One of our main duties is to review the whole activity from time to time, to strengthen and improve what is good, and discover what is bad in order to reject it.

It goes without saying that we Communists esteem each other very highly, but when we meet together in conferences such as this, it is not for the purpose of extending bouquets and empty compliments, but to speak out openly and frankly; to subject all our work to thoroughgoing examination and criticism in order that errors may be discovered and overcome. You have the right to expect plain speaking from the Central Executive Committee. I feel quite confident that if some errors in your work are mentioned here in this discussion, if some of the mistakes that individual comrades made are pointed out in a friendly and brotherly, but nevertheless frank manner, as is the custom among Communists, that none of you will feel offended. The discussion is only for the purpose of improving our effectiveness and strengthening the party for the fight.

Our Valuable Experiences

The power of a disciplined party, founded on revolutionary principles, and concerning itself in a businesslike fashion with all aspects of the trade union struggle, has already begun to manifest itself. At the last convention of the Illinois miners, for example, everybody could see that the party is beginning to grow up, to stretch its shoulders, and take its place on the stage of events.[1]

---

[1] The *Daily Worker* gave prominent coverage to this weeklong convention of District 12 of the United Mine Workers (see *DW* from 20-29 May 1924). Though the *Daily Worker* correspondent was expelled from the convention by a vote of 234 to 169, the convention was portrayed as a big victory for "progressive" forces since district leader Frank Farrington was stripped of his appointive powers and the expelled militant Alex Howat received a much warmer reception than John L. Lewis.

Our party appeared there as the leader of the fight for the interests of the men in the mines. It was in the forefront, dealing the heaviest blows against the agents of the bourgeoisie, who have usurped the official positions in the miners union. The work of our comrades in this convention added greatly toward making the miners union a better union for the class struggle, thereby increasing the prestige of our party. That must be acknowledged at the very beginning.

In a whole series of trade union conventions held in recent months the same phenomenon was to be observed. Our small party, which only yesterday emerged from underground and began to collect the scattered forces of the revolutionary workers, was the storm center of the fight against reaction in the labor movement. We have not yet become the leader of the masses in the trade unions, but we have become the leader in the fight for their interests. The rest will follow in good time. Of this we can be confident.

It is no accident that our party is pushing forward everywhere and putting itself at the head of the struggle. The reason for this is that ours is the only party willing to fight for the immediate interests of the workers, and the only party standing for the solution of the labor problem by means of the revolutionary overthrow of capitalism. All of the interests of the working class, immediately and ultimately, are indissolubly bound up with the revolution. And if we make mistakes here and there, if we fail to take the fullest advantage of opportunities which arise in the course of the struggle, it is because our comrades in the unions, due mainly to inexperience, have not fully mastered the art of taking a practical stand on every question that arises, and relating it skillfully to the final aims of the movement.

Correcting Our Mistakes

To do practical work, and at the same time to deepen and extend the class consciousness of the workers, and lead them toward the struggle for power—this is the heart of our task in the trade unions. From this point of view an examination of events that transpired at the last convention of the Illinois miners will bring forth fruitful results. Our power will be multiplied at the next convention, if we frankly recognize the negative as well as the positive sides of our activity at the last one.

One of the main errors made by our comrades there was the failure to realize fully that the brazen scheme of class collaboration, presented to the convention in the report of Frank Farrington, revealed the political and ideological basis of all the corruption and betrayal of the whole bureaucracy of the United Mine Workers of America, from Lewis to Farrington. Our comrades should have attacked this report in the most militant fashion. They should have shot it to shreds on the ground that it represented the theory of the mutual interests of the coal diggers and the parasites who exploit them and fatten on their toil and misery. Against it they should have set up the principle of the class struggle, the theory of the salvation of the workers through uncompromising struggle against their exploiters.

Such a fight would have been a dagger aimed at the very heart of the corrupt and treacherous trade union bureaucracy, because it would have been aimed at the false system of ideas with which they poison the labor movement. Such a fight should have been seized upon as the best means of opening the eyes of the miners, and making them see their real problem. All the other fights in the convention, the fight over the appointive power, the fight for better legislation in union affairs, for the reinstatement of Howat, etc., should have been regarded by our comrades, and explained to the delegates, as related to the basic fight for the principle of the class struggle, and subordinate to it. This would have been the best means of awakening the honest rank and file delegates, and of binding them more closely to us.

Another error at the convention occurred in the handling of the resolution on the recognition of Soviet Russia. Here again the principle of the class struggle was involved. The Farrington machine played a clever game with the delegates on this resolution, by calling for the recognition of Soviet Russia in one paragraph, and then nullifying the whole effect of the resolution by adding the qualification that Soviet Russia should recognize certain obligations—the very obligations which the capitalist governments of the world have been vainly trying for six years to impose upon her. Our comrades made the mistake of thinking that the question of formal recognition of Soviet Russia was the real issue, and of considering such a resolution a victory for us.

This was entirely too "statesmanlike." We are for the recognition of Soviet Russia, because it is a working class state, and because we recognize that the interests of the working class all over the world are bound up with it. The recognition of Soviet Russia is for us an issue of the class struggle, and we should have made the fight purely on that basis, and hammered home again to the delegates the idea that the solidarity of labor, the worldwide union of the working class in the fight for the overthrow of capitalism, must be accepted as the guiding principle of the labor movement. We might have failed to get a majority of the convention if we had put the fight on this basis, just as we might have failed to get a majority in a clear-cut class struggle fight against Farrington's scheme of class collaboration, but that is a secondary matter. We would have brought the principle to the front. We would have clarified the minds of many of the delegates, and tied them more closely to us. It is not the formal victory but the fight that is important.

Inadequate Organization

From the same point of view the inadequate development of the left wing caucus at the convention should be pointed out. Some comrades objected to these caucuses on the ground that Farrington's spies might be present and learn something in advance about the fights we intended to make in the convention. This attitude is erroneous. It is the result of overcaution and too much concern for immediate legislative and technical victories. Moreover, it represents, to a certain extent, an unconscious yielding to the position of the reactionary officials who naturally resent any attempt to organize the rank and file against them. This question goes much deeper than appears at first glance. The failure to organize the left wing delegates at the convention into a fighting body, if carried to its logical conclusion, would lead to the failure to organize the left wing forces throughout the union. It means giving up, under pressure of the officialdom, the right to organize the Trade Union Educational League. "Don't make a molehill into a mountain," is a good maxim; but it is just as good if we turn it around and say to the comrades who are willing to concede this small point: "Don't make a mountain into a molehill." If we are making a serious fight to break the control of the trade union bureaucracy we must not neglect to organize our troops.

Our fight for the conquest of the union is at bottom a fight to organize the rank and file workers together with us on the basis of the class struggle. Therefore, they must be enlightened as to our aims and plans.

Conventions should be regarded as the best occasions to advance this process. The conventions afford us the opportunity of coming into close contact with rank and file delegates, of combatting by discussion and argument their prejudices and misconceptions, and of uniting them with us into an organized body to fight for the regeneration of the labor movement. The left wing caucus is necessary for this work.

It is far more important to us if we get acquainted with ten new workers and make them a part of the organized fight, than if we pass a dozen resolutions in the convention by an accidental majority.

The conscious support of the workers is what we want. We are fighting for their minds and hearts. Do not forget that, comrades. The officialdom can turn our best resolutions into scraps of paper. They can retain office by stealing elections, but they cannot take away from us the workers we have won over to our way of thinking and fighting. The officials can maintain themselves in power, for a time, by a thousand tricks and fraudulent practices. But once we have won the masses over to our side, we can snap our fingers at them. The control of the unions means for us the control of the masses. This, and this alone, will insure our final victory.

Communists and Union Offices

I want to pass over now to another question which will become more and more important as our strength develops in the trade unions. It has confronted us already a number of times. That is the question of comrades holding office in the unions and becoming candidates for office. This may become one of our greatest dangers, and one of the greatest sources of corruption of party members, if we do not properly estimate this question and take a resolute stand on it at the very beginning.

In the discussions which took place here today, we heard the remark made by one of the comrades that our struggle in the unions is a struggle for strategic positions. This is a one-sided view and if we allow it to stand alone, we will fall into a serious error. We must adopt the point of view that our struggle is a struggle to develop the class consciousness of the rank and file workers and to win them over to the principle of the revolutionary struggle against capitalism under the leadership of our party.

If we will connect the fight for strategic positions with this broad political aim and subordinate it to this aim, we will be on safe ground. Otherwise, we will be confronted with the spectacle of party members regarding the fight for office as an end in itself; of evading or putting aside questions of principle with which the masses are not familiar; of scheming and calculating too closely in order to get into office. Of course the comrades will justify all this on the ground that once they get into office they will be able to do big things for the party. But quite often we will be apt to find the very comrades who adopt this method of getting into office falling into the habit of continuing it in order to hold the office. They will thereby degenerate into mere office-holders and office-hunters. They will lose the confidence and respect of the militant rank and file workers, and our party, which stands responsible for them, will have its prestige greatly injured.

Strategic positions, however, are very important and we must not take a doctrinaire view in regard to them. The opinion expressed here by one comrade that men become petty-bourgeois in their interests and outlook as soon as they are elected to office and that, therefore, we should have nothing to do with office, is not correct. It is true that official position, especially in the American trade union movement, has led many men in the past to corruption and betrayal of the workers, but that does not say that Communists must be corrupted. We have to hold the conception that a true Communist can go anywhere the party sends him and do anything, and still remain a Communist—still remain true to the working class. Comrade Lenin was an official. He had more power than Frank Farrington, but he did not become like Frank Farrington. The guarantee against corruption of party members who become officials is that they remain close to the party and that they base their fight for office on the support of the rank and file for the policy of the class struggle, and do not become too expedient and too "clever"—do not try to "sneak" into office by soft-pedaling and pussy-footing on questions of principle which may be unpopular, but which Communists, nevertheless, are duty bound to stand for.

A Party of Struggle

Our party is a party of rank and file revolutionary workers, a party of revolutionary struggle against capitalism and all its works, and we expect comrades who are put into official positions to retain that fundamental conception and carry it out in all their official work. They must not allow themselves to be influenced by their positions into an attitude of overcaution. Above all, they must not acquire an "official" psychology, and fail to do their duty by the party for fear of jeopardizing their positions. We do not put Communists into office in order that they may do less for the party, but more.

The atmosphere of American trade union officialdom is a fetid one. It is permeated through and through with customs and traditions of a non-proletarian character. Take care, you comrades who become officials, that you do not sink into this swamp. Remember always that you are Communists and hold on to your rebel Communist spirit. Do not succumb to the customs and traditions of office developed by the agents of the bourgeoisie, who have fastened themselves upon the labor movement in official positions, but take your own revolutionary ethics and customs with you.

Party Discipline

The question of party discipline becomes especially important in connection with comrades in official positions. Comrades so situated must tie themselves closely to the party, make themselves one with it, and regard the party always as their best friend. The close union of a Communist official with the party will be the best guarantee that he will be able to retain his revolutionary point of view and do his duty by the working class. The party expects even more discipline to be shown by comrades who become officials and leaders than by other members of the party. It does not fear even the biggest officials who go against the decisions of the party and follow a policy in conflict with it. Comrades who hold offices, no matter how important they may be, cannot act as independent individuals without being called to order by the party.

The Test of Our Work

We can sum up the whole question in a few words. We are not progressives, but revolutionists. Our role in the trade union movement is to organize the masses for the proletarian revolution and to lead them in the struggle for it. All of our daily work must be related to this, and subordinated to it. The test of our work can never be made by formal victories on paper, but by the development of class consciousness in the ranks of the workers, the degree of their organization on that basis and the increasing influence and leadership of our party. Strategic positions in the labor movement are of importance chiefly from the standpoint of enabling the party to advance and develop its work of revolutionizing the masses.

Let us be shrewd and practical by all means. Let us learn how to meet every question that arises in the union, in a realistic and businesslike manner. Let us become experts in the daily work of the unions, and in maneuvering for strategic positions, but let us also remember always the danger of degenerating into mere professional office seekers.

Active unionists, especially those who hold office, are beset by a thousand temptations to turn aside from the road of the class struggle. Only their close union with the party will enable them to overcome these temptations. With the assistance of the party they will learn how to serve the workers in the daily struggle and to connect all their activity with the task of leading the masses toward the final revolution. They will learn how to measure their progress at every step, not by formal victories on paper, but by the development of the class consciousness of the workers and the influence of the party, by the extent to which their activity inspires the workers with that spirit of determined struggle, which is the spirit of Communism.

Many difficulties will confront us in the task we have undertaken, but, with the assistance of the party and the International, we will solve them all. We will win over the masses to the side of Communism; we will wrest the labor movement from the hands of the agents of the bourgeoisie and convert them into mighty instruments for the proletarian revolution.

Communist Candidates and the Farmer-Labor Party

Published 29 July 1924

The following article was published in the Daily Worker. *In it Cannon justifies the Workers Party's sudden decision on July 8 to withdraw support from the Farmer-Labor Party candidates nominated at the St. Paul convention and instead run an election campaign in the name of the Workers Party. The Communist candidates were William Z. Foster for president and Benjamin Gitlow for vice president. The National Executive Committee of the Farmer-Labor Party, which was dominated by WP members, withdrew their candidates in favor of the Workers Party slate.*

Why should any Communist be surprised or shocked if the Communist Party decides to take part in elections under its own name? This is the natural thing to do, and is being done constantly by Communist parties in all parts of the world. To follow another course there must be a series of special circumstances which offer decided advantages to the party in making a joint campaign with other groups of workers.

The decision of our party to enter its own candidates in the elections this year has met with general approval throughout the party ranks. The judgment of the Central Executive Committee and the special party conference in taking this decisive step has been confirmed by the great majority of the comrades with whom we have had the opportunity to discuss the present situation and explain in detail the reasons for our action.

Some questions, however, are arising in certain sections of the party. A number of comrades have come forward with objections and criticism, and it is necessary to answer them.

Some comrades fear we have abandoned the united front. They consider that our action represents the victory of the two extreme wings in our party, who, strangely enough, have been meeting on common ground in opposition to our participation in the Farmer-Labor Party, although for quite different reasons. Other comrades, who have yet a somewhat unclear conception of the purposes of the united front and who have been unconsciously falling into the habit of regarding the Farmer-Labor Party as an end in itself, have written to the National Office in recent days, requesting further explanation of our action. The bold decision of our party to stand on its own feet in the present campaign and enter its own candidates has taken their breath away.

It is necessary to answer both of these criticisms fully and adequately. In this article we will take up some questions raised by a party branch in the West, from the latter standpoint, leaving a discussion of the tactical significance of our recent decision for a later article.

We have said a thousand times, and we repeat it again, that our labor party policy is based on the united front tactics laid down by the Communist International. In order for us to take part in the labor party instead of conducting an election campaign under our own name, we must be able to see decided advantages in it from the standpoint of Communism and the Communist Party. A first and necessary condition must be the participation in the movement of large bodies of other workers who are willing to make a common fight with us on the basis of the class struggle. In such circumstances, we have the advantage of coming into contact with a workers' mass movement, and if we have taken care to maintain the autonomy and independence of our party, we can do fruitful work therein for the principles of Communism. We can draw the masses of workers nearer to the Communist position, win them away from the false leadership of opportunist and progressive politicians and toward the leadership of our party. Only when all these conditions are present is it permissible to sacrifice even temporarily the tremendous advantage of putting up our own ticket, as is done in nearly every country in the world.

So much for the general theory underlying the labor party policy we have followed up to now.

Taking this theory as our basis, we were and are obliged to consider the concrete facts confronting us at every stage in the development of events. The statement of our party, printed in the *Daily Worker* on the day the candidacy of Foster and Gitlow was announced, correctly set forth the actual situation in the present campaign. Despite all our efforts to create a united front political movement under the banner of the Farmer-Labor Party on a national scale, we were not successful. The reasons for this failure are not far to seek. The basic reason, of course, is the almost complete domination of the organized labor movement by reactionary labor leaders and the labor aristocracy, which are opposed to independent political action by labor and to the class struggle in general. But besides this basic reason there were contributing factors which played an important part in killing the labor party in the present campaign. The treachery and cowardice of Fitzpatrick and his group in Chicago dealt the movement a heavy blow. The betrayal of the labor party movement by the Socialist Party played a part. On top of these, the tremendous sweep of the La Follette movement throughout the labor party generally had the effect of so neutralizing its class character as to make it impossible for us to hold any considerable section of it in line for a class fight on a national scale.

After the Cleveland convention of the CPPA we were confronted with the following facts:

1. There was not even one voice raised in the Cleveland convention against La Follette and for the Farmer-Labor Party. R.D. Cramer, who fought valiantly in the first Cleveland convention of the CPPA, sat mute in the convention of July 4th; Fitzpatrick had already gone back to the Gompers policy. William Mahoney, one of the outstanding pioneers in the labor party movement of the Northwest, swore allegiance to La Follette and to the movement that would not admit him as a delegate. Sidney Hillman was on the La Follette bandwagon. Even the Socialist Party, with Eugene V. Debs, surrendered unconditionally to La Follette, the petty-bourgeois politician, and cravenly gave up the fight for a labor party. Our hopes for a left wing at Cleveland which would fight for a labor party and join hands with the St. Paul Convention Committee on that issue did not materialize.

2. A large section even of the elements which took part in the St. Paul convention were unable to stand up against the tremendous pressure of the La Follette forces and capitulated to them. Even such pronounced Farmer-Laborites as William Mahoney of Minnesota, Kidwell of California, and many others who could be

mentioned, found it easier to betray the interests of the working class and the principles of the labor party than to fight against the permeation of the poisonous doctrine of La Folletteism into the class movement. They were afraid to take an unpopular stand, although the interests of the working class clearly demanded it.

We discussed the situation for many days and considered it from all angles. We took up the state of affairs in every single state and discussed them in detail.

Taking the principle of the united front, as briefly outlined above, as our basis, we put the question to ourselves this way: If we can see a substantial united front mass movement that can be organized on a national scale under the banner of the Farmer-Labor Party, we will participate in it and go through the campaign as a part of the united front, maintaining, of course, the right of independent criticism and agitation. On the other hand, if there is no united front and no mass movement, if the Farmer-Labor Party represents in reality nothing but the Communists and a circle of close sympathizers, then the very foundation for our participation in the movement on a united front basis is taken away. Under such circumstances, we are duty bound to raise our own revolutionary standard and fight in our own name in order that we may not be hampered in making the most out of the campaign for the Communist Party and the Communist principles, which, in the final analysis, is the objective of all our work. Our fight is a fight for Communism. All our activity must lead to this.

The conclusion we finally arrived at, on the basis of the facts staring us in the face, was that the Farmer-Labor united front in the present campaign does not exist. With the possible exception of a few states such as Minnesota, Montana and Washington, there is no appearance of a Farmer-Labor mass movement, able to stand up against the La Follette wave. And even in these places the movement is gravely endangered by enemies from within.

This judgment of the Central Executive Committee was confirmed by a special party conference of district organizers, federation secretaries, party editors, and a number of other leading comrades from various sections of the country. Events which have transpired since this decision only pile up the evidence mountain high, to prove the accuracy of our estimate of the situation.

In view of these facts, to have conducted the campaign under the banner of the Farmer-Labor Party would not have been to the best interests of our party, which are one and the same thing as the interests of the working class. It would have meant that the whole burden of the campaign on a national scale would have fallen on the shoulders of our party. We would have been obliged to do practically all the work for the Farmer-Labor Party and pay most of the expenses. With the exception of a circle of close sympathizers, who will support the Communist candidates just as readily as Farmer-Labor candidates in most cases, there would have been no one to help us, no united front, no mass movement.

Moreover, to conduct such a campaign under the name of the Farmer-Labor Party would have meant to moderate the propaganda and tone down the whole campaign. We would not have been able to utilize the campaign meetings to the best advantage to promote our party and its press. We would have been operating under a form of camouflage when the political situation cries aloud for a direct and open fight, for a frontal attack from a revolutionary class standpoint against La Folletteism, and all the traitors to the labor movement who are following in its wake.

In a word, we would have been making all the immediate sacrifices from the standpoint of our party that a united front movement entails, without having a united front in reality, without having a mass movement.

Under these conditions the Workers Party had no alternative but to raise its own revolutionary standard and make the fight alone. All the others go over to La Follette, but the Workers Party stands and fights. It is proven in this campaign, at the very beginning of the workers' independent political movement in America, as it will be proven in their final struggle, and at each decisive stage between then and now, that the Communist Party alone understands and defends the interests of the working class as a whole.

However, the principle of the united front, and the conditions under which we can and will take part in it, hold good now as before. The Workers Party has not retreated one inch from the ground which it has stood upon up till now in the labor party movement. It still stands for the creation of a broad labor party and will fight for it in the future as in the past. It will be the only party keeping the idea alive in the present campaign. Wherever there is a united front political movement embracing wider masses of the workers than we are able to draw around us for direct support of the Workers Party, we will take part in such a movement. We are ready and willing to do this now on a state scale, even though the conditions for such a movement do not exist on a national scale. In the state of Washington, for example, where we are of the opinion that the Farmer-Labor Party has some of the proportions of a mass movement, our policy will be to support the state ticket of the Farmer-Labor Party in the coming elections, providing it maintains its stand on a class basis and makes no alliances which will bring it under the leadership of petty-bourgeois politicians.

The Farmer-Labor Party of Washington is in no way jeopardized by the actions which we have taken on a national scale. If the leaders of the Farmer-Labor Party of Washington will stand their ground, the Workers Party will stand and fight with them. The same holds true in a few other states where there is a substantial state Farmer-Labor Party which will go through the campaign with its own candidates. The only condition we set up is that the Farmer-Labor Party must have some of the proportions of a mass movement, broader than the Workers Party and its close sympathizers.

We can understand how our decision to put Foster and Gitlow in the field may have taken some of the Labor Party leaders in the West by surprise. We were obliged to move quickly. Events were developing at a very rapid rate, and it was not possible for us to have lengthy and delayed consultations with Farmer-Labor people all over the country, much as we would have liked to do this, in order to come to a complete agreement with them before taking action.

The Workers Party has not betrayed the confidence of any sincere supporters of the Farmer-Labor movement. We stand now, as before, ready to go together with them in a common fight wherever it is possible to make a substantial showing. There is nothing in our recent decision to interfere with this.

There is another aspect to the question which it is necessary to speak about here. Their letter[1] seems to approach the question in all of its phases from the standpoint of the Farmer-Labor Party and from the standpoint of those Farmer-Labor leaders with whom we have been cooperating to a certain extent. We are sure that this attitude is an unconscious one and is the result merely of their far removal from the party center and of incomplete assimilation of the whole content of the united front tactic of the Communist International. But such an attitude puts the whole question on a false basis. Communists have to approach all these problems first of all from the standpoint of the Communist Party because it is the only party standing for the immediate and ultimate interests of the working class. Any activities we engage in that do not result in strengthening and building the Communist Party, in increasing its influence over the laboring masses and winning them away from the influence of all other groups and parties, does not serve the real interests of the working class as a whole. If we fail to do this, we fail to develop the instrument which is indispensable, not only for the final revolutionary victory of the workers, but also for all their immediate struggles which lead towards it—that is, an independent revolutionary party which stands up at all times for the interests of the working class as a whole and which leads the way at every stage of the fight.

If the united front fails in this, the united front is a failure and all our work is a failure.

The comrades of the western branch, lacking the complete information which determined our recent actions, found fault with what they considered a lack of frankness on the part of our party, and apparently have been influenced somewhat by the charges of our enemies that we have played some kind of a clever game with other groups in the Farmer-Labor movement.

There is no foundation for such an opinion. The Communist Party always draws up its policy independently of all other groups and parties, in accordance with what it considers to be for the best interests of the working class and the advancement of the revolutionary struggle. Of course this does not preclude an

---

[1] Cannon is answering a letter from a Western Workers Party branch critical of the party's new policy. No such letter accompanies this article in the *Daily Worker*.

agreement on a given line of action with other groups willing to make a sincere fight together with us. But we cannot put aside our own judgment when questions arise which so vitally affect the welfare of the working class as the present election campaign. There is no secret about what we have done or why we have done it. It is no breach of faith with any honest elements in the labor movement, but a proof of loyalty towards the movement as a whole.

The comrades seem to be somewhat concerned as to whether we have not done "grave injustice" to some of the leaders in the Farmer-Labor Party who have not completely understood and agreed with our action at first. Communists need not be so sensitive. It is incorrect to come to the conclusion that the subordination of our own party is always the correct thing to do. We have had to ask ourselves quite seriously a number of times if the many concessions and compromises we have been making in order to maintain the unity in the Farmer-Labor movement have not led a number of our own comrades to consider that the Communist Party is in its proper place only when it is sitting in the back seat. The true function of the Communist Party is not to "go along" but to go ahead.

The Communist International never tires of dinning into our ears that our first reaction to all political maneuvers must be this: How does it increase and extend the influence of the Communist Party over the laboring masses?

Comrade Zinoviev told us once at a session of the Enlarged Executive: "Do not forget that we are not merely a workers party; we have to be a shrewd workers party." Communists must never forget that we are dealing with all kinds of enemies in the labor movement, with all kinds of agents of the bourgeoisie, and with muddle-headed people who will lead the workers into the ditch if we allow their false conceptions to prevail.

We have to see to it that the Communist Party knows how to take advantage of every situation to strengthen the Communist influence over the masses and to strengthen the Communist Party. Only when we are doing this can we say that we are leading towards the real revolutionary struggle.

The proletarian revolution is the only solution of the labor problem and the Communist Party is the only party aiming at this goal. The Farmer-Labor Party, as such, does not do this and it cannot, under any circumstances, be regarded as an end in itself. Our work in the Farmer-Labor Party, in the united front in all its aspects, in fact, must be regarded by Communists as the Communist International regards it: a means of revolutionary agitation and mobilization. The German events and the verdict of the Communist International on them has settled this question for all time.

The Bolshevization of the Party

5 October 1924

Cannon delivered the following speech, in support of the "Bolshevization" campaign initiated by Zinoviev at the Comintern's Fifth Congress, to the New York Workers School. It was first published in the Workers Party theoretical journal, Workers Monthly, *November 1924.*

The founding of the Workers Party school in New York City has a great significance for the party and must be regarded as a real achievement. It is one of many signs that the American Communist movement, which already has five years of struggle behind it, is hammering itself into shape, overcoming its weaknesses, striving in real earnestness to throw off the encumbrances which it inherited from the past and to transform itself into a genuine party of Leninism.

We are well aware that our party is not yet a Bolshevik party in the complete sense of the term. But we can say that after five years we have succeeded in crystallizing at least a strong nucleus within the party which endeavors to adopt a real Leninist standpoint on every question which confronts the party. It is characteristic of such comrades that they regard the adherence of our party to the Communist International not as a formal affair, but as an inseparable part of its being, which shapes and colors all of its activities, something that penetrates into the very marrow of its bones. For them, the word of the Communist International is decisive in all party questions. It is as one of such comrades that I wish to speak here tonight.

The Fifth Congress of the Communist International has completed its work. It has examined and appraised the world situation. It has gone deeply into the experiences of all of the most important parties during the period since the Fourth Congress, as well as into the work of the International as a whole. The judgment finally arrived at has been compressed into a series of resolutions and theses which are now available for the Communist parties of the entire world. They constitute a clear guide for our future activities.

The Slogan of the Fifth Congress

The congress found that all of the parties of the International, with the exception of the Russian party, are still far short of the requirements of a Bolshevik party. The traditions, customs and habits of the past are like leaden weights on their feet. They lack the Bolshevik discipline, the iron hardness, the capacity for decisive action, the mobile form of organization and the strong theoretical foundation which a party of Leninism must have.

The congress demanded an energetic struggle against all these weaknesses and defects and the slogan of this struggle is "The Bolshevization of the party!"

Our educational work, as well as all other phases of our party life, must be carefully scrutinized and examined in the light of this slogan. When we come to speak of theory and theoretical work, we put our finger at once on one of the weakest spots in the American movement. This has always been the case. The American labor movement, in common with the labor movements of practically all the Anglo-Saxon countries, has a traditional indifference to theory. There is a widespread tendency to draw a line between theory and practice. The typical labor leader boasts of being a practical man who "has no time for theory." We encounter the same point of view quite often even in the ranks of our party.

Such a tendency is bound to lead the party into a blind alley. We must fight against it in a determined and organized manner. The party educational work must be organized in a systematic way and pushed forward with tenfold energy. Our educational work up to now has been practically negligible and that is all the more reason for making haste now.

Fundamental Importance of Theory

In connection with this work it is necessary continually to stress the fundamental importance of revolutionary theory. Comrade Lenin said, "Without a revolutionary theory, a revolutionary movement is impossible." These words must become a part of the consciousness of every member of the party. It must become obvious to all that the working class will be able to come into open collision with the capitalist order, to dismantle it and to set up in its place the Communist form of society—to accomplish the task which history has set for it—only if at every turn of the road, in every phase of the struggle, it is guided by a correct revolutionary theory.

The spectacle is familiar to all of us, of militant workers starting out with a great hatred of capitalist oppression and a will to fight against it, but drifting along, because of lack of knowledge of the capitalist system and of the means by which it may be overthrown, into a policy which leads them to actual support of the capitalist system. The participation of many thousands of discontented workers in the La Follette movement is an instance of this. We know that the typical labor leaders of America, who say they have no theory, carry out in actual practice the theory of the bourgeoisie and constitute strong pillars of support for the bourgeois system. There is no such thing as "no theory" in the labor movement. Two social systems are in conflict with each other, the capitalist system and the Communist. One must be guided either by the theory of revolution which leads to the Communist order of society or he will follow a line of action which leads to support of the present order. That is to say that, in effect, he adapts himself to the theory of the present order. "No theory" in the labor movement is the theory of the bourgeoisie.

Without revolutionary theory, the workers, even with the best will in the world, cannot fight the capitalist system successfully. This statement holds good, not merely in the question of the final revolutionary struggle for power, it applies equally in every aspect of the daily struggle. Workers who have no understanding of the theory of revolution cannot follow a consistent line of action that leads toward it. Behind every action aimed at the bourgeoisie, there must be the theory of the revolutionary overthrow of the bourgeoisie. False policies in the ranks of the workers, whereby even their own good will and energy is transformed into a force operating against their own interests, spring in the first place from false theory. Only by an understanding of the revolutionary nature of their struggle, and of the necessity of shaping their actions in the light of this theory and adapting them to the execution of it, can the workers follow a systematic policy of opposition to the bourgeoisie and of defense of their own interests. Revolutionary theory is not something separate from action, but is the guiding principle of all revolutionary action.

What "Bolshevization" Means

The Fifth Congress of the Communist International dealt with the mistakes made by various sections during the period between the Fourth and Fifth Congresses which, in the case of the German party, led to most disastrous results, and laid these mistakes at the door of incorrect theory, of deviation from the line of Marxism and Leninism. It declared that both the opportunistic errors of the right and the sectarian errors of the left represent deviations from the line of the Communist International, which is the embodiment of the theory of Marx and Lenin. The crisis in the German Communist Party, which became evident at the time of the October 1923 retreat, was declared by the Fifth Congress to be the result of the influence of the remnants of the old social-democratic ideology which still existed within the Communist Party of Germany. This also applies to our party and the remedy for this state of affairs, in the language of the propaganda thesis of the Fifth Congress, is to "Bolshevize the party!"

The propaganda thesis says: The Bolshevization of the party in this sense means the final ideological victory of Marxism and Leninism, or in other words, of Marxism in the period of imperialism and the epoch of the proletarian revolution, and to reject the Marxism of the Second International and the remnants of the elements of syndicalism.

The Bolshevization of the party, therefore, like all slogans of the Communist International, means not a mechanical formula, but a struggle. In this case it is a struggle against false ideology in the party. The Bolshevization of the party, for us, means the struggle for the conquest of the party for the ideology of Marxism and Leninism.

To quote again from the thesis: "The complete and rapid Bolshevizing of the Communist parties can be obtained in the process of the deliberate revolutionary activity of the sections of the Communist International, by more deeply hammering Marxism and Leninism into the consciousness of the Communist parties and the party members."

The Bolshevization of the party is a process and the means

towards the end is an ideological struggle. The Workers School, in common with all educational institutions set up by the party, must be a weapon for this struggle. Under no circumstances can we conceive of it as a neutral academy standing between the various tendencies and currents of the party, but as a fighting instrument against all deviations both to the right and to the left, and for the overcoming of the confusion of the party members and for the "hammering into the consciousness of the party and the party members, Marxism and Leninism."

Take Comintern Slogan Seriously

This conception imposes giant tasks upon the Workers School. There is much confusion in our ranks. This we must all admit frankly. Such a state of affairs is to be expected in a party which up to now has devoted little attention to theoretical work and which has had little revolutionary experience, but we must begin now in a determined fashion to cope with this condition and to overcome it.

A particularly dangerous form of confusion and irresponsibility, which we must conquer by frontal attack without delay, is the formal and even frivolous attitude which is sometimes manifested in regard to the relations of our party and our party members to the Communist International. We hear the Bolshevization of the party spoken of here and there as though it were a joke, not to be taken seriously. The very utterance of such a sentiment is in itself an evidence of theoretical weakness. Communists cannot take such a lighthearted attitude towards the Communist International. Let us say at the very beginning, and let everybody understand once and for all: The international organization of the revolutionary proletariat and the leadership of the World Congress is, in itself, an inseparable part of our theory. The very fact that any party members are able to regard the slogan of the Fifth Congress as a joke is a great proof of the need for this slogan in our party.

The Cause of Factionalism

If we examine closely the state of affairs within our party now, and for the five years that it has been in existence, we are bound to come to the conclusion, as did the Fifth Congress in regard to the International as a whole, that the internal conflicts and crises, as well as the mistakes made by the party in the field of its external activities, can be traced directly to ideological weakness, to the incomplete assimilation by the party of Marxism and Leninism. In other words it still carries with it the dead weight of the past and has not yet become a Bolshevik party.

The thesis on tactics of the Fifth Congress lays down five separate specifications which are the special features of a really Bolshevik party. One of them is the following:

"It (a Bolshevik party) must be a centralized party prohibiting factions, tendencies and groups. It must be a monolithic party hewn of one piece."

What shall we say of our party if we measure by this standard? From the very beginning, and even up to the present day, our party has been plagued with factions, tendencies and groups. At least one-half of the energy of the party has been expended in factional struggles, one after another. We have even grown into the habit of accepting this state of affairs as a normal condition. We have gone to the extent of putting a premium upon factionalism by giving factional representation in the important committees of the party.

Of course, this condition cannot be eliminated by formal decree. We cannot eliminate factions and factional struggles by declaring them undesirable. No, we shall make the first step toward eliminating factions, tendencies and groups, toward creating a monolithic party in the sense of the Fifth Congress declaration, only if at the beginning we recognize the basic cause of the condition, if we recognize that the existence in our party of factions, tendencies and groups runs directly counter to Leninism, to the Leninist conception of what a revolutionary proletarian party should be.

Then we will proceed, in true Leninist fashion, to overcome the difficulty. Not mechanically, not by organizational measures alone, but by an ideological and political struggle which has for its object the creation of a uniform and consistent proletarian class ideology in the party ranks. The problem of factions, tendencies and groups is not an organizational problem merely, it is a political problem and for political problems there are no mechanical solutions.

We must conceive of the Workers School as one of the best weapons in our hands for the fight to develop a uniform proletarian ideology in the party ranks and to overcome all deviations from it.

False Conceptions of Education

The American revolutionary movement has had in the past, and still has in many sections, even in a section of the party, queer and false conceptions of the nature of revolutionary education. We are all acquainted with that class of "educators" who reduce education to the study of books and separate the study of books from the conduct of the daily struggle. We know of that old school of "educators" whom we used to call the "surplus value" school, who imagined that if a worker learned something of the nature of the capitalist system of society, the process by which it exploits him and by which it expropriates the major product of his labor, that his education is complete.

We have no place for such a static and one-sided conception of revolutionary education. In all our work, the analysis of capitalist society and the study of the mechanics of capitalist exploitation must be directly and originally connected with the Marxian theory of the state and the process by which the proletariat will overthrow it and set up their own order of society. We must give short shrift to those pseudo-Marxists who convert Marxism into a "theory" separate from struggle. According to our conceptions, Marxism and Leninism constitute both the theory and practice of the proletarian revolution, and it is in this sense that the Workers School must teach Marxism, and must impart it to the students of the school.

Genuine Leninist education cannot by any means be separated from the daily activities and the daily struggles of the party. It must be organically connected with these struggles. No one can become a real Leninist if he studies in a glass case. We must discourage, and the Workers School must fight with all its means against, any such conception.

Education Must Be Partisan

Correct revolutionary education is partisan education. It must bear the stamp of Marx and Lenin, and no other stamp. Only the theory and teachings of Marxism and Leninism are revolutionary. They cannot be harmonized with any other theory, for no other theory is revolutionary. The Workers School cannot be natural or tolerant. It must scrutinize, ten times over, every item in its curriculum, and every utterance of its instructors from the standpoint of their adherence to the teachings of Marx and Lenin.

There is a phrase entitled "labor education" which is current in the labor movement. There is no such thing as "labor education." "Education" is given from the revolutionary standpoint of Marx and Lenin or it is "education" which leads to a conformity and an adaptation to the bourgeois order. This fact must never be lost sight of in any of our educational work. We must be intransigent in this conception of education and so must the Workers School. We must be "narrow-minded" and intolerant on this score, imparting knowledge or culture not from any "general" standpoint, which in the last analysis becomes the standpoint of the bourgeoisie, but from the standpoint only of Marxism and Leninism. There is a conception of this so-called labor education, in my opinion utterly false, which has become widespread. Scott Nearing recently expressed the opinion that the "united front" tactic should be applied in workers' schools.

Our answer to this point of view is that if there is one place where the united front should not be applied it is the field of education. According to our point of view, the only theory which correctly analyzes capitalist society and correctly maps out the road of the struggle for its overthrow is the theory of Marxism and Leninism. We cannot find a common meeting ground with any other theory or any other brand of education. The Workers School does not represent a united front in the field of education. The Workers School must be a partisan school, a weapon in the hands of the party for implanting the party ideology in the minds of the students who attend its classes.

Theory in Our Trade Union Work

I should like to deal now with the question of education in connection with our trade union activities. I speak with particular reference to the trade union activities because at the present time it is our main field of work, although the points made apply to all fields of activity in the daily struggle. Our party members in the trade unions are obliged to carry out widespread and many-sided activities, the sum total of which comprises a very large percentage of our party work. This is rightly so, because the trade unions are the basic and elementary organizations of the proletariat, and the success of our party, in its efforts to become a party of the masses, depends to a very large extent upon its ability to work in the trade unions and to follow out a correct policy in all of its work there.

To arrive at the correct policy in dealing with the complex problems which constantly come up in the trade unions, a firm grasp on theory is absolutely indispensable. However, theory is badly lacking in this field amongst the comrades in the ranks, who have to carry out the work.

The reason for this is obvious. The members who join our party directly from the trade unions come to it as a rule because they are drawn to the party in the daily struggle over immediate questions. They become convinced, by seeing our party in action and working with it, that it is a real party of the workers which fights for the immediate interests of the workers, and on that basis the workers come to the party. As a rule they do not go through a course of study before admission and do not inquire very deeply into the fundamental theory upon which the party's whole life and activity is founded.

Consequently, for our comrades in the trade unions to attempt to work out a line of tactics in relation to the employers, in relation to the reactionary labor leaders, progressive labor leaders and various other currents and tendencies in the trade union movement, and to coordinate everything with our general political aims, their own empiric experience is not a sufficient foundation. They are bound to become overpractical if they have no other guide, and to drift into tactics which lead them inevitably away from the revolutionary struggle. The Communists in the trade unions can be successful only if they approach all of their tasks from the standpoint of correct revolutionary theory and have all of their activities imbued with this theory.

Two serious errors manifest themselves in the party in connection with theory and practical work in the trade unions. On the one hand we are confronted, every now and then, with a prejudice on the part of the rank and file workers in the trade unions against theory and theoreticians and a resentment against any interference of this kind in their work. All the party leaders, especially the comrades leading our trade union work, have encountered this prejudice. On the other hand we frequently see comrades who have gained all their knowledge from books and who have had no experience in the actual struggle of the workers, especially comrades who can be classified under the general heading of "intellectuals," adopting a condescending and superior attitude towards the comrades who do the practical work of the party in the daily struggles in the unions. They take a pedagogical and supervisory attitude towards the trade union comrades and thus antagonize them and lose the possibility of influencing them and learning from them.

Both these attitudes are false, and in my opinion the Workers School must help the party to overcome them by systematic, persistent, and determined opposition to both. We must oppose the prejudice of some of the practical trade union comrades, who are new in the party and who have not yet assimilated its main theories, against theory and party workers theoretically trained. We must oppose and resist in the most determined fashion any tendency on their part to separate their work from the political and theoretical work of the party and to resent the introduction of theoretical and political questions into their discussion of the daily work in the unions. And likewise, to the comrades who have book knowledge only, we must make it clear that the theory of the party gets its life only when it is related to the practical daily struggle and becomes a part of the equipment of the comrades who carry on the struggle. They must learn how to approach the practical workers and collaborate with them in the most fraternal and comradely manner, and they must not under any circumstance adopt a superior and pedagogical attitude towards them. This very attitude in itself manifests an ideological defect. A Communist intellectual who cannot identify himself with the trade unionists in the party and make himself one with them is not worth his salt.

Organic Connection of Theory and Practice

The separation of theory and practice, the arbitrary line between theoretical work and practical work, the arbitrary division of activity into theoretical activity and practical activity, must be combatted and overcome. We must set up against it the conception of the organic connection between theoretical and practical work, and of fraternal collaboration between theoretically trained comrades and comrades carrying out the practical work in the daily struggle, especially in the trade union movement.

Our party, in common with the other parties of the International, is confronted by two dangers which militate against its effectiveness in the class struggle. One of the dangers is left sectarianism, which is a deviation from the line of Marxism and Leninism in the direction of syndicalism, and the other is right opportunism, which is defined in the Fifth Congress resolution as a deviation from Leninism in the direction of the emasculated Marxism of the Second International. These dangers can be overcome and the party remain on the right road only if it succeeds in carrying on a successful struggle against these deviations. Educational work is an important means to this end.

Educational work therefore is not a mere academic activity. In a certain sense it is a fight. It is a fight to overcome these dangers by building in the party ranks a true and firm and uniform proletarian ideology. It must help the party in the fight against right deviations without falling back into the error of deviations to the left. The Workers School must be for the party one of the most important means by which we impress in the minds of the party members a knowledge of Marxian and Leninist theory, of developing a respect for theory and an understanding of its fundamental importance, without falling into the error of teaching theory in an abstract manner and separating it from the daily activities of the party.

Our party must be at the same time a party of theory and a party of struggle, with theory and struggle closely interlocked and inseparable. Without allowing the party members to develop into mere fault-finders, the school must help them to acquire the faculty of criticism, of subjecting every action and every utterance of the party to criticism from the standpoint of its conformity to the basic theory of the movement. We do not want a party consisting half of critics and half of practical workers, but every party member must be at the same time a critic and a constructive worker.

The party must be a party of study and struggle. All the party members must be trained to become thinkers and doers. These conceptions carried out in actual practice will be the means whereby we can rapidly transform our party into a Communist Party in the true sense of the word.

Party Support for Educational Work

We have every reason to be proud of the response the Workers School has met in the ranks of the party membership of New York. The enthusiastic support it has already gained gives us the hope that our educational work, which we have so long neglected, can now be developed extensively and that all who are most active and alive in the party will join in the task of making it move forward.

The party members in New York should look upon the Workers School as their own institution, as their own party educational center which, by fraternal collaboration of all the comrades, can be built and maintained as a real leader in the fight for Leninist ideology in the party, in the fight to shake off the paralyzing inheritance of the past and to merge in the shortest possible time, through the process of careful study and vigorous struggle, into a party complying with the specifications of a Bolshevik party which were laid down by the Fifth Congress.

That is: "A central monolithic party hewn of one piece."

That is: "Essentially a revolutionary and Marxist party, undeviating, in spite of all circumstances proceeding towards the goal and making every effort to bring nearer the hour of the victory of the proletariat over the bourgeoisie."

The Minority Attitude Toward Our Election Campaign— A Warning Signal for the Party

Published 3 December 1924

The following article by Cannon attacks the views of the minority of the Central Executive Committee led by C.E. Ruthenberg. It was published in the Daily Worker.

Every Communist who can see straight knows that our election campaign this year, under our own banner, was one of the greatest and most significant achievements in the history of the party. And every Communist who has the right attitude toward his party is proud of that achievement; he wants every worker to know about it and to understand its great significance, and he will not try to minimize it.

The party did right to enter the elections under its own name. Our election campaign was a victory for the party. It strengthened the revolutionary morale of our membership and established our party as the only working class political party in America. This is our position, clearly stated in our theses.

The theses of the minority do not speak in such clear and emphatic terms about our election campaign.[1] They evade the issue. They completely evade one of the most important questions

[1] Differences in evaluation of the 1924 U.S. election results between the Foster-Cannon majority and the Ruthenberg minority emerged almost as soon as the polls closed. A Central Executive Committee plenum was called for November 21-22. Both the majority and the minority wrote documents for the meeting entitled "Thesis on the Political Situation and the Immediate Tasks of the Workers Party." The plenum authorized the publication of the counterposed theses and decreed *(continued)*

which must be answered before we can decide our line for the immediate future.

That question is:

Was the Central Executive Committee correct when it decided last July, against the opposition of comrades Lovestone, Engdahl and Browder, to withdraw support from the Farmer-Labor Party and to enter the elections under its own banner with its own candidates?

Why the Minority Theses Fail to Endorse Our Election Policy

The evasion of these questions by the Lovestone-Ruthenberg theses is no accident. The question was repeatedly discussed in the meetings of the Political Committee prior to the consideration of theses and the minority is fully aware of its importance and of its indissoluble connection with our future policy. The omission is conscious and deliberate. "There's a reason" for it.

That reason is as follows: At least a part of the minority group represented by comrade Lovestone, which has become the dominant part of the minority group—the part which determines the policy of the whole group—still maintains that the CEC was wrong and that we should have conducted the campaign under the banner of the Farmer-Labor Party. Comrade Browder has long since admitted his error, but in the meeting of the Executive Council of November 14, *both comrades Lovestone and Engdahl voted against the following resolution*:

> In view of the discussion that has arisen in the CEC over the results of the election and the results gained by the Workers Party participating in the election under its own name, the CEC considers it necessary to reaffirm its opinion that the decision of the CEC in its July meeting to withdraw its support of the national Farmer-Labor Party ticket and to enter its own candidates in the campaign was correct

---

the opening of internal discussion leading to a projected Workers Party conference in December (the conference was later postponed due to Comintern intervention). The theses of the minority, which Cannon refers to here, were signed by Ruthenberg, Lovestone, Bedacht, Engdahl and Gitlow and were published in the *Daily Worker*, 28 November 1924. The majority theses, signed by Foster, Cannon, Bittelman, Browder, Dunne, Burman and Abern, were published in the *Daily Worker*, 26 November 1924. The majority theses are not included in this book.

and the proposal of comrades Lovestone, Engdahl and Browder to continue the campaign under the banner of the Farmer-Labor Party was wrong.

The Minority Ridicules and Minimizes Our Election Campaign

Comrades Ruthenberg and Bedacht voted for the motion, but they must have done so with their tongues in their cheeks, for their whole attitude on the question of our election campaign is the same as comrade Lovestone's. That is, to persistently and systematically deride and belittle the achievements of the campaign in order to bolster up their theory that the Workers Party cannot do anything under its own name, but must find a substitute organization whenever there is practical agitational work to be carried on.

The arguments they now bring forward against the Workers Party attempting to lead united front struggles in its own name and in favor of assigning that role to a mythical "class farmer-labor party" are the same arguments used by comrade Lovestone in the meeting on July 8, against the Workers Party raising its own banner in the election campaign. Their theses are one long argument against our election policy. The attitude of the minority toward our election achievements and their attempt to belittle them is symptomatic of the falsity of their whole theory. It is a warning signal to the party.

The CEC theses do not overstate the case when they say bluntly that the policy of the minority leads to the liquidation of the Workers Party. Of course, no one will say that this is the conscious purpose of the minority. We are sure that the comrades of the minority have no other object than to advance the cause of Communism. But in their over-zeal to find a shortcut to the goal of a popular mass Communist party, they have already put their feet on a path that leads backward and not forward. "In dealing with questions of policy," said comrade Zinoviev at the Fifth Congress, "we have to consider objective effects and not subjective intentions." It is by this standard that we measure the policy of the minority and condemn it, and declare openly our firm intention to fight it to the death.

We do not need to wait for the comrades of the minority to

get control of the party and put their policy into effect in order to prove that it is a false policy. *The minority has already proven it, not only in words, but in deeds.*

Seven Facts Which Prove the Liquidation Tendency of the Minority Policy

On this point facts can speak for themselves. In order to bolster up their false and dangerous policy of demanding a farmer-labor party at all costs, right or wrong, "dead or alive," whether the workers are interested in it or not, the minority is forced to minimize and deprecate even the modest achievements of the Workers Party and to invest the "class farmer-labor party" with virtues it does not and cannot possess—unless it is a genuine Communist party. The minority has already started out on this course, as the following facts bear witness:

1. In order to minimize before the CI the showing made by the party in the election campaign, the minority proposed in the CEC meeting of November 14 to answer the Communist International's inquiry about our vote in the following words: "Workers Party vote very small; will not exceed 20,000." They took this stand at a time when we already knew that over 10,000 votes had been counted for us in New York City and the state of Minnesota alone, and when we already had evidence of wholesale fraud against us.

2. In order to minimize our election achievements before the party, the minority opposed and ridiculed the CEC estimate of 100,000 votes (including the votes stolen from us) and voted against our motion "That we issue a statement claiming 100,000 votes and citing incidents in which votes were stolen from us."

3. Comrade Ruthenberg had such lukewarm interest in getting the facts about the size of our vote that it took two meetings of the Political Committee and more than a week's delay before we could get a letter sent to all party units asking for reports of votes counted for us and evidence of fraud against us in order that we could prove the contentions of our official statement. Ordinary office routine work was given the right of way over this important matter.

4. Comrades Minor and Kruse, chief spokesmen of the minority in the recent Chicago membership meeting, ridiculed the

showing made by the party in the elections, comrade Minor sarcastically comparing it to the SLP.

5. Comrade Bedacht, at the same meeting, said, "Our party was less before the masses during the election campaign than at any time during the past two years."

6. Writing in the November *Workers Monthly*, comrade Ruthenberg attributes qualities to a "labor" party that only a Communist party can possess. He says: "A labor party speaks in the name of labor. It calls upon the workers for action. Or if it is a farmer-labor party it calls upon the workers and farmers and speaks in their name."

7. Writing in the December *Workers Monthly*, comrade Ruthenberg associates "class political action" exclusively with the farmer-labor party. We, who believe the Workers Party represents "class political action," are disdainfully swept aside in the following words: "A group in our party, under the leadership of comrade Foster, is of the opinion that the movement towards class political action by labor is dead and that, therefore, the Workers Party must abandon the slogan 'For a class farmer-labor party'."

The Struggle Against "Farmer-Laborism" Is Only Beginning

The struggle between the Central Executive Committee and the minority over the question of future policy is only beginning. The party has not yet had time to study the two theses. But already the comrades of the minority have given us seven concrete examples of the objective effects of their good intentions to build a mass Communist party "quickly" by means of the magic formula of a "class farmer-labor party." And this is only the beginning.

So false is their policy and so far afield will they be compelled to go to defend it, that before the discussion period has come to a close, the whole party will be able to understand, on the basis of evidence which the comrades of the *minority* will supply, that their policy would lead the party into the swamp.

The minority thesis fails to say the party did right to raise its own banner in the election campaign because the comrades of the minority have no enthusiasm over the great historical significance of the banner of Communism having been raised for the first time in a national election in America, and because it must belittle and deride the great achievements of our party in the campaign in order to convince the party and the Communist International that the Workers Party is a failure, that it cannot speak to the masses in its own name, and must, therefore, hide itself behind another organization and another name.

The comrades of the minority have started out on a false path, but the party will not follow them. When the party has studied and discussed the question and considered the objective effects of the false policy of the minority it will give such a decisive answer that "Farmer-Labor Communism" will never raise its head again in the Workers Party.

Lovestone Quotes Mahoney

Published 8 December 1924

The following article by Cannon was published in the Daily Worker.

The more the party controversy is brought out into the open, and the more the minority is compelled to defend its position, the more does the shallow opportunism of both the minority position and its advocates become revealed. In my previous article, I showed how the false policy of the minority had already led them, in seven concrete instances, to a non-Communist attitude toward our election campaign.

I can now add another example, more clear, more obvious, and more damning than the others. The latest and worst example is given to the party by comrade Lovestone in his article in the *Daily Worker* of December 3. This is only natural, since the policy of the minority is the policy of Lovestone and is the logical outcome of his opposition to the Workers Party entering the election campaign under its own name in the July meeting of the CEC.

"If you give a finger to opportunism," said Zinoviev, in speaking of Serrati, "you will soon have to give your whole hand." Comrade Lovestone has not given his whole hand as yet. But, in his article in the *Daily Worker* of December 3, he adds another finger to the one he gave last July. At the rate he is traveling to the right, and if the more stable elements of the minority do not call him to order, we may expect that he will soon give his whole hand—and his head, too.

From the very beginning of the discussion, the CEC, placing itself on the ground of reality, has put one insistent question to the advocates of "an intensified campaign for a class farmer-labor party." That question is: Where is the sentiment amongst the working masses for this so-called "class" party? Time and again we have begged them to tell us in what trade unions, in what cities, states or localities this sentiment exists and how it is manifesting itself.

Up till December 3, the minority made no answer. Oh, yes, comrade Ruthenberg answered. His answer was a formula. He told us, in effect: "The contradictions of capitalism will intensify the class antagonisms. The capitalist state power will be used against the workers and the latter will be driven to independent political action. Therefore, we must build a 'class farmer-labor party.' This is a fundamental of Marxism. Please do not press the question any further."

But it soon became evident that the sophomoric essays of comrade Ruthenberg were not satisfying the party. The party wanted facts, and not merely formulas. In the ranks of the minority itself voices began to be raised: "Give us some facts about the actual sentiment for a 'class farmer-labor party' so that we can at least answer the merciless attacks of those comrades who say there is no mass sentiment for it."

Comrade Lovestone Takes the Stand and Introduces Mahoney's Editorial as "Exhibit A"

At this juncture comrade Lovestone stepped into the breach. The question of facts was no problem for him, for is he not an expert "research worker" and "fact-finder" as well as an expert and experienced witness?[1] He took the witness stand, so to speak, in his article of December 3, to "give evidence." He had "run down" the elusive sentiment for a "class farmer-labor party,"

---

[1] Cannon is here alluding to the fact that Lovestone served as a witness in the trial of Harry M. Winitsky in March 1920. Winitsky, executive secretary of the CPA, was one of the first Communists prosecuted in New York in the aftermath of the Palmer Raids. Lovestone, under threat of prosecution himself, testified after being granted immunity by the state. Many Communists strongly disapproved of Lovestone's actions and a cloud formed over his head; for a time he was barred from party leadership. Ruthenberg asserted that he had ordered Lovestone to testify as a matter of party policy, and Lovestone was evidently cleared of wrongdoing by an internal UCP investigation in December 1920. Nonetheless, his testimony was raised during the Goose Caucus/Liquidators faction fight in early 1922, and Foster raised it again during the faction fight in 1924-25.

After Cannon wrote this article, around the time of the Fifth ECCI plenum in the spring of 1925, the Control Commission of the Comintern investigated the matter and evidently cleared Lovestone again of any wrongdoing. Ruthenberg, Lovestone and Pepper requested that the Control Commission's decision not be publicized at the time since Lovestone was still under indictment in Michigan and Pennsylvania.

captured it, and brought it into court with him.

What is this evidence? First and foremost, it is a quotation from the Minnesota *Trade Union Advocate*, edited by William Mahoney.

Think of it!

After all our experience with this renegade and faker, after his treacherous performances at the St. Paul convention and since, comrade Lovestone still wants us to put faith in him and rely on him as an ally in the fight for a "class" movement.

Basing his conclusions solely on the quotations from Mahoney, comrade Lovestone says: "It is only natural that the first tangible crystallization of disillusionment with La Folletteism should manifest itself in Minnesota....It is only a matter of time when similar manifestations will be displayed in other sections of the farmer-labor movement."

Let us examine the black record of this "ally" whom comrade Lovestone has found. Let us see how much the party can depend on this "first tangible disillusionment with La Folletteism."

The whole story cannot be told here. Mahoney's treachery multiplies daily and only a resident of St. Paul can keep track of it. But we all—including comrade Lovestone—know enough facts to take his measure and estimate him properly. Let me set down here a few outstanding facts about Mahoney which are known to us:

1. On the very day that comrade Lovestone's article appeared in the *Daily Worker*, and on the day following, a news story from Minneapolis also appeared containing the information that the Hennepin County Central Committee of the Farmer-Labor Federation, with the full support of Mahoney, had expelled the delegates of the Workers Party.

The news story in the *Daily Worker* of December 4, signed by comrade C.A. Hathaway, our district organizer, says:

> Mahoney, in his speech after the motion was carried, stated that the Farmer-Labor Federation of Minnesota was essentially a non-partisan organization having no goal aside from its immediate aims for social reform.
>
> In conversation after the meeting he repudiated all the progressive ideas previously held and even went so far as to condemn the workers and peasants government of Russia. He further stated that at the state convention to be held in the near future that the Federation would have to take steps to rid itself of the "troublesome" left wing.

Lovestone's Quotation From Mahoney Throws a Searchlight on His Opportunistic Policy

2. This present attitude of Mahoney is no temporary aberration. It is the logical outcome of a long and consistent series of betrayals which are known to us, *and known to comrade Lovestone.* Here are a few of them:

(a) Mahoney fought for La Follette before, during, and after the St. Paul convention.

(b) Mahoney fought in the arrangements committee which met on the eve of the St. Paul convention for a resolution excluding the delegates of the Workers Party.

(c) At the Cleveland conference of the CPPA Mahoney swore allegiance to La Follette and repudiated the St. Paul convention.

(d) Mahoney supported Oscar Keller, the Republican candidate for Congress in St. Paul, and fought against comrade Emme, the candidate of the Farmer-Labor Party.[2]

More evidence can be cited by our Minnesota comrades to prove the systematic treachery of this faker and renegade. But the facts set forth above are more than enough to show that he is no friend of a "class farmer-labor party," no friend of the Communists, and *no ally for us.*

Mahoney serves one good purpose, however. His introduction into the party controversy as "Exhibit A" for comrade Lovestone's policy is sufficient to prove that comrade Lovestone's policy is no good, that it is built in quicksand, that it is opportunistic in the worst and most dangerous sense of the term, and that it

---

[2] While the Workers Party ran Foster for U.S. president and Gitlow for vice president, it ran candidates for state and local office in only a few states (e.g., New York, where Cannon was the party candidate for governor). In Minnesota, Washington and South Dakota, the Workers Party supported local candidates of the state Farmer-Labor parties. Julius F. Emme, a member of the machinists union and an open Workers Party supporter, was the Minnesota Farmer-Labor Party candidate for U.S. Congress in the Fourth Congressional District of St. Paul. According to the 6 November 1924 *Daily Worker,* Emme polled over 13,000 votes though he lost the election; Emil Youngdahl, a Communist who was FLP candidate for the Minnesota legislature, won his seat with 4,483 votes. Youngdahl served in the legislature until 1933 and he remained active in Minnesota Farmer-Labor politics. The *Daily Worker* (21 January 1927) referred to him as a "former Communist." Emme quit the Workers Party around 1925. In the early 1930s he was the organizer of the Minnesota State Employees Association and a supporter of the Trotskyists.

would lead the party to the "united front from the top only," to "maneuvers" around the conference table with "farmer-labor" fakers, and, consequently, to the degeneration of the Workers Party.

Lovestone Finds Sentiment for the "Class Farmer-Labor Party" Even in the Camp of Coolidge

Another word about Minnesota before we pass over to "Exhibit B"—the Farmer-Labor leaders of Washington.

Comrade Lovestone found sentiment for his "class farmer-labor party" in the most strange and unexpected places. First he found it in the camp of La Follette embodied in the person of William Mahoney. Next he found it in the camp of Coolidge!

The fact that the Farmer-Labor Party of Minnesota jumped down La Follette's throat and insisted upon being swallowed, digested, and excremented does not mean, according to comrade Lovestone, that it suffered any serious injury. It was a "mere election union" and it emerged from the bowels of La Follette in better shape than ever, strong enough to go to Coolidge and repeat the process. Read this piece of evidence for the "class farmer-labor party" submitted by comrade Lovestone:

> Least of all does it follow that such a campaign alliance (comrade Lovestone still has that "election alliance" in his head, as I shall prove in another article—JPC) means the uprooting of the idea and sentiment for a farmer-labor party....For instance, in Minnesota, Magnus Johnson and Olson, running on the Farmer-Labor Party ticket, polled a higher vote than La Follette. The majority by which La Follette, running on an independent ticket, was beaten by Coolidge was much larger than the majority by which those running on the Farmer-Labor Party ticket were beaten.

This is telling evidence indeed!

Do you comprehend the situation? There were, it appears, some tens of thousands of workers in Minnesota who were hot-foot for a "class" party. Therefore, they couldn't bring themselves to vote for La Follette. Comrade Foster, the candidate of the Workers Party, was on the ballot, but he wouldn't do for them. They, like the minority, wanted "independent class political action." They, like the minority, wanted a "class party that would fight the battles of the workers and farmers." This, of course, eliminated the Workers Party.

What were these desperate supporters of the "class party" to do? They couldn't vote for La Follette since he represented no class party. Foster was out of the question since the Workers Party has no class at all when it appears under its own name. Then something truly remarkable happened. These workers and farmers of Minnesota executed a stroke of grand strategy. They showed such proficiency in the difficult art of going north by running south that they deserve to have their names appended as honorary signatories to the minority theses.

These dauntless proletarians of the plains voted for Coolidge! By this master stroke they accomplished three things: first, they proved that "the La Follette movement is disintegrating"; second, they got their "class" party; and third, they provided the minority with an argument in favor of their theses. It is as good as any argument the minority has.

Lovestone Condones the Treachery of the Farmer-Labor Leaders of Washington

One more quotation from comrade Lovestone's article will complete the proof that his conception of "an intensified campaign for a class farmer-labor party" is an opportunistic conception of the "united front from the top only" by means of negotiations and conferences with reformist leaders of reformist organizations. Moreover, it will show that he condemns our Communist action in entering the Workers Party in the election campaign under its own banner because it alienated some of these reformist leaders.

Comrade Lovestone's "Exhibit B" is the Farmer-Labor Party of Washington, a reformist party, predominantly agrarian and based on individual membership. Comrade Lovestone is very indulgent towards this so-called party. He says it "merely endorsed La Follette and Wheeler."

The leaders of this party attacked and denounced the Workers Party throughout the campaign, but comrade Lovestone does not seem to hold that against them. It was all our fault!

Read what he says in his article in the *Daily Worker*, the official organ of the Workers (Communist) Party of America, on December 3:

> More than that. There is good reason to believe that the leaders of this Farmer-Labor Party would likely never have sought to secure the endorsement of their organization for La Follette or be tempted to

> drive their followers into the La Follette election camp if the Workers Party had not cut itself loose from the national Farmer-Labor Party on July 10. The bungling manner in which we handled our change in policy then was especially harmful.

Here in plain words we have the *real* policy of comrade Lovestone, which is the policy of the minority. The evasive, double-meaning language of the minority theses is put aside. The mask of Marxian phraseology is torn off and the party has an opportunity to see the ugly face of opportunism that hid behind it.

The minority theses speak very vaguely and evasively about the means to be employed to form the "political united front" by organizing a "class farmer-labor party." Comrade Lovestone makes the matter clear.

We will "handle" the reformist leaders of reformist organizations more carefully. We will not make again the stupid blunder of raising our own party's banner in the elections. We will see what the "leaders" want us to do and do it. Then these leaders will not "be tempted to drive their followers into the La Follette election camp."

These leaders, who according to comrade Lovestone are, after all, not so bad, delivered their organization to La Follette, they "drove their followers into the La Follette election camp," and they maligned and denounced our party and its candidates. But why did they make these trifling errors? Because "the Workers Party cut itself loose from the Farmer-Labor Party on July 10."

* * *

Comrade Ruthenberg complains because we are not observing the amenities of parliamentary debate, and he raises a special "point of order" against the term "Farmer-Labor Communism." But he is criticizing us from the wrong side. We believe that when the party considers all the implications of comrade Lovestone's article, it will say that the word "Communism" should be eliminated entirely from the definition of his policy.

The party and the CI will say this policy is "farmer-laborism." And they will kill it, too!

The CEC, the Minority and Comrade Lore: How the Minority "Fought" Lore When They Controlled the Party

Published 11 December 1924

The following article by Cannon was published in the Daily Worker. *It attacks the record of the Central Executive Committee minority led by C.E. Ruthenberg in combatting the ideas of Ludwig Lore. The question had become an issue in the faction struggle because the Comintern had directed the Workers Party leadership to wage an ideological campaign against Lore's views. Lore was a supporter of the Foster-Cannon CEC majority at this time.*

The outstanding characteristic of the right wing always and everywhere is its political cowardice. This has been demonstrated so often in the international Communist movement that it can be laid down as an axiom. Opportunism is so foreign to Communism that it instinctively feels itself to be an intruder and tries to conceal its identity. The right wing never has the courage to stand up and fight directly for its policy, but tries by devious ways, by indirection, and by shifting issues, to advance its influence and smuggle in its policy.

At least a tendency in this direction is manifested in the article of comrade Ruthenberg in the *Daily Worker* of December 6. In this article comrade Ruthenberg runs away from the central and immediate issue of the "class farmer-labor party," which has already been so badly shattered in the party discussion. He attempts to divert the discussion from the real issue of our present and future policy in regard to the labor party question to the question of who was right and who was wrong in the past on a number of questions. By raising the issue of the opportunistic errors of comrade Lore he evidently hopes to avoid further discussion of the opportunistic policy the minority sponsors now.

We welcome the occasion to discuss this issue of "Loreism" openly before the party. But we will not oblige comrade Ruthenberg by separating it from the present issue of the opportunistic policy of the minority on the "class farmer-labor party." On the contrary, we will link them up together and show that the attitude of the minority toward the opportunistic errors of Lore has been itself, from first to last, an example of opportunism.

The Lore question has a history and to deal with it adequately and get the true perspective we must go back a little. Comrade Lore's mistakes did not begin since the present Central Executive Committee took office. As comrade Olgin points out in the *Daily Worker* of December 6, they began in the early days of the Comintern.[1] They arose from a faulty conception of some of the essential elements of Leninism and for that reason they have been repeated in a quite systematic manner.

The Lore of this year is no more out of harmony with the main line of the Communist International than the Lore of last year, when the Pepper-Lovestone-Ruthenberg group were in control of the party. In fact, as I shall prove in these articles, comrade Lore is today closer to the Comintern than ever before. As a result of the CI decision, and the ideological struggle of the CEC, he has publicly admitted a number of his past errors, which is the first necessary step towards correcting them. This does not please the minority, but we are sure it pleases the Comintern.

Therefore, let us have a real and thorough discussion of the Lore question. Let us review it at least for the past two years. Such a retrospect will reveal some very interesting facts.

---

[1] Moissaye Olgin wrote a three-part series entitled "Lore and the Comintern" which was published in successive issues of the Saturday *Daily Worker* magazine supplement, beginning 6 December and ending 20 December 1924. In this series Olgin quoted from Lore's *Volkszeitung* articles to prove that Lore had (1) supported Serrati against the Comintern; (2) defended Paul Levi even after he had been expelled from the German party; (3) opposed trying to organize a workers revolution in Germany in 1923; (4) defended Trotsky's right to criticize the Stalin majority of the Russian party; (5) criticized the offensive policy of the Italian Communist Party as having led to the victory of fascism; (6) written sympathetically of the MacDonald Labour Party government in England; (7) been openly critical of what he saw as the frequent tactical zigzags by Zinoviev's Comintern. This evidence, concluded Olgin, was more than enough to brand Lore an opportunist and a centrist.

The theses of the minority say:

"Contrary to the decision of the Communist International, the Foster-Cannon group, in place of carrying on a struggle against the tendency, has maintained an organizational alliance with it."

Comrade Ruthenberg repeats these accusations in practically the same words.

In these articles I will not only show the falsity of both these accusations, but I will prove the following:

1. The Pepper-Ruthenberg group itself had both an organizational and political alliance with comrade Lore.

2. The Pepper-Ruthenberg group never once uttered a word of criticism of comrade Lore, to say nothing of making a fight against his ideas, during the whole year in which they controlled the party, although some of his greatest mistakes were made during that time.

3. The Pepper-Ruthenberg group did not utter a word of criticism of comrade Lore during the last party convention, but, on the contrary, sought his help in their fight against us.

4. Their "fight" against Lore began only after the last party convention, not as an honest ideological struggle, but as a factional maneuver against the CEC.

The Minority Attitude Toward Lore When They Controlled the Party

In the hectic days of 1923, the year of the boom, when the party was buying gold bricks right and left, comrade Lore was in high favor with the CEC. He was handled with the greatest tact and consideration, and his advice and support were always sought whenever a question of policy was to be considered. Comrade Lore was carried around—so to speak—like a basket of eggshells. I never saw a grown man handled with more tender concern.

If I may be pardoned a few personal allusions, which are introduced not in any sense as a complaint but merely by way of illustration, I might cite the fact—to show the high favor enjoyed by comrade Lore—that he was drawn into the Political Committee when I was excluded from it, and that he was appointed a member of the CEC steering committee at the July 3 convention in Chicago which I was denied the right to attend, being assigned to speak at a picnic in Portland, Oregon on that historic occasion.

After July Third

After "July 3" the CEC returned to New York with the "Federated Farmer-Labor Party" in its briefcase. The letter of the Young Communist International to the Young Workers League of America quotes Karl Radek, who wrote the last CI thesis on America, as having said in the American Commission: "The Federated Farmer-Labor Party is seven-eighths a fantasy." What the other one-eighth consisted of, the letter does not say.

In the August meeting of the CEC, comrades Foster, Bittelman and myself began to ask a few questions about this "fantasy"; but comrade Lore supported it. Perhaps I do him an injustice. Comrade Lore's attitude, as I recall it, was about as follows: "We've got it, so we have to keep it."

At this meeting the "August Theses," the most curious melange of opportunism and confusion ever pressed into one document, was adopted. Foster, Bittelman and myself voted against it. Comrade Lore voted for it and his support was most gratefully accepted. Comrade Lore was one of comrade Pepper's famous "majority." I mention this merely as a matter of history.

Up till the time of this meeting comrade Foster had also been generally supporting the original experiments of comrade Pepper in the political laboratory and had consequently enjoyed a certain respect in the CEC. In fact, comrade Foster was highly regarded. He was immune from all criticism, and, as long as he did not attempt to assert himself in the CEC, was given the title, not only of "leader of the party," but "leader of the whole American working class."

When the attempt on his life was made in Chicago, *The Worker* carried a two-line streamer head, written by comrade Pepper, running across the entire first page. "The capitalists want to kill Foster! *Workers! We Must Defend Our Leader!*"[2]

---

[2] This was the front-page headline of *The Worker* of 8 September 1923. The lead article, written by John Pepper, reported: "A small group of gunmen burst into the Carmen's Auditorium in Chicago and fired three shots at William Z. Foster. He was speaking to thousands of members of the International Ladies' Garment

(continued)

The Attempt to Destroy Foster

But when it became apparent that comrade Foster was not becoming reconciled to the FFLP "fantasy," and that he was beginning to assert his right and duty to participate actively in the party leadership, the leading group in the CEC, which had formerly been heaping such fulsome flattery upon him, turned on him in fury. They set out to destroy him, to "kill" him, to rob him of his great prestige and undermine his authority in the party.

The leading group in the CEC suddenly discovered that comrade Foster was a "syndicalist," a "trade unionist," that is to say, no good. A subtle campaign in the party press against "non-Communist and syndicalist tendencies" held by unnamed comrades was accomplished by a systematic whispering campaign of slander and character assassination in the party ranks against Foster and the Chicago trade union comrades generally. Some of comrade Lore's greatest errors were made during this period—his estimation of events in Germany and the party crisis there—but the CEC took no notice. It was too busy fighting the "trade unionists."

This campaign to destroy Foster and the group closely associated with him continued right up to the last party convention and was the one big issue there.

The convention divided into two camps over the resolution introduced by Pepper and Ruthenberg, which had for its object the putting of the whole blame for the July 3 debacle upon Foster and the Chicago trade union comrades, who were standing up in the Chicago unions under the heaviest blows of the reactionaries and bearing the whole brunt of the fight for the party.

Workers' Union who had gathered to protest against the splitting tactics of the reactionary union officials in expelling from the union seven members of the Trade Union Educational League."

According to subsequent issues of *The Worker*, the gunmen were never caught or identified; the bourgeois press belittled the attempted assassination by claiming that the Workers Party had hired the gunmen as a publicity stunt. Foster does not mention the incident in his *History of the Communist Party of the United States*, though he does mention being kidnapped by Colorado Rangers and held for several days during the 1922 railway shopmen's strike. *The Worker* (19 August 1922) also ran a front-page headline on the kidnapping incident.

In the CEC meeting held on the eve of the convention, *and in the convention itself, comrade Lore voted for the resolution of Pepper and Ruthenberg.*

The overwhelming majority of the convention delegates, however, revolted against this monstrous piece of political crookedness and swept those who sponsored it out of power in the party.

What Happened in the Last Party Convention?

The minority have been making the statement, and still repeat it, that the present CEC gained the majority at the last party convention by making "an alliance" with the Lore group, and that this alliance is still maintained.

Here are the facts:

1. The majority of the present CEC appeared at the last party convention as a distinct and independent group, having its own policy on every disputed question that came before the convention.

2. On all questions we had a clear majority of the delegates from the beginning of the convention to the end.

3. We made no compromise on any question of policy with any group or individual in any way, shape or form. We specifically refused all proposals of the Lore group to change or modify our attitude toward the "third party alliance." (In this we were wrong, but we fought honestly for our wrong position.)

4. The Pepper-Ruthenberg group, in its desperate efforts to get the support of the Lore group for their fight against Foster and the Chicago trade union group, went to unheard-of lengths. *They withdrew the entire section of their thesis dealing with the "third party alliance" in order to avoid a collision with the Lore group.* In addition to this they centered their whole fight, during the entire convention, on the Chicago "trade union group" and had not a single word of criticism for comrade Lore.

5. Our group received from the convention a clear majority of the CEC members, independent of both other groups. That majority has stood unshaken until the present day, firmly united, on the rock bottom foundation of common policy, constantly drawing a line between itself and the Lore group, as well as the Lovestone-Ruthenberg group, on questions of policy.

The present majority of the CEC has a policy of its own and

fights for that policy. It had no alliance with any other group, organizational or otherwise, at the party convention and has no such alliance now.

The above constitutes a record of facts which no one can deny. It shows that comrade Lore was politically and organizationally united with the Pepper-Ruthenberg group at the time this group was leading the CEC. The record shows that comrade Lore was highly honored by the former CEC, being drawn into the Political Committee and appointed to the Steering Committee at the July 3 convention in Chicago. *It shows that the former CEC sought the support of comrade Lore at the convention, that it received this support on the main issue of the convention and that it made no criticism of Lore there.* And it shows that some of comrade Lore's greatest errors, which the CI has pointed out, were made during the administration of the former CEC and passed over in silence.

During the entire year that the present minority controlled the party, up to and throughout the party convention, their "ideological struggle" against comrade Lore's ideas was—not a word of criticism, not one single article, nor speech, nor motion. Their "fight" against comrade Lore, which comrade Ruthenberg now demands so virtuously, was—an organizational and political alliance with him against the "trade unionist Communists."

In my next article I will prove that the great fight of the minority on "Loreism" since the last convention is not now and never has been primarily directed against the wrong tendency of comrade Lore.[3] On the contrary, it has been directed against the CEC. This *indirect* means of attacking the CEC under cover of a fight against "Loreism," is merely a continuation of the last year's direct attempt to destroy comrade Foster and the group around him, and is organically connected with it. The raising of the Lore issue by the minority, *after the convention,* was merely a shift in *tactics* to serve the purposes of unscrupulous factionalism. The real target was not the wrong tendencies of Lore, but the Communist CEC which has nothing in common with these tendencies.

---

[3] Cannon did not publish a second article on this subject.

How to Organize and Conduct a Study Class

Published 13 December 1924

Cannon was the educational director of the Workers Party when he published this article in the Daily Worker *magazine supplement.*

The problem of educational work is many-sided. Enthusiasm for this work among the party members must be aroused and maintained. A general recognition of its fundamental importance must be established. It must be organically connected with the life and struggles of the party, and must not become academic and sterile. And it must be conducted in a systematic manner, becoming an established part of the life of the party throughout the year. This last will not just "happen." It will take much work and the introduction of correct organizational and technical principles. All our theories will come to nothing if our educational apparatus does not function properly.

Many classes have landed on the rocks because they were not conducted properly. One of the most frequent inquiries we have received from comrades who are undertaking party educational work is: "What is the best way to conduct a study class?" It is the purpose of this article to give an answer to this question based on the collective experience in the field of educational work from which a few general principles can be extracted.

Let us begin at the beginning and proceed step by step. When the responsible party committee in the given localities has decided to establish a class, let us say, for example, in the "ABC of Communism," the next move must be to appoint a leader for the class. This leader must understand that the class will not move of itself, but must be organized and directed from beginning to end, otherwise it will fall to pieces. The comrade in charge of the class must then proceed to enroll students, having them register for the class and making sure he has a sufficient number who agree in advance to attend the classes before he sets the time for calling it. As soon as a sufficient number of students have been enrolled, a date is set for the first class and all the students are notified.

At this point we should speak a word about the danger of haphazardness in the attendance at the classes on the part of any of the students. The party committee must decide that the attendance at class once a week, or more frequently, as the case may be, is a part of the member's party duty and should excuse him from party obligations for those nights. The systematic and regular attendance at class by all students must be constantly stressed, and the party committee and the leader of the class must constantly fight against the tendency, which always grows up, to regard the study class as a series of lectures at which one can "drop in" whenever he feels like it. Good results can only be obtained when the class is an organized body and is regularly attended by the same students.

Methods of Conducting Classes

The methods of conducting the classes which have proved most successful from past experience can be roughly divided into two general methods. These methods may be modified and varied in many ways, according to local circumstances, experience and qualifications of the teacher, etc.

These two methods are:

1. The lecture-question method.
2. The method of reading from and discussing the text in the class.

The Lecture-Question Method. This is the method most frequently employed by experienced teachers, and one which yields the most satisfactory results if qualified comrades can be found to conduct the class along this line. The use of this method presupposes that the teacher, who is himself thoroughly familiar with the subject matter of the text, possesses some ability and experience as a lecturer. It is not necessary, however, for him to be a professional. The average Communist who has a firm grasp of his subject will find that with a little practice he can succeed in holding the attention of a class.

Under this method the teacher delivers a lecture for the

period of about one hour on some phase of the general subjects dealt with in the text. In addition he requires the students to read, outside the class, in connection with his lecture, certain portions of the text and sometimes portions of other books which deal with the same subject. When the class comes together for the second time it is opened with a question period of about thirty minutes during which the lecturer quizzes the students on the subject matter of the previous week's lecture and the reading in connection with it. It is best to have a short recess at the end of the question period in order to get a fresh start for the lecture. A lecture of about an hour then completes the evening's work. Again the students are referred to sections of the text for reading in connection with the lecture. The same procedure is then followed at each successive meeting of the class until the end of the course.

When this method is employed it is not advisable to have indiscriminate discussion in the class, as this will almost invariably divert the attention of the class from the immediate subject in hand and destroy the possibility of consecutive instruction. For a teacher to conduct a class according to this method he must take it firmly in hand, establish his authority at the very beginning, and maintain it throughout the course. Nothing is more fatal to the success of such a class than for the opinion to grow up amongst some of the students that the teacher knows less then they do about the subject. For he will then be unable to maintain the proper discipline in the class and hold it to its course. Whenever a study class, organized for the purpose of consecutive study of a certain aspect of Communist theory or tactics, begins to resolve itself into a group for general discussion or a debating society, its early demise can be confidently expected.

Reading and Discussing the Text. This method also works out very well, especially in elementary classes. In this method, as in all others, however, the first prerequisite is a class leader who takes a responsible attitude towards the work and who takes it upon himself to organize and lead the class and hold it down to the matter in hand. This class leader should by all means thoroughly study the text before the class commences and make himself master of it.

The class conducted according to this method proceeds by

the class leader calling upon the students, one after another, to read a few sentences or a paragraph from the text. After each student finishes reading the part assigned to him, the leader asks the student who has read the passage to explain it in his own words. If he fails to bring out the meaning clearly or interprets the passage incorrectly, the question is directed to other students, the leader himself finally intervening to clarify the matter if necessary.

Proceeding along this line the class will cover a chapter or so of the text each evening. Before the reading commences each time, the leader should conduct a brief quiz of the class on the part of the text dealt with on the preceding evening in order to bring out the points clearly for the second time, refresh the memory of the students, and connect the preceding class with the one about to begin.

In the course of a few months, proceeding along this line, the class will get through the "ABC of Communism" and will have acquired a grasp of the fundamental theories of the movement. Moreover, if the class has been conducted successfully, if it has had the good fortune to have a leader that can inspire confidence and enthusiasm and who can hold it together as an organized body in spite of all difficulties, the students of the class, or at least a large part of them, will emerge from their first course of training with a strong will and spirit to acquire more knowledge and thereby equip themselves better to become worthy fighters in the cause of Communism.

The success of the study class work is to a very large extent dependent upon organization, leadership and class discipline. It should start on time and stop on time each evening. It must not accommodate itself to casual students or chronic late-comers. It should not degenerate into a mere discussion group over the general problems of the movement but must confine itself in a disciplined manner to the specific subjects dealt with in the course. It should be conducted in a businesslike fashion from start to finish, students being enrolled and the roll called each evening. Above all it should have a leader who, notwithstanding lack of previous experience, will take his task so seriously as to thoroughly master the subject himself. Then he will be able to establish sufficient authority in the class to lead it step by step to the end of the course.

A Year of Party Progress

Being a Record of Difficulties Overcome, of Party Achievements, and the Part Played Therein by the CEC and by the Minority

Published 27 December 1924

The following article defends the record of the Central Executive Committee majority against the criticisms of the minority led by party executive secretary C.E. Ruthenberg. It was signed by Cannon, William Z. Foster and Alexander Bittelman, and published in the Daily Worker *magazine supplement.*

The minority in their articles have challenged the leadership of the CEC majority. The minority charged us with lack of initiative and aggressiveness. The farmer-labor opportunists of the minority are attempting to make a case against the CEC majority for its alleged failure to foresee events and precipitate developments in the class struggle. This compels us to make a reply which will show the membership the real achievements of the party under the leadership of the present CEC.

In making our reply, we will be guided by the following considerations. First, truthfulness to facts and reality. Second, proper regard for the history of our party and for the objective conditions that were confronting our work during the past year. And, third, Leninist objectivity and mercilessness in the estimation of past performances, in admitting our own mistakes and in drawing lessons therefore for our future work.

Dangerous Inflation

This article deals with the term of office of the present Central Executive Committee, i.e., the period between January and December of 1924. It was a year full of difficulties for our party and its leadership. To mention only a few of these difficulties: the collapse of the third party alliance, the big sweep to La Follette, the breakdown of the arrangements perfected by the St. Paul convention, the change in our election policy, the bitter war of the reactionaries against our membership and sympathizers in trade unions, and, last but not least, the remnants of the internal factional struggle with an organized caucus of the minority functioning throughout the country and with the main executive office of the party, the office of executive secretary, in the hands of the minority opposition.

It was a difficult year for our party. The split of July 3 placed us in a state of isolation which threatened for a while to cut off most of our connections in the labor movement. Then came the La Follette sweep which shattered badly the basis of our farmer-labor operations. On top of this, we had to change our major policy, the third party alliance, and adjust ourselves quickly to the changed situation.

In addition to all these very serious obstacles to progress in our work, we had to be constantly on guard and at war against a peculiar state of mind of our organization which, for lack of a better name, we shall call the spirit of inflation. By this we mean disregard for objective facts and reality, dangerous self-conceit as to the strength and abilities of our party, the worship of empty phrases, and a grave lack of realism, practicability and Leninist objectivity. This inflationist spirit is the spirit of the minority.

Our party was dangerously inflated with this spirit of emptiness and fictitiousness. Conscious of this danger for quite a long time, we knew that no greater service could be rendered to our party than to deflate the party from the non-realistic, non-critical and non-Communist notions cultivated by the minority, to bring the party back to earth, making it a real, effective instrument in the class struggle. To this vital task the Central Executive Committee devoted itself in all earnestness, and today, we claim, our party is much more realistic, much more practical and, consequently, much more effective in its work than it has ever been before. The period of wild maneuvers based exclusively upon a policy of bluff, the practice of initiating campaigns and movements having no other result than an increased production of party circulars, the theory of measuring the effectiveness of Communist policy by the amount of publicity space and by the size of headlines appearing in the capitalist press, which was so typical of the former CEC, the days of such leadership, we hope, are gone forever.

The Workers Party in the Elections

As a legacy of the day of "grand maneuvers," the present Central Executive majority, immediately upon assuming office, found itself inextricably involved in the pursuit of an immediate political objective, which was totally beyond the power of our party to achieve under the prevailing circumstances. We mean the objective of creating a united farmer-labor party in the presidential elections and thereby defeating the La Follette influence upon the so-called class farmer-labor movement.

The present CEC did everything that was possible to achieve that objective. In doing so we were continually hampered by the minority in the CEC which was bent upon putting into effect the August Theses, that is, the creation of a farmer-labor party on the basis of the united front from above, instead of a real united front from the bottom with the broad farmer-labor movement upon the basis of an immediate program of partial demands. Beginning with the first meeting of the present CEC in January and up until May, our principal political efforts were directed towards one end, a national farmer-labor ticket and party as against the third party La Follette ticket. In this effort we were defeated through no fault of our own.

Why? Our answer is because La Folletteism was stronger among the masses than Communism, because petty bourgeois illusions (which mean La Folletteism) were and still are dominating the minds of the farmer-labor movement. When the old CEC, in its opportunistic rush for leadership, decided that we must set up a farmer-labor party as against a third party, it set for our party an impossible task. The present CEC majority did not realize the impossibility of this task until the June 17 convention. The situation became quite clear after the July 4 conference of the CPPA. Then grasping the situation with initiative, we cut loose from the fiction of a farmer-labor ticket and entered the elections as the Workers Party.

This represented a profound change in tactics. The party

should realize that it required courage, quick Communist thinking and much determination to make the decision and to carry it out successfully. The decision of July 8 placed the Workers Party in the elections under its own name and with its own program and candidates, thereby extricating our party from the intolerable position of compromise and opportunism involved in supporting a fictitious farmer-labor ticket. This decision we consider one of the major accomplishments of the present CEC. It was carried through in the face of bitter opposition by comrade Lovestone, minority leader, whose policy would have sacrificed the interests of the Workers Party for the fake farmer-labor party.

Were we right or wrong in putting the Workers Party in the elections under its own name? Did we or did we not manifest initiative, firmness and correct Communist understanding when we changed our policy on July 8? The party has already given the answer. Everyone in our ranks, except the incorrigible farmer-laborites, are convinced that our party made an excellent showing in the election campaign and greatly increased its prestige among the toiling masses.

Popularizing Our Program on Unemployment

It was through the second national conference of the TUEL and upon the initiative of our industrial department that our party made known for the first time its program and tactics for the organization of the unemployed. Sometime later the old CEC (now the minority), in line with its lack of sense for reality and understanding of concrete situations, proposed to immediately begin the actual organization of councils of unemployed, thereby through premature organizational steps endangering the success of what is bound to become a great movement.

Luckily for our party and for its unemployment program these premature organizational steps were not taken. The present CEC, after adopting a complete policy on unemployment at its March meeting, proceeded to popularize the issue, our unemployment program and proposed methods of organization. By instruction of the CEC majority the question of unemployment was made one of the major issues in every campaign carried on by our party on the economic and political field. In spite of all provocations of the minority, the CEC refused to begin prematurely the actual organization of councils of unemployed which because the situation was not ripe, would have resulted in complete failure, thereby wasting the efforts of the WP and discrediting a powerful organizational slogan for future use.

Our struggle against unemployment is still in its propaganda stage. During the election campaign alone the party distributed a quarter of a million leaflets on unemployment and sold 20,000 copies of a pamphlet written by comrade Browder. We are effectively propagating our demands for the unemployed and slogan of organization, thereby preparing the ground for organization work which we propose to start the moment conditions become ripe for it.

Teaching Our Party Methods of Organization

The present CEC has devoted a great deal of its attention to problems of organization, which were neglected by the former CEC. We realize that policies, programs and resolutions alone, even when correct, do not themselves build a party. When we assumed office we found that the party was totally out of balance as regards the various phases of its activities, and that systematic recruiting of new members was a matter not appreciated by the minority. The conception that the old CEC had of organization was mainly that of writing articles once in a while in the press.

We set to work to infiltrate into our party a few of the basic principles of Communist organization. At the March meeting of the CEC we adopted a statement on party activities by comrade Foster. It was an attempt to give our party a clear picture of a balanced program of party work, which proved very successful in educating our party to a better understanding of the principles of Communist organization.

This was followed up with the program of action finally adopted by the CEC at its full meeting in July. The party is well acquainted with the contents of this program. It was outlined and submitted to the CEC by the majority—the minority contributed nothing to its make-up—and was thereupon brought to our membership in a number of joint membership meetings in every large center. This program of action, with all that it stood for, was a real achievement of our party under the leadership of the present CEC.[1]

The comrades will recall the nature of the program. It included our election policy and the means of organizing the campaign in every one of its phases, political, organizational and financial. It provided for a systematic campaign to build the Workers Party through campaigns for new members. It outlined a program for the building and strengthening of the *Daily Worker.* It covered in a most thorough manner our immediate tasks on the industrial field, and also the question of shop nuclei. It laid particular stress on the unemployment situation and our program for it. It contained a special section on educational work.

It was a program not only of what to do but also of how to do it. It called for the most thorough departmentalization, from the bottom up, of every unit of the party in accord with the various specialized activities contained in the program. It also provided for an effective system of checkup and control to secure the systematic carrying out of the program of action. This program is progressively being put into operation. Insofar as our party is functioning and moving forward, it is doing so under the direction of and in line with the program of action of the CEC.

Establishing a Real Industrial Department

Another major accomplishment of the party during the past year was the establishment and perfection by the present CEC of a real Industrial Department. This department is a vital organ of our party. Through its policies, connections and machinery, our party is reaching out into the depths of the American labor movement and is establishing contact with the most elementary struggles of the organized workers. It is a real department, with subdivisions being established in every unit of the party, functioning under the direct supervision of a national committee and a national director, which in their turn are supervised and directed by the Central Executive Committee. For the first time the district

---

[1] This program of action was published in the *Daily Worker* magazine supplement of 19 July 1924. The *DW* reported that it had been adopted unanimously by the CEC at its meeting of July 8-9.

executive committees and other party units are taking serious hold of the industrial work as regular work of our party.

The department is carrying on its work in accord with a definite program, the program of the Trade Union Educational League, which is the industrial program of our party. This new program of the TUEL was submitted some six months ago by comrade Foster to the RILU and was accepted unanimously with a few additions by comrades Lozovsky, Johnson [Carl Johnson, also known as Charles E. Scott] and Dunne. On the basis of this industrial program of the party, which in many respects is a model program for the development of militant left wings in reactionary trade unions, the militants in the American unions are carrying on their work.

During the past year our comrades and sympathizers in the unions had to withstand and resist the most terrific onslaughts of the bureaucracy. In nearly every industry the left wing was compelled to carry on a bitter struggle for life, and in these struggles the industrial department of the party played a leading part. In the recent elections in the miners union and in the carpenters union the left wing was exceptionally well organized and carried on an intensive propaganda for the policies of the TUEL. The Communist strength within these unions is constantly growing. The result of these efforts shows that the left wing in such industries as mining, garments, building, transportation, metal and food is at present more definitely crystallized, more conscious of its aims and better organized now than ever before for continuing the struggle to revolutionize the trade unions.

In preparation for the El Paso convention of the AFL the Industrial Department submitted to the CEC a thorough and well-considered program. It dealt with every important issue in the labor movement, such as a general labor congress to consist of representatives of trade unions, workers' political parties, shop committees, the unemployed, etc., for the purpose of consolidating the ranks of labor politically and industrially and to launch a militant attack on the capitalist system; the recognition of Soviet Russia; abolition of racial discrimination against the Negroes; nationalization of the mines and railroads; amalgamation of the trade unions; organization of and relief for the unemployed;

demand that all the forces in the Pan-American Federation of Labor be mobilized for a struggle against American imperialism; condemnation of imperialist schemes against China; demand that the RILU plan for international unity be endorsed and the solidarity of labor be achieved; protest against criminal syndicalism laws, against the deportation of Oates, Mahler, Moran and Nigra;[2] the organization of the youth; release of Mooney, Billings, Ford, Suhr, Rangel, Cline, Sacco, Vanzetti and other political prisoners; condemnation of the Ku Klux Klan and American Legion.

This program was designed to serve as a basis of action in the trade unions to rally the masses to the left wing. Special mention should be made of the resolution "For a Labor Congress," which contains a practical program of partial demands, all of which respond to immediate burning needs of the masses, and which provides for united front action by the organized labor movement in alliance with the Workers Party. It is highly significant that all the minority contributed to making up a program for the AFL convention was a motion to add the opportunist slogan "For a 'class' farmer-labor party." They violently objected to fighting in the convention for the Workers Party.

In connection with this we must mention the convention of the Pan-American Federation of Labor held in Mexico City, Mexico. The party had its representative, comrade Johnstone, in the field with a definite program of policy and organization designed to achieve two aims. One, to promote and unify the left wing movement in the trade unions of North, Central and South America under the leadership of the RILU. Two, to coordinate the activities of the Communist parties of the United States and Mexico for common struggle against American imperialism in Latin America. The only improvement the minority could suggest to our Pan-American program was to insert some additional

---

[2] Joseph Oates, Herbert Mahler, William Moran and Pietro Nigra were all IWW men who had been tried and convicted with Big Bill Haywood in the infamous 1918 Chicago Trial. They were released as part of a general amnesty for IWW prisoners in 1923, but since they were all non-citizens their cases were turned over to the U.S. Secretary of Labor, who threatened to deport them.

commas, semicolons and incidentally an additional word.

It must be stated in passing that the minority exhibited a woeful lack of consistency and imagination when they failed to propose a Pan-American farmer-labor party as an amendment to our program. But that may come yet. It is also noteworthy that although the CEC adopted a Pan-American program upon the report of comrade Lovestone sometime in May, the executive secretary could find no better use for it than to put it in his files. Now, however, the CEC has taken the matter into its hands and is determined to see that its program is carried into effect.

Educational Activities

This was a field sadly neglected by the former CEC, who could see nothing but the Farmer-Labor Party campaign. We realized the burning need for systematic Bolshevist education in the party and at the first opportunity established a special educational department with a responsible national director, comrade Cannon, and a committee under the supervision of the CEC.

Already the party is realizing the beneficial results of the activities of the Educational Department. There have been established party schools and classes in New York, Chicago, Philadelphia and Boston, also a large network of elementary study classes in the ABC of Communism throughout the country. There are also in operation circuit study classes in the districts of Ohio, Illinois and Pennsylvania. Provisions have been made by the Educational Department for the publication of a library of Communism to contain theoretical books on the fundamentals of Leninism.

We realize that this is only a beginning, but a beginning in the right direction and with proper regard for the immediate needs of the party. The present CEC intends to remain true to its conception of a balanced program of party activities in which Bolshevist education occupies an important place.

Thesis and Work on Shop Nuclei

It was the present CEC that made the first earnest attempt to place the shop nuclei proposition as an immediate organizational task of the party.[3] Thanks to our efforts, a practical way has been found for the application of the principle of shop nuclei to the specific conditions of our own party. This practical program is embodied in a special thesis recently adopted by the CEC. This shop nuclei thesis on the most complicated and difficult organizational question confronting our party was worked out by the majority.

Months ago we set out to begin to educate our party membership to the necessity of starting the reorganization on the shop nuclei basis. Soon afterwards the first organizational steps were actually taken by our Chicago district. At present the situation is ripe enough for similar steps in a number of other districts where there is enough concentration of our members in industry to permit such action.

Strengthening the Communist Morale and Understanding of our Membership

Another major achievement of our party during the past year was the general strengthening of the morale and Communist understanding of our membership. This was no easy task to accomplish in the face of an organized minority caucus functioning throughout the country in flagrant violation of Comintern decisions, ever since the 1923 party convention and until this very hour.

The CEC majority has been working on the theory of discipline advocated by Lenin and practiced by the CI. This theory is that the basis of Communist discipline is confidence of the membership in the leading men and committees of the party and that this confidence can be won only in one way, namely, by the ability of the party to develop and apply correct political strategy and tactics. To win the confidence of the membership in our ability to give the party correct Communist leadership—this was the great ambition of the present CEC. It was for this reason that representatives of the CEC frequently addressed joint membership

---

[3] The Comintern's Bolshevization campaign, inaugurated in 1924, decreed that the basic unit of organization of all Communist parties was to be the shop or factory cell (nucleus).

meetings to familiarize the party with the plans and objectives of the CEC. And in every such instance the CEC received the almost unanimous approval of the rank and file of the party.

We attempted on numerous occasions to liquidate the organized illegal opposition of the minority. It was comrade Foster who immediately upon his return from Russia made a motion in the CEC providing for a special committee, consisting of an equal number of representatives of the CEC and of the minority, to remove the factional basis of our disagreements and to liquidate the organized opposition of the minority. We met the minority more than halfway. We conceded them a number of important organization appointments as an indication of our willingness to work with them on the basis of mutual confidence; we submitted our program of action, a major achievement of our party, not directly to the CEC, but first to the minority group in order that they might identify themselves with it and thus share in the credit of initiating the program. We regret to say that the minority, although always willing to accept our concessions, never for a moment relinquished its caucus organization and systematic opposition. This fact, together with the additional fact that the executive secretary of the party belonged to the minority opposition, made it very difficult for the CEC to put into effect more fully all its policies and decisions. The latest attempt to pacify the opposition was initiated by comrade Cannon on the eve of the party discussion, with the idea of removing if possible the purely factional sting from differences of opinion on policy. We proposed informal discussions with the minority of the immediate political tasks of the party in order to ascertain whether or not a common basis of policy could be found, but the minority was more intent upon discussing the make-up of the next CEC and similar questions of party control than problems of policy. This made it impossible for us to proceed, because we held to the Bolshevist principle that the basis of unity in a Communist party is agreement on policy and not the arbitrary division of organizational control. The minority, however, thought otherwise; consequently our latest attempt to liquidate the organized minority opposition came to naught. A further reason is now clear: the minority is one of the right wing tendencies in the party.

But the party as a whole, if not the minority, responded

splendidly to every effort of the CEC to improve the morale and understanding of the organization. The membership particularly appreciated the readiness of the CEC to admit mistakes and to correct them quickly, something that the minority never dares to do, even in the case of their pet third party alliance which was rejected by the Communist International. Till this very day the minority cannot muster the courage to say whether the Comintern was right or wrong.

In our ideological struggle against the remnants of the Two and a Half International we have been making steady progress, despite the numerous tactless provocations of the minority, which went as far as supplying misinformation to the CEC. We adhered strictly to the tactics of the CI, applied to Serrati, Smeral and many others, which was to defeat these Two and a Half International tendencies ideologically, to prove them wrong and politically bankrupt in the eyes of the membership, to win all the proletarian elements of the party to the point of view of the CI, and to compel the carrying out of the policies of the CI when necessary even by means of disciplinary measures. Together with the CI we realized that the Bolshevization of our party is not a one-act affair, to be accomplished overnight by means of senseless persecutions, but a process of education and merciless ideological struggle against Menshevism, opportunism and centrism. This was the policy of the CEC majority carried out daily in every phase of its activities. We fought to the best of our abilities every deviation from the CI policies, such as the remnants of the ideology of the Two and a Half International, the right wing farmer-laborist tendency, as well as those temporary deviations of which we ourselves have been guilty. We strained all our efforts to draw into party leadership, to bring to the fore, all the proletarian elements of the party, the active workers from the shops. And in contradistinction from the pseudo-intellectuals of the minority, we believe that our movement is essentially a proletarian movement and that its ideology and psychology must be permeated with that of the class-conscious revolutionary proletariat.

As a result of these efforts our party is now ideologically more homogeneous than ever before in its history. The attendance at branch meetings is now better, the internal life of our branches is richer and more intensive. The dues payments have never been so high as they are at present. Our party is continually growing in numbers. We are getting better organized and more closely knit together. All this makes us feel confident that our party is now on the right road to become an important factor in the everyday struggles of the American workers.

The *Daily Worker*

A major achievement of the CEC has been the management and operation of the *Daily Worker*. Instead of founding only our daily paper with the fund raised last year, as was planned by the former CEC, we have purchased a building to house the *Daily Worker* and the national office of the party as well, and have established a modern and complete printing plant to take care of all the party's printing. The management of the mechanical department of this plant as well as the office end has been economical and efficient in the extreme, to the end that the deficit of the *Daily Worker* for 1924 is much lower than we had dared to hope (only $20,000).

But it was not this phase of the work which brought the party its greatest gains. Nor have the education and propaganda values of the *Daily Worker* been its chief advantages. It has been in the field of organization that the *Daily Worker* has brought us the greatest benefits. For due to the planful organizational methods used in the *Daily Worker*, the organizing of the army of agents, we have developed a rich field for making new mass contacts. Instead of a haphazard attempt at building circulation, an organized army of subscription agents is being developed who are not simply sub hustlers, but actually rapidly developing, capable organizers for the party. The formalizing of this organization into the *Daily Worker* builders is another step in advance which is already yielding further results.

Centralizing the Party Press

The decentralized state of our party press, which the CEC inherited from its preceding administration, was an outrage and a nuisance. The *Weekly Worker* was printed in one place and edited and managed in another. The *Liberator*, *Labor Herald*, and *Soviet Russia Pictorial* all had separate editorial staffs and administration.

The party Literature Department had another. As long ago as last January the CEC decided to eliminate this waste and inefficiency.

The first step was the amalgamation of the three monthly magazines into the *Workers Monthly.* Thus the party has one monthly official organ instead of three, and instead of three editors and two assistants, there is only one editor. The *Daily Worker* has taken charge of the management of the *Workers Monthly,* and with the addition of one office girl to its staff, it does the work formerly done by the three business administrations which employed from four to five persons. The resultant saving to our party in wages alone amounts to over $12,000 a year.

But the monetary saving is not the only nor by any means the greatest achievement. The centralizing of the production of our monthly with the *Daily Worker* makes it possible to produce both a better daily and a better monthly. The centralizing of the distribution makes it easier to increase the circulation of both the *Daily Worker* and the *Workers Monthly.*

The CEC has now decided to centralize in a similar manner the party's Literature Department, so that beginning the first of the year, the *Daily Worker* will be charged with the administration and distribution of this important arm of our party. This will not only make new savings for the party, but also because of centralizing of the selling machinery the party will for the first time begin really to permeate the working class with Communist books and pamphlets.

Shortcomings to Be Overcome

We should not close our eyes to a number of shortcomings in our activities. Some of our language sections are not as yet sufficiently close to the party organization. Communist work among women employed in industry, among the Negro masses, and among the agricultural workers and poor farmers has hardly begun. This much, however, must be placed on record, that the present CEC majority succeeded in relieving the party of several very harmful notions of the minority regarding the policies and forms of organization to be applied by our party in its work among women, the Negroes, and the agricultural proletariat, at the same time formulating correct policies for our future work.

The party is now fully equipped to proceed successfully in these comparatively new fields of activity.

United Front Activities

One of the signs that our party is finally beginning to get the proper perspective in the estimation of events and in formulating its policies is the recent decision of the CEC to establish a permanent commission on the united front. The duty of this commission, which is a subcommittee of the CEC, is to continually survey the field of class struggle and to formulate for the CEC policies and plans of organization for united front campaigns on the basis of immediate burning issues in the life of the toiling masses.

At present we are beginning to develop such united front campaigns against child labor, and for the release of Sacco and Vanzetti. The subcommittee is preparing the outlines of policy and organization for a campaign against the so-called criminal syndicalism laws and for the release of class war prisoners. It is our intention, in accord with the decisions of the Fifth Congress of the CI, to seize upon every burning issue in the life of the masses, for united front action against the capitalists and against their agents in the labor movement. This plan to systematize the united front campaign was entirely the work of the CEC majority.

The Party Discussion

We want the party to remember that it was the present CEC that created the opportunity for our membership to discuss thoroughly and express itself on our immediate tasks. The whole plan for conducting the party discussion was presented by the CEC majority. We took the greatest care to so organize the discussion as to secure the maximum freedom of expression for the minority and to crystallize opinion for all views and tendencies in the party. Last year, on the contrary, when we were in the minority, we were denied by the Pepper group even the right to defend our policies in the various district conventions.

To us the party is the party membership. The success of the party depends upon the consciousness, initiative, and activity of every party member. The present CEC fully realizes that the strength of a Communist party rests mainly on the Bolshevist quality of its rank and file and leadership and upon the bonds of mutual confidence that exist between the two. We are therefore determined to do all in our power to deepen the Bolshevist quality of our party as a whole, and to strengthen the existing bonds of mutual confidence between the party membership and the party leadership.

The minority has challenged the leadership of the CEC majority. In reply we say, let the record speak. We do not propose to follow in the footsteps of the minority and to bluff the party into the belief that under our leadership the party has already conquered the world. Instead, we will ask the party membership to examine our actual achievements. The party will then see that it has been making continual progress despite all difficulties, that we have extended our influence and strengthened our organization, and that now we are making an effort to rid the party completely of the old spirit of inflation and farmer-laboristic opportunism. We are on the right road to building the Workers Party into a mass Communist party.

A Statement on Two and a Half Internationalism

Published 27 December 1924

The following article attacks the Central Executive Committee minority led by C.E. Ruthenberg for hampering the struggle against Ludwig Lore, who was at the time the editor of the party's German-language paper, the Volkszeitung, *and leader of an important group of trade unionists in the New York Workers Party. The article was published in the* Daily Worker *magazine supplement and was signed by Cannon, William Z. Foster, Alexander Bittelman, Earl Browder, Fahle Burman, William F. Dunne and Martin Abern—the entire CEC majority minus Lore.*

In view of the present situation in the party, we find it necessary to make a statement regarding our struggle to eradicate the Two and a Half International tendencies in our party.

In its recent decision on the Farmer-Labor Party, the Comintern pointed out the existence in our party of remnants of the ideology of the Two and a Half International, as exemplified by some of the writings of comrade Lore. The CI called upon us to wage a sharp ideological struggle against these tendencies. This the CEC has done and will continue to do until the entire party is completely won over to the point of view of Leninism and the CI. These efforts of the CEC to defeat ideologically the Two and a Half International tendencies were hampered and weakened by the tactics of the minority opposition.

Our tactics for combatting the remnants of the ideology of the Two and a Half International in our party were the same as the tactics applied by the CI in other Communist parties, notably in the cases of Serrati in Italy and Smeral in Czechoslovakia. These tactics can be grouped under the following three heads: (1) to defeat ideologically and politically these tendencies, to prove them wrong in the eyes of our membership and followers; (2) to strengthen in our party the ideology and prestige of Leninism and of the CI; (3) to compel under all circumstances full execution of every party member and every party unit of all decisions of the CI and of the CEC even by means of disciplinary measures. These principles have been successfully applied by the Comintern.

In pursuit of these aims the present CEC took sharp issue with the remnants of the ideology of the Two and a Half International when these manifested themselves in the activities of some of our comrades in the industrial field in the printers union, in the needle trades, in the miners union, and in several other labor organizations. In all instances the CEC immediately sent its representatives to instruct and direct these comrades to the Leninist point of view. The CEC took prompt action in every single instance when the *Volkszeitung* or any other party organ manifested deviations from the CI line of policy.

Through its educational department the CEC laid the basis for spreading Leninist ideology among our membership. Our party schools, study classes, and our press have been utilized in every possible way, through articles by comrades Zinoviev, Stalin, Kamenev and others to strengthen the Bolshevist ideology of our party. By a recent decision of the CEC the powerful speeches by comrades Kamenev and Stalin against Trotskyism were ordered printed in pamphlet form.

It was also by a decision of the CEC that comrade Olgin wrote his series of three articles explaining the decision of the CI regarding the deviations of comrade Lore. All these efforts have contributed greatly towards the Bolshevization of our party.

In this ideological campaign we have been persistently hampered by the minority opposition. *The tactics proposed by the minority always tended to crystallize the tendency of the Two and a Half International and not to dissolve it or break it up. Every move of the minority strengthened the position of this tendency.* The minority carried on a senseless campaign of petty personal persecution, going to the extent of furnishing misinformation to the CEC on two important occasions, whose only effect was to create sympathy for and strengthen the prestige of those who have been charged by the CI as manifesting remnants of the ideology of the Two and a Half International.

Not in a single instance did the leaders of the minority under their own names take issue publicly in the party press with any individual of this tendency inside or outside of our party. This was done, however, by members of the majority, as witness the above mentioned articles by Olgin, the debate of Foster against Nearing, Cannon's speech in the Workers School in New York on the Bolshevization of our party which was ordered published in the *Workers Monthly*, and the articles by Bittelman against Salutsky and Boudin.

The minority felt no responsibility for the welfare of the party. For this reason they were continually trying to provoke the CEC to such action as would create a crisis in the party, if not an actual split, and thereby strengthen the very tendencies which it is our duty to combat. All through the year the minority by their foolish tactics have been building up the Two and a Half International tendency. Now they are strengthening the right wing of the party generally by their advocacy of an opportunistic farmer-labor party policy.

The minority showed its utter disregard for the CI decisions by maintaining a permanent caucus throughout the country at the very time when the CI was fighting militantly against such manifestations of Trotskyism in the Russian and other parties.

The inevitable result of such a reckless policy as the minority proposes would be a disastrous split, which would cost the party large numbers of valuable proletarian elements, and which would strengthen the Two and a Half International tendencies. On the other hand, the policy of the CEC, which is the policy of the Comintern, will Bolshevize these proletarian elements and stamp out anti-Leninist deviations.

Ours is a young party, it has many unripe elements within it, and the task of Bolshevizing them is a difficult one. It can only be accomplished along the lines now being followed by the CEC, that is by a patient, persistent, intelligent, strategical, determined, relentless application of the principles of Leninism.

Controversial Questions in the Workers Party of America

ca. February-March 1925

The following article by Cannon and William Z. Foster is evidently an early draft of an article published under the title "The American Question" in both the German- and Russian-language editions of the Communist International *No. 3 (1925), which appeared around the time of the Fifth Plenum of the Comintern Executive Committee in March-April 1925. The plenum was to rule on the disputed questions in the Workers Party, and an article by American minority leader C.E. Ruthenberg was also published in the same journal. This unpublished English-language draft manuscript of the Foster-Cannon article is from the Max Shachtman Collection in the Tamiment Institute Library, New York University, and appears here by permission of the Institute.*

While the published German/Russian version and the English draft of this article are for the most part similar, there are a few substantive differences. The published version eliminates some of the direct attacks on John Pepper, and also omits the direct statement: "The split at the Chicago July 3rd, 1923 convention was disastrous." Moreover, in the German/Russian version the final three sections of the article, which deal with the internal factional situation in the Workers Party, are missing. Instead, a much shorter section on the Workers Party's internal situation is incorporated in the middle of the article. This section notes that the Foster-Cannon group's "tactics consist of carrying out active ideological struggle against Two and a Half Internationalist tendencies in the Workers Party. The group has published many articles condemning and rejecting these right-wing deviations. It has consistently taken a position against every manifestation of Trotskyism." Such a bald statement of anti-Trotskyism is missing from the English draft.

Economic and Political Situation

In the United States the capitalists have succeeded, since the Civil War, in keeping control over the various social classes, petty bourgeoisie, farmers, workers, etc., through the two big parties, Republican and Democratic. These parties are completely dominated by the big capitalists and are used to further their interests at the expense of the other classes following their lead. In the past 50 years sections of the petty bourgeoisie, farmers and workers have made various attempts to break the domination of the two capitalist parties and to establish a third party. Such breakaway movements have been most intense during industrial and agricultural crises. The most important of them were the Greenback Movement of the 1870s, the People's Party of the 1890s, and the Roosevelt Progressive Party of 1912. But all these movements failed to establish a third party. The economic driving power behind them was insufficient.

The outstanding feature of the present political situation in the United States is the development of another movement of the petty bourgeoisie, farmers and workers against the two old parties. This is the La Follette third party movement. It originates in the agricultural and industrial crisis, and in the continued intensification of capitalist exploitation. The petty bourgeoisie find themselves confronted by ruthless combinations of capital which are rooting out competition in every field of production and distribution. The farmers are faced by powerful capitalist monopolies, which on the one hand rob them of their products, and on the other charge them exorbitant prices for all manufactured commodities. They are being progressively impoverished and expropriated. In 1920, 38 percent of all American farmers were tenants, and 37 percent of those who technically owned their farms were encumbered by mortgages amounting to $3,356 on an average. Tenancy and the mortgage system are developing rapidly, especially during the past few years. In 1910 the mortgage debts of the United States amounted to $1,727,172,983, and by 1920 it had increased to $4,003,767,192. During 1922 about 1,200,000 persons left the farms and went to the cities.

The workers are under still greater pressure from capitalism. The bulk of them lack the elemental necessities of life. It is only the small fringe of well-organized skilled workers in the building trades, the printing industry, and on the railroads, etc., who receive the high wages that have been so widely advertised. In 1922 the railroad union leaders maintained that full-time wages of the organized skilled shop mechanics could not purchase the vital necessities necessary to maintain their families at even the lowest level of safety. The shop mechanics' wages, which have since been heavily cut, amounted to only $1,884.90 per year as against $2,303.99 per year called for in the budget of living issued by the United States Department of Labor. In 1924 the average wage throughout the United States was only $25 per week, or $1,300 per year. The unskilled workers in the industries live in real poverty, and as for the millions of agricultural workers, they are the most bitterly exploited and have the lowest standard of living. Unemployment is a constant scourge of the workers. In 1922 there were 6,000,000 out of work. It is estimated that there are at least 1,500,000 constantly unemployed. There are no state doles. The workers are denied practically all say in the control of industry and in the establishment of their own working conditions. Of the approximately 30,000,000 wage workers, only 3,500,000 are organized, and the existence of even their weak organizations is constantly threatened by the open shop drive of the employers.

The Republican and Democratic parties are the instruments of big capital and are devoted to its service. The government, whether controlled by either party, discriminates against the petty bourgeoisie by favoring concentrated industry and by choking out competition everywhere. It harasses the farmers by high tariffs and by general support of the farmers' immediate enemies, the meatpackers, bankers, railroad owners, etc. It crushes the workers strikes with injunctions, police and troops, and it openly assists the employers in their constant "open shop" drives. In 1920 it was the Democratic Attorney General, Palmer, who secured a federal injunction against the 600,000 coal miners, denying them the right to strike, and in 1922, it was the Republican Attorney General, Daugherty, who got an injunction against the 400,000 striking railroad mechanics. The government, whether Republican or Democrat, shifts the burden of the World War debt from the shoulders of the capitalists to those of the workers. Consequent upon this inevitable failure to represent the interests of these classes, the two old parties are seething with discontent. Masses of petty bourgeoisie, farmers and workers are becoming disillusioned with them and are tending to break away and to form a new party. This mass movement is the so-called La Follette third party movement.

The present third party movement, under the pressure of the agricultural and industrial crisis, has been definitely crystallizing for the past several years. Its organization point, loose and vague, was the La Follette group of the so-called progressives in Congress. Most of these came from the western agricultural states, as a result of the work of the Non-Partisan League and other farmer organizations, and the trade unions. In 1918 the trade unions began to become active in the third party movement, expressing themselves for a "labor party," although conceiving it in the sense of a petty bourgeois third party. The Chicago Federation of Labor and other bodies declared for a "labor party." In the next couple of years the federations in Michigan, Wisconsin, Illinois, Pennsylvania, etc., together with several national unions, also favored the movement. In 1920 the labor party group, headed by John Fitzpatrick of Chicago, held a national convention. Many farmers also came. The convention launched the Farmer-Labor Party of the United States, an alliance of workers and farmers, and put up as its candidate for president Parley Parker Christensen. At this convention the "Committee of 48," a loose grouping of petty bourgeois elements, participated. Third parties, calling themselves Farmer-Labor Partics, sprang up in Minnesota, Washington, South Dakota, Colorado, etc. The Gompers bureaucracy bitterly opposed the whole movement, being firmly attached to the policy of supporting "friends" on the tickets of the two old parties.

In February 1922, at Chicago, a fresh development took place by the organization of the Conference for Progressive Political Action. The basis of this organization was the 16 railroad unions. Around them rallied practically all the labor unions, farmers organizations and Farmer-Labor Parties that favored breaking from the two old parties. The Socialist Party also participated. Many expected that the CPPA would definitely launch the looked-for third party, but its leaders were too weak. In December 1922, the CPPA went on record for a modified form of the old Gompers non-partisan policy. The Farmer-Labor Party of the U.S. then split from it and many other organizations dropped away. The

CPPA became a skeleton. The whole third party movement was checked.

With the approach of the presidential elections in 1924, the demand for a third party flared up afresh. It was given impetus by the agricultural crisis which through 1922 and 1923 was intense, and by the slowing down of industry and the discharge of hundreds of thousands of workers in the winter of 1923-24. The Conference for Progressive Political Action called a convention for July 4th in Cleveland. La Follette assumed active leadership of the whole movement. At the July 4th convention he announced himself as candidate for president of the United States on an independent ticket without actually forming a party. Immediately after the July 4th convention, practically every organization in the country, except the Workers Party, that favored independent political action rallied to his support. Gompers gave La Follette the endorsement of the American Federation of Labor, and Debs hailed him as a champion of the workers. The petty bourgeois united front was quite complete, from La Follette to Gompers and Debs.

The election campaign was one of the most sharply contested in the history of the United States. The capitalist press attacked La Follette viciously. Although merely demanding government ownership of the railroads and water power and government regulation of other key industries, his program was bitterly denounced as Bolshevistic and destructive of all organized government. The capitalists told the workers that if they voted for La Follette factories would be immediately closed. A lessening of the agricultural and industrial crisis also adversely effected the La Follette movement. About September 1924, an improvement set in in the conditions of agriculture and industry. Due to world shortage of wheat the prices of that and other grains went to record figures, and the spirit of revolt amongst the farmers began to evaporate. The industries also began to pick up somewhat with increased production, which is continuing up to the present, and which has partially reduced the unemployment of the workers.

Consequent upon this terrorization of the workers and the lessening of the agricultural and industrial crisis, Coolidge won a sweeping victory at the polls. Whereas the supporters of La

Follette had expected the latter to carry enough states to prevent either Coolidge or Davis from getting a majority of the electoral votes and thus to throw the election into Congress, he succeeded in carrying only Wisconsin. This came as a big defeat to many of the labor bureaucrats and their followers in the La Follette movement. They lost their enthusiasm for a third party. Gompers and the AFL declared emphatically for the old non-partisan policy, and the railroad unions, backbone of the CPPA, did the same. The crystallization of the third party received a setback.

The Farmer-Labor Policy of the Workers Party

In the development of this mass movement the Workers Party took a most active part. For two and a half years, beginning early in 1922 with the slogan of "For a Farmer-Labor Party," it carried on a vigorous campaign to tear loose the masses of workers and poor farmers from the petty bourgeois leadership of La Follette and to organize them into a separate party. But these efforts were futile so far as creating a party was concerned. The first attempt to launch the so-called "class" farmer-labor party took place on July 3rd, 1923. This convention was held on a united front basis with the Workers Party and the Farmer-Labor Party of the United States, headed by John Fitzpatrick. Many organizations, trade unions, cooperatives, fraternal societies, which in the previous campaign had endorsed the farmer-labor party slogan as in some degree expressing their demand for a third party, sent delegates. About half a million workers and a scattering of farmers were represented. The Workers Party demanded the immediate formation of a new Federated Farmer-Labor Party. The Farmer-Labor Party of the United States was opposed and a split took place. The control of the convention fell into the hands of the Workers Party which then launched the Federated Farmer-Labor Party, based upon trade unions, cooperatives and other proletarian bodies.

The FFLP was stillborn. The masses immediately fell away from it. They wanted a petty bourgeois third party movement, not a semi-Communist "class" party of only workers and poor farmers. The Workers Party made a desperate effort to breathe the breath of life into the FFLP, expending great energy and resources upon it, but this effort failed completely. The masses would have nothing to do with the FFLP. It did not become a mass organization which could be used as a feeder for the WP. On the contrary, it became a rival tending to liquidate the Workers Party. It consisted of only the Workers Party and its closest sympathizing organizations. It was merely a "united front with ourselves," a distortion of the united front tactics peculiar to America. Thus we had practically two Communist parties, that is, the Workers Party and the Federated Farmer-Labor Party. The situation became so intolerable that the FFLP, which the Pepper-Ruthenberg group hailed as one of the greatest achievements of the world Communist movement, had to be abandoned.

Somewhat staggered by the failure of the Federated Farmer-Labor Party, the Workers Party nevertheless launched a fresh attempt to found the so-called "class" farmer-labor party. This culminated in the convention in St. Paul on June 17th, 1924. By this time the La Follette leaders were rapidly organizing their forces for the national elections in November. Foreseeing the danger of the absorption of the Farmer-Labor elements by the La Follette movement for a third party, the Workers Party proposed then an alliance be made between the two movements. This was the so-called "third party alliance." The outcome of it would have been that both movements, or rather the two sections of the one movement, as it later proved, would have endorsed La Follette. But the Comintern correctly forbade the "third party alliance," declaring that it would make of the Workers Party a tail for the petty bourgeois kite.

The La Follette leaders sharply attacked the St. Paul convention as being dominated by the Communists. They called upon the masses to rally to their convention on July 4th. Their call found a ready response. Practically all the trade unions, farmers organizations and other bodies which had supported the slogan, "For a 'class' farmer-labor party," joined the mass movement towards them. Consequently the June 17th convention was practically cut to pieces. It consisted merely of Communists, their close sympathizers, and a scattering of lukewarm trade unionists and farmers. Nevertheless, in a determined effort to give life to the slogan they had propagated for over two years, the WP delegates, who controlled the convention, launched a new party, the National Farmer-Labor Party, and placed in the field its candidates for president and vice president, MacDonald and Bouck.

But this party collapsed even more quickly than did the Federated Farmer-Labor Party. With the AFL, the railroad unions, the Socialist Party, and the state Farmer-Labor Parties all over the country gone to La Follette, the National Farmer-Labor Party was isolated. Comprising only Communists and close sympathizers, it was another case of a "united front with ourselves." This placed the Workers Party in a most difficult situation. To have gone through the campaign supporting MacDonald and Bouck would have been to gravely sacrifice the interests of the Workers Party by shoving it into the background and bringing the skeleton Communistic National Farmer-Labor Party to the fore. The Workers Party would have furnished all the resources and done all of the work, but got none of the credit. And in return the National Farmer-Labor Party could not have brought greater masses under its influence than the Workers Party could by campaigning directly under its own name. It was only another Communist Party. Hence the Central Executive Committee threw overboard the make-believe mass National Farmer-Labor Party and placed in the field its own candidates, Foster and Gitlow. Thus, after a two and a half year campaign for the farmer-labor party in the midst of the developing third party movement, the Workers Party was unable to get together enough of a "class" farmer-labor party to make it possible to run it in the election campaign. The movement had no mass support. The action of the CEC was received with enthusiasm all through the Workers Party.

These experiences made several facts stand forth, clear and indisputable, which must be taken into consideration in the working out of the united front policies of the Workers Party. The first is that the Workers Party greatly overestimated the degree of class consciousness of the workers in its campaign for a "class" farmer-labor party. Their support of the La Follette movement showed that the masses are still intensely petty bourgeois in their ideology. In fact, in order to get the support of the AFL and the trade unions generally, La Follette had to go to the right by dropping his demands for the recognition of Soviet Russia. These masses are not ripe for a "class" farmer-labor party such as the Workers Party advocated. Their wholesale flocking to the standard of La Follette proved this. Another important factor is that our every attempt to build a middle-of-the-road farmer-labor party between the Workers Party and the La Follette movement resulted merely in the creation of a new Communist labor party, only Communists and sympathizers joining it. Such a party must be a rival and liquidator of the Workers Party. The elements that become disillusioned with La Folletteism at the present stage of development are advanced enough either to be brought directly into the Workers Party as members or to come under its influence through the united front maneuvers upon the basis of concrete issues of the everyday struggles.

In the early phases of its farmer-labor party campaign, the Workers Party gained much valuable publicity and experience, but attempts to form farmer-labor parties prematurely led to very costly splits and isolation. The split at the Chicago July 3rd, 1923 convention was disastrous. The Trade Union Educational League had developed many valuable rank and file connections in the trade unions. These were used as the basis for the farmer-labor party campaign. When the split took place and the FFLP was formed, these sympathizers, who were not ready for such a step, broke away from the Communists not only on the farmer-labor question, but also for the amalgamation, unemployment and other campaigns being carried on by the party in the unions. This split practically broke the connections of the Workers Party in the trade unions and threw the center of gravity of the farmer-labor party movement among the farmers. The Pepper-Ruthenberg group (then the majority) practically abandoned work in the trade unions and concentrated their efforts on the farmers. The present majority, comprising principally the trade union elements in the Workers Party, objected to this shifting of gravity from the industrial workers to the farmers. A bitter controversy developed, which will be outlined further along.

The ill-fated National Farmer-Labor Party, formed at the St. Paul June 17th, 1924 convention, cut off more valuable connections of the party in the mass organizations. The present isolation of the Workers Party and the crippling of the Trade Union Educational League are due to the ill-advised attempts to found the "class" farmer-labor party of industrial workers and poor farmers in the absence of mass sentiment for such a party. This policy is a policy of "putschism," which, under the formula of "contact with the masses," leads in actual practice to isolation and sectarianism.

The Present Controversy Over the Farmer-Labor Party Policy

Just before the November elections a sharp division developed in the Central Executive Committee of the Workers Party on the question of the farmer-labor party policy. The majority group took a determined stand against any further attempts to form caricature farmer-labor parties and declared for a true united front policy of putting forward concrete and understandable slogans based on the everyday struggles of the workers. The minority group took the position that now more than ever the campaign for the "class" farmer-labor party had to be pushed.

The controversy was then laid before the membership for discussion. Mass membership meetings were held in all the important party centers. These gave a substantial majority vote for the theses of the CEC majority.[1] New York, Chicago, Boston, Philadelphia, Pittsburgh, Minneapolis and other large party centers voted for the majority theses. The reports in the *Daily Worker* show that in the 50 cities voting, the majority theses received 2,400 votes and the minority 1,590. All the important cities that had been active in the farmer-labor party campaign voted without exception for the majority theses. The Young Workers League also strongly supported the majority theses.

The central question in the present controversy is whether or not we shall organize the Workers Party forces in the trade unions and other proletarian organizations into a Communistic labor party. The minority champions such a program. The majority opposes it, insisting that wherever the labor party movement takes shape it must have a broad mass character. The controversy over this central issue has gone on with varying degrees of intensity since the organization of the Federated Farmer-Labor Party in July 1923. This has brought about a sharp factional situation, in which the minority has seized upon practically every party policy to utilize for factional purposes. But all the issues in the present

[1] Both the Foster-Cannon majority and the Ruthenberg-Lovestone minority had written theses on the tasks of the Workers Party. See note, pp. 244-245.

dispute revolve around the central question of whether or not the Workers Party shall organize a left wing farmer-labor party.

The theoretical expression of the minority policy of organizing a Communistic labor party was first given in the August (1923) Theses, which still remain the guiding principle of the minority in their farmer-labor policy. These theses were written in support of the Federated Farmer-Labor Party. The formation of this party was a tactical mistake. But instead of admitting it and realigning the Workers Party policies accordingly, comrades Pepper and Ruthenberg wrote theses to justify its existence. These were the so-called August Theses, in which they developed the theory of several competing labor parties in the United States. According to this theory the minority proposes to break off such sections of the labor movement as respond to the "class" farmer-labor party slogan and to combine them into a farmer-labor party, a party under the leadership of the Communists, with the object of transforming this hodgepodge into a "mass Communist party." The August Theses say:

> In America we have a number of political groups which fight for influence within the trade union movement. The attempt to gain influence upon the workers assumes the organizational expression of forming various labor parties. The Socialist Party tries to form a labor party. The old Farmer-Labor Party tries to form another labor party. The Workers Party has helped in the formation of the Federated Farmer-Labor Party. It is simply a dogmatic statement to decree that it is against the rules of the game for several labor parties to attempt to exist in one country.

And again:

> It is our duty to attempt through very careful, cautious propaganda and systematic campaigns to transform the Federated into a mass Communist party.

The CEC minority (now the majority) opposed the policy of organizing the Communists and sympathizers into a left wing Communist labor party which was bound to be a rival party and a liquidating influence for the Workers Party. We stated our general position in our thesis of November 1923, as follows:

> The organization of premature and artificial labor parties, as the theses of the majority (Pepper-Ruthenberg group) virtually propose, makes a caricature out of the very idea of the labor party and runs

> the danger of discrediting it. The Workers Party cannot assume the responsibility of such undertakings without injuring its standing in the eyes of the workers.

And further:

> Our position is not based on the assumption that the entire labor movement must join the labor party at once or that even a majority is necessary. But we hold that wherever it is formed, it must unite the labor party forces and have a genuine mass character.

Regarding the theory of transforming the Federated into a mass Communist party, our November 1923 thesis said:

> The August Theses make the argument that the Federated Farmer-Labor Party can be developed into a mass Communist party. There is no foundation for such an assertion. The conditions for the building of a mass Communist party are the existence of a closely knit Communist nucleus operating within the broadest mass organizations of the workers, permeating them with its doctrines and sweeping the most advanced of them into its ranks. The Workers Party is such a Communist nucleus and the naturally developing labor party movement is such a mass organization. By working within this mass organization and pushing it forward, the Workers Party is bound to expand and extend its influence. The organization of the FFLP does not facilitate this development, but interferes with it. Wherever it takes organizational form it separates the Communists and their closest sympathizers from the main body of the movement and creates the conditions for a sectarian Communist party controlling a sectarian labor party.

In the present phase of the 18-months-long controversy over the organization of a Communist farmer-labor party, the CEC minority reiterates its determination to form such a party by the following typical statement of policy in its latest theses:

> We shall mobilize all the "class" farmer-labor elements with which we have contact and which are now affiliated to the La Follette Progressive organization for the campaign against this as a liberal third capitalist party and not a labor party and to have them raise the slogan of a class farmer-labor party and split away from the La Follette movement.

As against this conception of organizing a "left class farmer-labor party," the CEC majority reaffirms its previous position that the labor party can be formed only if it is based on the broad organizations of the masses. The experience of the past two and a half years conclusively shows that no sentiment exists among the workers for the formation of such a "class" farmer-labor party, as against the La Follette third party movement. Hence, under existing conditions, a campaign for the formation of the farmer-labor party is out of the realm of practical politics. In this regard our latest theses say:

> The fundamental conditions determining the attitude of our party toward the farmer-labor movement are the same now as at the beginning of our experience in this field on the basis of united front tactics of the Communist International. At the time when the farmer-labor movement was developing a mass character, moving in the direction of an independent party, it was correct for our party itself to raise the slogan of "a farmer-labor party" and participate actively in the movement for it. When, as became apparent in July 1924, and as it is apparent now, the idea of a farmer-labor party lacks mass support and appeal among industrial workers and poor farmers, the basic reasons for our support of this movement are not in existence. The Workers Party, therefore, cannot advantageously promulgate the slogan of "a farmer-labor party" at the present time. The further development of the class struggle may eventually again create a mass sentiment for the formation of a farmer-labor party. In such case the Workers Party may find it advantageous to again raise the slogan for such a party and actively participate in the movement for it. Our attitude towards it will depend on the advantages it offers to the Workers Party from the standpoint of promoting independent political action on a mass scale and of building the Workers Party into a mass Communist party.

The CEC majority position is against the organization of a left wing farmer-labor party, a rival of the Workers Party, and is in favor of concrete, united front struggle around living issues in the workers' lives. This policy is based upon the realistic appreciation of the present situation in America. Our experience during the past two and a half years, and especially during the recent elections, demonstrates that the political development of the American workers is much more elementary than we had calculated in our farmer-labor party campaign. They are still bound ideologically to the bourgeoisie and petty bourgeoisie. Even those workers prepared to break with the two parties of big capital are merely transferring their allegiance to the petty bourgeoisie. Their class consciousness is only faintly dawning. Their conception of independent political action is that of a petty bourgeois third party movement, as is evidenced by the fact that practically all those labor organizations which had endorsed resolutions for a farmer-labor party supported La Follette in the elections without considering it any retrogression from their previous stand. In fact, many of the state sections of the La Follette movement, ideologically and organizationally bound to it, call themselves Farmer-Labor Parties: for example, Minnesota, South Dakota, Montana, Washington, etc. There is no considerable body of workers anywhere, outside of the Workers Party itself, who stand clearly for the organization of a "class" farmer-labor party, or who would respond to such a slogan and join such a party.

United front slogans must be of such a nature as to appeal to wide masses of the workers. They must be concrete and understandable, and capable of enabling the party to set a mass movement into motion. Under present conditions in America the main campaign of the party must be the effort to lead the workers and poor farmers into action and struggle on the basis of concrete burning questions affecting their daily lives. The Workers Party, while concentrating its main energies on its efforts to draw the unions as organizations into economic and political united front struggles over concrete issues, should advocate the idea of the trade unions entering into political action independently as organizations, and of their forming an alliance with the tenant and mortgage farmers under the leadership of the workers. But the slogan of the labor party should be put forth in an organizational sense only in those circumstances where it has or is capable of developing mass support. It should not be used in such a sense as to exaggerate the role and possibilities of a labor party or to obscure the identity and leading role of the Workers Party. The labor party should be formed only under conditions where it secures genuine mass support from the unions. The creation of so-called "left wing" labor parties, which amount in practice to little more than the Workers Party and its closely sympathizing unions, is a caricature of the labor party idea and is inadmissible.

In order to start the backward American masses towards the political struggle along class lines, it is necessary to begin with concrete and understandable slogans which propose united front struggles with the Workers Party over the most burning and pressing issues in their daily life. The basis of the CEC majority policy is to develop a series of campaigns along this line. The object of these campaigns is first to get the masses in motion, and second to formulate the questions in such a way as will bring the masses into collision with the petty bourgeois political leaders, and thus accelerate the process of disillusionment with these politicians and draw the workers nearer to the Workers Party as the practical leader in the daily fight as well as the herald of the Communist revolution. The present slackening in the industrial and agricultural crisis in the United States cannot prevent the development of such united front struggles on concrete issues. The ever-increasing exploitation of the workers by the capitalist system with its recurring and deepening crises furnishes the fertile soil for such movements.

One of the chief problems of the Workers Party is to find organizational bases broad enough to set the masses into motion behind the united front slogans. One means is for the Workers Party, as such, to initiate united front movements directly with the workers organizations. In the United States, the Workers Party has had much success with this direct method. Under the slogan of "protection for foreign-born workers," it set up united front movements directly with many trade unions, fraternal societies, etc., and carried on an extensive and effective campaign against the proposed laws limiting the rights of these workers, thereby greatly enhancing the prestige and influence of the Workers Party and winning for it many valuable proletarian elements. Similarly, in defending the Communists arrested at the Bridgman, Michigan underground convention, the Workers Party made a highly successful united front campaign. Also the Friends of Soviet Russia, a united front movement for Russian famine relief and recognition, extended the influence of the Workers Party widely amongst diverse proletarian organizations. The TUEL campaign for amalgamation of the trade unions, which was endorsed by fully half of the American labor movement, was a fertile field for the extension of Communist influence and organization. And during the recent campaign for the adoption of an amendment to the United States Constitution opening the way for legislation to restrict child labor, the Workers Party carried on wide agitation on a united front basis. In Omaha, for example, the effectiveness of such tactics was manifested. Under the direct leadership of the Workers Party many of the most important trade unions were rallied to fight for the child labor amendment. These unions were all active participants in the La Follette movement and they could not have been rallied by a movement to unite them into a "class" farmer-labor party.

The Workers Party must utilize every opportunity to develop such united front movements directly with the trade unions and other proletarian organizations. For this purpose, every living issue in the class struggle must be seized upon, including fights against unemployment, wage cuts, syndicalism laws, injunctions in labor disputes, use of troops and police in strikes, imperialism, the Dawes Plan, for defense of political prisoners, international trade union unity, amalgamation, defense of Negro workers, during election campaigns, etc. All these issues furnish the opportunity to mobilize the masses and to throw them into the political struggle under the leadership of the Communists. They enable the Workers Party to appear in fact as well as in theory the real leader of the working class in its struggles.

But the Workers Party cannot rely entirely upon such movements started upon its own initiative and under its own leadership. The Communists must also penetrate all the mass organizations of the workers, participate in all their struggles, and there fight for the WP slogans. Communist delegates from trade unions must work within the Conference for Progressive Political Action and the other so-called non-partisan political committees of the trade unions for the program of the party. These committees are taking on more importance as the trade unions go deeper into politics. They have always furnished the backbone of the labor section of the La Follette movement. Often they have considerable rank and file character, as in the case of the CPPA and the Workingmen's Non-Partisan Political League of Minnesota. At the recent convention of the AFL it was decided to make the non-partisan committees permanent and to extend their functions.

At the convention of the CPPA recently held in Chicago, the trade unions again demonstrated their stubborn allegiance to the non-partisan committee system. Two plans were before the convention to form parties, the La Follette group proposing a third party based on individual membership, and the Socialists proposing a labor party after the British model. The railroad unions rejected both plans and left the convention, declaring categorically in favor of their non-partisan method. The La Follette group arranged to call a convention to found a third party, and the Socialists, receiving practically no support for their labor party proposal, abandoned their fight for it on a national scale and decided to resume their former independent policy. The refusal of the railroad unions, however, to commit themselves definitely to the organization of a third party does not signify their break with the La Follette movement. Through their so-called non-partisan committees, the bulk of them will in the future, as in the past, support the La Follette movement, whether it expresses itself in the new party or as the left wing of the two old parties. The trade unions have persistently refused to affiliate themselves either to "class" labor parties or third parties. The Farmer-Labor Party of the United States (Fitzpatrick), the Federated Farmer-Labor Party and the National Farmer-Labor Party (both Communist), and the American Labor Party (Socialist) all failed to develop mass trade union support and have all passed out of existence.

During the recent national election campaign and immediately afterwards, the Workers Party did not participate on a large scale in the CPPA. This was because it was the very heart of the La Follette movement, and effective participation in it was impossible without endorsing its petty bourgeois candidates. But with the CPPA organizationally independent of the La Follette movement (even if dominated by La Follette sentiment), the effective penetration of it by Communist delegates from trade unions becomes much more feasible. These committees will be a battleground for the various tendencies in the labor movement. In this struggle the aim of the Workers Party must be to win the support of the masses represented in these committees for its various united front campaigns, during elections, during strikes, and for every burning issue in the labor movement.

It is only by work deep among the masses along united front lines, by movements launched upon its own initiative and by penetration of movements outside of its direct control, that the Workers Party will come to be recognized as the real leader of the working class and will build itself into a mass Communist party. The minority policy of organizing a left wing "class" farmer-labor party is full of danger to the Workers Party, and the overwhelming majority of our party is irreconcilably opposed to it. It is an opportunistic policy tending to isolate and liquidate the Workers Party.

As the basis for its drive to organize a left wing farmer-labor party, the CEC minority enormously overestimates the degree and tempo of revolutionary development in the United States. In his article in the October 1923 *Liberator* comrade Pepper wrote:

> I came to the conclusion that we are facing a deepgoing revolution, not a proletarian revolution, but a La Follette revolution. I stated that in this revolution the working class will free itself from the rule of the Gompers bureaucracy, will acquire a class consciousness on a national scale. I can add that this period will produce the mass Communist party. We should not forget for a moment this general revolutionary situation.

And in the September 1923 *Liberator,* in an article entitled "Facing the Third American Revolution," he said:

> Politics today has become a mass occupation. The basis of American conservative democracy was the inert mass of the farmers. This basis is now collapsing. The last reserve of capitalism in America was the 8,000,000 Negroes in the South. This last reserve is in the act of deserting....The Negroes in the South are making an unarmed Spartacus uprising.

In line with this extravagant estimate of the political situation in general goes an equally extravagant estimate of the role and extent of the movement for a farmer-labor party. They look upon such a party as the one means of bringing the masses into political struggle on a united front basis. They hold it to be practically fundamental to Communist strategy to build such a party. They also overestimate the influence of the Communists amongst the masses, in their eagerness to discover mass sentiment behind their slogan for a "class" farmer-labor party. Says comrade Pepper in the *Inprecorr* of September 27, 1923: "The laboring masses considered the Communists as their leaders, and they expect us to show them the best ways and means of fighting against the capitalists and the capitalist government."

As a result of their general overestimation of the revolutionary development in the United States, the Pepper-Ruthenberg minority, when in control of the Workers Party, led it into a whole series of opportunistic adventures. One of these was the August Theses theory of tearing away a section of the labor movement in the shape of the Federated Farmer-Labor Party, and then turning it into a mass Communist party. Another was the famous third party alliance with the La Follette movement, which projected an opportunistic spirit into our party. Still another was the wild chase after the farmer.

In the question of the farmers we come upon the second of the fundamental points of dispute between the CEC majority and minority. The first relates to the matter of mass support for the labor party. The majority takes the position that before the labor party can be organized, there must be a mass demand for it amongst the workers, and it must be primarily based upon the trade unions. The minority, on the other hand, holds the theory that the left wing forces in the labor movement should be combined into a labor party, a theory which translated into actual practice means the formation of a second Communist Party. In the second question, that of the farmers, the position of the majority is that in the labor party, the industrial workers just play the leading role, with the farmers occupying a minor position. The Pepper-Ruthenberg minority, while paying lip service to this second conception, in actual practice base their farmer-labor party principally upon the farmers.

This tendency of the minority became particularly pronounced after the split at the July 1923 convention, where the Federated Farmer-Labor Party was formed. This split broke the connections of the Workers Party with the masses of industrial workers apparently favoring a labor party. Then, largely forgetting that the industrial workers must of necessity be the base of our party activity, the minority, at that time controlling the party, shifted the center of gravity to the farmers. Work among the trade unions was neglected and all efforts were concentrated upon the farmers. In order to theoretically justify this policy, the trade unions were systematically minimized as mere organizations of labor aristocrats. In his thesis presented to the American Commission in Moscow, in May 1924, comrade Pepper stated the problem as follows:

> Shall we make an alliance with the labor aristocracy, which today socially and politically is the closest ally of imperialism, or shall we, in the name of the proletarian workers, make an alliance with the farmers, who today are beginning to fight against imperialism, although in a confused and hesitating manner?

He describes his group as the section of the party which "stresses the necessity of the alliance with the farmers," as against the Foster-Cannon group, "which emphasizes the necessity of an alliance with the labor aristocracy." By "labor aristocracy," comrade Pepper means the present trade union movement of America. The same tendency to base the farmer-labor party movement upon the farmers is manifested in the latest theses of the Pepper-Ruthenberg group, in which there is cited, as mass support for the "class" farmer-labor party, the Farmer-Labor Parties in the agricultural states of Minnesota, North Dakota, Montana, Colorado, South Dakota and Washington. All these parties are made up overwhelmingly of farmers, and they are all part of the La Follette movement. The minority theses cited only one party of industrial workers, a skeleton Farmer-Labor Party in Washington County, Pennsylvania.

In the midst of the opportunistic adventures of the Pepper-Ruthenberg group amongst the farmers, the present majority of the CEC sounded a note of warning against this shifting of the base of the party activities from the workers to the farmers, and fought against this tendency. We stated our general position in the November 1923 thesis as follows:

> Important as the revolt of the bankrupt farmers is in the present political situation, and necessary as it is that a close alliance be cemented between the exploited farmers and the industrial workers, there is a great danger in the tendency, displayed by the CEC majority (Pepper-Ruthenberg group), to base their labor party policy upon the farmers' revolt, and to relegate the role of the industrial workers to second place.

In the American Commission in Moscow, in May 1924, the CEC majority reiterated its position on the question of the farmers as follows:

> It shall be sharply called to the attention of the Workers Party that the importance of the farmers as a revolutionary factor must not be overestimated. The backbone of the Communist movement must be the industrial workers. The party shall be instructed to turn its attention more to work in the big industrial centers, rather than so much in the agricultural districts.

The minority conception embraces two political parties: one, the near-Communist farmer-labor party, to carry on an opportunistic struggle amongst the masses over their everyday burning questions, and the other, the Workers Party, to appear before the masses primarily in the role of advocate of Communist principles in the abstract and the ultimate proletarian revolution. In order to justify the campaign for the "class" farmer-labor party, the minority constantly exaggerates the extent of that movement. On October 3, 1923, when it was definitely known to the Central Executive Committee that the Federated Farmer-Labor Party was little more than an organization on paper, comrades Pepper and Ruthenberg submitted to the Comintern and Profintern the following inexcusably exaggerated report of the strength of that party:

> The figures show that comrade Foster's statement, that the Federated Farmer-Labor Party is simply the Workers Party under another name, is untrue. The Federated Farmer-Labor Party is everywhere at least 20 times as strong as the Workers Party. In New York, 60,000 and only 3,000 party members; in Buffalo, 60,000 and only 200 party members; in Minnesota 120,000 and only 2,000 party members; in Washington County, Pennsylvania 20,000 and only 100 party members; in Los Angeles 11,000 and only 100 party members. The Federated Farmer-Labor Party is the most important organ of the united front of our party. It plays the same role as the industrial councils (*Betriebsräte*) movement in Germany.

The minority comrades have an opportunistic conception of the role of the farmer-labor party. They speak of it as a party which will "fight the battles of the working class," and associate "independent class political action" in their theses exclusively with the farmer-labor party. In his booklet, "For a Labor Party," comrade Pepper goes so far as to raise the slogan, "The Labor Party or the Capitalist Dictatorship."

As a complement to this policy of grossly exaggerating the role and extent of the farmer-labor party movement, the minority also follows a policy of minimizing the influence of the Workers Party as such. The reverse of the campaign for the farmer-labor party policy in the Workers Party is a constant propaganda to show how little the Workers Party can accomplish in its own name. A characteristic statement of this defeatist attitude occurs in the article by comrade Amter in the *Inprecorr* of January 27, 1925: "To contend that the Workers Party can become a mass Communist party in a country like the United States where the workers and poor farmers have little consciousness, is utopian."

During the recent election campaign, this tendency to minimize the Workers Party and to shove it into the background came sharply into evidence. The minority followers, still mourning over the demise of the stillborn National Farmer-Labor Party, whose candidates MacDonald and Bouck had to be withdrawn, took but little interest in the election campaign under the banner of the Workers Party. When the election returns began to come in, the minority leaders, apparently eager to show that the Workers Party could not make any show directly under its own flag, and thereby to stress the necessity for a farmer-labor party, proposed to cable the Comintern an estimate of the vote which was only half as large as that which the official counters, after a wholesale stealing of votes, conceded to our party. This deliberate minimizing of the showing made by the Workers Party under its own name, as compared with the widely exaggerated reports sent to the Comintern regarding the Federated Farmer-Labor Party, give a real indication of the comparative importance attached to these organizations by the CEC minority. This attitude shows quite clearly that the policy of the minority leads to liquidation.

The American party is confronted with the most serious and complicated problems. In order for it to find its way along the right path, it is necessary that the whole political situation be re-examined in the light of developments and the experiences of the party. The party cannot live and grow until it clearly recognizes the opportunistic and liquidationist tendencies inherent in the farmer-labor party conceptions of the minority and rejects them resolutely. A halt must be called to the tendency to minimize and subordinate the Workers Party, to hide its name and to create a substitute and rival party by the propagation of the cure-all slogan of a "class" farmer-labor party. The party must overcome opportunism without falling back into the sterile rigidity which characterized the first year of its existence. This requires a sober analysis of the objective situation, and the elaboration of the tactics which take into account the present stage of development of the workers and the relative strength of the party. A first condition for healthy development of the party is the manifold extension of activities within the trade unions and other mass organizations of the workers. The party must penetrate deeply into the labor movement and draw the workers around it. This cannot be done by means of the magic "class" farmer-labor party slogan, but by means of concrete struggles around living issues on the basis of the united front. There are no short cuts to a popular mass Communist party in America. Realistic work and struggle over a period of years is the only road to that goal. The majority of the CEC and the overwhelming majority of the Workers Party stand on this position.

Factionalism in the Workers Party

At the present time there is a factional situation in the Workers Party which seriously hampers the functioning and development of the party. The worst feature of this is the struggle between two groups, majority and minority, which should constitute a single leading group of the party. This fight originated in 1923 in the dispute over the role to be played by the Federated Farmer-Labor Party. In November of that year the present majority of the party, then the minority, agreed with the Pepper-Ruthenberg group on interpretation of their theses which would prevent the FFLP from being developed into a left wing Communist labor party by splitting the labor party forces. Believing that the difficulty was properly adjusted, we exacted no organizational guarantees whatever from the then majority. Almost immediately afterwards, comrade Pepper, in violation of the agreement, launched into a bitter factional attack against our group, to which we had no opportunity in the party press to reply before the convention was held.[2] In the convention the overwhelming majority of the delegates revolted against the Pepper-Ruthenberg group, largely because of their factional activities and their attempts to

---

[2] This is evidently a reference to Pepper's article "How Not to Make the United Front," which was published in *The Worker*, 22 December 1923. Pepper attacked the Chicago District Committee, which included prominent Foster-Cannon supporters like Swabeck, Johnstone and Browder, for making a united front "only with the Fitzpatrick-Nockels group of leaders" and refusing to challenge Fitzpatrick's leadership of the Chicago AFL—both before and after the July 3 convention.

The Third Convention of the Workers Party, held 30 December 1923 to 1 January 1924, issued a statement on the Chicago united front (published in *The Worker*, 12 January 1924) which exonerated the Chicago leadership: "The majority resolution declares that the District Committee in its practice did not direct any criticism against the Fitzpatrick group. This was largely true. But in so doing the District Committee merely followed the policy which the CEC is following in Minnesota, Detroit and everywhere else where we have some semblance of a united front. If this policy was wrong, the CEC was entirely responsible...."

justify their errors by putting the blame for them on others who were not responsible.

At the sessions of the American Commission in Moscow in 1924, we urged that efforts be made to amalgamate the two groups, and our proposition was accepted by the commission and embodied in its decision. Immediately upon our delegates' return to America we proposed amalgamation with the Pepper-Ruthenberg group. Agreement was reached over the immediate tasks confronting the party, and in the reorganization of the party personnel made at the time, involving seven positions, the four most important were given to the minority, and every assurance was also given to the minority of our desire to consolidate with them and work harmoniously together.

We believed that the party was about to achieve unity and the elimination of the factional fight when there arrived a letter from comrade Pepper. This letter, which was broadcast in the party and the Young Workers League through underground methods, grossly misrepresented the decisions of the American Commission and incited the minority to a continuation of the factional fight. The result was to deepen and intensify the factional situation. The minority was stimulated to continue its illegal factional organization, based primarily on a number of language federations, and to extend it throughout the party. Every party problem was seized upon and exploited from a factional standpoint. A typical example of this was the question of unemployment. At the very moment when the minority were demanding the formation of unemployment councils and making a big issue of it throughout the party because the majority refused to form such councils until such a time as unemployment had developed to sufficient mass character to give these councils real meaning, comrade Ruthenberg, secretary of the party and a leader of the minority, had in his possession letters, from a number of district organizers who were supporting the minority, which declared it would be impossible to organize unemployment councils in their districts under the prevailing conditions, and urging that the attempt should not be made.

Despite repeated demonstrations that the minority is opposed by the overwhelming majority of the membership, they are obsessed with the ambition to secure complete control of the party organization, to the exclusion of the present majority group. This is the rock upon which our attempts to amalgamate with them have been wrecked. Their attitude was characteristically expressed by comrade Ruthenberg in his demand to the present American Commission that the control of the party be handed over to his group. Our proposals for the liquidation of the factional fight, which is doing so much injury to our party, are contained in our recommendations to the American Commission, which are appended to this document.[3]

Two and a Half International Tendencies in the Party

One of the worst features of the factional fight in the Workers Party is the reckless and irresponsible manner in which the minority has approached the question of the liquidation of Two and a Half International tendencies in the Workers Party. The decision of the American Commission of last year correctly called attention to the existence of a tendency toward Two and a Half Internationalism in the Workers Party, especially as exemplified by the writings of comrade Lore, and called upon the CEC to make an ideological campaign against it. The CEC majority fully agreed with this standpoint and proceeded along the lines laid down by the letter of the Comintern.

The CEC majority has written and spoken openly and continually against this group and tendency. The following examples can be cited:

1. The CEC theses declare against it and call for its liquidation.
2. Foster's polemics against Nearing (*Daily Worker* magazine, 10 and 17 May 1924).
3. Bittelman's articles against Salutsky (*DW* magazine, 15 April 1924) and Boudin (*DW* magazine, 9 August 1924).
4. Cannon's speech at New York Workers School (*Workers Monthly*, November 1924).

[3] The Cannon-Foster recommendations are not published here, as for the most part they are repetitive of other material. The recommendations end with a final section entitled "Liquidation of the Factional Fight," which is appended to the end of this article.

5. Cannon's speech at party conference of coal miners (*DW* magazine, 2 August 1924).
6. CEC resolution on role of New York Workers School (introduced by Cannon and printed in the *DW*).[4]
7. Olgin's articles on "Lore and the Comintern" (written by direction of CEC and printed in *DW* magazine).[5]
8. Bittelman's speech at convention of German Federation (*DW*, 4 December 1924).
9. CEC resolution against Wicks, minority leader, who supported the arch-reactionary Lynch for president of Typographical Union (printed in *DW*, 21 August 1924).
10. CEC decisions and resolutions against right wing fractions in South Slavic and Czecho-Slovak federations (printed in *DW*).[6]

The minority completely overlooked the political and ideological problems involved in this question and took it up from a purely factional standpoint. They hampered the ideological campaign of the CEC against this tendency and only succeeded in strengthening and consolidating the Lore group by stupid and obviously factional organizational proposals and petty persecutions. During the time the minority had control of the party they worked hand in hand with Lore against the bona fide proletarian Communist elements represented by the present majority. They drew Lore into the Political Committee of the CEC and at the same time excluded Cannon and Bittelman. They appointed Lore to the Steering Committee (in charge of the Communist fraction) of the July 3rd convention which formed the FFLP while refusing to allow Cannon to attend it even as a delegate. They never once so much as criticized Lore during the entire year, and during the last party convention they never once raised the issue of the opportunist errors of Lore, but concentrated their whole fight

---

4 We could not find this resolution in the *Daily Worker.*

5 See note, page 258.

6 The CEC statement condemning the Board of Directors of the Czecho-Slovak Federation's official paper, *Spravedlnost,* for splitting from the Workers Party, was published in the 28 July 1924 *DW.* The CEC decision on the South Slavic Federation, published in the *DW* magazine supplement on 29 March 1924, upheld the Federation Bureau in its struggle against the former editors of the Federation's journal, who had quit the party charging the Bureau with financial malfeasance.

with the support of Lore against the present majority. During the days of the German October and the party crisis attendant upon it, Lore in the *Volkszeitung* supported Brandler against the left wing. The Pepper-Ruthenberg CEC did not object to this for the very good reason that comrade Pepper, who was the leader of the CEC, was himself a supporter of Brandler.

Lore has made the statement a hundred times that Pepper expressed his approval of the attitude of Lore on the Brandler question. In *The Liberator* for November 1923, comrade Pepper wrote the following, in his article entitled "The New Wave of World Revolution":

> In the past year we have seen the three most outstanding mass successes of the united front tactic: an international united front of the transport workers; the united front of the German Communists and Social Democratic workers in Saxony; the formation of the Federated Farmer-Labor Party in the United States.

and

> The left Socialist-Communist government in Saxony is the nucleus of the future Soviet Government of Germany.

and

> In Germany the deciding battle of the class struggle of workers and capitalists will assume the form of a struggle and war between two state powers—between counter-revolutionary Bavaria and revolutionary Saxony.[7]

In addition to this, comrade Lore's article "analyzing the German events" was featured and given the most prominent

---

[7] Both the ECCI and the German party leadership only belatedly took note of the revolutionary situation in Germany in 1923. The plan worked out in Moscow in September called for the insurrection to begin in Saxony, where the German Communist Party (KPD) would enter into the Social Democratic (SPD) government which already depended on KPD support. It was hoped that entry into the Saxon government would give the KPD access to arms.

Party chairman Heinrich Brandler was one of three KPD ministers who joined the Saxon government on October 10; a few days later the KPD also entered into a coalition government with the SPD in Thuringia. On October 20 the KPD leadership decided to organize a general strike and insurrection. However the SPD refused to go along with the plan. When an SPD-dominated conference of factory delegates at Chemnitz, whose endorsement of the KPD strike call was supposed to signal the beginning of the insurrection, also refused to go along, Brandler called off the insurrection. The ECCI representatives in Germany backed his decision.

(continued)

position on the front page of *The Worker* at that time. One can easily see in all these incidents that the Pepper-Ruthenberg group, which today makes Loreism its main issue, had nothing to say against Lore at that time.

The question of the Two and a Half International tendencies constitutes a serious problem for the party. It can be solved by the Comintern laying down the correct tactics for the liquidation of this group and tendency, and by the repudiation of the adventurous and reckless policy of the minority which merely exploits the question for factional purposes. The CEC majority is carrying out a systematic struggle against this tendency and it demands that the minority cooperate in the campaign and not sabotage it.

For us it is a problem not simply of Lore but of the workers who sympathize with him and his policy to a certain extent. Valuable proletarian elements, among them some of the most active and influential party members in the New York trade unions, are, to a certain extent, under the influence of the Lore group. This is very largely the result of their reaction to the destructive factionalism and anti-trade-union practices of the minority. The aim must be to win these valuable proletarian elements over to complete support of the CEC and the Comintern by a careful and intelligent and systematic struggle against the opportunist tendencies of the Lore group, which will separate the workers from it and isolate the leaders who persist in their errors. It would be the

---

The German army marched into Saxony and deposed the SPD-KPD government on October 23; the Thuringian government was also deposed. In November the KPD was declared illegal (the prohibition lasted until March 1924).

In a letter to the German party written soon after these events, the ECCI noted: "We here in Moscow, as you must be well aware, regarded the entry of the Communists into the Saxon government only as a military-strategic maneuver. You turned it into a political bloc with the 'left' Social Democrats, which tied your hands. We thought of your entry into the Saxon government as a way of winning a jumping-off ground from which to deploy the forces of our armies. You turned participation in the Saxon cabinet into a banal parliamentary coalition with the Social Democrats. The result was our political defeat."

The ECCI later made Brandler the scapegoat for the defeat and endorsed a new "left" KPD leadership led by Ruth Fischer and Arkadi Maslow. Lore had not only supported Brandler in this affair, but denied that a revolution was possible in Germany in 1923.

greatest folly to precipitate a premature split which would lose them for the party.

The Question of Party Work in the Trade Unions

Another angle to the factional situation which is particularly harmful to the Workers Party is the manner in which the Pepper-Ruthenberg minority is hampering the work of the party within the trade unions. The trade unionist members of the party have made particularly strong opposition to the formation of a "left wing" Communist farmer-labor party, realizing that among other evil effects it would isolate the Workers Party in the trade unions. The minority have therefore directed the brunt of their attack against the trade unionists and the Trade Union Educational League. This attack was begun in the August Theses when comrades Pepper and Ruthenberg launched a long and bitter polemic against the comrades most active in the trade unions. This has been followed up by systematic, if disguised, opposition to the work in the trade unions. Charges of Gompersism and syndicalism are set afloat in the party, the tendency of which is to weaken the trade union work. An effort is made to set aside the trade unionists as a special group in the party and to play off against them the large percentage of the party membership who do not belong to the trade unions.

The party is now carrying on its trade union work under great difficulties. The trade unions have just suffered the most tremendous defeat in their history, in the period from 1919 to 1924. Whole sections of them have been wiped out. The officialdom, refusing to reorganize the unions and to adopt a policy of class struggle, have introduced elaborate plans of class collaboration, and have declared ruthless war against the left wing as part of this plan of betraying the workers to the capitalists. The Trade Union Educational League has been driven underground in practically every trade union in the United States. In addition to these handicaps many valuable connections were lost in the trade unions through the Federated Farmer-Labor Party split and the sweep of the La Follette movement. In the face of this difficult situation the factional fight of the minority against the trade unionists in the party is especially disastrous to the trade union work of the party.

The irresponsible attitude of the minority towards the trade union work arises primarily out of the non-proletarian past and lack of trade union experience of the minority leaders. They have no real appreciation of the importance of trade union work. Before the present factional fight developed and when they were in control of the party, their policy was to leave the mapping out and execution of policies in the trade unions to the men making up the present majority of the CEC. They were uncritical and indifferent. When the split took place after the July 1923 convention of the FFLP, the Pepper-Ruthenberg lack of appreciation for an understanding of the work in the trade unions took a new turn. The tacit support of the Trade Union Educational League came to an end and a campaign of carping criticism and passionate opposition developed. The Pepper-Ruthenberg group submitted an industrial program to the convention of the Workers Party in January 1924. This "program" indicates their complete lack of understanding of trade union work. Its principal features were proposals to drop the TUEL slogans for amalgamation and the organization of the unorganized.

The minority plan said about amalgamation of the trade unions, "Neither the workers of the unorganized industries nor the hundreds of thousands of organized workers are interested in any organizational improvement of the existing craft unions. Our vigorous campaign for amalgamation was in place for the period of prosperity and it helped to stir up great sections of organized labor." As for the organization of the unorganized, the minority program said, "Our slogan, 'Organize the Unorganized,' was a proper slogan during a period of complete employment, increasing wages and decreasing hours." For hours the minority members urged the dropping of these important slogans. They ignored completely that the campaigns to organize the unorganized and to consolidate the trade unions must be continued constantly, especially during industrial depressions, which was exactly when the minority proposed to drop them. In such trade union work as they take part in, the minority displayed strong right wing tendencies, a case in point being the endorsement by H.M. Wicks, a prominent member, of James Lynch for president of the Typographical Union. Lynch is one of the most notorious reactionaries in the trade unions, and Wicks' action, for which he was publicly censured in the party press, demoralized the left wing in the printing trades.

The majority of the CEC has a keen appreciation of the basic importance of trade union work. Without the deep permeation of the trade union movement and the widespread organization of Communist fractions, the party cannot exercise real influence over the masses. The fundamental condition for the solution of the recent factional situation and for the health and growth of the party is a clear statement from the Comintern on the necessity of trade union work and the liquidation of anti-trade-union tendencies in the Workers Party.

Appendix:

From *Recommendations to the American Commission*
by Cannon and William Z. Foster

The factional controversies in the Workers Party, which arose out of the complicated situation in America, have been exaggerated and intensified to such a degree by the minority under the stimulation and direction of comrade Pepper, that they now constitute a major problem of the party. The reckless and irresponsible factional conduct of the minority not only paralyzes the activity of the party, but actually threatens its unity. The Comintern decision will facilitate the liquidation of the factional fights by embodying the following points:

a) A clear statement on the question of united front tactics in general, as applied to the United States.

b) A specific condemnation of the theory of organizing a left wing Communist labor party and of transforming it into a mass Communist party, also a rejection of the general forming of "paper" organizations under the guise of the united front.

c) Renewed efforts to amalgamate the leading groups of the CEC on the basis of the decision of the Comintern.

d) A substantial number of new proletarian elements, workers actually employed in the shops and who are active members of trade unions, shall be drawn into the CEC and systematic efforts be made to train and develop proletarian leaders.

e) Caucuses and factions shall be dissolved and prohibited, and the practice of circulating underground "documents" in the party shall be condemned.

f) Energetic work with regard to the concrete aspects of Bolshevizing the party referred to above, liquidation of the Two and a Half International tendencies, reorganization of the party on the basis of shop nuclei, centralization of the party, proletarianizing the CEC and party educational work.

g) The trade union work must be developed and intensified on a manifold scale. All party members must join the trade unions and start faction fights against the bureaucrats. The anti-trade-union tendency in the party must be categorically condemned.

h) Point out the necessity for party leaders to frankly admit mistakes in policy. There is a danger to the party in the tendency to cover up past mistakes by posturing present theories to fit them, which hinders the party from turning back from a wrong path once it has entered it.

Pepper: Menace to Party Unity

13 February 1925

The following is an unpublished transcript of Cannon's remarks to a session of the American Commission which convened in Moscow before the Fifth Plenum of the Executive Committee of the Communist International. The American party had appointed a delegation of four to the plenum—two from each faction. But in Moscow the Ruthenberg minority attempted to have Pepper, who was then resident in Moscow, recognized as an additional American delegate. The dispute was eventually resolved by adding two new delegates—Pepper for the minority and John Williamson of the Young Workers League for the majority.

I think the question is not so much a formal question, it is a question of representation here in Moscow and of the Commission determining who represents the party here. I agree with comrade Kuusinen that the Pepper question is a part of the trouble in our party. What we object to is this typical example of comrade Pepper's maneuvers, of trying to get in three delegates for the minority against two for the majority. When comrade Pepper was in America he wanted to appear as representative of the CI. In Moscow he wants to appear as representative of our party. Comrade Pepper seems to have created the impression in Moscow that he represents our party. We want to establish the fact that our party has nothing to do with Pepper as a representative in Moscow, and anything he has to say here in no way speaks for our party.

The motion proposed by comrade Lozovsky would be acceptable to us—that there should be two reporters from each side. We object that the minority send Ruthenberg and Lovestone and we send Foster and myself, and then they try to get Pepper in because he is here already, and say it is not fair to put him out.

We can settle the question by letting the minority have two representatives and we will have two representatives.

* * *

At the last Commission to consider the American question, the CEC majority made an official request for the removal of Pepper from America. If this is not complete, if Pepper still has some strings on the American party, we here today make a further demand for the severance of those strings from the American party, because he is a constant menace to the unity of the party. The speech comrade Pepper made here just a minute ago gives a key to the work he has done in our party. What does he say about Foster? He compares him to Gompers. He has tried to stir up the most remote sections of the party against Foster on the ground that he is another Gompers. In this way he has created an extremely bitter situation. He comes here and says, I am not a hundred percent American, I am a poor immigrant. This may not mean very much here, but in America it is a good way to stir up a large portion of our foreign-born members and set them against the American leaders of the party. This creates strong nationalistic tendencies. I tell you here that if the CI does not remove Pepper from our party you will never have peace in it. He is a menace to the unity of our party. He incites the foreign workers in the party against us. We want the Commission to understand clearly that Pepper does not represent the American party, cannot, and never will by our consent.

The Situation Is Different in America

30 March 1925

The following remarks by Cannon to the third session of the Fifth Plenum of the Communist International were published in International Press Correspondence, *16 April 1925.*

The problem of Bolshevization in America has certain concrete aspects: The problem is concurrent with the problem of organizing the party, for we are *at the beginning of the task of forming a Communist party in America,* and the situation is different from the countries of Europe. We never had a revolutionary mass movement in America and have few traditions and experiences to draw upon. We have a large proletariat in America, but the party has only 20,000 members of which only 2,000 are in the English-speaking organizations. The American proletariat is politically very backward and the most elementary tasks are necessary in the attempt to set it in motion.

We must develop the propaganda of Marxist-Leninist theory. In this sense I agree with comrade Bela Kun's report. The party developed from two sources—the Socialist Party, which never had any Marxian theory, and the syndicalist organizations, which also neglected theoretical questions. But in training a cadre of functionaries we must be careful not to train functionaries separate from the masses. We must be careful with the term professional revolutionaries—they must be workshop revolutionaries primarily. From the Central Committee to the lowest organization the party must attain a more working class character. The tendency toward dilettantism and careerism must be combatted.

We have two fundamental problems: (1) *trade union work* and (2) *shop nuclei organization.* Trade union work has been more or less neglected because the weakness of the trade unions made the work very difficult. We must combat the tendency to neglect this work, and instead must actually help to build up the trade unions themselves. The second problem, that of organizing shop nuclei, is very important although its solution does not alone solve the problem of Bolshevization.

Our main difficulties are: (1) we are *a small party in a big industrial country*; (2) the *trade union movement is very weak*; (3) *our party is divided into foreign-language groups*, each with its own national apparatus, and each tending toward specializing in the problems peculiar to the group. The language federation form of organization is absolutely incompatible with a Bolshevist organization. We must have a centralized form of organization or we will never be a Bolshevist party.

Now as to the *question of the labor party*. It is not quite correct to compare our situation with that of England. The British Labour Party is an old party, and is supported by the entire trade union movement. The British trade union movement is much stronger than the American movement. There is no labor party in America. All attempts to create one in the past two years have been disastrous failures. The organized American workers are not yet class-conscious enough to develop a labor party on a mass basis, founded on the trade unions, and we want no other kind. We want no Communist labor party, for such a party will become a small group separated from the masses. A real mass labor party based on the trade unions, and not restricted to Communists, will be a great step forward, and in forming such a party we can learn from the experiences of the past two years. Such a labor party must be (1) a mass organization; (2) based on the trade unions; (3) a general labor movement in which the Communists can work, but in which they will not lose their identity. Under present conditions there can be no question of organizing such a labor party. The thing for us to do now is to conduct agitation and propaganda based on the concrete immediate problems of the workers and to raise the issue of independent political action and an independent party in connection with them. We must bring the workers into conflict with the petty-bourgeois ideas. It would be premature to form a labor party now, and even dangerous, for we would quickly become isolated from this growing mass labor movement. We know this from our own experience of the past two years, and especially in connection with the Federated Farmer-Labor Party and the St. Paul convention. We hope for the assistance of our Russian comrades, so that our movement will not be derailed and sidetracked and will not become the victim of experimental theories. Concrete issues are in the foreground of our problems. The American workers still follow the parties of big capital or the petty-bourgeois movement of La Follette. We must reach the masses and set them into motion in the class struggle. Our means for doing this is *united front struggles* on the basis of the concrete immediate problems of the workers.

We Must Acknowledge Our Mistake, But We Want No Fake Labor Party

5 April 1925

The following is an uncorrected and unpublished transcript of Cannon's remarks to the sixth session of the American Commission which convened around the Fifth Plenum of the Executive Committee of the Communist International. The Commission's decision favored the Ruthenberg minority in insisting on the necessity of continued agitation for a labor party in America.

I will try to be brief and just touch a couple of the main points. First, I want to state also with comrade Foster that the general line of the resolution is acceptable to the majority, that we could work on the basis of it with those remarks that he made. In making this statement, I think the majority is duly bound to state, as comrade Foster stated, that we must acknowledge our mistakes in our abandonment of the labor party and discarding the slogan altogether. We mean to take up the spirit of the resolution and make a real campaign for the labor party. However, we think it is incorrect to make the premise of the resolution depend so much upon the happenings of the CPPA convention because the facts are not quite as stated here, and it might have a tendency to cause a confusion in the minds of our membership in America if the impression is made that the conclusions are drawn from this statement of facts.[1] For example, it must be borne in mind first that the railroad unions which were the backbone of the CPPA left the conference not in protest against a third party, in favor of the labor party, but in protest against a third party in

[1] Cannon is here referring to events at the CPPA's February 1925 convention held in Chicago. See "Controversial Questions in the Workers Party of America," pp. 302-303.

favor of non-partisan action. When the vote which comrade Ruthenberg stated of 93 to 64 occurred over the resolution of admitting affiliated organizations it was directed primarily at the exclusion of the Socialist Party as an autonomous party. I want to quote here a report of the *Daily Worker* of the composition of the CPPA after the departure of the railroad unions, that is the railroad organizations:

> The credentials committee report showed that labor representation to the convention was practically nonexistent. A half dozen local labor bodies, three state federations had sent credentials, but the delegates were not present. The rest were from the Socialist Party, state committees of the CPPA and an array of "progressive" groups of doubtful standing with the officialdom of the Amalgamated, ILGWU, and Furriers' Union.

We must bear in mind the great practice in America in which we communists also have become quite expert of late of packing all kinds of delegates in a convention and it is a great mistake to think that the 63 votes cast there represented a real labor sentiment. It represented the Socialist Party and the Socialist Party influence only. Now, in proof of my statement that the resolution was carried against the affiliated organizations, and aimed against the Socialist Party, I wish to quote this report of the *Daily Worker*:

> Hillquit was asked a direct question by one of the delegates as to the willingness of the Socialist Party to lose its identity in the new party....The "progressives" were plain spoken. McKaig of Idaho said, "The socialists have got to forget their party if they want a progressive party."

We must not conclude, and it would be very erroneous if we should let the Comintern make a decision based upon a statement of facts which are not correct.

To pass over to one more point about the question of whether we shall state in the resolution the formation of a party of 500,000.[2] Comrade Ruthenberg said that Foster is afraid of the

---

[2] The final text of the Comintern resolution as published in the *Daily Worker*, 19 May 1925, included the following passage: "It may be that the mass support for the idea of the labor party will reveal itself so strongly in some cities and even in some states, that organizational measures can be taken without further hesitation. The formation of the national labor party should be advised against until at least 500,000 organized workers are definitely won over to it."

500,000 figure. We are not afraid of a labor party of 500,000. We will be enthusiastically in support of a labor party of 500,000. What we are afraid of is another Federated Farmer-Labor Party. We are afraid of a fictitious membership in the organization and we want to safeguard ourselves against it. Why is it necessary, comrades? The comrades of the minority representing the point of view for the federated organization have never been able to bring themselves to admit that this was not a real labor party. The figures of the Federated Farmer-Labor Party were 500,000 or even 600,000 at the July 1923 convention. And, comrades, we must decide here now—we are starting off on a new leaf—we must have a clear understanding, and it must be put in the decision that it will be a real labor party, and not a fake caricature organization.

Comrade Ruthenberg said that they never stood for this kind of a federated party. Let me quote from the August Theses, which say the following:

> We should create such local labor parties whenever they will have a size in the ratio of 10 to 1 to the membership of the Workers Party.

When we objected to this, when we did not want such a caricature party, they said to us, you want the whole labor movement before you are willing to form a labor party. But this is not so, I want to quote from our thesis of November 1923, which is as follows:

> Our position is not based on the assumption that the entire labor movement must join the labor party at once, or that even a majority is necessary. But we hold that wherever it is formed, it must unite the labor party forces and have a genuine mass character.

We stand on this platform today and in my conversations with comrades of the Commission I think this is the meaning and intention of the Commission, and I think it should be stated very clearly in the resolution, and our amendment which clarifies and implies this point should be accepted. Comrade Ruthenberg says that the test of our attitude towards the resolution of a labor party campaign is the acceptance of the 500,000 statement. No, I think it is better to say our test, as mentioned by comrade Foster, is that we shall consult the Comintern when the time comes for the actual formation of a party, and it shall be done only by the consent and cooperation of the Comintern. On the one hand it is a guarantee that there will be no fake caricature party formed, and on the other hand it is a guarantee that there will be a party formed when there will be a substantial mass basis for it, regardless of the attitude of the bureaucracy of the trade unions.

One point more, comrade Ruthenberg stated it. I think in the main it is correct. And we can get together with comrade Piatnitsky's Organization Department, and set up special organizational measures which we can agree upon.

Proposal on Comrade Pepper

6 April 1925

The following is an uncorrected and unpublished transcript of some of Cannon's remarks at the seventh session of the American Commission which convened around the Fifth Plenum of the Executive Committee of the Communist International.

I want to suggest an amendment to the organizational proposals. This deals with the section relating to comrade Pepper, which is as follows:

> In particular the Executive Committee wishes to state that it considers a personal campaign carried on between and against comrade Pepper and other leading comrades, is uncalled for, firstly because comrade Pepper is needed for other work in the Comintern, and has no intention to return to the United States, and secondly, because it needlessly injures the standing and effectivencss of these comrades. The Executive Committee knows that comrade Pepper during his brief stay in America performed political services for the Workers Party, for which he deserves praise.[1]

I bring this here before the whole commission and propose it for the consideration of the small commission.

---

1 Cannon's proposal was adopted with minor amendment. The wording of the final resolution as published in the *Daily Worker*, 19 May 1925, was as follows: "In particular, the Executive Committee must point out that it regards a campaign conducted against comrade Pepper as absolutely uncalled for, all the more since, firstly, comrade Pepper himself has no intention of returning to work in the Workers Party, and secondly, the Executive Committee desires to use his energies for other important tasks. The Executive Committee knows that comrade Pepper during his brief stay in America performed services for the Workers Party for which he deserves praise. The Executive Committee demands that all personal polemics between the two sides should cease."

Struggle Over Leadership of the ILD

26 June 1925

The following is an excerpt from the minutes of the Executive Council (Political Committee), the leading committee of the Workers Party. At this time, the Cannon-Foster faction controlled the Council and was able to prevail over the Ruthenberg-Lovestone minority in the struggle for leadership of the International Labor Defense.

Present: Abern, Bittelman, Burman, Cannon, Bedacht, Lovestone, Ruthenberg. Later: Engdahl and Dunne.

International Labor Defense

Comrade Cannon submitted copies of the resolutions to be introduced at the International Labor Defense conference which were approved together with the reporters of the various resolutions.

Copy of the constitution as approved by the subcommittee was also submitted. The minority report of comrade Ruthenberg to strike out the section of the constitution providing for the organization of branches as part of the basic organization of the International Labor Defense.

After discussion the vote was taken resulting as follows:

For the Ruthenberg motion to strike out:
Ruthenberg, Lovestone and Bedacht.
Against: Bittelman, Cannon, Abern, Burman.

The steering committee as decided upon by the subcommittee consisting of Dunne, Gitlow and Cannon was approved.

The Executive Committee recommended that comrade Cannon be chairman of the conference.

Comrade Ruthenberg submitted the report that a non-party member be designated as chairman.

Voting in favor of the minority report:
Ruthenberg, Lovestone, Bedacht.
Voting against: Bittelman, Abern, Burman, Cannon.

The subcommittee recommended that the steering committee be given full power to act for the CEC in the conference. The recommendation was approved unanimously.

The committee recommended that comrade Cannon be elected secretary of the Labor Defense. Comrade Ruthenberg submitted a minority report that comrade Bedacht be the secretary.

Voting in favor of the recommendation of the committee:
Abern, Burman, Bittelman, Cannon.
Voting for comrade Bedacht:
Lovestone, Ruthenberg, Bedacht.

Comrade Cannon submitted the following recommendations:

1. That the National Committee consist of a clear majority of party members.
2. That the Executive Committee consist of all or nearly all party members.
3. That the CEC decide definitely on the National Committee and Executive Committee at the meeting tomorrow.

After discussion comrade Cannon submitted the motion:

That the Executive Committee consist of 3/4 party members which was adopted unanimously.

ILD Will Grow Quickly

15 July 1925

Cannon addressed the following letter, written on the stationery of the newly founded International Labor Defense, to Eugene V. Debs in Terre Haute, Indiana.

Dear Comrade Debs:

I was very much gratified indeed to receive your letter of July 10th confirming your previous endorsement of the ILD.

The launching of such a movement as this has been in my mind for many years and the response it is getting from all sections of the working class, especially from men like yourself who have been in prison or who are confined there now, gives me confidence that the movement will grow quickly and will become a real power for the defense of persecuted workers and for the support of their dependents. The need for such a movement as the ILD is even greater than we had at first anticipated. Since the holding of the National Conference on June 28th and its attendant publicity we have been receiving letters almost every day from unknown and neglected prisoners and their families, and heavy obligations are piling upon us. That only means that we must work harder and broaden the scope of our activities to arouse the labor movement to unity and action in behalf of its persecuted fighters.

The main problem as I see it is to construct the ILD on the broadest possible basis. To conduct the work in a non-partisan and non-sectarian manner and finally establish the impression by our deeds that the ILD is the defender of every worker persecuted for his activities in the class struggle, without any exceptions and without regard to his affiliations. It is my aim to direct the work along this line. The whole National Conference was animated by this spirit and I am sure it is yours too.

I appreciate the fact that your time is fully occupied for the remaining months of the year. But in spite of this I trust that you will find the way to assist us by a certain minimum of active participation in the work of the ILD.

I will keep in touch with you and inform you regularly of the developments and problems of the organization and will greatly appreciate your advice and suggestions. It would be especially valuable if you could find time to write us a short article which we could send out in our press service. And if you happen to be in Chicago in the near future I would like very much to have a talk with you about the work.

Our main energy is concentrated at present on the building of the organization. Our plan is to launch it on a big scale by holding local conferences in all the main cities of the country simultaneously on Sunday September 13th, at which time local units will be established. Mass meetings are to be held in all these cities in the evening following the conference. If we carry out this project successfully it ought to have an electrical effect upon the movement.

Copies of our press service will be sent to you regularly. Will keep you informed about the progress of our organizational campaigns as well as of the other activities which we are developing.

Best wishes to you,

Fraternally yours,
International Labor Defense
J.P. Cannon
Executive Secretary

Cannon Replies to Henry Askeli

Published 8 August 1925

The following article by Cannon was published in the Daily Worker *magazine supplement. It replies to "Are the Finns Social Democrats?", an article by Finnish-Language Federation leader Henry Askeli published in the same journal. Askeli's article took issue with "rumors" within the Workers Party that the Finns supported Lore's "Two and a Half International tendency"; he wrote particularly bitterly against the "slanders" and "character assassins" of the Ruthenberg-led Central Executive Committee minority.*

In the preceding period the Superior branch of the Finnish Federation, which numbered among its members many Federation leaders, had published two articles critical of the Central Executive Committee in the party's Finnish-language press. These statements protested the levying of an assessment on party members to pay for the upcoming party convention, questioned the wisdom of the recent Comintern decision on the American question, and demanded further discussion on the issues in dispute in the party. A CEC condemnation of the Finnish statements was published in the Daily Worker, *1 August 1925.*

The Workers Party Fourth Convention instructed the Finnish Federation to remove Askeli from the editorial staff of the Federation's paper.

Comrade Askeli's article follows the two statements published by the Finnish branch of Superior and is directly related to them. The Central Executive Committee has declared that these statements contained a non-Communist tendency and represented the beginning of an ideological preparation for a split in the party. Comrade Askeli's article is another manifestation of this sentiment. It shows the same tendency in a clearer form and forces us to draw the conclusion that it amounts to an attempt to substitute a program of his own for the program of the party and the Communist International. At the moment when the serious Communist workers are striving to unify their ranks on the platform of the Communist International, comrade Askeli comes forward with an attack on the Communist International. Such propaganda tends to discredit the Communist International before the membership.

Comrade Askeli has presented a platform without one sound Communist plank in it. No one can accept this platform without first throwing away the platform of the party and the Communist International. The loyal followers of the Communist International in the party, and especially those in the Finnish Federation, have no choice but to take up at once the most resolute struggle against the political platform of comrade Askeli. The unity and integrity of the party demand such a struggle.

Incitement Against the CI

The Communist International is the most priceless acquisition of the revolutionary proletariat of the world. The authority of the Communist International is the surest guarantee that the unity of our party will be preserved and strengthened, that disintegrating opportunism will not be allowed to get a strong foothold, that mistakes will be corrected and that faltering leadership will be assisted, strengthened and equipped for its tasks. To make a breach between the party and the Comintern is the aim of those elements in all countries who shrink from the implications of a policy of determined revolutionary struggle. Comrade Askeli is following a policy which leads in this direction. His attack is directed first of all and above all at the authority of the Communist International. He opposes in a more or less direct way all the propositions put before the party by the Communist International in its recent decisions. He then unites his opposition to the various specific proposals of the Communist International into a complete and systematic opposition with the declaration that he wants a Central Executive Committee with sufficient "nerve" and "responsibility" to "settle questions without foolishly appealing to higher bodies on every little question." The practice of the Central Executive Committee in turning to the Communist International for advice and guidance and for the solution of disputed questions apparently does not commend itself to comrade Askeli. He regards it as "hesitation, indecision and a vacillating policy," which, he says, is "destructive and must be done away with."

What is such talk but incitement against the Communist International? And what could be its effect but to lead to a break between the party and the Communist International? To let the party become the prey of disintegrating tendencies and render it powerless?

Loreism

With such an attitude of general opposition to the Communist International, it is quite logical for comrade Askeli to find himself out of line with its specific decisions on the situation in our party. The Comintern has put before the party as one of its most important tasks the liquidation of the opportunist ideology of Loreism. Comrade Askeli has nothing to say on this question, except to deny the accusations of sympathy with Loreism. The open statement and direct attack on Loreism which all leading comrades should make without hesitation or evasion is lacking. On the contrary the article makes many concessions to Loreism.

Comrade Askeli says the Finnish Federation got rid of the right wing elements and the ideology of the Two and a Half International at the time of the split with the Socialist Party. We are confident that the overwhelming majority of the membership of the Finnish Federation will demonstrate that they have broken so decisively with this ideology that no one will be able to lead them back to it. But in the light of this article we cannot be so confident of comrade Askeli. A remnant of this ideology has found its way into his article.

The Labor Party

Our most important political question is the question of the labor party. The future growth and development of our party is indissolubly bound up with the solution of this problem. The first decisive steps of the American workers in constituting themselves as a class, and entering the political arena as such, will be taken through the medium of a labor party. The solution of the labor party problem is therefore of incalculable importance. It is in fact the key to the American labor movement. Every member of the party must understand this.

The Enlarged Executive Committee of the Communist International has solved the labor party problem, correcting the past mistakes of all groups in the party and laying down a clear political line for the immediate future. It is of the utmost importance that every leading comrade take a clear and unequivocal stand on this question. Mistaken conceptions of the past must be openly acknowledged and resolutely put aside. The whole party, as one man, must consciously swing its energy into the labor party movement according to the policy of the Communist International. In order to make this possible all leading comrades in the party and in the federations must have a unified point of view. A negative or halfhearted attitude is not permissible.

Comrade Askeli confines his remarks on this question to a couple of sentences that only serve to confuse the issue. He speaks of the questions of the third party alliance, the farmer-labor party and the present labor party policy of the party, making no distinction between them. He throws them all into one pot, labels them all "maneuvers" to be avoided and then concludes with the assertion that "99 percent of our membership is against that kind of policy." Such a method of presenting the question can only confuse the comrades.

"Maneuvers"

Political adventurism, maneuvers that are not based on a true analysis of all the factors in the given situation, are very dangerous for a party. But to proceed from this premise to a rejection of all maneuvers is to falsify and distort the Leninist standpoint. One of the most incorrect and harmful aspects of Loreism is its opposition to maneuvers and its undialectic conception which arbitrarily separates organization and propaganda from action and maneuvers. Askeli makes this error when he says, "We are strong for organization and education. Maneuvers do not, in our opinion, make the Workers Party." This conception is wrong. A fighting Communist party cannot be built upon it.

Organization and propaganda, actions and maneuvers, must be united in an organic whole. Without ability to maneuver there is no capacity for action and no real Communist party. The paralyzing dogma of "no maneuvers" must be eliminated from our conception at all costs. The great leaders and teachers of Leninism are constantly pressing this idea as a life and death struggle to the Communist parties. Only recently, the Executive Committee

GROUP OF MICHIGAN DEFENDANTS JUST AFTER THE BRIDGMAN RAID

Those in the picture are, left to right (top row): O'Flaherty, Erickson, Lambkin, Dunne, Mihelic, Bail, Reynolds, Ashworth; (bottom row): Talentire, Harrison, Bechtold, Nordling, Ruthenberg, Krumbein, Lerner, Sullivan, McMillan. "Ashworth" later turned out to be Francis Morrow, a stool pigeon who testified in the Foster and Ruthenberg trials.

1. August 1922

2. From left to right: Bill Dunne, Tom O'Flaherty, Bill Haywood and Jim Cannon. Probably in Moscow, spring 1925.

3. English-speaking delegates at Comintern's Fourth Congress, 1922. On floor: Otto Huiswoud, Rose Pastor Stokes. Second row: Arne Swabeck (far left), Anna Louise Strong (second from right), Alexander Trachtenberg (far right). Back row: Martin Abern (second from left), James P. Cannon (fourth from left).

4.
C.E. Ruthenberg (left) and Isaac E. Ferguson before their imprisonment in New York for sedition, 1920.

5.
William Weinstone (left) and Bertram Wolfe, 1919.

6. *Jay Lovestone, 1920s.*

7. *Jack Johnstone, 1922.*

8. *Clarence Hathaway, 1925.*

9. *Alexander Bittelman, 1927.*

10.
Founding conference of the ILD, June 1925: Jim Cannon (left) with George Maurer, secretary of the Labor Defense Council, which merged into ILD.

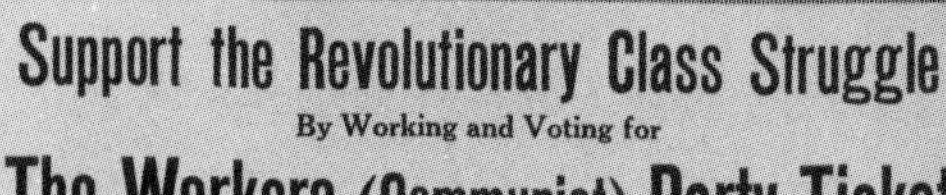

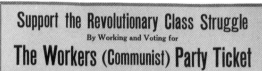

Support the Revolutionary Class Struggle

By Working and Voting for

The Workers (Communist) Party Ticket

For President:
WILLIAM Z. FOSTER

For Vice-President
BENJAMIN GITLOW

For Independent Political Action Through a Mass Party of Workers and Farmers
Make the Government and Industry Pay the Unemployed Union Wages
For Recognition of Soviet Russia
For a Workers and Farmers Government
For Nationalization of the Great Industries

Make Your Contribution to the Communist Campaign Fund

Workers Party of America,
1113 W. Washington Blvd.,
Chicago, Ill.

I enclose herewith $.................................. for the Workers Party Campaign Fund.

Name .... Address ....

11.
Workers Party campaign flyer for 1924 presidential elections.

12. Founding congress of Profintern, July 1921.

13. Executive Bureau of Profintern, 1924.
Left to right: C.E. Johnson (U.S.); Josef Hais (Czech.); A. Kalnin (USSR); Tom Mann (Britain); A. Lozovsky (USSR); W.Z. Foster (U.S.); Andrés Nin (Spain); A. Herclet (France). M. Hammer (Germany) and G. Germanetto (Italy) are absent.

14.
At Comintern's Fifth World Congress, 1924: Leon Trotsky (left) with delegate from French colonies and Vietnamese delegate Nguyen Ai Quoc (Ho Chi Minh).

15.
Leon Trotsky (left) with Arne Swabeck, in Prinkipo, Turkey, 1933.

Beginning of the march to the White House, Washington, D. C. in a protest demonstration against American military invasion of Nicaragua, arranged by the All-America Anti-Imperialist League. In the demonstration 104 were arrested, 87 later fined $5.00 apiece. The defense of those involved was conducted by the International Labor Defense. In the picture above, front row left to right, Manuel Gomez, secretary of the League with offices at 39 Union Square, New York, Max Shachtman, editor of the "Labor Defender" and Sylvan A. Pollack of the "Daily Worker".

16. Spring 1927.

17. *Martin Abern*

18. *Rose Karsner, 1925.*

BULLETIN No. 1.

Published by INDEPENDENT COMMUNIST LEAGUE of Boston

Single Copy — 5c | DECEMBER — 1928 | $3.00 per hundred

APPEAL FOR HELP!

Communists exiled to Siberia ! Communists starving on fifteen dollars a month ! Communists freezing for want of clothing and shoes ! Veterans of the October Revolution condemned to die the long Siberian Death !

No. The Roylists have not returned to power. No Czar sits on his murderous throne. Then what has happened?

These men have opposed dictatorship without previous party discussion. They could not be outargued, so they had to be framed up and deported.

Whether you agree with them or not — would you treat them thus? If you feel that it is not yet time for these men to die, it is your duty to keep them alive.

Comrade Yoffe killed himself because he felt helpless to keep up the fight against the rule of Stalin. We must rush to the support of our persecuted comrades to save them from such a fate. Already thruout the world the opposition is growing. These brave Russian Comrades, who would rather die than submit to factional terrorism, must be kept alive !

Send contributions to Dr. A. F. Konikow, 857 Beacon Street, Boston, Mass.

INDEPENDENT COMMUNIST LEAGUE

Secretary, Dr. ANTOINETTE F. KONIKOW
Organiser, L. SCHLOSBERG
Treasurer, EVA WEINER
Fin. Sec'y, CELIA COPPERSTEIN

P. S. Contributions are also needed to help our organization to keep you posted on news concerning the opposition in Soviet Russia and in our country.

WHAT IS WRONG WITH THE COMMUNIST PARTY ?

Certainly the principles of the Communist Party are not wrong. The Dictatorship of the Proletariat, as a transition to Communism, the effective work against capitalism and its conscious and unconscious supporters, the expose of the Socialist Party — these are the strength and glory of the Communist movement.

Then what is wrong? So deeply wrong that it is bound to become dangerous to the movement. What is the reason that so many communists find it impossible to work for communism within the party. The great sore growing larger and deeper in the communist movement is its form of organization carried over from the time of the Russian revolution; namely, the centralized democracy NOW without democracy, the strict discipline NOW without previous discussion, the power acquired by a faction of the Communist Party of Soviet Russia to demand obedience not only in Soviet Russia, but all over the world.

HOW DID THE PRESENT LEADERSHIP OF THE R. C. P. ATTAIN SUCH POWER?

First, because the Workers of the World look upon them as the direct followers of Lenin, because upon their heads rests yet the halo of the October revolution. All achievements of Soviet Russia for the last ten years are considered to be their work. In fact, the workers identified them, just as they do themselves, with the Russian revolution and with Soviet Russia. Whoever is against that faction is accused of being against the October revolution and against Soviet Russia. History made the Russian Communist Party, in the eyes of the workers of the world, the representatives of Soviet Russia, but in reality they represent only a faction in the R. C. P., which knows how to control its own Party and the Comintern. In the first year of the Soviet government all comrades of the executive committee had their say however deeply they differed. There were no bosses at that time and Lenin attained his influence only through the strength of his arguments and his deep knowledge, certainly not by mechanical control. This has changed since Zinovieff became secretary of the Comintern.

HOW IS THE R. C. P. AND ALL OTHER COMMUNIST PARTIES CONTROLLED BY ONE FACTION?

He, Zinovieff, was the first to establish boss rule. When he was removed the comrades all over the world gave a sigh of relief, finding out soon that there was only a change of power, Stalin having taken his place. The Russian Communist Party is ruled now by the Stalin-Bucharin faction through the application of the so-called centralized democracy, or rather "simplified democracy", as a Russian comrade satirically characterized it. He says the general secretary of the party appoints the secretary of the state organization and so downward till the nucleus is reached. Then starts the movement in the opposite direction.

The secretaries of the nuclei "elect" the secretaries of the higher units who have appointed them; these "elect" the secretaries of the next higher unit, (naturally those who have appointed them) and so it goes on till the secretaries of the districts or Goubernias are reached. They form the party conference, who certainly "elected" Stalin as the secretary of the party. The same "simplified democracy" holds good for the organizations of the Comintern and the organizations of all other Communist parties. The ruling factions can perpetuate themselves through perfect control of the party press and all avenues of information. If the majority of any Communist party proves unsuitable to the Comintern, "simplified democracy" at once begins to work. In other words, the Comintern appoints the comrades satsifactory to themselves.

19. *Antoinette Konikow (right). First issue of* Bulletin *of the Independent Communist League of Boston, December 1928.*

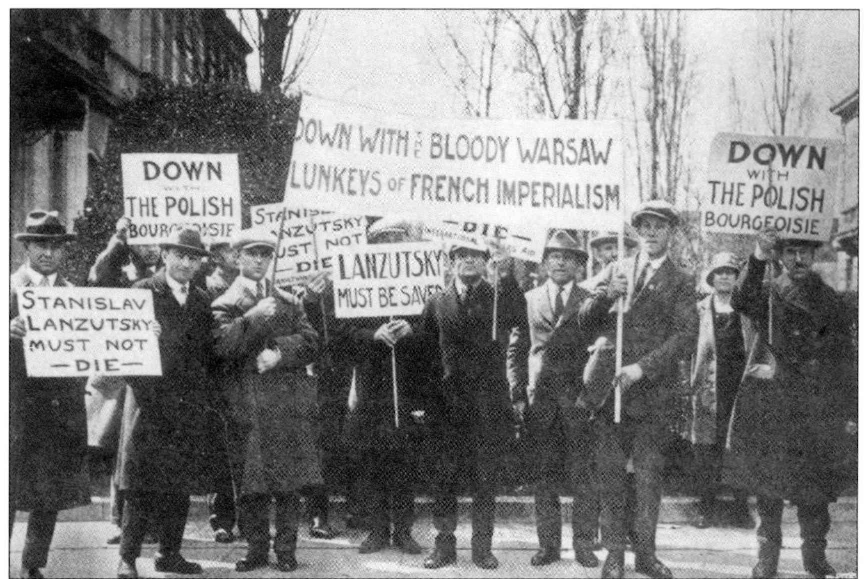

20. March 1925: Protest against white terror in Poland and threatened execution of Stanislav Lanzutsky, Communist member of Polish parliament. Demonstration in front of Polish embassy in Washington was part of national campaign.

21. Spring 1928: Workers Party picket in Washington, D.C., against U.S. intervention in Nicaragua.

22. Communist-supported garment workers leaders, New York, 1929. From left to right: Philip Goodman, Charles Zimmerman, Ben Gold, Louis Hyman.

23. Militant pickets during Communist-led New York garment workers strike, 1926.

24. *Above: James P. Cannon giving report to Second Conference of the International Labor Defense, September 1926. Elizabeth Gurley Flynn is seated next to Cannon. Below: Group of delegates to conference. Cannon and Flynn are standing at middle left of second row.*

25. *Funeral procession for Sacco and Vanzetti, Boston, August 1927.*

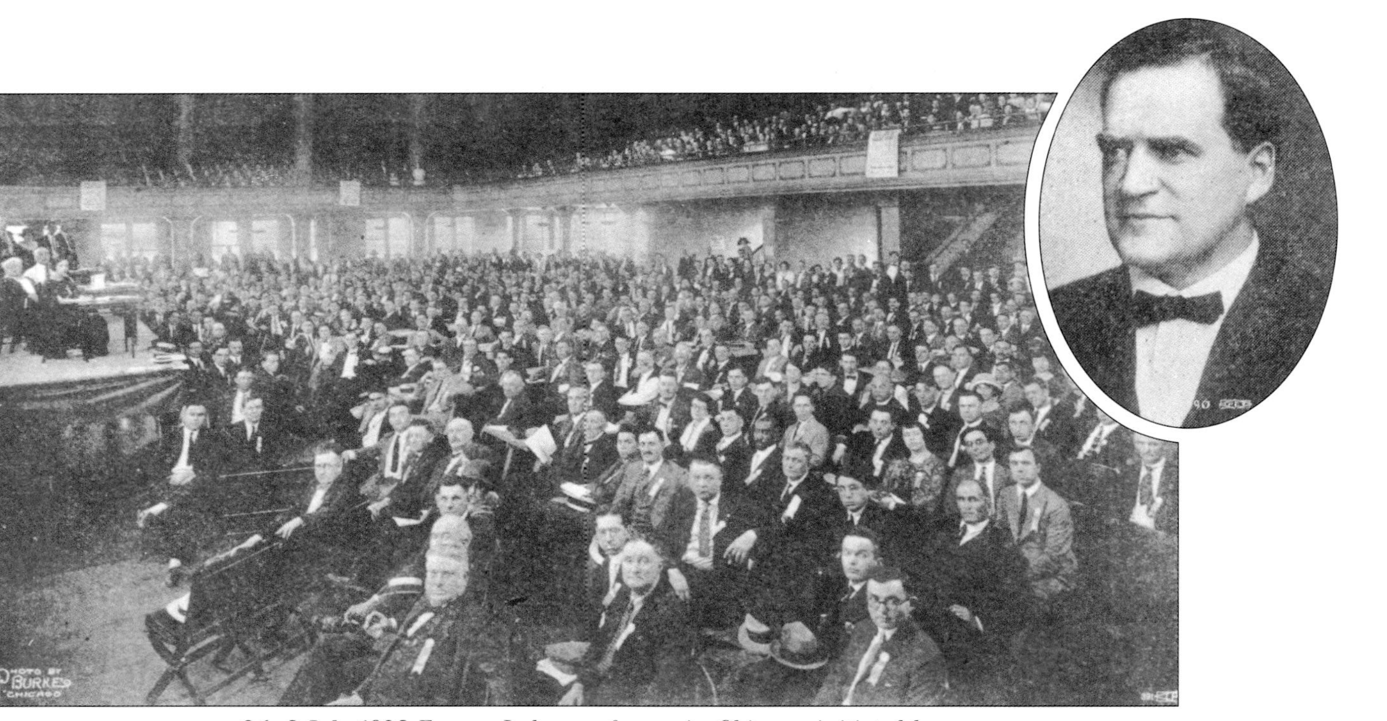

26. 3 July 1923 Farmer-Labor conference in Chicago, initiated by Chicago Federation of Labor leader John Fitzpatrick (inset).

One of Three Food Relief Stations Supported by the INTERNATIONAL WORKERS' AID.

In Passaic, New Jersey

Where the sun shines upon dire want and misery—18,000 men, women, and young workers are on the picket line—they have been there for twelve long weeks, in active combat against starvation wages. They do not fear police clubs, tear gas, imprisonment—but

They Must Have Food!

60,000 human beings depend upon their fellow workers and friends to help them keep the wolf from the door—while they are fighting for a living wage and the right to be organized.

The Bosses Say—STARVE THEM INTO SUBMISSION!

The I. W. A. Says—FEED THEM ONTO VICTORY!

Cut Out This Slip and Mail with Your Contribution. DO IT NOW!

INTERNATIONAL WORKERS' AID,
1553 W. Madison St., Chicago, Ill.
National Office.

Dear Friends: Enclosed find $............ as a contribution for Passaic textile strike relief.

Signed............ Address............

City............ State............

27. *Communist-led strike of textile workers in Passaic, New Jersey, 1926, drew support from all over U.S. The Workers Party organized massive relief effort.*

28. A group of arrested mine pickets following release by Pennsylvania police, spring 1928. Kansas miners leader Alexander Howat (inset), who often allied with Communists in the miners' union in the 1920s.

of the Communist International was obliged to adopt a special resolution against the doctrine of "no maneuvers" which was threatening to paralyze the Communist Party of Germany and which had already led it to the most serious errors in connection with the question of the monarchy. "The Communist Party of Germany must learn how to maneuver," said the resolution of the Communist International.[1] Our party must also learn and in order to do so it must reject the standpoint which is presented by the article of comrade Askeli.

Shop Nuclei

The Bolshevization of the party implies reorganization on the basis of shop nuclei. Our party is confronted with colossal difficulties in this respect on account of its small membership and many national divisions. The success of our campaign to construct the party on the shop nuclei basis requires the active, conscious and wholehearted support of the leading comrades of the various federations. Comrade Askeli does not give such support. He gives the shop nuclei form of organization only a negative endorsement and attempts to discredit it in advance with the statement that he favors it, "not so much that it is practical, tried and true, but because theoretically it appears practical and true and this must be shown." The transformation of our party from the social-democratic form of organization to the Communist form of organization, built in the workshops, will never be accomplished by such a skeptical attitude. The position of comrade Askeli

[1] In the presidential elections in Germany at the end of March 1925 the Communist International, fearful that the right-wing monarchist, Prussian Field Marshal Paul von Hindenburg, would be elected if the working-class vote was split, had advocated that the German Communist Party withdraw its candidate after the first round and support that of the Social Democrats. But the German Central Committee opposed the tactic. The Social Democrats withdrew their candidate in any case, in favor of the candidate of the bourgeois Center Party. Hindenburg won the election.

In July Zinoviev had sent a letter to the Tenth Congress of the German Communist Party, urging the party to reject the "ultraleft fever" and recognize the temporary stabilization of capitalism in Germany. But the German leadership under Ruth Fischer and Arkadi Maslow remained recalcitrant. On 29 July 1925 the ECCI Presidium decided to begin its campaign to remove the Fischer-Maslow leadership.

amounts to *opposition to shop nuclei,* under the flag of lip service to it. The party must oppose and reject this standpoint.

The Federation Question

The Communist International and the Central Executive Committee of our party have come to the definite conclusion that the existence of separate language federations must be done away with. The language federations must be fused into a single centralized party. The organization letter of the Communist International gives detailed and specific instructions on this question; and the resolution of the Parity Commission takes a clear and definite stand for the complete centralization of the party and the complete abolition of the present federation form of the organization. The energetic carrying out of these resolutions is an indispensable part of the process of Bolshevizing the party.

On this vital question as well as on all the others raised in his article, comrade Askeli takes a wrong stand. The letter of the Communist International and the resolution of the Parity Commission provide for the reconstruction of the present language branches as non-partisan workers' clubs. The proposal of comrade Askeli to maintain the federations on a national scale, "working independently under the ideological leadership of the Workers Party," would tend, in our opinion, to separate still more the federations from the party and reduce the control of the party over them to a fiction.

Factionalism

There exists in the party a sentiment against factionalism and factional groupings. Comrade Askeli appears to be attempting to play upon this sentiment and to exploit it for his own factional purpose. The decision of the Comintern demands the liquidation of factionalism and calls for the unity of the party on the basis of the political platform of the Communist International. Comrade Askeli would make it impossible to accomplish this result. Under cover of acceptance of the first half of this provision, his article reads like an attempt to prevent the unification of the party and to create a new faction of his own on a non-Communist platform. The members of the Finnish Federation who are against factionalism must be on their guard and not allow anyone to maneuver them into a faction against the party and the Comintern.

"History"

We would like to find some part of comrade Askeli's platform on which we could agree, but this is impossible. The platform is wrong from start to finish. Even the "history" which comrade Askeli recites is presented in a false light. He attempts to throw aspersions upon the glorious past of our party and to take credit to himself for remaining in the Socialist Party after the split.[2] It is quite true that the left wing made a tactical error in allowing the reactionary leaders of the Socialist Party to force the split too quickly. And it can also be admitted that the first programs of our party contained some leftist mistakes. But in spite of all, the fundamental line of division at the time of the split, which completely overshadowed all minor, tactical questions, was between revolutionary Communists and reformist social democrats; and it is no credit to anyone who, at the decisive moment, remained in the ranks of the Socialist Party. In such a situation, one who has a clear Communist position always unites with the Communists, even though he disagrees with their tactics. This is a fundamental principle.

We do not mean by these remarks to bring up the past in such a way as to cast any reflection on the comrades now in our ranks who took the wrong position in the historical days when the revolutionary vanguard in America was first organizing itself into a party. We know very well that many who remained in the Socialist Party at the time of the split and who later joined our ranks have done and are doing good work for Communism. The error of the past has been made good many times over and now has only historical significance. It is quite unnecessary to refer to it again, and we would be among the last to do so. But when the history of the party is considered, one

---

[2] The Finnish Federation had remained in the Socialist Party after the bulk of the Communist forces split in 1919. The Finns did not unite with the Communists until 1921, when they joined the Workers Party as part of the Workers' Council group.

should relate the past events in their true perspective. Comrade Askeli fails to do this.

The Federation Split of 1914

We take issue with another part of comrade Askeli's "history" —the part dealing with the split in the Finnish Federation in 1914. Moreover, we are of the opinion that the narrow attitude manifested by comrade Askeli may explain, to a certain degree, the reason we have not had greater success in healing the effects of that split and in winning over to Communism the Finnish workers who have fallen under the influence of anarcho-syndicalism.[3]

The platform of the syndicalist group in 1914 was politically incorrect, but so was the platform of the Socialists. A true explanation of the emergence of syndicalism and anarcho-syndicalism as a phenomenon in the labor movement is impossible unless one understands and clearly states that pre-war syndicalism represented an extreme reaction against reformist, parliamentary socialism. Reformist socialism is the father of syndicalism. This is the way to explain the split of 1914 and to show to the syndicalist workers that the Communist Party and the Communist conception of political action have nothing in common with the Socialist Party and the Socialist conception of political action against which they made a justifiable revolt, which led them to extreme and unsound doctrines.

The Communist Party and its Finnish section ought to represent, at least to a certain extent, a union of the best proletarian elements from the Socialist Party and the syndicalist movement. The Communist International was of this opinion when it invited the IWW as well as the left wing of the Socialist Party to send delegates to its First Congress. The Communist International declared many times that the progress of the Communist parties

---

[3] The Finnish Federation was not immune to the anarcho-syndicalism which swept the Socialist Party left wing from 1911 to 1914. During a strike by Michigan copper miners in 1914, pro-IWW sentiment grew rapidly among the Finns. The syndicalist wing actually took over a number of Finnish branches and, briefly, the Federation's paper, *Työmies* (The Worker), before being expelled by the reformist Federation leadership.

would be measured in a large degree by their success in winning over the syndicalist workers to the platform of Communism.

Many of the best revolutionary syndicalists responded to the Communist International and are in its ranks today. They are fully entitled to be placed on an equal footing with the revolutionary workers who came from the Socialist Party, without recriminations with regard to the past being brought up against them. Comrade Askeli has no right to give such a one-sided account of the old fight and to ridicule and attack them in such a bureaucratic and intolerant manner.

Anarcho-syndicalism still finds too much support among the Finnish workers in America. It is one of the most urgent tasks of the Finnish section of our party to win over the Finnish syndicalist workers to the platform of Communism and to draw the best of them into the party. This task can be carried out successfully only on the condition that we adopt the correct Communist policy on this question and reject the policy of comrade Askeli.

Fight for the Party

The great constructive work performed by the comrades in the Finnish Federation is known and appreciated by the party. The organizing genius of the Finnish comrades is responsible for many achievements from which the party has much to learn. We know that many of the greatest undertakings of the party, such as, for example, the establishment and maintenance of the *Daily Worker*, would hardly have been possible without the loyal support and generous sacrifice of the Finnish comrades. These facts are so well known as to need no special mention.

Comrade Askeli allows himself to present even these facts in the wrong way. In some of his language he creates the impression of an attempt to arouse among the Finnish comrades a federation patriotism as against a party patriotism, and to set them against the party on nationalistic grounds. The sharp criticism which the party directs against such non-Communistic policies as those put up by comrade Askeli are twisted around by him and made to appear as attacks against the Finnish Federation and against the Finnish comrades as such. The Finnish Communists are bound to repulse such methods.

Any attempt to make a breach between the party and the

Communist International and to lay the basis for a split must be fought against by every Communist. The whole party must mobilize itself for quick and resolute action to defeat such designs, which, if allowed to gain headway, would endanger all the achievements of the past six years.

The efforts of comrade Askeli to put himself up as the spokesman of the Finnish members of the party and to identify them with his program does not by any means signify that this is really the case. We are absolutely confident that the overwhelming majority of the members of the Finnish Federation will reject the program of Askeli without hesitation and in such a decisive manner that Askeli and those disposed to support him will be compelled to abandon their plans. The Bureau of the Finnish Federation has set an example to the whole membership by its resolute and determined stand in support of the party. The interests of Communism demand that the Finnish branches of the party follow the example of the Bureau and repudiate the policies of comrade Askeli and those who share his views. We are confident this will be done.

The Achievements of the Parity Commission

Published 11 August 1925

The following article by Cannon appeared in the Daily Worker. *The Comintern Executive Committee's Fifth Plenum decision on the American question had mandated an early party convention to settle the question of party leadership. In the meantime a Parity Commission was established to decide all disputed questions. The Parity Commission included Foster, Cannon and Bittelman for the majority and Ruthenberg, Lovestone and Bedacht for the minority. Comintern representative S.I. Gusev was the nominally "neutral" commission chairman.*

The Parity Commission commenced its work at a moment when the party was facing a most serious crisis. The majority and minority groups had crystallized themselves into the most rigid formation throughout the party. The positive aspects of the factional fight had exhausted themselves and disintegration was setting in. Party activity was paralyzed. The authority of party leadership was becoming undermined and was being replaced by factional leadership. In this favorable soil the right wing danger was growing, and the struggle against it was being subordinated to the struggle between the majority and minority. The situation in Cleveland was warning the party like an alarm bell of the danger of a split.[1]

In this desperate crisis the Parity Commission was constituted and commenced its sessions. The party members, wearied of the

[1] The Cleveland party organization was at the time fairly evenly divided between the Foster-Cannon majority and the Ruthenberg minority. Beginning in March, when the Workers Party leadership was still in Moscow at the ECCI plenum, the majority and minority members of the Cleveland Executive Committee and Cleveland Yiddish-language branch had engaged in a series of mutual suspensions and expulsions, resulting in a virtual split in the Cleveland party. See "Declaration of the Parity Commission," *DW*, 28 July 1925.

factional fight and fearful of its possible consequences, turned their attention toward the Parity Commission. Six years of party experience had taught the most responsible comrades in the party to fear splits and to guard the unity of the party at all costs. They looked with hope to the Parity Commission to find a solution which would turn the party back from the danger of a split, consolidate the Communist forces in the fight against Loreism and put the party on the road to unity.

The most urgent tasks of the Parity Commission were to save the party from the danger of a split, to unite all Communist elements in the fight against Loreism, to lay the foundation for the liquidation of factionalism, and to prepare the party to direct its energy, which is now being consumed by factionalism, into constructive work in all fields.

How did the Parity Commission deal with these tasks and to what extent did it accomplish them? The best way to answer this question is to review its proceedings and their results.

It was to be expected, in view of the general situation in the party, that a somewhat factional atmosphere should characterize the first sessions. This was accentuated by the fact that disputes over organizational and factional questions were taken up for consideration first. These conflicts brought many sharp clashes which made mutual agreement impossible. It was impossible for the two groups which had been engaged in the struggle for such a long period to see organizational and factional questions from the same standpoint. The factional situation made a solution of these problems very difficult.

However, consciousness of the seriousness in the party and of the grave responsibility resting upon us finally made concessions possible. Unanimity on the disputed factional and organizational questions was finally reached by means of compromises and concessions when mutual agreement was lacking. We believe this was the best course to follow under the circumstances. Factional interests were injured by some of these decisions, but the advantage to the party of a settlement of all disputes with the authority of unanimous decisions outweighed these considerations. The stabilizing effect on the party of the organizational decisions of the commission is proof of the correctness of this view.

While the settlement of the organizational questions marked

a certain progress in the work of the Parity Commission, the crucial test came when the political resolutions were to be considered. Serious differences on these resolutions would have made unanimity impossible and would have canceled much of the practical value of the other decisions. Since political platforms are the only basis on which factional groupings can stand for any length of time, the consideration of the political resolutions of the two groups in the Central Executive Committee had to determine the question whether the foundation could be laid for the liquidation of the factional fight between the majority and minority and their unification on a common platform in the fight against Loreism. The political resolutions, which were all unanimously adopted, are the answer to this question.

The discussion over the political resolutions was conducted in an atmosphere considerably moderated. Each group brought forward its own resolutions on all the questions. A study of the resolutions showed differences only in construction and phrasing, but no serious differences in policy. Therefore it became possible in each case, either by taking one resolution as the basis and amending it, or by combining the two resolutions, to reach unanimous agreement. Serious controversy did not arise over a single point of principle or tactics. It became obvious that the two groups in the Central Executive Committee, which have been fighting over political questions with more or less intensity for the past two years, would be able to go to the convention with a common platform.

After the long factional fight, which had virtually developed to the point of two parties within the party, and, consequently, to the danger of a split, the two groups, with the assistance of the Comintern, were finally able to adopt a common political platform dealing with all party questions, external and internal. This common platform is not the product of compromise, but of agreement on all fundamental points. In the face of this political agreement, the unification of the two groups becomes possible and necessary. Anyone who would now attempt to continue or to aggravate the factional fight would take upon himself a grave responsibility indeed.

The unanimous resolutions of the Parity Commission have laid the foundations for unity but they have not liquidated the struggle between the two groups. It would be utopian to expect that the groupings could be dissolved on the eve of the party convention or that a preconvention struggle could be entirely eliminated, since the question of leadership is not yet decided. Besides, the complete liquidation of the factional fight is beyond the power of the Parity Commission. That can be accomplished only by the party members of both groups, especially the leading members, cooperating in good faith with the Parity Commission and striving to put its resolutions into life.

The Parity Commission has enabled the two groups to take the first real step toward unity. They must take the next step themselves by basing themselves on its resolutions and by consciously striving for unity. The way to do this is to put the main energy into the fight against Loreism; to subordinate factional interests to party interests; to emphasize the fundamental points of agreement more than the minor points of disagreement; to lay more stress on plans for future work than on recriminations over past disputes.

The party must concentrate its energies upon the big tasks confronting it. Loreism must be fought against and liquidated politically and organizationally. The party must be reorganized on a shop and street nuclei basis, its apparatus must be centralized and federations merged into the party. The party must extend its political horizon, broaden its base of activities and plunge into constructive work. The theoretical level of the party must be raised by systematic Leninist education.

These tasks can be accomplished if the resolutions of the Parity Commission are sincerely accepted and carried out and the Communist forces become unified. Enormous achievements are possible for the party when it unites its ranks and throws its energy into constructive work. The Parity Commission has laid the foundation for this unity. Now we must build upon it.

Our Party and the Communist International

4 October 1925

The following speech by Cannon was delivered to the national convention of the Communist Party's youth group, the Young Workers League, and published in the Daily Worker *on 8 October 1925.*

The Foster-Cannon faction had won the majority of delegates to the Workers Party's Fourth Convention in late August 1925. However, a cable from the Communist International arrived in the middle of the convention: it declared that the Ruthenberg group was more "loyal" to the Comintern and "closer to its views." It also demanded that the Ruthenberg group be given at least 40 percent of the seats on the new Central Executive Committee.

Foster and Cannon disagreed over how to respond to this cable, as Cannon describes in this speech. Cannon's views carried the day within the Foster-Cannon faction. The CEC which was selected contained an equal number of Ruthenberg-Lovestone and Cannon-Foster supporters, as well as a representative of the Comintern. After the convention, the Comintern representative, S.I. Gusev, announced his intention of voting with Ruthenberg-Lovestone, thus giving the former minority the majority of the CEC.

Foster sought to appeal the Comintern decision after the convention. Cannon disagreed with Foster's course, and this speech marks the final split between the two. Foster's speech to the YWL convention, which defended his appeal of the CI decision, was published in the Daily Worker *along with Cannon's.*

Comrade Chairman and Comrades:

The youth league is meeting in this national convention just at a time of a particularly serious crisis in the party, and I am speaking here as one of the party representatives under circumstances which I think must be known to you comrades.

As a result of the decision of the last convention, and the decision of the Communist International, the Central Executive

Committee leadership is represented by the group which, prior to the party convention, was the minority, and which, as you know, I do not belong to. So in speaking here tonight I am doing so after consultation with the delegation of the Central Executive Committee, not as a direct representative of the Central Executive Committee, but I am speaking by permission of the Central Executive Committee in my own name, and in the name of a large number of comrades whose views coincide with mine.

The situation of the party requires very clear statements from us, and I propose here to make these statements. I propose to give the party and the Comintern an answer to every question, which they have a right to ask us in this situation.

I said the party is in a crisis, and we all know this. In my opinion, it is a crisis of Bolshevization. Our party is going through the travail of accelerated development towards a real Bolshevist party. It is the process of "The Birth of a Communist Party" of which comrade Zinoviev once wrote. The party appears to be torn into all kinds of groups, factions and subfactions as a result of this process.

The problem before the party, above all others, or rather embracing all others, is the problem of Bolshevization. And it is clear that the central question in the problem of Bolshevization is now the question of the relations of the party to the Communist International.

Bolshevization, without a correct estimate of the relations of the party and the party leaders to the Communist International, is merely an empty phrase. Bolshevization program or Bolshevization resolutions that do not take into account the full significance of the fact that we are members of the world Communist party, with international leadership, do not contain the real essence of Bolshevization.

Because of the peculiar nature of the present situation, and because of the rapid changes which have taken place in the party leadership, it is manifestly the duty of those comrades who prior to the convention composed the majority group to make known their attitude towards the party crisis, and their proposals for its solution.

I think it is known to nearly all comrades in the party, as it has been known for some time to the members of the former majority, that the former majority group is itself in the process of the deepest crisis. This crisis within the group of the former majority is a part of the crisis in the party. For that reason it is the concern of the party, and should be made known to it. Factions can have no interests of their own in a Communist party. They have to be related to the interests of the party.

Within the group of the former majority there has been in recent times a very thoroughgoing discussion. Very strong pressure has been put upon one section by another section. This pressure has had certain effects. But these effects have not been sufficiently decisive. Therefore it is necessary for the group of the former majority to have more pressure put upon it, from the outside, directly before the whole party. My speech here tonight has this purpose.

So I am going to discuss the question before the Young Workers League convention, not merely for the YWL, but for the party, since this convention is a forum before the whole party. I am going to speak about the situation which has developed within the ranks of the former majority. When I say this, I want to inform you in advance that if any comrade expects to hear me relate any private conversations, "secrets," scandals, or petty gossip, or anything of this sort, he will be disappointed. I will confine my remarks entirely to the questions which have political significance and a political content, which are known to all the leading comrades of the group and which are of concern to the party.

Comrade Green [Gusev] in his article in the *Daily Worker* the other day made the statement that the differences within the group of the former majority are not less serious than the differences between the former majority and the former minority. I want to testify here to the accuracy of this estimate.

The differences within the former majority are as serious as were those between the two former factions. Differences arose at the convention and have been intensifying since the convention. But these differences which came to the surface in the convention crisis, and which have intensified since then, were themselves the outgrowth of old differences, and were foreshadowed by the old differences. And all of these differences have become synthesized and concentrated now into one, big predominant question.

That question is this: *the role of the Communist International and the relations of our party and our party leaders to the Communist International.*

In the controversy in the group over this question, a conflict has developed between comrade Foster and myself. And in connection with the remarks I make on this I want to remind the comrades of my long collaboration with comrade Foster.

Some of the greatest forward steps of the party have been brought about as the result of this collaboration, together with some other comrades. As far back as 1921 and 1922, this collaboration made it possible simultaneously to develop the trade union work on a broad scale and to organize the legal party. These achievements laid the basis for the party to become a factor in the labor movement. Comrade Foster played a tremendous role in all of this, and I collaborated with him and with other comrades. And if we now come to the point where our differences are so sharp that there appears to be no possibility to reconcile them—and we are at such a point—it is not without great pain to those who were part of the collaboration.

On receipt of the Communist International telegram, a profound crisis was immediately precipitated in the group of the former majority at the party convention. The immediate difference appeared to arise over two separate propositions put before the caucus: one by comrade Foster and one by comrade Dunne and myself. Comrade Foster's original proposition was that we should accept only a minority of the Central Executive Committee, and that he should not participate, and that the organization of the new Central Executive Committee in fact should be carried out by the representative of the Communist International, and not by us who were the majority at the convention. Our counterproposition was that we, the majority, should organize the Central Executive Committee. At first I proposed an even division, half and half, and later it was modified to include the representative of the Communist International, on his suggestion. The difference was not technical but political. It was a difference in attitude towards the decision and towards the situation created by it. I considered that comrade Foster's proposition had serious objective consequences. I considered that if we, as a majority of the convention, should refuse to organize the new Central Executive Committee, or that in any event comrade Foster should not go into the new Central Executive Committee, it could not be interpreted in any other way than that we were rejecting responsibility for the Central Executive Committee. This would mean that the party would be thrown into a crisis in which the Central Executive Committee would be deprived of the assistance and support which it would require from us to pull the party through the crisis.

Our proposition was based on the opinion that the situation was such in the party, precipitated by the decision, that we were obliged, if we wish to save the party from demoralization, to take responsibility to the full limit of the possibilities under the provisions of the decision.

We held a discussion in the caucus for two days, and in this discussion I pointed out, together with other comrades, the objective consequences of the attitude shown by comrade Foster.

We stated there that comrade Foster's proposition would create a condition making it impossible for the party to work, or for the Central Executive Committee to lead it or control it; and that this would bring us inevitably not only into conflict with the Central Executive Committee, but into conflict with the Communist International, since the decision of the Communist International was the main factor; that consequently, regardless of the intention of the comrades, the whole objective tendency would be for all elements in the party who are in any degree actively or passively in opposition to the Communist International to rally around our standpoint, and enmesh us more and more into a position of opposition, which would inevitably develop into opposition to the Communist International.

And it was because we had such a deep conviction that this line would lead in this direction that we spoke ultimatively with great determination in the caucus. The tendency represented by comrade Foster met the most powerful opposition; it met opposition from the very backbone of the former majority group.

Comrades from all sections of the country, the leading, most responsible and most influential comrades, took a decided stand against it, and the final result was that a majority voted in favor of our proposal. We were then willing to consider the difference which arose over the Communist International decision as liquidated on the basis of the adoption of our policy, which was a decisive policy of responsibility for the party.

But this policy of responsibility for the party did not develop as the policy of comrade Foster after the convention. We were no sooner out of this crisis than we immediately plunged into a new crisis in the group, that is, amongst the comrades who belonged to the former group. This conflict was organically connected with the conflict at the convention. It was over the appeal to the Communist International.

It has been stated here by comrade Bedacht, and I think it is known to every Communist, that it is not only the right of a Communist who disagrees with a decision of the Communist International to appeal for a reconsideration, but it is his duty to do so. It is the duty of any Communist who thinks the Communist International needs more information on any question to furnish this information.

I disagree totally with the implications of comrade Stachel's statements here that an appeal to the Communist International is in itself in any sense a violation of Communist rights. However, there are two sides to this question of appealing to the Communist International.

On the one hand it is the duty, not merely the right, of comrades to appeal to the Communist International. On the other hand it is impermissible for them, when they are appealing to the Communist International, to appeal at the same time to the party, because that negates the whole principle involved in the appeal to the Communist International. An appeal to the party on the basis of an appeal to the Communist International is nothing less than an attempt to put the party in a position of opposition to the decision of the Communist International. No matter what is one's intention, this is the objective effect. Therefore we opposed the tendency that developed within our group to present resolutions to the party organizations endorsing the appeal of the former majority to the Communist International.

What was this conditioned upon? To us it was very clear, after a little consideration, that if the group of the former majority would present such a motion to a meeting of the party, it could only be adopted on the condition that the comrades present would be convinced that the appeal was justified and valid. In other words, they would have to be convinced that the decision was an error. In order to accomplish this it would be necessary, and would follow, in spite of all intentions, that propaganda and agitation would be made to convince party comrades that the decision of the Communist International is wrong. This is not permissible, because this is appealing in the party to the opinion and viewpoint that the Communist International decision was made with snap judgment, or made without due consideration. This in itself has an inevitable tendency to discredit the Communist International before the party comrades, to break down faith in the Communist International decisions. It is a step away from the Communist International. This was the position we took.

It is significant, in confirmation of my statements that this conflict over the question of the appeal had an organic connection with the convention conflict, that the alignment of comrades on this question was identically the same as the one in the convention caucus, with only a change here and there by comrades who had not understood the real question involved.

A very severe crisis developed which made it impossible to agree to a unified policy. I am sorry to say that comrades in several parts of the country, under influence of the policy which was sponsored and given support by comrade Foster, were misled into taking what I consider some false steps. These comrades who had a certain resentment against the Communist International decision began to speak quite openly against it.

Efforts within the group to compel the comrades to abandon this policy were not successful. In the New York membership meeting, as was reported in the *Daily Worker*, and as I have been informed by personal letters, some comrades of the former majority, who have been members of the party for many years, and who surely know the fundamental basis of our relations to the Communist International, allowed themselves to be placed in an impossible position. Before a membership meeting of the rank and file of the party they criticized the decision of the Communist

International. Also I read in the *Daily Worker* that similar occurrences took place in Boston.[1] The reports of the New York membership meeting greatly sharpened the crisis. It showed clearly the dangerous line that was being followed. We did not react so much in antagonism to the comrades in New York and Boston (we are confident they will quickly correct their error) as we did to the leading comrades of our former group, especially comrade Foster, because we held them to be responsible for having allowed such a situation to prevail.

We held it to be a result of the policy which they sponsored, and we decided to take drastic action to check the tendency developing amongst our comrades, as a result of the policy, to get themselves into contradiction with the decision of the Communist International. That policy proved itself to be completely wrong, completely bankrupt, and very dangerous for the party and for the movement.

We held a discussion with the comrades and presented to them in an ultimative fashion the demand that the appeal should not be made an issue in the party in any way. The comrades finally agreed to this.

But in spite of the agreement, the discussions we had with the YWL delegates seemed to center entirely around the question of the appeal. The whole discussion of the activities and the future line of the comrades seemed to hinge around this question, and proposals were made that the comrades of the YWL should come into the convention of the YWL and make a motion to endorse the appeal to the Communist International.

It was clearly demonstrated in these discussions that the acceptance of our policy was only a formal acceptance. Comrade Foster and those who supported him continued the attempt to have the essence of their policy prevail. This made further col-

---

[1] The October 4 *Daily Worker* published a report of the New York membership meeting held on September 25. William Z. Foster had called the CI decision "unexpected and unwarranted" but he advocated that it be carried out, pending appeal. Joseph Zack, Philip Aronberg and Charles Krumbein openly attacked the decision and refused to vote for it. In the Boston membership meeting George Kraska openly attacked both Zinoviev and the CI decision, according to the *Daily Worker* of October 6. Cannon was the only one to vote against condemning Kraska in the Political Committee meeting on October 9.

laboration with them impossible for us.

Further collaboration is impossible between those having our standpoint towards the relations of the party and its leaders to the Communist International, and comrades who persist in this other policy.

After this, during the few days we have been here, we have had many discussions with the youth. I personally attach tremendous importance to the convention of the YWL and to the comrades who are delegates here. So much importance that I have devoted my time almost entirely since the comrades arrived in town to discussions with them and to attempts to see to it that these comrades should not, under any circumstances, be placed in a position where they would be forming a political platform on the basis of opposition to the decision of the Communist International. The comrades representing the viewpoint of comrade Foster persisted day after day in their efforts to convince the comrades of the YWL of their position; and so persistent have these comrades been, that we were obliged to spend this entire day and all last night discussing the question with these young comrades to beat down this propaganda and this attempt to get comrades agitated on this fundamentally false basis. It was only at five o'clock this evening that we finally confirmed our victory in the YWL delegation. These comrades took their position, definitely and categorically, for our policy.

We came to the decision finally that in view of the violation of the prior agreement, these comrades who are delegates should not only take a position in the caucus against this policy, but that they should take a position openly in the convention condemning any attempts to agitate the party or the league on the question of the appeal, to discredit the decision of the Communist International, or to put up the appeal as a political platform of opposition in the party. And thanks to comrades Williamson and Shachtman, who fought side by side with me from start to finish, the YWL comrades have been led away from this false path and have unanimously adopted what I think is the correct position on the question of the relations of the party to the Communist International.

For us the question has come to the point where we could not be satisfied any longer, in view of our duties to the party and to the Communist International, with having a private understanding within a private conference. The question has come to the point for us now where we feel obliged and duty bound to take an open stand before the party in repudiation of the policy of comrade Foster, and to call openly on all comrades in the party who are willing to be influenced by us to follow our policy and not allow themselves to be maneuvered or pushed or led into any other policy on the question of the appeal to the Communist International.

This naturally brings about a very serious situation in the party on the question of our relations to comrade Foster. I personally hope that comrade Foster will be convinced and that he will turn back from the path he has drifted into.

Comrade Foster has played an important role in the party, and he has given much to the party, as we all know, and I am sure that now if comrade Foster will turn back from this course he can lay the basis for still greater work in the future. But on the other hand, if comrade Foster persists in the line that he followed even up to today, in my opinion, he will lose his influence in the party. Comrade Foster will find that he is more and more in conflict with all the best Communist elements in the party who have collaborated with him up till now.

At the convention caucus our policy was called a policy of responsibility. Now what do we mean by responsibility? We do not mean merely, comrades, that we shall accept party positions and discharge the functions of these positions, although this is important. What we mean by responsibility which must be taken by the comrades of the former majority is that we must take political responsibility to help in the solution of the crisis in the party. We must take responsibility to try to pull the party out of the crisis, to unify it, to complete the liquidation of the right wing within the party and to set it firmly on the path to Bolshevization. This is what responsibility means. Responsibility for us includes the criticism of the party in the proper time and place, and within limits of party discipline, as the conditions may make it necessary.

We do not believe the situation in the party is of such a superficial nature that it can be solved easily and quickly. Comrade Bedacht, as we know, is a very violent comrade. He spoke here tonight very violently. But I am afraid comrade Bedacht underestimates, at least in a slight degree, the deep seriousness of the problem in the party. In my opinion it is necessary for us to understand that mechanical measures have definite limitations. Mechanical methods of solving political problems have always to me appeared defective. I have learned this by experience in the party as well as by study. I do not believe that the crisis can be liquidated by persecution and terrorism of comrades.

We all know there is a certain dissatisfaction amongst some comrades. But I say it is impermissible for leaders of the party—whether they belong to the present official leadership or whether their leadership accrues from their influence within the party as the result of their past party work—it is impermissible for them to allow this sentiment to drift in the party, because it can drift only in one direction. We cannot permit ourselves to enter into propaganda, either openly in a party meeting or privately in discussion with the rank and file comrades, which continually questions the Communist International decision, and represents it as the result of false information.

I don't think it is necessary to argue so much here as we did in the private discussions, since the problem has been liquidated for our comrades who are delegates. We have been fighting comrades adopting these tactics (and there were some comrades, I am sorry to say, with whom I have long been associated, some of them even before the organization of the party, in the revolutionary labor movement, and in constant collaboration), and it is no pleasure to be in such sharp conflict with them. But we have reminded these comrades, and we want to remind them now before the party, that everyone in the Comintern who wound up in the camp of the social democrats began his opposition to the Communist International with statements such as we have been hearing lately. Comrades, regardless of intentions, in politics every action has its own logic; every action has an objective result, and it leads in a certain direction.

The policy adopted in the convention caucus by comrade Foster, which was adhered to even after it was formally defeated, led to making the Communist International appeal an issue. And this in turn led some comrades in the membership meeting openly to criticize the decision of the Communist International. Each step led in the same direction and that direction is the wrong one.

I think it is our duty now to come out and say openly before the party that we are going to strive with all our power, and with all our energy, to see to it that not a single Communist is led any longer in that direction; that he shall turn back if he has already taken such steps.

We have some opinions in regard to the solution of the present crisis in the party. We believe it requires a united front of all the Communist elements against the right wing, and against the right wing tendencies. When I say a united front against the right wing, I say it in the sense of the decision of the Communist International plenum of last April, and which has not been fully carried out up till now.

We think the crisis requires that comrades, especially leading comrades, do not forget what the CI called attention to in Germany: the necessity for a real Bolshevist self-criticism, which has not been practiced up to now. We think it requires a liquidation of the policy of refusing to admit mistakes or of admitting mistakes in such a way as to justify them. The party leaders have to begin to speak openly to the party and to the CI about everything that has been done wrongly, in order that the party and the CI can enable us to get straight.

And, finally, our opinion of the thing that is necessary for the liquidation of the party crisis is the firm establishment of real Communist relations between the party and the CI, a complete break with the whole tradition of diplomatizing with the CI; a complete break with the whole tendency to regard the CI as something outside the party putting pressure on the party or the party leadership. We must develop the understanding that the party and the CI are one inseparable whole. We must have frank and open dealing with the executive of the CI and with the party; comrades must say the same thing in the party as they say in Moscow, and vice versa.

I, for one, and the comrades associated with me, and they are a considerable number, intend to follow this policy.

On Trade-Union Policy

10 October 1925

These motions by Cannon, as well as the statement by Cannon and William F. Dunne which follows, are taken from the minutes of the Workers Party Political Committee meeting of 10 October 1925.

In the period immediately following his break with Foster, Cannon generally blocked with the Ruthenberg-Lovestone group, especially on trade-union policy. At issue here was the policy the TUEL-led left wing was to follow at the upcoming convention of the International Ladies' Garment Workers' Union in Philadelphia.

The ILGWU was an important union, claiming over 91,000 members in 1924, most of them in the New York area. Earlier in 1925 the social-democratic Sigman leadership had suspended the three large New York locals which were led by TUEL members. The locals had banded together into a Joint Action Committee which continued to function as a union and collect dues, retaining the allegiance of the overwhelming majority of New York ILGWU members. Sigman had been forced to reinstate the suspended locals and call a special convention of the union for November in Philadelphia. In the period preceding the convention, Sigman forced out some of the more anti-Communist officials of his bureaucracy, in the hope of making a deal with the left wing, which had entered into negotiations with him.

The TUEL was being run at the time by Foster's lieutenant Jack Johnstone, since Foster had left for Moscow to appeal the Comintern's cable to the party's Fourth Convention. In collaboration with the leaders of the party's needle trades fraction, Johnstone exaggerated the significance of the division in the Sigman machine, advocating that the left wing make a deal with Sigman. Johnstone's written proposal insisted that if the left wing failed to win a majority of delegates to the convention, **"attempts must be made to continue the split among the reactionaries, through carefully considered tactics**. *If that split continues, under these conditions, making it impossible for anyone to form an administration* *for the union with a solid majority of the delegates behind it, the left wing shall negotiate for organizational guarantees, which will completely protect it in the control of its present positions...* ***under which conditions it will give conditional support to a mixed administration for the union until the next convention.*** *" (emphasis in original)*

Cannon and Dunne vigorously opposed this policy, as well as the idea that the left wing should seek a deal with Sigman's vice president, David Dubinsky. But they also submitted the statement which follows, protesting the attempts of the Ruthenberg majority to undercut Foster's Trade Union Department.

Motions

1. That we establish, now, definitely, as is our policy, that we will have no united front, direct or indirect, with the Sigman forces—either before the convention or during the convention.
2. If the comrades in New York consider it necessary to give partial or indirect support to Dubinsky they shall furnish the CEC with more complete and explicit information as to the reasons for it.
3. In the event of such a course being decided upon, support must be given openly and with complete explanation to the workers as to the reasons for it.
4. The CEC does not support the policy of giving indirect support to Dubinsky by, on the one hand, not nominating left wing candidates and, on the other hand, telling the workers to vote for Dubinsky's slate.
5. If it is established that Local 89 takes a semi-progressive stand, the CEC is in favor of a united front minimum program with them against the reactionaries.[1]

[1] The Political Committee did not act on Cannon's motions at this meeting. Instead, it adopted Ruthenberg's proposal that action on the issue be deferred pending receipt of more information. At a meeting of the Political Committee on October 12, at which Cannon was not present, a report by Gitlow was read, indicating that negotiations with Sigman were continuing. Motions by Ruthenberg and Dunne demanding that this policy cease were passed unanimously. A motion by Dunne rejecting any kind of deal with Dubinsky in Local 10 also passed unanimously. However, this latter motion was reversed at a Political Committee meeting on October 24, after Gitlow objected that the left wing would lose control of the New York Joint Board if they did not make the deal. Cannon and Dunne were the only Political Committee members to vote against the agreement with Dubinsky.

Statement

We wish to again remind the Political Committee of the wrong path into which we are drifting in handling trade union work. The Trade Union Department is not given sufficient initiative and is not functioning properly. Trade union questions are constantly being taken up in the Political Committee before the Trade Union Department has had the opportunity to consider them and formulate recommendations. As a corollary to this practice the comrades in charge of our work in the field are failing to supply the Trade Union Department with copies of their reports and proposals. A continuation of these practices will have the inevitable result of practically liquidating the Trade Union Department. Since the CEC has already clearly established the necessity of an active and functioning Trade Union Department we are of the opinion that it should take definite steps to ensure it. To this end we propose the following motions, some of which have been previously adopted, but not fully carried out.

1. The Trade Union Department shall meet regularly and formulate recommendations on all important questions of policy for the Political Committee.
2. All material on current trade union problems (or copies of same) shall be supplied to the Trade Union Department.
3. All comrades in charge of party trade union work in the field shall be again instructed to report regularly to the secretary of the Trade Union Department, and to send him copies of all reports on their work which are sent direct to the CEC.
4. The Political Committee should have the recommendations of the Trade Union Department on all trade union questions before taking final action on them, except in cases of emergency where immediate political decisions are necessary.

Unify the Party!

Published 16 November 1925

The following resolution was adopted by the Political Committee and published in the Daily Worker, *which also announced that Ruthenberg and Cannon would address party membership meetings around the country in order to secure support for it. The resolution was signed by Max Bedacht, Cannon, William F. Dunne, Jay Lovestone, C.E. Ruthenberg and the National Executive Committee of the Young Workers League. William Z. Foster was the only Political Committee member who did not sign it. The Foster faction retained control of the party's Chicago District Committee, which voted down the resolution by a vote of nine to eight on November 28. According to a Foster faction circular dated 3 December 1925, the Political Committee majority was forced to postpone voting on the resolution in Chicago membership meetings while it sought support in other districts.*

1. The beginning of the process of Bolshevizing our party has created a very critical situation for the party. Certain right wing elements are opposing the reorganization of the party and this attitude finds encouragement in the attack made by Lore and his followers against the Communist International and the party.[1] Elements outside of the party, counting on this situation, are encouraging those opposing the Bolshevization to leave the party and to make a stand against the Communist International. The party for more than a year has been engaged in an inner factional struggle over the question of the correct line of policy and leadership of the party. The remnants of factionalism carried over from the preconvention period have not yet been liquidated. This fac-

[1] Lore had been expelled from the Workers Party at the August convention for opposition to Bolshevization and "open opposition and hostility to the party and the Communist International."

tional struggle, while an expression of the growth of Communist understanding within the party, has seriously affected the party work among the broad masses of industrial workers and exploited farmers, so that there has been an actual falling off of the effectiveness of the party in mobilizing these masses for the class struggle against the capitalists. The policy followed by a section of the former majority under the leadership of comrade Foster objectively leads away from the Communist International and thus provides a rallying point for the right wing of the party. This policy, if not changed, will do great harm to the party.

2. That section of the former majority which supported the policy of comrades Cannon, Dunne and others was right in making an energetic and determined struggle against the policies of comrade Foster. In openly combatting the policy of comrade Foster they gave a warning to the party as to the direction in which this policy was leading. The struggle within the former majority group over the question of the relation of the party and the party leaders to the Communist International has resulted in a definite and open split in the former majority group. This process is not, however, completed. Many comrades who at first followed the policy sponsored by comrade Foster since the convention are beginning to change their course. Continuous efforts must be made to clarify the situation in order to assist these comrades to completely adopt the platform of the Communist International and Central Executive Committee.

The Basis of Unified Leadership

3. The former differences on political questions have been settled by the decisions of the Parity Commission and the national convention of the party. There is therefore no longer any reason for political groupings in the party on the basis of former differences. The decision of the party convention, the decision of the Communist International delivered to the convention, and the events since the convention have broken down the old divisions and created new ones. The party leadership must reflect all these decisions and events and must be based upon them. It must represent a unification of all those who follow and fight for the political line of the Communist International. The party situation requires the unification of all groups within the party which stand for the line of the Communist International and for the unity of the party. The remnants of the factional struggle within the party must be quickly liquidated and the whole party drawn into the work among the masses. At the present time, when the opposition to Bolshevization and reorganization is developing, when Lore and Salutsky are renewing and intensifying their attacks on the Communist International, when the Socialists are gleefully speaking of the "disintegration" of the Communist movement in America, it becomes obligatory to effect the unification of the party. It would be an error to maintain old factional groupings or to form new ones. This would weaken the struggle for unity and Bolshevization and would objectively strengthen the tendencies which are mobilizing to resist it. Under these conditions the interests of the party imperatively demand the unification of all members of the party who are for the Communist International, and their united struggle for the party and the Communist International.

The Party's Immediate Tasks

The basis for the unification of the party is a common energetic struggle to carry out the following main tasks of the party:

A. *Energetic* support of the Bolshevization of the party through (1) carrying through the reorganization of the party on the basis of shop nuclei and street nuclei (international branches) in the shortest possible time; (2) the organization and mobilization of the membership for work in the trade unions through a campaign to have all the members of the party become members of the trade unions and the systematic organization of active trade union fractions; (3) an energetic struggle against the right wing and opportunistic deviations and, as part of this struggle, the development of a systematic Marxist-Leninist education to raise the theoretical level of the party; (4) the Central Executive Committee will subject its policies and actions in all fields to constant review and criticism. This prerequisite to Bolshevization has not been practiced by the party up till now.

Our Trade Union Activities

B. The trade union policy of the party must be fundamentally revised and our work in this field reoriented according to the line laid down by the Communist International and the Profintern. Vacillating tactics which oscillate between opportunism and leftism must be replaced by sure and confident Leninist tactics which combine firm principle with the greatest flexibility and adaptability to concrete problems. The trade union work of the party must be unified with the general political work of the party. We must make the aim of our trade union work the revolutionizing of the trade unions and the drawing of the organized workers into the struggle against the capitalists as a class. The building of a firm and centralized structure of party trade union fractions must be carried on with greater energy and a clear distinction must be made between the party fractions and the general left wing movement. The party must assist the organization of the left wing in the trade unions on a broad basis and aim to combine all the progressive and opposition elements into a bloc. The official name of such a bloc is of secondary importance. The party must not hesitate at the measures necessary to prevent the narrowing down of the organized left wing movement to the Communists and their close sympathizers.

The Labor Party Campaign

C. The struggle for a labor party must be again brought to the forefront of the party work and for this purpose the party must develop a program for the 1926 election which will again mobilize the whole party for a systematic campaign to achieve this purpose. The campaign for the defense of the Soviet Union against imperialism, work among the Negro workers, work among the women, must be connected with the campaign for a labor party and must serve to create the sentiment for and aid in the actual establishment of a labor party.

Work Among the Masses

D. The great task before the Workers (Communist) Party at the present time is to unite the party and mobilize all its forces for work in the class struggle. The energy of the party members must be thrown into mass work in all fields. Activity among the masses as a prerequisite to Bolshevization must be drilled into the consciousness of every party member. The party must fight with all its power and with every necessary strategy against the attempt to isolate it and throw its energy back upon itself. The party must also conduct a resolute struggle against the tendency to construe "party work" only in the sense of inner party work as well as against the tendency to make an artificial separation between mass work and inner party work.

Unite in Support of This Program

4. The policy of the Central Executive Committee is to draw the entire party into the work of carrying out the decisions of the national convention and to give every member of the party the opportunity to work for the party, make it a real force among the masses, draw the whole party into constructive work for the building up of the party and wipe out all factional lines. All comrades who accept this platform must be given full and complete opportunity to participate in party work and responsibility, according to their ability and without any discrimination.

5. The Central Executive Committee welcomes the stand in favor of unity and the progress already made by the Young Workers (Communist) League towards the liquidation of factionalism and the unification of forces. The National Executive Committee of the league now joins in the adoption of the resolution of the Central Executive Committee of the party as the basis for the continued work and for the complete unification of the league.

6. The Central Executive Committee calls upon all units of the party and the Young Workers League to seriously study and consider this resolution and to adopt it as their platform. The adoption of this resolution on the party situation by the Central Executive Committee, the District Executive Committee, City Central Committee, and in the shop nuclei and branches should be the signal for the wiping out of all factional lines and united work of all supporters of the Communist International for the building up of the party.

Broaden the TUEL

18 March 1926

The following summary of remarks by Cannon is taken from an unpublished document entitled "Minutes of the Discussion on the American Question." The discussion evidently took place in Moscow after the conclusion of the Sixth Plenum of the Executive Committee of the Communist International, held 17 February-15 March 1926. An American Commission had been convened in Moscow in connection with the plenum. The commission decreed that the Foster group should retain control of the Workers Party's trade-union work even though the Ruthenberg faction had the majority on the party's Central Executive Committee, and it also insisted that the Trade Union Educational League be broadened into a united-front organization. This "Discussion on the American Question" was evidently called to discuss implementing the commission decision. Present were A. Lozovsky, head of the Red International of Labor Unions, William Z. Foster, William F. Dunne, Cannon, Earl Browder, Max Bedacht and John Williamson of the Young Workers League.

We must approach the problem from the new situation as laid down in the CI resolution. Everything decided here must be based on this resolution and not on any interpretation of it by one or the other side. No decision made here should reflect previous party conflicts. The program of the TUEL should not be a political program; it shall bear no party characteristics. The TUEL is a united front organ; its program must therefore be broad enough for all the left wing elements. The program should have the following characteristics: it should be short and concise; it must contain such concrete points as the policy of the class struggle, the labor party, the organization of the unorganized, trade union democracy. The company unions shall be dealt with in connection with the organization of the unorganized.

There seems to be no conflict of concepts on the question of the progressives. As many of the progressive elements as possible should be drawn into the league on the basis of the minimum program. Those of the progressives who are not yet prepared to follow the minimum program can be won over and worked with on the basis of definite concrete measures.

The next period is a transition period, for the league is now in comparative isolation. The new development can be realized only gradually. If we don't realize it in a short time it should not be construed as a failure. It is clear that the TUEL must have an organ of its own, which shall reflect the minimum program of the TUEL and not that of the party. The process of broadening the league must be a gradual one; from the top it will be reflected in the organ, from the bottom in our work in the various industries and localities. Of course, we cannot separate this from the program of the party. If we take the CI resolution as a basis we shall achieve our aim.

As to the party situation. The first necessity is *peace in the party*: the party must do more serious trade union work; the Foster majority in the Trade Union Commission is to be construed as a real leadership; the functionaries selected for trade union work are to be chosen according to their capabilities. The only possible victory will be the broadening of the TUEL. All points of dispute must be subordinated to this central aim.

Our World Party at Work

A Summary of the Proceedings of the Enlarged Executive of the Communist International

Published 27 May 1926

The following article by Cannon about the work of the Comintern Executive Committee's Sixth Plenum was published in the Daily Worker.

The material of the sessions of the Enlarged Executive Committee of the Communist International, including the resolutions and speeches, are now available in the English language. It is one of the foremost duties of all active party members to study these documents most attentively and to draw from them the necessary conclusions for the correct orientation of our party.

The material is so voluminous, and the subjects dealt with are so many and varied, that an adequate survey of the work of the plenum cannot be given in a single article. The most that can be done is to give an outline and to indicate the main points. Such an outline would be of some value if it would stimulate party comrades to an earnest study of the resolutions and discussions entire. Such is the purpose of this article.

The main points dealt with in the document of the plenum are as follows:

1. The plenum confirmed the judgment pronounced a year ago in regard to the partial and relative stabilization of capitalism in Europe, which brought with it a retardation of the development of the proletarian revolution. The Comintern estimate of the so-called stabilization of course has nothing in common with that of the social democrats, who imagine that capitalism has been reconstituted for another hundred years. On the contrary, the

Comintern maintains its premise that the capitalist system has not recovered from the effects of the World War and the sharpening of its inner contradictions and will not recover. International proletarian revolution remains the perspective of the Comintern.

2. The tactics of the Comintern, based upon the estimate of the economic and political situation, have their center of gravity in the fight for winning other social democratic and non-party workers to the side of Communism through the tactics of the united front. All attempts of certain left elements to reject or stultify the united front tactics have been completely repudiated. It was clearly established that the united front tactic is the indisputable weapon of the Communist parties in carrying out their historic task of mobilizing the masses for the struggle against capitalism, and of leading them by degrees to the platform of Communism.

3. The main slogans of the plenum were: "To the masses!" "Go deeper into the unions." "Establish connections with workers everywhere, in all fields of activity and struggle!" "Identify the Communist Party with all the life and activity of the working class!" "Guard against isolation as well as against lack of principle!"

4. The necessity of establishing connections and influence amongst the working masses, especially in this period of retarded revolutionary development, puts before the Communist parties as a life and death question the necessity to struggle against and completely annihilate the ultraleftist and sectarian tendencies which would lead the party to isolation. The main struggle of the plenum was conducted against the ultraleftist tendencies. This does not signify, by any means, however, that the Comintern "is going to the right," as some people have attempted to maintain. It was pointed out in all the discussions that this would be a completely false estimate of the policy of the Comintern. It is not a question of substituting left digressions with right deviations, but of putting the fight against deviations concretely in each case and of maintaining the clear Leninist line, which does not recognize the legitimacy of either right or left tendencies in Communism.

The right danger still exists and will be fought against by the Comintern. In the French party, for example, the right danger is the greatest danger now, although the plenum was obliged also to combat "left" tendencies there.

But for most of the parties under the present conditions (and this applies also for America, where the connection with the workers is still weak), the greatest danger is sectarianism, which would deprive the party of the possibility of gaining influence amongst the masses. The thinly disguised attempt to form an international left fraction only emphasizes the danger. The main emphasis in most cases at present must be placed on the struggle against this ultraleft tendency, but this can only be carried on successfully if the parties at the same time repulse the right elements.

5. The struggle for influence over the masses, through the tactics of the united front, naturally finds its most important field in the trade union movement, since the trade unions are the elementary and principal mass organizations of the workers. The fight for world trade union unity, in which substantial successes have already been gained by the Comintern and Profintern, remains as before in the very foreground of the struggle. The necessity of increasing manyfold the activities and the practical work of the Communists in the trade unions was strongly emphasized.

6. Following along the same general line of the united front tactic to win influence for the parties among the working masses, the plenum raised one of its most important questions, the question of Communist work in non-party mass organizations of all kinds. This question occupied a special place on the agenda and much time and attention was devoted to discussion of the ways of working in this field. The narrow conception of party work, in the sense of only internal party work, was isolated in this plenum like a complete stranger. It was made very clear that party work is also, and even principally, work outside of the party, amongst non-party masses. Great stress was laid upon the necessity of giving concrete organizational forms to the sympathetic sentiment towards Communism and towards the Russian Revolution, which has been developed through propagandistic work. Of all the existing non-party mass organizations, the International Red Aid was declared to be the one having first claim upon the members of the Communist Party.[1]

In connection with this question of non-party mass organizations it is worthwhile to quote the following paragraph from the resolution adopted by the plenum:

> Party executives should not overlook the fact that a considerable number of our party members in all the capitalist countries have not yet fully understood the obligations as emphasized by the Third World Congress, under which every Communist is to do his share of work, and also that they consider as party work only work which is within the Communist Party organization. Therefore it is essential to impress on every member of a party nucleus, of a Communist fraction, that his work among non-party social democrats, syndicalist workers—in factories, trade unions, cooperatives, workers' sports organizations, working women's organizations, sympathizing mass organizations, and also among the peasantry—is also party work, and that for the majority of party members it must even be considered as the most important part of party work. They should be careful not to lose their identity among the masses, but should deport themselves as revolutionary organizers of mass activity.

7. Considerable attention was given at this plenum to the question of internal policies and tasks of the Comintern and of the national sections. The Comintern remains as before the centralized world organization with international leadership.

But on the initiative of the Russian delegation a resolution was adopted declaring for more independence and *self-activity* of the national parties. The parties have to stand on their own feet more—select their own leaders, etc. The leadership of the Communist International must assume a more collective character through the real and actual participation in the work of the ECCI to a much greater extent than before by the foremost representatives of the important national parties.

---

[1] The International Red Aid, also widely known by its Russian acronym MOPR, was founded in 1922 out of a successful international campaign to aid the victims of white terror in Poland. Its aim was to aid "the imprisoned and persecuted fighters for the revolution," and it greatly expanded its international scope in 1924-25. Rose Karsner was the American delegate to MOPR's second international conference, held in connection with the ECCI's Fifth Plenum in March-April 1925. It was in Moscow at that time that Cannon and Bill Haywood first discussed founding an American section of the organization, the International Labor Defense.

Above all, the central committees of the parties must master the task of maintaining their leadership by virtue of their own abilities and influence, and must not rely too much on the support of the Executive Committee of the Comintern. Comrade Zinoviev said:

> Moscow has broad shoulders....Now is the time to say to all our parties: "More independence." Nearly every party has had its own experience, its achievements, and errors. Now is the time for more independence and not simply for waiting to hear from Moscow. When I say this, my words have nothing in common with the anti-Moscow and right elements, for such an attitude is tantamount to a denial of proletarian dictatorship. Such moods among the ultraleft and right are enthusiastically welcomed by the bourgeoisie and social democracy. I realize that sometimes these moods have their origin in a strong nationalist feeling, and comrade Lenin has always warned us of this danger.

Hand in hand with the policy of greater independence for the national sections goes the policy of greater responsibility by them for the leadership of the Comintern as a whole. The resolution of the plenum on this question makes it incumbent upon the larger sections of the Communist International, the German, French, Czech and Italian sections, to appoint two representatives each, and of other larger parties (including the Oriental and American parties) one representative each, who will participate in the work of the Executive Committee of the Communist International for a period of at least six months after the enlarged executives.

8. After the lessons drawn by the plenum from the experiences of the various parties in dealing with internal party questions, there cannot be any doubt that in all the parties (and especially in America where the party is as yet comparatively small and weak) a real genuine party democracy must be established unconditionally and without delay. The practice of controlling parties by mechanical means, of setting up military factional regimes, of excluding qualified comrades from participation in party work and leadership—all these practices have ended in complete bankruptcy everywhere and have brought a number of parties to the danger of disintegration and smash-up. The classic illustration of this was in the German party. But in the French party, and in a number of others, the same mechanical methods brought the same evil results. These practices have everywhere led towards isolation of the leadership from the party membership, and consequently to the isolation of the party from the masses. Control of the party apparatus alone is not leadership. Only those who are able to lead the parties politically and ideologically and morally have any legitimate claim to leadership in the future.

9. A striking feature of the plenum was the prominence of the Oriental questions and of much greater participation than ever before of representatives of Oriental parties and revolutionary movements. In contradistinction to the Second International, which bases itself upon the upper strata of the working class in "civilized" countries, the Communist International had representatives at its sessions of all the oppressed and exploited people from all parts of the world. The presence at the session of the delegates from the so-called backward countries and the exploited colonies of the world imperialists, working hand in hand with the representatives of the revolutionary workers in the highly developed capitalist countries, was a living and most convincing proof that the Communist International is in reality a world party of all the oppressed and exploited people of the earth, fighting as an international army for the international proletarian revolution.

The United Front at Passaic

Published June 1926

The following article by Cannon was published in the Labor Defender, *monthly journal of the International Labor Defense. The strike of textile workers in Passaic, New Jersey had begun in January 1926. It was led by the United Front Committee of Textile Workers, organized by a young Workers Party member named Albert Weisbord. In August the official AFL union, the United Textile Workers, agreed to take over leadership of the strike, but only on condition that Weisbord withdraw from the strike leadership. The Workers Party agreed to these terms. The strike was settled four months later on terms that amounted to a defeat.*

The Passaic strike started out as a local dispute between textile workers and the mill owners over a cut in wages, but it developed into a historic battle in the class struggle. Other issues of fundamental importance for all the workers of America came into the foreground and dominated the struggle, along with the issue of wages. Other forces besides those directly involved at the beginning were brought into play. Passaic became a battleground with the whole country looking on or taking part, according to their interests.

The 16,000 textile workers would have had the bosses licked long ago if it had been a simple fight between the two. But the mill bosses had powerful friends who came to their aid. They used the public authority on their side as though it were something they carried around in their pocket. This was an eye-opener for the workers, most of whom had been under the impression that America is a free country where a working man has got a chance and where the government belongs to the people.

The bosses, with the help of the public officials and the courts, would have crushed the strike by this time if the thing had stopped there. But something happened that the bosses and perhaps the bulk of the workers never figured on. The strikers also had found powerful friends who put protecting arms around them. Everything that is alive in the labor movement is taking a hand in Passaic. They can't starve out the strikers at Passaic because the workers throughout the country won't let them. Money and food flows into the strikers' relief committee in a steady stream. They can't suppress the rights of the strikers and railroad the leaders either; at least, not without a fight of such proportions as they never dreamed of when they started their reign of terror.

Passaic used to be a drab mill town, with workers unorganized and fearfully exploited. It is something infinitely bigger and better today.

When you say Passaic nowadays, everybody knows what you mean. Passaic means monstrous exploitation. Passaic means the public officials, the courts, the police and the governor of the state all lined up on the side of the bosses and giving everybody a blunt and simple answer to the question: Who owns the government? Passaic means armored cars, police clubs, gas bombs and injunctions. Passaic means the solidarity of the capitalists and control of the government by them.

But now there is another side to Passaic. Passaic also means heroic and determined struggle. It means the inexhaustible resources of courage and endurance that lie deep in the working class. It means admiration, sympathy and support from workers far and near. Passaic means the united front. It means union. It means leadership of integrity and skill. Passaic means Weisbord. It means the awakening solidarity of labor.

At the time this article is being written, the Passaic strike is entering its 17th week with ranks unbroken. It is no longer an isolated local affair. Large sections of the labor movement throughout the country have already taken a hand in it. The heroic struggle of the Passaic textile workers against heavy odds has impressed itself so strongly on the rank and file of the labor movement that it has become very difficult for anyone to oppose them. Even those who tried to do so at first—those who tried to disown it as an "outlaw" strike—had to change front. The Passaic strikers have fought so well and have been led so skillfully as to compel the admiration and support of the labor movement.

They have received help of a substantial kind already. But

from the looks of things more and greater help will be needed, especially after the strike is settled and its dramatic incidents are no longer news items for the first page. For the bosses, through their political hirelings, are plotting to take revenge on the workers who have dealt them such a heavy blow. They are especially determined to "get" Albert Weisbord, the organizer of the strike and the soul of the movement. Three indictments have been brought against him, and they aim to railroad him to the penitentiary for a long term if they can put it over quietly.

But we confidently believe they will fail in this conspiracy just as they have failed to break the strike by means of terrorism and suppression. All their brutalities in the strike have reacted against them and produced a contrary effect to the one they counted on. The police terrorism did not break the spirit of the strikers; it only made them more stubborn and determined. It educated them as to the actual role of the government. Moreover, it aroused ever wider and deeper strata of other workers and brought them into active solidarity with the strikers of Passaic and with all that their struggle stands for.

If we realize the issues involved, the frame-up against the strike leaders will have the same result. It must be our aim to accomplish this result and frustrate the conspiracy. Our ILD, which has already played its part in the strike, will have the main responsibility of organizing the protest movement.

The Passaic strike marks a milestone in the development of the American working class. It is a mighty and inspiring spectacle. This is the verdict of all who have seen it in action. It incorporates all the best traditions of the militant movement. It embodies all the old and tried methods of industrial struggle welded together with many ideas that are new and great. The mass picketing, the singing, the militancy and the industrial form of organization which characterized the great strikes led by the IWW in the textile industry are used in Passaic. Together with these go the new ideas of the united front, the flexible tactics, the establishment of connections with all labor and sympathizing elements, and the constant effort to broaden the base of support and to make room for all who really want to help.

Elizabeth Gurley Flynn is there, representing in her person the experience and militancy of the old fights and pouring it all freely into the strike. Bob Dunn, one of the leaders of the great organization attempt of 1919, Norman Thomas helping in the fight to maintain free speech and assemblage for the strikers, Esther Lowell of the Federated Press, and many others of various political views are part of the united front at Passaic.

Weisbord and a group of others like him, Jack Rubenstein, Lena Chernenko, Nancy Sandowsky, the new and young ones, knit the whole body together and dominate it with their spirit. America has never before seen a strike like Passaic. The best of the old and the new are fused together there.

Courage and militancy of the rank and file; flexibility, skill and integrity of the leadership—that is Passaic. The bosses have been outmaneuvered at every turn.

The Passaic strike teaches over again in a most impressive manner an old lesson well known to experienced militants. That lesson is the part played by the state authority in conflicts between workers and bosses. The experiences at Passaic are also demonstrating the absolute necessity for a permanently organized and always ready non-partisan labor defense organization which we had in mind when we founded the ILD last June. The ILD has played its part in Passaic and will play a yet bigger one before the fight is over.

Any worker who has learned the ABC of the class struggle can tell you that the state authorities—the courts, police, etc.—side with the bosses in time of struggle. This is a settled and correct theory which has been confirmed a thousand times in practice. But it is not often that they do it so brazenly and ferociously and in such open defiance of their own laws as they have done it in Passaic.

The picket line, the living symbol of the power of the strike and its greatest weapon, was the first target of the "impartial servants of the people." Streams of ice cold water were turned on the picketers one bitter winter day. Men, women and children were knocked down by policemen's clubs without even a pretext of legal justification. Tear gas bombs were thrown into crowds of strikers, and in the confusion and panic that followed they were ridden down by mounted police. Oh, some great lessons in "democratic government" were taught at Passaic!

Two hundred sixty-four strikers were arrested on various

charges, most of them for peaceful picketing, in cynical disregard of a state law recently passed which expressly legalizes it. Lena Chernenko and Nancy Sandowsky, two of the moving spirits of the picket line, together with a number of others were arrested and rearrested as fast as bail could be provided. Jack Rubenstein, one of the most active militants, was arrested, beaten up, indicted and held on $10,000 bail. One striker died as a result of a police clubbing.

The police terrorists made no political discrimination. It didn't matter what one's political or other opinions might be, if he was in the strike or for the strike, he fell afoul of the "law" at Passaic. Norman Thomas was arrested and indicted for attempting to speak at a meeting in a free speech test. Robert W. Dunn of the Civil Liberties Union got the same treatment for walking on the picket line after an ignorant sheriff had read the "riot act" and proclaimed what he called "martial law." Esther Lowell of the Federated Press helped a woman to her feet after she had been knocked down by a policeman's club. She went to jail for it. Injunctions were issued forbidding practically everything.

To cap the climax of the reign of terror, Weisbord was arrested. Three indictments were quickly brought against him and it took $30,000 and a great deal of outside pressure to get him out on bail pending trial.

Our ILD is on the job at Passaic. Not a single striker went into court without our lawyer to defend him. There was not a single conviction that was not appealed. Nobody had to remain in jail more than a few days for lack of bail. The New York Emergency Strike Relief Committee, with Mrs. Michaelson as secretary, took charge of this end of the work and collected bail to the amount of $83,150. The American Civil Liberties Union harassed the power-drunk authorities with "free speech" tests and tried hard to blow the breath of life into the half-dead body of "civil liberty." A great wave of protest spread through the labor movement and even the most conservative labor leaders were compelled to give expression to it. This powerful and many-sided support of the embattled strikers had its effect and the authorities were compelled to beat a retreat, at least for the time being.

But there cannot be the least doubt that they are determining at all costs to get revenge on comrade Weisbord, "the outside agitator" who is "responsible for all the trouble," and put him safely away for a long term in prison. Nothing short of a powerful, nationwide and united defense and protest movement will be able to save him for the great and necessary work he is doing and has yet to do.

We realized from the first moment the tremendous importance for the militant labor movement of the Weisbord case. And we understood fully that a narrow, limited or partisan defense would not avail against the powerful forces that are determined to get him out of the way. Therefore, the International Labor Defense in its first manifesto called for a united front of all sections of the labor movement for the defense of Weisbord, Thomas, Dunn, Lowell, Rubenstein and all the others arrested in the strike.

The most gratifying success has already been achieved in this project. Unity of action and coordination of effort of all forces directly involved in the Passaic fight was accomplished at a conference held in New York City on April 22, of representatives of the United Front Committee of Textile Workers, the International Labor Defense, the American Civil Liberties Union, the League for Industrial Democracy, the Emergency Strike Relief Committee of New York, the Passaic Strikers' Relief Committee and the Federated Press.

At this conference a Joint Committee was formed to coordinate the work of the various participating organizations and to ensure complete unity of action. Elizabeth Gurley Flynn was elected secretary of the Joint Committee and the other members are Albert Weisbord, Forrest Bailley, Norman Thomas, James P. Cannon, Mrs. Michaelson, Alfred Wagenknecht, Art Shields and Robert W. Dunn.

By decision of the conference the International Labor Defense will conduct the defense of all the arrested strikers, strike leaders and pickets, while the American Civil Liberties Union will have charge of all cases directly involving the issues of free speech and civil liberties. The International Labor Defense will collect a defense fund by authority of the Joint Committee and will be responsible for all expenses involved in the defense. Each organization represented at the conference agreed to give moral and financial support to the tasks undertaken by both the ILD and the American Civil Liberties Union.

As a demonstration of the unification of forces in the common fight, a mass meeting under the auspices of the Joint Committee was held in the New Star Casino, New York, on April 28, with Albert Weisbord, Elizabeth Gurley Flynn, Robert W. Dunn, Norman Thomas and James P. Cannon as the speakers. It was an enthusiastic but deeply serious demonstration, a united front in the real sense of the word, and a most promising beginning of what must and will be developed into a broad and powerful protest movement in behalf of comrade Weisbord and those who stand in jeopardy with him.

The Passaic fighters are worthy of such a movement. They are the representatives of the new life and spirit which are beginning to manifest themselves in the labor movement of America. They will stand up in the court as the symbols of the right of the workers to organize and fight for better and freer lives. They signify the mighty idea of the united front not merely in theory, but in practice. "They crammed the doctrine into deed." Let us do likewise in our fight for them.

For Industrial Groups on a Broader Basis Than the TUEL

29 October 1926

The following motions were presented by Cannon to a Political Committee meeting on 29 October 1926. They were counterposed to a plan for the reorganization of the party's trade-union work which William Z. Foster submitted to the same meeting. Foster's plan called for new, industrywide, united-front organizations with "progressive" trade unionists in three cities: Kansas City, Buffalo and Minneapolis. Elsewhere Foster advocated maintaining the Trade Union Educational League as a centralized trade-union opposition organized across industrial and craft union lines.

Cannon and William F. Dunne united with the C.E. Ruthenberg-led majority to defeat Foster's plan. Cannon's motions were adopted unanimously—Foster even voted in favor, insisting that Cannon's motions were not in conflict with his original plan. The Political Committee also adopted a motion by Ruthenberg which insisted that "further investigation and effort should be made to organize progressive blocs."

1. That we proceed in all cases with the organization of the industrial groups on a broader basis than the TUEL wherever possible.
2. That in cases where it is not possible at present to organize broader general left wing groups than the TUEL, the TUEL shall be maintained as the local center.
3. That we shall strive to develop local industrial groups towards centralization on a local scale.
4. That where the TUEL is maintained in the meantime as the centralized organization, it shall be conceived as an instrument to hasten the development of the industrial groups towards local centralization on a broader scale than the TUEL.
5. When the conditions mature for the centralization of the industrial groups locally, that the TUEL shall be merged into the newly formed group.

Conference on Moderating Factionalism

7 February 1927

The following is an unpublished and unsigned summary by someone in the Ruthenberg camp of a conversation between Cannon, C.E. Ruthenberg and Ruthenberg's key factional lieutenants, Max Bedacht and Jay Lovestone. Since his return from Moscow in the spring of 1926 Cannon had been operating separately from both the Ruthenberg CEC majority and the minority led by William Z. Foster. Cannon was campaigning for an end to factionalism in the party and he had won William Weinstone, New York district secretary and a former Ruthenberg supporter, over to his group on that basis.

Ruthenberg did not have the chance to act on the desire to moderate factionalism which he expressed in this conversation. He died suddenly on 2 March 1927. Ruthenberg's death triggered an explosion of factional maneuvering for control of the leading party committees, with Lovestone assuming leadership of the Ruthenberg faction.

Ruthenberg: "The Political Committee meeting of Friday shows a drift and a marked tendency toward a sharp factional situation in the party. If such meetings continue we will have a sharp fight. If this goes further it means an open fight. In our opinion an open fight will endanger very seriously the party and all its work. For instance:

1. It will hurt us in our ability to meet the offensive launched against us by the reactionary trade union leaders.
2. It will weaken our connection with progressives.
3. It would undermine our work with the progressives.
4. It would destroy our campaign in the mining union and other organizations.

We must find a way of avoiding a fight. We want to know what is your attitude and what steps you think are necessary to avoid this fight."

Cannon: "I feel the same way about it as you do. My opinion is nothing new. My position has not changed since I have come back from the Sixth Plenum. I stand on the same platform—genuine unity. The section elections in Chicago (five out of the six largest sections elected majorities on the executive committees giving full support to the CEC) are a contributing immediate cause for the sharpening of the factional situation.[1] At least this is so for the Fosterites but not for us." Says he has been disturbed about the proceedings of the Committee in recent weeks particularly as to the question of the control of the party apparatus. The present majority is factional. In the last Polcom meeting he may have spoken a little too sharply about this matter but his speech was substantially an attack on this factional control only. Personally not in favor of a fight now.

Ruthenberg: Recites a number of facts indicating that we are not following a policy of elimination of Fosterites or Cannonites and mentions Baker, Johnstone, Dunne, Abern and others as being given and offered responsible party work. He says he is getting a feeling that some are developing an attitude of pure opposition to the appointment of any party member who was associated with the former Ruthenberg group. The question before us is what can be done.

Cannon: Emphasizes that he feels that the Committee is working on the basis of a definite hard bloc within it limiting the work of others. The situation in the Polcom must be corrected—that is the basic thing. Says we made an error in the procedure of electing Gitlow while Foster was absent and not waiting for Foster.[2]

---

[1] The party had been reorganized under the Bolshevization campaign. Party cells (nuclei) in each city were grouped into sub-sections and sections for the purposes of membership meetings and elections.

[2] On January 20 the Ruthenberg majority on the Polcom had pushed through the appointment of Benjamin Gitlow as head of the New York Needle Trades Committee of the TUEL, replacing Joseph Zack. Foster was not present at the meeting, but his lieutenant, Johnstone, had proposed that a secretariat of Gitlow, Zack and Aronberg be appointed instead. Cannon supported Johnstone's proposal.

The leadership of the party's needle trades work was a particularly sensitive issue since the TUEL fraction had been leading the New York local International Ladies' Garment Workers' Union. A bitter, militant six-month strike had just gone down in defeat. In December the national union leadership under Morris Sigman had stepped in, suspended the New York union leadership, and settled the strike on unfavorable terms.

He supports in principle the policy that the Trade Union Committee should handle trade union appointments. We made an error in working otherwise since this gives Foster similar ground of complaint.

Ruthenberg: "In retrospect," he said, "we can concede that we made an error as to procedure in handling the Gitlow case. It would have been better had we worked otherwise." He recites the fact that Zack sent a letter insisting on immediate action before a certain date.

Cannon: "It was a big mistake to give Foster such grounds for a fight. It was bad for us, speaking for myself and those working with me, that we have to be put in the position where we must support Foster in such a fight. He might interpret our support as meaning something else. We have heard that the New York District Executive Committee is against Gitlow." He doesn't know the reasons for the change of Zack to Gitlow. He is surprised to see a fight develop over this.

Lovestone: Recites the facts as to the developments at the plenum and the conduct of the Fosterites being extremely factional. The chief aim of the opposition at the plenum was to discredit the American CEC. "The elections in Chicago are not a cause of the factional attitude of the Fosterites but an answer of the members to the factional practices against the CEC. Foster's real reason for opposition to Gitlow was given to me by himself in Indianapolis when he said 'Do you think I am going to surrender a hundred thousand workers to Gitlow'." Examines facts of campaign launched against Pepper by the Fosterite opposition. Declares that he is hopeful of a party settlement. Examines Foster's analysis of the objective conditions showing the danger in the points he emphasizes as leading him either to hopeless pessimism for the existence of a party or to a conclusion which would afford a theoretical basis for narrow sectarianism. Insists that we have frank discussions in these meetings.

Ruthenberg: Answers the hinted united front differences as indicated by Cannon in his previous remarks. Cites the danger of an anti-party attitude as indicated in the refusal of some comrades in

Minneapolis to permit the party to issue a statement to the workers on the farmer-labor development.[3]

Cannon: Feels isolation for the party on the basis of some of the errors made in executing united front policy. Cites such errors as the selection of Weisbord for the tour, the insistence on the party being in the Foreign Born Council, the question of the All American Anti-Imperialist League, etc. Says a whole wrong tendency in these united front policies.[4]

Bedacht: Admits the existence of groupings in the party but he says there is no fundamental or basic differences. He is convinced that we may have potential differences but these potential differences should not be confused with immediate existing real differences. "Why do we have groupings in the party? As Jay said, very often it is due to a tendency to go into a struggle for power over every difference of opinion. As long as you have such groupings as we have today existing there will also be the other effect of making a power question out of every difference. There is a tendency to exaggerate differences under such conditions. Cannon speaks of right and left dangers. He cannot cite typical examples of such dangers. Today we do not have in the American party a crystallized right or left tendency. There is no outstanding individual leader for such tendencies. It is true, there may be individual inclinations. Some of us tend to make errors of a right character, others of a left character. (Interruption by Lovestone: "As Bittelman would say, I tend to make errors of a right character.") But we have no definite conscious forces driving the party to the right

---

[3] A conference of the Minnesota Farmer-Labor Association on January 17 had approved a Workers Party-initiated motion calling for a national conference to found a labor party to run in the 1928 U.S. elections. At a Political Committee meeting on January 20 Ruthenberg had been particularly concerned to push this development as a big gain for the Communists.

[4] The controversial Passaic strike leader Albert Weisbord was sent on national tour for the Workers Party in 1927. Foster had wanted him to tour under the auspices of a "National Committee for Organizing Textile Workers," according to the minutes of the Political Committee meeting of 21 September 1926. Early in 1926 the party had been active in creating a national Council for the Protection of the Foreign Born, while in 1925 it had formed the All American Anti-Imperialist League. The AAAIL had headquarters in Chicago and was led by Cannon faction supporter Manuel Gomez. Max Shachtman was acting secretary of the AAAIL in Gomez's absence. It claimed sections in 11 countries and published a monthly Spanish organ, *El Libertador*, in Mexico.

or the left. The use of such expressions as ultraleftists in so careless a manner is only a result of existence of groupings which have no basis for existence. If Gitlow is ultraleft then it is a sin of our whole Central Executive Committee. Every one of us. What is the picture of the party today? A number of groups fighting for leadership. In analyzing the real significance of the 14-point document presented by Bittelman—Bittelman may now try to deny but the central point is—was the letter proposed by Bittelman sent to the party or not?[5] All right, it was not sent, that is the answer. When we discuss leadership we must discuss the question of the hegemony in any collective leadership. Who will have the hegemony in any collective leadership in the party? Will it be those comrades whose line is generally symbolized by Foster or will it be those generally symbolized by Ruthenberg? We ought to have an agreement as to this question. We should have a frank discussion in the CEC and Polcom. This is the question."

Cannon: "These questions we have been having are all right. They have their value. But we should not think that unanimity is necessary for having unity. I do not like to see the same majority all the time in the Polcom. We cannot continue a closed group and at the same time dissolve other groups." He had the same problem when he was a member of the old majority. It isn't so easy to deal with Foster on the question of groupings. Says if we had dealt with the group problem in the way he suggested it would have been possible for us to dissolve the Foster group. We being the majority must take certain advances. We must depend more on certain agreements as to the main line in order to maintain our leadership. Believes that factionalism is played out and the party will not stand for anyone starting a factional fight.

Ruthenberg: Weisbord reported the same reaction of the party to factionalism as you mention.

---

[5] While in Moscow attending the Seventh Plenum of the ECCI in November-December 1926, Bittelman had written a document entitled "Points to Be Dealt with in Letter by Presidium to American Party." The document detailed 14 points, including a critique of the party's handling of the Passaic strike. Evidently Earl Browder, who was resident in Moscow at the time, helped to draft the document. There was no American Commission convened in connection with the Seventh Plenum, and the ECCI apparently rejected Bittelman's critique.

Cannon: Generally these are true but it depends who will start the factional fight. Categorically declares he rejects the theory of hereditary leadership in the party. Claims that Foster and we have this conception of leadership.

Ruthenberg: Declares he was the only one to be against this group method of working but today he has changed his mind as a matter of self-defense.

Cannon: Declares that if we had dropped our closed organization then Foster would not have been able to maintain his opposition. Foster himself is a practical fellow and would then have to come along since he would lose support and would see that he has no possibility of getting anything out of maintaining an opposition.

Ruthenberg: Such a hope is the basis of Foster's present attack.

Cannon: Declares that the dominating viewpoint in the Ruthenberg group is the factional control of the party. Emphasizes that he has been very peaceful.

Ruthenberg: Tells Cannon that we are planning a conference with Foster to discuss the same problems. "Foster's fight or anybody else's fight today would not be a fight to correct the errors of the CEC but to replace the CEC on the basis of factional issues. We will face such methods frankly and use our power if necessary."

Cannon: Doesn't agree that party is facing the alternative of Ruthenberg group or the Foster group. Believes in collective leadership. All comrades having ability should contribute. Doesn't agree to the theory of four comrades in the Polcom constituting the leadership in the party. Feels he has ideas but is discouraged by the fact that he feels that he must always convince four or lose.[6] We are operating on a group basis, therefore we have been narrowing the apparatus. Fights the Shklar appointment and bitterly criticizes the method of getting him elected district organizer in Boston.

Ruthenberg: There are two roads before the party. One is the test of power, two is the group working together. The last Polcom

6 The Political Committee at the time consisted of seven members: Ruthenberg, Lovestone, Bedacht, Gitlow, Foster, Bittelman and Cannon.

meeting was road number one. Such a situation would mean an early convention. It would mean a fight for power. If it becomes a fight for power we would fight. The second road would mean that we work out matters beforehand before coming to a Polcom meeting. Maybe it would be a good idea to have you, Foster and myself get together before a Polcom and lay a basis for agreement. The question is, will we have a convention without a factional fight? A convention is necessary this year, within the next six months say. Can we come to an agreement beforehand? Can we work out in advance the organizational and political questions? Perhaps it would be best if we had a general discussion in the CEC without new motions dealing with the whole situation.

Cannon: Suggests that we first arrive at an agreement on the united front line. Criticizes our inner party line. Complains as to persecution of Fisher in the South Slavic case.[7]

Ruthenberg: This involves difficulties in removing other comrades who now have party work. If there would be an opening I have no objection to Fisher being placed.

Lovestone: Emphasizes that all those opposed to the Central Executive Committee or its policies should not be entrusted with serious responsible party work. Opposition to CEC no qualification for work in our party. Fisher works overtime to destroy CEC. This means to create factionalism in the party. Such comrades should not be given work until they change their behavior.

Cannon: "We have the question of the Finnish secretary. Your tactics in the Finnish Federation will bring about a break between the center and left bloc. This will strengthen the right."

Ruthenberg: Declares the same Finnish Bureau as elected at last Finnish conference stands. No new majority was created. CEC does not actually have the majority of the Bureau.

---

[7] According to a report by the 1925 Parity Commission there were two warring groups in the South Slavic Federation, the Fisher group and the Novak group. The Fisher group supported the Foster-Cannon faction while the Novak group, which had a majority on the Federation Bureau, supported the Ruthenberg faction. The Bureau majority removed Fisher as editor of the Federation paper, *Radnik*, and tried to drum him out of the organization. For more details see the Cannon-Weinstone "Theses on the Party Factional Situation," pp. 437-438.

Bedacht: Cannot see any difference between what Cannon calls a left and a center in the Finnish Federation. Says Cannon works mechanically on the center idea. Our experiences and the CI's attitude show that it is a correct policy at the outset in establishing these big workers clubs to have the same secretary handle the work of the fraction and the clubs. We must control through the individual.

Cannon: Criticizes the procedure through which the Finnish Workers Club secretary choice was arrived at. We cannot measure the Finnish Federation with the same standards that we measure other federations of the party. They are not so well developed. We cannot lead the Finnish Federation with Goose Caucus elements. You will not isolate the right wing in that way.

Bedacht: "What do you mean by your collective leadership concept?" Examines the theory of taking chances. Is not correct position. It is not for the leading group to take chances. If they make a mistake no one can rectify it. It means the whole party makes a mistake. That is a mechanical viewpoint. Theoretically the minority has nothing to lose. It should be the one to take chances. (Cannon interrupts: "I disagree with your idea that you have the responsibility of the party.") "Yes, we have. We have shown that we can avoid factionalism. Let us discuss the whole question of leaders thoroughly. Is your formless collective leadership possible or desirable? This is wrong. It is an anti-Leninist concept. In such a collective leadership there must be an outstanding general line." Declares he is convinced by objections of Foster's at the last plenum, also by many of his writings, that he is not a Leninist, that he is not a Marxist. "Do you want his line to be outstanding in the collective leadership?" Declares that he is convinced that a collective leadership with Foster's hegemony would be bad for the party. It is an undesirable condition for the party leadership, therefore the collective leadership slogan you raise does not meet the case. Agrees that a closed group is not good. Reminds Cannon of conference he held with him in 1922 returning from Moscow for the need of a real group leadership. Group leadership is not necessarily exclusive. That is the kind of group leadership we want.

Cannon: Don't let us discuss this too abstractly.

Bedacht: No, I am discussing very concretely. The issue is Foster vs. Ruthenberg. The name is not a question. The question is Communism.

Cannon: What is the difference but your practice always works out factional. The Ruthenberg group in my opinion is not a finished product. It has contradictory elements within it. It has some indispensable elements in it. I cannot conceive a party leadership without you three comrades. Some are useful only negatively. You have negative elements in your group. The useful tendency should be towards a fusion of all those qualified for leadership in the party. Only in such a situation can we avoid factionalism. He does not consider Puro, Minor or Engdahl seriously for leadership. As long as we maintain a rigid line such amalgamation is impossible. Believes the Committee has gone backwards since the Sixth Plenum. Does not believe in factional fight as a solution. Dynastic struggles for power of the kind we have had is no road for the party to travel. Suppose Foster gets a majority—this is no solution. In New York we have had progress towards real unity. New forces are developing in the party for leadership. The real task for the party leadership is consciously to foster this process of merger and fusion of the best elements. Until recently we have had no differences except as to inner line but recently we have been developing differences with you on the united front policy. This is due to the fact that you yield to pressure from your negative elements. Believes that our strength in the party is based on many language blocs that have a leftist outlook such as the South Slavic fraction. One of the great weaknesses of the Ruthenberg group is that it is based too much on these elements. It is true that the leftists have no leadership. You comrades are no ultraleftists but the leftists tend to throw their support to you. Your unity with us was a forward step because it tended to counterbalance these elements in your lines. Your disunity with us was bad, that is why the federation blocs could not stand for your unity with us. The ultraleftists may have no leadership, but by attaching themselves to other groups they can exercise pressure on these groups and question their policies.

Lovestone: We will continue this discussion later.

Meeting adjourned.

For the Liquidation of Factionalism

6 May 1927

The following is an unpublished transcript of a speech by Cannon to a plenum of the Workers Party's Central Executive Committee. As part of the factional maneuvering following C.E. Ruthenberg's death, Jay Lovestone delayed the convening of this plenum as long as he could, knowing that Cannon and William Weinstone had won William Z. Foster's agreement to vote for Weinstone as party secretary. Rather than submit to the new Cannon-Weinstone-Foster CEC majority, Lovestone and his factional lieutenant Benjamin Gitlow fled the plenum early in order to hurry to Moscow to seek support for Lovestone's own bid for party leadership. The Comintern had requested that the party send a delegation to Moscow to discuss the party factional situation and to participate in the upcoming Eighth Plenum of the ECCI.

Comrade Chairman and Comrades:

I think it should be agreed by everybody that the plenum of the Central Committee, which was so long deferred, has already proven to be of great value for the party, particularly in this respect—and this is the most important thing of all—that it has established more clearly the political attitude of the various groups and comrades in the Central Committee and their perspectives on the future work, and it is possible now for us to approach the problem of unity and leadership with more knowledge of how we are to proceed.

I wish to say on behalf of those comrades with whom I am associated, and who hold the same views, comrades Weinstone, Dunne, Ballam, Abern, Swabeck, Reynolds and Gomez, that on our part, we have a clearer perception of the party situation and of the attitude of the various groups than we had before and we are in a better position now to determine our attitude towards them. This applies with particular reference to the majority of the

Polcom, which has been going through a process of reorientation in the period of recent weeks and months, and which has established at the plenum its new line more clearly.

Our attitude towards the question of party leadership and towards party unity is naturally regulated and determined by the things which have been established in this plenum and about which I will speak in the course of my remarks.

Our attitude expressed previously remains fundamentally the same, modified and adapted to the developments of the plenum.

I would like to take up first of all, in order to make our own position clear on the various points, the question of the "offensive against the party and our tasks," and try to establish some perspectives on the future development. I believe both the other groups have been somewhat deficient in this respect.

What is this drive against the party and the left wing, and what is its relation to the general struggle between the workers and the capitalists? What is the meaning of the united front between the government, the employers, the labor bureaucracy and the Socialist Party?

On the part of the bureaucrats I think we can all agree that it is on the one hand an attempt to divert the attention from their own bankruptcy as leaders of the workers and that they are acting in this whole situation as agents of the capitalists. It is essential for us to see the situation, not as a static affair, but to see it as a process, and look in this very process for the perspective of new struggles and new alignments which will create new bases of operation for the party.

It is a part of the "worker-employer cooperation" policy by means of which the bureaucracy aim first of all to maintain their own positions; secondly, *to remove those elements who fight to maintain the unions and maintain the position gained by the workers in the previous period from 1919 and the war*; thirdly, it is a move to evade the implications and consequences of the attack of the capitalists on the unions. Likewise, it is undeniable that the successes of the party in the organization of the unorganized, in conducting strikes, in Passaic, in United Mine Workers, needle trades, etc., have given impetus to this drive against the party.

We do not see the bureaucrats as a homogenous body engaged in direct and permanent contractual relations with the bosses. We see them also under the pressure of a process in which they are confronted with certain alternatives. Under the pressure of the general drive of the capitalists against the unions, the bureaucrats are confronted with the alternative of surrendering entirely all struggles against the capitalists and of entrenching themselves more securely in the various business enterprises of the unions, or of preparing and organizing the resistance against the open shop campaign of the bosses.

They are confronted with a contradiction in this sense, that regardless of their desire to come to an agreement with the bosses, the bosses are not always ready to come to an agreement with them to establish "stable" class collaboration relations between the unions and the bosses. The bosses are much more "unreasonable" than the bureaucrats and are not willing to stop at the point of "class collaboration." Their drive against the unions goes ahead, and in this process, under pressure of the masses, even the blackest reactionaries are compelled to make certain gestures of struggle.

For example, the situation in the United Mine Workers of America. The open fight of the operators against the miners union is a part of this whole campaign. It is impossible to get a clear picture of the drive against the party and the left wing without taking into account this fact, that despite the willingness of Lewis to come to "class collaboration" agreement with the operators, the latter have launched an offensive directly against the union. The fight against the party and left wing is an inextricable part of the fight against the unions.

Take the automobile campaign, decided upon by the AFL convention, even though it was a mere gesture. Consider the fact that the AFL Executive Council rejected the affiliation of the Passaic strikers, and then was compelled to reverse this decision at the convention of the AFL under the pressure of the masses. These things show, comrades, that the bureaucrats are not able to act as a homogenous body with a clear and definite orientation and policy, but that they themselves are in the midst of a demoralization and disorganization as a general result of the attack of the bosses which began against the unions in 1922. The offensive against the Communists and the left wing by the bureaucrats serves as a smokescreen, behind which they intend to carry out their retreat before capital. It is further designed to break the morale of the rank and file and thus make it easier to consummate their program of surrender and impose it on the unions. It also serves, in this stage of American imperialism, as the basis of the united front between the capitalists, the government and the reactionary bureaucrats against all fighting elements in the trade union movement.

This confronts the party, as all must agree, with the necessity of increasing the trade union work and organizing a broad left wing. Everyone who speaks will say that. The problem is not merely that the party has the will to do this and adopts or proposes certain things more or less obviously necessary, such as organization of the unorganized and so on. The important thing for us here in the plenum is to establish, insofar as we can, what features of this fight against the party and the left wing in themselves create a contradiction which will assist the work of the party in organizing the unorganized and creating a broad left wing.

It is necessary to understand that within the camp of the bureaucrats there is not a unanimous policy. There is a certain lack of enthusiasm for the fight in certain sections of the "upper strata" of the labor movement and its officialdom. We know, and it is reported here by comrade Lovestone, correctly I think, that Green has shown a somewhat more wavering policy than that of Woll. We know such people as Maurer, Brophy, etc., are in no way enthusiastic supporters of this policy and that the general weakness of the fight, the lack of funds, etc., shows that it has not yet been possible to mobilize the complete united strength of the labor officialdom in this fight against us. What we maintain is that the dialectics of this struggle are opening new possibilities for the party and it is from this standpoint that we make special criticism against the resolution of the Polcom, which, we think, has not sufficiently established this. First of all, the misgivings, lack of enthusiasm, wavering and even opposition in certain sections of the bureaucracy in itself creates possibilities for the party to maneuver. But more important is the fact that the developing offensive against the unions and the resultant struggles will create new bases for the broadening of the left wing. They will bring new masses of workers into the struggle and will therefore be the means, if properly exploited, by which this attack against the party and the left wing will be defeated and a broader left wing developed.

Let us consider for a moment the effects of this drive on the bureaucrats. The blackest section of the bureaucracy, which is collaborating so openly with the bosses and the government, is giving up all possibilities of leading any struggles of the workers against the employers, but this is not by any means stopping the struggle. The direct struggle of the employers against the workers proceeds, as we see, for example, in the United Mine Workers. We see Lewis on the one hand, and Brophy on the other hand. We see new alignments and struggles looming up inevitably in America on a broader scale than ever before.

We do not see this merely in fantasy, but in facts which have been reported. The facts, for example, that in the United Mine Workers convention in Illinois the left wing and the progressive delegates have shown an unexpected strength, in the fact that the possibility has arisen in recent days of creating a new movement in the miners union on the basis of a fight against the fraudulent election practices of Lewis and on the basis of a claim that the presidency belongs to Brophy. The Political Committee had sufficient facts to adopt a policy calling for a reconstitution of the left and progressive committee around Brophy on the issue of claiming the election in the United Mine Workers was stolen by Lewis, and of connecting this claim for presidency by Brophy with the bringing forward in an aggressive way of the strike policy of the progressive bloc. One must be dull indeed, and pessimistic besides, not to see the dynamic possibilities in the present situation in the UMW.

Here we come to sharp issue with the majority of the Polcom from the standpoint of their lack of perspective on this situation. I want to refer now to the differences which arose on this question in the Polcom. In this union which is engaged in a life and death struggle against the bosses, in which the bosses are driving to destroy the union, wherein there is a movement growing in the rank and file, where possibilities exist to recreate the leadership of the progressive bloc on a broader basis than before, we brought forward the idea, rather comrade Foster brought forward the proposition, that we should get this movement under way at once, with the objective of a conference of the left wing.

Now, is there anything utopian about the idea that we should aim for a conference of the left wing in the miners union? I say that in a union engaged in such a life and death struggle, in a union where we claim a majority voted for the opposition, and with the new ferment now going on, a conference of the progressive bloc should be regarded as an elementary aim to strive for. The Polcom could not see this.[1]

I will refer to the discussion as I recall it. We spoke of a conference of the left wing as an objective. The Polcom, with its new orientation, which I do not hesitate to say is a right orientation, rose up in alarm at the proposition. Despite the fact that the proposal did not provide for the calling of a conference but merely for the perspective of a conference, despite the fact that it was qualified by several motions, two by Foster and another one by me, that the actual calling of the conference was to be decided upon later, we met with a tremendous barrage of resistance from the majority of the Polcom.

We think this attitude is directly connected with their lack of perspective in the development of the process of this fight. We believe this attitude shows a lack of a grasp of the dynamics of this fight against the left wing as part of the fight against the unions. We were treated there by comrade Wolfe to an analogy between calling a conference of the left wing—and I repeat that the calling of a conference of the left wing only marks the elementary stage of the real fight against the bureaucrats—comrade Wolfe drew an analogy between our proposal and talk of developing a

---

[1] Throughout 1923-26 John L. Lewis had engaged in a concerted campaign to destroy the substantial TUEL influence in the United Mine Workers. Communists and their supporters had been expelled from the union in droves. In April 1926 the UMW Executive Board declared the Workers Party a "dual" organization. Any participation in party activities, including distribution of the *Daily Worker*, was grounds for expulsion. Lewis was afraid of losing control of the union: the annual UMW convention was postponed until after union elections called for December 1926.

With most leading party members purged from the union, Jay Lovestone had approached dissident District 2 leader John Brophy through his assistant, Powers Hapgood. The Communists agreed to support Brophy's candidacy for union president on a "Save the Union" ticket, while keeping the Workers Party and its politics in the background. Nonetheless, Lewis waged a vicious redbaiting campaign against Brophy and declared himself the victor in the election by a substantial margin.

Johnstone, Lovestone and Dunne constituted the "Committee of 3" which led the Workers Party intervention at the UMW convention in early 1927. Thirty-seven party members were convention delegates, most of them from District 5. The intervention was discussed at the Political Committee meeting of 27 January 1927,

(continued)

demonstration into an armed insurrection. They seem to see the idea of a conference of the left wing in a union engaged in a life and death struggle, where we have a majority voting for the opposition, and where the rank and file is in ferment—they see that as a utopia. For my part, I do not characterize that reaction as a part of the leftism of the past year. On the contrary, I think it shows on one hand not only lack of perspective on the processes at work, but it shows fundamentally something even more dangerous, *a lack of faith in the masses*, a lack of faith that the miners, under pressure of a life and death fight, will find ways and means to break through the iron ring of the reactionaries and hold an elementary conference of their own forces.

While we have always opposed premature conferences, fake conferences and things of that sort, we do not consider the idea of a conference of the left wing in the UMW as a remote or utopian idea, by any means. It is the duty of a Communist leadership, surveying the conditions as they really are, to see this perspective and drive towards it.

We see the starting of a process of differentiation in the bureaucracy. We do not see this differentiation so clearly now as we will see it later. Some of the bureaucrats, under the pressure of the masses, will be compelled to take part in the fight against the bosses to maintain the unions and even to help us to organize

---

where Johnstone complained that "instead of us criticizing the progressives, they criticized us in a progressive meeting for not fighting hard enough. And our fraction didn't." Johnstone also complained that Brophy, while "close to us," also did not fight hard enough against Lewis.

Despite this, the Polcom generally agreed with Lovestone that this had been "the most important trade union convention that has been held in years," and they resolved to continue the campaign against the Lewis leadership. While the Communists claimed massive vote fraud in the UMW elections, Brophy was still loath to confront Lewis in the convention's aftermath. Lovestone wanted to maintain the alliance with Brophy at any cost, but Foster argued in the Political Committee meeting of 8 April 1927 that "our entire orientation in the mining situation must be changed towards Howat's type rather than towards Brophy."

Eventually Brophy agreed to a campaign to challenge the UMW election results. Foster's motions establishing the campaign, submitted to the Political Committee meeting on 5 May 1927, included one that "we proceed to develop sentiment against Lewis with the end of eventually calling an open conference of the UMW provided the course of the movement would indicate that such a conference would be justified." The Lovestone majority voted down this motion. They also voted down Cannon's amendment stipulating that the decision to call the conference be made later.

the unorganized. Others will go still further the other way and this will create new alignments, new problems for our work, and new possibilities. Basing ourselves always fundamentally upon the masses, we can, at the same time, to a certain extent, find allies in the bureaucracy, and make use of them.

We maintain that if anyone stands here in this plenum and says that he can give a complete, precise, correct line for our party in this situation, he is deceiving himself. We have no real orientation on these problems of our trade union work. We have not sufficiently studied the means and methods of penetrating the entrenched unions under the new conditions.

We do not yet know enough about the different policies of the bureaucrats, as we have learned in the debate here. There are differences between them. We have Lovestone on the one hand speaking on the differences of orientation in the Executive Council of the AFL. We do not see anything about this in the resolution. We have heard other comrades express views about it. So we are really only beginning to get an approach to this problem.

We do not know enough about the whole situation, and one of the reasons is that this is the first time in six months that we have had a plenum of the party. There is another reason why we were not sufficiently oriented, that is the faction situation in the party, which hampers objective inquiry and discussion.

I maintain that the situation in the labor movement—the changes that take place, the growth of class collaboration, the drive of the bosses against the workers' unions directly, as well as the drive against the left wing and Communists—*this represents a turning point in the American labor movement, and consequently a turning point in our party work in the unions.*

We do not have sufficient orientation on these new tasks. What are the reasons for that? First of all, the unstable situation in the party and the unstable leadership which cannot provide normal processes of discussion. Second, the factional situation in the party, which is evident in spite of the optimistic assurance given by the majority of the Polcom, and for which the majority of the Polcom is primarily responsible. We have a situation in the party where the real political discussions take place in caucuses instead of in the regular party organs. This is the first time in six months that we have aired the problems before the party organization.

We are only now beginning. We have no material, no discussion. Can you imagine, comrades, in the circumstances of the party's great strike experiences of the past year, we have had no real survey of our shortcomings in the needle trades situation? There we have the most serious, complicated and difficult problem, not only in regard to the attack on the party as a whole, but also in regard to the internal situation of the party in the needle trades work. Our position has been weakened in this tremendous fight by reason of the fact that many of the leading comrades of the party in the needle trades have a clear and definite opportunist deviation and they are sheltered in it by the majority of the Polcom.

That is one of the most serious phases of the offensive against us in the needle trades. Our leading staff in the needle trades has rightist tendencies, yet there is not sufficient discussion and criticism, not sufficient struggle against it. And for this the majority of the Polcom is directly responsible. Let me take up for you a series of incidents in this connection which I think the plenum should know about and which the comrades of the majority of the Polcom ought to explain:

First of all, we had, out of a clear sky, a short time ago a change in the administration of our committee in the needle trades.[2] I want to give a picture of four stages of development which have helped undermine our position in the fight against the bureaucrats in the needle trades.

First stage: the removal of comrade Zack as secretary of the Needle Trades Committee. When I cite this I don't want to associate myself entirely with the point of view of comrade Zack. I do not agree with him on some questions of tactics and I think the whole party knows this; but I recognize in Zack a comrade who wants to fight for the party against those who want to undermine the party and weaken it for their own purposes in the needle trades. He was removed on the ground that he could not get the cooperation of the opportunistically inclined leading comrades in the needle trades.

Second, against the alternative proposal to create a secretariat of three, which I supported, we were confronted with the appoint-

---

[2] See note 2, page 384.

ment of comrade Gitlow, who apparently was acceptable to the opportunistic comrades in the needle trades, at least he was nominated by them.

The third development was that this whole group of opportunistic comrades in a body joined the Lovestone caucus in the party in recent weeks and have become enthusiastic promoters of comrade Lovestone's candidacy for general secretary of the party.

Fourth, there is no discussion or criticism against these comrades in the needle trades, neither in the Polcom report nor resolutions. Instead they go back to August last year and pick out an isolated sentence, or rather half-sentence, of comrade Swabeck's report to a district meeting and serve it up in distorted form as the basis of the political discussion of the Polcom. I hope the Polcom reporters will take the time to answer and explain these quotations.

We have had no discussion or evaluation of the Passaic strike. No examination of experiences, no conclusions drawn, no perspective laid out, nothing except a foolish pamphlet by Weisbord, and still more foolish speeches by Weisbord. All this is part of our lack of orientation. And when we take into account our position as the leaders and guiding spirits of the left wing, the critical situation of the labor movement as a whole, when we realize that what we do and what we decide and the tactics that we pursue may determine to a large extent the course of the labor movement itself, we must realize that it is time for us to begin serious work of orientation on trade union problems.

I said that the capitalists are not ready to accept class collaboration. The capitalists want the open shop and the elimination of the unions, and it is the greatest error to regard class collaboration as a fixed and final stage in this development. You want evidence of that? Take the miners union, the garment workers union, the lockout of the plumbers union in Brooklyn; take the fact that here in Chicago one of the largest printing plants employing 300 printers went to an open shop basis in recent weeks.

The fact of the matter is that the logic of the class struggle is entirely against any stable relations between capital and labor, and when the unions surrender a fighting policy in favor of class collaboration, they only give the bosses ground for new encroachments. This has already begun and is to be seen in the instance I have pointed out. But the Polcom evidently does not see it because in their resolution they point out no such perspective or possibilities of this development.

All we have from the Polcom is a black picture of pessimism. Our work is more difficult than ever! Not a ray of light ahead! The Polcom shows a tremendous weakness in this resolution from that standpoint.

They do not see the whole picture. They mention the drive of Lewis against the party and left wing in the UMW, but evidently they do not see as part of the same process *the drive of the bosses against the UMW which in itself is creating the base for the broadening of the organization of the left wing.* Lewis tried in every way to come to an agreement with the bosses for class collaboration agreements. He has made eleven different and important concessions in the past four years in order to establish "stable relations" with the bosses. For example, he began the war on the Communists in 1923. He took all class struggle phraseology out of the union's constitution, he abolished the checkoff in Anthracite and smuggled a form of arbitration into the agreement. In the last negotiations he offered district agreements. The open attack against the union and the lockout is the answer of the bosses to all of these overtures of Lewis.

I deny that class collaboration represents a fixed stage in the struggle. It represents only a stage in a process. Now the bureaucracy, in our opinion, is before the alternative of giving up the position of the unions entirely or taking up the defensive and even an offensive struggle. And herein we want to state the point of view that the tactics of the bureaucracy and reactionary workers will not be uniform by any means.

Some of the bureaucrats will unquestionably be compelled under pressure of the masses to take a stand which will be a gesture of struggle. And this in itself will create new possibilities which we can exploit in our work for the organization of the unorganized and the broadening of the left wing. These processes will work somewhat like that attitude of Brophy in the United Mine Workers union. The attitude of Brophy is an illustration of it.

And we also are of the opinion, on the basis of the fact that the capitalists will not stop with the class collaboration agreements, but will proceed from there to direct attacks on many of the unions, besides other factors making for movement in the masses, we are of the opinion that a new period of strike activity will begin.

A whole new situation will open up and prospects will appear which the resolution of the Polcom does not deal with at all. It leaves only a pessimistic and negative outlook.

On the trade union work of the party, I want to make a few remarks. Factionalism in the party and the lack of criticism has greatly affected this work. As a result of the general lack of orientation we are quite often a step behind and do not see clearly the implications of the fights we undertake.

We do not see clearly the implications of the needle trades situation, the general offensive, the miners conference, etc. There has been a lack of examination and revision of the steps we have taken. We work too much on the basis of formulae instead of dialectic processes of struggle. We have been confining ourselves to mere dogmatic denunciations of the class collaboration schemes and do not occupy ourselves sufficiently with the positive methods of struggle against it.

I want to make certain criticisms of the TUEL, and in making them I want to emphasize the fact that I make them from no factional attitude. First of all we reject absolutely the position that the situation we are in, the attitude of the bureaucracy and disappearance of radical unions, the trend of the labor movement to the right, dictates a TUEL comprising merely Communists and sympathizers.

On the contrary, our analysis of the symptoms and perspectives point in the opposite direction. We see forces at work in addition to our own wishes, making for new alignments and new struggles, creating bases for a broader TUEL. We have to prepare ourselves for that. We must understand the dialectic processes at work in the labor movement and base our plans upon them. We must work for a broader left wing to include all elements who will fight to preserve and modernize the unions as fighting organs against capital.

The dividing line between lefts and progressives must not be dogmatic and schematic. The real test is action more than formal program. The whole distinguishing characteristic of the entire movement of opposition outside of the Communist Party is the lack of clearness and consistency. The test is struggle and action. Furthermore, in recruiting the left wing and in establishing the line of demarcation between the left and progressive elements, we must distinguish between leaders and on the basis of their actions more than on the basis of their formal programs. And by all means we have to distinguish between leaders and workers in recruiting our left wing in the trade union movement and apply a different criterion to them. Here also the real test is action.

Again I emphasize the fact that the criticism I make is from a general party viewpoint, and not from a factional viewpoint. I believe that the TUEL is too narrow from the standpoint of the labor movement at present. I believe we put too much emphasis on schematic formulations, not enough on the dynamics of the struggle. I believe there is too strong a tendency to seek the dividing line which excludes workers from the left wing and not enough in the opposite direction, that is, to find the workers whom we can make qualified for the left wing. We must work out tactics for the fight against class collaboration, within the framework of class collaboration, in those industries where it is in operation.

Finally, I am going to make still more serious criticism. The TUEL is not only too narrow from the standpoint of the labor movement, but the TUEL is too narrow from the standpoint of the party. The party as a whole is not in the TUEL enough, and you may apply the blame and the criticism for this wherever you will. You may say that on the one hand there is a coolness or lack of enthusiasm for the TUEL in some sections of the party. On the other hand there is a certain monopolistic attitude on the part of some other comrades in regard to the TUEL work. I believe this is fatal to the TUEL. I believe that no program, however correct, will be able to make the TUEL the organ which it must and can become until the party as a party, much more than now, is inside of the TUEL and functioning in its apparatus. Factional passivity is equally fatal. A monopolistic attitude on the part of some comrades and passivity of other sections of the party—each of these spell death to the TUEL and any difference of attitude in the party towards the TUEL, regardless of who is correct from a formal standpoint, means isolation of the TUEL from the party membership, means the stagnation of the TUEL.

I think that the TUEL and its apparatus, as well as the trade union apparatus of the party, must become much more the concern of the party as a whole. In that, a certain decision of the CI on the division of labor has laid down a correct line. The basis is correct from an immediate standpoint, but from the standpoint of a permanent situation it is wrong. It should be the conscious aim of the party in its development to completely pass over this period of any division between political work and trade union work.

We are opposed to all theories and practices of a special trade union group in the party as well as all the implications of such a theory.

I want to go over the report of the Polcom and the resolution of the Polcom and to make the remark that I made before, that comrade Lovestone, in his analysis on the question of the united front, has not only abandoned the entire leadership of comrade Ruthenberg. He has not only thrown overboard the somewhat leftist orientation of the Polcom but has bent the stick backward. I agree with those comrades who have drawn the conclusion that the Polcom today in its orientation has a different line from the Polcom of the past year. This is established both in the meetings of the Polcom and in this plenum discussion and resolution.

I believe this resolution, when compared with comrade Lovestone's speech, represents a contradiction. I believe that this resolution, when compared with comrade Lovestone's speech, is an illustration of the conflicting lines within the majority of the Polcom. I believe that in this resolution we do not see the same tendency as in the Lovestone line. I think that the majority of the Polcom has conflicting tendencies within it. If any comrade thinks I am in error, I hope he will explain and prove it. In the present majority of the Polcom there is a conflict of tendencies, which will grow more and more apparent as the work develops, between the old line of a year ago led by comrade Ruthenberg and comrade Bedacht, and the new line represented by comrades Lovestone and Wolfe. I make the statement here that the Polcom in the past year, on the question of the united front and a number of other questions, under the leadership of comrade Ruthenberg expressed theoretically most of all by comrade Bedacht, represented a somewhat leftist orientation, and I maintain that since the death of comrade Ruthenberg, under the leadership of comrades Lovestone and Wolfe there is a bending of the stick backward. This is a most serious political statement, and nobody but a fool or a cynic can take this as a jest. Answer it politically and refute it if you can.

We have other contradictions in the line of Bedacht and Lovestone. The conflict between the line of Bedacht and the line of Lovestone reminds us of the advice once given to a man in the Bible: "Don't let your right hand know what your left hand is doing."

We say there are errors in the resolution of the Polcom, basic errors. First of all, we say this resolution is pessimistic, in this sense—that it gives no outlook, no perspective of new developments and new struggles creating a basis for a broadening of the left wing of the organization. It says that our work is more difficult than ever before under the drive against us. Speaking from a general standpoint, we say that is not correct. On the contrary, we say that the dialectics of the fight against the unions, of the drive against the Communists as a part of the drive against the unions, is in itself creating conditions and contradictions making more favorable the developments and the broadening of our left wing in the struggle. The resolution sees a static bureaucracy. We see a process of differentiation within the bureaucracy, in which are already indications of new alignments in the unions. You see growing difficulties in the work; we see growing possibilities.

The contradiction between the report of Lovestone and the resolution of Bedacht is especially interesting on the question of differentiation within the bureaucracy. It is quite characteristic of comrade Lovestone that he should see these things and point out that they have already been shown to a certain extent in the Executive Council of the AFL, and it is likewise characteristic of comrade Bedacht that he did not see them. On this question, Lovestone is apt to see too much and Bedacht to see nothing.

Comrade Bedacht makes a statement here in his resolutions about the bureaucracy. He says the trade union bureaucracy is the most powerful base of the capitalists in the labor movement. I want to know what this statement means. Do you mean to say that the trade union bureaucracy is a homogeneous static body which consciously serves as a basis of the capitalists? We say that this very bureaucracy will become instruments of the left wing against the capitalists in the fight to preserve the unions and for the organization of the unorganized. We point to the instances of Brophy and Maurer—and there are more Brophys and Maurers—who by our tactics and strategy have become instruments to fight in certain instances against the capitalists.

The resolution does not see this. It is very characteristic that it is made by comrade Bedacht and not by comrade Lovestone. In the question of the left wing, this resolution of our Political Committee says we must build a left wing. Well, I think we can take a vote and be unanimous on that point. We are all for the left wing and for the organization of the unorganized. But how are we going to build it and what forces are going to work on our side? On this the resolution is silent. Therefore the whole talk of the resolution dealing with the left wing is a hollow phrase. It does not show from where and in what dynamic process the left wing will be recruited and built on a broader basis.

We do, and we reiterate our position that out of the very drive against the party and the left wing in the unions, there will be developed new bases for building the left wing, new alignments, in which part of the very bureaucrats under the pressure of the masses will become instruments of the left wing. The resolution of the Polcom presented by comrade Bedacht paints only a picture of hardship, of difficulty, the blackest pessimism with no perspective, no analytical approach, while we on the contrary do see perspectives and draw conclusions from them.

I want to go over to the speech of comrade Wolfe, and to preface my remarks on this point by saying that I was one of those here who listened with the greatest attention to the remarks of comrade Wolfe. I believe that comrade Wolfe, jointly with comrade Lovestone if subordinate, is a bearer of the new orientation of our majority of the Polcom. And I listened very seriously and very attentively. I want to say, comrade Wolfe—and I wish the remarks I make here will be taken seriously with the understanding that I say them with a real feeling of responsibility. I am not here to make irresponsible charges or accusations.

I say the speech of comrade Wolfe was one of the worst speeches I have listened to since the foundation of our party. I say that the foremost duty of a leader of the party is to be a teacher of the party, that anyone, particularly an influential or able comrade, who resorts to misrepresentation, who confuses issues, and who above all evades the serious political charges, such as those made by comrade Weinstone, and covers them up, as comrade Wolfe did, is misleading and confusing the party.

Lenin said: "A demagogue is the greatest enemy of the working class." And I say doubly, demagogy is the greatest danger to our party.

I am going to answer the speech of comrade Wolfe point by point, and I will establish the thesis that it was not the speech of a political leader trying to clarify and explain and teach the comrades, but it was the speech of a comrade trying to confuse and cover the issues, with evasions and demagogy. For this purpose I will take up the speech of comrade Wolfe point by point.

First of all, comrade Wolfe said that comrade Foster does not want an alliance with comrade Weinstone, but the other way around, that Weinstone wants an alliance with comrade Foster. Comrade Wolfe knows that is not true. If it were true, there would be no reason to deny it. It is merely a clever attempt to transpose words and to confuse the real question of the relationship of the Foster group and the group of comrade Weinstone and myself. Comrade Wolfe knows that up to now the policy of our group has not been to seek an alliance with Foster. He knows on the other hand that Foster has made more or less open propositions for such an alliance. I do not say this as a criticism of comrade Foster. I am not one of those to put the Foster group in an outlaw category. I say the single consideration for a political relationship between our group and the Foster group, for closer cooperation, or even a combination of forces, is the question of the line of the party. That is the consideration. There is nothing personal about it. The political line is the deciding thing. I say, however, we will not trade off any principles for the sake of an alliance with comrade Foster. We will not say that we were "misled" into the old fight against Foster, as Lovestone said yesterday. We will take full political responsibility for our past attitude towards comrade Foster, and, furthermore, say that if the conditions arise for a principled fight with the Foster group in the future, as they did in the past, we will not evade it. Our attitude will be determined by their line.

I maintain, comrade Wolfe, that you evaded and confused the real question presented by comrade Weinstone on the 1924 and 1928 elections. On the one hand, Weinstone made the statement that if there is to be no mass labor party in 1928 and we all agree that chances for this are small, our party, while continuing naturally the fight for the labor party, must begin to orient to the idea that it must present its own candidates in the 1928 elections. Upon what does he base this proposition? On the theory that we will not put up a labor party ticket unless we have a mass basis for it. And then he made the serious accusation that the reason perhaps that Lovestone was silent on the question of our own candidates in 1928 was that, although he says that there are slight chances for a mass labor party, he would be willing to take a narrow labor party, a MacDonald-Bouck labor party which he stood for in 1924.

If you are performing your duty as a teacher of the party, you would explain whether this is so or not so. You would answer the serious accusation which you know, if it is true, will provoke a more serious, more determined struggle in the party. We fought with Lovestone on this question in the party and in Moscow, and he has never yet admitted he was wrong in wanting to support the Bouck-MacDonald "labor party" in 1924 instead of putting up our own candidates. We want to know whether you acknowledge it now or retreat from that position. When you say that it is too trivial to answer, you are evading a most serious question. If we cannot have a mass labor party in 1928, will you form a narrow labor party? You are duty bound to explain this thing. It is never too late to put forward our own ticket, but nevertheless it is never too early to foresee the probabilities and orient and prepare the party accordingly.

I want to cite another illustration. The position presented by comrade Weinstone, as Wolfe knows, merely meant to prepare the party for an eventual actuality that we will have no mass labor party in 1928, which we all see now. You distort that into a proposition on the part of Weinstone to abandon the idea of a labor party. You know that if the prospects and possibilities exist for a labor party, Weinstone said we can orient ourselves and organize that sentiment. We are for that. When you compare Weinstone's statement, that if the prospects are against the formation of a mass labor party in 1928 we must orient our party to put up its own ticket, with the Socialist Party's "day of mourning" for Sacco and Vanzetti, you are deliberately distorting and misrepresenting the position of Weinstone. Such methods are responsible for the fact that the party members do not get a clear teaching from the leaders of the party. They get only demagogy and misrepresentation.

Weinstone said the majority of the Polcom is characterized by a lack of principle in its relations to the party. A most serious accusation indeed! I agree with him and I do not make this as a blank charge. I will give reasons, point by point.

Why was "bourgeoisification" left out of the resolution? You must explain this. You have been going up and down the party since the death of comrade Ruthenberg with one of the most highly organized and venomous campaigns in the history of the party against Foster and "Fosterism" on the grounds that he advocates the idea that the American working class is becoming "bourgeoisified." This is a most serious political accusation and, if that is the case, you have to make it the center for discussion at the plenum and have the Foster group establish whether it is so or not. But when you came to the plenum apparently you were not quite sure what the situation would be between the groups, and consequently you were not quite sure what stand to take.

You were not quite sure, although a very short while ago you had established as your principal line that the Lovestone group must unite with the so-called Cannon group to save the party from Foster and Fosterism. When this proposal failed to work out, you began to orient to the idea of uniting with Foster to save the party from Cannon. And that is why when you came to the plenum you were not sure where to deal your blows and you forgot another principle and left out of your resolution the question of "bourgeoisification" about which you were so agitated in recent weeks. What is this but lack of principle? On the first day after the death of comrade Ruthenberg, Lovestone told me that we must unite against Foster because "we have not changed our attitude a bit about him." Yet in his speech yesterday, he threw away the fight against Fosterism and blamed it on Cannon. He said he was "misled" by Cannon. Why, to use some of the phraseology and terminology introduced in the plenum by comrade Gitlow, I would say the speech of comrade Lovestone was not flirtation with Foster. This was solicitation of Foster. And it is very unfortunate for comrade Lovestone that comrade Foster, if not in words, at least in attitude, repulsed these ardent advances so coldly and indifferently.

This is a serious charge that the Lovestone group is an unprincipled group which changes from day to day in its attitude to the groups in the party. One day he denounces Foster and the next day he denounces Cannon and asks for unity with Foster against him. Explain that, if you can, and show us what principle is involved in these gyrations.

Now I go on further, comrade Wolfe, and say that you resorted to misrepresentation and demagogy on the question of the united front. Comrade Weinstone said that we had many criticisms of the old Political Committee, before the death of comrade Ruthenberg, on the question of the united front. I say it here. I say that the tactics of the party in the past year established by the Polcom on the question of the united front showed a tendency towards the left, a tendency of putting the party forward as an organization with interests of its own, a tendency to demand that the party must be represented in its own name directly in all united fronts.

We see Lovestone come here as representative of this Polcom and present an entirely different tactical line on the united front. We say that the line presented by comrade Lovestone cannot be criticized fundamentally. We say it is a change of line, a correction of line. Comrade Weinstone made that charge and you, Wolfe, know that it is true. And you, Stachel, know that it is true, that it is a change of line. That our old criticisms on the united front of the past year do not apply to this line and we cannot honestly attack the line on the united front presented by Lovestone on the same basis that we did during the last year. But how do you educate the party? There is only one way of educating the party, and that is when you change a position, especially a position of the leadership of the party, you explain that change to the party and give the reasons, so that the party will understand it and not make the old errors again. Comrade Wolfe, you in your speech covered up this change. You did not acknowledge it or explain it, and you shifted the whole question to a discussion of alleged personal errors of Weinstone. I say if everything you said against Weinstone were true, and if you brought in 20 more errors of Weinstone, you do not answer the fundamental charge which we ask you again to answer: that the Polcom has changed its line on the united front, that it has not given any reasons for it, that it has not explained it to the party and is covering it up and maintaining that there is no change. That is not Leninist leadership. That is lack of principle.

Comrade Wolfe spoke about the "Nine Points" and mentioned one of them and said that they had been abandoned. I can assure you, comrade Wolfe, that you have been too optimistic on this question. Later I will speak upon it. I just want to mention one point in passing, that Wolfe centered his attack upon the proposal to create in the Polcom an advisory committee of three, one from each group, to consider matters before decisions of the Polcom, to facilitate mutual agreements and modify the factional intensity. You attack this as though this were a crime against the party. I tell you, comrade Wolfe, that this point of the "Nine Points" you will yet adopt. In fact you have already adopted it, but not officially. Every time there is anything serious in the party you have to talk to a representative of the Foster group and a representative of our group. When you try to represent our proposal for an informal body, without powers, as setting up an instrument against the Polcom, you are distorting the question. And when you reject the idea of one of the Lovestone group, one of the Foster group, and one of our group meeting informally to discuss disputed questions, you are rejecting the idea of any attempt to find a common political line in the party. You are rejecting the idea of unity, no matter how much you speak about it.

Something with respect to the party bulletin. You know that no one proposed a board to censor articles but merely to agree on the tone and character of them. You misrepresented that. You call that criminal hypocrisy. Our idea was to prevent the possibility of the discussion in the bulletin taking the form of 1924.

In comrade Wolfe's speech, last night, we had a shocking spectacle of a party leader making the charge, before a roomful of comrades, many of them rank and file workers, that we are keeping you here so that you can't go out and do anti-war work! Such a speech as that would call forth a unanimous protest from the meeting in any Communist party that established the necessity of principled conduct of leaders. It is only because the party, as a result of so many months of factional fights, heterogeneous groupings, and corrupt factional practices, is so saturated with cynicism and lack of Communist approach to these questions that we could tolerate such a remark as that in a party meeting. Everybody in the party is for anti-war work and when you try to put us in such a position you resort to the lowest form of demagogy. Comrades, the task of the party leaders is to pull the party out of this morass and unify it and set it to its revolutionary task. One of the foremost tasks of the party is to establish the necessity of principled conduct of party leaders. That they do not corrupt the party, resort to demagogy, and confuse and misrepresent questions to the party. That they have a principled line for which they work and when they change or correct it they explain it to the party. That is what is necessary in the party.

I want to take up some of the criticisms made by the Foster group, particularly the Sacco-Vanzetti campaign.[3] On this question, in my opinion, the Foster group made a very, very serious error, the failure to take into account the concrete realities of the problems of the Sacco-Vanzetti movement. I believe that if we had agreed to the line of the Foster group on this question, the destruction of the ILD in the labor movement might easily have resulted. Here is the situation. It is not an ordinary issue which you can fight to your heart's content. It requires the most delicate and tactful approach. First of all, two men are in danger of death. They are not Communists, but anarchists. Their committee is composed of anarchists bitterly hostile to us and to a certain

[3] Within the Political Committee Bittelman and Foster were vocal opponents of the ILD's conduct in the Sacco and Vanzetti campaign in early 1927. After the Massachusetts Supreme Court rejected Sacco and Vanzetti's appeal in April, Bittelman insisted that the party issue a national strike call. Cannon counterposed an ILD propaganda campaign, leading to a national Sacco and Vanzetti conference, and his proposal passed in the Political Committee meeting of April 7. But the anarchist-led Boston Sacco and Vanzetti defense committee refused to go along with a national conference. In the Political Committee meeting of 21 April 1927, Cannon deflected Foster and Bittelman's demands that there be a national conference in any case, and more trade-union involvement in the campaign, by referring the issue to a subcommittee of Wolfe, Cannon and Foster.

extent under the influence of the worst enemies in the labor movement.

This committee is composed of elements politically hostile to the party and looking for the opportunity to destroy and discredit the party. And yet you propose that the ILD go over the head of this committee, giving this committee the slightest basis for the charge that we disrupt the movement. The whole reactionary labor press and the fakers would take up the hue and cry that the Communists are disrupting the movement. I believe the proposal of the Foster group would have led to the most serious consequences. If your proposition meant anything, it meant to go over the head of the Boston committee and organize a national conference with or without their consent. This we cannot do under the present circumstances if we have any regard for realities. And when you finally qualified your motion by saying we should go as far as possible without an open break with the Boston committee, you abandoned the whole position, because that is the line we have been following.

Now some of the criticisms made by the Foster group against the Polcom I agree with and some I disagree with. And I believe it is my duty to state those I do agree with as well as those that I disagree with, since we are aiming for clarification. We must have the perspective of unifying the leadership, for there is no point in concealing agreements or disagreements. If we are aiming toward unity on policy we must not overlook real difficulties or set up false ones. Our conception of the party is not a schematic combination of two or more groups against others. It is the establishment, with the help of the CI, of a common line for collaboration of all leading and able comrades on the basis of the line. That is my idea and I am by no means one of those people who are compelled to change their attitude from day to day because I am looking for different combinations.

I believe that when Foster stated that the majority of the Polcom opposed building the TUEL he was wrong. It is my honest opinion that since the return from Moscow a year ago, such a charge is unfounded. I think it is wrong for you to drag up issues which were considered before the last decision of the CI, because there will never be any way of finding a common ground if you do that. At the last session of the CI all the propositions were presented there. I say the right thing is to take that decision as a starting, because if you go back in the history of the party you will find differences on every issue, not only between groups but within groups.

I do not believe that the Polcom has sabotaged the trade union work. I believe there was a real disposition on the part of the Polcom as a whole to support this work and I believe the party has been showing progress in trade union work because of that fact.

I believe when he says we failed to build the left wing he makes a criticism that applies to all equally. Comrade Foster states that the Polcom is sabotaging *Labor Unity*. I believe that there was indifference and passivity. On the other hand, that *Labor Unity* is organized on a very narrow basis. And I believe that the decision to have *Labor Unity* up for discussion in the Polcom with the prospect of revamping and remodeling it, with the idea of mobilizing the party behind it, will be successful. Our attitude on the question of "bourgeoisification"—we have never made this the issue against Foster, because we have no documents or concrete proof of such an attitude of comrade Foster. If Foster stands for this, if it is established in a document, then you have something concrete to base your attack upon. But in the absence of presentation of any such point of view of "bourgeoisification" in a clear and definite form, we see no possibility to educate the party on the basis of rumors and gossip. Our discussions must proceed from the basis of established facts. The same rule should apply on the question of the famous "head-on collision" which comrade Foster raises as a counter-bogey to "bourgeoisification," and in much the same way.

My recollection of this question, borne out by the records of the Polcom, is the following: At the first consideration of this question a wrong line was adopted but the decision was unanimous. At the second meeting, Foster raised the question of reversing the position and I supported him. Comrade Ruthenberg retreated from the former position and a new course was taken.

Do we have to fight over errors that are openly rejected and acknowledged? The fight over errors is only if somebody persists in them and develops a systematic line from them. We have got to quit fighting in the party over errors which are corrected and done with. I would like to have here the speech of comrade Stalin against Zinoviev and Trotsky on this point. He said everybody makes errors. The errors you fight upon are those which are persisted in and developed into a line. When errors are made and dropped, then it is useless to continue to fight against the comrades responsible. Otherwise you have a permanent factional fight. The fact that comrade Ruthenberg changed his position and that no one now defends the original motions is a sufficient reason to discontinue the controversy over them.

I would like to say a few remarks about Akron. Akron was a case where errors were multiplied at a rate and speed of which comrade Amter alone would be capable. He showed such incompetency for practical mass work that comrade Amter, in a normally functioning party, would be relieved of that post and assigned to another one. If our Polcom majority were free from its own factional contradictions, they would support that point of view. Unfortunately, it is not free and the party, particularly the Akron section, must suffer.

A few remarks on the criticism of our group. For a year and a half comrade Foster has been confronting us with a false accusation. Ever since the "big split" in the old majority group, which in my opinion was a good split, which helped serve the cause of the unification of the party, and which comrade Lovestone objectively repudiated yesterday and which I will never repudiate—we have been confronted with the charge that we were against taking power in the unions. If there were no factionalism in the party such a ridiculous charge would never be made. I do not believe that Foster believes it. I want to say that I don't believe it. I don't believe that there is anybody in this room or in this party who is more in favor of taking power in the unions than we are.

We are opposed to the fight for office for the sake of office, and particularly opposed to certain corrupt practices in the needle trades on the part of some elements of our left wing, and we say, Foster, that when you attack us on the ground of being opposed to taking office in the unions, you are objectively supporting those elements and tendencies in the needle trades which the party has fought in the past and must fight in the future. The factional misrepresentation of the Foster group against us on this question is a blow at the party.

Our group, in common with every group in the party, is prepared to resort to every strategy and method in line with the methods of Communists to conquer power in the unions. On the question of the Philadelphia convention, I believe the formulation made by the Polcom was subject to misrepresentation and was misrepresented. And, by the way, it is very interesting to see such an attitude towards party responsibility that although I have only one vote in the Polcom and was not the author of the resolution in question, yet I am credited with the trade union policy of the CEC at that time, and the personal responsibility for the resolution.[4]

Yesterday Lovestone accused me of misleading the Polcom majority on the fight with Foster, and today the Foster group accuses me of misleading the Polcom majority on the trade union question. They make out a case of "undue influence" which appears to be slightly exaggerated.

The basic line of the Polcom resolution, drafted by Ruthenberg, was correct. Its formulation was not wrong but faulty. It was subject to misrepresentation and the Foster group, for factional reasons, has misrepresented it.

The resolution was primarily aimed against those corrupt practices which would undermine our left wing in the needle trades, and I will never let anybody swerve me away from that principal question to the question of one incidental or tactical

---

[4] The policy of the Workers Party fraction at the International Ladies' Garment Workers' Union special convention which began in Philadelphia on 30 November 1925 was the source of significant controversy. See Cannon's motions on the subject, pp. 359-360. We have not been able to locate minutes of the Political Committee meetings which discussed policy during the convention.

At the convention, the social-democratic Sigman leadership retained a narrow majority of 154 to 110, but only because the voting procedure favored the small locals controlled by the right wing. At first Sigman tried to woo the left-wing New York locals, demanding and obtaining from the New York governor the release of union member and WP leader Benjamin Gitlow, who had been jailed again on an old state criminal syndicalism charge. However, in mid-convention Sigman changed his tune and refused to abide by a previous agreement which committed him to a union referendum on the issue of proportional representation for

(continued)

decision. The fundamental thing that we were and are driving against is the tendency to substitute maneuvers and deals with the blackest fakers for mobilization of the masses on the basis of the class struggle. At that time we were confronted with the brilliant idea of a *combination with Sigman,* and we said to them that you must at all costs keep up your criticism and attack against Sigman or you will demoralize and destroy the left wing. They entered into secret negotiations with Sigman and discontinued the attack and criticism against him. We said we were not going to allow it. That is the fundamental principle involved and the Polcom resolution struck against it. You are doing a wrong service to the party, Foster, when you distort the meaning of our fight even though we made errors in formulation. The party will not be educated and corruption will not be overcome by such methods.

Comrade Wolfe yesterday referred to the document of "Nine Points," which represents a point of view on the internal line of the party arrived at by a number of comrades coming from different groups in the party, having for their purpose the unification of the party. I might say, in prefacing my remarks on this point, that they were not formally presented to the party before, because we did not have the opportunity. The plenum was delayed, and I want to say in further explanation that since the time of the drafting of these "Nine Points," especially since the discussion in the

---

locals at future union conventions. In response, the left wing walked out of the convention.

Workers Party members comprised 52 out of the total of 110 left-wing delegates, but Louis Hyman, who had led the walkout, was not a party member. Dunne and Gitlow were the party steering committee on the spot, and they demanded that the left wing go back, with Dunne insisting that, if necessary, "You will crawl back on your belly!" The left wing went back. See Irving Howe and Lewis Coser, *The American Communist Party* (New York: Frederick A. Prager, 1962), 245-251.

In a report on the convention in *Workers Monthly* (February 1926), Dunne evaluated the behavior of the Workers Party's fraction as follows:

> "Its convention actions were a weird mixture of leftism and opportunism—leftism in that it followed an objectively splitting policy until the last day of the convention, opportunism in that this splitting policy was based on the naive belief that the Sigman machine was sincere enough in its unity maneuvers to make substantial concessions to the left wing in order to avoid a split in the union."

plenum, we have to make a certain amplification and modification of the point of view outlined in the document.

We have to underscore more the question of political differences between the groups which were not so clearly established then as now. The question of the internal policy is to a certain extent even overshadowed by the question of external policy at the plenum, and the question of arriving at the unification of the party here as a prerequisite, the liquidation of these differences manifested here. With the help of the CI, this can be done, we hope. Then it should be possible to achieve unity.

If the comrades will indulge me, since this question has been brought up, I am prepared to introduce the "Nine Points" in the name of our group, with the explanation which I spoke of before, and take full responsibility for them.

First of all, I want to explain they are an outline, by no means a program, but a preparatory outline which we thought would lay the basis for beginning the process of unifying the leadership. Some comrades have said we are looking for a "Mulligan unity," a general scramble of all the groups regardless of the differences existing. They don't know what they are talking about. We want unity on the basis of a clearly established political line and those who have tried unity with us in the past ought to know that. For us, policy is the determining factor and everything proceeds from that.

We have a situation in the party of permanently organized factions existing in times of struggle over differences as well as in time of unanimous resolutions, and we are trying to find a way to break the party out of it.

I will read the nine points with these words of explanation:

1. In order that the party may effectively cope with its problems in the class struggle, the party leadership must accomplish the liquidation of factionalism and the unification of the party on the basis of correct policy without factions.

2. Each group contains qualities and elements necessary for the party. The problem of party unity therefore cannot be solved by the elimination from effective participation in the party leadership of any of the groups. Neither can it be solved, with the present relation of forces and composition of the groups, by the control of the party by any one of the existing groups operating on factional lines, or by any combination of two groups and not a third.

3. The control of the party by the former majority group represented a factional deadlock; the former majority was unable to unify the party. The present majority of the Political Committee likewise failed to unify the party, notwithstanding its greater opportunities.

4. Neither of the factions was able to defeat the other decisively and establish a sufficiently stable majority. They were not able to work together harmoniously or to unite. They presented the party with the prospect of permanent factional struggle, continually hampering the development of the party work.

5. The experience shows that neither one of the factions as now constituted is able to lead the party alone and overcome the factional impasse. This arises out of the whole inner party situation. It is anomalous for a Bolshevik party to have factional groupings within which there are political divisions on issues of prime importance, while the groups cross each other in support of major political questions, and yet these groups retain their separate factional identity, cohesion and discipline. This rapidly degenerates into a condition of factional bankruptcy. The heterogeneous composition of the factions and the stubborn maintenance of permanent factional organization leads to factional corruption and unprincipledness.

6. The factional slogans that one or the other faction as now constituted must exercise "hegemony" or "form the basic element" of the leadership in the present circumstances are untenable. The party must now recognize the necessity for collective leadership. All the groups can contribute to this collective leadership and all the leading forces must come together and work consciously to establish it. The stable, collective leadership of the party will be further evolved in the process of the party unification and consolidation and the development of the party's leadership of the masses in the class struggle.

7. The dissolution of the existing factions is a necessary prerequisite for the unification of the party. The disintegration of the factions is directly connected with the process of integration and growth of the party. The idea of party must take precedence over the idea of factions. Party leadership must replace faction leadership. Loyalty to the party must prevail over loyalty to the factions. Not the mechanical combination or "amalgamation" of factions, but their liquidation, is the path to genuine party unity.

8. As first steps towards this end, we believe it is necessary to devise measures which by their nature would tend to liquidate within a reasonable period the factional groupings and practices, as well as such general party practices as are a hindrance to the unification and centralization of the party. As a beginning, we submit the following proposals:

a. It is proposed to establish as an informal and unofficial body an *advisory committee* to be composed of three members, one from each group as presently constituted. Its duty and task would be constantly to consult upon policies and measures with a view of forming a harmonious line of action and avoiding factional friction. The advisory committee should hold regular meetings twice a week as a minimum, which meetings should be considered as preparatory to the meetings of the Polcom. In case of failure to hold any such regular meeting, it may be convoked by any one of the three members.

b. The practice of the groups holding separate caucus meetings, where party questions are discussed and binding decisions arrived at, is a matter of general party knowledge. As a means of changing the irrational forms of the present factional practices and of leading towards the ultimate liquidation of the factions, it is proposed that the existing groups agree upon the following procedure.

1. For the next immediate period of approximately two months to permit representatives of the other two groups to come to every general caucus meeting of the third group for the purpose of presenting their position on the question under consideration.
2. Should this practice work satisfactorily, to extend it for the next period so as to permit such representatives not only to present their position, but also to remain and take part in the discussion in the caucus meeting.

c. As steps preparatory to a truly representative convention of the party the following proposals are made:

1. The establishment of a party bulletin to be devoted entirely to information and discussion on party matters. An editorial board to be formed on a parity basis whose duty it will be to pass unanimously on the discussion articles. All articles must be signed and can be accepted only as the position of the individual comrade signing the article. No article to be accepted that is either the presentation of the position of a faction or directed against the presumable position of another faction.
2. The organization of a truly representative and constructive party convention. To this end, the convention should be called only after all possibilities have been exhausted for the reaching of at least a tentative agreement on the main political line of the party.
3. As a safeguard against factional manipulations and mechanical suppression, the party convention should be organized on the basis of proportional representation and the creation of national, district and local convention committees on a parity basis.

9. The foregoing propositions are submitted to the Polcom as initial steps for the accomplishment of the aim set forth in Paragraph 1. They are submitted at the same time to each individual member of the CEC for consideration. Each member of the CEC is herewith requested to express his position in writing with regard to all these propositions. Acceptance or rejection may refer to the document as a whole or to single proposals. In either case, each CEC member is invited to express his reasons in writing for the rejection of any or all of the proposals and to offer alternatives.

Those who reject our proposals must point to another way. Can you unify the party on the basis of a monopoly of leadership by the comrades in the Lovestone group? To put that question here at the plenum is to answer it in the negative.

If there is one thing fatally doomed in the party, it is the idea that any one existing faction can maintain a monopoly of the leadership of the party. Is it not a fact that when the former majority controlled the party, we had a factional deadlock? Do we want to return to that? We say: no, we do not want to go back to that.

On the other hand, we say the present majority of the Polcom likewise failed to unify the party.

Do you maintain that the party is unified? One who wants to speak this way is refuted by this very plenum where such strong forces are represented in opposition to the Polcom. When you say that the party is unified you are either deceiving yourself or the party.

The party is in a dangerous factional situation, so much so that the Communist International has found it necessary to call a delegation consisting of representatives of all these groups in the party to Moscow. We have to recognize conditions as they exist and find a way out.

We should recognize that neither of the factions was able to defeat the other decisively. They were not able to work together harmoniously or to unite. That is a fact. They offer a perspective of permanent factional fight. One year the Ruthenberg group is getting a majority. Next the Ruthenberg group is the opposition and regaining the majority. Then the Foster group is the opposition and fighting for the majority.

There is a consistent "two-party system" in the party, so well established that neither group denies the right of the other group to exist. I have never yet heard the Foster group complain that the Ruthenberg group is maintaining a faction or the Ruthenberg group complain that the Foster group maintains a faction. It is only since comrades have revolted against both and try to break up the condition of permanent factions and form a group to fight for this idea that the comrades of the other "established" groups complain of factional organization. By some secret method of reasoning known only to themselves they have arrived at the conclusion that it is entirely right to have two groups in the party but entirely wrong to have a third group appear.

Why must we have factions in the Communist Party? Why must we always have two groups in the party? Upon what principle of Leninism is this theory founded? If there is no such principle, if on the contrary the permanent maintenance of two separate factions is against Leninist principles, we ask the other groups to show the party a solution for the deadlock.

In connection with this document, comrades, we also submitted some practical propositions to facilitate the unification process. We have caucuses and faction meetings going on all the time, as everybody knows, and participated in by all active comrades. We know that in these caucuses things are said and accusations are made to prejudice and poison comrades against others that would never be said if the other comrades of the other faction were there to answer. The tone of the plenum here is very different from that of faction meetings because if one makes irresponsible charges or accusations the comrade is here to answer them.

We propose that when the groups call the faction meetings that they permit a leading comrade of the other groups to come and state his point of view. It is easy to see that such a proceeding would change the character of the caucuses and break down the rigid group lines and lead toward the substitution of general party meetings for one-sided caucus discussions. We stand by these proposals and state that the proposals will yet be carried out. We will not solve the problem of unity by the *combination of factions*, but by the *liquidation of factions.*

Since the remark was made about unity between myself and Weinstone, I want to say a few words about it. In my opinion, it should be regarded as a natural and correct development. It is based upon the fact that we each, independently and under different circumstances and in different factions, came to a common standpoint on political grounds.

I believe we have arrived at a common attitude towards the problems of the party, and particularly about the necessity for party unity as a prerequisite for the further development of the party.

Now, a good deal was made here about the "Ballam" question. The fact that Cannon and Ballam are together is regarded by some people as a violation of the established factional code. I want to say here, for myself at least, that I stand by this step we have taken. If, after eight years, during which we were never together, always in opposite factions, with the sharpest personal feelings—if after eight years, Ballam and Cannon can find a common standpoint and unite, it should not be regarded as something foolish but as a matter of the greatest significance. It shows that the development of the unification of the party is drawing together Communists who have had longstanding fights. It is not enough to be able to fight over principled differences. Communists must also be able to unite when the differences are settled.

I believe it is the right thing for Communists to do, when they have no more serious differences, to quit fighting. And if I have been fighting Ballam, and he me, for eight years, and we have no differences now on serious questions, why should we not get together? Do we have to fight for the next eight years in order to prove that we are not pacifists?

My opinion is that this idea will grow in the ranks of the party, *the idea that permanent, personal factional fights and factional feuds* can be replaced by a higher order of struggle, in other words, that the faction fights based on outworn issues, on questions of two or three years ago, on prejudices, traditions and factional interests, can be replaced by political struggles in which comrades take their positions objectively on the question as it arises, and then when the issue is decided, abandon the fight and work unitedly together.

That is what we are standing for. We put before this body here our point of view and we ask you comrades to give serious consideration to our opinion. Our opinion is this: that while we have differences between the three groups, while these differences have to be discussed before the CI and settled, yet we must go to the CI with this idea, that we are not going to try to find a basis for further fights but a basis for coming together of all the leading elements in the party.

We say with real conviction that if there is good will and good faith the three groups can, with the help of the CI, find a common platform. The CI can correct us all on every field where we are wrong and we can come back and lead the party unitedly.

You cannot lead the party on any other basis. You cannot develop the party without unity. Certainly you cannot develop the party by unity of Cannon, Weinstone and Foster against the Lovestone group, and by all means you cannot unify the party with Lovestone and Wolfe against Foster, Bittelman, Johnstone, Krumbein, Aronberg, Cannon, Weinstone, Dunne, Ballam, Abern, Reynolds, Swabeck. Not a combination of factions but the unification of the party and collective leadership—this is our aim.

We must aim for unity. We must have a will for unity. Laugh at our proposals if you want to. Say they are "infantile." Say that the expressions and plans for unity are utopian. We answer you, only because the party is mired in factionalism, only because it is not yet oriented towards the real need for unity, is it possible to find anything strange or ridiculous in the demand for unity. We fight for the idea of unity on a common political line. We fight for the idea that factions are to be replaced by party, that faction loyalty is to be replaced by party loyalty, that political fights are to be carried to conclusions and settled, and not resolved into permanent groups and cliques.

That is what we stand for here and that is what we will fight for before the Comintern.

Theses on the Party Factional Situation

ca. May 1927

The following are three sections excerpted from lengthy, unpublished, undated and unsigned theses, apparently written by Cannon and William Weinstone for submission to the American Commission which was convened in Moscow to resolve the question of the American party leadership in the aftermath of the sudden death of general secretary C.E. Ruthenberg. The commission was appointed toward the end of the Eighth Plenum of the Executive Committee of the Communist International, held 18-30 May 1927. Cannon and Weinstone were included among the American plenum delegates only after the Comintern overruled Lovestone's attempt to exclude them. They arrived in Moscow on the last day of the plenum.

Party Reorganization and General Party Work

The following statement is an amplification of the resolution of the CI on the reorganization, a brief examination of the shortcomings in the general party work politically and organizationally.

It must be stated at the very outset that the entire party work has been influenced and affected by the factional struggle within the party that has put an obnoxious impression upon every phase of party work, blurring and obliterating the necessary political crystallization of party thought by means of exchange of opinions and hampering as well the thorough reorganization of the party along the lines pointed out in the resolution of the CI.

For a correct situation of the state of our party organizationally there must be stressed the necessity of examining our present party cadres taking into consideration all the losses sustained after the reorganization on the one hand and the net results gained from the new membership drive (Ruthenberg Drive) on the other. This examination must include the following points:

a) The district distribution of the party membership.

b) The distribution of party membership with regard to industry (heavy industry, light industry, which light industry, proportions, etc.).
c) The distribution of the party membership along language lines and a special occupational investigation in each of them.
d) A new statistical investigation of the trade union affiliation of the party membership.
e) An examination into the circulation of the entire party press with its language divisions.
f) The utilization and distribution of party functionaries.

There must also be examined the question of how far the party has advanced towards centralization and integration into one ideological and organizational unit responding to all actual party problems and participating in the carrying through of all directions of the party.

The practice observed in the life of the smaller party units clearly shows that a good number of them stand altogether aloof from party problems and activities. There is the noteworthy deficiency in our general political and agitprop work which brings with it the absolutely insufficient manner in which the party membership participates in the political and other experiences of the party which, until now, have been reflected only at the very top of the party organization. The main fault of the situation lies in the fact that this very top of the party itself has not taken the trouble of evaluating in a halfway sufficient manner its political experience.

As a proof of this statement we must underline the absolutely important fact that the party has done practically nothing in order to clarify the question of the character and possibilities of a third party movement nor has it attempted to analyze how far the organization of the labor party is related to this third party problem. No analysis has been made of the La Follette movement and its failure.

Similarly the party has not endeavored to evaluate its political experience in such cases where it has presented its own candidates independently. Despite the fact that the results of elections show a remarkable disproportion between the mass influence that we are able to obtain and count upon in various cases when we call upon the masses for support (protest meetings, etc.), and the net numerical election results that are obviously much smaller, we have not tried to find the reason for such disproportion. The usual explanation that our sympathizers are not eligible to vote is superficial and, besides, untrue. Moreover, we have yet the facts of rather remarkable local attainments in such cases as in Massachusetts, California, and North Dakota, but we have not paid political attention to these phenomena.

Further proof of our deficiencies in the political work is the manner in which we have dealt with the question of the farm crisis and its political implications in general, with respect to our possibilities in particular. In this connection the fact must be underlined that the party has not indicated in any manner what course it has taken toward a member of the party in the legislature of North Dakota.[1] This incident has passed without the slightest response from the party that apparently has not only failed to broaden its basis in North Dakota in consequence of this fact, but has apparently failed even to keep up a necessary and sufficient political connection with this isolated party post.

There has been in the past too frequent presentation of new slogans without sufficient attempt at their realization. Happily this practice is slowly disappearing now, without, however, being substituted by any systematic plan of the activization and politicalization of the party. The tendency of individual manifestos and individual directions instead of manifestos and directions of the party must be eliminated.

---

[1] An article entitled "North Dakota's Communist Legislator" in the *Workers Monthly* (April 1925) described one A.C. Miller as the "first Communist farmer to be elected to a legislative body in the U.S." Miller, the son of a refugee from the German Revolution of 1848, had been a member of the Socialist Party. He joined the Workers Party in 1923. The article did not mention what party slate he ran on.

The Workers Party did not run candidates in the North Dakota state elections in either 1924 or 1926. It supported the slate of the North Dakota Farmer-Labor Party in the 1926 local elections (it also supported the candidates of state Farmer-Labor parties in Montana, Minnesota, Washington and South Dakota). The North Dakota Farmer-Labor Party was founded in December 1925 in Bismarck, where the Workers Party agricultural organizer, Alfred Knutson, lived. Knutson was editor of the *United Farmer*, journal of the American Farmers Educational League, American affiliate of the Comintern's Peasant International. He was a supporter of the Lovestone faction.

A part of the fault in the political work of the party lies in the deficiencies of its agitprop department. It has been fully realized by the party circles that this department has not fulfilled its tasks. There has not been any central activity that would place the various organizations of the party in contact with the political line of the party. Moreover, the issuance of party literature was conducted in an incidental and at times absolutely factional manner.

The recent moving of the party organ [*Daily Worker*] to New York while the party leadership remains in Chicago has created a situation where there exists decentralization and dislocation of the political work of the party that in the long run must create very obnoxious results for the further political work of the party. In this connection must be undertaken a general reorganization of the entire party press that would be in line with the program of Americanization presented in the later points.

The theoretical organ of the party has to be reorganized in order to serve truly the ideological needs of the party. As it is at present, it presents a picture of a casual and superficial character.

The Americanization of the party in the Bolshevist sense. A clear-cut program of Americanization has to be put through. This is necessitated by the fact that for reasons growing out of its origin and composition, the party during its entire history has been influenced by a tendency to adopt tactics, methods of work and general practices which were not sufficiently grounded in a realistic survey of the objective circumstances in which the party must carry on its work, and the stage and tempo of the class development of the American workers. A whole series and system of errors which have hampered the development of the party can be traced to this source. The "Americanization" of the party in the Bolshevist sense of the word is a task which must now be taken up in earnest and progressively accomplished. This slogan must pass from the stage of formal resolutions and be more concretely defined and applied.

The party must be oriented upon the facts and realities of the class struggle in America. The party tasks and slogans must be formulated more concretely on the basis of the American economic and political situation internally and externally.

The tactic of the united front must be conceived not as an abstraction but as an approach to the masses in accordance with all the possibilities and peculiarities of the present stage of working class development in America.

The party leadership must develop the logical implications of the reorganization of the party to the end that all party members become active and conscious participants in the general party activities and tasks. The fusion of the various nationalities in the party with the native and English-speaking members in common activities must be accelerated.

The language sections of the party, in their daily activities, their propaganda and press, must, to a much greater degree than heretofore, react to the class struggle in America. The tendencies towards isolation of the members of the language sections of the party from the general party work and the limitation of their activity to workers and organizations of their own nationality alone must be overcome by systematic educational efforts of the leading organs of the party, particularly of the language bureaus. The "home country" ideology must be replaced by planful working out of American revolutionary class consciousness penetrating into all sections of the American working class.

The party press of all languages must become politically and ideologically centralized under the leadership of the central party organs and bear a uniform general character. They must devote themselves primarily to the living issues of the class struggle in America and become real organizers of the workers in the struggle.

The party must study and take into account the traditions and psychology of the American workers. It must learn how to approach the workers and speak a language in its propaganda which is comprehensible to them. The party terminology must be simplified and revised from this standpoint.

More attention must be devoted to the native American workers and much greater efforts must be made to attract them to the party. The workers in the party who are in contact with the masses, particularly those who are closely connected with the trade unions, must be deliberately encouraged and assisted to play a more prominent and decisive role in the leading organs of the party in all of its subdivisions. The continuity of the American revolutionary movement and the connection of the party with the movements which preceded it must be established in the propaganda of the party. Special care must be devoted to the building up, the preservation and the appropriation for the party of the revolutionary traditions of the American working class.

The Party Press: In respect to the press there must be created a special press committee in which the editors of the various party organs should participate under the direction of the committee. The duty of the press committee will be to unify the character of the party press by:

a) Placing identical articles on general political and industrial problems of the party in all language papers.
b) The control of the language press as far as their "national" ideology and policy is concerned and the placing in the central organ as well as interchange in the language press of such material as sheds light upon the particular "national" question and the particular language bureau in the respective fields of activity.
c) The accumulation in the party press of such material appearing in the language press particularly of workers' correspondence that sheds light upon the industrial and shop conditions of the workers.

Similarly a press fund must be established that should be created upon a basis of contributions from all undertakings for the sustenance of the various party organs and should serve as a steady reservoir from which to strengthen this or another financially weak party organ.

Party Organization Department: There must be called into life the nonexistent organization department of the CEC whose duty it shall be to centralize the entire strictly organizational work of the party under the direction of the Polcom. The organization department must investigate *all* district and other reports on organization work of the party as well as check up on those party units that do not report upon their activities. It must further report to the Polcom on all failures of the various organizations to put into life the directions of the party. It must further elaborate an organization plan for the systematic work of the party subjecting it to constant revision on the basis of actual experience.

A competent party member must be entrusted with initiating systematic research work along the lines of party needs offering thus a basis for a clearer understanding of the problem of the party.

Negro Work: In the field of Negro work, the party has failed to realize the opportunities which presented themselves due to the weak and largely unorganized American Negro Labor Congress. The influx of Negroes into industry, the formation of large industrial centers of Negroes in the North, East and West, the growing interest among Negroes in the liberation movements in the colonies and semicolonial countries, the growth of the Soviet Union, the industrialization of the South, provide fertile fields for organization of Negroes into trade unions and for more extensive struggle of the Negroes for equal rights under the influence of our party. For this purpose it is necessary to establish a functioning center for Negro work, and for reorganization of the American Negro Labor Congress, as well as the endeavor to link up our work closer with the existing Negro organization through common united front campaigns and through the establishment of interracial labor committees. The organization of Negro workers into trade unions and the Negro tenant and poor farmers into farmers organizations and tenant leagues is an important task of our work. The linking up of Negro labor with white labor and Negro farmers with white farmers in the general movement of the workers must be always borne in mind. The establishing of a central organ appearing regularly is a task which must be hastened without delay.

Women's Work: The party in various districts, particularly in the New York district, has made important strides forward in women's work. The apathy and disinterestedness towards this field of activities has been wearing off. The party's progress in this work has been hindered by the lack of a center for this work in the CEC. It is necessary to speedily establish this center and to direct our attention not only for the organization of housewives (in which some successes have been achieved) but in the organization of the factory working women through the formation of women's delegate conferences, and drawing the working women into the political struggle of the working class. The establishment of women's factory correspondents conferences is a useful step in this direction. Systematic and persistent organization of the party apparatus for women's work by the CEC and districts must be speedily accomplished as a condition for the development of our women's work.

Young Workers League: The party is faced with the task of building a Young Workers League which shall have numerical strength at least double that of the party. The YWL must be converted into a powerful reservoir of strength for the party.

Even though the masses of young workers in this country are still politically apathetic and under the ideological influence of the bourgeoisie, the objective conditions for the building of a mass Young Communist League exist: the young workers are the most exploited part of the working class.

In the past not sufficient attention was paid to the development of the YWL into a genuine youth organization and its tendency was to merely become a sectarian section of the party. This reflex on the mass activities of the YWL had a still more marked influence on the internal life of the league. This can be seen in the fact that the majority of the league membership is foreign-born, about 65 percent of the members are party members and the social composition of the league is still bad. Though with the development of the unification process in the league and the conscious reorientation of the league towards the young workers in the factories a slight improvement can be seen in the national and social composition.

The party is the political leader of the YWL and the YWL must support the CEC of the party and be enrolled in all its campaigns. Within these campaigns the YWL with the help of the party develops the special youth aspects. Though the party is the political leader of the YWL and enrolls the league in all its campaigns, it does not mean that the league must merely be occupied with high politics and the details of the tactical lines of the party. On the contrary, it must be occupied more with the daily questions of the life of the youth in America.

The party must give added attention to the league by helping it become a broad and open organization accessible to all young workers. The YWL must understand how to apply broad and flexible methods and forms which take into consideration the present stage of development of the class consciousness of the working youth. Its agitation and propaganda must be simple and attractive, and all its activities must tend in the direction of Americanizing and proletarianizing the league in a Bolshevist sense.

Only through the rigid application of these tasks will the YWL be set well on the road towards becoming a mass Young Communist League of the American working class youth. An ideological campaign shall be carried on throughout the party to acquaint the members with the role and special problems of the YWL.

Internal Party Situation

In the party at the present time we are confronted with a factional situation which has grown very acute in recent months.

The main reasons for the factional condition are as follows:

1. Differences over questions of external policy as indicated in the theses of the three groups.

2. A tendency toward permanent factional organization on the part of both the Lovestone and Foster groups which has been leading to a "two-party system"—two parties in one.

3. The factional regime established in the party by the Lovestone group which has been a barrier to the unification of the party.

The Lovestone group which for the past 21 months has controlled the party apparatus has failed in the task of unifying the party leadership and liquidating the factionalism. This failure stands out all the more conspicuously in view of the fact that at the May and November plenums (1926) unanimous political resolutions to which all groups contributed were adopted, and in view of the further fact that during the past year the CEC did not have to contend with a factional opposition obstructing the work.

The present majority was given exceptional opportunities to unite the party. An examination of the facts proving its failure and the reasons which contributed to this result will throw light on the question of whether this faction in the future can be depended on to overcome the factional divisions and unite the collective leadership of the party.

The "Unity Resolution" of November, by which the majority of the Polcom united with the Cannon-Dunne group on the basis of a common platform, was recognized by the CI and by the large majority of the party membership as a progressive step toward the breakdown of the old factional divisions and the unification of the party. In spite of the common platform agreed upon, this "unity" was soon broken. It could not succeed for the principal reason that it was conceived and entered into by the Lovestone group as a factional maneuver. The resolution was not accepted and carried out in good faith. The Lovestone group all the time maintained a separate faction and followed a policy of discrimination against the other signatories to the unity resolution, and continued "unity negotiating" with the Foster group and the Cannon-Dunne group, attempting to play one against the other, without sincere intentions in regard to either. Such practices, which are fully established by fact and documents, broke up the process of unification which was commenced by the adoption of the unity resolution.

The factional course embarked upon by the Lovestone group during the past year artificially prevented any actual developments toward unity and consolidation and rendered an eventual outbreak of factional struggle inevitable. This course estranged and repulsed the Cannon-Dunne group in the Central Committee, helped to justify and strengthen the maintenance of the Foster group and facilitated its consolidation as an opposition. And, finally, the Lovestone group, having failed to effect a stable unity with any part of the former majority, brought about a split in its own ranks.

This split was caused by:

1. Opposition within the group, led by Weinstone, to the tendency of the Lovestone group of maintaining narrow factional groupings and especially the underestimation of the necessity of drawing American and trade unionist elements into effective leadership of the party and establishing a condition of closest cooperation and collective activity with such elements of the party.

2. The determination to transfer the struggle for unity, which had been carried on within the group for more than a year, openly to the party and CI.

3. Opposition to the vacillating external policy of the group in following a tendency to the left, particularly in questions of the united front, and, on the other hand, overemphasis on per-

sonal relations (Lovestone) with leaders of the miners union, and unprincipled relations with party right wing elements in New York.

4. This conflict existed for a long time in the group. Shortly before the death of comrade Ruthenberg attempts were being made to adjust the differences in agreement with the other groups. The irresponsible policy of comrade Lovestone broke up all these efforts and forced matters to the point of a split.

The Factional Regime of the Lovestone Group

The factional regime of the Lovestone group can be fully proven by an abundance of indisputable facts, among which are the following:

1. Maintaining permanent caucus organization in the Political Committee and deciding all important questions in private meetings before the official meetings of the Political Committee, thus reducing the latter body to a "rubber stamp" for caucus decisions and depriving other members of the Polcom of any real and decisive participation. This practice became so well established that decisions of the caucus were frequently carried out without the formality of approval by the Polcom.

2. The Lovestone group developed the theory of permanent factional control by the faction as now constituted and made no real efforts for actual fusion with other elements.

3. Systematic and excessive factionalism in organization questions, language sections, etc.

a) Appointment of poorly qualified district organizers in Boston, Philadelphia, and Seattle. Refusal to take any action to correct gross errors of district organizer in Cleveland.

b) Supported unprincipled and ultrafactional group in leadership of South Slavic section against other groups having more correct policy, greater ability and support of great majority of membership. This group, the Novak-Zinich group, went so far as to issue factional circulars against their opponents calling them "fascists," "blackshirts" and the like. They went to the extent of organizing a campaign to expel comrade Fisher, one of the oldest and best leaders of the South Slavic section, on the charge that he is "not a Communist," and they published an article by comrade Fisher in which his own meaning had been changed and new material inserted which completely distorted his position and put him in a false position before the membership. In spite of these outrageous methods, the Lovestone group, having a majority of the Polcom, consistently supported the Novak-Zinich group, gave them control of the section by mechanical and artificial means, and denied the other comrades any redress.

c) The Lovestone group deliberately intervened to prevent and break up a natural and healthy process of unification taking place between the factions in the Young Workers League under the inspiration and guidance of the YCI.[2] The Lovestone group insisted on the permanent maintenance of a faction in the YWL and has even resorted to direct and mechanical organizational interference to prevent a majority of the National Executive Committee of the YWL from carrying out decisions to facilitate the unity.

d) The Lovestone group entered into a factional alliance with the party right wing in the needle trades and makes unnecessary organizational concessions to them. The removal of Zack as secretary of the Needle Trade Committee and appointment of Gitlow was a part of this policy. At the last meeting of the Polcom the majority refused repeated demands and voted down all motions to reject the candidacy of comrade Wortis (one of the most prominent representatives of the right tendency) as secretary during the impending new strike of the Furriers.

e) Followed a narrow factional policy in the organization questions in the Finnish section basing itself entirely on the small faction of the old ultraleft in the section, repulsing and breaking up the bloc with the center, and creating a dangerous ferment of

---

2 The leadership of the Young Communist International had developed an interest in the American faction fight because of the influence of N. Nasanov. Nasanov, a young Russian Communist who had been working in China, was sent to the United States as punishment after he signed a letter critical of the policy of the Chinese Communist Party in March 1927. Under his tutelage a "Unity Caucus" had been founded to end factionalism in the Young Workers League.

Nasanov later played a role in the discussions on the American Negro question at the Sixth Congress of the Comintern in 1928. He was killed in the Stalin purges. Nasanov's letter from China, which was coauthored with N. Fokine and A. Albrecht, was published as an appendix in Leon Trotsky's *Problems of the Chinese Revolution* (New York: Pioneer Publishers, 1932), 397-492.

discontent and dissatisfaction throughout the section by a policy of organizational removals and discriminations.

f) A policy of the Jewish section which has kept up artificially a state of acute crisis for the past year.[3]

g) Attempt to break up the personnel of the party apparatus in New York where a genuine unity policy was being carried out and a real process of unification taking place.

h) Factional exploitation of the death of comrade Ruthenberg and the Ruthenberg Drive: 1) factional articles of Lovestone, Bedacht, Minor, etc.; 2) factional organization of memorial meetings, sending Bedacht and Zam for caucus work on memorial meetings tour and excluding Foster, Cannon and others; 3) presenting Ruthenberg by these means as leader of faction and not of party; 4) inferentially trying to weaken and minimize all the other leaders of the party.

---

3 The majority of the Jewish Federation leadership had been supporters of Ludwig Lore and the Foster-Cannon faction. After the Ruthenberg-Lovestone group won party leadership at the Fourth Convention in August 1925, they deposed the old majority of the Jewish Federation Bureau, installing a majority of their own faction supporters under the leadership of Benjamin Lifshitz. There followed a year of factional infighting, with the Political Committee often fighting over issues like the editorship of Federation newspapers and Communist work within the Jewish organization, the Workmen's Circle.

Letter to the American Commission

16 June 1927

The following is an unpublished letter signed by Cannon, William Z. Foster and William Weinstone. It was written in Moscow and submitted to the American Commission which continued deliberation in Moscow after the conclusion of the Eighth Plenum of the Comintern's Executive Committee. The letter reflected a new factional bloc formed in Moscow between the Cannon-Weinstone forces and the Foster faction.

Dear Comrades:

We are herewith submitting for your consideration a number of concrete points which we think should be included in the resolution of the commission on the American question. Our viewpoints on these and other questions have been further elaborated in the speeches and documents presented to the commission.

1. War Danger and the Party Tasks

The most vital and immediate task of the party is to combat the war danger to the Soviet Union and the intervention in China in which Great Britain is playing the leading provocative role.[1] The party must concentrate its full force to oppose the war pro-

---

[1] The advance of Chiang Kai-shek's nationalist army in China throughout 1926 had led to a deterioration in relations between the Soviet Union and Great Britain. The Chinese Communists had entered Chiang's Kuomintang, which was admitted as a sympathizing section of the Comintern in early 1926 against the sole dissenting vote of Leon Trotsky.

When Chiang occupied Nanking on 24 March 1927, British and American gunboats anchored in the Yangtze River shelled the city, killing 12 and wounding many more. In May, the London offices of Arcos, the Soviet trading company, were raided and diplomatic relations were broken. Communist parties the world over embarked on a campaign to prevent imperialist intervention in China and against the war danger to the Soviet Union. Meanwhile Chiang turned on his

(continued)

gram against the Soviet Union. The party must emphasize Britain's role as the leading aggressor against both the Soviet Union and China. At the same time, the party must avoid any tendency to conduct the struggle in such a way as to obscure the aggressive role of American imperialism or slacken up in its attack upon it. Any slogans which place American imperialism as the "cat's paw" of Britain or as the guileless victims of British intrigue in China can afflict the party with pacifist illusions and weaken its power to combat these illusions in the masses. More emphasis must also be placed upon anti-imperialist work in Latin America and the campaign against the present war danger must be intimately linked up with the course of American imperialism in Latin American countries. In all struggles of the workers, the relations of imperialist policies of American and world imperialism to these struggles must be pointed out, particularly with regard to the danger of an imperialist war against the Soviet Union.

2. The Offensive Against the Party

In their efforts to still further swell their already enormous profits and to consolidate their control of industry and the government, the capitalists in the United States are now carrying on a general offensive against the working class. Their offensive manifests itself chiefly by a widespread introduction of the speedup system in industry, by smashing trade unions (miners, needle trades, etc.) and by the company unionizing of others (railroads, etc.), wage-cutting campaigns (miners) and by the passage of legislation violently hostile to the interests of the workers.

As part of this offensive the employers are aggressively attack-

---

erstwhile Communist allies. In March and April, Chiang's army massacred thousands of workers and Communists who had seized control of Shanghai.

During this campaign the *Daily Worker* continually portrayed the American role in China as that of unwitting tool of British imperialism. The China campaign had been debated in the Political Committee on 21 April 1927. Cannon was the only one to vote for the following motion, which he had introduced:

> "In all agitation and demonstrations the attack against British imperialism is to be absolutely subordinated to the attacks against American imperialism—to apply to both demonstrations before the embassies and agitation generally. All demonstrations before the British embassies shall be held only in connection with general demonstrations against American imperialism and subordinated to such general demonstrations."

ing our party, which alone is able to give leadership to the masses and which seeks to unite them for the struggle against the reactionary employers and the reactionary trade union leaders. Although the offensive against the left wing tends to develop in other directions, the weight of it is delivered in the trade unions, through the instrumentality of the trade union bureaucracy. Thus develops the present campaign of expulsions and gangster tactics which have reached their high point in the mining and needle industries.

The combined attack of the bosses, the government and the labor bureaucracy which is concentrated in the needle trades under the direct leadership of the AFL has a profound significance and must be resisted with all our strength.

To resist the offensive of the employers and bureaucrats and to turn it into a counteroffensive of the workers, our party must develop its fighting qualities to the utmost. This makes necessary the elimination of the factional struggle and a thorough unification of the party, the intensification of the campaign for the recruitment of new members for the party, especially in the heavy industries, and the activization of the party in all its campaigns among the workers.

3. Effects of Imperialism on the American Workers

The party must develop a stronger and more effective ideological campaign against the class collaboration illusions now being spread by the employers and their agents, the trade union leaders, in connection with the corruption of upper strata of the workers by imperialism.

The party must make a thorough analysis of the entire movement characterized by company unions, the new wage policy, trade union capitalism, employees stockholding, etc., in order that the fraudulent claims can be more effectively exposed. This movement constitutes a specifically American type of reformism, against which a strong and sustained ideological struggle must be carried on by the party.

As part of the fight against the bureaucracy on the issue of trade union business enterprises, the demand must be raised for their complete separation from the union and for their reorganization on a cooperative basis.

4. The United Front

The united front remains the major tactic of the party in its efforts to gain contact with and win support of the masses. In the united front activities, the party has the twofold task which is inseparably bound together. On the one hand to get the backward American workers into action for their class needs and on the other hand to consolidate the party and increase its influence.

In all questions involving the case of the united front tactics it is necessary to bear in mind the specific American conditions under which the party must operate (strength of American capitalism, weak class ideology, extremely reactionary labor bureaucracy with its brazen capitalist viewpoint, comparatively unpolitical attitude of the masses and the comparative weakness of the party).

These conditions dictate that the party must not mechanically apply the united front method, but must react to flexible forms adapted to the specific situation in setting up the united fronts. The party must avoid a policy which hides the face of the party and it must fight aggressively for participation in the united fronts under its own name. The party must avoid carrying this policy of pressing for open affiliation to the point of a split, or to a condition of narrowing the united front merely to the party and its close sympathizcrs.

5. The Trade Union Question

The central problem before the party in beating back the offensive of the reactionaries and gaining new strength and influence in the struggle is the building of a broad left wing movement within the unions in which the party will be the driving force and which will be an instrument for revolutionizing the labor movement. In the period which has elapsed since the last decision of the ECCI on this question, despite opportunities and a number of successes in our trade union work, the task of giving organized form to the left wing in the TUEL has not received sufficient support from the party and thus has made insufficient progress. The next period in the labor movement holds out good prospects for progress in this work and the party must devote more attention to the trade union work and concentrate its efforts to firmly establish the left wing.

The work of organizing the TUEL and its industrial and local sections under various names must be pushed forward energetically. The TUEL as the organization of the left wing should and must comprise not merely party members and close sympathizers, but should embrace all honest elements willing to fight and preserve the unions as organs of struggle against the capitalists.

The TUEL must be organized immediately on as broad a basis as possible in all industrial centers and unions on an action program comprising: organization of the unorganized, democratization of the unions, amalgamation, a labor party, and an aggressive struggle against the employers. Such organizations as can be created shall be used as the instruments for the development and organization of opposition movements. Active support should be given to the league's paper, *Labor Unity. Labor Unity* must be broadened somewhat in its general character, more non-party contributors enlisted and non-party elements drawn into the editorial staff. The TUEL should serve as the connecting link between the party and the broader opposition movements. In recruiting members into the TUEL, the ideological backwardness of the American workers should be kept in mind and their readiness to struggle against the bosses and the reactionaries should be the main criterion. Distinction should also be made between the rank and file workers and officials in determining the question of membership in the TUEL.

The party and TUEL must establish connections with the progressive elements who accept certain parts of the left wing program and who are honestly in conflict with the reactionaries on questions of policy. Every opportunity must be taken to come to agreements with these elements for joint struggles on various issues. Such united front agreements and all divisions and splits which occur in the ranks of the labor officialdom must be utilized to create a broader base for the left wing and strengthen the position of the party.

Care must be taken, however, to avoid illusions in regard to the role of the progressives and all relations with them must be accompanied with criticism of such a nature as to press them into more determined and militant struggles and to bring out clearly the role of the party and the TUEL and to popularize them in the fight.

Especial care must be taken to avoid illusions regarding the black reactionaries posing as the progressive opposition for the moment, and "supporting" them in such a way as to compromise the party and the left wing. Communists must come to the front as leaders of workers in actual struggles and take advantage of all opportunities to gain leading positions in the unions, without allowing this fight to degenerate into an unprincipled scramble for offices.

Organization of the Unorganized: Increased activity in the work of organizing the unorganized workers, the masses of unskilled and semi-skilled, is a foremost necessity. This work bears a direct connection with the work within the existing unions and must not be separated from it. The two activities are parts of one task which supplement and strengthen each other. Every success in the work of organizing new bodies of workers and of conducting strikes in hitherto unorganized industries has a deeply stimulating effect on the existing unions. To the extent that we succeed in bringing new masses of workers, particularly the unskilled, into the trade unions, the base for the revolutionary left wing is strengthened. On the other hand, every inch of ground gained in the established unions, every strategic post secured, every division in the officialdom, exploited with correct tactics, facilitates and strengthens the work of reaching the unorganized workers and drawing them into the unions.

The drift of the bureaucracy to the right and the weakening of the trade union movement in its most proletarian section such as the miners, coupled with the development of an extensive expulsion policy and the suppression of democracy in the unions, creates leftist illusions that nothing can be done in the trade unions and that a general policy must be adopted for the organization of dual and independent unions. The decision should clearly state the policy regarding dual and independent unionism and, while combatting dualistic illusions, it should also warn against the right tendency to so fear splits in the unions that militant action becomes impossible. The party should work energetically in all existing unions, seeking to amalgamate and democratize them, to organize the unorganized into them and to build them into real fighting bodies. In industries, however, where there are no unions, or where the existing unions are hopelessly decrepit and block the organization of the workers, it is the party duty to organize the unorganized masses into the unions and in connection with this procedure fight to affiliate them, with proper guarantees against the betrayal of the workers, to the AFL or independent mass unions. In the event of mass expulsions, as a general policy, the expelled organizations should firmly consolidate themselves, claiming to be the original organizations and continuing the fight for unity on the basis of such an amalgamation as will protect the interests of the workers as a whole. The actual formation of independent organizations in such cases has to be determined according to the concrete circumstances.

The Miners Strike: The present miners strike, the outcome of which will have a profound effect upon the entire labor movement, must be supported by the party in every possible way and the forces of the party mobilized to influence its course to the greatest degree possible.[2] The united front with the opposition elements must be strengthened and developed while all efforts are made to overcome their prejudices against an exposure and fight against the Lewis machine during the strike.

The miners union is in a deep crisis. The militancy of the rank and file of the union must be counted upon to assert itself under the attack of the mine operators and the party tactic regulated accordingly. The reconstitution of the committee of the opposition bloc in the fight to claim the legal election of Brophy and the connection of this fight with the agitation for the strike program of the opposition and especially emphasizing the organization of the non-union fields is the right tactic in the situation. With proper safeguards against expulsion, this new agitation in addition to the program already adopted by the party should have

---

[2] One hundred fifty thousand miners had been locked out by the coal operators in the Central Competitive Field (Western Pennsylvania, Ohio, Indiana and Illinois) on 1 April 1927. The lockout followed the expiration of the "Jacksonville agreement," which John L. Lewis had negotiated in early 1924. Under the agreement the coal operators had agreed to preserve the $7.50-a-day wage rate, but demand for coal continued to plummet and the operators demanded wage cuts even before the end of 1924. The union had been broken at a number of important companies even before the 1927 strike, which was a long and losing one.

as an objective the organization of a national conference of the opposition with the aim of consolidating its forces, clarifying its program and strengthening its authority over the masses in the union.

The lack of systematically organized party fractions, the absence of definite organization of the left wing and of the general opposition, except in the form of committees at the top, and the failure to draw outstanding non-party militants more directly into the leadership of the left wing, are outstanding weaknesses in our work in the miners unions. A miners paper must be published, the opposition bloc consolidated, and a firm organization of the left wing built within it.

6. Americanization of the Party in the Communist Sense

The American party must strive more conscientiously to "Americanize" itself in the Bolshevist sense. It must make greater efforts to centralize the apparatus, to draw the language sections into closer contact with the general political work of the party. This must take place with particular reference to the press, which must be placed under more direct supervision of the party committees, and a regular exchange of the material must be established. At the same time there is to be no slackening of the work among the foreign-born workers.

The party must seek to draw more American workers into the party and into the leadership of the party. A systematic and persistent effort must be made in this regard.

7. The Labor Party and Parliamentary Election Campaign

The party should be instructed to at once begin the organization of a national committee and local committees of left wing and progressive trade unionists to advocate and work for the eventual formation of a labor party. Such committees will be an important bridge to the building of a left wing in the trade unions.

The party must pay more attention to parliamentary election campaigns, which have a great significance for the American party in its task of connecting itself with and reacting to the American life and class struggle. Better organizations and preparation of the election campaigns and much greater general participation of the party members in this work is an absolute necessity. The party must make its influence felt in the election periods and make the most of the opportunities to establish connections with the workers, by approaching them with an election program based on the burning issues of the class struggle.

8. Negro Work

In the field of Negro work the party has failed to realize the opportunities which presented themselves due to the weak and largely unorganized American Negro Labor Congress and the sectarian and factional tactics employed in its work. The influx of Negroes into industry, the formation of large industrial centers of Negroes in the North, East and West, the industrialization of the South, the growing interest of Negroes in the liberation movements in the colonies and semicolonial countries, provide fertile fields for organization of Negroes for more extensive struggle for social rights, for organization into trade unions under the influence of the party. For this purpose it is necessary to establish a functioning center for Negro work and a regularly appearing organ and for the organization of the Negro Labor Congress upon a broader basis, as well as endeavoring to link up our work closer with the existing Negro labor organizations through united front campaigns. At the same time attention must be given to the organization of Negro tenant and poor farmers into tenant leagues and farmer organizations, linking these up with the white labor and farmer organizations and with the general movement of the workers.

9. Women's Work

The party in various districts, particularly in the New York district, has made important strides forward in women's work. The apathy and disinterestedness towards this field of activities has been wearing off. The party's progress in this work has been hindered by the lack of a center for this work in the CEC. It is necessary to speedily establish this center and to direct our attention not only for the organization of housewives (in which some successes have been achieved) but in the organization of the factory working women through the formation of women's delegate conferences, and drawing the working women into the political struggle of the working class. The party must definitely orient itself in the field of the working woman in the factories. The establishment of women's factory correspondents conferences is a useful step in this direction. Systematic and persistent organization of the party apparatus for women's work by the CEC and districts must be speedily accomplished as a condition for the development of our women's work.

10. Young Workers League

1) The party must build a mass YWL even bigger organizationally than the party.

2) For this the party must on one hand give closer political direction to the YWL than in the past and on the other hand help the YWL develop its special youth initiative so that it does not merely become a sectarian section of the party.

3) The league must in its strategy and tactics cope with the relatively backward American working class youth: a) more open organization in pursuing broad and flexible tactics, b) must be Americanized and proletarianized, must orient itself deliberately to American young workers in heavy industries and large shops, c) must simplify its agitation and propaganda and institute lighter features in proper proportions.

4) The party must help the unification process now going on in the league.

11. The Internal Party Situation

On the internal party situation the resolution should reiterate and emphasize the great danger to the development of the party of further factional struggles, which was already pointed out in the resolution of the Sixth Plenum of the ECCI. The basis of the factional divisions in the party has been outlived to a very large extent and the big task now is to accelerate the process of consolidation and unity of the party. A collective leadership must be established which includes the strongest forces of the three groups.

The leadership of the party must not be constructed on a narrow factional basis. An attitude must be taken towards the various groups of harmonious collaboration and full right to participate in the activities and work of the party on such a basis as will facilitate consolidation and unity. All attempts to establish factional monopoly of the party apparatus and to carry out a program of removals and displacements of qualified party workers can only lead to greater narrowness and aggravated factional struggle.

The factional regime of the Lovestone group, its theories of permanent factional organization with the role of "hegemony" over the party, and its refusal to work with the other groups on a basis of equality, must be condemned as the principal barrier to party unity and consolidation. The alliance of the Lovestone group with the right wing must be dissolved unconditionally.

Organization steps to further the aim of unity and consolidation shall be taken as follows:

1. The plenum of the Central Committee shall meet immediately after the return of the delegation and reconstitute the Political Bureau with nine members, three representatives from each group, and elect a secretariat of three, one from each group.

2. The date of the convention shall be postponed to September 10, in order to give adequate time for the organization and preparation of the convention after the return of the delegation and for a thorough party discussion.

3. The convention elections to be held on the basis of proportional representation from the nuclei to the national convention and proportional representation to apply also in the selection of the district committees.

4. The sending of a representative of the ECCI to America.

5. The convention preparation, organization and discussion to be conducted by a committee of four, two representatives of the Lovestone group and one representative from each of the opposition groups in collaboration with the representative of the ECCI.

6. Comrade Hathaway to be appointed as joint representative of the party to the ECCI until the party convention.

7. Organizational changes and removals carried out in the New York district and elsewhere since the last plenum of the Central Committee to be canceled immediately and all comrades reinstated in their positions.

8. A declaration shall be made refuting the claims that com-

rade Dunne's mandate as a member of the ECCI (alternate) has been revoked.

9. All nuclei which have been in continuous functioning existence since June 1 shall be entitled to send delegates to the section or city conventions on the basis of one delegate for each ten members.

10. YWL members shall not be transferred into the party in the period between June 1 and the convention elections.

11. The unfounded report now being circulated through the party to the effect that comrade Foster proposed the removal of comrades Ruthenberg and Bedacht from the Polburo shall be refuted by the committee.

With Communist greetings,
J.P. Cannon
Wm. Z. Foster
William Weinstone

Report from Moscow

26 June 1927

The following is an unpublished internal circular of the Cannon faction, of unknown authorship, addressed to faction supporters in the Workers Party. It contains excerpts of reports from Moscow by Cannon and Weinstone.

Dear Comrade:

The following is the latest information received from our comrades abroad in letters written during the first week in June, with some comments added. While you may note interviews with only two of the leading comrades of the Comintern, this is because the information was sent us shortly after the arrival of our delegates. All reports from our comrades are in quotations.

Interview with Kuusinen

"We talked with him, discussing the whole situation thoroughly in a conversation of two to three hours. He made a special note of the fact that the right elements have entered the Lovestone group as the older Communist elements left it. He said Lovestone could not take the place of Ruthenberg and that collective leadership must now be established."

"He expressed himself in favor of a secretariat of three—one from each group—and also strongly indicated, although he did not say so directly, that the Polcom should be reorganized. He discussed this at some length with us and asked what our proposition was on this point. We proposed 3-3-3."

"He then asked whether such an arrangement would lead toward stability or whether a new faction fight would develop between the three groups for domination. He also asked whether it would be best to decide the organizational questions here or to let it go to a convention. We said we had nothing against a convention if a free discussion could be had and organizational safeguards established to prevent factional manipulation of the elections. He said it was self-understood that this must be done and indicated that the convention would be postponed at least two-three months."

"We took up the question of the claim made by the Lovestone group that the failure to call Dunne to the plenum as a member of the ECCI was intended as a repudiation of our group and as a slap at him personally.[1] He said this was not the case, that the Secretariat had made an error in not stating in the cable that Dunne, as a member of the ECCI, had the unquestionable right to come, but that since so many were coming and since his point of view was to be represented by Weinstone and Cannon, that it would not be advisable for him to come also to this plenum. *He said they would make a declaration on this question.*"

Ewert, the Political Leader of the German Party

"He will probably take an active part in the commission. He is for collective leadership, and seems to think our group needs to gain greater strength and cohesion before it can undertake the danger of blurring its line by losing its identity in a bloc (referring to the bloc with the Foster group). He gave us some very interesting history of the development of the groups in the German party. His group went through an evolution much the same as we are going through."

"It was originally a part of the German Left. Split from the Left early in 1923, but was not strong enough to maintain an independent position and was swallowed up by the Brandler majority. After the October collapse, it took up an independent position (not going back to the Left) and maintained it until the downfall of the Fischer-Maslow regime when it united with a

[1] In the Political Committee meeting of 25 April 1927, Lovestone read a cable from the Comintern which requested that Gitlow, Lovestone and Foster be the American delegation to the ECCI's Eighth Plenum. The cable deemed the presence of Cannon and Weinstone "desirable" and didn't even mention William F. Dunne, who had been elected alternate member of the ECCI at the Fifth World Congress in 1924. Cannon introduced (and was the only one to vote for) a motion noting that Dunne, as a member of the ECCI, had a right to go to the plenum.

section of the Left to form the present leadership of the party."

"His attitude, implied more than expressed, is that we have a big part to play as a group in the future development of the party —*if we are Bolsheviks enough to establish a clear line and stick to it.* He said, 'A middle group is either buffer or Bolshevik! Buffer groups do not cut much ice here'."

"The way that the Polcom attempted to exclude us from the delegation made a bad impression here. It was intended from the first that we should come and all the impressions in America that our group is disregarded here have no foundation so far as we have been able to discover."

The comrades will remember the manner in which the Lovestone group made use of cables received from the Comintern for their own factional purposes, attempting to interpret them to mean that the CI did not want our delegates to come, but the CI was decisive. It ordered that the plenum be held and it also ordered that our delegates come.

"Weinstone was selected by the Comintern Organization Department to make a co-report on the organizational situation in the party."

"The American delegation before the arrival of Foster and ourselves voted to send Minor home after the plenum, and to elect Pepper in his place as a member of the Presidium. We have opened up a fight on this. We have already succeeded in postponing this question to the Presidium."

"The British delegation said they would not support the proposition to make Pepper the representative of the American party or to send him back to America. Kuusinen also said that he would be opposed to Pepper coming to America or representing the party in the Presidium or writing more factional letters to America."

Since these actions, the Polcom majority of our party has decided to recall Minor, and appoint Pepper American representative over our protest and the protests of the comrades of the Foster group. This appointment is contrary to the CI decision on democratization, which specifies that each party must send real representatives who are members of the party and functioning in the party. The appointment is also extremely factional. We cabled a joint appeal together with the Foster group. It is clear that the real intention of the Lovestone group is to bring Pepper back to America only for the purpose of helping bolster up their group.

The Chinese Policy

"The position of the Lovestone group on the Chinese question causes a great deal of amusement here, especially the editorials in the *Daily Worker*, the poem *The Eagle and the Lion*, the resolution passed at the New York mass meeting—all of which put America in the position of being influenced and misled by Great Britain.[2] This position and the slogan 'America is the cat's paw of England' are regarded as a wrong line and a tendency towards the right in the direction of the pacifists. The main line of the plenum resolution on the Chinese question is 'Fight your own imperialism first and foremost'."

Our policy on the Chinese question is linked up with the entire question of the role of American imperialism and the decisions of our party in fighting it, as well as the more general question of basing ourselves upon the development of the international class struggle rather than upon secondary factors such as the divisions in the enemy ranks—divisions which must be utilized but which cannot be allowed to obscure our main task—that of fighting American imperialism. Our policy has proven correct.

The Bloc with the Foster Group

We are again quoting from the letters from our delegates, letters written shortly after their arrival in Moscow.

---

[2] See note pp. 440-441 for background on the Lovestoneites' anti-British tilt in the China campaign. A resolution adopted by a party-initiated "Hands Off China" rally in New York's Union Square on May 7 noted that "our government under the influence of Great Britain and in contradiction to its declared policy is virtually waging war against the Chinese people," and demanded that "our government refuse to follow Great Britain in its imperialist policy of bribery, corruption, and the use of armed force in China..." (*DW*, 9 May 1927).

The poem *The Lion and the Eagle: More Fact Than Fable* by Adolf Wolfe, published in the *DW* on May 7, was of a piece, though perhaps more of an example of the Lovestone view of literature:

"Yonder, where the Yangtze flows,
Where wakened China restless grows,
The Yankee eagle stoops to trail
Behind the British lion's tail...
The spectacle must give the chill
To the glorious ghosts of Bunker Hill..."

"The general attitude of the Profintern and YCI leading comrades is against the Lovestone group and for a bloc between our group and the Foster group, formed in such a way that there is no step backward from the present position we have reached and that our political weight in the party is increased.[3] They all take the position that the splits in the two old groups and the unity of the two revolting sections, Cannon and Weinstone, represent a forward step which must not be lost or compromised. They also maintain that a Foster leadership or the reconstitution of the Foster group on the old basis is not desirable. They think in terms of a *bloc* which would be somewhat of an extension of our line at the plenum with a working agreement on party work and questions, where a common line can be found without obscuring the line of our group or going to the point of *organizational fusion.* This is a modification of and retreat from their earlier ideas of the bloc and is based on a more thorough comprehension and recognition of the positive and progressive role of the middle group."

"Our position and aims here proceed from the stand taken at the plenum. We will not retreat an inch from that position under any circumstances. We aim to take one step further along the progressive course followed up to now and to concentrate our blows upon the Lovestone regime while drawing, at the same time, a clear line between our position and that of the Foster group. Here as before, we will be willing to come to an agreement with the Foster group on those points upon which we can find a common standpoint."

"There is much sentiment here for the bloc between our group and the Foster group to form a majority and take over the party. We believe it is wrong to imagine that a complete unity can be established at once after the bitter struggle and with a number of disputed questions remaining. We do not believe in 'unity maneuvers' and will not undertake any joint agreements with the Foster group which we do not have a reasonable assurance of

---

[3] The Young Communist International was supporting the "Unity Caucus" in the Young Workers League, see note page 438. The Profintern under Lozovsky usually supported the Foster faction.

being able to carry out. There is not sufficient confidence between the groups to contemplate, at the present time, more than an agreement to work together and try to reduce friction to a minimum. This we are ready to undertake and propose that we proceed step by step, being sure of our ground as we go. We cited the factional monopoly attitude in the trade union apparatus, the bringing up of fake issues and the factional aggressions against us while the 'unity maneuvers' were being carried on, as barriers to the establishment of the necessary confidence to consider anything further than the one or two steps forward in the direction of close cooperation."

"Foster made the same arguments with which we became familiar in the recent months."

"Everybody in Moscow apparently is against the idea of the Foster group leading the party alone and practically all who discuss the bloc with us do it from two standpoints: 1) the absolute necessity of taking the party leadership away from the Lovestone group, 2) that the developments of the party will not be in favor of a Foster domination of the bloc. We agree with the first point —that is, we are firmly convinced that the Lovestone group has no future possibilities to properly lead and unite the party. In regard to the second point we are not afraid that the Foster group will be able to politically dominate the combination. But on the other hand we have had experience with the Foster group and with the question of unity from which we have learned a few things."

"Also we believe it is absolutely necessary in the next period to establish the identity and position of our group more clearly before the party, to broaden and consolidate it and accomplish a firmer cohesion in its ranks in order that it will be the more able to exert a decisive influence for our aims—including the aim of breaking down factional organizations and traditions and uniting the party."

"At the conference with Foster tonight the following agreements were arrived at:

"1. To make a joint stand for a Polcom on the basis of 3-3-3 with Cannon, Weinstone, and Dunne to be designated as our candidates.

"2. To make a joint stand for a secretariat instead of a single secretary as at present.

"3. Each group to have the right to designate its own candidate.

"It should be understood as follows:

"1. An acceptance by Foster of the propositions and proportions of representation already presented by us to Kuusinen.

"2. An application of the policy we have always stood for, namely that we are in favor of a working agreement with either or both the other groups on any or all points where common agreement can be reached and under conditions which give none of the groups a majority."

It is clear that:

"The agreements reached tonight are in full conformity with the line of the 'Nine Points'."[4]

"It is clear that the Comintern desires the bloc with our group and the Foster group and that this also indicates a lack of faith by the Comintern in the ability of the Lovestone group to lead the party alone. The American Commission favors collective leadership as opposed to hegemony. The fact that the Lovestone group persists in its attitude that it alone must lead the party, which to them means factionally controlling the party, makes the bloc necessary as the only possible present step towards complete party unification. We have proven our readiness and our serious desire to extend this step to include all three groups. The Lovestone group has rejected this."

The Lovestone group claims hegemony of the party for its group and states that any other view is a social-democratic deviation. At the present period none of the existing groups can lead the party alone. The fullest cooperation of all is required. The Lovestone group contains only a small minority of the active leading elements in the party. Its factional control has become a detriment to the growth of the party. Hence our proposal of doing away with absolute and decisive control of one group is a correct

---

[4] Cannon and Weinstone had jointly drawn up a nine-point "Outline of Statement on the Liquidation of Factionalism and the Unification of the Party." Cannon read the entire text during his speech to the May 1927 CEC plenum, see pages 419-422.

step towards the elimination of factionalism and unification of the party and towards the establishment of real collective leadership.

To lay this basis is a task of the bloc. It does not eliminate the principal difference existing between the two groups in the bloc. The Foster group as yet has not shown any inclination to change its trade union line, which is its main line. In the thesis presented by Foster the group states that it is for a broad left wing. Its concrete policies in some instances have the effect of narrowing the left wing movement to comprise merely Communists and sympathizers. Its policy often results in drawing schematic dividing lines between left wing and progressives. Our view was, and remains, that the real test is action more than formal programs. In the present backward state of the American trade union movement, the character of the left wing is determined by the degree of development and may vary in the different unions. For this reason, we fought for a change of the TUEL program. It was changed. Our practical policy must always be so constructed that it allows for the broadest inclusion into the present left wing of all those who are ready to fight the bureaucracy on a class basis and we must then proceed to permeate such broad movements with a real left wing ideology. We must also work out tactics for a fight against class collaboration within the framework of class collaboration itself, where it is in operation, as well as the general struggle against class collaboration theories.

Recall the statement of comrade Ewert on buffer or Bolshevik groups. A buffer group merely stands between two groups and loses its identity and disappears. Our line is clear. We will maintain our independence of our group within the bloc. We maintain the line we have followed and the right to criticize and fight for correct policies. We must build our middle group as a guarantee to fight for complete unification of the party and for a correct external party policy.

As an evidence of the further extension of the factional monopoly of the Lovestone group and to what conditions it will lead the party, we cite the recent reorganization of the New York District Political Bureau by the majority of the party Polcom. Formerly the New York District Political Bureau consisted of four members from the Lovestone group, three from the Foster group, and two from the middle group. The latter were Weinstone, and

Don from the YWL. The YWL, under the control of the Lovestone group, removed Don. Two members of the Lovestone group were put on the Political Bureau in place of the two members of the middle group, Weinstone and Don. In addition, comrade Ballam was removed from the District Secretariat. This whole manipulation is in complete defiance of the CI decision given prior to the plenum, stating that there should be no removals or changes until the party convention.

The idea of collective leadership of the party as opposed to Lovestone hegemony and monopoly is being endorsed by the Comintern. The question, however, as to whether the actual proportion of the selection of the Polcom will be settled in Moscow by decision or referred to the convention of the party, for working out, is not the important thing. The important thing is not so much the mechanics, but that collective leadership is the policy of the Comintern. We are perfectly satisfied to have a convention but we want our comrades to be on the job against factional manipulation of the apparatus by the Lovestone group.

All indications from Moscow are that the unity line established in the YWL will be completely endorsed by the YCI and the unity group in the YWL upheld strongly as against the factionalism of the Zam-Lovestone group in the league. We are for the further development of the unity group in the league, which is continuing its work of drawing more and more comrades towards the policy of the YCI.

Urge the comrades to prepare energetically for the forthcoming convention. Organize your forces in every unit of the party. Prepare to struggle against factional monopoly of the party, ideologically and organizationally. Work and fight for the unification of the party on the correct political line.

We must prepare our comrades for party responsibility more intensively than ever. We must energetically Bolshevize our comrades and inculcate in them, more than ever, a sense of loyalty, discipline and duty to the party, to the CI and to the working class.

Lovestone Faction an Obstacle to Party Unity

ca. June 1927

The following are partial, uncorrected, undated and unpublished transcripts of Cannon's remarks to several sessions of the American Commission appointed toward the end of the Eighth Plenum of the Executive Committee of the Communist International. The commission issued a "Resolution on the American Question" which was endorsed by the Presidium of the ECCI on 1 July 1927. Both the Cannon-Weinstone-Foster bloc and the Lovestone faction initially claimed victory with the ECCI resolution. But in the all-out factional battle for control of the Workers Party which followed the ECCI decision, the Lovestone group managed, with the aid of the Comintern, to gain the upper hand. They won a majority of the delegates to the party's Fifth Convention, held 31 August-7 September 1927.

Comrade Chairman and Comrades:

Since the time is limited it is obvious that I will not be able to deal with all the questions. I will only take some, particularly the internal party questions and the points of difference. We proceed here on the standpoint that the old factions in the party have been to a large extent outlived and that the problem we have is the problem to accelerate the process of breaking down the old divisions and forming the leadership on a broader and more collective basis than was possible before. We regard the course through which our group has passed as a part of this process: beginning with the split—first in the former majority group and second with the split which recently occurred in the Lovestone group represented by comrade Weinstone—then the combination of these two elements together to fight for the idea of unity and collective leadership in the party. We are of the opinion that the main line we followed throughout this course has been correct and in line with the natural development of the party and we stand by it.

We believe also that the problem now is to take a decisive, progressive step further in the direction of greater unity. We have this position and comrade Foster, having spoken for this in his speech—we agree with him on this point—and we thus speak here for a closer working together and a unity with the Foster group.

Comrade Pepper inquired as to who constituted our group. It is quite well known in the American party that our group is represented by one-third of the Central Committee. It consists of old revolutionaries of 15 to 20 years experience and is well known to all those who know the American movement. It is supported by strong sections in the party as well as in the Young Workers League, in the trade union work, etc. For example, the leading comrades in the Detroit Federation of Labor; in Minneapolis and in St. Paul the leading fractions of the party in the Central Labor Union; the leader of the left wing in the Chicago Federation of Labor; and a large number of influential functionaries in the party as well as in the Young Workers League have supported our standpoint.

I think we have two proposals before the commission. One is the proposal presented by our group which is also presented by comrade Foster and is the standpoint of the opposition in general in the party now, i.e., that we shall form a leadership on a collective basis drawing in the most responsible and qualified elements from the three groups in the party. We have the alternative proposition submitted in the speeches of Lovestone and Gitlow which in substance amounts to a proposal to unify the party by smashing the opposition groups. The very way in which they presented the question draws this conclusion. They try to picture the party situation as a situation of unity. Everything is all right in the party—only a little trouble on top with some disgruntled elements. The fact that these disgruntled elements are represented in such force that they represent a majority of the Central Committee, that they are such responsible and influential people as those who are representing the opposition here—who are by no means strangers either to the Comintern or to the party—this seems to have no significance to the Lovestone group. We are merely some disgruntled people and in their entire presentation they do not offer any proposal whereby they could come to an agreement with us.

Their policy is to smash the opposition group. Therefore, I present to the commission this question: Can the Lovestone group lead a unity of the party? We say it cannot. We have all kinds of experiences, evidences, practices, the composition of the group and the relation of the forces to judge by. We say a combination of forces is necessary to lead the party. The Lovestone group cannot be entrusted with the monopoly of the leadership of the party for various reasons of policy both external and internal.

I want to state a few of the errors and mistakes which the Lovestone group has made and will make in the future unless there is a creative or a balanced leadership.

I will take the question of China and the question of the war danger which has already been presented by comrade Weinstone. On this question, just precisely as we warned the comrades in the Polcom—it was not a question of agitation against Great Britain; it was not a question of pointing out the role of Great Britain as the chief instigator in China and the general war danger. It was a question of combining in the proper form the agitation against Great Britain with the attack against our own powerful imperialism. That was not done in the correct way. Precisely as I warned the comrades, we carried through the agitation to such a point as to barely leave a dividing line between our party and the pacifists. When they are able to carry out demonstrations against Great Britain and to adopt resolutions in which there is no denunciation of imperialism in demonstrations controlled by our party—we say they are going over to the wrong line. The opposition raised this question in the Polcom at the time and when comrade Lovestone says that I made motions in the Polcom demanding the quite obvious policy that they should connect all agitation against Great Britain with the fight against our own imperialism—I say that is correct and when we return home I will make some more motions of this obvious character and see that it is done.

We criticized the Lovestone group for its policy in the miners union; that in the midst of this big upheaval, this life and death struggle by the unions, they could not see the ferment in the masses and were not sufficiently awake to justify the orientation towards a national conference of the opposition. They threw up their hands in horror at the very idea of such a perspective and that also is a part of their lack of sensitivity to the developments of the labor movement.

They cannot lead the party alone because they have too close relations with the right wing in the party. They have entered into too many obligations with them and they even appear here with a letter of recommendation from one of the supporters of Lore. They have to rely on such philistines to do their work.

* * *

The Lovestone group must be compelled to break its relations with the right wing in New York, and to unite itself with more reliable and more consistent Communist elements as represented in the opposition. It must be taken into account, comrades, that it was precisely in the period when the Lovestone group was splitting with such elements, led by Weinstone, who were among the founders of the party and most reliable elements of the party, that in the same period the Lovestone group was carrying out an alliance with the right wing, and admitting into their group every single one of the prominent leaders of the Lore group without exception. We criticize them because they do not approach in the proper spirit the proletarian and trade union elements in the party. They do not know how to unite with the Foster group which is an absolute necessity in the next stage of the party.

We are not willing to trust the Lovestone group with the monopoly of leadership because of its irresponsible attitude towards the party signalized, for example, by such an incident as occurred when comrade Lovestone, when he was general secretary of the party, left a meeting of the plenum of the Central Committee without an explanation. We say that such an attitude towards the party cannot be supported.

The Lovestone group, in the period in which it entered into unity with our group, conducted itself in an irresponsible and unprincipled and factional manner. It played with this big idea of unity—which is the biggest idea confronting the party—as a factional maneuver and not as a Communist, straightforward and political development necessary for the future of the party, and this can be substantiated by absolute evidence, with documents and facts to satisfy anyone who has doubts about it. For example, comrades, at the time that we were presumably working in unity with a common platform, comrade Lovestone was capable of writing in the following way: [citation not included in transcript].

This is the attitude towards party comrades which has made unity difficult for the Lovestone group to achieve.

A few days after we had entered into the unity resolution on the common platform, and had declared to the party that we were standing together as a united majority in the Central Executive Committee, Lovestone writes to Ballam the following week in the same language: [citation not included in transcript]. This was comrade Lovestone's attitude to the unity resolution.

Now further evidence of the irresponsible factionalism of the Lovestone group is contained in material received from America even in the period since we have come to Moscow. The Lovestone group in the Political Committee has refused to carry out the agreement made at the plenum, viz.: to appoint a commission to investigate the critical situation in the South Slavic Federation. The Lovestone group in the Central Committee has called a membership meeting in Boston to discuss the internal party situation without authorization of the Political Committee. They have removed comrade Dunne from the District Executive Committee of the New York district; they have removed Ballam from the Secretariat; they have added two candidates to the DEC of New York; they have changed the majority in the DEC Political Committee of New York in the period since we came to Moscow attempting to decide the question of unity.

A further criticism of the Lovestone group is connected with the Pepper question. On this question, as well as some others, I will ask the indulgence of the commission to speak a little longer as was granted to all the other comrades.

Comrades, I want to speak in the most impersonal way and serious way about the question of comrade Pepper, not as a person, but as a problem—as an artificially added problem to our other difficulties in America. We have noted in the period since we came to Moscow a still greater sharpening of the factional relations of the Political Committee under the instruction of comrade Lovestone. We have noted that at several periods in the party when the groups were approaching towards unity, we have received some letter from comrade Pepper to the party; some new maneuver, some new scheme whereby the factional fires were intensified, and we turn to the comrades of the Executive

Committee of the Communist International with a very direct request in the interests of the normal, natural and healthy development of the American party to relieve our party of this unnecessary difficulty, and let us contend with those difficulties which the objective circumstances in America make necessary.

[The transcript records that comrade Kuusinen interrupted Cannon at this point.]

I am sorry that the regulations became strict only when I began, because the things which I say have to be said and to be heard, and if not now, they will be heard later....

*　*　*

Since I have only five minutes I want to take up one point which I think is of special necessity to make clear: our attitude towards the groups on the question of leadership. In regards to the Foster group, as was stated in our speech by Weinstone the first day, we have maintained certain criticisms, some of which still remain. On the whole, however, in the past the differences between our group and the Foster group have grown less, and still further at this plenum, and especially after the discussion in the Profintern. We are of the opinion that the Foster group is politically necessary to the leadership of our party, not merely as trade unionists. During the past year we have maintained the policy of unity towards the Foster group but it has not succeeded because of the presence of the hangovers of the last fight. We believe that for the leadership of the party the road lies toward the Foster group through closer collaboration, more and closer work leading toward unity. We are ready to work together with the Foster group. We reject and condemn the hostile and factional attitude maintained by the majority of the Polburo, particularly since the death of Ruthenberg, toward the Foster group. We have points in common with both groups. We are ready to work with the Polburo on the same basis as we lay down here. But we say that this attitude of the Lovestone group of solving the question of unity by smashing the other groups, we say that they take the responsibility of continuing the factional fight. We say that it lies in the direction of breaking down the faction lines, the faction organizations, toward a genuine collective leadership. We believe that any attempt to solve the problem of leadership on the basis of the narrow Lovestone faction would only result in further and more difficulties which we know will lead not only to a more narrow leadership but a further split in the Lovestone group, as there is already a strong sentiment to split the Lovestone group further. And any attempt on this basis would turn the party backward.

Comrade Engdahl, in his very hostile speech in the same tone as Lovestone, Pepper and Gitlow's speeches, stated that no one disproves the fact that the Lovestone group has a majority. We must reject this idea. We state that the attempts to represent the section elections in Chicago, New York and other places as a faction victory of the Lovestone group is an attempt to practice fraud. (Interjection by Engdahl: "A victory for the party.") That has been your attitude—the party, you are the party, we are the interlopers—and it is because you have this attitude that you did not succeed in unifying the party. I hope that we made our position clear upon this point and along that line we are going to work in the future.

* * *

Comrades, the opposition groups are in agreement with the political line of the resolution on all points covered by it and believe that it provides a basis both for the progressive liquidation of the factional situation and for the development of party work, and especially the tasks imposed upon it by present conditions. We are in agreement with the emphasis placed upon the war danger, on the question of bourgeoisification. We believe that the resolution has provided the party with a clarified explanation of this problem which was threatening to become a serious obstacle to the party unification. We agree entirely with this section, both as to the character of the section and the emphasis placed upon various points, etc.[1]

---

[1] The section on bourgeoisification in the final resolution, dated 1 July 1927 and published in the *DW* on 3 August 1927, read in part:

> "American imperialism is still in a position to provide for a large section of the working class a comparatively high standard of living. In comparison with the position of the workers in European capitalist countries, the American working class as a whole still occupies a privileged position. What Engels wrote to Marx in 1858 about the bourgeoisification of the British proletariat may be applied to a certain extent even today to the American working class: 'The English

(continued)

On the trade union question we believe the resolution provides a basis for the complete liquidation of the controversies which have existed in the party which have been at the bottom of very much of the faction friction during the past two years. We are of the opinion that the resolution being proposed now provides a settlement of the important disputes on this field so that we can go back with united activities covering all aspects of the trade union question in the future.

On the question of the internal line of the party, I believe also that the resolution has recognized the actual state of affairs in the party and has prescribed the necessary measures accurately. The big task of the party leaders is unification. It is fully established in the resolution and we believe it is correct, that the problem of the party leadership, the problem of overcoming factionalism, has not to be solved by an annihilation of any group but by their absorption. The prerequisites for this are established by the fact that on all the important political questions there is either unanimity or sufficient agreement to work, and the means of closely working together and cooperating with the work of the party, leaving no basis for the retention of factional groupings and factional fighting. This is our standpoint. We believe the resolution is absolutely correct when it says that the groupings "are outlived now and block the further development of the party." This is the standpoint we have had previously and we will continue to hold this view in the future.

On this basis of this political line, as embodied in the resolution, as well as on the internal questions, comrade Weinstone and myself have come to an understanding to work closer together already with the Foster group as we have previously informed the commission. We think we should point out what this signifies so there can be no misunderstanding. First, it is an agreement to

---

proletariat is actually becoming more and more bourgeois, so much so that it appears that this most bourgeois of all nations evidently wants to bring things about to the point where it will have a bourgeois aristocracy and bourgeois proletariat alongside of the bourgeoisie. Of course this is to a certain extent natural on the part of a nation exploiting the whole world'."

While insisting that American imperialism "*still is not powerful enough to corrupt the entire working class,*" the resolution went on to call on the party to "carry on an energetic struggle against this bourgeoisification."

work closer together, in closer harmony, in collaboration and endeavoring to come together without friction. The question of our working together is especially facilitated by the fact that disagreements on the trade unions questions, which in the past have been a source of friction, have been liquidated by the resolution.[2]

We are in agreement with the necessity of collective leadership and against the theory that any group in the party at the present time and under present conditions should have the hegemony. Before the resolution was adopted we presented these points to the commission pointing out that the basis for unity had been arrived at on political grounds. Therefore, we see no reason to continue the fight and we propose to abandon it. We offer and propose to take the same attitude towards the Lovestone group. The agreement which we have reached, to work together, is in no way a proposal to fight against the Lovestone group if they will agree to work with us. On the contrary, it is at the same time a proposal to unite with them on the same grounds. It is not our intention to go back to any of the old forms, or form new ones, but on the contrary, to take steps for the formation of a collective leadership without factions. We believe the remarks made by comrade Lovestone on this point are already an indication and a threat against the new opposition groups which we hope will be corrected in further discussion. We hereby declare for unity and harmonious collaboration with the Lovestone group on the basis of the resolution presented. We do not speak here for fight on any grounds except opposition to the resolution. We believe the next thing necessary now to sincerely develop and carry out the line of the resolution is a united attitude on the part of the Lovestone group which up to now has been lacking. Especially on the theory of hegemony. They must be prepared to meet us on the same grounds that we offer to meet them.

---

2 The resolution endorsed Foster's position by insisting that the party "support the TUEL to a much greater extent than hitherto." But it endorsed the Cannon-Dunne position in insisting that the TUEL be a broad united-front organization. Moreover, the resolution represented a major break with Foster's policy of only working within AFL unions, declaring that "the party should not limit itself only to the work in the existing trade unions." It also called for a party campaign to organize the unorganized.

In order to realize in the closest possible way the objectives outlined in the resolution we believe the organizational guarantees are necessary and must be insisted upon. This arises out of the experiences of the past which put us in a position where the organization of a convention with a lot of factional friction and suspicion can become possible only if there are sufficient organizational guarantees for free discussion, free elections, etc., as provided in the resolution. Any attempt to weaken the organizational guarantees set up in the resolution, in our opinion, weakens the resolution itself.

I wish to add just one word of a personal nature on the criticism of comrade Dunne in the resolution. The records of the Polcom and of the party show that on all these points upon which comrade Dunne is criticized, I have disagreed with him and voted in the contrary way. However, I am willing to state that a certain responsibility should be made against me to the effect that I did not criticize him in a sharp enough manner in view of the fact that we were working together. I am willing to have such a statement in the resolution.[3]

---

3 The resolution raised a number of criticisms of the party's trade-union cadre, accusing the needle trades leaders, Wortis and Zimmerman, of "right deviations," and Joseph Zack of wanting to abandon the AFL. It was particularly harsh against William F. Dunne:

> "Other deviations manifested themselves in the case of comrade W.F. Dunne who sized up the possibility of the struggle of the workers in a pessimistic manner and through such estimations arrived at false conclusions. Among such deviations are proposals imposing limitations on the leading role of the TUEL in certain cases and intending to take the initiative out of the hands of the TUEL. Comrade Dunne has also in an article in the *Daily Worker* of March 24th, 1927, made the impermissible attempt to differentiate between the reactionary Green and the reactionary Woll, both leaders of the AFL, in favor of Green."

It appears that most of the CEC joined Dunne in differentiating between Woll and Green—see Cannon's speech to the May CEC plenum, page 395.

The Red Month of November

For the Third Annual Conference of the International Labor Defense

Published November 1927

The following article by Cannon was published in the Labor Defender, *monthly journal of the International Labor Defense.*

A red stream runs through the month of November, marking in its course many struggles of the working class of this country, here with defeat, there with victory, always with inspiring record of working class courage, exemplary in its noble devotion to the cause of the oppressed, magnificent incidents of solidarity and self-sacrifice, instructive milestones along the difficult road to liberation. It is a record to sharpen the hatred of labor to jailers and assassins, to increase the respect and pride we have for our fighters.

On the eleventh day of November 1887, Albert R. Parsons, August Spies, Adolph Fischer and George Engel were hung on the scaffold of Cook County.[1] Louis Lingg was either murdered or committed suicide in the death cell. Other of their comrades were sent to serve long terms in prison. They were heroes of an early day. They were the pioneers of the eight-hour day movement, and their crime was so heinous in the eyes of the master class that nothing but their blood would satisfy the vampires whose profits and power they menaced.

On November 19, 1915, a worker was stood up against the stone wall of the penitentiary at Salt Lake City. At the command, the firing squad sent its deadly bullets through the body of Joe

[1] These are the Haymarket martyrs, who were executed after being framed up on charges of bombing the police contingent at an 1886 demonstration for the eight-hour day in Haymarket Square, Chicago.

Hill. We know why Joe Hill died, and it was not because of the "murder" he was charged with committing. We know that Joe Hill died for the class he fought for, for whom he composed his rebel songs, whom he organized to break their chains. Member of the IWW, a migratory worker who tasted the lash of exploitation in railroad and construction work, in the harvest fields and the lumber camps, he combined shrewd common sense with a vision of the future society where workers are not legally murdered behind tall stone walls to keep out the protests of the labor movement.

A year later, the black reaction took its toll again. Ten score of workers, on their way by steamer from Seattle to Everett for a free speech fight, were ambushed from the dock by power- and whisky-drunk deputies. Fusillades were fired into the gay and determined group from every direction. The workers, cornered by the hidden "heroes," fought back against tremendous odds. When the last shot had been fired, and the last note of *Hold the Fort* had died away, the workers counted Felix Baran, John Looney, Hugo Gerlot, Abraham Rabinowitz and Gustav Johnson among their martyred dead. Others were swept away by the sea. Scores were frightfully wounded. Frenchman, Irishman, German, Jew and Swede—all gave their lives in the fight.[2] To this day, and for many days to come, the workers pledge themselves to these brave spirits in the words of the Northwest rebels: *We never forget!*

Centralia on November 11th, 1919. The attack on the IWW hall by the businessmen's uniformed mob, and the kidnapping of Wesley Everest to be diabolically tortured, mutilated, suffering a dozen deaths in one before he was hung and shot. And the aftermath: the farcical trial and conviction of Eugene Barnett, John Lamb, Bland, McInerney and their fellow workers for a crime that should have been charged to their enemies. The Centralia IWW are still in prison at Walla Walla, victims of capitalist vengeance.

November 7, 1917! The rising of tens of millions, the liberation of all the Russias! The opening of a new epoch for all the exploited and oppressed is marked by this day of the seizure of

---

[2] Most of those killed were IWW members, and the incident became known as the Everett Massacre.

power by the Russian workers and peasants. Who but the working class could maintain its power for ten years in the face of such obstacles and poisonous opposition! The brush of revolution has covered one-sixth of the earth with the red of freedom, and it sweeps on inexorably over the rest of the world.

It is no accident that the Third Annual Conference of International Labor Defense is being held on the fortieth anniversary of the execution of the Haymarket martyrs. The day was deliberately chosen to commemorate this historic episode in the American class struggle, and to work in a manner that will enable the ILD to carry the Haymarket tradition forward in the building of a powerful class defense movement.

It is only a little over a year now since the close of the Second Annual Conference of International Labor Defense but the events of this period have confirmed many times over the basic idea of a non-partisan working class defense movement which is the rock upon which the ILD is being built.

Whatever skepticism existed about International Labor Defense must now have disappeared in the past year, particularly since the last conference. When the ILD got into its full stride, as it did in the great agitation for Sacco and Vanzetti, there was no need for further proof that there was a strong necessity for such a movement and that its right to existence and support could not be challenged.

In the Sacco-Vanzetti case, the ILD brought out with cameo clearness the main lines of its program. The first of these was unity of all working class forces. In the Sacco-Vanzetti conference it initiated could be found an all-embracing reflection of all elements in the labor movement: Communists, Socialists, anarchists, syndicalists, members of the American Federation of Labor and of the IWW and other independent unions, and scores of fraternal organizations. Even when slanderous attacks were launched against the ILD and attempts made to split the united movement, the International Labor Defense continued to forge forward with patient persistence for unified action.

Secondly, the reliance upon the class movement of the workers. We pointed out incessantly that the Sacco-Vanzetti case was an instance of class persecution and not an accidental case of the "miscarriage of justice." We drew therefrom the conclusion that only the class action of the workers for whom Sacco and Vanzetti were being groomed to die could save them from such a fate. The history of the many Sacco-Vanzetti cases of the past decades in this country confirmed our belief that militant workers could expect no "justice" from capitalist courts and judges, and that their vindication could be guaranteed only by the workers movement.

The Sacco-Vanzetti case was not only tied up with the other cases before the American workers, but also with the militant traditions of the American workers. Among the greatest of these is the tradition of the Haymarket martyrs, whose history contains so many points that are similar to the history of their blood brothers of two score years later. They represent the spirit of courageous struggle for the cause of the working class, the spirit of self-sacrifice, the spirit of defiance to the mad capitalist class that hung them in Cook County jail.

The Third Annual Conference of the ILD will honor the memory of the Haymarket martyrs by meeting on their fortieth anniversary and making their great tradition its own.

The necessity for the defense movement is shown not only by those fighters of the past and those still in prison, the Mooneys, Billingses, Barnetts, McNamaras and others, but by those who are about to be sent there—or to the electric chair—the miners in Cheswick, the Michigan Communists, the New York Italian workers Greco and Carillo, the furriers and ladies' garment workers in New York and Chicago and others in other parts of the country.[3] To defend them is also to defend the labor movement, the working class.

Let the working class of America ring with our fighting slo-

---

[3] More than 20 miners were arrested in Cheswick, Pennsylvania after the state police viciously broke up a protest meeting on the eve of the execution of Sacco and Vanzetti, beating many of the participants. One of the state cossacks was shot and killed in the melee.

Calogero Greco and Donato Carillo were two anti-fascist workers accused of murdering two members of the Fascist League of North America in the Bronx on Memorial Day, 1927; they were acquitted in early 1928.

Many New York furriers and garment workers faced charges as a result of militant strikes in 1926.

For Michigan Communist cases, see glossary.

gan: Build a wall of labor defense against the frame-up system! We want to make the Third Annual Conference of International Labor Defense a sounding board for this militant appeal.

Red November is for our heroes and martyrs, for our battles and for our victories! On with the glorious struggle for liberation, for the freedom of the workers from the prisons of capitalism and from the greater prison which is capitalism!

Workers Entering New Path of Struggle

5 February 1928

The following is an unpublished transcript of a speech by Cannon to a plenum of the Workers Party's Central Executive Committee. It was at this plenum that Cannon refused to speak in support of Trotsky's expulsion from the Soviet party, despite the urgings of his chief factional lieutenant, William F. Dunne. Later, Cannon discussed his doubts on the issue with Canadian party leader Maurice Spector, who also attended the plenum.

Comrade Chairman and Comrades:

It is a good omen not only that the Central Committee is meeting at the right time in view of the big changes taking place in the labor movement, but that the Political Committee is able to come to the plenum with theses unanimously agreed upon and with the prospect that the Central Committee as a whole will accept the theses unanimously.[1]

In my opinion the theses properly estimate the new turn of events and lay down the main line of the correct policy for the party. It will be our task here to emphasize, and immediately after the plenum it will be the task of the Political Committee to bring home to all the members of the party, the fact that membership in this party of ours is beginning to acquire a significance that has not been fully felt up to now.

We are entering a turning point in the American class struggle. The American workers are faced with war danger and actual war, with the beginnings of mass unemployment, and with an industrial depression leading towards a crisis. A crisis in the labor movement is already at hand and new waves of struggle are loom-

[1] The theses were not published in the *Daily Worker.* Instead, Jay Lovestone's report to the plenum was published in nine installments, beginning February 7.

ing up before the American masses, when our party as the vanguard of the masses will have to prove its mettle in the struggle and fight, when every member of the party will be called upon to apply in practice all the knowledge he has gained both by experience and by study in our movement.

In the time that is allotted to me I shall deal briefly only with a few main points, some of which have already been discussed but which I may supplement.

I want to say a few words about the labor party in connection with the forthcoming presidential campaign. The fact that in addition to the new factors in the objective situation we are facing a national presidential campaign gives a special significance to this plenum. We know that the prospects for the formation of a labor party of sufficient mass character, with sufficient base in the industrial labor movement in America, for the forthcoming election campaign are remote. On the contrary, I think it is agreed that from present indications and prospects, and without deep changes which cannot now be counted on, we must recognize that we will be obliged to enter into the forthcoming campaign under our own party banner.

In my opinion, it is necessary to speak thus concretely now. It is necessary to begin already to make our party members understand, as many of them do not yet understand fully, that we are a political party in the complete sense of the word, that we take part in election campaigns and that we will get a great test and great opportunity in the campaign of 1928.

We speak of the labor party as having its base primarily in the industrial proletariat. No other labor party will serve. One of the organizational steps towards the building of such a party that has been stressed in our Political Committee repeatedly especially in the past year has been the building of trade union committees as preliminary steps. It was pointed out in the address of comrade Lovestone and it is also mentioned in the theses that we did not succeed yet in making our comrades in the lower ranks and districts work speedily and consistently with this task. And to this must be attributed, to a certain extent at least, the organizational weaknesses of the labor party, which lags behind the sentiment for it. The theses point out that the sentiment of the laboring masses for a labor party goes far ahead of the actual organization of the forces to fight for it. And we must catalog as one of the errors of our party a slackness in pushing the organization of trade union committees for the labor party. This is to be remedied, I hope, in the future.

When we enter the campaign under our own banner, we will naturally come into sharp collision not only with the big parties of the bourgeoisie, but again with the enemy that parades as a labor party, the Socialist Party. It must be repeated again and again as one of the important tactical conclusions for us to draw in view of the fact that a new wave of struggle is imminent, that in this period radicalism amongst the workers will grow and strengthen and that elements will arise in the ranks of the Socialist Party who will seek to capture those workers with pseudo-radical talk. Therefore, we must understand not only the necessity for a head-on fight with absolute lack of consideration against the Socialist Party as such but also against the pseudo-left wings in the Socialist Party. Dr. Thomas, Mr. Maurer, and all others, although they are not of one type, who under the cloak of radical phrases seek to divert the discontented workers into the Socialist Party, must meet the most merciless exposure and attack from our party.

Turning to another problem of fundamental importance which was stressed in the main political report by comrade Lovestone but which was elaborated at great length by comrade Foster—the problem of the crisis in the trade union movement and the tactical conclusions with regard to the organization of the unorganized and the work in the trade unions.

I want to say in other words and perhaps with somewhat different emphasis that we must make our party members and all sympathizers of the party in the labor movement understand that the Communist Party, in view of certain changes in circumstances and conditions, is putting more emphasis than before upon the direct organization of the unorganized workers and is clinging less to any form of fetishism with regard to independent or dual unionism.

However, we must not allow the impression to get abroad that we have altered our basic trade union policy. Clearness and precision is absolutely necessary here. Our comrades must be fortified tactically and ideologically on this question. They must be prepared to refute all arguments of professional dual unionists and independent unionists to the effect that the Communist Party has come to its senses, has changed its policies and adopted their line.

Comrade Foster pointed out in the Polcom that we must recognize a fundamental difference in the relation of forces between now and 1921 and 1922. We must recognize the tremendous weakening of the apparatus of the trade unions in many of the important industries. We must recognize further that many of these unions, under the straitjacket of reactionary bureaucratic control, have gone further and further to the right, towards the line of bourgeois ideology. The prospects of these unions, in many cases, serving as the mechanism of decisive struggles and strikes is far less than it was in 1922. And if we are to serve our real purpose, if we are to act as the vanguard of the masses in these coming struggles, we must be prepared in many cases to actually offer to the masses leadership and forms of organization not circumscribed and bounded by the old forms.

This is not for us a change of policy, because the Communist Party says that the center of gravity is where the struggling masses are. That was true when we emphasized with especial sharpness the necessity to keep within the form of these unions when they serve as the main centers of the mass struggle and it is just as properly applied when we say the masses of workers who are outside of these unions must be reached and organized, forming new unions where the old ones cannot or will not serve.

I would like to add my voice in this connection to those who spoke against the danger of taking an extreme position, against the danger which has been a popular one in the American movement as long as I can recollect—the danger of running over to new formulas and panaceas. In view of the traditions that we have in the American movement, we will have to recognize a danger. Our emphasis on direct organization of the unorganized will be construed as a fundamental change in our tactics and an excuse for running off to new forms and grandiose experiments and deserting our basic work in the trade unions.

Anyone who thinks that the trade unions of America, backward as they are, betrayed by the agents of the capitalists as they are, weakened as they are, anyone who thinks that these unions are not going to play a tremendous role in the class struggles of

America does not know the ABC of the labor movement.

Our party understands that. And I think we will not put the question as though it were a matter of building new unions as against working in the existing unions; of organizing the unorganized instead of working within the present organized ranks of the American labor movement. We put the problem as one part of the unifying whole, of working within the existing unions with greater energy than before while building new unions if necessary, to lead the masses in struggle in certain cases, all as part of one tactic and one problem.

I believe that there is unanimity on this question within our leading committees although there are shadings of emphasis here and there. I think the mean between the divergent positions of those comrades who want to emphasize or shade here or there results in a harmonious balance and the arrival at a correct line in the last analysis.

A few words on the IWW, which has become again a problem as a result of the Colorado strike.[2] First of all, for us it is not a problem of the IWW alone, because on the trade union side it cannot be isolated from the problem of the entire labor movement. On the ideological side, the attitude towards the IWW involves some fundamental principled questions. In the broader sense, the IWW is a labor union and a political party at the same time, though not very successful in either role. As a part of the trade union problem of the party we must not look at the IWW with blind eyes as some comrades in the East are apt to do and fail to see it altogether; neither should we exaggerate the size and role and significance of the IWW.

We can say that the Colorado strike brought about no reason for any basic change in our policy. We always had the theory,

---

[2] While the UMW was half-heartedly waging a losing strike in the East, the Industrial Workers of the World led close to 10,000 Colorado miners out on strike beginning 17 October 1927. Picketing in defiance of a state ban, the IWW waged a militant fight against the bloody Colorado coal companies. In November six miners were killed when the state police opened fire on a miners' demonstration at the Columbine mine. But the IWW had won higher wages and union recognition when the strike ended on 17 February 1928.

On 23 November 1927 the Colorado strike had been discussed in the party's

(continued)

since we first corrected our trade union line after the leftist debacle of our early years, that we had to work within the IWW wherever it had workers organized in the ranks, form united fronts with them, work within the ranks of the IWW members and try to lead them in the direction of Communism. That remains our basic attitude while rejecting the fantastic theory of building an entire new labor movement in America as against the existing unions, now more than ever before.

Many comrades even in our own ranks have had their vision obscured by the Colorado strike, and when party members adopt a false conclusion you can be sure that many workers are also reflecting this false conclusion.

In the miners union, some comrades who wearied of the stubborn struggle have shown tendencies to look to the IWW as a short cut to an ideal union. Such a point of view must be more decisively rejected. A greater folly cannot be imagined. We have to master the tactic of working within the IWW in cases where they have serious bodies of workers, of joining them and cooperating with them, while at the same time we fight persistently against their false teachings on the general field of theory as well as in tactical questions of the labor movement. We combined these two tasks in our work in the Colorado strike better than ever before.

We have a right to congratulate ourselves upon the fact that even in this far Western outpost our party was able to have a nucleus of loyal Communists on the job, working directly in the IWW and through various other committees and organizations,

---

Political Committee. Bill Dunne submitted a statement on the strike, which began as follows:

> "1. The Colorado situation in its relation to the whole struggle of the coal miners and the American working class in general has been entirely underestimated by our party.
>
> "2. The IWW has not only picked up and appropriated the class struggle tradition of the Colorado workers, but has added a new tradition to it as a result of their state-wide struggle and the recent shooting at the Columbine mine."

Dunne went on to list the party's failings, which included not sending a reporter to Colorado and allowing Hugo Oehler, the Kansas City District Organizer who had gone to Colorado and been arrested for strike support activities, to languish in jail because he could not pay the $2,500 bail. Subsequently the party threw significant resources into supporting the strike.

who were able to get real influence amongst the strikers, penetrating into the ranks of the IWW and gaining prestige with the members while continually fighting against the false line of the IWW leadership. The lessons and experiences of the Colorado strike, amended and corrected as a result of the critical examination by our Central Committee, will be a guiding line for the future tactics regarding the IWW.

There is another side to the IWW which always interested me greatly. I asked myself many times since we formed the Communist Party, how does it come that the Leninist party which always has as its foundation the most exploited and militant workers, allowed so many good proletarian fighters in the West to fall into the hands of syndicalists and anarcho-syndicalists. I always felt there was a weakness in the tactics of the party, that it had not learned to combine the ideological fight against syndicalism with the task of fighting side by side with the syndicalist workers and winning them to the party.

We are learning that today. The Colorado strike shows that they can no longer speak, as they attempted to speak in the past, of our party as one which stands aloof from this type of workers and does not know how to approach them and make them feel at home in its ranks. The Colorado strike is proving that we are learning how to deal with this big problem of winning over to our side all the best elements of the syndicalist movement of the West.

I want to say a few words on the party organization. The party organization, in the period when we are facing big struggles, the apparatus of the party, the personnel, the activity of party members within the party, all this takes on a special significance. If we do not have a firm and strongly disciplined apparatus of the party, we will not be able to carry out our tasks in the coming struggle. We will have to consider this very carefully. The whole Political Committee will have to consider with greater attention than ever before the problem of strengthening the party organization in the sense of selecting comrades very carefully from the standpoint of experience and ability for work in the party apparatus. One of the first things we will have to strengthen will be the district organizations, which are very weak. There is too big a gap between the central organization and district organizations, too big a difference between the quality and ability of the material mobilized for work in the center of the party and that utilized and available for the work of the districts. It will be one of our main problems to strengthen the apparatus of the district organizations. Failure to do this will prove to be very costly in the period of greater struggles.

A few words on party membership, on the question of how many members we have. First of all, let me make a remark which I believe will express the sentiment of every member of the Central Committee. Facing the big fights and big struggles before us, everybody has a sound optimistic attitude on the question of the party responding to its obligations in the coming fights. We look forward to a healthy growth in our party membership. But I believe we must be careful to have an exact knowledge at the same time of what our forces consist of. Otherwise, we are apt to exaggerate our possibilities and come to certain defeat. I got the impression from comrade Lovestone's report that our party membership is approximately the same now as it was at the time of reorganization. Comrade Lovestone in his concluding remarks may elaborate on this point but it appears to me that a certain discrepancy exists. My recollection is that we had 16,000 dues-paying members at the time of the 1925 convention, averaging over the six months time before the reorganization. We know there was a lot of material amongst these 16,000 members then that was not 100 percent utilizable in a more tightly organized party, and it was to be expected that some would drop out in the reorganization. But if the figures I have at hand are correct, we have sustained a heavy loss. I have some of the financial reports furnished by the Secretariat in the months of August, September, October, November and December, from which it appears the average dues payment for the period is for 6,731 members. The initiation fees show a total of initiations of 541 in those four months. That does not represent our actual strength, not even our actual organizational strength. It represents the actual dues-paying members of our party. If these figures are supplemented by some later ones showing a more favorable side, I would be glad if comrade Lovestone would clarify this point so that we will know exactly where we stand on the question of members.

I want to make a small remark also on another organizational point. In the period since the convention our party Secretariat has become a very important institution.[3] It has naturally taken up a number of functions of an important character, even going perhaps a step too far, taking over a number of the normal functions of the Political Committee, and in such actions as selecting a chairman of the plenum. If in the coming period the Secretariat is going to play an especially important political role and act as a sort of substitute for the Political Committee in important questions, I would make the suggestion for the consideration of the comrades to broaden the composition of the Secretariat to a slight extent.

(Interjection: "What do you mean?")

I mean that if the Secretariat is to assume important political functions it should be made broader, more representative and consequently stronger and more authoritative.

Now, comrades, on the question of errors. We made some. Comrade Lovestone speaking on the theses pointed out a number of them. The important ones are those from which we can draw conclusions of importance to us in the immediate future. We ought to discriminate and to pick out only those errors which might have a bearing upon the future, because an incidental error here and there does not mean much.

I would emphasize one, it might be two, mistakes in the miners campaign. One is we procrastinated and delayed too much with the idea of organizing the conference of the left wing in the miners union. We had in this a certain remnant of the tactic which is reminiscent of a period of less tension—the habit of overcaution. We were too late with relief. We made some errors of showing the party face here and there.[4]

---

[3] In August 1925 the Fourth Convention of the Workers Party had elected a Secretariat consisting of Ruthenberg, Lovestone and Cannon. The Foster faction was not represented, and in 1926 an ECCI decision on the American question abolished the institution. But it was revived after Lovestone won his victory at the party's Fifth Convention: Lovestone, Gitlow and Foster were the members.

[4] See note pp. 397-398 for background on the fight in the Political Committee over calling a national convention of the miners opposition. These differences were evidently overcome, because the Political Committee meeting on 2 November 1927 unanimously passed Foster's motion "that we, through our progressive contacts, sound out these leading progressives at once as to their attitude regarding the calling of a conference." John Brophy and Powers Hapgood agreed to go

(continued)

(Interjection by comrade Stachel.)

When Bolsheviks get to the point when they can tell each other face to face what is the matter and not get nervous, they will be on the road to overcoming factionalism. We made errors in the past of the same character which we have to avoid in the future, the question of showing the party face. I have never been the most extreme on this point and I am not speaking now from a "leftist" standpoint. In the period of slow development of the struggle our approach to the workers must be by many roundabout methods. But in the coming period, just because we are facing struggles, just because we expect an increasing radicalism of the workers which will render them more accessible to Communist ideas, we must endeavor, wherever possible, to approach them directly and bring the party as a party into the foreground.

I could speak further on the mistakes in the miners campaign but I will refrain lest I call forth another interjection from comrade Stachel which would not have any bearing on this. I would rather save the time. It is merely to draw the conclusions of a general nature for future guidance that I have mentioned these matters here.

Now I will pass over to the discussion of a very interesting phenomenon. I want to deal a minute or two with the Panken case.[5] I use the term case in a clinical sense since it is quite clear there is some sickness here. It looked as though the "Panken policy" was going to be allowed to die until comrade Weinstone jumped on his horse and like Paul Revere rode to the rescue.

(Interjection by Weinstone: "It was not a revolutionary situation.")

No, and on reflection I don't think the Paul Revere analogy

---

along; Brophy remained chairman of the "Save the Union" Committee. A national conference was called for 1 April 1928 in Pittsburgh. Over 1,000 miners attended—most of them strikers. In early September 1927 the party had begun a campaign for relief for the striking miners in the Central Competitive Field, who had been on strike since early April.

[5] The Political Committee first discussed this issue on 12 October 1927, when Weinstone proposed that the Committee endorse the New York district policy of giving "qualified support" to the re-election of Socialist judge Jacob Panken. Cannon, Foster and Bittelman opposed the policy, while the Lovestone majority endorsed it, noting, however, that "criticism of the SP and Judge Panken has not been brought out sufficiently strong enough."

is a good one from another standpoint, because Paul Revere reached his destination and accomplished his aims whereas comrade Weinstone's horse stumbled before he got a good start.

(Interjection: "There were too many riding the horse.")

There were a good many riding that horse but some of them have already unloaded and others are willing to sell their seats very cheaply.

What was the Panken case? First of all, I want to say there is no ground for panic. I think the situation has been modified to a large extent, as is shown by the fact that the comrades did not put a defense of this policy in the theses. The amendment of comrade Dunne represents progress on his part and undoubtedly on the part of the others. What we want is clarification for future guidance. First of all, maybe you comrades don't know about the discussion which arose in the Polcom over the Panken policy. We were served up with some great reasons for voting for him. One of them that I can recollect, and it was explained here fully by the various defenders, was that we were engaged in the building of a "united front against reaction." This nonsense was dispersed amongst the comrades of New York as a reason for voting for Panken. This is not worth a nickel—when this "united front against reaction" contains the *New York World*, the Bar Association, and when the Republican Party offers to join it, where does the Communist Party fit in? Besides, it was not a revolution now, it was only a case of a yellow Socialist judge running in an East Side district in New York. Comrade Wolfe said that we were trying to draw mechanical conclusions from the CI decision on England and France.[6] He will remember that it was we who protested

[6] At this time the Comintern was just beginning a turn to the left, as Stalin prepared to move against Bukharin. In the initial stages Bukharin was forced to execute the turn, and in early November he signed a circular letter addressed to the Central Committees of all the Communist parties. This letter was attached to the minutes of the American Political Committee meeting of 30 November 1927. The letter gave a critique of recent rightist errors of the French and British parties, particularly their desire to give electoral support to reformist parties in coalition with bourgeois parties:

"In connection with these questions, attention must be devoted to the preparations for the general elections in Britain and France, in which countries the

(continued)

against the mechanical transference of examples when we heard the truly astonishing attempt to compare the issues in an election for a petty judgeship in New York with the Hindenburg election and the issue of monarchism in Germany.[7] The comrades had some very big and peculiar ideas on the Panken issue at the time. We do not hear much of these arguments now. I believe the united front against reaction forms a valid argument under certain circumstances but it was entirely out of place in the Panken case.

Nobody said that we should make a principled stand against it and nobody said that we should not vote for a Socialist under any circumstances. Comrade Wolfe was only trying to draw strength for a weak position and fighting a straw man when he imputed this position to us. We were told the workers would not understand us if we did not support Panken. This would surely be a good reason if it were really so because it is of the utmost importance that the workers understand our tactics. Would they understand why they should vote for Panken? In the middle of the garment workers struggle, with the issue burning in the hearts of the workers in the district, we were against the Panken maneuver.

What the district of New York should have done was to force the SP into the open on the question of organizing a labor ticket or not. By the failure of putting conditions in endorsing Panken, we allowed them to create the impression that they were the labor party. With our anxiety to execute a maneuver in grand style, we let the Socialist Party pose as a substitute for the labor party. My understanding of a united front in an election campaign is that we bargain with them, compel them to give concessions, to agree to certain programs and all things of this sort. We should never let them masquerade as a substitute for the labor party, which we must support because "the workers will not understand."

That is not all. One of the basic problems of dealing with the

---

question of relations with the USSR is particularly acute. It must be borne in mind that the ECCI regards the policy of supporting a Liberal-Labour bloc (Lloyd George and MacDonald) in Britain and the Left cartel in France as *radically wrong*, even if this support is advocated under the guise of assisting the USSR."

[7] See note page 337.

Socialist Party in New York is to break down the prejudice in the minds of the sympathetic workers that the Communist Party fights on the trade union field only and the Socialist Party on the political field—and they should support us in the unions and vote for the Socialist candidates. We have to establish the identity of the Communist Party as a political party in the full sense of the word. That was an additional reason why we should have put up our own candidate. Here we are in the midst of the great needle trades struggle, with the furriers and left wing garment workers concentrating their whole attention around the fight in the garment industry.

Our task in this election was to take this fight in the garment workers outside of the trade union sphere and bring it out in the political arena as one of our battle cries in this election—concentrating our fight against Panken as the representative of the reactionary and traitorous Socialist Party. In this very respect, it is interesting news that Panken is a likely candidate for president of the garment workers' union. The right wing is putting him forward as a man who gets the support from the black reactionaries and who to a certain extent is acceptable to the left wing. I think we should adopt the amendment proposed by comrade Bittelman, with which I am in agreement, to list the Panken policy as one of our mistakes.

There is one other point in this question that must be answered because it was brought up by comrade Weinstone. He said we had to support him because we were confronted with a "pendulum situation." I think comrade Weinstone has a weakness for pendulum situations.

(Interjection by comrade Weinstone: "Charity begins at home.")

I don't believe in charity. The pendulum is all right on the clock but the trouble with the pendulum in politics is that it never stops. It was said here by comrade Wolfe that the Panken case is not the "father" of the opportunist error in Boston[8]

---

[8] The minutes of the Political Committee meeting of 2 November 1927 contain the following point on the Boston elections:

"Comrade Dunne reported that Bearak has been endorsed by the Good Government Association for Mayor in Boston. Bearak is running on the Socialist ticket. *(continued)* because the latter came first in point of time. I do not know whether it is important to establish the date of the birth of the Panken atrocity, and to say just which is the father and which the son. I will only say they were related. If they were not father and son, they were brothers. (Laughter.)

The Panken case is very important because it affects our tactics and our attitude towards the SP in the coming campaign. I hope nobody then will propose similar policies because, as the theses say, this was under special circumstances and not a settled policy.

Now, comrades, in closing I want to again emphasize my agreement with the main line of the theses, especially with the conclusion that we are approaching a period of new struggles which are bound to affect the party line. The theses orient the party on this line. We are entering a new period in the development of the class struggle, in which we have to decide and determine where lies the greater danger. Will that danger be that of leftism, or opportunism? It is agreed that the greatest danger for the party in the coming period is the danger of conservatism, of overcaution in not responding and reacting quickly enough to situations. The party must be aggressive and determined to put itself at the head of the movement of the masses. At the same time we have to sound a warning against any running away towards the left. We must not underestimate the powerful resources of American capitalism, the sluggishness and the backwardness of the American workers. While putting emphasis on aggressiveness and quick action, we must see that we do not isolate ourselves from the workers by ill-considered actions and proposals.

The basic task is to equip the party ideologically and organizationally for the fight. And in connection with this task, the internal problems of the party acquire an especial significance—the problem of unity and consolidation of the party is a burning one.

"Comrade Lovestone stated that the question has been taken up previously and acted upon: that our comrades were instructed to present a workers' program to the Conference, and if Bearak accepted it we should support him, otherwise we would fight him. He did not accept and our comrades are now fighting him." Joseph Bearak, a well-known Socialist and labor attorney, was in fact an SP candidate for Boston City Council.

Under the circumstances it is more true now than before that the fundamental Communist cadres of the party must be welded together into a single block, that the Central Committee must be the real and only leader, and that the factions must be done away with. That is a prerequisite. Have we solved that problem already? I think not. The theses point out, a little too mildly perhaps, that in spite of headway, we have yet a long way to go, and call for new and more vigorous efforts for the unification of the party. I would underscore that section. It is of the utmost importance that from this plenum new and more vigorous efforts for the consolidation and unification of the party be made. In this connection I wish to emphasize the opinion that criticism and plain speaking are necessary, and from this standpoint I want to disagree again with the remarks of comrade Weinstone. He promised to speak plainly. But I will admit that I did not understand what he said, and to the extent that I did understand it, I did not agree with him. Comrade Weinstone, of course, in perfect good faith, spoke here as a sort of patriarch. The boys fought a little here and a little there, there was fault on both sides, they mustn't do it anymore and must unite. We must be more concrete. The plenum of the CEC is not a class in the Workers School. We are older, more hardened, more used to hard words, and can even stand a few blows in order to clarify matters. There have been factional errors in the appointments of party functionaries in the districts and language sections. And these errors should be spoken about, and not only spoken about, but they should be corrected, as a prerequisite for the speeding up of unity. It is no answer at all to say there was factionalism on both sides. The real blame goes to those who are responsible for these factional errors and have the power to correct them. What has hampered the progress of unification? I think there has been some error in a theoretical way. Some comrades evidently evolved the fantastic theory of solving the problem of party unity and party leadership by artificially picking here and there citizens for the unity (so to speak) and candidates for the leadership. To artificially permeate here and artificially "squeeze" there are not the proper methods of selecting a leadership which grows in struggles and fights. I think this theory of "squeezing" certain sections of the leadership, without political basis, is a very unprincipled one and will be unsuccessful. I contend that the progress of unification can only be hampered by such unprincipled maneuvers.

Comrade Wolfe had no ground to attack the speech of comrade Bittelman, whose remarks were mild. Bittelman said: "If you want I will give you a bill of particulars." And I could say if his is not big enough, then I can supplement it. He said, and I agree with him, that there were many instances, and it is only because we do not wish the plenum to occupy itself with organizational questions that he did not give them.

(Interjection: "Give the bill of particulars.")

Well, I could begin by saying that the removal of comrade Swabeck from his position as district organizer in Chicago was a factional action that did not benefit the party in Chicago. I can go further and say that the factional discrimination and persecution against the former political friends of the Weinstone group in the South Slav Federation has not helped the party in the Federation.[9] If Weinstone does not know it, then I know it. And I do not desert the comrades who are persecuted for the sole reason that they supported us in the past fight, and by silence approve the unfounded discrimination made against them.

Comrade Wolfe said there were no political differences of a fundamental character and therefore no protest should be made against discrimination in organization questions. This logic is upside-down. The absence of vital political differences makes factional discrimination all the more unprincipled and puts a heavier blame on those who persist in it. It is maintained that there are no more majorities and minorities in the Polcom. It is true that on a number of political questions, we did not vote on group lines, but I noticed that on all organization questions, there always happens to be a substantial majority, and I always find myself in the minority. That is the way the thing shows up in practice. I don't want to dwell too long on this point. I do not wish to switch the discussion away from the general problem of

---

[9] Max Bedacht replaced Swabeck as district organizer in Chicago after Lovestone's victory at the party's Fifth Convention in August 1927. For the situation in the South Slavic Federation, see note page 389.

party unity into the merits of this or that appointment. The theses speak of drawing new forces into the leadership, and into the entire apparatus of the party. This advice is always in order. But in the period when the party is going into struggle it must be doubly careful about throwing away the old and tried material, discarding qualified comrades, drawing lines of distinction against those who are faithful and loyal to the party and have no reason to be discriminated against. I want to make my point of view as clear as possible, so that when I get through speaking nobody will wonder what I think about the question of unity. My adherence to the cause of consolidating and unifying the leadership of the party and doing away with factions stands as before. I do not want to deny a measure of progress, but a certain degree of dissatisfaction—not a crisis, not a big revolt, not a revolution—with the rate of progress that we have made must be placed on record at the plenum.

The question of unity is bound up with the question of leadership, and the sooner we understand a few fundamental principles of Communist leadership, the better. Communist leaders must have certain prerequisites. They cannot be artificially manufactured or artificially put aside for any considerable length of time in the Communist movement. That is the lesson of the history of factionalism in the international movement, and the classic example is to be found in the development of the leadership in the German Communist Party. The sooner the party as a whole understands this, the quicker we will be able to pass over into a solution of this problem, and enter into the new battles with a really welded and single leadership of the party.

In conclusion, a few remarks of a summary nature. First, the theses, as unanimously adopted in the Polcom and unanimously adopted here, clearly analyze the new situation and draw correct conclusions. The theses will orient our party and prepare it for the new period. The conclusion of the theses that the workers are entering into a path of struggle puts upon us tremendous obligations as American revolutionists to make good, in fact and in the struggles, as the leaders of the working class. In this period we will record further betrayals and further collapse of all parties and ideologies in the labor movement, outside of the Communists.

The members of the Communist Party and its leadership will be tested in deeds. I want to express firm confidence that in the face of the big fights before us, our Communist Party, already nine years old, will unite and steel its ranks, discharge its obligations, and emerge from the test struggle bigger and stronger and more worthy to lead the workers to the final revolution.

Party Work and Accountability

Published March-April 1928

The following article by Cannon was published in the Workers Party's internal journal, Party Organizer.

At the recent party membership meeting in Philadelphia, one of the comrades drew attention to the failure of many party members to render accounts to the respective party committees on the execution of the work assigned to them, and asked how this condition could be remedied. This is a timely question and one deserving consideration by the party. The February plenum of the Central Committee estimated the sharpening economic situation and foresaw a period of increasing and expanding struggles of the workers. With the perspective before us, the problem of the tightening of the party machine and strengthening its capacity to shape and guide these struggles acquired a particular importance.

It is a well-known fact that Bolshevism clashes with reformism on organization questions no less decisively than on points of general politics. The looseness, laxity and general flabbiness which characterized all shades of opportunism in the realm of organization is alien to the Communist Party. Lenin would never tolerate the idea that party membership could be enjoyed by do-as-you-please people who took no part in the general work and activity of the party and gave no account of themselves to the party committees. It was over a section in the party constitution dealing precisely with this question that the formal break between the Bolsheviks and the Mensheviks took place in 1903. The differences today on these questions are no less marked.

The old Socialist parties, and all reformist organizations generally, are characterized by an active bureaucracy and a passive membership. The "business" of the organization is attended to by a small group of officials while the participation of the masses of the membership is largely formal and financial. It is obvious that this method and form of organization is not suitable for serious struggles in which the mass power of the workers must play the decisive role. Of course, this is not a defect in the eyes of the opportunists, since it is not their policy to struggle against capitalism but to adapt themselves to it.

The Communist Party, which organizes the proletarian vanguard for the revolutionary struggle, breaks with all these conceptions of organization and carries on a continuous struggle to extirpate their remnants from its ranks. Such a party must know its forces and be able to estimate correctly their capacities and mobilize them for action. The assignment of definite tasks to every party member and the construction of a whole network of responsible committees to supervise and regulate this work is the Communist organization principle. This leads to the construction of a flexible but strong party apparatus interwoven with the entire mass of the party members and drawing them all into active party work.

Fierce fights over these conflicting organization principles took place in the Russian labor movement prior to the revolution. The Mensheviks reviled those theories of Lenin and attacked the Bolsheviks as "apparatus men" and "committee workers." But thanks to their superior apparatus, as well as to their general political program, the Bolsheviks were able to annihilate the capitalist regime and with it the Mensheviks. In good time the same result will be recorded in America.

It goes without saying that our party, which is only gradually and painfully developing on the path of Bolshevism, suffers from the remnants of many old and false conceptions and practices, and the question propounded by the Philadelphia comrade draws attention to a common evil. A glaring disparity exists everywhere between the plans and decisions of the party committees and their practical execution. Passivity and indifference hamper the movements of the party everywhere like a growth of poison vines. This evil can never be completely eradicated. How to reduce it steadily and increasingly to the minimum is the problem.

This task has two sides. In the first place, especially now in the face of impending struggles which will tax all the capacities of the party, we should undertake a general tightening up of the party apparatus. The party committees and subcommittees must be galvanized into a more intense and better regulated activity and the practice of assigning specific work to party members and checking up on its performance must become more thorough and systematic. The practice of reporting on work done by the party members to the respective committees must be insisted on until it becomes the general and accepted order of things. Every party member must be trained in the habit of accounting for his specific work.

This pressure from the apparatus alone, however, will not solve the problem. Hand in hand with it must go a thoroughgoing campaign of education on Communist organization principles, together with widespread enlightenment on the party policies which are given life only by the multiform practical activities of the party members, and the reasons for them.

The key to successful mobilization for collective work is the permeation of the party members with enthusiasm and conviction. A general campaign of education within the party on these questions, reinforced by a proportional intensification of discipline and accounting, will go a long way toward solving the worst features of the present difficulties and equipping the party to play a more influential part in the impending battles of the American workers.

Organization of Propaganda Meetings

Published 14 May 1928

The following article by Cannon was published in the Daily Worker.

Communist tactics and methods of work, the placing of emphasis on this or that form of activity, are naturally regulated to a very large extent by the given situation and the stage of development. Communist propaganda and agitation through the medium of mass meetings are always in order, even after the seizure of political power, as we see in Russia where great attention and skill is devoted to this work. If the Russian party, which rules the country, has not found it advisable to dispense with such activities, it is fairly obvious that they have possibilities yet for us.

Propaganda Meetings Important

We in America are in that stage of development where the ideas of Communism have as yet penetrated only a very narrow fringe of the working class. The overwhelming masses have absolutely no conception of our aims beyond that false and distorted one furnished them by our enemies. The natural operation of the laws of capitalism will push the millions of American workers, now mental and spiritual captives of the ruling class, onto the path of class struggle and in the direction of their historic goal, regardless of their present understanding and will. It is our task as Communists, taking part in all the struggles of the workers, to accelerate this process by all means in our power and to impart to it the greatest possible degree of consciousness as it develops. For this an enormous amount of agitation and propaganda will be necessary. This work, of course, will take many and varied forms, but the spoken word, the public mass meeting, will play a great part. The day of the importance of propaganda meetings is by no means over; indeed, for our party the period just ahead of us must and will see a much greater emphasis placed upon them.

And in connection with this our party comrades will begin, for the first time, to devote serious attention to the technique of organizing propaganda meetings.

If we except the larger cities where we have staffs of professional party workers (and not all of them!) we must acknowledge that our party on the whole has not properly estimated the importance of this elementary revolutionary work, and consequently has not derived the maximum benefits which skillful organization would bring. For the most part, our comrades, who have become experts in a number of activities, remain hopeless amateurs in this field, although there is nothing involved except the assimilation and application of a few organizational rules and principles derived from the experience of the past.

The Socialist Party of pre-war days was far ahead of us on this score and knew how to organize propaganda meetings in such a way as to make them mighty instruments of agitation and inspiration. The speakers did not do all of this by any means. Organizational technique played the principal role in this work of the old Socialist Party. Would it be treason to Communism if we should borrow and learn from this experience? I think not. On the contrary, I would not be above "lifting" a few tricks of the art of propaganda anywhere they can be found and made serviceable for our revolutionary work. Aside from that, we are the rightful heirs of all that was sound and proletarian in the old Socialist Party and its accomplishments belong to us. We ought to study the old movement more attentively.

Rules for Organizing Meetings

I have had some experience as a speaker and even more as local organizer of meetings for other speakers. Like all who have had this experience, I have learned a number of rules and principles for the successful organization of meetings which I am going to enumerate here. These organizational rules and principles are bound up with a certain conception of the function and purpose of agitation and propaganda meetings which I think is a correct one.

They must be a recruiting ground for the organization. They must provide inspiration together with instruction. They must strengthen the morale of the comrades and leave them with a feeling of success and accomplishment, and they must provide revenue for the organization and not deficits. These things cannot be accomplished by the speaker alone. The organization of the meeting and the atmosphere in which it is held have an equal importance. A mediocre speech will often serve the purpose with the proper organization and atmosphere of the meeting, while a good speech will often be a heartbreaking failure without them. As a rule the measure of success is determined by the attention and skill devoted to the preparation and organization of the meeting along the following lines:

1. Put a committee in charge of the arrangements of the meeting with responsibility for different phases of the work definitely assigned to individual members.

2. Advertise the meeting widely. People won't come unless they know about it. A penny-pinching policy on advertising is absolutely fatal to success.

Mailing Lists

3. Build up and use a mailing list. This is one of the most important instruments of every local organization. It should contain the name of every member, sympathizer and prospective sympathizer, properly classified. Every name on it should receive notice of the meeting, and as many handbills or pluggers advertising the meeting as a two-cent stamp will carry. A local organizer who doesn't keep an up-to-date mailing list and use it constantly is working with one arm in a sling.

4. As a rule admission should be charged for the meetings and tickets should be sold in advance. The most extensive experience shows that more people attend meetings for which tickets are sold in advance and the financial returns from the meeting are much greater. There are exceptional circumstances where it is advisable to hold a free mass meeting, but the comrades who never want to charge admission on the ground that the workers are too poor to pay are victims of a false theory and a harmful prejudice. All experience speaks against them. Sell tickets in advance and send a number on credit to every name on your mailing list, using discretion as to the amount in each case. Don't be afraid someone will sell a few tickets and abscond with the money. This doesn't happen very often, and even then the

organization is the gainer for everyone who comes to the meeting on an unpaid ticket.

5. Always try for publicity for the meeting in the local capitalist papers as well as in the party and labor press. The best way to do this is to establish personal acquaintance with a reporter or staff member on each paper who handles labor news. There are few cities where small notices cannot be secured if real systematic efforts are made. Of course good-sized write-ups are secured only in rare cases and with the most prominent speakers, but it should be remembered that a small notice in a local capitalist paper reaches thousands of workers who do not read our own press.

6. Hire a hall with a seating capacity approximately the same as the size of the crowd you expect. This detail is of the utmost importance. Atmosphere is a great part of the meeting. A crowd of 200 lost in a hall with a seating capacity of 1,000 throws a chill over the meeting, takes the heart out of the speaker and leaves the crowd at the end with a feeling of failure and defeat. The same crowd of 200 with the same speaker comfortably filling or packing a smaller hall will produce a meeting with entirely opposite effects. Remember this rule: get a hall to fit the size of crowd you expect.

7. Select a chairman able to attend strictly to the business of supervising the meeting, making the necessary announcements and introducing the speaker. That's all! Many a promising meeting has been spoiled by a loquacious chairman who undertook to make the speaker's address for him in advance. This happens all too frequently, and local organizations which take their propaganda meetings seriously should put a stop to this harmful nonsense. It is better to offend the chairman by telling him bluntly that he talks too much, than to offend a whole audience by forcing them to hear a long speech they didn't come to hear.

And what about the speaker himself? Has he no rights at all? An old campaigner once expressed the sentiments of all speakers when he said that if he could get only one wish granted he would ask for a tongue-tied chairman.

8. Ushers should be selected in advance by the committee and they should be on hand early to escort people to the front seats as they arrive. Then latecomers will take the rear seats without disturbing the meeting. Without ushers the early arrivals

will invariably take the rear seats, leaving the front ones vacant.

Then it will happen just as invariably that others will straggle in all through the meeting and come gawking all over the front of the hall looking for a seat just at the time the speaker is working hardest to get the attention of the audience for what he considers a particularly impressive point. An efficient set of ushers is indispensable to a well-organized meeting.

9. In cool weather make certain beforehand that the hall is properly heated. This is necessary for the success of the meeting, the comfort of the audience and the health of the speaker. Such a detail would seem obvious, but I have never yet made a tour in wintertime without having at least one or two meetings in cold halls due to the negligence and thoughtlessness of the local committee, and I never yet saw a meeting held under such circumstances that could be called a success.

Sale of Literature

10. The selling of literature, taking collections and passing out application cards for new members are details which work themselves out best in actual practice without a uniform plan. The best results in selling literature from the platform are gained if one piece is concentrated on, leaving the rest for sale at the literature table near the door.

If the speaker is worth his salt, a meeting conducted along these lines will be a success and will strengthen the local organization morally, organizationally and financially, provided one final detail is not overlooked. That is: Quit on time and on the right note. Pace the meeting along and get it through quickly after the speech is over. Don't let it drag along and fizzle out until the audience gets tired and begins to leave of its own accord.

Attention to these practical details until they become a matter of routine in the organization of public meetings will bring rich returns to the party in the field of propaganda work.

Opening the Election Campaign

Published 5 June 1928

The following article by Cannon was published in the Daily Worker.

The awakening of all the leading forces of the party to the importance of the election campaign was demonstrated in the most dramatic and convincing manner by the national nominating convention. No one who took part in the convention or watched its three days' deliberations could have the slightest doubt that the party has at last made a real beginning with election activities.

It was our first national nominating convention, and for many new members and sympathizers it was the first effective demonstration of the party's national scope and organization. The convention itself and all the preparations for it were excellently organized and the high points effectively dramatized. This was no mere happenstance. The party machine is nine years old and the experience of our past work is bearing its fruit in every phase of party activity. The successful organization of all sides of the convention preparations augurs well for the 1928 campaign.

Party Growth Reflected

The convention reflected the growth and development of the movement in a striking manner. We have held many conventions in the past nine years. Even in the period when the party was outlawed, we held a number of underground conventions where as few as thirty or forty delegates from ten or twelve states struggled and argued for days over disputed points of the program.

The convention we have just held had 296 voting delegates from 39 states and the District of Columbia. In addition to that 150 fraternal delegates were present. Prominent and distinguished people in the labor and revolutionary movement, such as Anita Whitney and Lucy Parsons, gave added importance to the convention by their attendance. There was a strong delegation of Negroes, strengthening the fraternal bonds of solidarity between the races in the common fight. Striking miners, textile workers and the embattled needle trades workers were there, as well as delegates from the solid South and the Far West. The composition of the convention deserves a special article. It showed a picture of a national organization.

The character of the delegations and the burning issues of the class struggle dealt with in the platform and the speeches were convincing proof that the Communist Party does not approach the election campaign from the standpoint of the capitalist and reformist parties. The election is for us a field of the class struggle and we raise there the issues and slogans which animate the struggles of the workers on every front, developing them further and tying them together.

The success of the convention was so pronounced as to justify the opinion that we are nearing the accomplishment of a most essential task, that is, to establish our position as a political party in the general and national sense of the word. In recent years, the party has developed greatly along the line of partial and sectional struggles of the workers. It is now gathering its forces for a general fight on the broader field. Herein lies the great significance of the turning point marked by the opening of our national election campaign.

The party has already made a good name for itself as a fighter for the interests of the workers on the economic field. The hatred and fear of the exploiters and all their labor agents for us is the outcome of the heavy blows we have dealt them.

Communists Heart of Mine Struggle

Many workers have a good opinion of our work in the trade unions and think it represents the sum total of our activity. We made a good fight at Passaic. We, together with the workers, fought and are fighting the bosses, the police, the AFL and SP traitors to a standstill in the needle trades. At the present time our party is the heart and soul of the epic struggle of the coal miners.

Some erroneous conclusions have been drawn from these activities, partly because our work in the past has been somewhat one-sided. Many workers who see our party in these fights and who support it in them have not yet come to recognize us as a general political party, fighting effectively in the political arena.

Is it not a fact that many workers in New York who support us in the needle trades against the Socialist Party traitors vote for these same charlatans on election day? What is the explanation of this anomaly? It arises primarily from our failure up to now, because of the passivity of the party members in this respect, to make a sufficient impression in the election field, with the result that we are regarded in some circles of the sympathizing workers as a "trade union party" only. This confusion must be overcome in the 1928 campaign. It is one of our great tasks in the coming election period to deal a death blow to all such misconceptions. The convention was a big help to this end.

The convention dramatized the entrance of the party into the presidential campaign and focused the attention of the party on it even more effectively than we had dared to hope. The lackadaisical approach to this form of work which has been so noticeable in the past was entirely lacking. The spontaneous enthusiasm which greeted nomination of our candidates Foster and Gitlow and other high points of the convention was inspiring to see. It swept over the whole gathering and took possession of all. The comrades who attempted to prolong it unduly and artificially, however, should be reproved for their overzeal. Gold needs no gilt and proletarian enthusiasm needs no claque.

With our great nominating convention as the starting point, we must now proceed to the development of our election activity with all forces and all speed. The entire work of the party in the elections must be organized as a fighting campaign, discarding all routine and desultory methods. The regular apparatus of the party must be keyed up for this task and, as with all campaigns, a special auxiliary apparatus throughout the party, from top to bottom, must be constructed.

We should aim high, because the prospects and possibilities are great. The election campaign this year ought to bring out all the latent powers and resources of the party, concentrating them all for the first time in a single general struggle. We should aim at tenfold greater propaganda with hundreds of speakers, with thousands of meetings on the street corners, and with our participation in the campaign dramatized in every possible way.

The Communist parties of Germany, France and Poland have utilized the elections this year to extend and consolidate their influence. The elections gave a remarkable demonstration of the stability and growing strength of Communism in Europe and showed that Communists know how to exploit elections in the capitalist state for revolutionary purposes.

For us in America the election campaign, as a means of revolutionary propaganda and mobilization for struggle, has an extraordinary significance. It offers us the opportunity to bring the message of Communism and its platform of daily struggle to tens of thousands of workers and farmers with whom we have not yet established contact and who know nothing of our aims.

The party must see this opportunity clearly and mobilize all of its forces for the fight. The nominating convention showed that all the leading circles of the party are ready to plunge into the work of the campaign with energy and confidence. It remains now to carry the message of the convention to all the party ranks and inspire them with its spirit and enthusiasm.

I Will Go to the Sixth Congress

13 June 1928

Cannon inserted the following statement into the minutes of the Political Committee meeting of 13 June 1928 in response to his nomination as a delegate to the Comintern's Sixth World Congress, which was to be held in Moscow from 17 July to 1 September 1928. The delegation elected at the meeting included all the major party faction leaders, including Cannon.

I have been of the opinion that the big campaigns the party is now engaged in, some of which are in a critical condition, make it highly inadvisable for a large delegation of Polcom members to leave for the Congress, and have been of the opinion that I personally would not go, but in view of the fact that practically all of the leading comrades are going there, I think it is necessary also for me to accept the nomination.

The Voice of the Communist Movement

Published 26 June 1928

The following article by Cannon was published in the Daily Worker. *Cannon had submitted it three weeks prior to its publication, and on June 27 he wrote a letter to the Political Committee protesting the paper's delay in publishing it.*

At a recent meeting of the Political Committee of our party the report of the management of the *Daily Worker* was the first point on the agenda. It was not a new subject for us. The material difficulties of our paper have become an old story.

We have to admit that the leading committee of the party, overburdened with duties and responsibilities, has often taken the existence of our paper too much for granted and has not always given it the direct supervision and support, technically and politically, which its place as the voice of the party demands. This negligence has been reflected in the party circles also and we all share the blame.

At the meeting of the Political Committee to which I have referred, however, a changing attitude was shown and a new note of interest and concern for all the affairs of the paper was struck. I was especially sensitive to this new current because I had come back from my tour of the country with a higher regard for our daily organ and a greater appreciation of its worth to the movement than I had ever felt before.[1]

---

[1] Cannon was on national tour in March and April, speaking on "The American Frame-Up System." It was his first national tour since 1924.

The *Daily Worker* was in almost continual financial crisis in the late 1920s. On 2 June 1928 its front-page headline read: "Grave Crisis May Close *Daily Worker* Soon." The lead article reported that an ultimatum from the printer required the paper to raise $10,000 in two weeks, or close. The first Political Committee meeting to discuss the crisis was held on 14 May 1928. The *DW* Management Committee proposed a number of measures, including cutting the editorial payroll from $500 to $400. Cannon opposed this measure, but he lost the vote.

The *Daily* in Danger

The report of the management gave the whole committee new realization that greater attention and support from the entire party is a life and death question for the paper. Those who were present there know that the alarming notice of danger which has again been issued to the readers of the paper is no "wolf" cry, but a statement of actual facts.

The discussion on the report naturally covered a wide field and dealt with the various aspects of the *Daily*, since they are all bound together and are all part of one general problem. The discussion culminated in a motion to consider the political, technical and financial strengthening of the *Daily Worker* as one of the party's foremost immediate tasks.

This was a necessary and a highly significant decision. It is true we have passed similar motions before which remained only on paper, but the recognition of the overshadowing importance of our central organ is growing and there is reason to believe this motion will bring positive results.

It is time now, in the light of the motion and the exigencies of the moment, to review the whole question of our leading organ openly before the party in order that the party membership will participate in the work of giving life and substance to the motion.

Long before we started to publish the *Daily* we were many times admonished by the Executive Committee of the Communist International, and by Lenin personally, that we must take up this heavy task at all costs. Lenin often said that the publication of a national, daily political organ was one of the first prerequisites for the consolidation of a real political party. His maxim that such a paper should be "the collective propagandist, agitator and organizer of the movement" is familiar to most Communists.

Our paper, despite weaknesses and shortcomings, is fulfilling this role to a much greater degree than many of us realize. Its great authority and influence is especially to be noted by one who travels the country and sees the movement as a whole. The *Daily* shapes the ideological unity of the party and gives a lead to the entire left wing movement on all decisive questions, even in the farthest outposts of the class struggle and the remotest sections of our vast country.

It is needless to say that the *Daily* is highly valued by the party members and is the staff of life to the militants in every field of the labor struggle. The comrades in the field are of the opinion that the paper is improving in many respects. This does not mean that they are blind to its faults. They criticize it with a freedom and often with a sharpness which one only employs toward an institution he feels to be his own.

The party members know that the staff of the *Daily* performs miracles with the resources at hand and with the inadequate support they receive. When we criticize the paper it should be understood that we are criticizing the party. The faults of our daily are the faults of the movement and they can be overcome only insofar as they are freely discussed and the improvement of the paper becomes the collective responsibility of its supporters. The readers of a Communist newspaper must help edit it as well as finance and circulate it.

Needs of *Daily*

In line with the resolution of the Political Committee for the political and technical strengthening of the paper, I wish to set forth a few ideas of what our daily organ needs and will gain with the help of the workers who maintain it.

A stronger staff, from a Communist political standpoint, is one of the first prerequisites to the execution of the decision of the Political Committee. The staff as a whole must be nearer to the party and, for the most part at least, have a stronger background of party experience and political understanding. It is true that newspaper work is a trade for which certain technical qualifications are more or less necessary. It is also true, however, that Communist journalism can be successfully practiced only by those who have a certain minimum of acquaintance with the principles of Communism and the history of the labor movement. Workers can be trained for these tasks. It is easier, as a rule, to make a journalist out of a Communist than to make a Communist out of a journalist.

Worker Correspondence

Worker correspondence—letters from workers in the shops and in the fire of struggle—are the cornerstone of proletarian journalism. We have made but little headway in encouraging and training workers to write for our paper despite the efforts which have been made. More hammering along this line, more deliberate and systematic stimulation and organization of worker correspondence is a necessity.

Our paper should have more articles of a political and general nature and should not be confined to the groove of any established "newspaper" standard. We should not fear to blaze a new trail in form as well as in substance and to make a pattern of our own. We must have more features in the paper, especially light and interesting features, as a balance to the heavier material. The tabloids which have broken away from the old newspaper models consist mainly of light features. Without copying their substance we can learn from their technique. Too much emphasis cannot be placed on this point if we really want to extend our circulation and reach new strata of workers.

The staff of the *Daily* is short-handed and overworked, and underpaid to a scandalous degree. The lack of material resources prevents proper and necessary division of labor.

It has already been acknowledged by the leading party committee that the *Daily* has been greatly handicapped by the limited number of qualified party representatives assigned to work on the paper. Important matters are too frequently entrusted to politically inexperienced reporters, or still worse, we depend on reports of the Federated Press, with their inevitable liberalistic bias. Our *Daily* badly needs, in addition to the present staff, a Washington correspondent and one or two political feature reporters who can be sent out to report important events, from a convention of a political party to a strike or a labor convention, with the assurance that he will draw the correct political inferences as well as tell the story in a readable and interesting way.

The style of our paper must be such as to make every incident in the class struggle an inspiration to the workers for further endeavors. The more accurate it is in handling facts, the more the readers depend on the truth of its accounts, the better will it succeed with this aim. Issues and events of the class struggle must be played up, not played down, but irresponsible exaggeration, which defeats itself, is a fault to be avoided. A reputation for reliability is one of the greatest assets of any publication. The more the workers learn to depend on the truth of our reports the greater will our real influence grow.

A Communist paper cannot take any other journalistic form for its model, least of all in determining the make-up of its staff. Journalists employed on capitalist and reformist papers are merely journalists. They are disconnected from life and struggle, and become mere functionaries of a machine without any connection with its motive forces. That is why they almost always become good-for-nothing cynics, mere craftsmen whose trade is barren words.

Bureaucracy and routine are to a certain extent inherent in the trade of journalism, but they are alien to a Communist newspaper. The staff must be directly and organically connected with general party activities and mass struggles of the workers, and the contents, style and tone of the paper must be a true reflection of this party and labor life.

Our *Daily* which, in spite of enormous difficulties and many shortcomings, has nobly fulfilled its role of guide and voice of the movement for more than four years, is again in the direst straits.

We know that the appeal of the Management Committee was prompted by imminent danger to the life of the paper and we must stake everything on the hope and confidence that the loyalty and self-sacrifice of the workers who love the *Daily Worker* will pull it through the present crisis.

For the future we must aim to put a stronger and broader foundation under the paper. The resolution of the Political Committee showed the way for this and, it is to be hoped, will lead to a closer unity of the *Daily Worker* and its editorial and business staff with the entire party and the left movement of the workers of which it is the voice.

If the greater prominence which the affairs of the *Daily* are to have on the agenda of the CEC, as indicated in the resolution, is reflected in the party ranks, there can be no doubt that the new resources and energies drawn into the work for the paper will firmly establish and safeguard its future.

Trade-Union Questions

Published July 1928

The following article by Cannon was published in the Workers Party's theoretical journal, The Communist. *It supports criticisms of the Workers Party's trade-union work made by the head of the Red International of Labor Unions, A. Lozovsky, at the ECCI's Ninth Plenum in February 1928 and at the RILU's Fourth Congress, held in March-April 1928. Lozovsky attacked the American trade-union policy as the Comintern began its turn toward the ultraleftism of the "Third Period." Both the Foster faction and the Lovestone majority of the Political Committee at first resisted this turn. In particular, they opposed Lozovsky's view that the American party had been "dancing a quadrille the whole time around the AFL and its various unions." Lozovsky's view did coincide, for the moment, with the longstanding position of the Cannon faction.*

Cannon wanted his article printed in the Daily Worker, *but the Political Committee voted on June 9 that it could only be published there if Foster wrote a reply. Not surprisingly, Foster did not choose to publicly attack Lozovsky. Cannon had to be content with publication in* The Communist.

At the plenary meeting of the Central Executive Committee held in the last week of May 1928, the trade union question was the center of the discussion. This was inevitable.

Big changes are taking place in the labor movement. We have gone through big struggles in the trade union field which call for an evaluation of the experiences gained and the drawing of inferences as a guide to future work. The recent World Congress of the Red International of Labor Unions adopted a resolution on America, and our trade union policies and work have recently come in for sharp criticism from comrade Lozovsky in his speeches at the recent congress of the Red International of Labor Unions and in special articles in the press.

Comrade Lozovsky's speeches and articles were so sharp in

tone and so drastic in condemnation as to set the party buzzing and even to provide our opponents with a basis for discussion and moralization. Some comrades reacted quickly to these criticisms and attempted to dispute their validity. The plenum of the CEC hummed with a discussion of the questions raised by these criticisms, and the discussion there was only a beginning. A thorough consideration of all aspects of the trade union question in America is the order of the day.

Perspectives

The first point is the question of perspective. Where are we going, what are the factors in the situation, and what is the general trend? Clarification on this point is necessary first. Confusion, or the reconciling of conflicting perspectives in one thesis or resolution, is a source of errors and of conflict between programs and practices. Such a state of affairs is intolerable.

The trade union resolution adopted at the May plenum of the CEC quotes from and reaffirms the estimate of the February plenum on the growing industrial depression and its radicalizing effects upon the workers. This outlook is entirely correct.

The resolution predicts a growing unrest of the workers and sees a prospect of big struggles, particularly in fields where the workers are unorganized, such as the automobile, rubber, textile and meatpacking industries. Great masses of workers are employed in these industries, they are fiercely exploited, the existing trade unions offer them no protection, and their mood for struggle is growing.

These factors determine our orientation. The only possible line for the Communist Party in the present situation is to calculate upon a growing unrest of the workers and an increasing will to struggle and to put the main emphasis and center of gravity in its trade union work on the organization of the unorganized and the preparation for strikes.

The Decline of the Old Unions

In recent years, the AFL unions, retreating before the assaults of the employers, have been declining in numbers and narrowing their base even more to skilled workers. The smashing of such unions as the steel workers, packinghouse workers and railroad shop crafts has robbed the AFL of a large mass of unskilled and semi-skilled workers who were a source of strength and a reservoir of militancy. This has wrought a profound change in its basic composition. The disintegration of the United Mine Workers union tremendously accelerates this process and raises very sharply the whole question of the future course and development of the American labor movement.

One of the hallmarks of the AFL unions under the leadership of the dominant bureaucrats has been an absolute incapacity for struggle against the open shop offensive. The policy of resistance has been replaced by the theory and practice of retreat and surrender; the "labor" leaders appeal for the right of the old organizations to exist in company-unionized form, by consent of the employers, as agencies of efficient production.

This course corresponds with the policy of the ruling bureaucracy. These bosses of the unions not only present no fighting program for the safeguarding of the unions, but openly and systematically sabotage every impulse in this direction coming from the rank and file. Their crusade against the Communists and the left wing is a part of their policy of erecting barriers against the unskilled and unorganized workers and of stamping out the remnants of militancy in the existing unions in order, as they hope, to render them acceptable to the employers.

A degeneration of class spirit in the old unions is the inevitable outcome of such a course. An inability to defend the existing unions and labor standards and an incapacity to organize the unorganized workers—the key to the future of organized labor in America—follow from it.

The Crisis in the Labor Movement

The American labor movement today is in a profound crisis. Our estimation of trade union problems and the formulation of tactics must proceed from this premise.

The crisis in the labor movement consists in the fact that the trade unions are being broken up by the growing offensive of the bosses and the black treachery and anti-proletarian policy of the official trade union leadership. The unions are decreasing in membership, narrowing down more and more to a caste of skilled workers and growing more incapable of defending the existing standards and of organizing the unorganized and unskilled.

The crisis in the trade unions must be taken together with the position of the American working class as a whole, the increasing pressure put upon the masses of unorganized workers in the basic industries and their reaction to it. Failure to proceed from this general standpoint will lead to false and one-sided conclusions.

The growing unrest of the workers in many industries and their increasing readiness for struggle brook no delay. The future of the American labor movement is bound up with this question. The prospect of big struggles is on the agenda of the proximate future and for these struggles organization forms must be provided.

The existing unions, manned and officered by agents of the bosses, will not provide these forms and will not organize the unorganized masses for struggle. On the contrary, the present trade union officialdom will strive in every way to prevent the organization of these workers and will develop even more open and notorious methods of treachery against them in the coming battles.

The old faker-ridden unions failed to organize the workers in the preceding years of prosperity. With their narrowing base and increasing tendency to become guilds of labor aristocrats, and with the reactionary leaders tightening their death grip upon them, they will serve even less as the medium of organizing the masses of unskilled and unorganized in the period that lies ahead.

Organization of the Unorganized

No two opinions on this question can be allowed. We must face this issue squarely and give a clear and definite answer. Otherwise the formulation of correct tactics for the left wing—one of the most decisive factors in the future development of the American labor movement—will be impossible.

It is the historic task of the Communist Party and the left wing to organize the unorganized masses of workers, forming new unions without hesitation in all cases where the old unions do not exist or cannot function as real organs of struggle. This does not stand in contradiction to the continuation and intensification of our work within the old unions, even the most reactionary, but is bound up with it in one task. We are not confronted with the question of "either one or the other," but of combining the two together in a united policy. The real tactical question facing the left wing is the question of emphasis, of center of gravity, in trade union work in the period at hand. That emphasis belongs undoubtedly to the work of organizing the masses of unskilled and semi-skilled workers in the heavier industries who are now unorganized, who are destined to play the decisive role in the class struggle and whom the trade union bureaucracy cannot and will not organize.

Comrade Lozovsky's Criticism

Has the party been following the right line in these vital questions up till now? Were the critical remarks of comrade Lozovsky justified by actual facts?

Conflicting answers have been given to these questions, but I am of the opinion that if we face the matter objectively and with an eye to the elaboration of the correct tactics for the future, a conflict on these points can arise only between those who have conflicting views on the main problems of our trade union work. In any case, the questions must be answered because our future work cannot be separated entirely from the past.

No one can accuse comrade Lozovsky of over-politeness or of understatement of the faults of the party's trade union work. He accused the party straight out of appealing to "the leaders of the reformist trade unions to organize the unorganized, save the unions, lead strikes, etc.," and he says we have been hampered by a false interpretation of united front tactics and a "fetish of dual unionism" which prevented us from starting to form new unions of unorganized workers.

There is no doubt that some of comrade Lozovsky's criticisms were couched in exaggerated terms, and some of them do not correspond literally to the facts as we know them. But there is likewise no doubt that his strictures contain a good kernel of truth and that they, together with the resolution of the Red

International congress, have helped the party decisively in overcoming inertia and straightening its line on this important question.

Resolutions and Practice

It is true, if we want to be formalistic, we can point to resolutions adopted at various times during the past year to show that we understood the right line on the organization of the unorganized and provided for everything. But the trouble with us has been a lethargy in taking the decisive steps to put our resolutions into practice when opportunities presented themselves—and this is precisely the main point of comrade Lozovsky's criticism.

It is easy to cite objective difficulties as a reason for our slackness in attempting to organize new unions in new fields or in fields where the old unions are disintegrating. The difficulties are many and easy to enumerate—but this, in my opinion, only begs the question. The point at issue is not simply how much we succeeded with the work of organizing the unorganized into new unions, but how much we really tried where we had the chance and how much we were held back by inhibitions and reservations regarding the full import of our own resolutions.

Why were we asleep in Colorado, allowing the IWW to monopolize the organization of the coal miners and to introduce new elements of confusion and reaction into the miners' situation? Why did we not begin a year ago at least to form the nucleus of a new union of the unorganized miners in the coal fields of Western Pennsylvania whom the Lewis machine deserted and betrayed—and thus prepare a foundation for the strike attempted there in April of this year? And why was there a delay of a whole year after the beginning of the coal strike before the left wing held its open national conference because of the possible implications of such a direct challenge to the Lewis machine?[1]

The argument that we were behind in these matters only because of the lack of forces does not hold water. That might be an explanation of failure if we had really made the attempt.

---

[1] See note pp. 480-481, on the Colorado IWW strike. Note 4, pp. 484-485, deals with the fight over calling a national conference of the opposition in the miners union.

The true answer must be sought in a certain disparity between our resolutions on the trade union question and our actual practice, in a certain hesitancy in carrying them out in their full implications.

The criticism of comrade Lozovsky and the resolution of the Red International congress have stimulated us to close this gap. The trade union resolution adopted at the plenum of the Central Executive Committee is absolutely right when it says our failure to make greater progress with the actual building of new organizations can be explained, among other obvious reasons, by "a slowness of our party in orienting itself to a situation which has demanded a more decided emphasis on independent unionism."

Self-Criticism

Of course the dogmatists of independent unionism, in principle and at all costs, now step forward with the claim that they were always right and we were always wrong. That was to be expected because it is a long time since they have had anything to talk about. But their words are just as hollow now as they have been in the past. The Communist Party, with its correct tactics, has been in the center of practically every fight of the workers of America in recent years while the tactics of these dogmatists of separatism have sidetracked them from the living movements and mass struggles of the workers and converted their organizations into isolated sects.

I think some comrades are inclined to attach undue importance to the arguments of these sectarians. To cite their propaganda as a reason for soft-pedaling an open and straightforward review and discussion of our experiences and problems would lead us astray entirely. The fear of "what our opponents will say" has often been a refuge from self-criticism and an obstacle to the elaboration of correct tactics. It is our task to examine our problems and to practice self-criticism in the true Bolshevik manner, disregarding the apostles of isolation and all other opponents of our policy.

Work in the Old Unions

The trade union resolution adopted by the CEC is a necessary supplement to the resolution of the Red International and is not in contradiction to it.[2] Both resolutions proceed from the same perspective of a sharpening of the class struggle with more frequent clashes between the workers and the capitalists. Both resolutions assign the decisive role to the unorganized workers in the basic industries and orient their policy accordingly.

The resolution of the CEC gives a necessary and more elaborate analysis of the situation within the existing unions and calls for an intensification of our work within them to win the rank and file workers away from the control of the reactionaries.

Increased and intensified work within the old unions must go hand in hand with the organization of the unorganized. There can be no question of abandoning the work in the old unions and neither comrade Lozovsky nor any leading or influential member of the party has proposed that. No doubt such a sentiment could develop in the rank and file of the left wing, with its tradition in this respect, if it were given any encouragement. Such encouragement must not be given and all signs of such tendencies must be combatted, for the three million workers organized in the existing unions are not to be surrendered to the bureaucrats. These workers, with our help, will carry on battles in spite of their traitorous leaders.

The Question of Emphasis

The real question here is one of emphasis. The articles of comrade Lozovsky, the resolution of the Red International and the resolution of the CEC all put the emphasis in the present situation where it belongs: on the organization of the unorganized into new unions. To place the emphasis at the moment on the other side, to raise a scare about abandoning the work in the old unions where none exists, or to deny that the party has been remiss on the question of organizing the unorganized, might easily, in their objective consequences, become a cover for again distorting the main line and putting the center of gravity in the wrong place.

---

2 In sharp contrast to the February plenum, the May CEC plenum was not even mentioned in the *Daily Worker*, which published neither the resolution nor any of the speeches made there.

The obstacles in the path of organizing the workers in the basic industries of America are truly enormous, and the present forces at our disposal are small. There is no need to minimize the difficulties; they will multiply and confront us at every turn. The state power of capitalism will obstruct the new union movement with the fiercest persecution, and the workers will soon find that they are not done with the treacheries of the labor fakers when they seek to form new unions.

Between the decision to organize the unorganized masses and the actual formation and consolidation of new unions lies a long and stony road. But history has laid out that task for the Communist Party and the left wing, and we must begin the work in earnest.

Against the Opportunism of the Lovestone Majority

25 July 1928

The following transcript of Cannon's remarks to the Sixth World Congress of the Communist International was published in International Press Correspondence, *11 August 1928. The Cannon faction had cemented its bloc with the Foster group, submitting a joint document to the American Commission on "The Right Danger in the American Party." Meanwhile, Cannon obtained a copy of Leon Trotsky's critique of the Comintern's draft program, which won him to Trotsky's Left Opposition.*

Comrades, the draft thesis of comrade Bukharin calls for a stronger struggle against reformist tendencies by the Communist parties. This policy, which is correct on an international scale, also applies to America despite the attempts to "exclude" America from this international policy and set it aside as an exception. There is a right danger in America and this right danger is accentuated by the opportunistic policy of the majority of the Central Committee—the Lovestone-Pepper group.[1]

The conditions of the present period of American imperialism create the possibilities and the prospects of growing struggles of the American workers, and provide our party with abundant opportunities to press forward as the leader of these struggles. The growing world antagonisms, the mass unemployment, attacks on the workers, rationalization, wage cuts and so forth are features of the present situation in America. There is a deep crisis within the labor movement in America, which is being seriously weakened and undermined under the blows of the employers and the treachery of the bureaucrats. On the other side, as a reaction

[1] Pepper had returned to the U.S. in March 1928, though he had evidently been ordered to Korea by the Communist International. He actively participated in the deliberations of the Political Committee, using the name Swift.

to these circumstances, there is a growing series of struggles of the workers and a readiness for struggle on the part of the semi-skilled and unskilled masses.

In the face of this deepening discontent of the workers, of their readiness for struggle, the majority of the Central Committee has an overcautious attitude. It has a conservative outlook and policy which it pursues in every sphere of party work. This policy of the Central Committee of the party is paralyzing it in the midst of the greatest opportunities of its career.

In a document which we have presented to the American Commission, we have enumerated the situation in great detail. I want to point out a few of the particular and general errors of the Central Committee of the party proceeding from its wrong analysis and its failure to draw the correct conclusions.

In this changing of the class struggle in America, the beginning of the sharpening of the objective conditions and the passing of the workers over from the period of apathy to the period of fight, all members of the Central Committee have shown certain confusion and have been guilty of certain errors. The minority has made some errors, but there is a deep distinction in this respect: that our errors have been incidental, they have been recognized and are being corrected, whereas the majority has followed a consistent wrong line and adheres to it to this very day.

Let me cite one of the basic errors of the Central Committee showing its false estimate of the Socialist Party and its calculations upon a left wing within it which would help us to fight for a labor party. At the time when the Socialist Party had reached a state of its most complete degeneration and was merging itself openly with the American Federation of Labor bureaucracy, the police and the government in the fight against the workers—our Central Committee was capable of such a proposal that we send members of the Communist Party into the Socialist Party to "bore from within."[2]

---

[2] The proposal to enter the Socialist Party was discussed in the Political Committee on 14 December 1927. Cannon had put forward the following motion:

"1. Under the present circumstances our main tasks with regard to the SP are to establish more clearly and sharply the independent ideology of our party as against the SP, to strengthen the morale and antagonism of our party members in the fight against the SP, and to overcome any tendencies objectively leading

(continued)

That was not merely an incidental or isolated error—it flowed from the wholly false conception, and the motions of the minority to reject such a policy as absolutely false were defeated by the Polcom. Following from such a conception, we had the "Panken policy" of our party. In New York City, there is a Socialist judge named Panken, and he has been a judge for long years and is a typical social democrat, that is to say, an enemy of the workers. When he came up for election our party conceived the brilliant policy of voting for Mr. Panken in the election. We fought against that, but our fight was unsuccessful. They said the Panken election was a question of "a united front against reaction."

Who composed this "united front"? First of all the Socialist Party and then the Republican Party of New York City endorsed Mr. Panken to show that they had confidence in him.

The same thing happened in Boston in the Bearak case and in Milwaukee where the proposals were made not to put up our own candidates against Mr. Victor Berger, the Socialist chairman of the Socialist Party of America.

Not only in the sphere of the estimate of the Socialist Party and tactics regarding it has our party majority followed a false and stubbornly opportunistic line, but the same thing has been done in the field of trade unionism. The American Federation of Labor is steadily declining and becoming restricted to a caste of highly skilled workers. The mass unions of the AFL are being broken up. For a number of years this policy has been going on and the trade union leadership has merged more and more with the whole governmental apparatus and capitalist machine in general. The obvious conclusion is, orient the party's policy on the organizing of the unskilled masses into new unions. The RILU and Comintern have been hammering upon the party with this line. The minority of the party has pressed for this. But the biggest

---

towards the recognition of the SP as a bona fide workers organization in which the Communists can play the role of the left wing.

"2. Our tactics should be centered on a frontal attack against the SP all along the line combined with united front maneuvers with left-inclined sections of the SP, that under present conditions it is not tactically correct to send party members into the SP."

Cannon's motion lost, though Lovestone was forced to back away from his original proposal.

obstacle to the party proceeding to do this duty is precisely the delaying, the hesitancy, the opportunistic policy of the majority of the Central Committee of the party.

One can cite a number of instances beginning with the mine strike; at the beginning of this strike more than a year ago a project for the holding of a national left wing conference was made by the minority as a prelude to the organization of the struggle to wrest the control from the Lewis gang, which is now taking place. This was rejected by the Central Committee as a "dual union policy" and was delayed for eleven months. The strike was a year old and had spent its force before our party organized the national conference of the left wing, the prelude to the formation of the new union. In a number of fields, opportunities have been presented to the party to organize new unions which have not been grasped. Is that merely incidental? No. That failure proceeds also from the conservative estimate that they make of the situation in America and of the prospects for struggle.

We say there is no more stubborn resistance anywhere in the International to the resolutions of the last congress of the RILU than in the leadership of our party. The same conservativeness before the power of American capitalism and the bureaucratic American Federation of Labor paralyzes the party in this as in all other fields, and it all proceeds from this false estimate and incapacity to lead the party in the period of growing struggles.

In the election campaign we have the same thing: a hesitancy, delay, refusal to enter our party candidates until after the Socialist Party was already in the field, a calculation as far back as March that there might yet be a labor party in America for the 1928 elections. The labor party has been envisioned as the leader of the masses. A whole series of articles has appeared in the *Daily Worker* referring to the labor party as the "emancipating force" of the American masses and the only hope of the workers. In the united front, in the trade union work, in cooperatives, in women's work—touch any phase of party activities and you find the same thread of opportunistic policy I have mentioned in these other cases.

And what does the leadership of the party do in the face of this? They denied the existence of the right danger in America. In the plenum of the party, held only last May, not one single word was mentioned in the political resolution or in the political reports against the right danger, and the whole debate was a polemic against those comrades who are criticizing the party from the standpoint of the policy of the Comintern and RILU. The majority of our party has consolidated itself into a close-bound faction, with all the discredited remnants of the Lore group, with all the right wing and opportunistic elements of the party. They deny that there is any such right danger.

They cover up their opportunistic policy by misrepresentations of the position of the minority of the Central Committee and then fight against the straw men set up by these misrepresentations. We had an example of it from this tribune only yesterday in the person of the internationally known exponent of correct political policies, comrade Pepper. He read out of our document words that were not in it and then polemicized against the words which were not in our document. He spoke for nearly an hour against us on the ground that we say American imperialism is "already on the decline"—when we say nothing of the sort, as our document shows. And one might ask, are such methods possible in the Communist International?

We have in America big objective possibilities. We have possibilities before our party to put itself at the head of great struggles of the workers. They are already in progress and they are growing. Strikes are imminent in a number of great industries and this situation calls for a resolute, clear, aggressive Communist policy. The opportunities of the party to establish itself as a real leader of the masses are paralyzed by the leadership of the party, by its opportunistic outlook, by its fight against precisely those comrades who want to straighten out the line of the party. The Communist International must correct the right errors in the party and establish guarantees of the carrying out of the correct policy.

Our struggle is for a correct Communist policy which will give the party the opportunity to make the most of the great objective possibilities in the present and immediate future situations.

I Stand on My Record

27 October 1928

The following are excerpts from the uncorrected transcript of the interrogation of Cannon at the Workers Party Political Committee meeting of 27 October 1928, at which Cannon, Max Shachtman and Martin Abern were expelled for Trotskyism. The meeting was the culmination of more than a week of "investigation" of the three, who had been accused by William Z. Foster, Alexander Bittelman and Philip Aronberg on October 16 of trying to organize a Trotskyist faction.

Cannon and his two lieutenants were removed from their posts in the International Labor Defense at a Political Committee meeting on October 16. At that meeting Cannon temporized, as he did when questioned again on October 19. It was only on October 27 that he, Abern and Shachtman admitted they were Trotskyists and submitted their statement, "For the Russian Opposition," which declared that "The Opposition in the Communist Party of the Soviet Union led by L.D. Trotsky has been fighting for the unity of the Comintern and all its sections on the basis of the victory of Leninism. The correctness of the position taken by the Russian Opposition over a period of five years of struggle has been fully confirmed by events." The document went on to support Trotsky's struggle for internal party democracy, his opposition to Stalin's program of "socialism in one country," Trotsky's economic program for the Soviet Union, his struggle against the Anglo-Russian Trade Union Committee and his struggle against the Comintern's disastrous policy in China.

The Political Committee asked Cannon very little about the substance of his positions. In his questioning of Cannon, Bittelman is obviously at pains to dissociate the Foster group from their former factional allies. We publish here only those sections where Cannon reflects on the history of his faction in the Workers Party. Transcripts of all the Cannon interrogation sessions were mimeoed and attached to the Political Committee minutes.

Bittelman: Comrade Cannon, would you say today that it was correct for you in 1926 to unite with Lovestone and carry on a campaign in the party against Fosterism and Foster as the main danger in the party?

Cannon: At that moment, it was correct. In general, I stand upon the platform which I stood on then. In general, the position we took in this whole fight I stand on now.

Bittelman: But I am concerned in clearing up a particular question. Was it correct for you to unite with Lovestone then and initiate a campaign and jointly carry it out against Fosterism and Foster in the party?

Cannon: I have answered several times that in general, all the actions of our group taken in that period since the struggle arose in the 1925 convention have been in the main correct.

Bittelman: Why did you, comrade Cannon, advocate a split in the minority in Moscow?

Cannon: I did not advocate a split in the minority in Moscow.

Bittelman: You did not advocate a split. Why did you advocate a theory that the danger in the minority comes from the left?

Cannon: I believe this is correct as a general theoretical formula, that a group which is fighting as a left wing against a right wing in the party, inevitably would have a tendency to attract to it ultraleft elements, rather than right elements who would naturally gravitate towards the right wing. I believe such a formula is borne out by the history of political struggles, particularly throughout the life of the Comintern, and I believe it applies vice versa and I was not alone in that opinion; comrades Hathaway, Dunne, Gomez and others were of the same opinion.

Bittelman: In other words, you still maintain that when a group in our party, speaking concretely, the minority, the danger which the minority itself suffers comes from the left?

Cannon: I believe there will be more danger for a left wing to attract ultraleft elements rather than right elements.

Bittelman: And these ultraleft dangers are more serious than the right, in your opinion?

Cannon: I believe there is a danger of getting off the track to the left, rather than to the right.

Bittelman: Why did you propose to the comrades of the former Foster group in Moscow the formation of a new group with possibly comrade Weinstone and others, as possible allies?

Cannon: That is not true. I did not make such a proposition. I am prepared, if the body wishes, to explain what actually transpired out of which this fiction arose, although I don't think it has any special bearing, but I have no fear to answer that question. In fact I will volunteer to answer. I am not one of those who in the time of new alignments base much political significance on private conversations and caucus secrets and so forth. I have nothing but contempt for this type of politician. I think that the attitude of responsible political leaders has to rest itself upon political acts, documents, speeches, articles, etc. And I have always undertaken to estimate comrades in this manner, not on the basis of private conversations. As a matter of fact, I have always conducted an educational struggle among the comrades with whom I have been associated against this philistine method, and the reason is quite clear to any responsible leader—because it is impossible to establish any political facts by private conversations which lead only to denials and mutual recriminations and present the issue of veracity between comrades and poison the atmosphere and make political discussions impossible. I believe only tenth-rate politicians are capable of conducting polemics on this basis. It is known to comrade Bittelman and others that within the minority in Moscow, I conducted a struggle against the idea that the minority, as at present constituted, is sufficiently broad-based to lead the party. I did not conceive of a small faction, but a group which would broaden itself sufficiently to lead the party and that naturally presupposes alignments with elements of the Lovestone group which is now in control. The discussion concerning Weinstone arose as follows: that I had a conversation with Foster, which I reported to some of the comrades that have been offering themselves for leadership and told them that I was highly pleased with Foster's expression in which he stated that he also was of the opinion that we did not have a sufficiently broad group and that we must have such an attitude towards Weinstone of possible future alliances. I think that it would be an absurdity to believe that on the basis of the minority as constituted in Moscow, it would be possible to exclude all other comrades in the party and that is the basis of the rumor that I had advocated a new group. If I had, I should not hesitate to say so. It is only a question of facts. I did not see any intelligent basis for an arbitrary decision to form a new group as I believe a new group should proceed from a serious political basis.

Bittelman: In discussing Weinstone at that time, with whomever you discussed it, you knew that Weinstone stands for a definite political line in the party and belongs to the Lovestone group and the minority was fighting in Moscow the right danger in the party. How, on what consistent political basis, could you, would you, consider a leading member of the right wing as a candidate for possible future relations?

Cannon: I estimate political leaders not only by the immediate political position they take, but over a period, and by that one is able to estimate, to a certain extent, what new positions may exist in the future. I think it was no accident, for instance, that Weinstone stood with us a year ago. I think it proceeded from a certain political attitude, and that he helped us to fight the Lovestone group a year ago, and I think it would be no accident in the future, if Weinstone changes his present position.

...

Lovestone: Do you think you were right in March 1924 when the question of Trotskyism came before the party in your objecting then to condemn Trotskyism and support the position of the CEC of the CPSU?

Cannon: I do not recall the exact form of the motion. As I recalled it, I objected to a position being taken until documents had been received. I think it was entirely correct to ask for the documents before we took a position.

Lovestone: You state that the Central Committee has been mechanically foisted on the party by the ECCI. On what basis do you make that statement?

Cannon: On the basis of the decisions taken a year ago, which denied the CEC the right to reconstruct the Polcom and to elect its own officers, and by the subsequent decisions which have been more or less a confirmation of that attitude.

Lovestone: Do you question the authority of the last party convention in the election of the CEC?

Cannon: No.

Lovestone: Do you think there was anything done in the way of arrangements of that convention to lend any support to your conclusion that the present leadership was mechanically foisted on the party?

Cannon: Yes, I do. I think first the instructions of the ECCI denying the Central Committee the right to reorganize the Political Committee and leaving the apparatus in control of the Lovestone faction. Secondly, the supplementary decision.[1] Thirdly, the telegram sent to the party against the opposition. Fourthly, the factional support given to the Lovestone faction by comrade Ewert, the representative of the Comintern, was also in this direction, also comrade Ewert's arbitrary denial of our right for contests in the election. All of these things helped to shape the present composition of the party leadership.

...

Bittelman: I would like to ask a couple of questions. I will ask comrade Cannon. In 1925, comrade Cannon, you were primarily instrumental in splitting the former Foster group, which was then the majority of the Central Committee and was controlling the party convention in 1925, and by splitting the then majority of the party known as the Foster group, you are primarily responsible for enabling what is now known as the Lovestone group to get control of the party, which they have held since then. Do you say in the light of your present experience that this split was a mistake?

Cannon: On our part, no. On the part of the Foster group, yes. First of all I was not the one who proposed to turn over the lead-

[1] In addition to the official 1927 resolution on the American question, there was an "Agreement for the Carrying Out of the Resolution on the American Question Adopted by the Presidium of the Executive Committee of the ECCI." It was signed by Lovestone, Gitlow, Pepper, Cannon, Foster and Weinstone, and sealed by the ECCI. The agreement stipulated a number of measures to be taken in organizing the Workers Party's Fifth Convention, including the ratio for election of delegates (one delegate for every five members at the district level, one for every 200 members at the national convention) and the proportion of minority seats on the incoming Central Committee (at least 13 out of 35).

ership of the party to what was then the Ruthenberg group; that came from the Foster group and I opposed it.

Aronberg: Your proposal was carried.

Cannon: To make the position straight, let me state that the proposal of the Foster group was that Foster retire from the Central Committee, become a private citizen of the party and turn over the party to the Ruthenberg-Lovestone group. My proposal was that we construct the Central Committee on a parity basis, which was carried out with this amendment as a concession to Foster, who proposed Green [Gusev] be the impartial representative, which I was not for but conceded as a concession.

Bittelman: So you still think it was correct to split the group?

Cannon: The split arose later, on principled questions, and I am willing to state any time that we were right in principle in this fight and we don't give up our fight.

...

Minor: How far back in point of party history do you see a consistent line in your position and struggles in the party leading to your present position?

Cannon: In general, my whole record.

Minor: You consider that it extends back to the struggles which began in the Polcom of the party in 1923?

Cannon: Before that. Back to the time when we formed the party. Back to years and years of revolutionary record before that.

...

Swift [Pepper]: But you yourself said that in Moscow you abstained from voting on the decision of the Sixth Congress on the Trotsky question but you never mentioned that in the delegation, in any meeting of our delegation. How do you explain that? Is that a fair and frank attitude towards the party?

Cannon: It is my practice to come to the party with definite proposals. Always has been. I think that is correct.

Wagenknecht: Knowing as you do that the Foster-Bittelman group intends to carry on a serious struggle in the American party against the right wing danger, are you not really trying to organize a new right wing group in the American party under the cloak of leftist phrases, objectively giving support to the right wing in the party and the Communist International, thereby vitiating the struggle against the right wing danger?

Cannon: I have stated, I think in the document, our estimate of the situation. I believe that the position taken by the opposition logically and inevitably leads it to the platform which we espouse. I believe that an opposition group that tries to stand between these two bases on fundamental principled questions cannot exist. I believe the opposition has one of two paths of adopting the inevitable implications of its platform or giving up this platform and becoming camp followers of the present leadership, and there are definite indications already that this process is true.

Swift: You mean the second one.

Cannon: No, both processes are true. When principled questions are presented in their full implications, I don't think it is possible to stand in between. I stated in the document that the logical banner bearers against Trotsky are the present leaders of the party, that the aspirations of the Foster group to seize this banner for themselves to secure thereby their organization positions can succeed only insofar as they give up their opposition attitude and adopt the platform in its entirety of the present majority of the party, and I make this prediction for the stenographic record: That one will see this process very quickly beginning, and that some of those who have shouted very loudly against us in the very recent period under the banner of the opposition will find it impossible to continue along this line and will have to take one attitude or the other.

...

Stachel: Isn't it a fact, comrade Cannon, that since the first discussion on Trotsky, throughout all the discussions we have had in the party here, that you have never spoken on the question? At a meeting of the plenum of the Central Committee or at any party membership meeting?

Cannon: That is true.

Stachel: Do you think that the fact that you have never spoken, although you have always voted for the motions of the Central Committee, has something to do with the fact that you had doubts on the question throughout this period?

Cannon: Yes.

. . .

Appendix 1

Cannon's Collaborators

Cannon cited the important campaigns in which the Workers Party was involved when he explained his reluctance to go to Moscow for the Comintern's Sixth World Congress in the summer of 1928. Cannon was justifiably worried—the entire top leadership was scheduled to attend the Congress. But the party had just launched a U.S. presidential election campaign. Communist organizers had mobilized massive support among the miners, and building on the success of the April 1 "Save the Union" convention, they had launched a call for a national convention in Pittsburgh in September to organize a new miners union. Over 26,000 cotton mill workers in New Bedford, Massachusetts were out on strike against a proposed 10 percent wage cut, under the leadership of a party-organized Textile Mills Committee, and the International Labor Defense had just launched a national campaign for the release of Mooney and Billings.

As is apparent from the material we publish in this appendix, leading Cannon faction members were concerned with pushing forward the real work of the party in the summer of 1928 rather than in the factional games-playing and posturing that occupied most of the rest of the second-string factionalists appointed to the interim Political Committee. Martin Abern was representative of the Cannon faction on this Political Committee; Cannon had tried, unsuccessfully, to have Shachtman appointed as well. Arne Swabeck also played a big role in the debates at the top of the party that summer. He had been appointed a party field organizer in late 1927, and from March 1928 he had special responsibility for the miners work.

International Labor Defense Activities (1 January-1 July 1928)

by Martin Abern

23 July 1928

Almost as soon as the delegation left for Moscow in early June, Lovestone's factional lieutenants opened an attack on the ILD. At the Political Committee meeting on June 2, Benjamin Gitlow, who was acting secretary in Lovestone's absence, noted that he had been getting a lot of "complaints" about the ILD. Gitlow demanded a report from Abern. Abern's report, published below, was attached to the minutes of the PC meeting of July 23. Gitlow was unable to make factional hay with it: the PC adopted the report unanimously, including the previously controversial proposal for founding a Jewish section of the ILD.

Report represents period of intense and varied activities and campaigns. According to applications received by national office, 70 new branches organized since January 1st, averaging 20 members each. Hungarian and Italian sections organized and developed. Among important activities are:

A. National tour in 35 cities and nearly 50 meetings against American frame-up system by James P. Cannon, coupled with three-month subscription drive for *Labor Defender*. Tour also laid basis for Mooney and Billings campaign and Centralia prisoners campaign.[1] California district conference held during tour at San Francisco to lay basis for campaigns. Highly successful tour.

B. Illustrated lecture tour by Max Shachtman, editor *Labor Defender*, on "Revolution and Counterrevolution in China" in 28 cities. Successful tour and demonstrated value of illustrated forms of propaganda.

C. National tour against Polish fascism by David Bogen, special Hromada representative.[2] Special committee against Polish

---

[1] See "The Red Month of November," page 472, for an account of the IWW Centralia prisoners. See glossary for Mooney and Billings.

[2] Hromada was the acronym of the White Russian [Byelorussian] Workers Party, whose leaders were then on trial in Vilnius.

fascism with ILD as main force organized for campaign and tour. Several hundred dollars raised for Polish prisoners.

D. Special campaigns, consular protests, etc. on behalf of Béla Kun and special trains in Italy organized.[3] Still continuing.

E. Circularization in campaign to provide books for labor prisoners had special dramatic and propaganda appeal and value. Plan now adopted, by German Red Aid.

F. Amongst literature issued was:

1. Eight-page folder, Bonita, Mendola, Moleski Case, selling at one penny. 20,000 copies.[4]
2. Four-page leaflet, "What Is International Labor Defense," 150,000 in English, 20,000 in Italian and by arrangement with Jewish section in Chicago an edition in Yiddish.

G. Bonita, Mendola, Moleski Defense. Special defense committee with ILD as main force organized. National office had representative in field almost continuously. Aided in raising funds and expended some $700 directly in the case.

H. *Labor Defender*. The circulation of the *Labor Defender* as a result of a systematic development of policy and campaign has grown phenomenally since January 1st. Briefly, the circulation has increased from 10,000 in January to 22,000 with the July issue, a special Mooney-Billings issue. The subscriptions have increased from 1,500 to 5,500. The bundle increases have been from 8,500 to 16,500. The 22,000 circulation (printing is only according to actual orders) is a circulation greater than the combined circulation of the *Daily Worker*, *Labor Unity*, and *The Communist* combined, which are representative organs in other important fields.

Our analysis shows that this development toward swiftly increasing circulation will continue and we have set 30,000 as our January 1, 1929 goal. For informative purposes we might state that we propose to maintain the lower 10¢ retail price of the magazine

---

[3] The June 1928 *Labor Defender* reported that Béla Kun had been arrested by the Austrian government in Vienna, and that he was being threatened with deportation to Hungary. Evidently he was soon released.

[4] Sam Bonita was president of UMW Local 1703 in Pittston, in the Pennsylvania Anthracite region. He had shot and killed a local UMW district official, Frank Agaty, after Agaty attacked him in the district union office in the midst of a heated dispute about a pit closing. Bonita was charged with murder, as were fellow local members Steven Mendola and Adam Moleski, who had gone to the union offices with Bonita and participated in the argument.

and, therefore, we must continue publication as yet at a slight loss till the magazine's circulation grows a bit more. There is, however, a much higher cost involved in publishing a labor pictorial than other kinds of publications. The circulation which is being attained by the *Labor Defender* is, we suggest, also a base for and demonstration that, with a systematic organization drive and policy, the circulation of labor publications can be substantially increased. Also the party should be in a position to utilize the membership increase of ILD and the *Labor Defender* increase in circulation for party membership increase also.

The ILD is also conducting at the present time a number of campaigns. Among these are:

1. The Miners' Defense campaign. The hundreds of arrests in various sections of the coal regions have confronted the ILD with special problems. In addition to the activities conducted on behalf of the Colorado Miners' Defense and the Bonita, Mendola, Moleski defense in the Anthracite coal regions, the main miners' defense activity exists in Ohio, Pennsylvania, West Virginia and Illinois. The National Office thus far has borne the major cost in financing the defense of the miners. In addition, in the Ohio and West Virginia territory a special Miners' Defense drive with the issuance of a special Miners' Defense stamp has been carried on through the Cleveland secretary in order to spread the raising of funds. Rather than a special National Miners' Defense drive which might affect the relief work, the ILD entered into a special week for relief and defense of the miners, with the National Miners' Relief Committee, for the week of July 22nd to July 29th, and which, it is expected, will thereby make it possible to cover the cost for miners' defense cases.

2. In the New Bedford textile strike there are some 72 cases of textile workers on hand. The National Office has helped to defray costs in the textile region, but in an endeavor to meet the actual needs, a special textile defense and relief week is being conducted from July 15th to 22nd. In the New Bedford cases there have occurred errors in policy, which matters were dealt with by the party elsewhere.

The National Office has sent comrades to Pittsburgh from time to time to aid and advise in the work. The National Office had a full-time worker in Colorado also during the period of the strike. The *Labor Defender* has steadily dealt with the miners' and textile strikes as the major campaigns and has called for support. The *Labor Defender* has been circulated widely in the mining regions and also is being conducted and extended in the textile regions. From reports coming to the National Office from various ILD locals, much money and relief in the form of clothes, etc., has gone directly to the National Miners' Relief Committee or the Workers International Relief, and here and there the impression has prevailed that funds sent to the relief organizations also covered defense. The National Office has tried to clarify always the functions of relief and defense work.[5]

3. A major campaign which ILD hopes to develop into the largest campaign in its history is the campaign now being conducted for the release of Tom Mooney and Warren Billings. This campaign is already gaining impetus swiftly. The labor press is using our material more extensively and even the capitalist press, including the *New York World*, the *New York Telegram* and the *New York Graphic*, mentioning only the New York papers, have used our pictures and press material, and there has been editorial comment. Criticism might be made at this point of some sections of the party press which hardly carry, if at all, the ILD press material. A program and motions on the Tom Mooney and Warren Billings campaign is herein proposed, many points of which have already been executed.

4. Another major campaign is the campaign for the release of the Centralia prisoners, for which a program and motions are also herein proposed. This campaign is well under way and the ILD has taken leadership. The prisoners themselves, their closest adviser, Elmer Smith, and one group of the IWW is working closely with us. The other section is now being compelled to recognize the ILD as the main force in the drive, although this group headed by Payne has fought the ILD steadily.[6] A special provi-

---

5 The party's miners relief work was organized under the auspices of the Workers International Relief, not the ILD. The WIR was an international organization with headquarters in Berlin. Founded in 1921 to organize economic aid for Soviet Russia, the WIR expanded its scope in 1923 to include organizing material aid for workers struggles the world over.

6 Elmer Smith was one of the original Centralia defendants. He later studied law and became the lawyer and spokesman for the Centralia prisoners. C.E. Payne was a vocal anti-Communist in the IWW, and he remained active in the organization into the 1950s.

sional committee is in existence for this campaign, developing more, to begin with, in the Northwest states. The press, generally, has been quick to pick up material on the Centralia campaign. The *Labor Defender* naturally is now also devoting considerable space to these above two campaigns.

Finances. Since January 1st to approximately July 1st, about $15,000 has been expended by ILD for the numerous defense cases, prisoners' relief, bail costs, etc. Of this amount approximately $4,000 has been paid directly and the cost borne wholly by the local ILD organizations. The remaining $11,000 expenses have been paid by the National Office directly and indirectly. Of this $11,000 approximately $8,000 has been paid out in cash by the National Office and $3,000, approximately, has been borne by the National Office in the application of local accounts to the *Labor Defender*, etc. Our reserve fund for the various cases has now been depleted and this naturally affects our immediate situation, particularly among the miners and textile workers, but which we hope the Textile Relief and Defense Drive and the Miners' Relief and Defense Drive will overcome.

Among the major expenditures since January 1st has been over $2,100 for the Woodlawn, Pa. steel workers' case which involves the right of the legal existence of the Workers (Communist) Party of America in Pennsylvania. This case must now be taken to the State Supreme Court and another $1,500 must immediately be raised for the printing of the records and lawyers' fees. The outcome of this case will almost inevitably be a defeat in the courts, but nevertheless we are thus far proposing to carry it to the United States Supreme Court. In the Cheswick, Pa. coal miners' cases arising out of a Sacco-Vanzetti demonstration, we have expended over $600 since January 1st.[7]

Monthly prisoners' and family relief has approximated $3,000. The Bonita case expenditures have been over $700. Bail premiums and interest thereon, etc., have been about $1,500. $210

[7] Woodlawn, Pennsylvania was a company town, property of the James and Laughlin Steel Company. In 1926 the local police had raided the home of Tom Zima and confiscated "seditious" Workers Party literature in Croatian. Zima and three co-workers were later indicted under the state anti-sedition act. They were convicted and sentenced to five years. The conviction had just been upheld by the Superior Court in Pennsylvania. For the Cheswick case see note page 474.

has been sent in recent weeks for textile defense and over $500 has been expended in connection with the Ohio, Pennsylvania and West Virginia cases, and of course the remaining legal fees and expenses therewith are yet to be met.

The Minerich anti-injunction case, it is planned, will be carried to the United States Supreme Court.[8] Deportation cases, anti-imperialist and anti-militarist cases, etc., etc., make up other large costs. We have just succeeded in canceling the bonds on about 150 of the Passaic cases with the exception of Weisbord's, and for this there must be an immediate expenditure of $725 for lawyers' fees and costs and the payment of an additional $3,000 approximately as premiums on the bonds to the surety company.

This makes up briefly some of the activities of the ILD. In addition we are now taking steps in connection with the Michigan cases in an endeavor to bring the cases to an issue in one manner or another.

There has been no decision as yet relative to the organization of a Jewish section of the ILD upon which motions are herein proposed.

The American Civil Liberties Union has cooperated in the Woodlawn, Cheswick, and Passaic cases, but in the first two cases, there will be no further joint action, to all reports, since from the ACLU standpoint the civil liberties aspect no longer enters.

The locals throughout the country are doing excellent work in the varied defense activities, and on the whole there has been splendid cooperation between the locals and the National Office.

---

[8] Anthony Minerich had been convicted of violating an anti-picketing injunction in the state of Ohio during the miners strike. He was sentenced to 45 days in jail, but appealed the conviction. In December, Alfred Wagenknecht, who became secretary of the ILD after Cannon's expulsion, recommended that the case not be appealed to the Supreme Court.

On the Textile Situation

by Arne Swabeck

23 July 1928

This letter from Arne Swabeck to Benjamin Gitlow was also attached to the minutes of the July 23 Political Committee meeting. In the letter Swabeck objects to the party's too precipitous move toward founding a new textile workers union. Pushed by the emerging Third Period dual-unionist line of the Communist International, in June the party had transformed the New Bedford Textile Mills Committee into the New Bedford Textile Workers Union. But the Committee's support, which had been strong among New Bedford's largely unskilled Portuguese workers, was already fading. The AFL textile union, which had retained the allegiance of the skilled, white, male craft workers, had accepted a compromise deal of a 5 percent wage cut, undercutting the party's organizing drive. Nonetheless, Gitlow adamantly defended the party's policy against Swabeck, and the party transformed the New Bedford Textile Workers Union into the National Textile Workers Union at a conference held September 22-23.

Dear Comrade Gitlow:

Reading in the Polcom minutes the decisions made in regard to the organization of a new textile workers union, I fear that there are some serious errors in the policy adopted and in the tactics to be applied in carrying out this task.

In considering the general situation in the textile industry I believe the following factors should be definitely taken into account:

First, the general migration of the industry to the South into up-to-date equipped mills, highly competitive, with low wages; a migration which has now reached the point of half of the spindles and possibly two-thirds of the activities being in the South.

Secondly, the process of rationalization now going on in the textile mills in the North, particularly in New England.

Thirdly, the fact that some unions already exist, the United Textile Workers of America being the dominant one; truly a moribund organization but yet having shown lately some capability of amalgamation of textile unions, under domination of reactionaries. It has also shown some signs of activities.

Fourthly, our contacts among textile workers at present appear to be rather limited and organization certainly less. In the South no organization within which we have a basis, and apparently no contacts. In the silk mills in the Pennsylvania Anthracite region, apparently little or no contacts and no organization within which we have a basis. In New England and nearby states in several points local organizations or mill committees, some of a high quality. Yet neither our actual local organizations nor our contacts could be claimed to be very broad in scope when we consider an industry of about one million workers.

The first three factors mentioned are by no means arguments against a new union. On the contrary, they serve to accentuate the necessity of such a step. The correctness of the building of a new textile workers union I believe is unquestionable. But these factors do emphasize the necessity of correct policies and tactics being applied in building this union. The fourth factor, I believe, particularly serves to suggest certain changes in our policy.

For instance, I believe our first task in organizing this new union should be to greatly intensify our activities in all textile centers for the building of local unions, mill committees and actual live contacts, this work to reach a sufficient organizational basis before the final step of launching the national union is taken. Meanwhile the local organizations, mill committees and contacts should have some sort of affiliation to a center to be created.

Further, I believe it necessary to consider the possibility of utilizing the conference called for September 22 as a means of creating such a national center to stimulate and intensify the further work of building and strengthening local organizations, mill committees and contacts everywhere to a point where the national union can be successfully launched.

These few points mentioned in this letter are by no means exhaustive or even sufficient as a basis to fully consider policy and tactics to be applied in building the new textile workers union, but I believe they do warrant a more thorough examination by the Polcom of the needs of the present situation and I would urge that the whole matter be again discussed.

Report on the Mining Situation

by Arne Swabeck

8 August 1928

Arne Swabeck's report on the meeting of the national committee of the National Miners' Convention Arrangements Committee, held in Pittsburgh on July 24-25, is published below, as are the proposals for furthering the miners campaign, which he and Alfred Wagenknecht jointly submitted to the PC. Both the report and the motions were attached to the minutes of the Political Committee meeting of August 8. The PC did not act on either, but referred both to the "Mining Committee."

The party had begun the move toward founding a new union in the mining industry a few months earlier than it did in textile. On May 16 Foster submitted to the PC a series of proposals which insisted, "our definite immediate goal must be to win away from Lewis in open struggle the masses of organized miners. This inevitably means a split. For this our comrades must be steeled." Foster advocated organizing a series of regional miners conventions that would build toward a national convention to found a new union, and his proposals were unanimously adopted by the Political Committee. The "Save the Union" conference held in May in Illinois' District 12 voted to "remove" the District UMW president, Fishwick, and to set up a new district office where locals should send dues.

While the primary motivation for advocating a new miners union was the shifting line of the Communist International (the Profintern's Fourth Congress motion on the American question, which called for the TUEL to transform itself into "the basic organization for the organization of the unorganized," was appended to the minutes of the same PC meeting which adopted the call for a split with Lewis), the new line also reflected the sharp decline of the UMW in the industry. Production had fallen from 970 million tons to 383 million tons between 1923 and 1931, and union membership had fallen from 450,000 to 150,000 in the 1920s. The UMW was threatened with extinction in the bituminous coal fields. In the face of the losing strike in the Central Competitive Field, Lewis had abandoned the attempt to enforce the Jacksonville scale of $7.50 per day—he was negotiating wage agreements district by district, based on "existing wages." But however militant, most of the "Save the Union" support came from miners who were no longer working. The movement *had less support in the higher-grade "hard" coal Anthracite region of Pennsylvania, which was insulated from the industry's general decline by lack of competition.*

The Pittsburgh meeting was held soon after Lewis had abandoned any pretense of saving the Jacksonville scale. The meeting decided to call on all UMW locals to break with the Lewis machine, pay no more dues to Lewis, affiliate to the National Arrangements Committee, and send delegates to the founding convention of the new miners union, set for September.

The meeting of the national committee of Pittsburgh, held July 26th, was successful. It had two main purposes: first to make our policy clear, and secondly to work up more activity for the national convention. While the first purpose may not have been fulfilled as completely as desired, due to the little discussion, the second purpose was particularly well taken care of. Several meetings were also held with the Illinois and Anthracite delegations: with the Illinois delegation particularly with a view to organizing mass resistance to wage cuts, to fight to break the locals away from the machine and to fight the checkoff, and secure a substantial delegation as well; with the Anthracite delegation, particularly with a view to better coordinate our forces there. Matters of both delegations were fully taken care of.

In Illinois the first conference called of organizers and leading elements had 16 attending. Policy for Illinois in accord with national line was adopted. Delegates were all ready for fight. Organizers were sent to the field, mass meetings organized and special efforts made to break the locals away immediately which are under our control. Negotiations are still going on between the operators and the Fishwick machine. Wage cuts will follow and there are reports that the operators fight the checkoff. The sentiment throughout Illinois has become very favorable due to the abandonment of the Jacksonville scale and there is a new fighting spirit developing. In Indiana, similar arrangements have been made for the future activities, negotiations between the machine and the operators have been broken off, pending settlement in Illinois. In Kentucky, we are establishing a number of connections. A conference has been held, participated in by delegates from more than a dozen mines, with good prospects.

The Chicago District Committee has decided to remove Simons

from position of industrial organizer and appoint comrade Feingold in his place. This is harmful to the miners campaign, since comrade Feingold lacks experience as a party organizer and is not familiar with the situation.[9]

In the strike areas, the operators have flatly refused to enter into any negotiations with the old machine; there are some prospects of our obtaining a settlement in Avella, but generally speaking, the greatest danger is disintegration because the checkoff is gone, the old union is practically wiped out and it is very difficult to actually have the retreat in face of the lost strike become an organized one. None of the locals have as yet affiliated with the National Arrangements Committee, and in view of the great dangers of disintegration and the necessity of our forces and locals supporting us being kept intact, both where we have control and where we have a minority it is necessary that we greatly intensify the carrying out of our policy and actually affiliate locals and groups with the National Arrangements Committee, so that we may maintain organization.

In the unorganized territory, we are making headway slowly. We have a total of 55 organized groups beginning to function as embryo unions.

In the Anthracite, the forces under Brennan's control are fighting recognition of the Boylan machine and are discussing strike against recognition.[10] There is some anti-Communist sentiment amongst a number of our supporters there for the new union.

Only 12 local unions throughout the field have so far elected delegates to the national convention and it is necessary that every source be mobilized to greatly intensify our campaign to make the convention a success.

The coming United Mine Workers elections nominations, which have to be in before August 26th, have been considered by

---

[9] The minutes of the Political Committee meeting do not record whether or not Feingold, who was presumably a Lovestone faction supporter, remained industrial organizer of the Chicago District. "Simons" is probably Bud Simons, who was later active as a Communist organizer in the auto workers union.

[10] Brennan, a UMW official in the Anthracite region, had been part of the Communist-led anti-Lewis bloc in the period leading up to the UMW convention in early 1927. But Brennan "simply collapsed at the convention," according to Johnstone's report to the 27 January 1927 Political Committee meeting.

the Pittsburgh Committee and proposals for policy are submitted. Likewise in regards to the declaration of war upon the Communists by the bureaucracy of the American Federation of Labor.

* * *

Motions by Swabeck and Wagenknecht on the Mining Situation

In view of the present great importance of our activities in the Illinois and Indiana coal fields in regards to the inevitable wage cuts resulting from the abandonment of the Jacksonville agreement, the possibility of a mass movement against such wage cuts, the necessity of breaking the local unions away from the Lewis-Fishwick machine and organization for the national convention, the Polcom disapproves the action of the Chicago DEC in removing comrade Simons from the position of industrial organizer and replacing him with comrade Feingold. It is harmful to make such changes at the present time. Comrade Feingold lacks the necessary qualification and experience as a party organizer to fill this position now, and he is entirely unfamiliar with the problems confronting our party in the mining campaign. Comrade Simons is more qualified, has a greater experience as a party organizer and is more familiar with our mining campaign problems. The Polcom therefore recommends to the Chicago DEC to reverse its action and again place comrade Simons as the industrial organizer of the district.

In view of the present great danger of disintegration of the local organizations still existing in the strike areas of Districts 2, 5 and 6,[11] we shall intensify our activities to carry out the policy adopted by the Polcom by the following measures:

1. The Polcom calls to the attention of leading comrades in the mining field, particularly in Districts 5 and 6, that there has been a serious shortcoming in carrying out the policies laid down in the following respects: insufficient efforts to make the retreat in face of the lost strike an organized one, failing to pursue the

[11] The Workers Party divided the country into 15 districts for the purposes of internal administration. District 2 was headquartered in New York City, District 5 in Pittsburgh and District 6 in Cleveland.

campaign for breaking the locals away from the Lewis machine and have them affiliate with the National Miners Convention Arrangements Committee, since not one local has affiliated as yet.
2. In all locals where we have a majority steps shall be taken immediately to have them affiliate with the National Miners Convention Arrangements Committee, to be given charters and dues cards (temporary).
3. In locals where we are still a minority we shall be guided by the size of the minority and conditions obtaining whether the local resumes work under an agreement with the coal operators.
4. Where our minority is a fairly substantial one and no agreement exists, the minority shall be given a charter and dues cards (temporary) and function as a local union affiliated with the National Miners Convention Arrangements Committee, endeavoring to organize all the miners in the locality within this local.
5. Where our minority is too small, whether or not an agreement exists, they shall function as organized left wing groups, but be given dues cards, working within the local to win the majority and affect no split until after the convention unless such minorities become majorities.
6. More efforts shall be made to have the striking miners return in an organized manner and have our forces give real leadership at this moment. The party shall give all possible support to carry out the decisions of the Pittsburgh Committee to place an organizer in each subdistrict within these districts, each to be in full charge of their territory and establish functioning left wing blocs in every mining camp, and further to call conferences in each district of progressive elements to better carry our policies into effect, preceding this conference the party fractions to meet for the same purpose. These conferences to have as broad a character as possible.
7. In the event of a strike of the Brennan forces in the Anthracite against recognition of the Boylan administration, our policy shall be to throw our forces fully into this strike but completely carry out our own independent line as already laid down by the Polcom, intensifying our efforts to swing the local unions under control of this group into participation in the building of the new miners union. Simultaneously we shall inject the issues of the economic needs of the Anthracite miners, such as the abolition of

the contractor system, etc., and demand that the strike be carried on on these issues as well.

8. In view of the anti-Communist tendencies and propaganda of the supporters of our movement in the Anthracite, the Gaffney group and others, the party shall use all possible efforts to combat and correct these wrong views. Our comrades in the leadership of the new union movement shall personally try to convince these elements of their wrong position and our party units in the Anthracite shall carry on a systematic campaign to show the role of the Communists in this, as in other struggles, as the real champions of the working class. The party Agitprop Department to give special attention to this situation and work out the necessary measures.

9. At the earliest possible date a party membership conference shall be held in the Anthracite to take up this question, together with the general problems of our mining campaign.

10. In order to increase our efforts for mass participation in the coming national convention, there being now only four weeks left with altogether too little of a campaign carried on, comrades Minerich and Watt shall return to the center as soon as possible and comrade Wagenknecht be assigned to give all possible assistance to work up an intensive campaign for selection of delegates by the local unions everywhere, and assist in other matters necessary to make the convention a success.

11. For the present nomination and later elections of national, district and subdistrict officials of the United Mine Workers, our attitude shall be opposition to any participation in general. Our counter action shall be propaganda and organization for the new union wherever our supporters still remain within the old union. For the Anthracite district and subdistrict elections, action shall be taken in each instance after a survey of the situation has been made.

12. The Polcom calls to the attention of comrade Jakira that acceptance of the proposal for us to nominate a slate for the coming United Mine Workers of America national elections at this time would be a complete negation of our whole line of policy in the mining situation.

13. In regards to the declaration of war upon the Communists by the AFL bureaucracy, we shall adopt the recommendation of

the Pittsburgh Committee that the party and the TUEL begin an extensive propaganda campaign of mass meetings, etc., to acquaint union labor with the Lewis sellout and the need for organizing new unions in the mining industry, the textile industry and the organization of the unorganized, thus waging a counter-offensive against the attacks of this bureaucracy.

Attack on the National Miners' Union Convention

by Martin Abern

18 September 1928

We publish below Abern's report as assistant secretary of the ILD on the organization's activities at the September convention which founded the National Miners' Union. The report was attached to the Political Committee minutes of October 12. Six hundred seventy-five delegates assembled in Pittsburgh on September 9, but they were unable to meet there. John L. Lewis had fought the "Save the Union" movement with every means at his disposal, including colluding with the coal companies in blacklisting supporters. Now his thugs violently attacked the Pittsburgh meeting. More than 125 delegates were arrested, and it was Abern as the on-the-spot representative of the ILD who organized the campaign to get them out of jail.

Dear Comrades:

The following is the report in brief of the defense work of the International Labor Defense, during the convention of the National Miners' Union at Pittsburgh, September 9th-11th.

At the party fraction meeting on the Saturday night preceding the opening of the convention, it became clear from the reports that were given that difficulties were to be expected from the Lewis machine, and that preparations should be made to make certain that the convention would be held. Arrangements were made that the ILD representative should be on hand on the morning of the convention before the Labor Lyceum, to take the necessary measures for defense, in case the convention was prevented from opening at the hall that morning, and in case of arrests, etc.

I was at the hall on Sunday morning at 8 o'clock, and the struggle between the Lewis gangsters and the forces representing the new National Miners' Union was already under way. During the course of the next half hour of the struggle, perhaps a thousand people accumulated in the street. The thugs and gangsters of the Lewis machine attempted to break down the doors, which were guarded by the National Miners forces. All their attempts to beat down the doors were unsuccessful due to the effective resistance of those who were defending the hall. Clubs, stones, blackjacks, knives and other weapons were being used by the Lewis thugs against the delegates. Stones flew in through the windows of the hall. I noted one individual on the outside, whose supporter he was I do not know, whose coat in the back was slashed clean, as if by a razor blade, and his back had a similar cut and blood was flowing freely. Provocation was to be noted on every direction, and whether there were not many bystanders who also received blows in the struggle is an open question; undoubtedly there were. The police did not arrive until almost 9 o'clock. At this time it must be mentioned that representatives of the National Miners' Union forces had visited the Superintendent of Police the day before, and had informed him that they intended to hold a convention. The police authorities gave no indication that they were ready to defend the rights of the men to hold their convention. This is to be noted now, in view of the fact that the police did not arrive until long after the struggle had begun, and is an indication that the police were definitely aware of the fact that trouble was going to ensue, and that the police were definitely fighting on behalf of the Lewis gangsters. This, of course, was to be expected. During the scuffling it was to be noted too that the police made no efforts to prevent forces from the National Miners' Union from being clubbed and beaten. The police clubs were by no means indiscriminate in their use, but quite definitely against the National Miners' Union forces. They were using their clubs quite freely. I do not need to dilate much on this point in my report. I wish, however, to make this observation. The forces of the National Miners' Union were protecting themselves effectively, and were beating back the thugs despite the fact that the latter were armed with weapons of all sorts. In my opinion, if the police had not interfered and taken the side of the gangsters, the forces of the National Miners' Union would have routed these elements and the convention would have proceeded at the Labor Lyceum. However, the role of the police as the allies of the reactionaries naturally asserted itself.

A number of the National Miners' Union forces and some of the gang elements were somewhat seriously injured, and taken to the hospital where they were given treatment, and then placed under arrest. One of these ten National Miners' Union supporters, however, Calemeri, was beaten insensible. I visited him at the hospital at a later date and his memory was completely gone. The doctor was unable to give any definite word that there were possibilities of recovery.

The police patrol loaded the men into the wagons and took them to the police station. Then those delegates inside of the hall were made to leave the hall. Delegates who were merely watching on the streets were arrested. Later, as the committee knows, truckloads of delegates who came to the hall were arrested by the police, who were at the hall.

A few minutes before the fight was finally over, and the police had loaded the delegates away, and the hall was cleared, we proceeded to telephone various attorneys in order to take the necessary steps for the release of the men, that they might be able to participate in the convention at a hall that had been previously arranged by the proper committee. My idea was immediately to have a conference of attorneys to work out the best ways and means for quick action. The Civil Liberties representative was with me, but he was very doubtful as to what course the Civil Liberties Union would pursue and was not ready to take the responsibility, until he had communicated and had definite word from the New York office. I told him, of course, that we would proceed under any conditions, since the ILD was concerned with getting the men out.

Attorney Allan Davis was secured over the phone and he proceeded to get in touch with the police station. I also got in touch with a young attorney, Ellenbogen, not known as yet to the Pittsburgh comrades, but whom I knew through our previous contacts with Isaac Ferguson, and I knew that he had certain capabilities and connections. We held a conference with him and attorney Roe, at the latter's office, where also representatives of the Civil Liberties Union, Nunn and Woltman, were present, and White and myself. Attorney Davis telephoned giving us some information as to the men who were arrested, but stated that he wished a $300.00 retainer fee. This of course was impossible and after a discussion Roe and Ellenbogen were retained with Ellenbogen to carry on the active work. Mr. Ellenbogen immediately got busy, visited the station, obtained the names of those who were under arrest and the charges that had been placed against them. It is important to note that the convention of the miners was charged with being a convention of the Communist Party and that in the charges all blame was placed against the National Miners' Union. The police blotter records stated that the struggle was a faction struggle and that those inside the hall had piled up sticks and stones and taken the offensive. This is again confirmation of the fact that the police were in alliance with the Lewis machine and the operators and were doing everything that they could to break up the convention of the National Miners' Union. The charge placed against the men was that of rioting, which constitutes a felony in the State of Pennsylvania. Consequently, despite all efforts, the police refused to set any bail for the men, and we were unable therefore to get any of the men out that day. However, arrangements were made for an early hearing at 8 o'clock in the morning. Our attorney, Mr. Ellenbogen, was of the opinion that heavy bail would be placed upon the leaders, if not all of the 22 who were first arrested, if the operators, the police and the Lewis machine were intent on framing some of the leaders immediately and keeping them in jail for the period of the convention. This placed us in a position of getting bail immediately and of arranging to get the main leaders out at once, since it was manifestly impossible to get all of the men out on bail immediately. Especially in view of the arrests which later took place at the various hotels where the miners were quartered.

At the conference with Nunn and Woltman, we also declared for a fight to establish the right of the convention to hold its conference in Pittsburgh. To work for this end, it was decided to organize immediately, that night, a delegation of liberal elements, preachers, lawyers, doctors, professors and other forces who would visit the Director of Public Safety and demand the right for the convention to hold its conference and to receive the fullest protection of the police. This of course was not to be organized in the name of the ILD but rather as a delegation of the kind outlined, "to protest in the name of the fair city of Pittsburgh." This delegation was quickly gotten together, and the next morning they visited the Director of Public Safety and made very emphatic demands, to such an extent that the Director of Public Safety was compelled to declare that the convention could be held.

The fullest publicity was given to this conference in all of the press, and undoubtedly it at least had the effect of breaking down the open enmity towards the National Miners' Union forces, and turning the tide against the Lewis machine and the police. This was to be noted subsequently in the attitude of some forces of the Pittsburgh press, particularly the paper *The Pittsburgh Press*, which declared that the forces whose desire is to hold a convention must have the fullest opportunity to do so, and that the police must not act as the allies of the Lewis forces. I do not detail on this, since it is merely one of the methods we employed in Pittsburgh, but it is an indication that the party should utilize and mobilize these forces more often in such struggles since they can exercise an indirect pressure and influence that we as the ILD or the party cannot hope to do in that manner. That this liberal delegation was mobilized so quickly is due mainly to the energetic efforts of Professor Nunn of Pittsburgh University, who is a live element and who should be utilized more than formerly by the Pittsburgh forces in their various struggles of this kind.

During the whole day on Sunday, delegates to the convention were being rounded up at their hotels and arrested and charged with inciting to riot. Lewis men accompanied the police to the various quarters and pointed out the delegates, and also attempted to provoke fights, to make it simpler for the police to have an excuse to arrest the delegates. In once instance, the Negro delegate Charles Fulp was badly beaten up and then he was charged with assaulting and resisting an officer! During the course of that Sunday, almost 125 delegates were arrested, thus posing a big problem for immediate action for the ILD.

I held a conference with Ellenbogen on the policy and tactics to be pursued at the hearing the following morning, and it was agreed to carry out the policy along the lines of the ILD. The Civil Liberties Union was out of the picture in the matter of defense. The Civil Liberties Union declared that they did not wish to follow a policy of bailing out these arrested miners but were interested in fighting out the issue for the right to hold a convention. While we, of course, proposed to carry on the struggle to hold a convention in Pittsburgh, we proposed to do it simultaneously with the immediate problem. We were concerned with getting the miners out of jail so that they could participate in the convention at the earliest moment; consequently, it was our intention to procure bail, to get the men out as fast as possible. The entire work, therefore, was left to the ILD.

Upon action of the steering committee, I also attended the convention of the miners union at East Pittsburgh on Sunday night, and addressed the convention on the work of the ILD, and what was being done to get the men out of prison, and gave them greetings and endorsement. I also took up other matters at the convention, as per the instructions of the steering committee.

On Monday morning, together with Attorney Ellenbogen and others, I attended the hearings at Police Station Court 1. The miners were brought out, indicted and given a hearing. There were two hearings; the first hearing was, as the magistrate put it, called to weed out the "good" ones. A number of the miners were thus released. During the entire proceedings, the magistrate indicated quite clearly that his sympathies were on the side of the reactionary Lewis officialdom, and that he would do everything he could against the new union forces. He attacked the Communists, the reds, the Bolsheviks, etc., viciously and declared that non-citizens had no business in this country, etc., etc. It was the usual kind of tirade against the labor movement put on by the stupid and ignorant capitalist police officials.

Representatives of the Lewis machine including lawyers, a number of officials, as well as an even larger number of Lewis gangsters, were present. The Lewis supporters were, of course, immediately released. It was obvious that an understanding had been arrived at beforehand.

The magistrate inquired of the delegate miners, whether they had any money and whether they were able to support themselves. Since naturally very few of them had, I had arranged for the attorney to state that every man would be taken care of during the course of his stay. Thereupon the magistrate stated, "All right." To avoid further attempts of the Lewis gangsters to gang up on our supporters, I arranged for the miners, as fast as they were released, to be taken in taxicabs to the National Miners Relief Office, and there also provided with money for food.

During the second hearing, the same day, the men after some questioning were either released, had fines placed upon them or were remanded to jail for the grand jury or federal hearing. The fines ranged from $5.00 to $25.00. Although it is generally the policy of the ILD not to pay fines, in this instance, it was agreed by the party committee that this be done, in order that we be able to get the miners, if possible, to the convention at the earliest possible moment. Therefore I paid the fines as fast as I was able to raise the money.

All of the men, therefore, of the 125 were released, except those who received fines. Some paid their fines immediately out of the money they had with them and the rest were taken out by me in the afternoon. Three men remained in jail, remanded to the grand jury according to the court on $1,000.00 bail, charged with rioting (and assault and battery upon an officer, in the case of Fulp). We proceeded to raise bail, but because of technical conditions it was not possible to get the men out that night. However, during the course of the night and the next morning, there was further consultation between our attorneys and the magistrate and other individuals, and in the morning these three were also released with a small fine placed against one of them. Of the 125 arrests that took place, every man was released outright or fines paid, within a space of 24 hours, with the exception of the three that had to remain an extra day.

As the men were being released and taken to the National Miners Relief Office, the police also set out to drive the delegates out of town, and declared that they could not remain. I immediately arranged for a conference of attorneys, of Porter of the Civil Liberties, Ellenbogen and others, to visit the Director of Public Safety, and the Chief of Police, and declared that we would resist any attempt to take the men out of town, that they had a perfect right to remain. It was stated finally that the men had a perfect right to remain in Pittsburgh as long as they pleased, so that this fact was also established. Nevertheless, under cover and through other pretexts the men who were released from jail were continually harassed by the police, and undoubtedly, though I do not have specific knowledge, many men were whisked out of town in this fashion. The police remained in the office of the National Miners Relief and at the railroad stations for quite some time, but later in the evening, I noticed that they had been removed. This second conference of liberal elements also served to establish, in the civil rights sense of capitalism, the right to hold a convention.

From a financial standpoint, the proceedings during those few days cost the ILD over $600: $250 for legal fees to Ellenbogen, fines, cost of food and taxis. The ILD will have to pay the entire amount itself, since the Civil Liberties Union regards itself as in no way obligated, since the cases were handled from the viewpoint and methods of the International Labor Defense.

I discussed, before leaving Pittsburgh, what the Civil Liberties Union might do in respect to some of the assaults. It is quite possible that the Civil Liberties Union will enter suit against the police who beat up Fulp. Its value will of course be mainly moral, if it is carried through.

In connection with the series of solidarity meetings which will be held by the National Miners' Union, both the ILD and the Civil Liberties Union will undertake to see that these meetings are held, and will take all necessary steps toward this end.

To summarize, I am of the opinion that the ILD carried on a very successful fight in Pittsburgh, and that the results speak for themselves. The changing attitude of the press is of significance for the future work, prestige and standing of the National Miners' Union in that territory. The operators, the Lewis machine and the police made a determined effort to smash the holding of the convention, and to smash the formation, in fact, of the union itself. They were completely unsuccessful despite their extreme methods of terror. They were unable to prevent the holding of the convention. They were unable to establish, even after their own methods and fashion, the illegality of the movement. They were unable to drive the forces away. At the earliest moment, the solidarity mass meeting by the union in Pittsburgh should be held, to establish there openly and strongly the stand of the National Miners' Union and its victory over the Lewis machine.

The union forces should immediately notify us when this will be held, so that we can take the necessary steps from our angle.

I also proposed to comrade White, the ILD secretary of Pittsburgh, that this was the period to try to gain organizational as well as political advantages for the ILD. I propose, therefore, that he organize immediately an affair or meeting on the strength of the work of the ILD in Pittsburgh in this convention struggle, and thereby also, in addition to the political and organizational possibilities, be able to raise the much-needed money to meet the cost of the cases. I proposed to comrade Jakira, the district organizer, that he give the fullest cooperation in this respect. It will be shameful to overlook this situation and not get results.

In my opinion, also, it is necessary to make a change of secretary for the Pittsburgh local. While comrade White is a good revolutionary and has the best of intentions, I do not believe that he is capable of meeting the situation of labor defense as it confronts us in Pittsburgh and vicinity. This was to be noted during the course of the struggle in Pittsburgh during these few days as well as from viewpoints and opinions which were given to us by various sources. The Pittsburgh local and vicinity should be one of the strongest sections of the ILD, yet it is one of the weakest. This can be remedied. If it is necessary to give additional reason on this matter, I will do so, but I think that the members of the Political Committee who were present at Pittsburgh and others will realize that everything that I am saying is absolutely correct and that a change is essential, and immediately. I also propose that the Polcom immediately authorize the National Office of the ILD to take steps to replace comrade White by another secretary.

* * *

P.S.: I understand that Calemeri, who is yet confined at the Passavent Hospital and whose memory is at present destroyed, is one of the best of the left wing forces. I visited him at the hospital and, while the doctors declared that they are not certain of recovery, it is quite possible that the efforts of the psychiatrists and other attentions may bring his memory around again. If so, he could be effectively used by the National Miners' Union forces at various meetings, in view of his experiences, and I propose this suggestion to the committee.

Letter to Lovestone

by Antoinette Konikow

2 November 1928

Antoinette Konikow was not a supporter of the Cannon faction, but she was one of the first within the American party to support the views of Trotsky's Left Opposition, and she had won a group of five Boston area party members to her views. Summoned to appear before the Political Committee after the expulsion of Cannon, Abern and Shachtman, she wrote a defiant protest letter to Jay Lovestone, which is published below. After reading Konikow's letter to the November 2 meeting of the Committee, Lovestone commented that "it is obvious from her letter that she is the worst kind of a Trotskyite, biologically as well as politically. The sooner that we throw her out the better for the party." Konikow, a medical doctor and a pioneer of birth control, was unanimously expelled by the Political Committee. She founded the Independent Communist League, which published her letter in its first Bulletin, *dated December 1928. Konikow's League merged forces with the expelled Cannon faction to found the Communist League of America in May 1929.*

Dear Comrade:

This sudden order to appear Friday noon in New York before the Political Committee is in line with your usual tricky policy. You know well that going to New York from Boston means quite an expense and that leaving my medical practice for several days involves a big financial loss. Why can't a local committee consider my case? Because they fear the indignation of the local comrades? Or you are not sure that the local committee would act against me with the desired decision? All you want is to be able to tell the rank and file you offered me a hearing and I refused to avail myself of the opportunity. According to the latest decision of the Comintern we should have full inner party democracy and inner party criticism. Why does this not apply to the Trotsky Opposition? Because a few faked resolutions were forced through our party organization by misrepresentation and terrorism? I did work for Trotsky's ideals and tried to arouse sentiment for the

Opposition in our party, and I consider I have the full right to do so according to the party's stand on inner party democracy. But it is useless to expect your committee to accept this viewpoint, for your leadership would not last long under rules of real democracy in our party. I consider that the party has taken an outrageously wrong standing on the Trotsky situation in Soviet Russia. This stand is a result of the servile submission to the Stalin faction.

It happens that I am one of these comrades of whom comrade Stalin in his answer to the American Trade Union Committee said, "Real Communists cannot be controlled from Moscow." I am willing to submit to discipline if a proposition had been given free discussion where both sides were equally given a chance to express themselves. Otherwise I consider it my right and duty to oppose wrongly imposed discipline.

Your decision about me is already made up and my statement will never reach the comrades until I see to it myself. It is good that you have not the power to take away my livelihood as it is done in Soviet Russia. As to besmirching of my name before the comrades, this is to be expected.

A comrade of thirty-nine years services in the socialist cause.

Dr. A.F. Konikow

Appendix 2

Report to the Political Committee on the Right Danger and Trotskyism

by Jack Stachel

25 December 1928

The following report by Jack Stachel to the Workers Party Political Committee was attached to the minutes of the PC meeting of December 25. On 23 December 1928 the home of Jim Cannon and Rose Karsner had been burglarized. The burglars, who had forced the lock with a jimmy, were evidently caught in the act. They left a room strewn with papers, but they managed to escape with a file of correspondence, account and receipt books, editorial material and manuscripts, as well as a partial list of subscribers to the new Trotskyist paper, the Militant. *There was never any real doubt as to the perpetrators—especially after photostats of some of the stolen correspondence appeared in the* Daily Worker. *This report confirms that the culprits were Lovestone's henchmen.*

Cannon publicized the incident in the 1 January 1929 Militant, *reporting that the Trotskyists had taken the precaution of keeping copies of some of the stolen material. Nonetheless, the Lovestone leadership used the names and information they acquired to intimidate potential supporters of Trotsky within the party. On 14 January 1929 the burglars returned and this time they stole everything.*

Stachel's report reveals the extent of interest within the party concerning the views of the expelled Trotskyists. But not everyone mentioned by Stachel as having contact with Cannon was expelled from the party, and not all those who were expelled joined the Trotskyist movement. At the December 25 meeting the Political Committee removed Bud Reynolds, William Schneiderman, George Saul and Joe Giganti from their posts and suspended them from the party. But Reynolds and Schneiderman remained in the Workers Party; only Saul and Giganti joined the Communist League of America. George Kraska, who had been condemned in 1925 for openly criticizing the Comintern, was expelled, but there is no record that he subsequently joined the CLA. S. Markizon, who was reported to be the wife of a Wilmington businessman, was also expelled; we have been able to find no record of her subsequent activities.

Stachel does not mention miners leader Joseph Angelo in his report, but the burglars had evidently found incriminating evidence against him. The Political Committee voted to hold his expulsion "in abeyance pending an effort to make him repudiate his whole Trotsky position and to isolate him from the miners." He was expelled from the party in 1929; he joined the CLA.

The strange case of George Mink deserves special mention. Stachel proudly reports the incriminating evidence against him, but Mink was not expelled. Alone among all those mentioned in Stachel's report, Mink's case was referred to the Secretariat "with full power to act." Mink had special status indeed; the minutes of the April 9 Political Committee meeting reveal that the Profintern had earlier **demanded** *that he be a member of the American delegation to its Fourth Congress in the spring of 1928. In Moscow he was recruited and trained for the GPU.*

In December 1928 Mink was head of the party's Seamen's Bureau. He was subsequently president of the Third Period CP's Marine Industrial Workers' Union. He was arrested in Copenhagen in 1935 on charges of attempted rape, but he was sentenced to 18 months in jail for espionage after the police found false passports and $3,000 in his hotel room. After his release, using the name Alfred Herz, he played a role in the Stalinists' murderous assault against the Trotskyists in Spain. The anarchist Carlo Tresca publicly denounced Mink as a GPU agent in February 1938, after the mysterious disappearance of longtime Communist Party member Juliet Stuart Poyntz. In 1940 Mink was rumored to be part of a team assigned to assassinate Trotsky in Mexico, but he had disappeared from sight and was never heard from again. Whether his masters in Moscow thought better of Mink's attempt to infiltrate the Trotskyist movement in 1928, or whether Lovestone's burglary upset their plans, will never be known.

The Cannon Opposition has within the last few days received a very serious blow at the hands of the Central Executive Committee; a blow which I think will weaken them considerably because we will to an extent disrupt their work organizationally and politically. Also because of the fact that we will be able to expose many of their agents that are still in the party. That to my mind is, at present, even more dangerous than the open Cannon supporters themselves. We have come into possession of certain information and documents to show the following situation.

It shows a very serious situation because it shows much wider ramifications than even we had expected. It shows that the Opposition poison is still within the party, working consciously through its agents and working in almost every district in a large number of cities. To date the Trotsky Opposition has established some sort of organization in at least 30 cities, including New York, Chicago, Boston, Philadelphia, Cleveland, Detroit, San Francisco, Akron and many other cities such as New Haven, Newark, St. Paul, Superior. In all of the 30 cities, some of their agents are still working under cover. We also find that in the mining field the situation is quite serious because they have some leading people working consciously and openly as party members. The Opposition press—of course, their figures are exaggerated—they printed on an average of 10,000 copies of the first issue, 7,500 of the second and a little less of the third issue, though they had additional orders. They have agents, and it is peculiar that many of those in the party who never sold a *Daily Worker* are making good agents for the *Militant*.

Next, Cannon, of course, is receiving funds from Eastman that are receipted received from L.T. Cannon is of course connected organizationally and politically with the international Trotskyists in all countries including the Soviet Union, France and particularly receiving direct instructions from the Urbahns group in Germany. One of the documents that I find I did not bring along, which should be read at the Secretariat tomorrow, is a very important letter from Urbahns to Cannon. One of the important things for us to know is that through the seamen here material is being shipped to the Trotskyites.

Now to what extent have they made headway in the United States? They have succeeded in getting quite a lot of recruits from, first of all, party members we know. Second, from the party members we do not know, and third, from people outside the party and those on the fringe of the party. Swabeck was not willing to take in doubtful elements. It came up also in connection with the South Slavs, whom Cannon instructed Swabeck to take in immediately. While calling themselves an Opposition inside the party, we find that their semi-monthly organ has a policy of taking in everybody and anybody.

We see the following: The Opposition organizing definitely. Organizing openly those that have been expelled and having meetings in the cities with their agents still members of the party. We have minutes of such meetings. In Connecticut they are planning to call a state conference sometime in January. They have quite a lot of followers. In New Haven in particular all their following is among non-party people. They have a following in Bridgeport. Also in Hartford and one or two other minor places in Connecticut.

Now as to their press. Of course, they are a little bit pressed for money, but I note that every time the issue has to come out, they receive a bulk sum marked L.T. because the receipt is attached to the Eastman letter. Financially they can still go on with the paper because they are receiving a regular subsidy. Every time about 300 dollars comes in and that pays for the issue. They have received quite a lot of money from Chicago and also from Connecticut, which has a lot of money. They have a certain individual named Herman who is giving large sums here in the city.[1] Also connections with different liberals who are giving them financial support. The perspective is, I think, they will be able to continue the paper for some time financially. Organizationally they are considering now a change of policy with regard to having some of their people come out in the open. Some of them are in favor of coming out after the party convention when "many of the Foster-Bittelman minority will be disappointed," etc., etc. Cannon seems to be inclined to immediately come out into the open, as his theory seems to be: a bird in the hand is worth two in the bush. He is moving in the direction of compelling people to come out into the open.

Concretely, we are in possession of quite a number of names of subscribers to the *Militant*, special lists of people that give and receive information. The list I think runs about 100 or so of the people who give and receive information. It includes some more or less leading comrades.

---

[1] This was probably Bill Herman, who was a carpenter and an early sympathizer and financial supporter of the Trotskyists.

Next there are some leading people that I want to deal with. First of all there is the question of the seamen, and I think this is perhaps the most serious situation we are facing. That is, the facts disclose that one who is now at the head of the Seamen's Bureau, George Mink, is an active supporter of the Cannon-Trotsky group. We have only two things to prove it. One, the official receipt book. Now we find that on November 12, Receipt No. 17, signed by Max Shachtman, 1114 Stratford Avenue, George Mink paid $1.00 for a subscription. We find, however, that on Receipt No. 11, there is no date, 1114 Stratford, $50.00 donation. The moment I saw this I did not believe that this was Mink. I remembered that he was transferred from Philadelphia in July. The same night I called him at the Seamen's Club. "Geo," I said. He said, "Yes." "I have some very confidential documents for you, what is your address?" "1114 Stratford." That is very clear. Now we have definitely established two or three things. We find, first of all, Urbahns' letter, two, the $50 donation and three, a sub. Urbahns' letter states that all letters are being shipped through the seamen.

That is number one. Next comes comrade Kraska, Boston, member of the Political Committee of the District. He writes the following letter to Cannon. *Militant* financial statement shows George Kraska, Boston, Mass. 50 copies No. 1 *Militant* $1.50. Letter dated October 31, 1928, 148 Seaver, Roxbury, Mass.:

> Dear Jim:
>
> Thanks for that information. As a true Communist I also feel that we must have more free discussion, that that is a healthy condition for a party. Would appreciate a copy of the Trotsky program, if you have one to spare.
>
> Before I take a definite stand one way or the other, I wish to know what's what. I fully realize what it may mean, but I cannot help it. This has been my position all along the line as you no doubt know it by this time.
>
> Keep up the fight and let us have a party that will not be afraid of any new thoughts. The joke is that Trotsky is a member of the party while those that agree with his program are expelled.
>
> Regards to Max and Marty.
>
> Signed: George Kraska
>
> Note the new address.

Now let us see. We have a financial statement to S. Markizon, 724 Madison Street, Wilmington, Delaware, five No. 2 *Militant*,

15¢, five No. 4 *Militant*, 15¢, total, 30¢. Also the following letter from Markizon:

November 8, 1928, Wilmington, Delaware
Comrade Cannon:

Please send me all information on hand so I will be better able to handle the matter here. If it would be possible for someone to come down to Wilmington, I wish you would please send someone here. I think it will help clear things up a bit as the pressure is rather strong although it is not direct. It comes from the YWL who are advised from above. So far I am able to get full details of what is going on but do not know how much longer I will be kept informed as I expect some changes to take place here as the D[istrict] O[rganizer] is after my skin, but as yet have not taken any action.

So please keep in touch with us so we will know how to act when the time comes.

The comrades here have been informed of the facts we have on hand; although they have not taken any stand, it will not be so easy to get them to act blindly as would have been the case before.

Comradely,
S. Markizon

Reply from Cannon dated December 4:

Dear Comrade Markizon:

In your letter of November 8th you neglected to give your address and this caused a delay in answering. We finally located your address on a list we have and hope this reaches you. In the meantime we have sent you copies of the paper and bulletins in care of another comrade and hope they reached you.

I wish you would let us know about the developments in Wilmington and whether any of the comrades protested against the expulsions. One of us can come down there if you think it will be advisable. Can you distribute a regular bundle of the *Militant*? We have a hard fight, but our cause is growing throughout the party.

Hoping to hear from you soon, I am

Yours fraternally

Now, in District 7, Detroit, Reynolds. We have a financial statement for the first issue of the *Militant*. Wm. Reynolds, 6626 Scotten, 25 copies, No. 1 *Militant*, 75¢. We have a letter from Reynolds to Cannon as follows (in handwriting):

Nov. 4
Dear Jim:

Got your circular letter and have since received copies of the statement and formalities incidental to your expulsion.

Your position came as a complete surprise to everyone in Detroit. I have spoken to all the leading comrades in the District and find them emphatically opposed to you.

I have shared the correct opinion or rather the "official attitude" on the Trotsky matter and think as you too must that whatever the merits of the Trotsky Opposition, there is a set attitude here or elsewhere that will be very hard to overcome.

I am anxious to see what your documents consist of and to learn from you the perspectives you base your course upon. Certainly there must be political currents developing internationally to move so cautious (or careful) a politician to so radical a departure.

I am leaving soon for California. I had not intended to attend the plenum. Now it seems almost imperative.

I will likely be confronted with a demand that I take a position at once. However, I intend to state that I want to hear all there is to be said before casting a vote.

I would like a letter from you and copies of the most important of the documents, if they can be had without too much trouble.

Regards to the girls and boys from Ruth and me.

Yours,
Bud

P.S. I will be at Apartment 403, 233 East Willis, Detroit until November 15. After that 1330 Ethel, Lincoln Park, Michigan.

We have a letter from Barney Mass to Cannon:[2]

December 3
James P. Cannon
Box 120, Madison Square Sta., NYC
Dear Jim:

Expelled Sunday at a meeting of the Polcom when I came out definitely supporting your position. I preferred charges against the Fosterites for caucusing with Hathaway before taking a stand on your expulsion. It was at Hathaway's caucus that they decided to break with you and support the CEC. I exposed their political cowardice

[2] The case of Barney Mass had been decided by the Polcom of the Detroit District; it was discussed by the national Political Committee at its meeting of 5 December 1928, where Lovestone read the following report from the Detroit district organizer:

> "In his statement Barney Mass openly declared himself in favor on all points of Cannon and against the decision of the CEC. After his statement which we will send in together with the whole investigation I made a motion that Barney Mass be expelled from the party. This motion was carried unanimously."

The Political Committee unanimously voted to sustain the action of the Detroit leadership.

and put them on record as endorsing the campaign of terrorizing the membership, believing there has been a genuine discussion in the party, admitting their ignorance on the issues involved in the Trotsky controversy.

There will be a few more expelled in the course of the week. I will inform you when it happens. My expulsion has revived interest and there is considerable commotion. When I was asked if the Trotskyites organized a new party, I replied that we considered ourselves an opposition of the party and would carry on our work in the class struggle and fight for our opinions in the party. I think that I am safe in saying that many of the rank and file Fosterites will not follow the decisions of the Hathaway caucus.

A couple of the Fosterites followed the statement that you issued with Aronberg and Costrell without understanding its significance, when Wolfe was addressing membership meetings on the CI Congress.[3] Hochberg was one of them but I surmise that Hathaway put him wise.

How is Dunne lining up? I understand that O'Flaherty will support you. Ruth is going to put up a fight in her shop nucleus and the other nuclei in her section before they put the skids under her.

I suppose that you have received my last letter.

As ever,
Barney Mass

District 8. Comrade Giganti, Secretary of the ILD. Following letter to Abern:

Chicago, November 4, 1928
Dear Marty:

I have received your letter together with the document. I had heard about the action taken by the Polcom through a New York friend of mine.

I read the document signed by you, Jim and Max, and find it immensely interesting. To tell you frankly, I do not really know the

---

[3] The *Daily Worker* of 2 October 1928 carried a statement signed by Cannon, Aronberg and Costrell, which read:

"In line with the position taken by the delegates representing the opposition at the World Congress we wish to place on record our disagreement with that section of the decision of the Political Secretariat of the ECCI which says the charges that the majority of the CEC followed a right line are unfounded. It is our opinion that the right line of the majority in the period prior to the departure of the delegation has been further confirmed in its course since that time....We demand an immediate cessation of the campaign of factional discrimination, persecution and suppression of the majority against the opposition."

The Foster faction was later much embarrassed by this joint statement.

position of Trotsky. Of course, I have read something about it, i.e., what his opponents say about him and his position, but that is all. I would be pleased to read his own writings on the discussions within the Russian party, as well as the documents that he is alleged to have presented to the delegates at the Sixth Congress.

From the way I understand things at present, I believe that the matter was handled wrong. I am speaking of your expulsions from the party. If it is true that Trotskyism is what they say it is, and if your line is admittedly Trotskyian, then certainly you should have been given the opportunity to lay the matter before the party in the next party discussion. I know Trotsky was not expelled so quickly by the Russian party.

This precipitous action looks *too much* like an attempt to shut off discussion and a quick and easy way of getting rid of an opposition. I consider the Lovestone group the most dangerous group that a Communist party has ever had the misfortune to be ruled by. The whole party is demoralized and before things can be bettered we must eliminate their stifling misgovernment.

The present minority is weak, getting weaker and more vacillating. This latest occurrence will have a tremendous effect in consolidating the Lovestone rule. You know that in the past I have never agreed with Jim's maneuvers. I think that history has proved them wrong. This is not to say that the Foster group has been always right. The opposition have been consistent bunglers. The immediate future will tell, I hope, whether a revolutionary movement will continue to exist in this country or whether it will have to be built anew, with new elements.

Hoping you will keep me in touch with anything new.

Best personal regard from Rose and me.

Joe

639 N. Central Park Ave., Apt. 2

District 13. Schneiderman, District Organizer of the Young Workers League. First of all we have a financial statement: Wm. Schneiderman, 210 27th Avenue, Apt. 5, San Francisco, ten No. 2 *Militant*, 30¢, ten No. 3 *Militant*, 30¢, total, 60¢. Letter dated November 15, 1928:

James P. Cannon
New York, NY:

I read your statement and would like to have you send me some of the material you mention.

Yours,
Wm. Schneiderman
210 27th Avenue, Apt. 5
San Francisco, California

Then we have the answer of Cannon as follows:

> November 30, 1928
>
> Dear comrade Schneiderman:
>
> We received your letter and have sent you a copy of the first number of our paper. Enclosed is a copy of the second number. We are bringing out "Criticism of the Program" by Trotsky in pamphlet form, of which the two installments appearing in the paper constitute less than one-half, and expect to have it ready in about two weeks. We also have a mass of other material dealing with the disputed questions, but can only print it gradually in the *Militant* and then in pamphlet form on account of the lack of money.
>
> I wish you would let us know your reactions after reading this material and whether you will take a stand against the expulsions. Our support from the League is proportionately greater than from the party. It is quite natural, as the younger comrades on the whole are more alert and sensitive to new issues and problems outside the official routine propaganda.
>
> Hoping to hear from you again,
>
> Yours fraternally

I also have a letter dated Dec. 30 to Glotzer. Documents disclose that Cannon and Spector worked together on the Trotsky business in Moscow.

Unfortunately, due to the fact that I gave comrade Lovestone three letters, I am not in a position to give here the most important letters. One is a letter from Cannon dated Dec. 20 to Swabeck dealing with the plenum. I gave this to Lovestone and believe this letter should be read at the Secretariat. There are matters contained which require action. Secondly, a letter from Urbahns and one from Eastman. These also I turned over to comrade Lovestone.

Also a list of those who actually support the Opposition. All the names are actual supporters like Malkin, Judd, Becker, etc.

Carlson, a member of the DEC of Seattle, Agitprop director and campaign manager of Los Angeles, California, without being transferred from Seattle and being suspended by the Seattle district. The National Office instructed the Los Angeles subdistrict to remove him. They were hesitant and never did. Instead he again left without permission and came to Chicago. Comrade Lovestone has the letter from Cannon to Swabeck which discloses the fact that Swabeck claims Carlson is with them 100 percent, and Cannon instructs Swabeck to make him come out with a statement at once. Otherwise we will make it appear that we expelled him for reasons other than his statement.

On George Saul. Letters from Saul showed clearly that he was uncertain and wavering on the situation. It appears from information that Saul has already definitely taken a stand for Cannon. He is a member of the Kansas District Committee and subdistrict organizer.

In regard to Lore and Cannon, Cannon is willing to work with Lore openly but is waiting until after the convention. Shachtman has seen Lore, but Cannon has not. Lore is opposed to being called the Opposition within the party, but wants to organize a separate party. Lore wants to fight against the CEC not as a right danger, but as opportunists.

* * *

(Stachel then made motions and the following summary.)

As I said at the outset, I think that it will be a very heavy blow to the supporters of Cannon. First of all, we have succeeded in getting information that will actually disrupt their work for some time.

Secondly, we succeeded in exposing many of their agents already, people who were very dangerous while they worked from the inside.

Thirdly, we have a list of all subscribers, etc. I do not think we should have a panicky policy. It is possible that we may find certain elements that also are serving as agents. Also certain wavering elements can be won over to the party. This is valuable information in weakening both their organizational activity, and secondly, we have certainly not given them any pleasure, but trouble. We have weakened them by exposing their methods and activities and we will concentrate on winning over certain elements for the party.

I think this calls to our attention the following. First of all I want to criticize the Central Committee on its daily organ. I want to say we are absolutely underestimating the role of their activity in the United States. The *Daily Worker* proves it. Why do we not carry on an ideological campaign. Comrade Minor will have to answer that. There is plenty of material that should be printed.

Photo Sources

1. *Workers Monthly*
2. *Labor Defender*
3. Ed Swabeck
4. *Revolutionary Radicalism*, report of New York State Senate Committee to Investigate Seditious Activities, 1920
5. Bertram D. Wolfe Papers, Hoover Institution Archives, Stanford University
6. Bertram D. Wolfe Papers, Hoover Institution Archives, Stanford University
7. *Labor Herald*
8. *Workers Monthly*
9. *Labor Defender*
10. *Workers Monthly*
11. *The Liberator*
12. *Labor Herald*
13. *Workers Monthly*
14. *Workers Monthly*
15. Ed Swabeck
16. *Labor Defender*
17. *Militant*
18. Walta Ross
19. *Militant* (Konikow); John Dwyer Collection, Wayne State University Archives of Labor and Urban Affairs (*Bulletin*).
20. *Workers Monthly*
21. *Labor Defender*
22. International Newsreel photo, ILD Collection, Schomberg Center for Research in Black Culture, The New York Public Library, Astor, Lenox and Tilden Foundations
23. International Ladies' Garment Workers' Union Archives, Labor-Management Documentation Center, Cornell University
24. *Labor Defender*
25. International Newsreel photo from *Labor Defender*
26. *Labor Herald*
27. International Newsreel photo in collection of American Labor Museum, Haledon, New Jersey; *Workers Monthly* (flyer)
28. *Labor Herald* (Howat); *Labor Defender* (miners)

Glossary

Abern, Martin (1898-1949) Joined SP youth, 1912; SP, 1915; IWW, 1916; CLP founding member, on CEC almost continuously from 1920; YWL national secretary, 1922-24; WP Chicago organizer, 1924-26; ILD assistant national secretary, 1926-28; delegate to CI Fourth Congress, 1922; member of Cannon faction; expelled from WP in 1928 for Trotskyism; founding member of CLA; split from Trotskyist movement with Max Shachtman in 1940.

Allen, Henry J. (1868-1950) Supporter of Progressive Party, 1912; Republican governor of Kansas, 1919-23; U.S. Senator from Kansas, 1929-30.

Amalgamation The merging of craft unions in particular industries to form industrial unions.

American Consolidated Trades Council (ACTC) Federation of independent black unions and groups in the Chicago building trades formed during WWI; persisted as organization at least into 1930s.

American Federation of Labor (AFL) Trade union federation, made up primarily of craft unions, founded in 1881. The AFL split in 1936, when John L. Lewis of the UMW and several other unions founded the Congress of Industrial Organizations (CIO) to organize unorganized workers along industrial rather than craft lines. The two organizations merged in 1955 to form the AFL-CIO.

American Labor Party of Greater New York Founded in 1919 by local union leaders in New York City, based on a program of "democratic control of industry and commerce." Also fielded candidates in 1920 statewide elections. In 1936 a different New York ALP was founded by Hillman and Dubinsky to support Roosevelt; this party split in 1944, one wing founding the Liberal Party, the other merging in 1948 into the Henry Wallace presidential campaign.

American Negro Labor Congress Workers Party vehicle for organizing black workers, 1925-30.

Amter, Israel (1881-1954) Professional musician, journalist; SP member in Denver; joined Communist movement in 1919; on WP CEC from

1922; leader in 1922 of Goose Caucus; member of Ruthenberg-Lovestone faction; representative to CI, 1923-24; Cleveland WP district organizer, late 1920s; later New York CP leader; arrested in 1951 under Smith Act.

Anglo-Russian Trade Union Unity Committee Founded in 1925 by Soviet trade unions and leaders of the British Trades Union Congress. Stalin upheld this alliance even as the British union tops liquidated the 1926 General Strike. The British walked out in 1927.

Aronberg, Philip Joined Communist movement, early 1920s; arrested at Bridgman convention, 1922; Foster faction lieutenant in WP; elected to CEC, 1927; member of Political Committee, summer of 1928.

Askeli, Henry Leader of SP Finnish language federation; joined WP with Finnish Federation and elected to CEC, 1921; editor of WP Finnish newspaper *Työmies* (The Worker); fired from post in 1924 after opposing reorganization of party's Finnish Federation in Bolshevization campaign; expelled by Political Committee as "hopeless right-winger" and "Trotskyist," November 1928; no evidence that he sympathized with Cannon.

Bailley, Forrest Socialist, ACLU member active in Sacco-Vanzetti and Passaic strike defense work.

Baker, Rudy Named Detroit district organizer of WP, 1926, upon recommendation of Foster; remained party organizer into early 1930s.

Ballam, John CPA founder in Massachusetts; CEC member from 1919; led 1921 opposition to formation of legal Workers Party; Ruthenberg-Lovestone faction member in WP; briefly supported Cannon's anti-factional group in 1926-27, then returned to Lovestone's faction.

Barnett, Eugene One of leaders of IWW prisoners convicted after American Legion lynch mob attack on IWW hall in Centralia, Washington, 1919; sentenced to 25-40 years in prison; his autobiography was serialized in *Labor Defender*, 1927.

Bedacht, Max (1883-1972) Active as social democrat in Switzerland, Austria and France; immigrated to U.S., 1908; edited German newspapers in Detroit and San Francisco; CLP founder, member of CEC; representative to CI, 1921; member of Ruthenberg-Lovestone faction, but renounced Lovestone in 1929; acting CP national secretary, 1929-30; expelled from CP in 1948 for "leftism," later reinstated.

Berger, Victor (1860-1929) Founding member of SP, 1901; member of SP NEC, 1901-23; leader of SP right wing, nominally opposed U.S. entry into WWI, held racist views of blacks and Asians; elected as first Socialist in U.S. Congress, 1910.

Berry, George L. (1882-1948) International president, Printing Pressmen's Union, 1907-48; was a major in U.S. military in WWI; narrowly missed being nominated as Democratic Party vice presidential candidate, 1924.

Billings, Warren K. (1893-1972) President, San Francisco shoe workers union; delegate to SF Labor Council; with Tom Mooney, falsely accused of planting bomb which killed ten people at 1916 "Preparedness Day" parade; convicted of manslaughter and sentenced to life; released from prison, 1939.

Bittelman, Alexander (1890-1982) Member of Jewish Bund in Russia, exiled to Siberia; immigrated to U.S., 1912; a leader of SP's Jewish Federation; a CPA founder and CEC member; remained in CPA even after Ruthenberg split in May 1920; briefly published journal *Communist Unity*, early 1921; leader of Communist Jewish Federation; became Foster's chief factional lieutenant, 1924-28; CI representative to India, 1929-31; head of party's Jewish Bureau during WWII; imprisoned for five years under Smith Act in 1950s; expelled from CP as "revisionist," 1959.

Bogdanov, Aleksandr A. (1873-1928) Early Bolshevik; led opposition which wanted to boycott elections to tsarist Duma in 1907; target of Lenin's 1908 work *Materialism and Empirio-Criticism*; quit party in 1911 but supported Bolshevik Revolution in 1917; member of Presidium of Soviet National Economic Council after 1917, as well as director of Socialist Academy of Social Sciences.

Bolshevization Campaign initiated by Zinoviev at CI Fifth Congress in 1924 to put an end to factions in all national sections and purge them of Trotskyists and other critical elements. It entailed the replacement of territorial party units by factory and street nuclei and the elimination of the foreign-language federations in the American party.

Bouck, William (1868-1945) President of Washington state Western Farmers Progressive Association, 1921; nominated as U.S. vice presidential candidate of Farmer-Labor movement at St. Paul convention in June 1924.

Boudin, Louis B. (1874-1952) Lawyer, Marxist author; a leader of SP left wing; co-editor of *Class Struggle*; opposed 1917 Bolshevik Revolution; broke with left wing when it split from SP in 1919; became noted legal scholar and labor attorney; strongly anti-communist after 1940.

Brandler, Heinrich (1881-1967) Leader of German CP during failed revolution of 1923; made a scapegoat by Zinoviev and Stalin, removed from leadership in 1924; expelled in 1929 for organizing a Bukharinite opposition.

Brennan, Martin (1896-1968) UMW member from 1912; president of Anthracite district in 1920s; candidate for UMW secretary-treasurer on Communist-supported "Save the Union" ticket, 1926.

Briggs, Cyril (1887-1966) West Indian who emigrated to U.S., 1905; reporter and editor for New York black newspaper *Amsterdam News*, 1912-18; forced to resign because of antiwar stand during WWI; editor of the *Crusader*, 1918-23; founder of ABB, fall 1919; one of first blacks to join Communist movement; editor of ANLC journal, *Negro Champion*, 1925-30; elected to CEC, 1928; expelled from CP for "Negro nationalist way of thinking," 1939; rejoined CP, 1948; leader of Los Angeles party, 1950s; editor of L.A. *Herald Dispatch*, late 1950s.

Brophy, John (1883-1963) President of UMW District 2 (Pennsylvania), 1916-26; leader of WP-supported Save the Union Committee and candidate for UMW president, 1926; broke with WP when it turned toward dual unionism in 1928; expelled from UMW; reconciled with UMW leader Lewis, 1933; CIO organizing director.

Browder, Earl (1891-1973) SP member, 1907-12; worked with Foster's Syndicalist League, 1912-15; rejoined SP as left-winger after Russian Revolution; editor with Cannon of *Workers' World*, 1919; in prison for conspiracy during founding of Communist movement; joined UCP, elected to CEC, 1921; headed American delegation to founding RILU congress, 1921; Foster faction lieutenant, 1924-28; in Moscow, 1926-27; worked for Comintern in Far East, 1927-28; American CP general secretary, 1930-45; expelled for "opportunism," 1946.

Budenny, Semyon (1883-1973) Sergeant major in tsarist army; joined Red Army in 1918 and Bolshevik Party in 1919; commander of First Cavalry during Civil War; one of few military figures to escape Stalin purges; commander in chief of Soviet cavalry, 1943-53.

Bukharin, Nikolai (1888-1938) Bolshevik from 1906; elected to Central Committee, 1917; editor of *Pravda*, 1918-26; head of Comintern, 1926-29; leader of right-wing Communists, allied with Stalin against Trotsky-Zinoviev Joint Opposition, 1926-28; ousted from leadership posts, 1929; *Izvestia* editor in chief, 1933-37; arrested, 1937; executed after third Moscow purge trial.

Burman, Fahle Western Federation of Miners official, 1911-14; member, carpenters union, 1914-24; joined SP, 1920; joined WP as secretary-treasurer of Finnish Federation, 1921; elected to WP CEC as supporter of Foster-Cannon group, 1923 and 1925 conventions.

Carlson, Oliver National secretary of SP youth from 1919; broke with SP and went to Moscow, 1921, where he helped to found YCI; founding

YWL member and national secretary upon return, 1922; representative to YCI in Moscow, 1923-24; founding CLA National Committee member in 1929, but suspended for indiscipline later that year; became teacher and author.

Central Executive Committee (CEC) Also known as the Central Committee, the leadership body of the Workers Party, elected at delegated national conventions.

Chaplin, Ralph (1887-1961) Radical artist, journalist and songwriter; author of labor anthem *Solidarity Forever*; joined IWW, 1913; tried and convicted with Haywood in 1918 Chicago trial and sentenced to 20 years; released on appeal in 1921, fled to USSR with Haywood but returned to prison in U.S.; released in 1923; remained active in IWW until 1936.

Chiang Kai-shek (1887-1975) Leader of Chinese Kuomintang's military arm from 1923; emerged as Kuomintang leader after Sun Yat-sen's death in 1925; ordered bloody Shanghai massacre of workers and Communists, April 1927; Chinese dictator until 1949 revolution; fled to Taiwan and established KMT dictatorship there.

Chicago Conference (July 3 Conference) The 3 July 1923 conference of the Farmer-Labor movement; dominated by WP supporters. "Progressive" union leaders, led by Chicago AFL president John Fitzpatrick, walked out after WP pushed through a resolution to organize the Federated Farmer-Labor Party.

Christensen, Parley Parker (1870-1954) Salt Lake City attorney and politician; member, Committee of 48; 1920 U.S. presidential candidate for FLP.

Cline, Charles IWW member; convicted of murder and sentenced to life in prison for participating with Jesus Rangel in 1913 guerrilla expedition from Texas to aid Mexican Revolution; pardoned in 1926; worked with ILD upon his release.

Comintern See "Communist International."

Committee of 48 Remnants of Theodore Roosevelt's Progressive Party who sought to get the Farmer-Labor movement to endorse La Follette for U.S. president.

The Communist Monthly theoretical organ of WP from 1927, when it replaced *Workers Monthly*, to 1944, when it was supplanted by *Political Affairs*.

Communist International (CI, or Comintern) Also known as Third International. International revolutionary organization founded on

Lenin's initiative in Moscow, 1919; national Communist parties were sections of the International. Underwent degeneration after 1923 as Stalin faction consolidated control of Soviet state; dissolved by Stalin in 1943.

Communist International Official organ of CI, published 1919-40.

Communist Labor Party (CLP) Founded 31 August 1919, led primarily by native-born U.S. Communists who unsuccessfully sought to remain in the SP to win over greater numbers of Socialists; fused in May 1920 with Ruthenberg group that split from CPA, forming UCP.

Communist League of America (CLA) Organization founded in 1929 by James P. Cannon and other Trotskyists expelled from the Workers Party.

Communist Party of America (CPA) Founded September 1919, dominated by former members of SP foreign-language federations who rejected further political struggle within the SP. It fused with the UCP in May 1921. This united underground organization, also called the CPA, was dissolved in April 1923 in favor of its public arm, the Workers Party.

Conference for Progressive Political Action (CPPA) Founded in 1922 by the leaders of the Machinists and other railway unions to support "progressive" candidates; Fitzpatrick's FLP split in December 1922 when CPPA refused to endorse call for labor party; CPPA endorsed La Follette for U.S. president in 1924.

Coolidge, Calvin (1872-1933) Republican President of U.S., 1923-29.

Costrell, H.I. Jewish Federation leader and Foster faction lieutenant in WP; sat on party's Political Committee in absence of most WP leaders during CI Sixth Congress in 1928.

Cramer, Robley D. Editor of AFL organ, *Minnesota Labor Review,* until retirement, 1962; ally of Mahoney in Minnesota FLP.

Daily Worker WP's daily newspaper from 1924. Remained organ of CP until 1955, when it resumed earlier name, *The Worker.*

Daugherty, Harry M. Republican Attorney General, 1921-24; Ohio crony of President Harding; two trials for conspiracy to defraud U.S. government ended in hung juries, 1926-27.

Davis, John W. (1873-1955) West Virginia Congressman, 1911-13; Democratic candidate in 1924 U.S. presidential elections.

Dawes Plan U.S.-sponsored restructuring of Germany's post-WWI reparations payments, adopted in 1924; named after its principal author, Charles G. Dawes (1865-1951). Dawes was also U.S. Vice President under Coolidge, 1924-29.

Debs, Eugene V. (1855-1926) Railway union leader, 1878-92; founder and leader of American Railway Union, 1892-94; SP founder and outstanding spokesman from 1901; member of IWW, 1905-08; five-time Socialist candidate for U.S. president, 1900-20; defended Bolshevik Revolution but refused to join Communist movement; member of ILD National Committee, 1925-26.

De Leon, Daniel (1852-1914) Joined SLP in 1890, became its main leader and theoretician; opposed working in reactionary AFL trade unions; helped to found IWW in 1905 though broke with it in 1908.

Don, Sam Also known as Sam Donchin; YCL leader in 1920s; came over with Weinstone to Cannon's faction to end factions in 1926; briefly *DW* editor in early 1930s, but removed when Browder became party leader.

Doty, Edward Alabama-born black plumber, leader of ACTC, Chicago; post commander of Chicago ABB, early 1920s; joined Communist movement, early 1920s; supporter of Ruthenberg-Lovestone faction in WP.

Dubinsky, David (1892-1982) Right-wing Socialist; ILGWU vice president, 1922-29, secretary-treasurer, 1929-32, president, 1932-66; a founder of CIO; co-founder of pro-Roosevelt American Labor Party, 1936.

Dunn, Robert W. (1895-1977) ACLU member who joined WP in early 1920s; founder and executive secretary of Labor Research Association, 1927-75; in CP through 1940s; ACLU Executive Committee, 1923-41.

Dunne, Vincent R. (1889-1970) Founding member, IWW; joined Communist movement in 1920; prominent Communist in Minneapolis labor movement; supporter of Cannon faction; expelled from WP as Trotskyist, 1928; founding member, CLA; central leader of 1934 Minneapolis Teamster strikes; imprisoned during WWII in Smith Act prosecution of Trotskyists.

Dunne, William F. (1887-1953) SP member from 1910 and union leader in Butte, Montana; joined CLP, 1919; WP CEC member, 1922-28; representative to CI, 1924-25; chairman, U.S. delegation to CI Fifth Congress, 1924, where he was elected alternate member of ECCI; elected to Comintern Organization Bureau at ECCI Fifth Plenum, 1925; *Daily Worker* co-editor, 1924-27; Cannon's chief factional lieutenant and collaborator, 1924-28, but remained in CP after Cannon's expulsion; expelled in 1946 for "left deviationism."

Eastman, Max (1883-1969) SP member and *Masses* editor from 1912; member of SP left wing and defender of Bolshevik Revolution; did not join Workers Party; publicized views of Trotsky's Left Opposition in U.S. in late 1920s; supported formation of CLA; turned to right during Moscow purge trials in 1930s; became right-wing *Reader's Digest* editor during WWII.

Engdahl, John Louis (1884-1932) SP member, 1907-20; a leader of Workers' Council group; WP CEC member from 1921; co-editor of *Daily Worker*, 1924-27; supporter of Ruthenberg-Lovestone faction; representative to CI, 1927-28; ILD leader after expulsion of Trotskyists.

Epstein, Shachno Co-editor of SP Jewish paper *Naye Welt* (New World), 1915-17; returned to Russia during 1917 Revolution; sent back to U.S. by CI in 1921 to educate Jewish Communists; edited Jewish Communist journals; returned to USSR in late 1920s, where he remained active until at least 1940.

Ewert, Arthur (1890-1959) Joined German SP, 1908; lived in Canada, 1914-19; returned to Germany and joined KPD, 1919; first elected to German CC, 1923; chaired American Commission of Eighth ECCI Plenum, May 1927, using name Braun; Comintern delegate to WP Fifth Convention, 1927, using name Grey; elected alternate member of ECCI at Comintern Sixth Congress, 1928; close to Bukharin; censured by Comintern in 1928 and removed from German leadership; worked for Comintern, mostly in Latin America, 1930-35; imprisoned in Brazil, 1935-45; amnestied, having lost his sanity, 1945; spent rest of life in East German mental institution.

Farmer-Labor Federation Minnesota formation founded by WPers and left-wing FLPers in September 1923; Communists purged in 1925.

Farmer-Labor Party (FLP) Founded as Labor Party in 1919 on initiative of John Fitzpatrick and allies in Chicago Federation of Labor. Name changed to FLP in 1920; sponsor of 3 July 1923 Chicago conference (see "Chicago Conference"). The Fitzpatrick FLP ceased to exist after July 1923. In June 1924 the St. Paul convention nominated a U.S. presidential slate on a "Farmer-Labor Party" ticket—the slate was withdrawn when the Workers Party nominated its own slate soon afterward.

Farrington, Frank (1873-1939) Head of UMW District 12 (Illinois), 1914-26, and opponent of union president Lewis; suspended from UMW for collusion with Peabody Coal Co., 1926; participant in 1930 convention of Reorganized UMW.

Federated Farmer-Labor Party (FFLP) Formed by WP supporters at 3 July 1923 Chicago conference after union "progressives" in FLP leadership walked out. Though based on the FLP's populist reform program, the FFLP lacked support outside the Communist movement and was abandoned soon after the 1924 St. Paul convention of the Farmer-Labor movement.

Federated Press Radical, labor-oriented news service founded in 1919 by Farmer-Labor activists; closely associated with the Communist movement from early 1920s; disbanded under impact of anti-Red witchhunt, 1956.

Ferguson, Isaac Chicago lawyer; joined SP, 1918; CPA founding CEC member and *Communist* editor, 1919-20; one of Ruthenberg's chief collaborators; imprisoned for sedition, 1920-22; quit Communist movement upon release; worked with ILD in late 1920s.

Fischer, Ruth (1895-1961) Founding member and leader of Austrian CP, 1918; member of German CP left wing from 1919; elected to Central Committee, 1923; promoted to co-leadership of party with Maslow after removal of Brandler, 1924; expelled from German CP, 1926; in exile in Paris after Hitler's coming to power in 1933; briefly member of Trotskyist movement, 1935; resided in U.S. from 1941; author of self-serving *Stalin and German Communism* (1948).

Fitzpatrick, John (1871-1946) President of Chicago Federation of Labor, 1906-46; opposed U.S. intervention in WWI; supported union amalgamation and U.S. diplomatic recognition of Soviet Republic; founder of Farmer-Labor Party; broke with Communist allies in 1923 and turned politically to the right.

Flynn, Elizabeth Gurley (1890-1964) Nationally known IWW activist and speaker from 1906; ILD chairman, 1927-30; ACLU national committee member from 1920 until 1940, when removed in anti-Communist purge; joined CP, 1937; imprisoned under Smith Act, 1955-57.

Ford, Henry (1863-1947) U.S. industrialist and founder of Ford Motor Company. In 1923-24 there was a strong movement to give Ford, a right-wing populist and anti-Semite, the Democratic presidential nomination.

Ford, Richard IWW organizer; arrested with Herman Suhr during 1913 Wheatfield, California hop pickers strike and framed up for murder of deputy sheriff; paroled in 1925 and immediately re-arrested for murder of county D.A. during same strike; acquitted, 1926.

Foster, William Z. (1881-1961) SP member, 1901-09; member of IWW, 1909-11; founded Syndicalist League to "bore from within" AFL, 1912; led 1919 Chicago meatpacking organizing drive and national steel strike; founded TUEL, 1920; delegate to first congress of RILU in Moscow, 1921; joined WP, 1921; member of CEC from 1922; leader of Communist trade-union work; CP chairman, 1945-57.

Fraina, Louis (1892-1953) Member of SLP, 1909-14; on editorial board of *New Review* and other SP left-wing journals from 1914; supported Bolsheviks before October Revolution; founding member of CPA, 1919; CPA international secretary and editor of *The Communist*; delegate to CI Second Congress, 1920; expelled by CI for financial malfeasance, 1922; began writing as Marxist economist under name of Lewis Corey from 1926; member of Lovestone organization, 1937-39; a founder and research director of early Americans for Democratic Action, 1940;

renounced Marxism in 1940; economics professor, Antioch College, 1942-51; threatened with deportation by U.S. government, 1950-53.

Garvey, Marcus (1887-1940) Jamaican-born black nationalist, founded UNIA in Harlem, 1917; arrested and charged by U.S. government with fraud in connection with his back-to-Africa steamship line, 1922; served two years in prison; deported to Jamaica, 1927; died in London.

George, Harrison Joined SP, 1910; IWW, 1913; convicted under Espionage Act during WWI and spent most of 1918-23 in prison; author of first IWW pamphlet in support of Soviet Russia, 1918; joined Communist movement secretly in 1919, but remained in IWW until 1924; Foster faction supporter; worked for RILU in late 1920s; participated in CP agricultural organizing in early 1930s; named editor of CP West Coast journal in 1938; expelled from CP with William Dunne in June 1946.

Giganti, Joseph Recruited to Communist movement in early 1920s by Abern; member of TUEL in barbers union; Chicago ILD secretary, 1928; Foster faction member; expelled from party for writing letter to Abern, 1928; joined CLA two years later; expelled from CLA along with Hugo Oehler in 1935.

Gitlow, Benjamin (1891-1965) Joined SP youth, 1907; SP, 1909; a CLP founder; jailed for criminal syndicalism, 1919-22; Goose Caucus member; trade-union authority for Ruthenberg faction; expelled with Lovestone, 1929; left Lovestone's group, 1933; was government "witness" during anti-Communist witchhunt trials in 1940s and 1950s.

Glotzer, Albert (b. 1908) Joined YWL, 1923; member Chicago YWL DEC; elected to national YWL Executive Committee, 1927; member of Cannon faction; expelled as Trotskyist, 1928; founding National Committee member of CLA; split along with Shachtman in 1940.

Gomez, Manuel Pseudonym for Charles Phillips; a founder of Mexican CP; delegate from Mexico to CI Second Congress, 1920; secretary for WP's All-American Anti-Imperialist League, 1925-28; member of Cannon faction; expelled from CP in 1929, but did not support Trotskyism.

Gompers, Samuel (1850-1924) AFL founder and leader from 1886 to his death.

Goose Caucus Name given to those who fought to maintain the "illegal" apparatus of the underground Communist Party alongside that of the legal Workers Party, 1922-23.

Grange Farmers movement founded in 1867 and peaking in 1876; promoted cooperatives and restrictions on monopolies; still exists as an organization of conservative farmers.

Greenback Party Organized in 1876 and renamed Greenback Labor Party in 1878; advocated an easy money policy, specifically that the government keep in circulation the devalued "greenback" currency issued to finance the Union in the Civil War; faded from scene, 1880s.

Green, William (1873-1952) UMW official from 1900; AFL president, 1924-52.

Gusev, Sergei I. (1874-1933) Bolshevik from 1903; member of Soviet military council during Civil War, where he sided with Stalin in disputes with Trotsky; CI representative to WP in 1925; helped put Ruthenberg-Lovestone faction in control of party; ECCI member, 1928-33.

Hapgood, Powers (1899-1949) Writer, union activist; a leader of UMW Save the Union Committee; delegate to 1930 Reorganized UMW convention; SP member from 1926; CIO organizer in several industries; Indiana CIO director, 1941-49.

Harding, Warren G. (1865-1923) U.S. Republican President, 1921-23; died in office.

Hardy, George (1884-1966) Seaman; IWW member from 1911; IWW general secretary, 1920-21; supported affiliation to RILU; expelled from IWW, 1922, and became a Communist; worked in England for RILU in late 1920s; remained CP member until his death.

Hathaway, Clarence (1894-1963) Briefly a member of sectarian Proletarian Party before joining Communist movement in early 1920s; official in Machinists union; a founder of Minnesota Farmer-Labor Federation; organizer of 1924 St. Paul convention; Cannon faction member; attended Lenin School in Moscow, 1926-28; led witchhunt against Cannon supporters after Cannon's expulsion from the party; *DW* editor, 1930s; expelled from CP, 1940; readmitted after WWII.

Haywood, Harry (1898-1985) Pseudonym of Harry Hall, Nebraska-born black American and WWI veteran, recruited to Communist movement by his brother; joined ABB in 1922, YWL in 1923, WP in 1925; student, University of the Toilers of the East, Moscow, 1926-27; first black American to study at Moscow Lenin School, 1927-30; delegate to Sixth CI Congress, 1928; first American to push Stalin's line of self-determination for blacks in Southern U.S. "black belt"; vice-chairman of CI Negro Commission, 1929-30; returned to U.S., 1930; trade-union organizer and leader of CP's Negro work, early 1930s; elected to CC, 1931; elected to PC, 1934; lost influence when party downplayed self-determination slogan during popular front period; fought in Spain, 1937; removed from PC and CC, 1938; active in Los Angeles CP, 1940s; expelled from CP, 1959; member of Maoist Communist Party (Marxist-Leninist), early 1970s.

Haywood, William D., "Big Bill" (1869-1928) Western Federation of Miners secretary-treasurer, 1900-08; an IWW founder, 1905; acquitted after 15 months in jail for 1905 murder of Idaho governor; SP organizer and spokesman, 1908-12; purged from SP leadership in 1913 for left-wing views; IWW general secretary from 1914; fled to Moscow in 1921 after being convicted under Espionage Act; died in Moscow, 1928.

Hill, Joe (1879-1915) Pseudonym for Joel Emmanuel Hoagland, Swedish immigrant worker; joined IWW around 1910, becoming its most prominent songwriter; organizer among Utah copper miners, 1913; framed up, charged with 1914 murder of Salt Lake City grocer and executed by firing squad, 1915.

Hillman, Sidney (1887-1946) Amalgamated Clothing Workers president, 1915-46; a CIO founder; helped to build pro-Roosevelt American Labor Party, 1936.

Hillquit, Morris (1869-1933) SLP member, 1890-99; an SP founder, 1901; centrist SP leader, who after 1904 directed party in alliance with Berger right wing; oversaw 1919 purge of tens of thousands of SP left-wing members; ILGWU general counsel, 1913-33.

Howat, Alexander (1876-1945) Head of UMW District 14 (Kansas), 1906-21; SP member; candidate for UMW vice president on anti-Lewis ticket, 1920; expelled from UMW by Lewis, 1921; sought reinstatement throughout 1920s; participated in Communist-supported Progressive International Committee in UMW, 1923; TUEL member; member of ILD national committee; reinstated by District 14 as president in late 1920s; president of Reorganized UMW, 1930; expelled from UMW, 1930; died an employee of city of Pittsburg, Kansas.

Huiswoud, Otto (1893-1961) Surinam-born black printer who joined American SP during WWI; one of first blacks to join Communist movement; member, ABB; delegate and chairman of Negro Commission at Comintern Fourth Congress, 1922; used pseudonym J. Billings in Moscow; supporter, Ruthenberg-Lovestone faction; abandoned Lovestone to remain in CP, 1929; opposed slogan of self-determination for American "black belt," 1928-30; worked in Europe for CI and RILU, 1930s; returned to U.S., 1939; instructor, Harlem People's School, 1940; returned to Surinam where he was interned, 1941; thereafter denied entry to U.S.; lived in Amsterdam, 1947-61.

Industrial Workers of the World (IWW) Founded in June 1905 by leaders of the SP, SLP and Western Federation of Miners as a revolutionary industrial union movement; faced severe government persecution for its leadership of many heroic, mostly losing strikes of mainly unskilled workers; declined in the aftermath of WWI and the Russian Revolution.

International Labor Defense (ILD) Organization created by the WP in 1925, on Cannon's initiative, to organize united-front defense for class-war prisoners, regardless of political affiliation.

International Press Correspondence (Inprecorr) An official organ of the CI, published at least weekly in the Soviet Union, Germany, Austria and Britain, beginning in 1921. In 1938 its name was changed to *World News and Views.*

Jakira, Abraham Goose Caucus leader, 1922; secretary of WP's Russian Federation and CEC member, 1922-23 and 1925-29; Lovestone supporter; Pittsburgh district organizer, late 1920s.

Johnson, Charles E. Also known as Charles Scott and Charles Jansen; Lettish-American Communist from Roxbury who performed many foreign assignments for CI and RILU in early 1920s; member of CI delegation to American party, spring 1921; American representative to RILU, 1924-25.

Johnson, Magnus (1871-1936) Minnesota farmer; Republican state legislator, 1915-23; leader of right wing of Minnesota FLP; FLP gubernatorial candidate, 1922 and 1926; elected to U.S. Senate in special election, 1923; lost Senate seat in 1924 election; U.S. Congressman, 1933-35.

Johnstone, Jack W. (1880-1942) IWW member from 1906. Supporter and associate of William Z. Foster from 1912, when he quit IWW in support of Foster's policy of "boring from within" AFL; organizer of 1917-19 campaign to organize meatpackers; co-founder of TUEL, 1920; joined Communist movement, 1920; one of Foster's chief lieutenants in WP; CI representative to Mexico, 1924-25, and India, 1929; Communist Party CC member, 1927-42.

Judd, Helen Member of Workers Party Chicago district Central Control Commission, 1928; expelled for opposing Glotzer's and Swabeck's expulsions from Workers Party; schoolteacher; founding member of CLA.

Kamenev, Leon B. (1883-1936) Bolshevik from 1903; CC member from 1917; allied with Stalin and Zinoviev against Trotsky, 1923-25; in Joint Opposition with Trotsky, 1926-27; capitulated to Stalin; executed after first Moscow Trial in 1936.

Karsner, Rose (1890-1968) Born Rose Greenberg in Rumania; immigrated to U.S. as a child; joined SP, 1908; secretary of Max Eastman's journal *Masses* during WWI; founding member of Communist movement; worked for Friends of Soviet Russia and Workers International Relief; her first husband, David Karsner, wrote authorized biography of Eugene V. Debs; she was Cannon's companion from 1924; assistant secretary of ILD; founding member of CLA; business manager of Trotskyist newspaper *Militant*; active in Trotskyist movement until her death.

Kautsky, Karl (1854-1938) Best-known theoretician of Socialist International in two decades before WWI; opposed Bolshevik Revolution; leader of "Two and a Half International," rejoining Second International in 1922.

Kerensky, Alexander F. (1881-1970) Leader of Russian Social Revolutionaries; minister of justice in first government formed after tsar was overthrown in February 1917; became Prime Minister in July 1917; his government was overthrown by Bolshevik Revolution in October.

Konikow, Antoinette (1869-1946) Joined Russian exile socialist organization, 1888; immigrated to U.S., 1893; member of SLP; founding member of SP, 1901; medical doctor and pioneer of birth control in U.S.; a founder of Communist movement, 1919; went to Soviet Union in 1926 as birth control specialist, afterwards she supported Trotsky's views in WP; formed Independent Communist League, a Trotskyist group in Boston, 1928; a CLA founder, active Trotskyist until her death.

Krumbein, Charles (1889-1947) Steamfitter active in Chicago labor movement; a CLP founder; imprisoned during Palmer Raids; Chicago WP industrial organizer and union delegate to Chicago Federation of Labor, 1921-23; Foster faction member; WP New York district organizer, 1924-25; attended Lenin School in Moscow, 1926-27; worked for CI, mainly in China, 1927-34; spent 15 months in U.S. prison in 1934-35 for using false passport; CP treasurer, 1938-47.

Kruse, William F. (1893-1980) Leader of SP youth; a leader of Workers' Council group; WP member from 1921; CEC member, 1922-29; Ruthenberg-Lovestone faction supporter; attended Lenin School in Moscow, 1926-27; expelled from party for refusing to denounce Lovestone, 1929; did not join Lovestone's new party.

Kun, Béla (1886-1939) Joined Bolsheviks in 1917 as Hungarian prisoner of war; founding leader of Hungarian CP, 1918; head of short-lived Hungarian Soviet Republic, 1919; leader of ultralefts in Comintern, 1921-23; ECCI member, 1921-37; arrested in Soviet Union, 1937; died in prison.

Kuomintang (KMT) Chinese bourgeois-nationalist party founded by Sun Yat-sen in 1912 and led after 1925 by Chiang Kai-shek. Ruling party of China until 1949 Revolution; it has continued to rule Taiwan since then.

Kuusinen, Otto (1881-1964) Prominent pre-war Finnish Social Democrat; attended CI founding congress; member of ECCI from 1921; presided over dissolution of Comintern, 1943; member of Soviet Politburo, 1952-53 and 1957-64.

Labor Defender Organ of the ILD, beginning in 1926 as a monthly edited by Max Shachtman. After 1928 it was edited by Louis Engdahl; frequency was reduced. Its name was changed to *Equal Justice*, 1937-42.

Labor Herald Organ of the TUEL, appearing from 1922 to 1924, edited by William Z. Foster and then Earl Browder. In November 1924 it was combined with *The Liberator* and *Soviet Russia Pictorial* to form *Workers Monthly*.

Labor Unity Monthly organ of the TUEL and its successor, the Trade Union Unity League, from 1927 to 1935. It was published as a weekly during most of 1929-31.

La Follette, Robert M. (1855-1925) Republican governor of Wisconsin, 1901-06; U.S. Senator, 1906-25; Progressive Party presidential candidate, 1924.

Lenin, V.I. (1870-1924) Founder of St. Petersburg League for the Emancipation of the Working Class, 1895; principal Bolshevik leader from 1903; leader of October Revolution in Russia, 1917; chairman of Soviet government, 1917-24; a founder and leader of Communist (Third) International until illness overtook him in 1922.

Levi, Paul (1883-1930) German CP founding member and party leader after 1919; expelled in April 1921 for publicly attacking party's adventurism in "March Action" that year; became Social Democratic parliamentarian; committed suicide in 1930.

Lewis, John L. (1880-1969) President of UMW, 1920-60; principal leader of CIO until 1940.

The Liberator From 1918 continuator of the *Masses*, radical monthly published by Max Eastman. After 1919 the magazine began to express the Communist line. In 1924 it merged with *Labor Herald* and *Soviet Russia Pictorial* to become *Workers Monthly*.

Little, Frank (1879-1917) Western Federation of Miners organizer from 1900; joined IWW, 1906; son of Cherokee Indian mother and Quaker father; organized IWW local of Japanese and Mexican agricultural workers in Fresno, California; helped found IWW Agricultural Workers Organization; elected IWW General Executive Board, 1914; brutally murdered during copper miners strike in Butte, Montana.

Lloyd George, David (1863-1945) Liberal Party Prime Minister of Britain, 1916-22.

Lore, Ludwig (1875-1942) German Social Democrat; immigrated to U.S., 1903; member of SP left wing and IWW; CLP founding member, on

CEC from 1921; led party's German language federation; defended Serrati and Levi against Comintern criticism, 1921; defended Trotsky, 1924; expelled from WP, 1925; briefly in Trotskyist movement, 1934-35.

Lovestone, Jay (1898-1990) Joined SP in 1917 while a student at City College of New York; founding CPA member, elected to CEC, 1919; WP CEC member 1922-29; became Ruthenberg's chief factional lieutenant; WP general secretary after Ruthenberg's death, 1927-29; expelled from WP, 1929; founded Communist Party Opposition, later renamed Independent Labor League, as section of Bukharinite International Right Opposition; disbanded organization, 1940; became anti-Communist AFL-CIO adviser, leading Cold Warrior and CIA collaborator.

Lowell, Esther Federated Press reporter from 1923; wife of Art Shields; joined *DW* staff, 1924.

Lozovsky, A. (1878-1952) Bolshevik from 1903; union leader in exile in Paris and Geneva after 1909; returned to Russia, 1917; expelled from Bolshevik Party, December 1917; rejoined, 1919; leader of Profintern, 1921-39; arrested during Stalin's 1949 anti-Semitic campaign and shot.

Lynch, James M. (1867-1930) Member of International Typographical Union from 1887; ITU president, 1900-14 and 1924-26; New York State labor commissioner, 1914-21.

MacDonald, Duncan Illinois UMW secretary-treasurer, 1912-17; elected Illinois Federation of Labor president, 1919; nominated as U.S. presidential candidate by St. Paul convention of Farmer-Labor movement, June 1924.

MacDonald, James Ramsay (1866-1937) British Labour Party leader and Prime Minister, 1924 and 1929-31; expelled from Labour Party in 1931, when he remained as Prime Minister (until 1935) in joint government of Conservatives, Liberals and some Labour politicians.

McKaig, Ray Leader of North Dakota state Grange; NPL organizer from 1916; sent to Idaho, 1917; also active in CPPA.

McKay, Claude (1890-1948) Black Jamaican-born poet and author, residing in U.S. and Europe from 1912; early figure of the Harlem Renaissance; collaborated with Sylvia Pankhurst's Communist *Workers' Dreadnought* in Britain, 1919; assistant editor of Max Eastman's *Liberator*, 1921; attended 1922 CI Fourth Congress where he spoke on black question in U.S.; turned to Catholicism in 1930s.

McNamara Brothers Iron workers union secretary-treasurer John J. McNamara and his brother James B. McNamara, both charged with killing 21 in dynamiting of *Los Angeles Times* building in 1910; induced by attorney Clarence Darrow to plead guilty to escape death penalty; sentenced to 15 years and life imprisonment, respectively.

Mahoney, William (1869-1952) Member of Printing Pressmen's Union from 1893; Socialist from 1896; editor, *Minnesota Union Advocate*, 1920-32; president of St. Paul Trades and Labor Assembly, 1919-32; collaborated with WP in forming Farmer-Labor Federation; broke with WP over latter's refusal to support La Follette; FLP mayor of St. Paul, 1932-34.

Malkin, Maurice CPA founding member active in Furriers' Union; expelled from WP as Trotskyist, 1928; imprisoned for participation in Furriers strike, 1929-30; repudiated CLA in October 1929 when ILD threatened to withdraw from his defense, but he retracted his statement a year later; expelled from CLA and rejoined CP, 1931; expelled from CP, 1937; anti-Communist witness before Congressional Dies Committee, 1939.

Maslow, Arkadi (1891-1941) Joined German CP, 1919; became leader of Berlin party left wing; promoted with Ruth Fischer to party leadership after Brandler's removal, 1924; expelled by CI, 1926; went into exile in France and Cuba after Hitler came to power in 1933.

Mass, Barney (later known as Barney Mayes) Auto worker expelled from WP as Trotskyist, 1928; active as Trotskyist in San Francisco labor movement in mid-1930s; quit Trotskyist movement in late 1930s and became AFL official.

Maurer, James (1864-1944) Plumbers and Steamfitters Union local official in Reading, Penn., 1886-1944; president of Penn. AFL, 1912-28; SLP member, 1898-1902; SP, 1902-36; CPPA National Committee, 1922.

Michigan Communist Cases Thirty-one Communists, including WP secretary C.E. Ruthenberg, arrested after the underground party's 1922 convention in Bridgman, Michigan and charged with criminal syndicalism. Foster's trial resulted in a hung jury. Ruthenberg was convicted and sentenced to three to ten years; he died just before the Supreme Court turned down his appeal. The charges against the rest were dropped in 1933.

Minerich, Anthony A leader of Communist work among miners, late 1920s; a leader of Detroit Hunger March, 1932.

Minor, Robert (1884-1952) Prominent political cartoonist; joined SP, 1907; joined UCP, 1920; Goose Caucus member; CEC member from 1921; delegate to CI Third Congress, 1921; American representative to Comintern, 1926-27; elected to Presidium at ECCI Seventh Plenum, December 1926; protégé of John Pepper; Ruthenberg faction authority on black question; *Daily Worker* editor, 1927-28; acting CP national secretary while Browder in prison, 1941; remained in CP until his death.

Mooney, Thomas J. (1882-1942) SP member from 1907; International Molders' Union activist, elected to San Francisco Labor Council, 1912;

framed up with Billings on charges of bombing SF "Preparedness Day" parade in 1916; execution stayed in 1918 due to international campaign; pardoned in 1939.

Nearing, Scott (1883-1983) Economist, teacher and author; member of SP, 1917-22; joined WP, 1926; member of ILD National Committee; expelled from party, 1930.

Nelson, Oscar (1884-1943) President, National Federation of Postal Clerks, 1910-13; vice president, Chicago Federation of Labor, 1910-35; Chicago alderman, 1923-35; switched from Democratic to Republican Party, 1927; Superior Court judge, 1935-43.

New Economic Policy (NEP) Program adopted by the Soviet government at the end of the Civil War in 1921, to revive the economy primarily by permitting the temporary development of market relations in the agricultural sector.

Non-Partisan League Farmer-based organization with a program of populist reforms; founded as offshoot of North Dakota SP in 1915; national headquarters moved to St. Paul in 1917; tried to take over apparatuses of both bourgeois parties, usually the Republicans; large component of Farmer-Labor movement, especially in Minnesota.

Oehler, Hugo (1903-1983) WP district organizer in Kansas City in late 1920s; Cannon faction supporter; visited New York soon after Cannon's expulsion and was won to Left Opposition but remained undercover in CP for over a year; helped lead CP's work in 1929 Gastonia textile strike; joined CLA, June 1930; formed sectarian opposition in CLA, 1934; expelled 1935; founded Revolutionary Workers League, which was active into 1950s.

O'Flaherty, Tom (1889-1936) Immigrated to U.S. from Ireland in 1912 and joined SP soon after; founding member of Communist movement; WP CEC member, 1921-22 and 1925-27; prominent journalist in *Daily Worker* and *Labor Defender*; Cannon faction supporter, expelled as Trotskyist, 1928; CLA founding member; left Trotskyist movement, 1931.

Ohio Socialist Weekly paper issued by the Socialist Party of Ohio beginning in 1917 and becoming, in November 1919, an organ of the CLP called *The Toiler.*

Olgin, Moissaye J. (1878-1939) Immigrated to U.S. from Russia, 1915; supported Mensheviks in 1917; joined WP in 1921 with SP Jewish Federation and Workers' Council; elected to CEC, 1922; editor of *Freiheit*, Jewish Federation organ; supported Lore until anti-Trotsky campaign of 1924; in 1935 wrote CP handbook, *Trotskyism: Counterrevolution in Disguise.*

Olson, Floyd (1891-1936) Minneapolis county prosecutor, 1920-30; Farmer-Labor Party candidate for governor, 1924 and 1930; Minnesota governor, 1930-36.

Palmer, A. Mitchell "Progressive" Democrat and U.S. Attorney General, 1919-20; initiator of "Palmer Raids" repression against IWW and Communist movement.

Pan-American Federation of Labor Initiated by AFL leadership in 1918, with secret U.S. government funding, to rally Latin American support for Washington's war aims. Continued to function through 1920s as a prop for U.S. foreign policy.

Panken, Jacob (1879-1968) Member of SP right wing and supporter of Hillquit; elected New York municipal judge on Socialist ticket, 1917; supported by New York WP in failed re-election bid, 1927.

Parsons, Lucy (1853?-1942) Early American anarchist; lifelong fighter for vindication of Haymarket martyrs (including her husband, Albert Parsons); IWW founding member; worked with Communists from mid-1920s to her death.

Party Organizer Internal CP organ appearing monthly 1927-38.

People's Party Also known as the Populist party, or movement; founded in 1892; advocated easy money and credit policies and government control of the railroads; strong mainly in the South and West; declined after 1896 when party supported the Democratic candidate for U.S. president, William Jennings Bryan.

Pepper, John (1886-1938) Name used by József Pogány, Budapest Social Democrat who helped lead failed Hungarian Revolution of 1919; upon defeat, fled to Moscow; sent to U.S., 1922; architect of WP's "labor party" policy, 1923-24; recalled to Moscow in 1924 but returned to U.S., 1928-29; oversaw expulsion of U.S. Trotskyists, 1928-29; recalled to Moscow and removed from CI posts, 1929; arrested during purge trials, 1937; executed.

Piatnitsky, Osip (1882-1939) Bolshevik from 1903; member of CC from 1920; named treasurer of Comintern in 1921; CI organization expert; member of ECCI, 1923-35; arrested, 1937; executed.

Poyntz, Juliet Stuart (1886-1937?) CPA founding member; university and labor educator; leading Lore supporter and sole delegate to vote against Lore's expulsion at 1925 WP convention; remained active in party until 1934; disappeared under mysterious circumstances in 1937, amid allegations of GPU involvement.

Profintern See "Red International of Labor Unions."

Progressive Mine Workers of America Organization formed by members of the UMW protesting wage reduction negotiated by John L. Lewis in southern Illinois, 1932; recognized as official AFL union after UMW broke with AFL, 1938; late 1930s national organizing drive failed to break UMW hold on miners; 18,000 members by end WWII; slowly declined after charter revoked by AFL when UMW briefly reaffiliated, 1946.

Progressive Party The formal name of Theodore Roosevelt's "Bull Moose" party, which split from the Republicans in 1912 on a program of moderate social reforms and the "constructive regulation" of capitalist competition. Also the name given to Robert La Follette's 1924 presidential campaign vehicle.

Proletarian Party Formed by the so-called "Michigan group," which broke from the CPA in 1920 rather than accept party control over its Proletarian University in Detroit; lived on as a small, independent sect to 1971.

Puro, Henry (1888-1981) Party name of Jon Wiita; immigrated to U.S. from Finland, 1905; worked in ore docks and mines in Minnesota; joined SP, 1907; one of leaders of Socialist Party's Finnish Federation; fled to Canada during WWI; returned to U.S. in 1923; worked on Finnish paper *Eteenpain* (Forward) in Mass.; became leader of WP Finnish Federation in 1927; head of CP agrarian work, 1930-34; *Eteenpain* editor, 1939-43; quit CP in 1943.

Radek, Karl (1885-1939) Active in Polish, Russian and German socialist movements from 1902; expelled from Rosa Luxemburg's Polish organization, 1911, and from the SPD, 1913; unsavory reputation; joined Bolsheviks in 1917; elected to CC, 1919; member ECCI, 1920-25; CI representative to German party, October 1923; member of Trotskyist opposition, 1924-29; expelled from party, 1927; repudiated Left Opposition's views, 1929; convicted in second Moscow Trial, 1937; died in internal exile.

Randolph, Asa Philip (1889-1979) Early black supporter of SP; editor of the *Messenger*, 1917; founder and first president of Brotherhood of Sleeping Car Porters, 1925-68; organized March on Washington Movement for black rights, 1941; elected vice president and executive council member of AFL-CIO at merger convention, 1955; a leader of 1963 civil rights march on Washington; founder and president of Negro American Labor Council, 1960-66; became supporter of New York Liberal Party.

Rangel, Jesus IWW member; leader of "Red Flag" guerrilla expedition from Texas to join Zapata peasant forces in Mexican Revolution, 1913; convicted of murder and sentenced to life in prison after expedition was attacked by U.S. forces.

Red International of Labor Unions (RILU) A federation of revolutionary-led trade unions associated with the Communist International; formed in Moscow in 1921 in opposition to the social-democratic trade-union federation, the "Amsterdam International."

Reed, John (1887-1920) Left-wing journalist contributing to *Masses* from 1913; author of *Ten Days That Shook the World,* eyewitness account of Bolshevik insurrection in Petrograd; joined SP as a Leninist, 1918; a founding member and leader of CLP, 1919; delegate to CI Second Congress, 1920; died in Russia that year.

Reynolds, William (Bud) Joined Communist movement in early 1920s; arrested at Bridgman Convention, 1922; Detroit WP leader and secretary of Detroit ILD; member of Cannon faction; elected to CEC, 1927; remained in CP; a leader of 1932 Detroit Hunger March.

Russell, Charles Edward (1860-1941) Prominent muckraking journalist; joined SP, 1908; one of founding members of NAACP, 1909; SP candidate for New York governor, 1910; candidate for New York City mayor, 1913; quit SP in 1917 in support of WWI; argued that war would bring "real socialism"; part of U.S. "peace" mission to Russia, 1917; editor of Non-Partisan League journal in early 1920s; in later years wrote poetry and biography.

Ruthenberg, Charles Emil (1882-1927) Joined SP, 1909; a leader of SP left wing; CPA national secretary, 1919; led group from CPA to fusion with CLP in May 1920; imprisoned for sedition, 1920-22; WP national secretary after release; allied with Pepper and Lovestone from 1923; died suddenly on 2 March 1927.

Rykov, Aleksey I. (1881-1938) Bolshevik from 1903; underground organizer in tsarist Russia for most of 1902-17; on Presidium of Moscow Soviet from 1917; first Commissar for Internal Affairs; head of Soviet government after Lenin died, 1924-30; part of party right wing around Bukharin; arrested with Bukharin in 1937 and convicted in third Moscow Trial; executed.

Sacco, Nicola (1891-1927) Anarchist worker framed up with Vanzetti for a 1920 murder and payroll robbery; executed by state of Massachusetts despite worldwide mass defense campaign in which ILD played prominent role.

St. John, Vincent (1876-1929) Western Federation of Miners strike leader and organizer; IWW founding member; IWW general secretary, 1908-14; leading proponent of "direct action," led fight to eliminate call for political action from IWW constitution; arrested during WWI government roundup of IWW members, and imprisoned for several years.

St. Paul Convention Farmer-Labor gathering of 17 June 1924, heavily organized by WP. Though most non-Communist delegates were prepared to support La Follette, the convention nominated MacDonald and Bouck as U.S. presidential and vice presidential candidates. Three weeks later these nominations were withdrawn and the WP fielded Foster and Gitlow as candidates.

Salutsky (Hardman), J.B. (1882-1968) Immigrated to U.S. from Russia, 1909; secretary, SP Jewish Federation, 1912-13; member of Workers' Council; joined WP in 1921, elected to CEC; expelled in 1923 for publicly criticizing the WP in his own *American Labor Monthly*; Amalgamated Clothing Workers education director, 1920-40; editor of ACW journal, 1940-44.

Saul, George ILD secretary in Denver, 1928; joined CLA and was active in its Detroit branch; expelled in 1935 along with Hugo Oehler.

Schneiderman, William (1905-1985) YWL founding member; joined WP, 1923; Cannon supporter, but remained in WP when Trotskyists were expelled, 1928; served as CP district organizer in California and other states until 1952, when he was jailed for five years under Smith Act.

Second International Also known as Socialist International; international organization of social democratic parties formed in 1889. After the leaderships of various national parties supported the war aims of their own governments in August 1914, Lenin called for a new, third International, which was formed in Moscow in 1919 as the Communist International. The Second International still exists as a federation of social-democratic and bourgeois parties.

Serrati, Giacinto Menotti (1874-1926) Member of Italian SP, 1892-1924, and leader of its left-wing "maximalist" faction; claimed support for Comintern but refused to break with reformists when CP was formed, 1921; joined Italian CP, 1924.

Shachtman, Max (1904-1972) Member of Workers' Council; joined WP, 1921; leader of Communist youth work, 1923-27; editor of *Labor Defender*, 1926-28; elected CEC alternate member, 1927; member of Cannon faction; expelled for Trotskyism, 1928; CLA founder and National Committee member; editor of U.S. Trotskyist publications; in 1940 led split in opposition to Trotskyist position of defense of Soviet Union, founding Workers Party, later renamed Independent Socialist League; dissolved ISL into SP right wing, 1958.

Sherman Anti-Trust Act Passed by U.S. Congress in 1890 ostensibly to curb monopolies, but frequently used as a legal basis for anti-strike injunctions and jailings of unionists, particularly in the 1920s.

Shields, Art IWW member to 1923; editor of *Industrial Solidarity*, 1921; Federated Press reporter from 1921; joined *DW* staff, 1924.

Sigman, Morris (1881-1931) Immigrated to U.S. from Russia, 1903; joined SLP's Socialist Trade and Labor Alliance, 1904; founding IWW member, 1905; joined International Ladies' Garment Workers' Union, 1908; ILGWU vice president, 1920-23; president, 1923-28.

Skoglund, Carl (1884-1960) Socialist union activist in Sweden from 1905; immigrated to U.S., 1912; joined SP, 1914; IWW member, 1917-21; joined Communist movement in 1920; WP industrial organizer, Minnesota district, from 1922; member of Cannon faction; expelled from WP, 1928; National Committee member of CLA from founding; president of Teamsters Local 544, 1938-40; jailed during WWII in Smith Act prosecution of Trotskyists; resisted government deportation attempts in 1950s.

Smeral, Bohumir (1880-1941) Member of Czech Social Democratic Party from 1897; elected to Central Committee, 1904; initially pro-Austria/Hungary in WWI, but moved left during war; by 1921, a leader of Czech CP; elected to ECCI, 1922; one of leaders of Stalinist Comintern until his death.

Socialist Labor Party (SLP) Founded in 1877 and led by Daniel De Leon from 1890. Emphasizing passive, legalistic propaganda to the exclusion of intervening in actual social struggles, the SLP became an isolated sect by the 1920s.

Socialist Party (SP) Founded in 1901 under leadership of Eugene Debs, Morris Hillquit and Victor Berger. U.S. section of Second International. Lost majority of members when left wing split off in 1919 to form Communist and Communist Labor parties, but remained active competitor of Workers Party.

Social Revolutionaries (SRs) A peasant-based party founded in Russia in 1900. Its right wing opposed the Russian Revolution, while the left wing briefly joined the Bolsheviks in a coalition government before going into armed opposition in 1918.

Spargo, John (1876-1966) British granite cutter who immigrated to U.S. in 1901; prominent SP propagandist; on right wing of party; wrote first full-length U.S. biography of Karl Marx; opposed SP policy of support to U.S. immigration restrictions; quit SP to support WWI, 1917; supported Coolidge for U.S. president, 1924; founded Bennington, Vermont Museum, 1927, and spent rest of life on its development.

Spartacist Journal of Spartacist League and its founders, left oppositionists expelled from Socialist Workers Party, 1963-64; currently theoretical journal of International Communist League (Fourth Internationalist).

Spector, Maurice (1898-1968) A founder of Canadian CP, 1921; national chairman, 1924-28; privately sympathized with Trotskyist opposition from 1924; delegate to CI Sixth Congress, 1928, where he was elected to ECCI; expelled from Canadian party for Trotskyism, 1928; founding member of CLA; leader of Canadian Trotskyists until he resigned from movement in 1939.

Stachel, Jack (1900-1965) SP member; joined WP, 1924; New York organization secretary, 1926-27; Lovestone supporter but briefly backed Cannon's anti-factional group in 1926-27; head of Organization Department, 1927; leader of CP trade-union work, 1932-35; CP national organization secretary, 1935-46; imprisoned under Smith Act for five years in 1950s.

Stalin, Joseph (1879-1953) Bolshevik from 1903; elected to CC, 1912; Russian CP general secretary from 1922; allied with Zinoviev and Kamenev, and defeated Trotsky in struggle for Soviet party control, 1923-24; developed nationalist theory of building "socialism in one country"; led bureaucratic degeneration of Russian Revolution; had most leading Communists of Lenin's time murdered.

Suhr, Herman IWW organizer; arrested with Richard Ford during 1913 Wheatfield, California hop pickers strike and framed up for murder of sheriff's deputy; released, 1926.

Swabeck, Arne (1890-1986) Danish immigrant and editor of SP Scandinavian weekly; IWW member, 1918-20; one of leaders of 1919 Seattle general strike; CLP founding member; CEC member from 1921; Chicago district party organizer; member of Cannon faction; expelled for Trotskyism, 1928; founding member, CLA; expelled as Maoist from Socialist Workers Party, 1967.

Third Period According to Stalinist theory expounded in 1929, the post-WWI periods of revolutionary upsurge (1917-23) and capitalist stabilization (1924-28) were to be followed by a "third period" of capitalist collapse and the victory of socialism. During this time (1929-33), the Comintern adopted sectarian and adventurist tactics.

Thomas, Norman (1884-1968) Presbyterian minister and "Christian Socialist"; SP member from 1918; leader of SP after Hillquit's death in 1933; six-time candidate for U.S. president on SP ticket, 1928-48.

The Toiler Weekly organ of Ohio CLP, succeeding *Ohio Socialist*; became organ of UCP; appeared 1919-22. After the formation of the Workers Party, it merged with *Workers' Council* to form *The Worker.*

Trade Union Educational League (TUEL) Founded by Foster in 1920 to promote industrial unionism within the AFL. After Foster joined the WP in late 1921, the TUEL was re-founded as the party's trade-union arm with a program calling for a workers republic, support for the Russian Revolution, affiliation with the Profintern; its program was watered down in 1926 and an attempt was made to transform it into an ongoing bloc with "progressives" in the trade unions; replaced as CP trade-union arm in 1929 by dual-unionist Trade Union Unity League.

Tresca, Carlo (1879-1943) Anarchist, strike activist; immigrated to U.S. from Italy, 1904; editor, *Il Martello* (The Hammer); jailed for one year for printing birth control advertisement, 1925; associate of Sacco and Vanzetti, collaborated with ILD in their defense; member of Dewey Commission of Inquiry into Moscow Trials; prominent anti-fascist; assassinated in New York during WWII.

Trotsky, Leon (1879-1940) Joined Russian socialist movement, 1897; after 1903 split did not belong to either Bolshevik or Menshevik faction; chairman of St. Petersburg Soviet in 1905 Revolution; exiled to Siberia; escaped abroad, 1907; returned to Russia, May 1917; leader of *Mezhrayonka* group; joined Bolshevik Party in July; as Bolshevik CC member and chairman of Petrograd Soviet, organized October insurrection; founder and organizer of Red Army; member of ECCI from 1920; leader of Left Opposition that fought Stalinist degeneration of Russian Revolution; expelled from Soviet CP, 1927; exiled by Stalin, 1929; founded Fourth International, 1938; died after being struck down by a Stalinist assassin in Mexico, 21 August 1940.

Two and a Half International An "International Association of Socialist Parties" led by Karl Kautsky that split to the left of the Second International in 1921 and reunited with it in 1923.

United Communist Party (UCP) Founded in May 1920 in fusion of CLP with a faction from CPA led by Ruthenberg. Fused with CPA to form unified underground Communist Party, May 1921.

Universal Negro Improvement Association (UNIA) Black nationalist organization established by Marcus Garvey in Harlem, 1917; advocated establishment of strong black nation in Africa and emigration of U.S. blacks to Africa; grew into mass organization in period of reaction following 1919 race riots; disintegrated after 1925, following Garvey's arrest and imprisonment.

Urbahns, Hugo (1890-1946) Leader of German left wing along with Fischer and Maslow; expelled as Zinoviev supporter, 1927; with Trotskyists, founded Leninbund, 1928; expelled Trotskyists from Leninbund, 1930; in exile in Sweden from 1933.

Uritsky, Mikhail S. (1873-1918) Sided with Mensheviks in 1903; internationalist in WWI and member of Trotsky's *Mezhrayonka* group; joined Bolsheviks, 1917, and was elected to CC; Left Communist and opponent of Brest-Litovsk peace; head of Petrograd Chekha, 1918; assassinated by SRs.

Vanzetti, Bartolomeo (1888-1927) Anarchist worker, Italian immigrant; framed up with Sacco for 1920 murder and payroll robbery; executed by state of Massachusetts despite mass international defense campaign in which ILD played prominent role.

Voice of Labor Weekly published in Chicago by William Z. Foster and other left-wing unionists, beginning in July 1921, and increasingly expressing a Communist viewpoint. At the end of 1923 it became *Farmer-Labor Voice.*

Volodarsky, V. (1890-1918) Member of Ukrainian Social Democratic Party from 1905; worked as tailor in U.S., 1913-17; collaborated on New York Russian-language journal *Novy Mir*; returned to Russia in 1917 and joined Trotsky's *Mezhrayonka,* then Bolsheviks; popular agitator; member of Presidium of Petrograd Soviet after October 1917; assassinated.

Wagenknecht, Alfred (1881-1956) SP member, 1900-19; a founder of CLP and its executive secretary; leader of Goose Caucus; supported Foster-Cannon faction, 1923-25; Foster faction supporter after 1925; chief WP fund-raiser; led unemployed work in early 1930s; stayed in CP until his death.

Walecki (Valetski), Henryk (1877-1938) Polish Socialist from 1898; a leader of Polish CP, 1920-21; Comintern official, 1921-37; Comintern representative to CPA's Bridgman Convention of 1922; arrested in Moscow, 1937; died in prison.

Walsh, Frank P. (1864-1939) Kansas City lawyer who became one of the most prominent labor lawyers in the U.S.; chairman of National Committee on Industrial Relations, 1913-15; editor and publisher of *Kansas City Post,* 1915-16; member of War Labor Relations Board, 1918; moved to New York in 1919; chairman of American Committee on Irish Independence; defended William Z. Foster against criminal syndicalism charges, 1920; La Follette Progressive, 1924; involved in Sacco and Vanzetti legal defense; founder of National Progressive League, 1932; became prominent New Deal Democrat; chairman of New York State Power Authority, 1931-39.

Watt, John J. Illinois miner and WP member; first president of National Miners' Union, 1928-30.

Weinstone, William (1897-1985) Socialist student leader at City College of New York; founding member of CPA; elected to CEC, 1921; New York district secretary of WP, 1925-28; WP CEC member, 1925-28;

Ruthenberg-Lovestone supporter, but backed Cannon anti-factional group in 1926-27; broke with Lovestone in 1929; editor of *Daily Worker,* 1931-32; convicted in 1953 under Smith Act and spent two years in jail.

Weisbord, Albert (1900-1977) SP youth leader, 1921-24; joined WP, 1924; Passaic strike organizer, 1926-27; Lovestone faction supporter; expelled from CP as Lovestoneite, 1929; led Communist League of Struggle, 1931-37.

Wheeler, Burton K. (1882-1975) Democratic U.S. Senator from Montana, 1923-47; Progressive Party vice presidential candidate, 1924.

White, John P. (1870-1934) UMW District 13 official, 1899-1907, 1909-12; UMW international vice president, 1907-09; UMW president, 1912-17; opposed attempt at 1912 UMW convention to recognize Socialist Party as political arm of working class; resigned from UMW to serve as adviser to National Fuel Administration during WWI; after war took management position with Haynes Power Company.

Whitney, Charlotte Anita (1867-1955) Joined SP, 1914; a founding member of CLP; a leading Communist in California until her death; arrested in 1919 under California criminal syndicalism law; conviction appealed in important ILD-supported test case; refused to seek pardon separate from IWW members convicted under same law; conviction upheld by Supreme Court; pardoned, 1928.

Wicks, Harry (1889?-1957) Capitalist agent in Socialist and Communist movements from 1919; SP member, 1915-19; member of Proletarian Party in 1920, but then joined underground Communist Party; led United Toilers split opposed to founding of Workers Party; joined Workers Party, 1922; Lovestone-Ruthenberg faction supporter; WP CEC member, 1922-23 and 1927-29; representative to Profintern, 1928-29; Comintern representative to Australia and Philippines, 1930-32; expelled as spy, 1938; joined Lovestone's Independent Labor League; cooperated with FBI in anti-Communist investigations.

Williamson, John (1903-1974) Seattle SLP member, 1918-21; WP member from 1922; YWL representative to WP CEC, 1924; national secretary of YWL, 1924-25; supporter of Cannon group, but remained in CP after Cannon's expulsion; spent nine months in Russia in 1928 and upon return was sent to Canada to root out Trotskyists; CP CC member from 1930; convicted in 1949 under Smith Act, served five years in prison; deported to Britain, 1955; remained active in British CP.

Wilson, Woodrow (1856-1924) Democratic President of U.S., 1913-20; led U.S. into WWI; after war championed League of Nations and Versailles Treaty, which was rejected by U.S. Senate.

Wolfe, Bertram D. (1896-1977) Member of SP left wing; CPA founder; fled rather than face Palmer Raid persecution; in Mexico, 1922-25; upon return acted as Lovestone lieutenant and "specialist" on Trotskyism; editor, *The Communist*, 1927; expelled from WP with Lovestone, 1929; member of Lovestone's organization until 1940; became anti-Communist writer; author of *Three Who Made A Revolution* (1948).

Woll, Matthew (1880-1956) President, International Photo-Engravers Union, 1906-29; AFL vice president, 1919-55; AFL-CIO vice president, 1955-56; known as bitter anti-Communist.

The Worker Weekly newspaper of Workers Party, 1922-24; successor to *The Toiler* and forerunner of *Daily Worker.*

Workers' Council A leftward-moving group in SP after 1919, originally calling itself the Committee for the Third International and publishing a biweekly paper called *Workers' Council*; fused with Communists to form WP in 1921.

Workers Monthly Official theoretical organ of Workers Party, beginning in 1924 as amalgamation of *Labor Herald, Liberator* and *Soviet Russia Pictorial*; replaced by *The Communist*, 1927.

Workers Party (WP) Founded in December 1921 as legal counterpart to underground Communist Party; was official name of U.S. Communists after underground party dissolved itself, April 1923. Its name was changed to Workers (Communist) Party in 1925 and Communist Party U.S.A. in 1929.

Workers Vanguard Present publication of Spartacist League/U.S., organization formed by left oppositionists expelled from the Socialist Workers Party, 1963-64.

Workers' World Weekly published in Kansas City, Missouri by left wing in Socialist Party of Kansas, 1919; edited by James P. Cannon and Earl Browder.

Wortis, Rose (1886-1958) A leading Communist activist in ILGWU; delegate to CI Fourth Congress, 1922; Lore supporter, 1922-25; Lovestone faction supporter, 1927-29.

Wrangel, General Peter Nikolaevich (1878-1928) Cavalry commander in tsarist army during WWI; general in counterrevolutionary White army in Caucasus, 1918-19; became commander in chief of White army, April 1920; defeated by Red Army in fall, 1920; leader of White émigré movement until his death.

Young Communist International (YCI) Youth section of Communist International; founded in Berlin, November 1919; continuation of Second International's Socialist Youth International, which had evolved to the left under impact of WWI and Russian Revolution; headquarters moved to Moscow, 1921; disbanded, 1943.

Young Workers League (YWL) The Communist youth organization founded in April 1922; name later changed to Young Communist League.

Zack, Joseph (1897-1963) CPA founding member; WP section organizer in Harlem, assigned to lead party's black work, 1921; member of Foster faction; elected to WP CEC, 1927; sent to Lenin School in Moscow, 1927; expelled from CP, early 1930s; briefly in Trotskyist movement, 1934; testified in anti-Communist witchhunt proceedings from 1938.

Zam, Herbert Joined SP youth, 1916; joined Communist movement, 1920; Lovestone supporter in YWL leadership; expelled from WP, 1929; left Lovestone organization and rejoined SP, 1934; resigned in late 1930s.

Zimmerman, Charles (1896-1983) Joined SP, 1917; joined Communist movement in 1920; leader with Rose Wortis of TUEL needle trades section; Lore supporter, 1922-25; Lovestone supporter, 1927-29; left party with Lovestone in 1929 and was member of Lovestone's organization; ILGWU vice president, 1934-72.

Zinoviev, Grigori Y. (1883-1936) Bolshevik from 1903; CC member from 1907; close collaborator of Lenin during WWI; Comintern head, 1919-26; allied with Stalin and Kamenev against Trotsky, 1923-25; Joint Opposition co-leader with Trotsky, 1926-27; capitulated to Stalin, 1928; imprisoned, 1935; executed in 1936 after being convicted in first Moscow Trial.

Bibliography of the Writings and Speeches of James P. Cannon 1912-1928

The following bibliography is a list of those articles, speeches and documents by James P. Cannon which we were able to locate, for the period from 1912 until Cannon's expulsion from the Workers Party in October 1928. Items are listed by date written, where known, or, more usually, by date of publication. Where the same article appeared in two different publications we have listed it only under the first publication date and title, followed by a reference to the second publication. Titles not in quotation marks have been given to unpublished manuscripts, letters and transcripts for descriptive purposes only. Articles in the *Daily Worker* which include substantial material by Cannon (e.g., lengthy quotations from his speeches, ILD statements signed by him) arc also listed.

For entries authored by Cannon along with others, all signers are listed immediately following the article title in the exact order in which they appeared in the original publication. While this volume contains motions and statements submitted by Cannon to the Workers Party Political Committee, we have not generally listed material from the Political Committee minutes in this bibliography. Nor have we listed statements issued by the Central Executive Committee during the time Cannon was a member, unless Cannon was explicitly listed as one of the signatories when the statement was published.

Beginning in January 1925 the *Daily Worker* published a New York City edition as well as its regular national edition. Articles often appeared in the New York edition one day later than in the national edition. In general we have used national edition dates for *Daily Worker* articles listed in this bibliography, but researchers should be aware that dates can vary by a day or more, depending on which edition of the *Daily Worker* is being consulted.

Entries which appear in this volume, even if only in excerpt, are indicated with an asterisk (*). An entry followed by the notation "(*Cannon Papers*)" indicates that the item can be found only in the James P. Cannon and Rose Karsner Papers, 1919-1974, Archives Division at the State Historical Society of Wisconsin; no photocopying is allowed from this collection until the year 2002. The notation "(in *Notebook*)" indicates entries that were also published in *Notebook of an Agitator* (New York: Pathfinder Press, 1973). The following abbreviations are used in the bibliography: *DW* for *Daily Worker* and *LD* for *Labor Defender.*

Pre-1919

"Seventh Convention, Harmonious Gathering of Young Men Fighting for Industrial Freedom," *Solidarity*, 28 September 1912.

"The Seventh IWW Convention," *International Socialist Review*, November 1912.

"Cannon Balls," *Solidarity*, 7 December 1912.

1919-20

"Statement of the Kansas Membership by the Temporary State Executive Committee of the Communist Labor Party," by Gertrude Crumb Harmon, W.H. Tilley, A.L. Kuntz, J.L. Crevitson, Effie Main, Ernest I. McNutt and J.P. Cannon, *Workers' World*, 26 September 1919.

Telegram to CLP National Office, in "Communist Labor Party National Office Bulletin," *Ohio Socialist*, 1 October 1919.

"The IWW at Philadelphia," *The Toiler*, 27 August 1920.*

"Another Renegade," *The Toiler*, 11 December 1920.*

1921

"The Story of Alex Howat," *The Liberator*, April 1921.*

"The Political Prisoners," *The Red Album*, May Day, 1921.*

"Who Can Save the Unions?" *The Toiler*, 7 May 1921.*

"Workers Party of America Born," speech given 23 December 1921, *Voice of Labor*, 6 January 1922 (also as "Greetings to the Convention," *The Toiler*, 7 January 1922).*

1922

"Open Letter to the Conference of Progressive Political Action," *The Worker*, 4 March 1922. Signed by James P. Cannon and Caleb Harrison for the Workers Party Central Executive Committee.

Letter to Frank Miner, 17 April 1922.

Letter to Albert Inkpin, *The Worker*, 22 April 1922.

"Proclamation of the Workers Party for International May Day, 1922," *The Worker*, 29 April 1922. Signed by James P. Cannon and Caleb Harrison for the Workers Party Central Executive Committee.

"The American Question," by J.P. Cannon, Max Bedacht and Arne Swabeck, n.d., ca. November 1922.*

1923

The Fifth Year of the Russian Revolution, Workers Party of America, New York, 1923.*

"Scott Nearing and the Workers Party," *The Worker*, 24 February 1923.

"What Kind of a Party?" *The Worker*, 3 March 1923.*

"Cannon Hits Morality of Kept Press," *The Worker*, 21 April 1923.

Letter to C.E. Ruthenberg, 25 May 1923.*

"The IWW and the International," *Voice of Labor*, 26 May and 2 June 1923.

"A Talk with Alex Howat," *Labor Herald*, June 1923.

"The Albany 'Conversion'," *The Worker*, 11 August 1923.

"Things as They Are," *The Worker*, 11 August 1923.

"Things as They Are—Words Versus Deeds," *The Worker*, 18 August 1923.

"The Workers Party Today—And Tomorrow," five-part series in *The Worker*, 25 August-22 September 1923.*

"Amalgamation—The Burning Question," *Voice of Labor*, 20 September 1923.*

"Party in Ohio Plans to Push Fight Forward," *The Worker*, 22 September 1923.

"Militants in 2nd TUEL Conference Pledge Struggle for Class War Victims," *The Worker*, 22 September 1923.

"The Communists in the Trade Unions," *Voice of Labor*, 5 October 1923.

"Statement on Our Labor Party Policy," by William Z. Foster and J.P. Cannon, November 1923.*

"The Russian Revolution—The Inspiring Force in the American Labor Movement," *The Worker*, 3 November 1923.

Letter to the 15th IWW Convention, IWW Convention Minutes, by James P. Cannon and Robert Minor, 13 November 1923.

"What Happened at Portland?" *The Worker*, 24 November 1923.*

"Lewis' Policies Victimize Maryland Miners," *Voice of Labor*, 30 November 1923.

"The IWW and the Red International of Labor Unions," *The Worker*, 1 December 1923.*

1924

"The IWW Convention," *Labor Herald*, January 1924.*

"Cannon Lauds Herrin Miners' Strike at Klan," *DW*, 12 February 1924.

"The St. Louis Conference of the CPPA," *Labor Herald*, March 1924.

"Reply to the Thesis of Comrades Lore and Olgin," by Alexander Bittelman and J.P. Cannon, *DW* magazine supplement, 12 April 1924.*

"Third Party Will Weaken Our Foe, Says Cannon," *DW*, 21 April 1924.

Letter to the Editors of the *Daily Worker*, *DW*, 22 April 1924.

Letter to Noah London, 24 April 1924.

Letter to Noah London, 29 April 1924 (*Cannon Papers*).

"St. Paul—June 17th," *Labor Herald*, May 1924.*

"New Party Industrial Registration," *DW*, 25 July 1924.

"Our Aims and Tactics in the Trade Unions," speech given 27 July 1924, *DW*, 2 August 1924.*

"Communist Candidates and the Farmer-Labor Party," *DW*, 29 July 1924.*

Letter to Rose Pastor Stokes, 4 August 1924.

"All Ready for the Industrial Registration," *DW*, 16 August 1924.

Letter to Rose Pastor Stokes, 28 August 1924.

Telegram to Kate Gitlow, 2 September 1924.

"Industrial Registration in Full Swing," *DW*, 6 September 1924.

"Cannon Calls on Thomas to Appear Oct. 2—Socialist Candidate Is Challenged to Debate," *DW*, 27 September 1924.

"Cannon Exposes Tammany Smith as Labor Foe," *DW*, 3 October 1924.

"The Bolshevization of the Party," speech given 5 October 1924, *Workers Monthly*, November 1924.*

"Many Indications that New York Socialists Are Deserting Thomas for Candidate of Tammany Hall," *DW*, 11 October 1924.

"Using the Party Registration," *DW*, 25 October 1924.

"Cannon Hits at Tweedledum and Tweedledee," *DW*, 30 October 1924.

"Developing the Party Educational Work," *DW* magazine supplement, 15 November 1924.

"Thesis on the Political Situation and the Immediate Tasks of the Workers Party," by Foster, Cannon, Bittelman, Browder, Dunne, Burman and Abern, *DW*, 26 November 1924.

"The Minority Attitude Toward Our Election Campaign—A Warning Signal for the Party," *DW*, 3 December 1924.*

"Lovestone Quotes Mahoney," *DW*, 8 December 1924.*

"The CEC, the Minority and Comrade Lore—How the Minority 'Fought' Lore When They Controlled the Party," *DW*, 11 December 1924.*

"How to Organize and Conduct a Study Class," *DW*, 13 December 1924.*

"A Year of Party Progress—Being a Record of Difficulties Overcome, of Party Achievements, and the Part Played Therein by the CEC and by the Minority," by William Z. Foster, James P. Cannon and A. Bittelman, *DW* magazine supplement, 27 December 1924.*

"A Statement on 2½ Internationalism," by Abern, Burman, Bittelman, Browder, Cannon, Dunne and Foster, *DW* magazine supplement, 27 December 1924.*

1925

"Origin and Structure of the TUEL," in pamphlet *Trade Unions in America*, Little Red Library No. 1, 1925.

"Controversial Questions in the Workers Party of America," by William Z. Foster and James P. Cannon, n.d., ca. February-March 1925 (also as "On the American Question" in the Russian- and German-language editions of *Communist International*, Volume 3, March 1925).*

Recommendations to the American Commission, by William Z. Foster and James P. Cannon, n.d., ca. February-March 1925.*

Remarks to American Commission, 13 February 1925.*

Remarks to American Commission, 8 March 1925.

Statement to American Commission, by Wm. Z. Foster and James P. Cannon, 28 March 1925.

Remarks to the ECCI Plenum, 30 March 1925, *International Press Correspondence*, 16 April 1925.*

Remarks to American Commission, 5 April 1925.*

Remarks to American Commission, 6 April 1925.*

"Statement of the CEC on Resolution of the ECCI," by Abern, Browder, Burman, Bittelman, Cannon, Dunne and Foster, *DW*, 19 May 1925.

"International Labor Defense Calls on All Organizations to Make Returns on Coupons Sent," *DW*, 7 July 1925.

Letter to Eugene V. Debs, 15 July 1925.*

"Cannon Replies to Henry Askeli," *DW* magazine supplement, 8 August 1925.*

"The Achievements of the Parity Commission," *DW*, 11 August 1925.*

"Workers Party Convention Organized—Cannon's Statement," *DW*, 25 August 1925.

"Our Party and the Communist International," speech given 4 October 1925, *DW*, 8 October 1925.*

"Policy on Anita Whitney Case," ILD circular dated 3 November 1925, *LD*, January 1926.

"Unify the Party!" by Max Bedacht, James P. Cannon, William F. Dunne, C.E. Ruthenberg and the National Executive Committee of the Young Workers League, *DW*, 16 November 1925.*

Letter to Comrades, 16 December 1925 (*Cannon Papers*).

1926

Telegram to Eugene V. Debs, 26 January 1926.

Remarks in Discussion on the American Question, 18 March 1926.*

"Defend Weisbord! Appeal to the Workers of America by the International Labor Defense," *DW*, 17 April 1926.

"'Free Weisbord!' Campaign On—ILD Gathers All Resources for Big Fight," *DW*, 18 April 1926.

"United Front in Passaic Defense," telegram to Political Committee, 22 April 1926.

"Statement of International Labor Defense on the Sacco-Vanzetti Case," *DW*, 14 May 1926.

"With All Our Strength for Sacco and Vanzetti," *DW*, 20 May 1926 (in *Notebook*).

"Our World Party at Work—A Summary of the Proceedings of the Enlarged Executive of the Communist International," *DW*, 27 May 1926.*

Letter to Eugene V. Debs, 27 May 1926.

"The United Front at Passaic," *LD*, June 1926.*

ILD Statement, in "Echo of Sacco, Vanzetti Move Stirs Congress," *DW*, 19 June 1926.

"Statement on the Question of Moving Party Headquarters and the *Daily Worker* to New York," n.d., ca. summer 1926 (*Cannon Papers*).

"Supplementary Statement to the Political Committee on the Question of Moving the Headquarters and *Daily Worker*," n.d., ca. summer 1926 (*Cannon Papers*).

"Frank Little, the Rebel—On the Ninth Anniversary of His Death," *LD*, August 1926 (in *Notebook*).

"Call for the Second Annual Conference of International Labor Defense," *LD*, August 1926.

"ILD Protests Imprisonment of Polish Workers," *DW*, 23 August 1926.

"The Cause That Passes Through a Prison," *LD*, September 1926 (in *Notebook*).

Telegram to Eugene V. Debs, by Elizabeth Gurley Flynn and James P. Cannon, 8 September 1926.

"The Second Annual Conference of the International Labor Defense," *LD*, October 1926.

"The Revolutionary Heritage of Eugene Victor Debs," *LD*, December 1926 (in *Notebook*).

"Shall the U.S. Government Be Mussolini's Bloodhound?" *DW*, 10 December 1926.

1927

"The Sormenti Case: A Challenge to American Labor," *LD*, January 1927.

"Who Can Save Sacco and Vanzetti?" *LD*, January 1927 (in *Notebook*).

Letter to Comrades, 10 January 1927 (*Cannon Papers*).

Letter to Comrades, 15 January 1927 (*Cannon Papers*).

"The International Campaign for Sacco and Vanzetti," *LD*, February 1927 (in *Notebook*).

Remarks in Cannon-Ruthenberg Conference on Moderating Factionalism, 7 February 1927.*

Telegram to Theodore Debs, 7 February 1927.

Letter to Theodore Debs, 16 February 1927.

"Resolution of the Central Committee on the Controversy in the Party Fraction in Relation to the Congress of the Co-operative League of America and Party Policy in the Co-operatives," submitted by Cannon and Ruthenberg to meeting of Political Committee, 24 February 1927.

"Our Tribute to the Memory of the Paris Commune," *LD*, March 1927.

"Ruthenberg Died at His Post," in "Workers' Leaders Mourn Ruthenberg," *DW*, 3 March 1927.

"Comrade C.E. Ruthenberg—General Secretary, Workers (Communist) Party," statement by Max Bedacht, Alexander Bittelman, J.P. Cannon, J. Louis Engdahl, Wm. Z. Foster, Benjamin Gitlow and Jay Lovestone, *DW*, 3 March 1927.

Protest Telegram to Communist International, by Cannon, Dunne, Ballam, Swabeck, Abern, Reynolds and Weinstone, n.d., but according to Draper, 23 March 1927.

"Charles E. Ruthenberg—A Tribute by the National Committee of International Labor Defense," *LD*, April 1927.

Draft telegram to William F. Dunne, 3 April 1927 (*Cannon Papers*).

"Ruthenberg, The Fighter—Passing of an American Pioneer," *DW*, 4 April 1927 (also in *LD*, April 1927, and in *Notebook*).

"Save Sacco and Vanzetti from Death! International Labor Defense Calls on All Labor to Protest," *DW*, 7 April 1927.

"Labor Rallies to Save Sacco and Vanzetti—From Supreme Court of Capital to Supreme Court of the Masses," *DW*, 9 April 1927 (also in *LD*, May 1927, and in *Notebook* as "From the Supreme Court of the Capitalists to the Supreme Court of the Laboring Masses").

Telegram (re: Hungarian repression), 12 April 1927 (*Cannon Papers*).

"ILD Warns of New Menace for Sacco, Vanzetti—Analyzes Attempts to Disrupt Campaign," *DW*, 4 May 1927.

Speech for the Liquidation of Factionalism, at CEC Plenum, 6 May 1927, which includes "Outline of Statement on Liquidation of Factionalism and Unification of the Party," submitted by Weinstone, Cannon, Dunne, Ballam, Abern, Swabeck, Reynolds and Gomez to Political Committee.*

Cannon-Weinstone Theses on the Party Factional Situation, n.d., ca. May 1927.*

"Life and Freedom for Sacco and Vanzetti!" *Labor Unity*, 15 May 1927.

Letter to Rose Karsner, 25 May 1927 (*Cannon Papers*).

"Sacco and Vanzetti Must Not Burn on the Electric Chair," *LD*, June 1927 (in *Notebook* as "A Speech for Sacco and Vanzetti").

Letter to American Commission, by J.P. Cannon, Wm. Z. Foster and William Weinstone, 16 June 1927.*

Report from Moscow, circular of Cannon faction, 26 June 1927.*

Remarks to American Commission, n.d., ca. June 1927.*

Telegram, signed by Bill (Foster), Jim (Cannon) and Will (Weinstone), 30 June 1927 (included in circular of "National Committee of Opposition Bloc," 1 July 1927).

"Agreement for the Carrying Out of the Resolution on the American Question Adopted by the Presidium of the Executive Committee of the Comintern," July 1927. Signed by Jay Lovestone, Benjamin Gitlow, John Pepper, J.P. Cannon, Wm. Z. Foster, Wm. W. Weinstone, A. Braun; sealed by ECCI.

"Death, Commutation or Freedom?" *DW*, 12 July 1927 (also in *LD*, July 1927, and in *Notebook*).

"Order Exile for 'Radnik' Editor; ILD Calls Aid—Zinich, Communist, Is Hated by Capitalists," *DW*, 15 August 1927.

"No Illusions," *DW*, 18 August 1927 (in *Notebook*).

"New Developments—New Dangers in the Sacco and Vanzetti Case," *DW*, 19 August 1927 (in *Notebook*).

"The Murder of Sacco and Vanzetti," *DW*, 24 August 1927 (in *Notebook*).

"Class Against Class in the Sacco and Vanzetti Case," *LD*, September 1927 (in *Notebook*).

"ILD Answers Felicani Slander; Socialists Curbed Mass Protest," *DW*, 2 September 1927.

"Militant Labor Urged by ILD to Save 'Daily'—Lauds Paper's Struggle for Sacco and Vanzetti," *DW*, 3 September 1927.

"International Labor Defense Meets Nov. 11th—Chicago Martyrs' Death Date Spurs Activity," *DW*, 30 September 1927.

"Call for the Third Annual Conference of International Labor Defense," *LD*, October 1927.

"Boston and Cheswick," *DW*, 3 October 1927.

"A Living Monument to Sacco and Vanzetti," *LD*, October 1927.

"The Cause of the Martyrs," *DW* magazine supplement, 8 October 1927 (in *Notebook*).

"A Christmas Fund of Our Own," *DW*, 17 October 1927 (in *Notebook*).

"The Red Month of November—For the Third Annual Conference of International Labor Defense," *LD*, November 1927.*

"Shall It Be Again? Yesterday, Sacco and Vanzetti—Today, Greco and Carillo," *DW*, 12 November 1927.

"The Third Conference of International Labor Defense," *LD*, December 1927.

1928

"Greco and Carillo on Trial," *LD*, January 1928.

"Vitality of the Revolutionary Press," *DW* magazine supplement, 13 January 1928.

"The Acquittal of Greco and Carillo," *LD*, February 1928.

Speech at Central Executive Committee Plenum, 5 February 1928.*

"Fun on Commerce St.—A Review of Gold's 'Hoboken Blues'," *DW*, 21 February 1928.

"The Daring Enterprise," *DW*, 28 February 1928.

"Party Work and Accountability," *Party Organizer*, Vol. 3, Nos. 3-4, March-April 1928 (also in *DW*, 23 March 1928, as "Tasks Face Every Workers Party Member").*

Telegram to Theodore Debs, 19 March 1928.

"The Workers Party and the 1928 Election Drive," *DW*, 24 March 1928.

"Points West—Impressions On The Road," *DW*, 24 March 1928.

Telegram to Theodore Debs, 24 March 1928.

"Colorado, the Realm of the Rockefellers," *DW*, 26 March 1928.

"A Fraternal Order for the U.S. Workers," *DW*, 30 March 1928.

"To Revive Case of Billings, Mooney, Frame-Up Victims—'Center on Masses,' Is Message From Cell," *DW*, 12 April 1928 (in *Notebook* as "Tom Mooney's Appeal").

"Labor Defense Cables Protest," *DW*, 10 May 1928.

"Organization of Propaganda Meetings," *DW*, 14 May 1928 (also in *Party Organizer*, Vol. 3, Nos. 5-6, May-June 1928).*

"Refute Slander of IWW Officials," *DW*, 16 May 1928.

"William D. Haywood—Soldier to the Last," *DW*, 22 May 1928 (in *Notebook*).

"Our Communist Nominating Convention," *DW*, 23 May 1928.

"A Visit with Billings at Folsom Prison—An Interview," *LD*, June 1928 (in *Notebook*).

"A Talk with the Centralia Prisoners—An Interview," *LD*, June 1928 (in *Notebook*).

"W.D. Haywood—A Pioneer of Revolutionary Unionism," *Labor Unity*, June 1928.

"Opening the Election Campaign," *DW*, 5 June 1928.*

"The Voice of the Communist Movement," *DW*, 26 June 1928.*

Letter to Political Committee, 27 June 1928.

"Trade-Union Questions," *The Communist*, July 1928.*

"The Right Danger in the American Party," minority resolution submitted to the Sixth World Congress of the Communist International by James P. Cannon, William Z. Foster, William F. Dunne, Alex Bittelman, J.W. Johnstone, Manuel Gomez and George Siskin, July 1928, serialized in the *Militant*, Nos. 1-5, November 1928-January 1929.

Remarks at Sixth World Congress, 25 July 1928, *International Press Correspondence*, 11 August 1928.*

"Statement of Cannon, Aronberg and Costrell," by J.P. Cannon, Philip Aronberg and H.L. Costrell, *DW*, 2 October 1928.

Index